CHINA'S POLITICAL SYSTEM

**Updates and supplements
to this book
can be downloaded here:
www.merics.org/polsys**

CHINA'S POLITICAL SYSTEM

Sebastian Heilmann (ed.)
Mercator Institute for China Studies (MERICS)

ROWMAN & LITTLEFIELD
Lanham • Boulder • New York • London

Published by Rowman & Littlefield
A wholly owned subsidiary of The Rowman & Littlefield Publishing Group, Inc.
4501 Forbes Boulevard, Suite 200, Lanham, Maryland 20706
www.rowman.com

Unit A, Whitacre Mews, 26-34 Stannary Street, London SE11 4AB

Copyright © 2017 by Rowman & Littlefield

Published in Cooperation with MERICS

British Library Cataloguing in Publication Information Available

Library of Congress Control Number: 2016955487
ISBN: 978-1-4422-7734-2 (cloth : alk. paper)
ISBN: 978-1-4422-7735-9 (paper)
ISBN: 978-1-4422-7736-6 (electronic)

♾™ The paper used in this publication meets the minimum requirements of American National Standard for Information Sciences—Permanence of Paper for Printed Library Materials, ANSI/NISO Z39.48-1992.

Printed in the United States of America

Table of contents

List of tables

List of figures

List of acronyms and abbreviations

ABC	Agricultural Bank of China
ACFAC	All-China Federation of Literary and Art Circles
ACFIC	All-China Federation of Industry and Commerce
ACFTU	All-China Federation of Trade Unions
ACWF	All-China Women's Federation
ADB	Asian Development Bank
APEC	Asia-Pacific Economic Cooperation
AQSIQ	General Administration of Quality Supervision, Inspection and Quarantine
AVIC	Aviation Industry Corporation of China
BOC	Bank of China
CAAM	China Association of Automobile Manufacturers
CAC	Cyberspace Administration of China
CAE	Chinese Academy of Engineering
CAS	Chinese Academy of Sciences
CASS	Chinese Academy of Social Sciences
CAST	China Association for Science and Technology
CAUPD	China Academy of Urban Planning and Design
CBRC	China Banking Regulatory Commission
CC	Central Committee
CCB	China Construction Bank
CCCMPS	Central Commission for Comprehensive Management of Public Security
CCDI	Central Commission for Discipline Inspection
CCP	Chinese Communist Party
CCTV	China Central Television
CDB	China Development Bank
CDRLSG	Central Comprehensively Deepening Reforms Leading Small Group
CEA	China Earthquake Administration
CEDA	China Enterprise Directors' Association
CEIC	Census and Economic Information Center
CEPA	Closer Economic Partnership Arrangement
CFDA	China Food and Drug Administration
CFELSG	Central Finance and Economy Leading Small Group
CGCA	China Group Companies Association
CIC	China Investment Corporation
CIRC	China Insurance Regulatory Commission
CIVTE	China Institute for Vocational and Technical Education

CMC	Central Military Commission
CNOOC	China National Offshore Oil Corporation
CNR	China North Locomotive and Rolling Stock Corporation
CNSC	Central National Security Commission
CNY	renminbi
CPPCC	Chinese People's Political Consultative Conference
CRC	China Railway Corporation
CRCC	China Railway Construction Corporation
CREC	China Railway Engineering Corporation
CSHRS	China Society for Human Rights Studies
CSILSG	Central Cyber Security and Informatization Leading Small Group
CSR	China South Locomotive and Rolling Stock Corporation
CSRC	China Securities Regulatory Commission
CSUS	China Society for Urban Studies
CVET	China Society of Vocational Education and Training
CYL	Communist Youth League
DM	disaster management
DRC	Development Research Center (under the State Council)
EMO	Emergency Management Office
ETIRI	Electronic Technology Information Research Institute
ExCo	Executive Council
FAW	First Automotive Works
FDI	foreign direct investment
FLEC	Fisheries Law Enforcement Command
GDP	gross domestic product
GDR	German Democratic Republic
GERD	gross domestic expenditures for R&D
GIZ	Gesellschaft für Internationale Zusammenarbeit
GONGO	government-organized nongovernmental organization
ICBC	Industrial and Commercial Bank of China
ICCPR	International Covenant on Civil and Political Rights
ICESCR	International Covenant on Economic, Social and Cultural Rights
ICG	International Crisis Group
ICT	information and communications technology
IFDI	inbound foreign direct investment
IMF	International Monetary Fund
INGO	international nongovernmental organization
IoT	Internet of Things
IPO	initial public offering
LegCo	Legislative Council
LSG	Leading Small Group

MEP	Ministry of Environmental Protection
MERICS	Mercator Institute for China Studies
MIIT	Ministry of Industry and Information Technology
MINT	mathematics, informatics, the natural sciences, and engineering
MOA	Ministry of Agriculture
MOCA	Ministry of Civil Affairs
MOE	Ministry of Education
MOF	Ministry of Finance
MOFA	Ministry of Foreign Affairs
MOFCOM	Ministry of Commerce
MOHRSS	Ministry of Human Resources and Social Security
MOHURD	Ministry of Housing and Urban-Rural Development
MOJ	Ministry of Justice
MOLSS	Ministry of Labor and Social Security
MOS	Ministry of Supervision
MOST	Ministry of Science and Technology
MOT	Ministry of Transport
MPA	Master's of Public Administration
MPS	Ministry of Public Security
MSS	Ministry of State Security
MWR	Ministry of Water Resources
NAO	National Audit Office
NBS	National Bureau of Statistics
NCDR	National Commission for Disaster Reduction
NDRC	National Development and Reform Commission
NGO	nongovernmental organization
NHFPC	National Health and Family Planning Commission
NIMBY	"not in my backyard"
NPC	National People's Congress
NSFC	National Science Foundation of China
NSSF	National Social Security Fund
OECD	Organisation for Economic Co-operation and Development
OFDI	outbound foreign direct investment
PAP	People's Armed Police
PBOC	People's Bank of China
PHCC	Patriotic Health Campaign Committee
PLA	People's Liberation Army
PLAN	People's Liberation Army Navy
PPC	Provincial People's Congress
PPP	purchasing power parity
PRC	People's Republic of China

R&D	research and development
ROC	Republic of China
SAC	Securities Association of China
SAFE	State Administration of Foreign Exchange
SAG	State Administration of Grain
SAIC	State Administration for Industry and Commerce
SAIC	Shanghai Automotive Industry Corporation
SAR	special administrative region
SARFT	State Administration of Radio, Film and Television
SARS	severe acute respiratory syndrome
SASAC	State-owned Assets Supervision and Administration Commission
SCOPSR	State Commission Office for Public Sector Reform
SEZ	special economic zone
SFA	State Forestry Administration
Sinopec	China Petroleum & Chemical Corporation
SIPRI	Stockholm International Peace Research Institute
SMEc	socialist market economy
SMS	short message services
SNWTP	South-to-North Water Transfer Project
SOA	State Oceanic Administration
SSAPS	State Supervisory Authority for Production Safety
TI	Transparency International
TVE	township and village enterprise
UNCHR	United Nations Commission on Human Rights
UNCTAD	United Nations Conference on Trade and Development
UNDP	United Nations Development Programme
UNESCAP	United Nations Economic and Social Commission for Asia and the Pacific
UNODC	United Nations Office on Drugs and Crime
UPSC	Urban Planning Society of China
USD	US Dollar
VAT	value-added tax
WHO	World Health Organization
WTO	World Trade Organization
WWF	World Wide Fund for Nature

Preface

The Chinese government is one of the most important actors in international affairs today. China's global economic and diplomatic presence is challenging the earlier dominance by the Western powers. As a result, many diplomats, journalists, and social scientists are coming to see the comprehensive program of national modernization for business, technology, and public administration implemented by the Chinese government in a new way, that is, as a constituent part of competition among different systems of government. Some commentators have even speculated that over time the Western model of market-based democracy may be permanently eclipsed by the growing economic and technological strength of authoritarian China.

Without any doubt, the Chinese political system has been able to exploit the opportunities of economic globalization with a degree of agility and stamina that almost no one would have expected. How has this in many ways rigid political and administrative system been able to adapt and to be innovative to such an extraordinary extent?

To thoroughly understand how the People's Republic of China (PRC) has grown in power requires a careful analysis of its political system. This includes how the system is formally organized (i.e., what institutions and organizations are integral parts of the system) and the processes involved (i.e., what are the interactions among political, business, and societal actors) to prepare, adopt, implement, review, and adjust authoritative decisions and policies. In the analysis of the political system this book focuses on the following substantive questions:

- To what extent can China's economic achievements be attributed to the country's political system and its policies?
- What are the effects of economic modernization and global economic integration on the Chinese political system?
- Is the Chinese political system capable of adapting to changing economic, technological, social, and international conditions?
- What kind of developmental potentials and risks are likely to shape the Chinese political system over the medium term?
- Do the Chinese political and economic systems provide viable approaches for other developing and emerging nations, thus giving rise to systemic competition with the Western market-based democracies?

The purpose of this book is not to take static snapshots of the current balance-of-power situation but rather to grasp the dynamic aspects of the political system, that is, its elasticity and sustainability. Only a political system that is able to adapt to changing socioeconomic conditions through policy innovation and institutional renewal will be able to cope with social and political tensions in a constructive way and to prevent a breakdown of the existing order. The extent to which the PRC political system can actually make such adaptations is the underlying theme of this book.

In the Chinese political system, central mechanisms of political communications (most strikingly, through propaganda and censorship), the setting and adjusting of political priorities (multi-year planning and target-setting through the cadre system—activities that differ from those in other polities), as well as the introduction of novel policies (typically by way of local policy experimentation) are based on the specific organizational and mobilization experiences of the Chinese Communist Party (CCP) during its long political history since the 1920s. This is also the case with respect to the party's mechanisms of policy enforcement, for instance, by way of vigorous campaigns and targeted repression. China's approach to governance is firmly rooted in, and facilitated by, the lack of checks and balances in the authoritarian party-state. From a comparative international and historical perspective, however, it is highly unusual how China's authoritarian institutions and instruments have adapted during the period of reform and opening since 1978–79 to match the new requirements for government activity, therefore leading to unexpected economic, social, and political outcomes that differ profoundly from the experiences of other one-party systems.

The purpose of this book is to provide readers with a broad yet subtle understanding of the preconditions, prospects, and risks associated with China's political development. Domestic power shifts are presented in a way to show how they are closely linked with economic, social, technological, and foreign policy changes. The chapters deal primarily with issues of political leadership, political institutions, and state–economy and state–society interactions. To introduce readers to how China's approach to governance works on the ground, the book also provides case studies on the creation, implementation, and adjustment of policies in specific issue areas, ranging from administrative reform and industrial and environmental policy to disaster management. The final chapter proposes some fundamental perspectives on Chinese development over time and outlines possible scenarios for the future.

The book is based on research work carried out over the past twenty-five years, comprehensive assessments of Chinese sources of information, and the latest international research on China. Our own research has benefited considerably from studies and suggestions by a host of colleagues who are too numerous to be listed here individually. Nevertheless, their work is specifically referred to in the text. We have deliberately chosen to dispense with footnotes, as it does not seem appropriate to cite a myriad of Chinese sources in an attempt to produce an overview of the political system (after all, in addition to researchers on China, the book is aimed at general audiences). Thus, in referring to works of major importance upon which we have drawn and that deal with the topics under discussion in greater depth, we have placed the authors' surnames and dates of publication in parentheses. These publications are listed in full in the bibliography at the end of the volume.

This book is not the work of a single author. Rather, it is the product of close cooperation among research associates and fellows at the Berlin-based Mercator Institute for China Studies (MERICS). I would like to express my great appreciation and gratitude to Marie Hoffmann, without whose passionate involvement and diligence the manuscript would never have been completed on time. The creative graphics were commendably created by Johannes Buckow. I am deeply grateful to my fellow researchers and colleagues at MERICS for working together so effectively to produce such a comprehensive volume. I would also like to thank the translation team, headed by Carl Carter, for its meticulous work. And, as in previous publication projects, I deeply appreciate and admire the copy-editing skills of Nancy Hearst at Harvard's Fairbank Center. It is a true pleasure to work with people who are so competent, energetic, and curious to learn about how China works.

Sebastian Heilmann

1 Analyzing Chinese politics

1.1 Historical foundations

Sebastian Heilmann

China is a fascinating country, both because of its long tradition as an immensely influential East Asian civilization and because of its rapidly growing global importance in the contemporary world. The legacy of China's history has had far-reaching effects on the attempts at political renewal undertaken during the Mao era (1949–76) and on the policy of reform and opening pursued by the Chinese government since 1978–79 (Klein 2007; Kuhn 2001). Nevertheless, the often-cited claim about China having a five-thousand-year history should not distract from a number of facts that lead one to question the notion of an uninterrupted tradition of statehood.

During most of its history, China's national territory encompassed only parts of what is now known as the People's Republic of China (PRC). Large regions, such as Tibet, Xinjiang (known as "East Turkestan" among the Uyghurs), and even the island of Taiwan, were incorporated into the Chinese Empire only temporarily or at a relatively late point in time, and do not belong to what is traditionally regarded as the heartland of Chinese culture. Furthermore, Chinese history has been repeatedly shaped by phases of territorial division, foreign dominance, disintegration, and major cultural, social, and technological upheavals. The widespread view of Chinese culture being unchanging or continuous fails to take into account these historical disruptions and fault lines (Gernet 1996; Osterhammel 1989; Rawski 2015).

1.1.1 Political destabilization in modern history

The encroachment by the Western powers in East Asia and Japan's rapid rise in the late nineteenth century destroyed the traditional self-image of imperial China as a culturally superior civilization at the center of the world order. The Chinese Empire proved to be unable to undergo political renewal and economic modernization in reaction to the foreign challenges and social unrest that it was confronting. The empire had completely collapsed by the time of the Revolution of 1911 and the proclamation of the Republic of China in 1912. For a period following these dramatic events the empire was broken up into a number of disparate regimes governed by warlords. Growing political rivalry between the Guomindang (or the Nationalist Party) and the Chinese Communist Party (CCP) in the 1920s led to violent clashes. This enmity was temporarily put aside and replaced by a period of superficial cooperation from 1937 to 1945 when China was challenged by war with Japan. However, the end of the Japanese occupation was followed by a bloody civil war, from which the CCP eventually emerged victorious in 1949. Led by Chiang Kai-shek (Jiang Jieshi), the Republic of China (ROC) (under the Nationalist Party) was forced to flee to the island of Taiwan, where it subsequently set up its own government. Today, Taiwan is still officially known as the Republic of China, even though the ROC actually no longer existed on the mainland after 1949. The problem of China being divided into two separately governed entities remains unresolved to this day.

When the PRC was founded on October 1, 1949, the new Communist leaders confronted seemingly insurmountable hurdles: the population, economy, and administrative sector had all suffered immeasurably due to the many years of armed conflict, first during the war against Japan and then during the civil war. In their daily lives people generally struggled for survival. Yet by the beginning of 1957, the CCP had managed to achieve a number of major accomplishments: a strong, centralized state ensured both national sovereignty and political unity; high economic growth and progress in terms of industrialization generally improved the livelihood of the people.

Ten years later, however, when the "Great Proletarian Cultural Revolution" was at its height, China was again on the verge of civil war as violent political clashes erupted and affected the state, the economy, and indeed the entire society. The country seemed to be on the brink of jeopardizing everything it had achieved in the early 1950s.

It was only after the death of the leader of the revolution, Mao Zedong, in 1976 that there occurred a fundamental change in direction. Beginning in the early 1980s, this period was characterized by exceptional economic dynamism, unusual from both a historical and an international perspective. The high rate of economic growth that China maintained for more than three and a half decades created conditions for a large share of the Chinese population to benefit from better living standards as well as for bringing about an enormous boost in the modernization of the industrial sector, infrastructure, education, technology, and military armaments, among others. At the same time, however, this rapid economic growth also produced some politically undesirable side-effects that have continued to threaten the stability of the system. These destabilizing factors range, among others, from social inequalities and widespread corruption to degradation of the environment (see Table 1.1.A).

Table 1.1.A

Important events in the history of the PRC, 1949-79

Period	Formative political and social events
1949–55	After the founding of the PRC in 1949, political and economic institutions are established, land reform is implemented, and the country enters a period of "socialist transformation."
1956–57	Agriculture is collectivized and private firms are taken over by the state; the "Hundred Flowers" Campaign is followed by the "Anti-Rightist" Campaign to silence government critics who dared to speak out during the "Hundred Flowers" Campaign.
1958–60	The establishment of "People's Communes" and the rash industrialization of the "Great Leap Forward" result in the catastrophic famine of 1959–61 (the "Three Bitter Years").
1959–63	A rift in relations with the Soviet Union due to fundamental conflicts over strategy, ideology, and power, thereby divides the socialist camp.
1961–65	Attempts at a partial restructuring of industrial and agricultural production exacerbate strains among party leaders.
1964 and thereafter	After the first Chinese atomic bomb is detonated in 1964, China becomes a nuclear power.
1966–76	Domestic conflicts and persecutions during the "Great Proletarian Cultural Revolution"; Mao Zedong dies in 1976.
1971 and thereafter	Rapprochement with the United States; the PRC obtains a permanent seat on the UN Security Council; China gains a stronger standing in the U.S.–USSR–Chinese "strategic triangle."
1976–78	Failed attempts to recentralize economic planning; conflicts between those loyal to Mao and the reformists.
Since 1978–79	Introduction of the policy of "reform and opening" at the Third Plenary Session of the Eleventh Central Committee of the CCP.

Based on Heilmann 2002.

© MERICS

1.1.2 Formative developments and traumatic experiences in recent history

Contemporary Chinese politics is saddled by a series of historical burdens that influence the behavior of the country's political representatives. It is impossible to gain a sound understanding of China's current problems unless the historical circumstances in which they arose are also taken into account (Schmidt-Glintzer 1997, 1999; Spence 1990; Vogelsang 2013). In the following section, several developments and traumatic experiences that have shaped the country will be outlined (see Table 1.1.B).

Table 1.1.B

Formative developments and traumatic experiences in China's recent history

	Development	Consequences and reactions
I	Very rapid population growth (esp. from 1750–1850 and 1950–90).	Poverty, famine, social unrest, and internal migration. Strict birth-control policy from the 1980s to 2013.
II	Repeated breakdown of law and order (beginning with the Taiping Uprising, 1850–64).	Primacy of domestic stability and unity. Harsh suppression of potentially destabilizing groups.
III	Military superiority of the Western powers and Japan (the "unequal treaties," the cession of territory, and China's "semi-colonial" status).	Destruction of China's self-image as a leading cultural "Middle Kingdom." Creation of a national victim complex and erratic nationalism.
IV	A conflict-ridden search for a workable modernization strategy (the Revolution of 1911, the May Fourth Movement of 1919, the Nanjing Republic, 1927–49).	National experiments to develop society, utopian in nature and devastating in practice, e.g., the "Great Leap Forward" and the "Great Proletarian Cultural Revolution."
V	Bid to regain a prominent position in the international system.	Achieving "comprehensive national strength" while refusing to compromise on territorial issues. Regional rivalry with Japan and strategic rivalry with the United States.

Based on Heilmann 2002.

© MERICS

The very high rate of population growth, a development that was to have particularly far-reaching consequences, began in the mid-eighteenth century. This trend was due to changes in the agricultural sector that were accompanied by periods of peace both at home and abroad. The increase in the size of the population confronted the government with numerous challenges that called for political countermeasures. The severity of the government's birth-control policy, which was a direct result of the population growth, has frequently been criticized. It has been in force since the 1980s but was relaxed somewhat in 2013 (Section 5.1.2). In October 2015, the controversial one-child restriction was abolished, even as the National Health and Family Planning Commission maintained that the birth-control regime would remain a "fundamental state policy."

The Chinese repeatedly experienced traumatic events after the existing political order collapsed; in the twentieth century alone, such events led to numerous famines, rampages of violence, and drastic economic setbacks: China's war with Japan, 1937–45; the civil war, 1945–49; the "Great Leap Forward," 1958–60; and the "Great Proletarian Cultural Revolution," 1966–76. Fears of the collapse of internal stability have had a strong influence on the political leadership over the years.

Another psychological factor that is frequently underestimated is the collective trauma experienced as a result of Western and Japanese military and economic superiority. Beginning at the end of the nineteenth century, this led to large sectors of the population developing a highly sensitive national consciousness that has been subject to political manipulation. The traditional Chinese self-image as the cultural and political center of the world—the "Middle Kingdom"—was truly destroyed. This traumatic experience left an indelible mark on the populace and it shaped attitudes toward both the West and Japan, as seen repeatedly even today in terms of Chinese foreign policy, in particular with respect to its territorial disputes with Japan and its rivalry with the United States.

Closely connected to these historical traumas and experiences has been the political leaders' ongoing search, with repeated setbacks, for a workable modernization strategy. Tragic social experiments of a catastrophic nature, such as the "Great Leap Forward"—a policy that resulted in the most serious famine in the entire twentieth century, with 20–40 million people dying of starvation (Yang Jisheng 2012)—and the "Great Proletarian Cultural Revolution"—with its social rifts verging on civil war—were the outcomes of radical experiments intended to bring about a new economic and political era.

1.1.3 Persistent and transformed political traditions

China's recent political history has not only been shaped by the country's own traditions and by domestic developments. In the twentieth century, in particular, "imported" notions of political order and organizational patterns have also had a considerable effect on Chinese politics. After the socialist revolution, ideologies originating in Europe and the Soviet Union became part and parcel of Chinese state doctrine. In practice, however, they underwent substantial changes and Chinese adaptations. What is the proportion of "inherited" characteristics to "imported" characteristics in the existing political order? For that matter also, what is the share of "Sinicized" elements in Marxism-Leninism?

The dominance of the Communist Party, which is not checked by any independent bodies to monitor its activities, is not only due to the typical characteristics of a Communist Party dictatorship, but also due to traditional Chinese concepts of social and political order. In the course of China's political history, no nationwide institutionalized constituencies or rival autonomous organizations (churches, regional authorities, etc.) were tolerated as legitimate counterweights within the existing order so as to create any form of a separation of powers such that existed in the West. Instead, the Emperor reigned supreme over the entire country, with unlimited authority.

In many ways, this autocratic tradition was retained by the Chinese Communists, but they used it to pursue their own political goals. The rather bewildering political dominance of Mao Zedong (in power from 1949 until his death in 1976) and of Deng Xiaoping (in power from 1978 until 1993, then no longer able to participate in the decision-making process due to health reasons [he died in 1997]) can largely be explained by the charismatic authority traditionally enjoyed by the Chinese Emperor. Both of these modern-day leaders generally steered the country from behind the scenes without having to depend on the support of any official bodies or formalized procedures. Xi Jinping's rapid assumption as the dominant party leader between 2012 and 2016 can also be attributed to this historical pattern of autocratic personal rule.

Nevertheless, disruptions in the development of steady patterns of political order and in the establishment of fundamental institutions are just as important as historical continuities. Such breaks were particularly obvious in connection with the socialist transformation of society during the Maoist period. The comparison provided in Table 1.1.C conveys the relationship between historical and socialist patterns and notions of political order in the PRC. The table reveals that a number of traditional patterns continue to exist in present-day China, whereas others have either been transformed by new patterns or have been completely abandoned.

Both traditional and socialist notions of order and organizational patterns have faced pressures since 1978-79 as a result of the economic and social upheavals precipitated by the government's reform and opening policy. The sweeping transformation of social life and the rapidly increasing influence of international patterns of economic organization and of Western models of a consumer society have created a difficult situation whereby the population is torn between traditional family values, collective socialist values, and individualistic values of a market-driven economy. Since the first decade of the twenty-first century, China's cultural and political histories have been attracting a growing amount of interest and have had a significant impact on cultural policy. Imperial China has now been rediscovered and revamped as an attractive and patriotic area of interest to provide a wealth of material for novels, movies, and video games. China's political leadership has put a great deal

Table 1.1.C

Notions of political order and organizational patterns:
Continuities and novel approaches (selected examples)

Basic patterns of the traditional order (late imperial era)	Novel approaches during the Maoist period (1949-76)	Novel approaches during the reform era (1978/79–present)
Social harmony and preservation of the traditional order.	Complete revision of the traditional order, with the aim of creating a "new man" through class struggle.	Reforms to gradually adapt to present-day requirements; borrowing of select elements from Chinese tradition.
People are not equal and they have different roles to play in society.	A vision of social equality (excluding "class ennemies").	Commitment to grant citizens equality before the law.
Absence of individual rights vis-à-vis state rights.	(Continuity.)	Administrative law to grant certain rights of defense against the state.
Moralistic political rhetoric; ritualized politics.	(Continuity.)	(Continuity.)
Absolute dominance of the emperor (personal rule).	One-party rule, under the de facto unlimited personal authority of Mao Zedong.	One-party rule; primarily collective leadership, currently under the strong personal authority of President Xi Jinping.
A centralized unitary state.	(Continuity.)	(Continuity.)
Policies are implemented by means of a bureaucratic hierarchy.	Policies are implemented via large-scale campaigns; bureaucratic institutions imitate the Soviet model; during the "Cultural Revolution" many bureaucratic entities are temporarily dismantled.	Policies are implemented by a fragmented bureaucracy; the introduction of an "entrepreneurial state," particularly at local levels.
The state ends at the county level; everything below the county level is self-governing.	A drastically enhanced state capacity down to the village level.	Partial erosion of the state's control capacity; efforts at using information technology to enhance mass surveillance.
Restrictions on private enterprise.	Suppression of private enterprise.	Broad expansion of private enterprise.
Suppression of heretical religious movements.	(Continuity.)	(Continuity.)
Political influence of high-ranking military officers only during periods of war.	High-ranking military officers play a key role in the CCP leadership.	The domestic role of high-ranking military officers is limited; military modernization.
Restrictions on international exchanges.	Isolationism from the capitalist world, and, beginning in 1960, from "Soviet revisionism."	Controlled opening to allow for commercial exchanges and international cooperation; economic and diplomatic engagement become increasingly global.

Based on Heilmann 2002.

© MERICS

of energy into channeling the population's interest in Confucian traditions to legitimate its current dominance and to propagate those values and notions of order that it deems politically desirable. The great pride in national traditions felt by many Chinese citizens today has been fostered by the cultural sector and the media for both commercial and political reasons.

Thus, since 1978–79 China's historical legacy has been combined with its socialist institutions and its market-oriented modernization to create a unique blend of interdependent factors that have shaped the political culture of the PRC. theses that simplify issues, such as Jenner's "tyranny of history" (1992), the "renaissance" of cultural traditions, the dominance of elements of Marxist ideology, or the "Great Leap" in the direction of Western capitalism, are unable to account for the many factors that currently influence both political and social development in China.

1.2 How China is portrayed in Western media

Kristin Shi-Kupfer

The varied, and at times contradictory, dynamics of China's national development present specific challenges for foreign journalists. Personnel resources allocated for media coverage of China vary greatly, depending on the institutional and economic capacities of the respective media institutions and corporations. According to information provided by the Chinese Ministry of Foreign Affairs, in January 2015 320 foreign media institutions were accredited in the PRC, stationing in China some 700 journalists from 50 different countries.

Foreigners who work in China and who also write their own blogs are an important source of information with respect to international media coverage of China and have come to represent strong competition for the accredited foreign correspondents. Some bloggers have acquired specialist knowledge of environmental or financial issues, for example, whereas others focus on selecting Chinese-language Internet articles and translating them for international audiences. Foreign bloggers who travel to some of the more remote provinces of China are often able to write about trends that foreign correspondents based in Beijing or Shanghai cannot cover, or at best can only cover sporadically.

Currently, it takes at least one year for the accreditation process to be completed for a foreign journalist to be stationed in China (this procedure takes place under the jurisdiction of the Chinese Ministry of Foreign Affairs). Since 2010, the ministry has threatened not to renew the accreditations of those journalists who are "overly negative" in their China coverage (such as writings on the personal wealth of top-level Chinese officials and their families). In 2012 and 2013, two foreign journalists were forced to leave the country at short notice because the ministry refused to renew their residence permits. In 2014, the China correspondent for the German weekly *Die Zeit* hurriedly left Beijing—escorted by members of the German Embassy—after being repeatedly interrogated by state-security officers regarding anti-government protests in Hong Kong and her Chinese assistant was detained. In December 2015, a French journalist was forced to leave China after questioning comparisons between Islamist violence and unrest among the Uyghur community in Xinjiang.

In the aftermath of the 2008 Olympic Games in Beijing, the Chinese government allowed foreign correspondents easier access to sources and information. Journalists no longer had to apply in advance to state authorities for permission to conduct interviews or to undertake field trips outside their place of residence. However, they were still required to apply for special permission to report from the Tibet Autonomous Region. Local police could also issue special regulations temporarily prohibiting media access to regions affected by unrest or natural disasters.

Nevertheless, access to official information and statements issued by authoritative bodies has improved somewhat due to the holding of regular press conferences and active media work by press officials and press departments of public institutions. Still, with the exception of when they hold formal press conferences, top-level Chinese politicians remain practically unreachable to the foreign media. Even when they are available, only limited questions are permitted and they must be vetted in advance.

According to reports by the Foreign Correspondents' Club of China, since the beginning of this decade state authorities and security forces have been exerting increasing pressures on Chinese sources and on Chinese employees of foreign correspondents. Officially, on the one hand, Chinese employees are only allowed to be recruited from licensed "personnel service corporations for diplomatic missions" (外交人员人事服务公司) and are required to report to these corporations on a regular basis about the activities of their foreign employers. Chinese journalists, on the other hand, are not allowed to work for foreign media, nor are they permitted to share any work-related information.

Allegations by government departments of one-sided, "negative," or "biased," media coverage of China are commonly made against foreign correspondents reporting on Chinese affairs. Foreign company representatives working in China and selected academic studies also point to the fact that external media coverage of China is mainly critical or imbalanced, focusing on the negative aspects of Chinese developments and failing to emphasize the more positive progress. Media coverage of China thus has a polarizing effect. Those who advocate more "positive coverage" argue that by increasing intercultural understanding, more favorable reporting helps to support and expand existing exchanges and to promote international trade and scientific cooperation. However, opponents point out that a central function of journalism, not only in democratic systems but also in China, is its remit to be critical of the regime and to expose problems so as to facilitate the formation of public and political opinions. At the same time, there are a number of media representatives who find it problematic that reports about China by foreign correspondents only focus on "conflicts, crises, and catastrophes" (Hanitzsch et al. 2011).

Indeed, a strongly "anti-Communist" stance is observed by Li and Lee (2013) in a study of how the anniversary of June Fourth—the date of the violent repression of the student-led protest movement in 1989—was covered by *The New York Times* and *The Washington Post*. These authors claim that the key U.S. media continued to be influenced by the "victory of capitalism and democracy" paradigm. In addition to ideological and political axioms, Western media coverage of China is also shaped by a one-sided definition of "Western modernism." According to Cao Qing (2012), only if China adopts core elements of modernism based on the "Western model" (i.e., markets, technology, and social insurance) will it be judged favorably by the Western media. As long as it openly rejects and violates the core principles and role models of "Western modernism" (democracy, rule of law, freedom of speech, and freedom of the press), China will remain an anomaly and a source of provocation (see Figure 1.2).

Figure 1.2

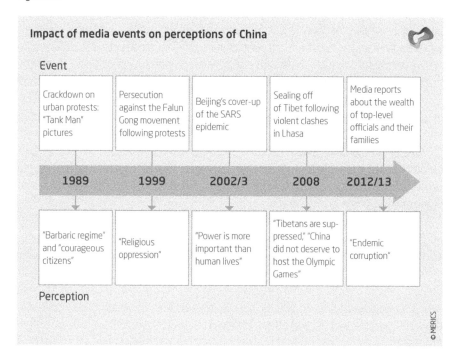

Impact of media events on perceptions of China

Event

| Crackdown on urban protests: "Tank Man" pictures | Persecution against the Falun Gong movement following protests | Beijing's cover-up of the SARS epidemic | Sealing off of Tibet following violent clashes in Lhasa | Media reports about the wealth of top-level officials and their families |

| 1989 | 1999 | 2002/3 | 2008 | 2012/13 |

| "Barbaric regime" and "courageous citizens" | "Religious oppression" | "Power is more important than human lives" | "Tibetans are suppressed," "China did not deserve to host the Olympic Games" | "Endemic corruption" |

Perception

© MERICS

1.3 Why China challenges popular assumptions

Matthias Stepan and Sebastian Heilmann

Perhaps more than any other country, the PRC presents social scientists with considerable challenges in attempting to identify universal laws—in other words, causal relationships that can be observed to a similar extent in the most varied of political or economic contexts, regardless of the specific regional or situational factors. Developments in China after the reform-and-opening policies were introduced in the early 1980s have often taken a course quite different from that expected by outside observers. For this reason, China represents a particularly significant "atypical case" and thus is a rewarding subject of research in comparative politics. In order to demonstrate the type of analytical challenges faced by those studying China, we have selected six common hypotheses about political systems and political change that are contested by developments in China:

Hypothesis 1: "A market economy and an authoritarian political regime cannot coexist on a sustainable basis. Economic openness and structural reforms inevitably lead to political reforms."

This hypothesis is supported in particular by research on political-regime change and democratic transition. The collapse of the Central and Eastern European systems that began at the end of the 1980s provides empirical evidence to support the assumption of interdependence between the political and economic orders: within a mere few years, the planned economies under authoritarian regimes were transformed into democratic market economies. In other words, the shifts in the political and economic systems were simultaneous. Many researchers had predicted a similar dual transformation of China's party-state as well (Pei Minxin 1994, 2006). Contrary to this assumption, however, despite the market-economy reforms and the opening up to global markets, there have been no profound political or institutional reforms in China (see Chapters 2 and 4).

Hypothesis 2: "A growing middle class is the driving force behind democratic change."

The growth of a middle class (with its increasing income/wealth, higher levels of education, better access to information, vested interests in legal security, and growing political participation) is considered by scholars of democracy to be a decisive indicator and a significant driving force behind the democratization of nation-states

(Huntington 1993). However, despite the vast increase in income, the improved levels of education, and the increased experience of traveling and studying abroad, members of China's urban middle class have thus far been more vocal in their focus on income and consumerism than in any calls for a political voice (see Chapter 5).

Hypothesis 3: "Growing income gaps and increasing inequalities lead to destabilization and ultimately to the collapse of authoritarian regimes."

An increase in social inequalities with regard to income and wealth has been identified as a key factor behind a weakening and breakdown of authoritarian political systems (Przeworski et al. 2000). In the late 1990s, the key conventional indicators of income and wealth inequalities in China had already exceeded the critical levels that typically lead to the onset of social destabilization, which is marked by widespread violent crime and recurrent social unrest. The predicted consequences of such social inequalities in China have not yet materialized and they appear to have had less of a destabilizing influence than they have had in other societies (Whyte 2010; see Chapter 5).

Hypothesis 4: "Central states that are organized hierarchically cannot respond flexibly to new challenges in national or international contexts."

The more heterogeneous the natural environment, economic structure, and living conditions are within a country, the more difficult it is to govern it centrally with uniform national laws. Based on this insight, researchers focusing on decentralization and federalism have concluded that it is beneficial to decentralize as many state functions as possible—not only to cater to the differing regional requirements, but also to enable a higher level of diversity and flexibility in the government system. However, according to the Chinese Constitution, the PRC is a centralized unitary state. The CCP is a hierarchically structured Leninist party, with strong central control. In spite of such centralism, the Chinese government system has demonstrated a remarkable capacity to adapt and to be creative in the face of extremely far-reaching and rapid economic, social, technological, and international developments (see Chapters 6 and 7).

Hypothesis 5: "Leninist party-states are not capable of learning and adapting."

Based on the experience from the collapse of the Leninist one-party states in Eastern Europe in the late 1980s and early 1990s, the ability of such parties to learn and adapt has been disputed by both researchers and the media. In recent decades, however, the CCP has proven to be surprisingly creative and adaptable in a number of highly complex policies: from the constant need to adapt in the wake of global-ization and the growth of international trade to the requirements for administrative reorganization as a consequence of the rapid urbanization and to the fostering and regulating of information technologies. However, structural adjustments—in the sense of establishing a system of checks and balances or widespread opportunities for the general public to have a say in politics—have not been implemented (see Chapters 2 and 3).

Hypothesis 6: "Chinese cultural tradition does not nurture individual creativity or technological innovation."

Moving beyond stereotypical and static arguments ("China's culture is shaped by a mixture of authoritarianism and collectivism and will never change"), one well-es-tablished direction in the field of China studies points to how traditional Confucian notions of order essentially validate hierarchical social and political structures: the individual is pigeonholed and subordinated regarding her roles, status, and behavior by prescribed constraints. China's education system has never fostered creativity and critical thinking—instead it favors acquisition of knowledge by repetition (rote learning of facts that can be regurgitated for standardized tests) and obedience to the party-state. Since the 1990s, the state's cultural and education policies have been actively promoting those cultural traditions (especially Confucianism and le-galism) that seem likely to legitimize the leadership of the Communist Party (Bell 2008). Only traditions that are supportive of the state and that are compatible with the current system of rule are trusted by the political leaders.

The numerous "minor traditions" with a religious content (Buddhism, Daoism, and Christianity) or even individualistic and anarchistic tendencies (Daoism and, in particular, the Stratagems) (see Senger 2002) either go beyond the boundaries of a "state-friendly" doctrine or stay below the radar screen. Popular traditions continue to have a striking effect on people's values and behavior as well as on their everyday language. They provide a strong driving force for autonomous, evasive, or atypical behavior and individual creativity, which are manifested in influential social groups. For example, China's private research companies and service-providers are among the most vigorous, least risk-averse, and creative worldwide innovators in the fields of information technology, communications science, and biotechnology.

There are entire groups and subcultures within China's urban society that are attempting to escape from official constraints with regard to order and assimila-tion by cultivating individual lifestyles, values, and religious activities. The "minor traditions" of evasion and self-assertion in the face of state and economic restric-tions remain unbroken in Chinese society and in the private economy; their chance of survival depends on their being able to avoid the radar of the state authorities at all cost. Therefore, individual creativity and autonomous lifestyles in the context of politics in China today are unlikely to be facilitated by open, noisy protests, but rather by clever evasiveness (see Chapter 5).

Outlook

The above conundrums and challenges provide a recurring point of reference throughout this volume. The correlations and interpretations need to accommodate an exceedingly dynamic and as yet open-ended transition process in a vast and extremely diverse country. Statistical and deterministic approaches are of limited use in such a rapidly changing and often contradictory context. Therefore, this book primarily utilizes terminology and explanatory concepts that are conducive to the specific dynamics in the PRC and modifies them where required, without losing sight of comparative perspectives and universally applicable observations.

1.4 Utilizing information and data from China

Sebastian Heilmann, Mikko Huotari, and Sandra Heep

Anyone intending to seriously study Chinese politics, economy, and society will confront numerous challenges. Understanding the paradigms of historical development, and in particular the idiosyncrasies of the language, is a major hurdle. In order to be able to analyze the PRC political system in proper detail, it is imperative to use Chinese-language sources and academic literature. The internal rules and transformation of the main political organization, the CCP, are impossible to comprehend without a thorough reading of party documents, which are often difficult to access, and without regular, face-to-face discussions. At the same time, the field of China studies must avoid a narrow perspective by adopting the Chinese internal perspective—a phenomenon referred to as the "Sinological trap"—and instead it must apply general concepts, methods, and theories of comparative politics or other systematic disciplines to the Chinese situation.

The variety of sources and academic literature written within China or about China has increased significantly since the start of the new millennium. Data and statistics with respect to many aspects of Chinese politics, economics, and society have generally become more readily accessible. The Internet has drastically increased the number of sources available worldwide and has come to play a key role as a research tool (important Internet sites are included in the reference list at the end of this volume). It is also considerably easier nowadays to obtain information—at least on topics that are not directly regarded as politically sensitive—through direct exchanges with Chinese officials, researchers, and citizens.

The analyses in this book are based on an extensive range of sources and academic literature, including:

- Chinese-language newspapers, journals, and documents studied systematically over many years.
- The results of regular field trips to various political centers and provinces of China that included personal background briefings and discussions with political insiders.
- Chinese-language contributions on the Internet, with a special focus on the plurality of values and controversial discussions in social media.
- International media coverage of China, the range and quality of which have improved considerably since the end of the 1990s.
- Studies containing valuable "insider" knowledge, as presented by Chinese social scientists. Although Chinese researchers cannot conduct independent research on politically sensitive topics (such as intra-party conflicts and decision-making, or on issues related to the broadly defined concept of "state security"), they are able to produce valuable, independent research studies in areas that are less politically charged (for instance, on economic, social, and technological policies).
- Results from some of the vibrant China studies programs on offer in the West, which benefit greatly from contributions by Chinese researchers who have been trained or have worked abroad.

However, there are still serious doubts about the reliability of official economic and social statistics on China (see Section 4.2). Average national indicators are not always representative due to the considerable regional variations. China's homogeneity is clearly a statistical invention and conceals the drastic differences among the various parts of the country (see Section 2.5, Section 4.9, Section 5.3, and Section 5.4).

In addition, statistics are still regarded by Chinese government departments as a central-level tool to control information, not only within China but also with respect to foreign governments and investors. The Chinese leadership systematically suppresses and manipulates information, especially in times of crisis. Politically sensitive data (for instance, on local debt, social protests, or the number of executions) remain secret or are only selectively accessible. The Communist Party's need to control information and communications is a fundamental problem facing the field of professional China studies. Additionally, Chinese colleagues are often constrained by political campaigns against Western values and influences on the media, research, education, nongovernmental organizations (NGOs), and academic exchanges.

1.5 Analytical approaches to Chinese politics

Mikko Huotari, Matthias Stepan, and Sebastian Heilmann

The fundamentals underpinning an analysis of China's political system are constantly changing. This permanent state of flux means that prevailing concepts and assumptions quickly lose their relevance. Research priorities are shifting and new analytical challenges are constantly arising. In the meantime, the discipline of political science continues to further develop, as do the conceptual and methodological tools employed in the field of China studies. In other words, analytical perspectives for studying political structures and processes in China are caught in the middle between discipline research and "area studies" research focusing on Asia or China.

Simply put, political science strives to identify generalizable laws (causal relationships) and apply universal, as opposed to case-specific or country-specific, concepts, theories, and methods. China studies, in contrast, which is an academic field requiring both language skills and sound knowledge of the country, tends to focus on determining those aspects of Chinese politics that are unique and that have evolved historically, corroborating its findings through field research and a comprehensive understanding of the situational context. The most productive and frequently used analyses of China exploit the links between the social sciences and China studies: methods, models, and theories of comparative politics are applied to China in order to examine similarities and distinctive features of developments in China in comparison with other contexts. At the same time, unexpected developmental interdependencies and particularities in the Chinese context are utilized to test and adapt theories used in the field of comparative politics.

Some of the teleological and normative assumptions of modernization theory and transition research have become obsolete ("from underdevelopment to Western modernity," "from dictatorship to democracy," and so on). Equally problematic are attempts to "indigenize" China studies ("China cannot be understood by applying Western categories of social science") and approaches that from the outset declare that Chinese politics is unique ("China is fundamentally different"). Case studies of specific configurations of actors and volatile political processes in individual policy domains must be systematically combined with analyses of overarching structures and institutions. This necessitates an ongoing questioning and fine-tuning of assumptions, concepts, and models. Simplistic and static dichotomies—for instance, democracy versus dictatorship, market economy versus planned economy—are thus of little use to make sense of the rapidly changing, multifaceted, and often contradictory features and driving forces behind China's contemporary evolution.

The following sections present a brief overview of six frequently used analytical perspectives, each of which make specific core assumptions and place different phenomena at the center of their respective research agendas.

1.5.1 Political culture and legitimacy

The first strand of research examines shifts in the normative foundations of political behavior. Analyses stressing the continuity of the political culture between traditional and modern China interpret political processes in modern-day China in terms of the continued influence of traditional Chinese culture, in particular that of Confucian culture. From this perspective, informal rules (for example, structures of patronage, relationships, and authority) that originated in Peking palace politics during the imperial period continue to have an impact behind the façade of the modern socialist state and in the political interactions between the government and the people. In this light, the continuity of cultural traditions carries greater weight than the CCP transformation of politics and society in recent decades. This approach helps to analyze political symbolism and rituals. Phenomena such as individual leadership styles, the role of the individual in Chinese law, or ritual forms of protest (such as protesters kneeling collectively for hours on end in front of government buildings in 1989) can be explained against the backdrop of Chinese tradition (Pye 1988; Wang Gungwu 2003; Wasserstrom/Perry 1994).

However, there is a problematic tendency for the culturalist approaches to treat Chinese politics in a static, singular, and circular manner. They often ignore the far-reaching political implications of the disintegration of traditional lifestyles, which are part of the broader comprehensive social and economic transformation. The most significant shortcoming of the politico-cultural perspective is that it labels political phenomena as "China-specific." It ignores the fact that phenomena such as the importance of patronage or the failings of the legal system can be observed to a similar extent in a number of other developing countries and political systems.

In contrast, more productive than assumptions about continuity are empirical analyses of the consequences of institutional changes and shifts in values over time. Studies on the adaptability of China's "resilient authoritarian system" (Nathan 2003) explain these changes by means of institutional mechanisms and discursive strategies that promote legitimacy and acceptance (Holbig/Gilley 2010; Schubert 2014). This perspective makes an important contribution to an understanding of the persistence and stability of authoritarian rule through new forms of political consultation, meritocratic elements in the Communist Party's cadre system, and ideological adjustments to emerging policy challenges. However, such approaches often implicitly equate the persistence of authoritarian rule and power (facilitated in some cases by state repression) with legitimacy (based on the consent of the governed).

1.5.2 Political elites and power struggles

This analytical perspective focuses on the regularities and system-wide implications of power and policy struggles among the political elite. Such political confrontations, along with the reorganization of intra-party groups and the formation of new groups, are deemed to be the driving forces behind political change. To a greater or lesser extent, power politics and ideological interests determine which members of the leadership will band together to form loose coalitions or entrenched "factions" if there is prevailing conflict. Disputes within the highest echelons of the party penetrate all the way down to the lowest levels of the party organization and generally lead to the losers being "purged" from the decision-making bodies.

Indeed, since the 1950s such conflicts have repeatedly led to abrupt changes of direction in the development of China's domestic politics. The reason for this rested with Mao Zedong's and Deng Xiaoping's leadership styles that were based on personal authority and informal decision-making processes, thereby preventing the establishment of institutionalized forms of political-conflict management and conflict resolution. Important contributions to this explanatory approach include works by Baum (1994), Fewsmith (2008) and Teiwes (1995), albeit with very different emphases. The strength of this approach lies in explaining—or even predicting—how decision-making processes and confrontations at the seat of power in Beijing are handled during times of major domestic crises (such as in 1989). These rules of political interaction are identified in this volume as an important element in the "crisis mode" of Chinese politics.

Where this perspective fails is that it concentrates on processes within the highest ranks of the leadership. As a result, independent developments at other levels of the political system—at the provincial-government level, within the ranks of the economic bureaucracy, or within society itself—tend to be ignored or underestimated. More recent studies highlight not only intra-party power struggles at the highest echelons of power and procedures within the provinces (Bo Zhiyue 2010) but also at the level of the economic bureaucracy and the financial sector (Shih 2008).

1.5.3 Civil society and bottom-up political change

Supporters of this perspective analyze Chinese politics not from the standpoint of the policy-makers in Beijing but from a "bottom-up" approach. They describe how social actors, groups, or associations are exploiting their newly gained space to maneuver in the economic and social contexts to exert their influence politically. Studies of this kind make a significant contribution to unveiling civic and political commitments outside of the CCP political structure. The results of this research provide empirical evidence showing that—contrary to popular belief abroad—the CCP does not have complete control over society. Self-organization, hidden resistance, and in some cases open protest against state authority are integral parts of political and social life in China. This opens up new avenues for "bottom-up" political change that, beginning in the society, is partly able to escape the control of the CCP.

The emergence of a Chinese "civil society" has been the subject of animated debates since the 1990s (see Section 5.4 and Section 5.5). The influence of a nascent civil society on policy making is illustrated by highlighting different population groups (Heberer 2003; Mertha 2008; Zhou 1996). In the 2000s, researchers examined the role of NGOs, protest movements (O'Brien 2008; O'Brien/Li 2006), and the emergence of a more independent general public that was intermittently encouraged by the rise of interactive digital media (Zheng Yongnian 2008).

The civil-society perspective has a significant amount of explanatory power with respect to political-power shifts, which are not adequately covered by the other analytical models since the latter tend to be oriented toward the elite. However, the shortcoming of this perspective is its tendency to overestimate the level of autonomy enjoyed by social groups in China today. It is important not to underestimate the ongoing significance of party-state control and party-business ties. The Communist Party has devised new methods to integrate private entrepreneurs (Dickson 2003) and foreign NGOs (Ho/Edmonds 2008) into state institutions. At the same time, state monitoring of communications and the public in digital networks has become more effective due to a series of technological innovations introduced after 2010 (see Section 5.6).

1.5.4 Bureaucratic bargaining

This perspective is based on empirical studies that show that bureaucratic rivalries have a significant impact on decision-making. Examples are mainly drawn from the fields of economic and fiscal policy. Below the most senior leadership levels, Chinese politics is characterized by a system of permanent bureaucratic bargaining among various actors within the state bureaucracy. There are intensive formal and informal channels of communications and interdependencies, both between ministries or commissions and between central and provincial authorities, which have a marked influence on the policy-formulation and policy-implementation processes. Taken from the perspective of "fragmented authoritarianism," the interests and interactions of bureaucratic organizations are accorded a crucial role in explaining the course of the Chinese economic reforms. Central contributions to this line of research have been presented by Duckett (2003), Lieberthal and Lampton (1992), Shirk (1993), and Yang Dali (2004).

The strongest explanatory force evolves from the bureaucratic, institutional approach in the field of economic regulation, since state institutional structures and restrictions are of vital importance to the transformation of the socialist state economy. Relationships between the central government and the provincial governments, which are often tense (Chung Jae Ho 2000), can also be explained in a differentiated manner. During phases of routine government activity, this approach makes plausible sense of many of the phenomena observed in Chinese politics. However, this research perspective fails to grasp how political decisions are formed during phases of acute domestic and foreign-policy crises. Examples are the intra-party clashes in 1989 or more recently during the financial crisis of 2007–9 (see the case study in Section 6.6). At such times, Chinese politics lapses into a special "crisis mode," characterized by extensive centralization, personalization, and ideologization of the decision-making process, with bureaucratic, institutionalized processes taking a backseat role.

1.5.5 Organizational learning

This perspective focuses on the ability of the Chinese governmental system to adapt through continuous learning, either from its own experiences or from international experiences. Seen thus, state organizations not only have a decisive influence on the continued development of the political, economic, and social systems in China, but they are also under constant pressures to adapt to the rapidly changing environment. Adjusting successfully to new contextual conditions and solving urgent challenges are the only ways to guarantee the competency and acceptance of the political system and to prevent the government from being outpaced or weakened by new developments (Göbel 2013). Rapid urbanization, the aging population, growing digitalization, and economic globalization are but a few of the fundamental challenges that are currently being confronted.

Whereas the interests of individual actors, of competing organizations, or of norms are at the center of the other approaches, the focus of this perspective is on the technical, bureaucratic processes, including leveraging and expanding state capacities and incorporating new scientific evidence. Technological innovations and IT applications play a central role here. Adjustment processes are typically initiated through experimental programs and pilot projects. In the course of the Chinese reform policies, targeted investigations and assessments of international experiences with different problem-solving methods assumed vital importance, particularly with respect to advancing the opening-up and globalization policies in a monitored, low-risk manner.

In particular, in the area of economic and technology policies, China's governmental system shows traits of a learning organization—it can thus be conceived of as a "learning authoritarian system." Localized, sometimes competing, experiments serve to test and implement new solutions and to facilitate learning within a hierarchical order ("experimentation under hierarchy"). Significant contributions to such an analytical perspective examine this form of learning in economic policy (Heilmann 2008), health (Wang Shaoguang 2009), administrative reforms (Göbel 2016), and rural and social policies (Ahlers 2014b). The weakness of the approach is that its technocratic focus often focuses on the internal views and actions of government bodies rather than on the direct impacts on sectors of the population.

1.5.6 Integrated political and economic analysis

Recent approaches to study the political economy of developments in China are playing a key role in current research in the field of China studies. These require an integrated analysis of the processes of political and economic change because an analytical separation of politics and economics obscures the key drivers behind political behavior, especially in states undergoing transformation. Two different analytical focuses can be identified. The first, starting from a more actor-oriented perspective, analyzes the incentives and constraints that influence political and economic actors and the resultant formal and informal "rules" that affect the interactions among these involved actors. Such approaches make an important contribution to our understanding of how political and economic changes are linked to the distribution of bargaining power and resources among various interest groups. Another strength of this perspective lies in its context-sensitive descriptions of reform incentives and strategies (decentralization, gradualism, and experimentation) as well as their political consequences. In this respect, the adaptation of political systems can be analyzed as an extensive, fiercely contested, and open-ended redistribution of property rights (Heilmann 2000; Naughton 2007; Xu Chenggang 2011).

A second group of approaches seeks to comprehend the complementarities or tensions among institutional regimes and the methods and extent of state intervention in the economic system (Kennedy 2011). Here a core question focuses on how companies, the financial system, and the labor market are coordinated. This research is persuasive in terms of its analyses of various regional forms of state intervention in China's economic system (Peck/Zhang 2013; Walter/Zhang 2012). Associated with this perspective are analyses that describe China as an example of state capitalism (McNally 2013), a regulatory state (Pearson 2011), or a modern developmental state (Breslin 2012). The search for a modern theory of state capitalism is also a reference point for central economic debates in China (Liu He 2014).

1.5.7 Combining analytical perspectives

The previous sections have outlined and described some of the most influential approaches in China studies (see Table 1.5). However, none of these perspectives can

Table 1.5

Analytical perspectives in the study of Chinese politics

Analytical perspective	Object of explanation	Explanatory factors
Political culture and legitimacy	Shifts, stability, and adaptation in the political micro-structures and in the system as a whole; repercussions on public perceptions	Shifts in the construction of norms and values that shape political interactions; legitimation processes and strategies
Political elites and power struggles	Patterns of power struggles and ideological disputes and their effects on policy making	Single actors (individuals) and their networks; personal preferences and tactics; allegiance to differing factions
Civil society and bottom-up political change	Potential influence of social groups on policy making; "bottom-up" democratization	Organizational forms and resources of various social actors (with the state merely providing the context); the role of protests, petitions, and appeals in social media
Bureaucratic bargaining	The impact of particular bureaucratic interests and conflicts on policy making	Conflicts of interest and consensus in negotiations among various groups of actors (organizations) within the state and party organizations
Organizational learning	Processes of adaptation of the Chinese state and the party apparatus to new societal, technological, and security challenges	Development and expansion of the state's capacity to master new challenges; adaptation of internationally tested solutions to suit the Chinese context
Integrated political and economic analysis	Dynamism or stagnation of processes of political/economic change	Incentives and constraints that shape individual and group behavior; interactions of different modes of economic governance; variable forms of state interventions

© MERICS

encompass every aspect relevant to the PRC political system. Although the choice of a specific analytical approach may be helpful for an individual research project, ultimately only a combination of the analytical approaches will do justice to the complexity of studies of Chinese politics. At a minimum, an open-minded attitude is necessary to appreciate and integrate the results from these overlapping and often conflicting research perspectives.

2 The Chinese Communist Party and state institutions

2.1 Socialist organizational and ideological features

Sebastian Heilmann, Lea Shih, and Sandra Heep

The formal organization of political institutions in the People's Republic of China (PRC) corresponds to that of a centralized socialist party dictatorship. Political rule is based on a cadre party—the Chinese Communist Party (CCP)—that is organized along the lines of Leninist principles and that possesses comprehensive powers in terms of decision-making and the ability to interfere in all aspects of political, administrative, economic, and social issues.

The key elements of the constitutional and governmental order of the PRC—dictatorship under the leadership of the CCP and a concentration of power rather than a division of power with respect to the executive, legislative, and judiciary functions—are based on the model of the former Soviet Union and Soviet influence. Although the formal structure of its institutions overlap to a certain extent with the Soviet model, in many ways the Chinese variant of the socialist system differs in terms of its organization and ideology.

2.1.1 Leninist organizational principles

The political and economic reordering of China after 1949 was modeled after the Soviet party-state. The Chinese Communists adopted the organizational principles of a cadre party and its leadership role in politics, society, and the economy from Lenin (1870–1924), the founder of the Communist party-state in the former Soviet Union. The party was conceived of as a centralized hierarchical organization for political mobilization and control. With its structure of party committees and party cells, it was intended to serve as the absolute decision-making and supervisory power in all sectors of the socialist system (government, the judiciary, industry, and public associations).

To this day, the personnel and organizational structures of the CCP form the main pillars of the ruling system in the PRC. Leading party cadres are situated at all key control points in the political system. With the aid of party committees and political commissars, who play a key role in the security bodies, the CCP holds a particularly tight grip over the police and the armed forces.

The following is a list of China's primary political-control institutions, which, in essence, can be traced back to Lenin:

- a centralized hierarchy of party bodies with supervisory responsibility over policy making, administration, the police, the judiciary, the military, the economy, and society;
- a CCP monopoly in matters regarding recruiting, deploying, and supervising leading personnel (the "cadre system") not only in party, government, and administrative bodies, but generally also in government-related economic enterprises and in state-controlled and state-financed organizations;
- an internal party discipline commission outside of the state judiciary that operates in accordance with political instructions and grants party cadres (as long as they have not been expelled from the party) de facto immunity from investigations by state judiciary bodies;
- ideological indoctrination and campaigns to discipline party members, to combat political "deviance" within the party, and to strictly forbid the formation of inner-party groups (i.e., a ban on factions);
- propaganda—party-guided, selective dissemination of information and active molding of public opinion—with the aid of traditional channels as with the new digital media, both of which are politically controlled;
- party-guided "mass organizations" (trade union, youth, and women's associations) acting as "transmission belts" for CCP policy.

Nevertheless, the features of the socialist system that were adopted from the Soviet model should not mask the numerous differences that arose from Chinese organizational and ideological innovations (see Table 2.1.A and Table 2.1.B).

Well into the 1990s, "units" (*danwei*) were considered one of the most important Chinese social-control features. Each citizen was assigned a basic unit at work, at home, or in the place where he or she was receiving training, and within this unit he or she was effectively monitored, supplied with essential goods and services, and, if necessary, disciplined. Because the entire urban population was generally included in this system, only a relatively small secret police apparatus was necessary to secure CCP rule. Mobility within China has increased since the 1990s, with the result that social control through the geographically fixed *danwei* system is no longer effective. Since then, the political leadership has intensified its expansion of the police and state-security organs and has stepped up installation of modern

Table 2.1.A

The Chinese variant of socialism: Basic organizational features

Organization and personnel controls under CCP rule	
Adopted from the Soviet model:	*Innovations from the Soviet model:*
• The Communist Party as the "advance guard" of the revolution and the working class • Party claims of absolute leadership and control • Parallel hierarchies of party and state organizations • The principle of "democratic centralism" • The *nomenklatura* system of cadre control • A strict ban on factions • Mass organizations acting as "transmission belts" for the Communist Party	• Concentration of power in the Politburo Standing Committee • Continued predominance of party bodies over government organs in decision-making processes* • The unchanged strong position of the Communist Party political commissars in the military* • A notably downsized party apparatus • A highly decentralized economic administration • Prior to the 1990s, primary social control in "basic units"; since the 1990s rapid expansion of police organs

Note: *In the Soviet system of the post-Stalin era, the role of party bodies was weakened in relation to that of the ministries, and the role of political commissars was diminished in relation to that of professional army commanders. See Gill 1994.
Based on Heilmann 2002.

© MERICS

surveillance technologies (including inner-city camera systems and equipment to monitor digital communications) (see Section 5.6).

The Chinese system of political leadership differs from the Soviet model in several important respects. For example, executive power is concentrated in the very small Politburo Standing Committee, which has consisted of from five to nine members (presently there are seven) who serve as the central decision-making body. The PRC also differs from the former Soviet Union in that its party committees wield more weight over government bodies in terms of decision-making processes. This has been increasingly the case since 2012. In addition, the size of the full-time party apparatus has been reduced since the 1980s and it now focuses primarily on political and organizational surveillance activities, particularly those affecting the cadre system and personnel policy, disciplinary surveillance and combatting corruption, media oversight and propaganda, as well as internal security and the secret services. Regular administrative and policy implementation has been transferred to state bodies.

The decentralization of economic administration as practiced in China since the 1950s seems to have had particularly far-reaching consequences to differentiate it from the former Soviet Union. In China's decentralized institutional environment, economic-reform experiments are more easily carried out than they were in the highly centralized planning system of the USSR. With the aid of a large number of regional economic-policy experiments, such as the special economic zones (SEZs) and the urban pilot projects, China has succeeded in phasing in market elements (see Chapter 4 for more details).

2.1.2 Ideology and legitimation in transition

After the Russian October Revolution of 1917, Marxism-Leninism spread primarily first among intellectual circles. The CCP referred to this "imported" ideology at its First National Party Congress, held in Shanghai in 1921. It propagated ideas of Marxism-Leninism combined with endeavors to achieve national liberation from the influence of the colonial powers and accompanied by a desire to achieve national modernization. Through interpretation and adaptation to Chinese circumstances, the ideology was gradually modified, resulting in its "Sinicization" (中国化) (see Table 2.1.B). Due to the special circumstances in China, such adaptations were inevitable because the Chinese Communists, unlike their Soviet counterparts, had had to struggle for almost three decades before achieving the victory of their revolution. Over the course of this time, in contrast to the situation in the Soviet mother party, the Chinese Communists found support primarily among farmers, and from the villages they were able to take over the cities. Their special skills consisted of mobilizing impoverished farmers for political ends that addressed the direct interests of a large proportion of the rural population: land reform, expropriation of the land of large landowners, and resistance to the Japanese occupation (Selden 1995).

The unique revolutionary experiences of the Chinese Communists appear in Mao Zedong's writings, which differ in major respects from the Marxist and Leninist ideologies. Beginning in 1945, Mao's writings were canonized by the CCP as "Mao Zedong Thought" (毛泽东思想) (Martin 1982). This is revealed, for example, by a downgrading of the working class in favor of the farmers and by an emphasis on revolutionary guerrilla warfare. From the Soviet perspective, the significance of the "mass line" in the revolutionary and ruling strategies (in which the party and the army guerrillas were regarded as "fish swimming in the sea of the people" [Mao Zedong 1937]) was also unorthodox.

In addition, Mao Zedong was a proponent of the concept of radical class conflict based on the assumption that even after a socialist state is established, "class enemies" will continue to exist in their long-term resistance through covert sabotage and they will attempt to undermine the revolution. During the 1960s, Mao went

Table 2.1.B

The Chinese variant of socialism: Fundamental ideological features

Sino-Marxism under CCP rule	
Adopted from the Soviet model:	*Deviations from the Soviet model:*
• Absorbing the fundamental ideological principles and terminology of Marxism-Leninism • Socialization of private property, industry, trade and commerce, and agriculture • Justifying extreme sanctions against political opponents ("enemies of the people," "counterrevolutionaries") • "Anti-imperialism" in international relations • The goal of achieving a conflict-free Communist society	*(I) Early phase (1921–50s):* • "Mao-Zedong Thought" elevated in 1945 to accompany Marxism-Leninism as the leading ideology; "Sinicization" of Marxism-Leninism • Emphasis on the rural foundation of the revolution; placing the role of the working class in perspective • Emphasis on revolutionary guerrilla warfare, including decentralized initiatives ("guerrilla policy style") • The "mass line": party-guided mass mobilization as a method to enforce policies *(II) Radical phase (1957–78):* • Temporary dismantling of judicial and bureaucratic organizations that are branded as "reactionary organs" • Radicalization of class conflict • Personality cult surrounding Mao Zedong • Criticism of Soviet "revisionism" and "hegemonism" *(III) Reform era (beginning in 1978):* • In contrast to Soviet "de-Stalinization," the absence of "de-Maoization": Mao's political accomplishments are officially assessed as "70 percent good." • Gradual ideological adaptations: lowering the importance of class conflict; "primary stage of socialism"; acceptance of market coordination and nonpublic forms of ownership • Maintaining Marxist-Maoist dialectics to define the "principal contradiction" and to determine the priorities for action accordingly

Based on Heilmann 2002.

© MERICS

so far as to suspect that "class enemies" had infiltrated the party, and he called on the people to expose "capitalist roaders within the party." As a result, such appeals during the Great Proletarian Cultural Revolution (1966–76) not only led to arbitrary political persecutions, but at times they also resulted in paralysis and the collapse of the party apparatus—developments that completely contradicted the Leninist principles that upheld the inviolable leadership role and unity of the party.

In the aftermath of the upheavals of the Cultural Revolution and the death of Mao Zedong in 1976, there were calls in the party and among the people for an ideological reorientation to serve as the foundation for the program of the "Four Modernizations," in agriculture, industry, national defense, and science and technology. The importance of class conflict was downgraded.

Under the leadership of Deng Xiaoping, the focal point of party work shifted to the socialist modernization of the economy and to the consolidation of party and state organizations. The "advance of Marxism-Leninism" in light of the requirements of China's economic modernization moved to the center of ideological debates. Together with Marxism-Leninism and "Mao Zedong Thought," "Deng Xiaoping Theory" was elevated to become one of the key components of CCP ideology.

Today, the CCP officially represents "socialism with Chinese characteristics" (中国特色社会主义), or "Sino-Marxism" (Senger 1994), not only distancing itself from the Soviet model but also seeking to reassess classical Marxism in terms of its significance for China's modernization. In 1987, and then again in 1997, the CCP National Party Congress determined that China was still at the "primary stage of socialism" (社会主义初级阶段) and that the transition to a developed socialist system was only possible after China reached the developmental level of an industrial country by the middle of the twenty-first century. The primary goals established by Deng Xiaoping were to develop the productive forces and to raise the people's standard of living: "Poverty is not socialism. To uphold socialism ... it is imperative first and foremost to eliminate poverty" (Deng Xiaoping 1987). In order to modernize the Chinese economy, reformers felt that capitalist market-economy methods were necessary. However, the values on which these methods are based, such as individualism and pluralist interests, were never acceptable to the CCP leadership because such "Western bourgeois" values and concepts are not compatible with either Chinese tradition or Marxist-Leninist ideology.

Marxist and Sino-Marxist ideological elements continue to heavily influence policy making and the CCP's justification for its rule. For example, social and sociopolitical priority shifts since 2003—particularly the program to build a "new socialist countryside" (社会主义新农村建设)—are justified by reference to Marxist solidarity standards that are bolstered by the guiding principles both of the traditional (the "harmonious society") (和谐社会) and the technocratic (the "scientific outlook on development") (科学发展观).

However, the CCP adapted to the new economic conditions by making ideological modifications during the course of the reforms that included the abandonment of a number of essential ideological principles. For example, the 16th National Communist Party Congress (November 2002), which upgraded private enterprise, private property, and private capital, effectively abandoned key elements of the Marxist-Leninist ideology, such as the abolition of private property, the elimination of private entrepreneurs and private capital, and opposition to the capitalist class. These ideological revisions have been sharply criticized on the Internet by orthodox Marxists both inside and outside the CCP (Heilmann, Schulte-Kulkmann, and Shih 2004).

Since 2002, the CCP has referred to itself in its party constitution as the vanguard not only of the Chinese working class but of all the people, i.e., the entire nation. The formula of the "Three Represents" (三个代表), which maintains that the CCP should represent the advanced social productive forces, advanced culture, and the fundamental interests of the overwhelming majority, was added to the party constitution as an additional "guide to action" (行动指南). In addition, the party constitution cites the realization of communism as the ultimate goal of the CCP. However, the immediate task is to "comprehensively build a moderately prosperous society" (小康社会). By the year 2020, China's gross domestic product (GDP) is expected to have quadrupled from that in the year 2000. At the same time, social inequalities, regional disparities, and structural distortions in the economy and society are expected to have been curbed.

The 17th National Communist Party Congress in October 2007 placed a stronger emphasis on social and environmental policy and on a search for modern bases of legitimacy. The guiding formulas (提法), propagated by CCP General Secretary and PRC President Hu Jintao, of the "scientific outlook on development" and a "harmonious society" were incorporated into the revised party constitution. The concept of a "scientific outlook on development," calling for economically, socially, and ecologically balanced and sustainable modernization, had already served as a guideline for the creation of the 11th Five-Year Plan (2006–2010). The concept of a "harmonious society," which harkens back to Confucian concepts of order, seeks to eliminate conflicts and to establish a social balance based on law, social and educational policy, and respect for people and nature.

An important special feature of Sino-Marxism is that the leadership and the analytical methodology are flexible and explicitly adaptable over time, rather than involving static and closed dogmatism (see Table 2.1.C). Officials must become familiar with the "position, perspective, and method of Marxism" (马克思主义立场观点方法), and then use this information in a manner that is appropriate to the situation at hand to analyze and solve practical problems. Officially, the "Marxist position" refers to the side of "the majority of the working people" and the "developing countries." The nature of the "Marxist perspective" must be strictly historical-materialistic and must focus on collective socioeconomic development rather than individual and

Table 2.1.C

Sino-Marxist methodology and its effects in political practice

Method	Analysis	Examples in Practice
Contradiction analysis.	Identifying and processing principal and secondary contradictions in stages.	Defining the focus of work; concentration of resources.
Contradiction synthesis.	Identifying a productive, politically advantageous coexistence (a temporary nonsolution) of contradictions.	"One country, two systems" (as in Hong Kong); "selectively utilizing what is foreign for China," "selectively utilizing Chinese traditions for modern-day China."
Class analysis.	Identifying dependency, exploitative, and oppressive relations within and among societies.	Rejecting foreign influence or "hegemonism;" rejecting "Western bourgeois" values.
Testing theory in practice.	Theory must be tested and developed in practice. Practical knowledge is more reliable than theoretical debates.	Experimental policy development in pilot projects and special zones; implementing policies "from point to surface."
Adopting foreign experiences.	Focused analysis and the use of experiences of others (including political opponents) as points of reference.	Instrumental learning of administration, technology, education, etc. from abroad; sending students and researchers overseas.

Based on Senger 1994, 2008.

© MERICS

specific interests or metaphysical and religious inclinations. The "Marxist method" addresses dialectics and teachings on contradictions, specifically defining and processing the "principal contradiction" (主要矛盾) that changes over the course of time and that determines the CCP "work focus" (工作重点) during each historical developmental phase (see Table 2.1.D).

Under the changed conditions of the twenty-first century, in addition to its economic and sociopolitical programs, nationalism plays a vital role in the self-legitimation of the CCP. In order to win political support, the party presents itself as the guardian of China's national sovereignty and dignity. "Patriotic education" is of key importance in the media and in education. In this respect, the political leadership has been taking advantage of the interest, among large sectors of the population,

Table 2.1.D

Definitions of the "principal contradiction" and the CCP "work focus"

Developmental stage	Principal contradiction	Work focus
1921–37	Proletariat/working class vs. exploiting/oppressor classes.	Class struggle directed against the capitalists and imperialists.
1937–45	China vs. Japan.	Struggle against Japan during the United Front.
1945–78	Proletariat/working classes vs. exploiting/oppressor classes.	Class struggle against the capitalists and imperialists.
From 1978	Material and cultural needs of the people vs. economic backwardness.	Economic, technological, and cultural modernization as a national task.

Based on Senger 1994, 2008.

© MERICS

in Chinese history and tradition, which has been growing since the end of the 1990s (Billioud 2007).

After Xi Jinping assumed power, the party's strategy of legitimation began to stress a reliance on nationalism. For example, immediately after his appointment as general secretary of the CCP in November 2012, Xi coined the guiding principle of the "China Dream" (中国梦), which he describes as "the great rejuvenation of the Chinese nation" (中华民族伟大复兴), whereby the party accomplishes its mission of liberating the Chinese people from poverty and oppression and once again transforms the country into a "wealthy and powerful nation." The "two centenary goals" (两个一百年奋斗目标) are the core elements of the "China Dream," as propagated by Xi Jinping (see Table 2.1.E).

Unlike the American dream, the China dream does not involve personal self-fulfillment. Instead, it emphasizes the strength of the nation as a prerequisite for collective welfare and individual happiness.

The CCP leadership under General Secretary Xi Jinping has far more aggressively than its predecessors rejected adoption of politically organized Western values and principles. Demands for constitutional democracy, human rights, and an independent civil society have been suppressed as attempts to undermine the party-state. Accordingly, in a document circulated in April 2013, the Central Committee

Table 2.1.E

The "two centenary goals"

By 2021 (the 100th anniversary of the founding of the CCP)	Comprehensive completion of a moderately prosperous society (全面建成小康社会)
By 2049 (the 100th anniversary of the founding of the PRC)	Completion of a prosperous and powerful, democratic, culturally highly advanced, harmonious, socialist, modernized state (建成富强、民主、文明、和谐的社会主义现代化国家)

© MERICS

(CC) of the CCP called on all party members to increase their vigilance regarding any ideological deviance from the party line (CCP CC General Office 2013a). At the same time, the party leadership silenced the growing number of critical voices, either by warning them or by arresting political activists, and subjecting traditional as well as digital media to heightened censorship.

By the end of 2014, Xi Jinping had formulated the priorities of party and government work that will be open to adaptation under his leadership—the so-called "Four Comprehensives" (四个全面): comprehensively completing construction of a moderately prosperous society (全面建成小康社会); comprehensively deepening reforms (全面深化改革); comprehensively governing the country according to law (全面依法治); and comprehensively strictly governing the party (全面从严治党).

Xi Jinping considered strictly governing the party to be a prerequisite for achieving the other goals. Hence, beginning in 2013 the party leadership embarked on an extensive anti-corruption campaign, which was explicitly directed against leading party cadres and their patronage networks (see Section 4.8). In addition, a "mass line" campaign was intended to heighten cadre awareness of the people's needs. For this purpose, cadres were required to spend more time engaging in exchanges with the people and taking part in repeated "self-criticisms" during group meetings. Large sectors of the population approved of the party leadership's efforts to combat graft. Since 2008 there have been repeated attempts by the CCP to anchor a canon of "core socialist principles" among the population (社会主义核心价值观)—literally, "core socialist values"). But these efforts have proved to be conspicuously short-lived and ineffective. Such officially propagated "values" appeared to be too remote from the reality of the lives of most Chinese (see Table 2.1.F); from the perspective of the people, the official party ideology no longer had any connection to everyday life.

Table 2.1.F

"Core socialist values," as propagated by the CCP	
Values and goals at the national and state levels (国家层面的价值目标).	Prosperity and power (富强), democracy (民主), cultural development (文明), and harmony (和谐).
Values and orientations at the societal level (社会层面的价值取向).	Freedom (自由), equality (平等), justice (公正), and rule by law (法治).
Values and norms on the level of individual citizens (公民个人层面的价值准则).	Patriotism (爱国), professional dedication (敬业), honesty (诚信), and friendliness (友善).

Based on CCP CC General Office 2013b.

© MERICS

Despite the dissemination of economic and commercial values in society and officialdom, fundamental elements of Sino-Marxism within the CCP continue to exhibit a practical efficiency as methods of analysis, communications, mobilization, and discipline. Western research and reporting on China have tended to underestimate or ignore these roles of ideology in China today. Nevertheless, under the pressures of the centrally guided party campaigns during Xi Jinping's first several years as general secretary, the political functions of Sino-Marxist ideology were re-emphasized to support the authority of the party center.

2.2 The constitution of the party-state

Sebastian Heilmann and Moritz Rudolf

The political order of the PRC was conceived of as an executive instrument of the party rather than as a constitutional state characterized by independent rules, accountabilities, restrictions of power, and controls. Key elements of the state institutions set forth in China's first constitution in 1954 adhered to the Soviet model, particularly the constitution of the Soviet Union of 1936 that had been enacted under Stalin. To this day, the following features remain the basic principles of the constitutional system of the PRC: the leading political role of the CCP; the comprehensive powers of the central government to intervene with respect to the regional leadership; a concentration of power (and hence an explicit rejection of political limitations on power among the executive, legislative, and judicial branches); and subordination of individual rights to collective interests.

2.2.1 A short constitutional history

From 1949 to 1954, the PRC was governed on the basis of the "Common Program" of the Chinese People's Political Consultative Conference (CPPCC), which incorporated a broad cooperative "United Front" of non-Communist forces. But when the First National People's Congress (NPC) convened in September 1954, the Common Program was cast aside and replaced by the first PRC Constitution.

Four constitutions have been enacted since the PRC was founded (in 1954, 1975, 1978, and 1982), each of which reflect the changing political objectives of the CCP. Whereas the constitutions of 1975 and 1978 highlighted the importance of class struggle, the present constitution of 1982 (of which key elements were modified in 1988, 1993, 1999, and 2004) is indicative of efforts to achieve socialist modernization of the economy and stabilization of state institutions.

In 1999, for the first time in the text of the PRC Constitution, the constitution explicitly states that the constitution "is the fundamental law of the state and has supreme legal authority." In addition, no organization shall be allowed to overstep the bounds set by the constitution and the laws. However, this stipulation contradicts the leading role of the CCP in the government, the economy, and society, as specified in the preamble to the constitution.

2.2.2 Key principles in the constitution

The constitution of 1982 is subdivided into a preamble and four chapters. The detailed preamble first assesses the "revolutionary struggle" of the "Chinese masses" in history, as seen from the perspective of the CCP. In addition, it formulates programmatic and political principles, which in 1993 and 1999 were amended to be in accord with the political lines of the time. Article 18 in the seventh paragraph of the preamble to the constitution was amended in 2004 to:

> "China will be in the primary stage of socialism for a long time to come. The basic task of the nation is to concentrate its effort on socialist modernization along the road of Chinese-style socialism. Under the leadership of the Communist Party of China and the guidance of Marxism-Leninism, Mao Zedong Thought, Deng Xiaoping Theory and the important thought of the Three 'Represents,' the Chinese people of all nationalities will

continue to adhere to the people's democratic dictatorship and the socialist road, persevere in reform and opening to the outside world, steadily improve socialist institutions,
develop the socialist market economy, develop socialist democracy, improve the socialist legal system and ... to build China into a socialist country that is prosperous, powerful,
democratic and culturally advanced."

In Chapter I, the "General Principles," it goes on to state:

"The People's Republic of China is a socialist state under the people's democratic dictatorship led by the working class and based on the alliance of workers and peasants. ...
Disruption of the socialist system by any organization or individual is prohibited" (Art. 1).
"All power in the People's Republic of China belongs to the people. The NPC and the local
people's congresses at various levels are the organs through which the people exercise
state power" (Art. 2).
"State organs of the People's Republic of China apply the principle of democratic centralism. ... All administrative, judicial and procuratorial organs of the State are created
by the people's congresses to which they are responsible and by which they are supervised" (Art. 3).
"All nationalities in the People's Republic of China are equal" (Art. 4).
"The People's Republic of China governs the country according to law and makes it a
socialist country under rule of law. ... No organization or individual is privileged to be
beyond the Constitution or other laws" (Art. 5).
"The State maintains public order and suppresses treasonable and other criminal activities that endanger State security; it penalizes criminal activities that endanger public
security and disrupt the socialist economy as well as other criminal activities; and it
punishes and reforms criminals" (Art. 28).

Key statements on "the fundamental rights and duties of citizens" can be found in
Chapter II:

"All citizens of the People's Republic of China are equal before the law" (Art. 33).
"Citizens of the People's Republic of China enjoy freedom of speech, of the press, of
assembly, of association, of procession, and of demonstration" (Art. 35).
"Citizens of the People's Republic of China enjoy freedom of religious belief" (Art. 36).
"The personal dignity of citizens of the People's Republic of China is inviolable" (Art. 38).
"Citizens of the People's Republic of China, in exercising their freedoms and rights, may
not infringe upon the interests of the State, of society or of the collective. ..." (Art. 51).

Finally, Chapter III contains details about the state structure. Compared to the provisions in the Mao-era constitution, these provisions are very detailed. They reflect
the party's interest since the end of the 1970s in consolidating the government ap-

paratus, which was severely weakened between 1966 and 1976 during the Cultural Revolution. (The most important state organs, responsibilities, and formal rules listed in the constitution are presented in detail in Sections 2.3 to Section 2.12 below.) At this point, an outline of several general distinctive features of the state bodies and procedures will suffice.

The *NPC* (Art. 57ff.), the legislative body, is indirectly elected every five years and is formally the "highest organ of state power." It convenes once a year for a plenary session. Due to its sheer size (there are almost 3,000 delegates), it is not an effective legislative body. The plenary session of the NPC is responsible, among other things, for revisions to the constitution (with approval by a two-thirds majority), for preparing and amending basic laws (by a simple majority), for election/removal of the president, and confirmation/removal of the most important members of other state bodies (including the supreme judicial organs), for examination and confirmation of the national budget, and for decision-making on war and peace (Arts. 62–64). According to the constitution, candidates for high-ranking government offices are elected by the NPC or by its Standing Committee. However, in reality the candidates are already selected and appointed—but not publicly—prior to the congress by the CCP organs.

With only 161 members (as of the First Plenary Session of the Twelfth National People's Congress, March 2013), the *Standing Committee of the NPC* (Arts. 65–78) serves as an "ersatz" parliament of the NPC. It convenes once every two months. The Standing Committee of the NPC enacts most laws and interprets the constitution and the laws (a separate committee was established to interpret the Basic Law of the Hong Kong Special Administrative Region [SAR]). When meetings of the NPC Standing Committee are not in session, it supervises the work of the state bodies, confirms the appointments of key members of the government, and makes decisions on ratifying international treaties and agreements and on declarations of war. Members of the Standing Committee of the NPC are not allowed to hold any office in other state bodies.

The *Chairman of the PRC,* referred to simply as "the President" (Arts. 79–84), who is allowed to serve a maximum of two five-year terms, engages in "affairs of state," which remain unspecified in the constitution. Since the 1990s, the office has effectively served diplomatic purposes and foreign-policy profiling of the CCP general secretary, who appears internationally not in his party role but rather as China's state president.

The *State Council,* that is, the Chinese central government, is defined in the constitution as the "executive body" of the NPC and as the "highest organ of state administration" (Art. 85). The *Premier,* or the head of the State Council, exercises a broad range of powers. His term of office is limited to two five-year periods.

The *Central Military Commission* (CMC), which is dealt with only briefly in the constitution (Arts. 93–94), "directs the Armed Forces of the country" (see Section 2.12).

The *local people's congresses and people's governments at all levels* (Arts. 95–111), i.e., the local organs of state power, have roles at their specific administrative levels that essentially correspond to those of the NPC at the national level. Only the delegates to the people's congresses at the county and township levels are elected directly. Standing committees are established from the county level and upward. The characteristic of the PRC as a unified state is clearly formulated in the constitution: local people's governments at all levels "are responsible and accountable to the state administrative organs at the next higher level, and they are state administrative organs" under the unified leadership of the State Council (Art. 110). The State Council can annul "inappropriate decisions" by local organs of state administration (Art. 89).

People's courts and people's procuratorates perform their duties "independently, in accordance with the provisions of law, not subject to interference by any administrative organ, public organization, or individual" (Arts. 126 and 131). At the same time, the judicial organs are accountable to the people's congresses, which in turn are responsible for appointing the leading judges and procuratorates (Arts. 128 and 133) (see Section 2.11).

Chapter IV of the constitution, citing Beijing as the capital city of the PRC, deals with state symbols and the national anthem. The national flag is red (symbolizing the revolution), with a large yellow star (symbolizing the CCP) surrounded in a semi-circle by four smaller yellow stars. Today, these four smaller stars are regarded as symbols of "the Chinese people." However, at the time of the establishment of the PRC in 1949, they represented the social forces that combined to form the "New Democracy": peasants, workers, the petty bourgeoisie, and the "patriotic capitalists." The national emblem of the PRC features the following against a red background: in the middle, Tiananmen, i.e., the gate of Heavenly Peace (because Mao Zedong proclaimed the founding of the PRC from Tiananmen, the Gate symbolizes the "invincible spirit of the Chinese people in the battle against imperialism and feudalism"), illuminated by the light of five stars (the party and the people), encircled by a wreath of ears of grain (a symbol of the peasantry), and below the ears of grain a cogwheel (a symbol of the working class). The national anthem of the PRC is the "March of the Volunteers," composed in 1935, which represents the determination of the Chinese people in their "struggle for liberation" from domestic and foreign oppression. These national symbols have carried the revolutionary symbolism of the early PRC into the twenty-first century.

2.2.3 Constitutional revisions

According to the constitution of the PRC, the NPC as the legislative body has authority to revise the constitution. In practice, initiatives and concrete suggestions for constitutional revisions originate with the top leadership of the CCP. To the present, the NPC has always approved such suggestions (but not without occasional votes of abstention or rejection). Constitutional revisions reflect changes in the political orientation of the party. The course of the economic reforms initiated by the Chinese leadership since 1978 is reflected in the text of the 1982 constitution as well as in its 1988, 1993, 1999, and 2004 revisions.

In 2004, the growing economic and social significance of private entrepreneurs made it necessary that the protection of their rights be included in the constitution. Following controversial prior discussions, the term the "Three Represents" (三个 代表), coined by former PRC president and CCP general secretary Jiang Zemin, was added to the preamble of the 2004 constitution. According to this concept, the CCP represents (1) the advanced social productive forces, (2) the progressive course of China's advanced culture, and (3) the fundamental interests of the majority. The CCP now encompasses all those contributing to the building of socialism, including private entrepreneurs. This is indicative of the transition of the CCP's self-image from a revolutionary-class party to a popular party with a claim to lead the modernization of the entire nation.

Protection of the private economy and of private property was significantly upgraded by explicit acknowledgment of support for the nonpublic economy, which was also included in the 2004 constitutional revisions. Under the constitutional amendment to Art. 11, the state now encourages and supports the private economy. The revision extends the scope of protection to the entirety of lawful private property and for the first time also includes protection of ownership of private enterprises and income from private investments. Additionally, claims to defense against expropriation by the state have been expanded. In Art. 13, persons whose property has been expropriated by the state are entitled to compensation. Additional revisions include political programs for building a social-security system (Art. 14) and for protecting human rights (Art. 33). The legal relevance of these constitutional revisions remain generally low, however, since there are no courts (such as a constitutional court) capable of taking legal actions to secure these constitutionally guaranteed rights (Schulte-Kulkmann, Shih, and Heilmann 2004).

2.2.4 The Communist Party as sovereign of the state

The system of political institutions that exists in the PRC has not been fundamentally affected by any of the constitutional revisions that until now have been enacted. The constitution of the PRC remains primarily a political document. There are insurmountable political barriers for any comprehensive structural changes: the power of the CCP and its cadres, which relies on the absence of a division of power and on virtually unlimited intervention, persists in spite of the rapid economic and social changes.

De facto, the CCP stands above the constitution and the people: the party, and not the people, is the sovereign of the state. Thus, in practice, the state constitution has limited impact regarding the formation of political will, conflict resolution, and decision-making.

2.3 The Chinese Communist Party

Sebastian Heilmann and Lea Shih

The paramount importance of the CCP in the PRC political system should already be apparent. The following sections analyze the party organization in more detail, focusing on the links between the party and the state as well as the CCP's power bases in the changing economic and social environments.

2.3.1 Party organization and party membership

In terms of its membership, the CCP is the largest political party in the world. By the end of 2014, the number of members totaled 87.79 million, that is, about 6.4 percent of the entire population (see Table 2.3.A for 2005–13 membership data). However, the steady increase in the number of members does not necessarily mean that all new party members are dedicated Marxists or disciplined Communists. Rather, the myriad of benefits from party membership, such as easier access to the public sector and state-owned enterprises (SOEs), preferential promotions, and inclusion in elite political networks, are significant motives for joining the CCP.

The CCP's organizational structure is highly homogeneous throughout the country. The central level has an organizational structure that is almost identical to that at the regional and local levels. At all levels, the Party Congresses (党的代表大会) are the supreme elected assembly, which must vote on the personnel composition of the Party Committees and the Discipline Inspection Commissions once every five years. The Party Committees then carry out the day-to-day business until the next Party Congress. A CCP grassroots organization can be established when three or more party members meet in one organization or at one location. At the end of 2014, there were about 4.36 million CCP grassroots organizations in rural townships and villages, in urban residential areas, and in government entities, SOEs, and other organizations. Such grassroots organizations also existed in 53 percent of all private companies.

Table 2.3.A

Membership structure of the CCP, 2005–13

	2005	2007	2009	2011	2013
Total no. of CCP members (million)	70.80	74.15	77.99	82.60	86.69
Applications for membership (million)	17.67	19.51	20.16	21.60	21.66
Female members (%)	19.2	20.4	21.7	23.3	24.3
Ethnic minority members (%)	6.4	6.5	6.6	6.7	6.9
Members younger than 35 years old (%)	23.3	23.3	23.7	25.0	25.8
Members with academic degrees (%)	29.0	32.4	35.7	38.6	41.6
Cadres in party and state organs (%)	No data available	7.5	8.5	8.5	8.4
Cadres in companies and service organizations (%)	No data available	No data available	No data available	No data available	11.6
Skilled workers, technicians (%)	No data available	No data available	No data available	No data available	5.8
Blue-collar workers and farmers (%)	43.7	41.5	39.7	38.6	38.1
Increase in membership compared to the previous year (%)	1.7	2.4	2.7	2.9	1.8
CCP members as a proportion of the total population (%)	5.4	5.6	5.8	6.1	6.3

Based on personnel statistics published by the CCP CC Organization Department; Heilmann 2002. © MERICS

The *Communist Youth League* (CYL) (共产主义青年团) plays an important role in raising the profile of prospective leading party cadres and acting as a springboard for their careers. In the course of CCP history, several CYL members who subsequently became Politburo members used their positions at the top of the CYL CC during the early stages of their careers to establish a network of friends and followers and to create veritable cliques as they climbed the party hierarchy. One prominent example is the network of former general secretary and president of the PRC, Hu Jintao (2002–12). Despite the relatively large number of registered CYL members (88.2 million at the end of 2014), the CYL leadership still complains about its passive grassroots organizations. In many villages, bureaucracies, enterprises, and schools, the CYL is unable to mobilize its members to participate in regular activities. Many young Chinese between the ages of 14 and 28 join the CYL only because they, or their parents, consider membership to be an advantage for their future career prospects.

At the same time, the CYL supervises the Young Pioneers (少年先锋队), a youth organization that reported a membership of 140 million in 2010. The Young Pioneers, children between the ages of 6 and 14, are primarily active in schools offering opportunities to participate in extracurricular group activities.

2.3.2 Party congresses and ballots

The *National Communist Party Congress* (中共全国代表大会) takes place once every five years and is a major political event: revisions of ideological principles, realignments of the national development strategy, and the composition of the CC, the Central Commission for Discipline Inspection (CCDI), and the CMC are all decided by this body (see Figure 2.3.A). The high-ranking leaders of the CCP carefully prepare in advance all of the proposals to be presented to the National Communist Party Congress for discussion and voting. Months of exploratory talks, consultations, and internal discussions dominate the run-up to each National Communist Party Congress, which takes place over the course of about one week.

The *CCP CC* (中共中央委员会), which is formally elected by the National Communist Party Congress, generally meets once or twice a year for a plenary session (全体会议). It is the central administrative and decision-making body of leading party, state, and military officials. Approval by the CCP CC is required for decisions about appointments to leading CCP positions as well as decisions on fundamental policy questions, ranging from constitutional changes to changes in economic development strategy. Organs of the CCP Center and central-government bodies are represented on the CCP CC by their respective heads. The provinces, the municipalities under the direct administration of the central government, and the autonomous regions are represented by their party secretaries and governors or mayors, while the military is represented by high-ranking officers and political commissars.

The 2012 CCP CC, which will remain in power until the next National Communist Party Congress to be held in 2017, consists of 205 full members and 171 alternate members (i.e., nonvoting members). More than one-half of the 2012 full members

Figure 2.3.A

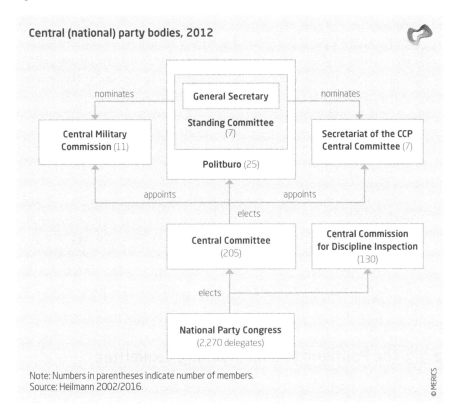

Central (national) party bodies, 2012

Note: Numbers in parentheses indicate number of members.
Source: Heilmann 2002/2016.

© MERICS

were newly appointed at the 18th National Communist Party Congress held in November 2012. The average age of members of the 18th CCP CC is 56.1. The People's Liberation Army (PLA) is represented by 40 officers, constituting about one-fifth of the total number of full members of the CCP CC. In addition, the CC also includes 25 senior managers of major SOEs who, as an economic interest group, wield considerable influence in Chinese politics.

In contrast to representatives of the state economy, not a single representative from a private company was elected to the 18th CCP CC, although the number of private entrepreneurs among the National Communist Party Congress delegates has increased since 2002; 28 private entrepreneurs participated in the 2012 National Communist Party Congress, including (for the very first time) a Chinese employee of a foreign company (a subsidiary of Siemens in Shanghai).

The National Communist Party Congress also elects the members of the *CCDI* (中央纪律检查委员会), which has a special status at party headquarters (as well as at lower levels of the party hierarchy). The CCDI is responsible for supervision of leading cadres in both party and government departments. In 1993 the commission was merged with the Ministry of Supervision to consolidate within a single organization supervision of both CCP cadres and cadres who do not belong to the CCP. The CCDI has repeatedly served as an extra-judicial body in spectacular corruption cases and has often led investigations into local corruption by sending delegations of high-ranking teams of investigators to SOEs or local governments. The commission is not only entitled to suspend the party membership of leading cadres (which means an end to their political careers and the loss of their jobs), but it can also make decisions about whether to pass the results of its investigations on to the judiciary, a step tantamount to beginning criminal proceedings against the suspects (see Section 4.8 for details regarding the extent of corruption in China and attempts to control it).

To the present, the military has been under the control of the *CMC* (中央军委), which holds a prominent position in the arrangement of political power and on which the party and military leaderships are equally represented. Its chairman is always the "top man" in the CCP: initially Mao Zedong, followed by Deng Xiaoping, then Jiang Zemin, Hu Jintao, and now Xi Jinping since 2012. Under the National Defense Law, the loyalty of the military is first and foremost to the party rather than to the constitution or the central government.

2.3.3 The Politburo and its Standing Committee

The highest decision-making and leadership bodies of the CCP are the *Politburo* (政治局), with 25 members since 2007) and the *Politburo Standing Committee* (常务委员会), which was reduced from nine members in 2007 to seven members in 2012) (see Table 2.3.B). The composition of the Politburo is settled by lengthy advance negotiations within the party leadership, and the names are then submitted for approval to the CCP CC (at its first plenary session immediately following the meeting of the National Communist Party Congress).

Twelve of the twenty-five Politburo members elected at the 18th National Communist Party Congress held concurrent posts as party secretaries or heads of government at the provincial levels. The PLA is represented by two generals. The remaining members held posts at party headquarters or in the State Council (central government). An unusual feature of the 2012 Politburo is that twelve of the members are either social-science or humanities graduates, thereby relaxing the previous conspicuous dominance of technocrats (understood in the Chinese context to be engineering or science graduates) (see Section 3.2).

The *Politburo Standing Committee* (政治局常务委员会) represents the leading body of the CCP and is composed of the highest-ranking, active party leaders in Beijing. At the head of the Standing Committee is the CCP general secretary, who

Table 2.3.B

National Communist Party Congresses and leading CCP bodies

Year	National Congress	Full members of the CCP CC	Full members of the Politburo	Members of the Politburo Standing Committee
1921	1st	–	3	–
1922	2nd	5*	–	–
1923	3rd	8*	3	–
1925	4th	10*	5	–
1927	5th	33	8	5
1928	6th	23	10	4–6
1945	7th	44	13	5
1956	8th	95	17	6
1969	9th	170	21	5
1973	10th	195	21	10
1977	11th	201	23	8
1982	12th	210	25	5
1987	13th	175	17	5
1992	14th	189	20	7
1997	15th	193	22	7
2002	16th	198	24	9
2007	17th	204	25	9
2012	18th	205	25	7

Note: * Called the Central Executive Committee at the time.

© MERICS

concurrently holds the office of president of the PRC and chairman of the CMC. In addition, the Standing Committee also includes the premier, the NPC chairman, the CPPCC chairman, and the head of the CCDI (see Chapter 3 on the political leadership).

The *CCP CC Secretariat* (中央书记处) prepares Politburo sessions and decisions, and supervises implementation of party resolutions. Key departments of the CCP Center are represented on the CCP CC Secretariat to ensure policy coordination among the various areas of responsibility. The CCP CC Secretariat is headed by a member of the Politburo Standing Committee rather than by the CCP general secretary: since November 2012, this position has been held by Liu Yunshan, who previously headed the CCP CC's Propaganda Department (2002–12). After Xi Jinping assumed office in the fall of 2012, the CCP CC Secretariat was expanded to include seven members. The head of the State Council General Office, who plays a key role in coordinating government activities, was also elected to the CCP CC Secretariat. Such overlapping tenures are designed to ensure tighter links between the CCP and the government.

2.3.4 Central working organs and Leading Small Groups

The organizational structure and functions of the CCP headquarters have been increasingly institutionalized since the 1990s. The internal organization and responsibilities are set out in organizational plans (Zou Ximing 1998) (see Table 2.3.C). Within the party system, there are official distinctions among the following:

- *working organs* (办事机构), which include the general offices of the party committees as well as the Departments of Organization, Propaganda, and United Front Work at the various levels of the party hierarchy, and
- *Central Leading Small Groups and commissions* (领导小组 or 委员会), which perform routine and ad hoc coordination as well as decision-making in specific policy areas.

Many of the working organs and leading party bodies that are responsible for specific overlapping areas (conventionally known as *kou* [口]), i.e., broad, inter-ministerial policy areas, such as financial and economic affairs, internal security and justice, ideology, and propaganda) are found at a reduced scale in the regional and municipal party systems. These party bodies generally consist of one member of the Politburo Standing Committee and relevant officials from the state, administrative, and judicial organs. As these bodies are responsible for producing guidelines and providing coordination in important policy areas, they wield considerable influence within the government system (see Chapter 3 for further details about this leadership system).

The *General Office* of the *CCP CC* (中央办公厅) is the lynchpin of ongoing activities at party headquarters. The responsibilities of the General Office include preparing for meetings, distributing and storing CCP CC documents, preparing information for leading party cadres, and providing personal security. The General Office also makes budget allocations for the various organs at party headquarters. Regional party committees send information and make requests to the party leadership via the CCP CC's General Office.

Table 2.3.C

The internal structure at the party center, 2014

Working organs of the CCP CC	Central commissions	Central Leading Small Groups
• General Office • Organization Department • Propaganda Department • International Liaison Department • United Front Work Department • Policy Research Office • Central Security Bureau (under the General Office)	• National Security • Political and Legal Affairs • Central Institutional Organization	• Comprehensively Deepening Reforms • Foreign Affairs Work • Finance and Economy • Cyber Security and Informatization • Party Building • Propaganda and Ideology • Rural Work • Taiwan Work

Organizations directly under the CCP CC (selected examples)

- Central Party School, and cadre institutes in Pudong (Shanghai), Yan'an, and Jinggangshan
- Publications (including the newspapers *Renmin ribao* [People's Daily] and *Guangming Daily*, and the journal *Qiushi* [Seeking Truth])
- Research institutes (including the Party History Research Center and the Documents Research Office)

Organizations supervised directly by party headquarters (selected examples)

- Communist Youth League (CYL)
- All-China Federation of Trade Unions (ACFTU)
- All-China Women's Federation (ACWF)
- All-China Federation of Literary and Art Circles (ACFLAC)
- China Association for Science and Technology (CAST)
- All-China Journalists Association
- State Administration of Radio, Film and Television (SARFT)
- All-China Federation of Industry and Commerce (ACFIC)

Based on Heilmann 2008.

© MERICS

Departments of the party center

The *Organization Department of the CCP CC* (中共中央组织部, or for short: 中组部) is responsible for cadre and organizational policy. It maintains personnel files for leading officials and cadre reserves at the central level, presents the Politburo with lists of potential candidates for leadership positions, develops proposals for procedural reforms within the party with regard to staffing and organization, and establishes binding measures for cadre training. The Organization Department is among the most sensitive bodies at the party center and therefore also the least willing to release information.

Training programs for high- and middle-ranking cadres at the various organizational levels of the CCP take place at the party schools. The *Central Party School* (中央党校) in Beijing has become a key forum for discussions of fundamental questions about domestic and foreign affairs as well as a think-tank for administrative reforms. Its courses, which are regularly attended by central and regional party cadres, provide an opportunity for cadres to meet one another. In 2005, the Central Party School established three subsidiaries ("cadre institutes"): one in the Pudong national experimentation zone (in Shanghai) and two in regions that are historically significant to the CCP, namely, Jinggangshan (in Jiangxi province) and Yan'an (in Shaanxi province). By taking courses offered at the party schools, chances for cadres to access the networks of the political leadership are improved.

The *Propaganda Department of the CCP CC*, also referred to as the "Publicity Department" (中共中央宣传部, or for short: 中宣部), is responsible for the CCP's propaganda work and information policy as well as for media regulation. The state media and publishing houses are bound by directives issued by the Propaganda Department, which also has personnel responsibility for managers in the media sector (see Section 5.6). The director of the Propaganda Department generally is also a member of the *Central Leading Small Group for Propaganda and Ideology* (中央宣传思想工作领导小组), which is headed by a member of the Politburo Standing Committee and comprises representatives of the key actors in the propaganda and media sectors. One aspect of propaganda work that is rapidly growing in significance is the monitoring of interactive digital media, which comes under the remit of the *Central Leading Group for Cyber Security and Informatization* (中央网络安全和信息化领导小组).

The *International Liaison Department of the CCP CC*, also known as the "International Department" (中共中央对外联络部, or for short: 中联部), is responsible for collaboration and dialogue with foreign political organizations. Prior to the 1980s, due to ideological reasons such collaborations were limited to dialogues with Communist or socialist parties. However, its links have since been expanded to include a wide range of foreign political parties, including socialists, social democrats, and conservative Christian parties. In particular, its relations with parties that have been involved in forming governments in key countries, or are likely to be so involved in the future, have been expanded. Staff are routinely rotated between the International Liaison Department and the Ministry of Foreign Affairs. If there are tensions or breakdowns in communications with regard to official diplomatic relations (as there were with Japan and Vietnam in 2013–14 on account of the intermittent territorial disputes), diplomats in the CCP's International Liaison Department are still able to maintain informal dialogues at the party level. Since the 1990s, the International

Liaison Department has repeatedly played a particularly active, semi-diplomatic role in relations with North Korea and Vietnam. In essence, the International Liaison Department is an important player in China's unofficial diplomacy.

The United Front Work Department of the CCP CC (中共中央统一战线工作部, or for short: 统战部) is responsible for maintaining contacts with the non-Communist forces that are required to collaborate closely with the CCP (especially China's "democratic" parties; ethnic minorities and religious groups; entrepreneurs and the All-China Federation of Industry and Commerce; and cooperating forces in Hong Kong, Macau, and Taiwan, including overseas Chinese). However, the United Front Work Department does not wield the same political influence as the other central departments.

Commissions at the party center

The *Central National Security Commission,* also referred to as the "National Security Council" (CNSC) (中央国家安全委员会), was established in November 2013 and is currently one of the largest commissions at the party center. It consolidates all the relevant security institutions, including the PLA, under the leadership of the CCP general secretary, with the objective of improving coordination and the exchange of information. The CNSC is responsible for the following: (1) planning and implementing internal and external national security strategies (including combating terrorism, separatism, and extremism, as well as cyber and data security); (2) refining the legal basis for state security; and (3) analyzing the principal security challenges. The CNSC serves as the party leadership's highest advisory and coordinating body for all security-related matters.

The *Political and Legal Affairs Commission* (政法委员会) exists as a permanent body not only at party headquarters but also at the provincial, city, and county levels. This commission is responsible for overseeing the police and the judiciary (see Section 2.11). The *Commission for Comprehensive Governance of Social Management* (社会管理综合治理委员会) is responsible for maintaining social stability and for taking preventative measures to counter social tensions and unrest; usually it is almost identical to the Political and Legal Affairs Commission in terms of its leadership and personnel.

The *Central Institutional Organization Commission* (also known as the "State Commission Office for Public Sector Reform," SCOPSR) (中央机构编制委员会, or for short: 中编委) is responsible for organizational planning and administrative reform at the various party and government levels. This commission defines position charts and clarifies the responsibilities of party and state bodies. It has become increasingly important due to the frequency of extensive reorganizations of government (generally every five years with the formation of a new government).

Central Leading Small Groups at the party center

The *Central Foreign Affairs Work Leading Small Group* (中央外事工作领导小组) and the *Central Taiwan Work Leading Small Group* (中央对台工作领导小组) are inter-ministerial coordination and decision-making bodies at party headquarters. Headed by the CCP general secretary since 1993, these Central Leading Small Groups are key players in Chinese foreign and Taiwan policy.

The *Central Finance and Economy Leading Small Group* (CFELSG) (中央财经领导小组) is responsible for developing guidelines for economic planning and economic-structural reforms, drawing on the expertise of a large number of government bodies and research institutes. The group is headed by the premier or by the CCP general secretary if the latter wishes to have a direct influence on economic policy. Due to its direct access to the highest levels of the CCP leadership, the high-ranking General Office of the CFELSG (understatedly referred to simply as "the Office" (中央财经领导小组办公室, or for short: 中财办) is currently one of the most influential advisory offices as well as the most important body for the direct preparation of decisions relating to China's economic policy.

The *Central Leading Small Group for Rural Work* (中央农村工作领导小组) is responsible for rural economic and social policy. Consisting of a small research and advisory team, it is occasionally supplemented by external officials and experts called in to formulate specific policy proposals. Between 2003 and 2005, this advisory team provided a significant stimulus to rural economic, fiscal, and health reforms as part of the program to build a "new socialist countryside."

In 2013 CCP General Secretary Xi Jinping established a new central Leading Small Group at the party center: the *Central Leading Small Group for Comprehensively Deepening Reforms* (中央全面深化改革领导小组). The group was set up specifically to implement the institutional and economic-restructuring program that had been approved by the CCP CC in November 2013 and is due to be completed by 2020. With a total of forty-three members from all relevant government departments, in 2015 this central Leading Small Group was the largest coordinating body at party headquarters (see also Section 3.4).

2.3.5 Overlap between party and state bodies

In Communist government systems, the party and the state are often almost indistinguishable from one another and, without exception, the CCP appoints personnel for leadership positions in both government and administrative bodies (see Figure 2.3.B). Moreover, decisions made by government bodies must follow those guidelines established by the parallel party committees or by the party groups (党组) established within the government bodies.

Figure 2.3.B

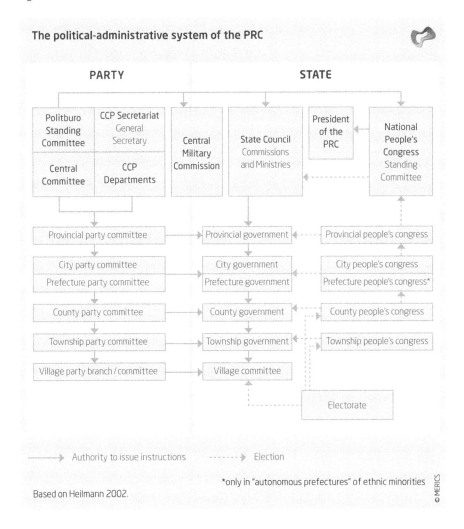

The political-administrative system of the PRC

To provide economic administration with more room for maneuver, and thereby to promote flexibility with regard to economic policy, in the mid-1980s Deng Xiaoping championed the separation of party and state (党政分开), and most economic powers were transferred from party bodies to government departments. However, although there were still Central Leading Small Groups on economic policy within the CCP, bodies mirroring the state's economic administration no longer existed. Party bodies with economic responsibilities focused on long-term economic planning, inter-ministerial coordination, and supervision of policy implementation. Political control of economic administration and SOEs remained fundamentally intact by virtue of the fact that the heads of the government authorities and the leading managers of the SOEs were concurrently the members of the party committees, and thus they could be appointed or removed from office within the framework of the CCP cadre system.

When it comes to controversial issues or matters of principle, party committees continue to enjoy a right to veto and authority to issue directives to the administration. Strategic areas, such as the cadre system, the judiciary and the security forces, and the military chain of command, are still under the direct control of party bodies. Organizational power at higher levels of the CCP is repeatedly demonstrated by systematic reorganizations and staff rotations, not only in regional governments but also in SOEs and military units.

2.3.6 Organizational decline and reform efforts

The powerful façades presented by official party institutions are unable to hide the porous foundations on which the cohesion of the CCP is built. The party center has dramatically admitted the CCP's weaknesses on a number of occasions: corruption, clique-building, and a lack of ideological orientation are common at all levels of the party organization.

These developments were caused and exacerbated by the economic reforms that were introduced by the CCP. Local party officials were expected to achieve high economic growth rates and to produce widespread increases in income levels. To a greater extent, however, they were unable to justify their power by means of the ideology propagated by party headquarters. Because the ideological appeals from party headquarters were no longer linked to purges as they were during the Mao era, they lost their effectiveness. The pursuit of individual interests became an integral part of the market-oriented economic transformation. Party officials found themselves in the middle of a rapid economic upturn. Based on their own initiatives and on measures in their particular areas of responsibility, they often helped promote companies and investments, while simultaneously exploiting the situation to their own benefit and to that of their families and their protégés. Economic reforms and political corruption proceeded hand-in-hand and became two inseparable aspects of the development process.

The 16th National Communist Party Congress in November 2002 permitted private entrepreneurs to join the party. The CCP thereby evolved into a business-friendly organization with a clear mission to stimulate the economy, a development that accompanied the rise of new social groups, even among its members. As a result, the CCP became more heterogeneous internally. The top party leadership thus had to manage a political balancing act between wealthy entrepreneurs (previously persecuted as "class enemies") and poorer segments of the population (the "proletariat" who previously had been privileged by CCP policies).

To avoid social differences becoming a political time bomb, since 1995 the CCP has been experimenting with the expansion of intra-party democracy. At local levels, for instance, limited competition for leading positions is allowed and there is greater scope for political participation by ordinary party members. At the 17th National Communist Party Congress in October 2007, General Secretary Hu Jintao announced that intra-party democracy would be the main focus of the work of the CCP for the next five years.

However, Hu's successor, Xi Jinping, terminated this reform initiative and prohibited expansion of local experiments to higher levels of the CCP. Instead, Xi expanded supervision and governance techniques adopted during the Mao era. In an education campaign extending from 2013 to 2015 and aimed at state and party cadres, Xi attempted to revive the traditions of the "mass line" and "self-criticism" in order to eliminate "formalism, bureaucratization, hedonism, and extravagance" from the minds of party officials. In particular, Xi initiated a vehement anti-corruption campaign that targeted top-level cadres ("tigers") as well as low-ranking functionaries ("flies"). By mid-June 2015, warnings, fines, and demotions had been handed out to almost 200,000 low-ranking party cadres, and by 2014 criminal proceedings had been brought against sixty-eight high-level officials.

It is highly doubtful whether a disciplined, corruption-free, and efficient party organization will successfully emerge as a result of such temporary political campaigns. As long as party officials are not subject to independent controls and they continue to possess far-reaching powers to intervene in administration and the economy, the institutional opportunities for corruption and abuses of power, and their underlying causes, will not be effectively stemmed.

2.3.7 The persistence of Leninist patterns of control

Leninist supervision and control bodies, originating during the period of the Chinese Revolution, may seem anachronistic in the context of modern China. However, they continue to exert a substantial influence over key areas of the political system. In particular, this applies to the supervision of cadres and party personnel (see Section 2.9.1 on the *nomenklatura* system), military policy (see Section 2.12 on the political commissar system), and internal security (see Section 2.11 on party control of the judiciary, police, and state-security bodies). Within the context of the cadre-management system, the Chinese party leadership clings resolutely to its comprehensive powers to appoint and dismiss leading party members. All of the important decision-making processes in the political system are dominated by the leading party bodies: the Politburo, the Central Leading Small Groups, the party committees, and the party groups.

The CCP remains the only organization through which one can obtain political power in China. As of the present, no other elites or organizational groups have emerged either from the economy or the society that can compete with the CCP or challenge its monopoly of power beyond the localities. The CCP has pursued a policy of coopting emerging social groups and associations, with the help of the state-controlled mass organizations (see Section 5.5). But politically undesirable groups are the targets of powerful repression (see Section 5.8). In reality, the CCP has lost control of clan associations, religious groups, and criminal gangs in some rural regions and city districts. However, thus far the political influence of these forces has rarely extended beyond a narrow regional limit. As a result, there are currently no organizations, associations, movements, or social forces on the horizon that might offer an alternative to CCP rule in China.

2.4 The central government

Sebastian Heilmann and Lea Shih

When the PRC was initially established, the state organs were perceived of simply as instruments for enforcing the will of the CCP. As the bureaucratic apparatus expanded, however, they gradually gained political influence in their own right. As a result of administrative consolidation and professionalization efforts, the autonomy and room to maneuver by government bodies increased during the reform period, particularly in the field of economic administration. Due to the centralist and unitary notions of order, which are explained by China's political history and the CCP's need for control, the central government is accorded considerable political weight and is not restricted by federalism or any system of checks and balances. Instead, government influence is only limited when it is confronted by regional special interests or creative drives that relativize its de facto authority.

2.4.1 The State Council and its inner cabinet

The work of the government at the national level is headed by the premier of the State Council (Wen Jiabao was premier from 2003 to 2013, and Li Keqiang has held the post since 2013). Candidates for senior government positions are nominated behind closed doors by the CCP's top leadership, and such appointments are approved by the NPC.

The *State Council Executive Meeting* (国务院常务会议), also known as the State Council Executive Committee, serves as the inner cabinet of the State Council. It convenes once a week and is made up of the ten highest-ranking State Council officials:

- the *Premier*, who directs the State Council and assumes overall responsibility for the work of the government;
- *four Vice-Premiers,* who are in charge of interdisciplinary political tasks: (1) socioeconomic development planning as well as fiscal, environmental, construction, land, and raw materials policies; (2) economic, technology, education, cultural, sport, and family-planning policies; (3) commercial, financial, banking, foreign-exchange, competition, and tourism policies; and (4) industrial, ICT, transportation, intellectual-property, and social-security policies;
- *four State Councilors,* who are responsible for coordinating noneconomic interdisciplinary tasks across ministerial boundaries: (1) national defense and military policy; (2) foreign policy and overseas Chinese policy; (3) police and justice; (4) rural society, disaster management, national minorities and religious policy, and water resources;
- the *Secretary General of the General Office of the State Council,* who has the rank of a state councilor, liaises with the premier and coordinates government work across departments.

The *State Council Plenary Meeting* (国务院全体会议), also known as the Full State Council, functions as the *outer cabinet,* which leads the twenty-five ministerial-level bodies of the State Council (commissions, ministries, the Central Bank, and the National Audit Office [NAO]; see Table 2.4.A). The plenary meeting generally convenes twice a year to discuss important issues related to work organization or the government work report delivered by the premier to the NPC. The plenary meeting is not a working group as such, but it serves as a point of communications for discussions on important issues related to government work.

The varying historical designations, such as "commission" or "ministry," do not indicate any difference in ranking. However, certain State Council organs play particularly prominent roles in government work due to their extensive supervisory and regulatory functions. The following section introduces some of the so-called "super ministries" or "super commissions" as well as important state organs at the ministerial level.

- The National Development and Reform Commission (NDRC) (国家发展改革委员会, or for short: 发改委), the successor to the former State Planning Commission, was given its present name in March 2003. Formally, the NDRC, a ministerial body under the State Council, is responsible for interdisciplinary tasks. In practical terms, however, the NDRC functions as an inter-ministerial planning and coordinating body for the national leadership and it collaborates especially closely with the CFELSG to devise a strategic framework for economic policy as well as to develop the multi-year plans. Traditionally, the director of the General Office of the CFELSG concurrently holds a leadership position in the NDRC.

The NDRC is also in charge of planning and supporting major supra-regional projects (such as developing China's western provinces or the Pearl River Delta region). In addition to its planning remit, the NDRC serves as an ad hoc coordination point for a number of policy areas. This special position is apparent from the wide range of departments within the NDRC mirroring the line ministries (for example, environment, health, and technology) that serve as points of contact and clearing centers for the relevant ministries in order to prepare special action programs for specific departments.

With regard to practical government work, the NDRC has a higher status than other ministries and regularly encroaches upon their departmental competencies. Such interference tends to lead to frequent disputes between the NDRC and individual ministries, and heads of government have repeatedly attempted to curtail the NDRC's interventions. Although its authority was strengthened in 2012 in terms of strategic planning, coordination, and crisis prevention, the NDRC's control over investment-approval processes for most mega-projects was transferred to the provincial governments. In effect, this meant that the NDRC lost some of its strategic influence with respect to economic and investment policy. However, its key tasks remain unchanged: planning, evaluating, and optimizing government programs; securing balanced, sustainable growth; and supervising market competition, income distribution, and pricing.

- *The Ministry of Commerce* (MOFCOM) (商务部) was also established in March 2003 as the result of the merger of the former State Economic and Trade Commission and the former Ministry of Foreign Trade and Economic Cooperation. MOFCOM plays a key role in developing the Chinese domestic market and regulating China's integration into the world economy. Foreign companies looking to make large-scale investments in China cannot bypass MOFCOM. When China's Anti-Monopoly Law entered into force in 2008, MOFCOM was empowered to enforce such anti-trust activities by investigating mergers and takeovers involving foreign investors. After 2013, anti-trust proceedings and sanctions became more significant and resulted in heavy penalties for companies with foreign investors. MOFCOM also cooperates with the NDRC to formulate China's national "investment catalogs." *The Catalog of Industries for Guiding Foreign Investment* (外商投资产业指导目录) was last published in 2015. These catalogs specify the industrial sectors and technology fields in which the government either welcomes foreign investors with open arms (such as the high-tech sector), encourage foreign investments with certain restrictions (e.g., the automobile industry only allows joint ventures with Chinese partners in order to facilitate technology transfers), or do not encourage any foreign investment (e.g., in industries that are sensitive either from a political or a military perspective). MOFCOM and the NDRC thus act as champions of national industry and technology policy. This role has been criticized by many foreign investors for being interventionist and/or protectionist since it limits access to the Chinese market and micro-manages all technology transfers.

- The *State-owned Assets Supervision and Administration Commission* (SASAC) (国务院国有资产监督管理委员会), established in March 2003, is a central supervisory body responsible for managing China's SOEs. As of 2015, SASAC supervised 112 companies under the central government, some of which were listed on the stock exchanges. Many of these companies have monopoly or oligopoly status in "strategic sectors" of the domestic market. The focus of the work of SASAC is to turn these companies into profitable and competitive "national champions" to compete in global markets. As a special organization (特设机构) under the State Council, SASAC enjoys an exceptional status that highlights the particular significance and complexity of state-owned assets supervision due to the conflicts of interest between its dual roles as both owner and regulator. Since the majority of SOEs (approximately 150,000 in 2013) are under the jurisdiction of China's regional governments, bodies responsible for state-owned assets supervision have also been set up at the provincial and municipal levels. These local SASACs play a key role in terms of designing and approving partial privatizations, stock market flotations, and foreign capital investments. After the Ministry of Finance (MOF) began claiming dividend payments from the profits of the SOEs in the 2010s, thus effectively assuming a public ownership role, SASAC was gradually forced to surrender its previous role as a passive shareholder in the SOEs and to concentrate increasingly on restructuring, regulatory, and supervisory tasks in the state sector.

- *The Ministry of Industry and Information Technology* (MIIT) (工业和信息化部), established in 2008, was the result of the merger of the Ministry of Posts and Telecommunications and the Ministry of Electronics Industry as well as the relevant departments in the former State Economic and Trade Commission. MIIT is responsible for technical (rather than content) regulation of the rapidly growing telecommunications, Internet, and software markets, and is one of the key bodies designing sector-specific industrial policy in China.

Key government agencies are also found among organs subordinate to the State Council that appear to have a lower status than the ministries. These include the national customs and fiscal authorities and the State Administration for Industry and Commerce (SAIC) (国家工商行政管理总局). The State Council Legislative Affairs

Table 2.4.A

The central government of the PRC, 2015

Inner cabinet (State Council Executive Meeting)

- Premier
- 4 Vice-Premiers
- 5 State Councilors (including the Secretary General of the State Council)

Outer cabinet (25 ministerial-level bodies of the State Council)

Macroeconomic coordination:
- National Development and Reform Commission
- Ministry of Finance
- Central Bank (People's Bank of China)

Comprehensive tasks with respect to economic regulation:
- Ministry of Commerce
- Ministry of Industry and Information Technology
- Ministry of Land and Resources

Special regulatory tasks:
- Ministry of Environmental Protection
- Ministry of Water Resources
- Ministry of Transport
- Ministry of Agriculture
- Ministry of Housing and Urban-Rural Development

Internal administrative affairs:
- Ministry of Supervision
- National Audit Office

Social affairs:
- National Health and Family Planning Commission
- Ministry of Human Resources and Social Security
- Ministry of Civil Affairs
- State Ethnic Affairs Commission

Education, science, and culture:
- Ministry of Education
- Ministry of Science and Technology
- Ministry of Culture

Security and justice:
- Ministry of Public Security (police)
- Ministry of State Security (intelligence)
- Ministry of Justice

Foreign affairs and defense:
- Ministry of Foreign Affairs
- Ministry of Defense

Ministerial-level economic supervisory organs with special status

- State-owned Assets Supervision and Administration Commission (*SASAC, since March 2003)
- China Banking Regulatory Commission (*CBRC, since April 2003)
- China Securities Regulatory Commission (*CSRC, since October 1992)
- China Insurance Regulatory Commission (*CIRC, since November 1998)

Ministerial-level research and advisory organs

- Development Research Center (*DRC, since 1985)
- Chinese Academy of Sciences (*CAS, since 1949)
- Chinese Academy of Social Sciences (*CASS, since 1977)
- Chinese Academy of Engineering (*CAE, since 1994)

Note: *These English acronyms are also widely used in China.
Based on Heilmann 1996, 2002, 2013.

© MERICS

Office plays a key role in legislative procedures. Of significant importance in terms of economic regulation are the supervisory commissions appointed by the State Council, such as the three regulatory commissions for banking, securities, and insurance that are responsible for the respective sectors of the financial system. These commissions have the same administrative rank as the ministries, but they are granted a special status that allows a departure from the usual *nomenklatura* system in terms of organizational, personnel, and salary matters, even enabling them in some cases to recruit top managers from Hong Kong.

Central to government work are the interdepartmental coordinating bodies, which are assembled by the premier or his deputies and bring together a small circle of relevant government members to discuss specific issues, ranging from the fight against poverty to climate change and food safety. Some of these interdepartmental coordinating bodies have remained in existence for a number of years and are indispensable to China's segmented state bureaucracy. Table 2.4.B presents a list of prominent and active coordinating bodies of the State Council, all of which are personally headed by the premier.

Table 2.4.B

Coordinating bodies of the State Council (国务院议事协调机构), under the leadership of the premier, 2014

- National Leading Small Group on Poverty Reduction and Development (since 1986)

- National Leading Small Group on Science, Technology, and Education (since 1998)

- National Leading Small Group on Climate Change, Energy Conservation, and Emissions Reduction (since 2007)

- Food Safety Commission of the State Council (since 2009)

- National Energy Commission (since 2010)

© MERICS

The central-government reorganizations, which took place in 1998, 2003, 2008, and 2013, involved a reduction in the plan-based ministerial structures and a simultaneous expansion of market-oriented bodies. The focus of this lengthy restructuring process has been to disband the industrial ministries and sectoral bureaucracies that were established in the 1950s based on the Soviet model. It is hoped that the reorganization will promote a reorientation toward the "socialist market economy" that was officially introduced in 1993 at the Third Plenary Session of the Fourteenth National Communist Party Congress and that is characterized by a separation of state regulatory bodies and commercial businesses. The demands for administrative adaptation both before and after China's accession to the World Trade Organization (WTO) in 2001 were seized upon by supporters of the radical reorganization measures as a decisive argument to overcome resistance from the established bureaucratic machinery. Since 2003, the goal has been to gradually direct the ministerial structure to provide better public services.

2.4.2 Party organs within the State Council

Embedded within the various ministries and government bodies, party organs play a pivotal role in the internal decision-making processes. The so-called party group (党组), which is made up of leading functionaries nominated by party headquarters and convenes at least once a week, forms the core of the decision-making process

Figure 2.4

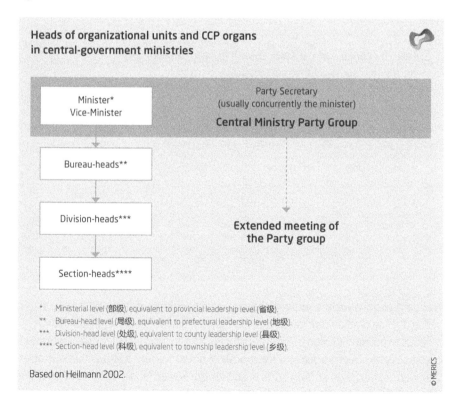

Heads of organizational units and CCP organs in central-government ministries

Minister*
Vice-Minister

Party Secretary
(usually concurrently the minister)
Central Ministry Party Group

Bureau-heads**

Division-heads***

**Extended meeting of
the Party group**

Section-heads****

* Ministerial level (部级), equivalent to provincial leadership level (省级).
** Bureau-head level (局级), equivalent to prefectural leadership level (地级).
*** Division-head level (处级), equivalent to county leadership level (县级).
**** Section-head level (科级), equivalent to township leadership level (乡级).

Based on Heilmann 2002.

© MERICS

in each ministry. The party secretary of the respective ministry leads the party group and usually concurrently serves as the minister. To discuss important broad issues, ranging from ministerial projects to internal reorganization, it is common for the party group to hold extended meetings (党组扩大会), to which the party members among the heads of the bureaus, divisions, and sections are summoned. The party committee (党委) of each ministry, comprising several dozen members, has limited strategic significance and meets at irregular intervals (see Figure 2.4).

Throughout the history of the PRC, cadres with ministerial status have also been members of the CCP, with only a very few exceptions. However, for better integration of highly qualified "democratic personages" and deputies from the various "democratic parties," since 2007 the position of minister of science and technology has been occupied by Wan Gang, a technical expert who is not a member of the CCP. Wan Gang spent ten years working in the R&D department at Audi in Germany before returning to China. As a "non-Communist" minister, Wan must maintain good personal working relations and close liaisons with the incumbent party secretary because he leads the central ministry party group, even though he is not permitted to attend its meetings since he is not a member of the CCP. Given this dual leadership system, the "non-Communist" minister and the ranking party secretary generally appear in public together when key ministerial programs are announced.

2.4.3 The unitary state and decentralization

Neither the party constitution nor the state constitution leave any doubt that the PRC is a centralized unitary state. The strong central seat of power in Beijing is responsible for safeguarding the country's unity; the regional party and state organs are required to carry out with utmost loyalty all orders issued by Beijing; and the central powers have effective mechanisms at their disposal to enforce their authority and to discipline any recalcitrant regional leaders.

Following its formal principles, the PRC might be reasonably expected to have a hierarchical command system that allows the central political leadership to crack down without restraint on lower-level administrative units. However, the dynamics of everyday political practice extend beyond the norms of the party constitution and the state constitution.

With several important exceptions (foreign affairs, defense, and taxation), there is no vertically integrated administrative organization in China to coherently carry out the instructions of the central government. Each administrative level has its own organizational structure that is formally identical to that of the next higher level. In fact, rather than the higher authorities issuing binding instructions to the lower authorities, they only issue nonbinding "professional recommendations" (业

务指导). This gives the lower-level authorities a certain degree of latitude in terms of policy implementation. However, it does not mean that there is a vertical division of power in China, as is common in federalist states. In the event of a dispute, the central government can revise or even revoke any decisions made at the lower levels. Leading party and state cadres are appointed and dismissed by the level immediately above them in the party hierarchy. After 2012, the central-government anti-corruption campaign led to a strengthening of the hierarchical controls and sanctioning mechanisms. Both the cadre system and the disciplinary supervision system provide the party organization with effective instruments to maintain centralized political decision-making power and authority to issue directives.

After the establishment of the PRC, there were repeated periods during which the ability of the party center to exert control was abruptly strengthened. This was particularly pronounced during the Great Leap Forward (1958–60) and during the peak phase of the Cultural Revolution (1966–69). At such times, regional initiatives were subject to fundamental restraints: ideologically charged political campaigns and recurrent waves of purges within the party apparatus insured that the regional leaders did not stray too far from the official line in terms of economic or social policy.

In the 1980s, after introduction of the policy of reform and opening by Deng Xiaoping, the ability of the central authorities to exert control was significantly reduced. To stem the influence of the centralized planning bureaucracy, Deng delegated some of Beijing's personnel decision-making powers to the provinces; at the same time, he gave local governments free rein with regard to economic policy. During critical phases of debate over domestic policy, Deng even depended on the personal interests of regional leaders in order to press ahead with the economic reforms against those dragging their feet in the central bureaucracy. Two examples include the introduction of the agricultural reforms in 1979 and Deng's high-profile trip to Southern China at the beginning of 1992. Susan Shirk (1993) strikingly describes this strategy as "playing to the provinces."

Strained relations between the central and regional governments in China's huge territorial state are a typical feature of the political system, with recurrent shifts back and forth between phases of strongly centralized policies to phases of heavily regionalized initiatives. Highly volatile interactions between Beijing and the regional governments—driven either by the willfulness or the weakness of the party leadership, or by internal or external crises—have resulted over time from the absence of reliable institutionalization. Economic dynamism and a willingness to experiment in China's authoritarian and bureaucratic system have profited time and time again from regional initiatives (see Chapter 6 for information on the policy-making process).

2.5 Provincial- and municipal-level governments

Dirk H. Schmidt and Sebastian Heilmann

The governmental and administrative structure in the PRC comprises four administrative tiers below the central-government level (see Figure 2.5) (Chung Jae Ho 2010). The organizational hierarchy of the CCP follows the same four-tier administrative structure, with party organs integrated at each level of the state organizational structure.

The provincial level (省级) comprises twenty-two provinces (省) (excluding Taiwan, which China officially counts as its twenty-third province), five autonomous regions (自治区), and four directly administered municipalities (直辖市): Beijing, Tianjin, Shanghai, and Chongqing.

The prefectural level (地级) is not explicitly mentioned in the constitution and is not a formal part of the administrative structure. It developed after 1949 in order to ease the administrative burdens on the higher-status provincial levels. As a consequence of urbanization, almost all cities in China are now prefectural-level cities (地级市), established as regional growth centers to radiate out to the surrounding rural areas. The two lowest levels of the state administrative structure are the county level (县级) and the township level (乡级, 镇级) (see Section 2.7).

There are also two special levels in the administrative system. The SARs of Hong Kong and Macau (see Section 2.6) are controlled by China's central government and are officially categorized as administrative units at the provincial level. However, the SAR Executive Councils (ExCos) have extensive autonomous decision-making powers and are not directly integrated into the CCP's hierarchal control system.

Another distinctive feature is the so-called "subprovincial level" (副省级), currently comprising fifteen "deputy-provincial cities," including selected provincial capitals and SEZs. In their capacity as supra-regional economic centers, these cities are granted by the central-government special administrative privileges with regard to economic development and regulation, and therefore they are more independent vis-à-vis their respective provincial governments.

2.5.1 Regional administrative organization

The administrative units of the PRC at the provincial level enjoy varying levels of political decision-making powers according to their policy areas, economic strength,

Figure 2.5

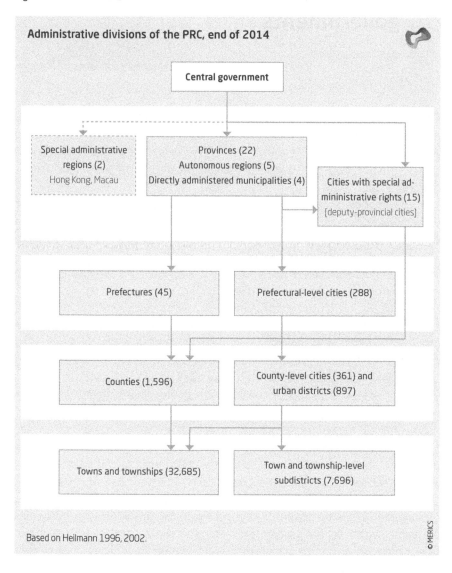

Administrative divisions of the PRC, end of 2014

Central government

Special administrative regions (2)
Hong Kong, Macau

Provinces (22)
Autonomous regions (5)
Directly administered municipalities (4)

Cities with special ad-mininistrative rights (15)
[deputy-provincial cities]

Prefectures (45)

Prefectural-level cities (288)

Counties (1,596)

County-level cities (361) and urban districts (897)

Towns and townships (32,685)

Town and township-level subdistricts (7,696)

Based on Heilmann 1996, 2002.

© MERICS

and bargaining power, but also depending on the links between the regional leadership and the decision-makers in Beijing (see Table 2.5.A).

In terms of economic and social policy, wealthy provinces and directly administered municipalities have extensive room to maneuver. However, the autonomous regions of Tibet, Inner Mongolia, Xinjiang, Ningxia, and Guangxi, created by the PRC for the ethnic minorities, effectively have less administrative autonomy because the

Table 2.5.A

Policy-making authority granted to regional governments

Administrative unit	Number	Degree of policy authority		
		Administra- tive reform	Economic development	Culture and education
Special administrative regions	2	autonomous	autonomous	autonomous
Directly administered municipalities	4	medium	medium to high*	medium
Provinces	22	medium	low to high*	medium
Autonomous regions	5	low	low to medium*	medium to high
Special economic zones	5	high	high	medium
National experimental zones	4	high	high	medium

Note: *Depending on the fiscal and economic resources available to the respective governments.

© MERICS

central government is suspicious of such politically sensitive regions, particularly Tibet and Xinjiang. Nevertheless, these areas are sources of essential raw materials and their governments are dependent on generous financial aid from the central government.

The SEZs play an important role in the development of Chinese foreign trade and in the acquisition of foreign direct investments. These export zones were originally established to attract foreign capital, serve as regional growth centers, and contribute to the development of new reform models. The first four SEZs (Shenzhen, Zhuhai, Shantou, and Xiamen) were established in 1979 and 1980 along China's southeast coast in the immediate vicinity of Hong Kong and Taiwan, partially with the political objective of increasing the latter's ties with the Chinese mainland. Hainan Island was granted SEZ status in 1988.

The Pudong New Area in Shanghai, which was established in 1990 with strong backing from the central government, was granted extensive special rights and now plays a key role in the Chinese banking sector and stock market. In the hierarchy of the state administrative divisions, the SEZs remain formally subordinate to the provincial-level governments. However, they are allowed plenty of room to maneuver with respect to export promotion, taxation, and regulation of local markets. Following China's admission to the WTO, which required the creation of a standardized economic regulatory framework for domestic and foreign companies, the SEZs lost many of their unique selling points. In 2005 and 2006, Pudong (Shanghai) and Binhai (Tianjin) were elevated to "national experimental zones for comprehensive reforms" (i.e., representing complementary reorganizations of the services sector, administration, and research/education, among others). Additionally, in 2007 the central government designated Chongqing and Chengdu as "national experimentation zones for integrating urban and rural development." It is hoped that these experimentation zones will play a pioneering role in China's transition to a "moderately prosperous society."

The structure, working practices, and competencies of Chinese provincial governments are based on the Chinese Constitution and the "Organic Law of the Local People's Congresses and the Local People's Governments of the PRC" (the latest version of which was drafted in 2004), and they follow the same basic setup as that of the central-government level (see Section 2.4).

The governor is the administrative head of the provincial government. Along with his deputies and the secretary general (as head of the General Office responsible for coordinating the work of the government), he is a member of the "executive meeting" (常务会议) of the provincial government. The governor and his deputies are elected by the Provincial People's Congress (PPC) for a term of five years. They are allocated working organs (工作部门), which operate as departments (厅), bureaus (局), offices (办公室), or commissions (委员会). The provincial authorities are responsible for steering and coordinating work in their respective fields of competency in the provincial county and municipal governments. If the executive meeting of the provincial government includes the leaders of these various organs, it is then known as a "plenary meeting" (全体会议).

As an executive organ of the PPC, the provincial government is responsible for implementing PPC decisions and is accountable to the PPC or its standing committee. At the same time, the provincial government is subject to the "unified leadership" of the State Council, which, according to the constitution, can at any time revoke "unsuitable" decisions made by the provincial governments. Public disputes between the central government and the provinces that can be documented are extremely rare; disagreements tend to be resolved quietly and informally before any final decisions are announced. However, the central-government ministries do not have the right to encroach upon the competencies of their counterparts at the provincial level; they are only allowed to provide "professional guidance."

In addition to the authorities named in Table 2.5.B, there are numerous other organs, either directly under the provincial government (省政府直属机构), such as the Statistical Bureau or the Fisheries Bureau, or under the supervision of individual provincial authorities (部门管理机构), such as the Price Office under the provincial Development and Reform Commission.

Table 2.5.B

**How a provincial government is structured
(based on the example of Jiangsu province, 2015)**

Executive Meeting of the Provincial Government
Governor
9 Vice-Governors
Secretary General

Plenary Meeting
Including the leaders of the 24 provincial authorities

Macroeconomic coordination:
• Development and Reform Commission
• Department of Finance

*Comprehensive tasks with respect
to economic regulation:*
• Department of Commerce
• Economy and Information Technology
  Commission
• Department of Land and Resources

Special regulatory tasks:
• Department of Environmental
  Protection
• Department of Water Resources
• Department of Transport
• Agricultural Commission
• Department of Housing and
  Urban-Rural Development

Internal administrative affairs:
• Supervision Department
• Audit Office

Social affairs:
• Department of Health
• Population and Family Planning
  Commission
• Department of Human Resources
  and Social Security
• Department of Civil Affairs
• Ethnic Affairs Commission

Education, science, and culture:
• Department of Education
• Department of Science and
  Technology
• Department of Culture

Security, justice:
• Department of Public Security
• Department of State Security
• Department of Justice

Foreign affairs:
• Foreign Affairs Office (including
  matters related to Hong Kong and
  Macau)

Based on Government of Jiangsu province (www.js.gov.cn): Accessed February 9, 2016.   © MERICS

2.5.2 Regional special interests

In light of the considerable variation in the level of socioeconomic development among China's provinces, the challenges presented by regional special interests hardly come as a surprise: in 2014 Guangdong province, with a population of more than 107 million, had a GDP of over CNY 6,781 billion (almost USD 1,030 billion) (NBS 2015b, 2015d). In comparison, at the same time Tibet, with a population of a little more than three million, produced a GDP of only CNY 92 billion (USD 14 billion). Whereas Guangdong exported as much as South Korea in 2010, exports from Qinghai province only reached the level of exports from Rwanda. This strong discrepancy in economic performance is not only a consequence of different geographical and historical backgrounds, but also the result of China's 1978 modernization program that gave provincial governments considerable latitude in order to stimulate regional economic initiatives (Donaldson 2010; see also Section 4.9).

The existence of regional special interests is reflected in the wide variety of political conflicts that exist at various levels, with arguments often arising between the central government and the provinces, between two or more provinces, or even internally within a single province. The most widely discussed conflicts are the tensions between the central government and the provinces: with a one-dimensional focus on rapid economic growth, a number of provincial governments have shown little interest in social and environmental needs, resulting in social inequalities, serious degradation of the environment, and short-term wastes of resources. Many regional governments have used the freedom granted to them as a result of the economic reforms to issue trade and tax regulations that do not conform to national guidelines and to safeguard their local markets against goods from other regions through radical protectionism.

In terms of the shaping of the reform policy, fundamental conflicts soon emerged among the provinces: coastal provinces had a keen interest in maintaining their prominent positions with respect to foreign-trade policy. Hence, economic recentralization and redistribution in favor of the interior regions were not in their interest. However, representatives of the interior provinces campaigned strongly to shift the central-government's regional policy in their favor (particularly with respect to major national investments to expand infrastructure or healthcare in the interior regions).

The political framework within the provinces changed as well. The governments of economically prosperous counties and newly established special economic and development zones became increasingly self-confident vis-à-vis the provincial authorities and actively represented the interests of their respective jurisdictions. The special privileges granted to deputy-provincial cities were a constant bone of contention, as these cities were able to negotiate directly with Beijing due to their autonomy with respect to national economic planning.

The central government is responsible for maintaining China's national macro-economic, social, and ecological stability as well as the country's political and administrative unity vis-à-vis the diverse special regional interests. At the same time, Beijing focuses on fostering integration and cooperation with regard to the domestic economy, narrowing regional developmental gaps, and diverting the national economy over the medium term to a sustainable growth pattern that is more strongly oriented toward domestic consumption.

When it comes to enforcing national development goals, regardless of the forces of regionalism, the central government can resort to special political instruments. Its personnel authority (in the form of the CCP cadre and discipline systems) allows the central political leadership to dismiss overly stubborn or corrupt provincial office-holders, thus thwarting the establishment of regional power bases and nepotistic structures. In a broad sense, however, the existence and functioning of local and regional party and government organs are still dependent on the central authorities. Formally, Beijing still retains unlimited organizational and legislative power. The internal organization and the division of power within the regional governments are essentially defined by the central government in Beijing. According to the state constitution, the State Council can, at any time, "annul inappropriate decisions and orders" issued by regional authorities (Art. 89). In practice, such interference in the work of regional governments is never publicized. Solutions are generally reached behind closed doors by delegations of top-ranking ministerial officials sent from Beijing.

With regard to economic growth, however, the central government cannot afford to silence the regional voices; only compromise and cooperation, not one-sided commands, will safeguard the progress and success of the economic reforms. A complex negotiating system has thus evolved, leading to extensive transformations of the functions of the central government and realignments in its relations with regional-government organs. The unique features of these new relations are revealed by the following: political debates about revenue and the division of power with regard to budgetary and fiscal policy; lobbying of the central government by the regional leaderships with the objective of attaining special economic provisions; attempts by Beijing to secure control over the regional governments by means of personnel reshufflings, by sending in inspection teams, or by creating additional administrative authorities (such as audit offices).

What is the precise framework for these negotiating processes that have been characteristic of relations between the central government and the regions? Special regional interests are not openly represented within the supreme decision-making party and state bodies, namely the CCP CC and the NPC Standing Committee. However, leading regional representatives issue statements of regional concern during informal discussions with central-government representatives or with individual ministries on the sidelines of CC or NPC meetings. Additional opportunities for dialogue between decision-makers from the central government and from the various regions are provided by frequent trips by top officials to the provinces. Furthermore, at all levels of the administrative system countless expert meetings are held on a daily basis, at which the ideas and interests of the central and regional bureaucracies are presented and decisions are prepared for presentation to the higher political levels.

Although these expert meetings generally focus on bureaucratic work, the Central Party School and the Chinese Academy of Governance (formerly, the National School of Administration) serve as key forums for policy coordination between national and regional decision-makers. With respect to formulating specific measures, the high-level workshops on specific policy fields that have been offered by the Chinese Academy of Governance since 1998 are especially relevant. Decision-makers and top officials from national and regional governmental departments and experts from research institutions are invited to participate and to provide input on the specific design and implementation of pending reform and legislative proposals. National ministries, which are responsible for formulating individual draft bills, are thus presented with the experiences, concerns, and proposals of the regional governments, resulting in a number of changes or revisions to key reform projects. The Chinese Academy of Governance has thus become one of the main forums for informal, high-level policy coordination between the central government and the regions.

2.5.3 Informal federalism?

The PRC continues to be a centralized state with a hierarchical one-party system. The central government in Beijing is responsible for all policy areas and all major structural decisions. What does not exist in China's system of governance is an organ to represent regional interests in Beijing, that is, a second parliamentary chamber.

However, as illustrated in the previous section, the political reality of consensus-building and decision-making between the central government and the regions is considerably more complex than the formal constitutional provisions would suggest. The special features of economic decentralization in China have been described as "market-preserving federalism" (Montinola, Qian, and Weingast 1995) or "de facto federalism" (Zheng Yongnian 2007). In contrast to formal constitutional federalism, these models emphasize two fundamental features.

First, economic and financial responsibilities, which are governed by informal political rules without constitutional validation, are subject to special distribution. The central government is essentially restricted to monetary policy and macroeconomic management and to preventing regional protectionist tendencies, but it cannot intervene in the system of decentralized economic regulation. Such a distribution of responsibilities provides strong incentives for interregional competition for corporate investments and for innovations boosted by market-friendly institutional terms. At the same time, such competition restricts each individual government's scope to prevent economic activities through arbitrary interventions or regulations that may obstruct the market. China's informal federalism thus leads to a restriction of central-government powers in terms of economic control, sets boundaries regarding the political levying of company profits, and, in so doing, alleviates some of the essential defects in China's political institutions.

Second, this type of informal federalism is characterized by unique political consensus-building through a process of permanent internal consultation and negotiation among parties at various levels—even, in some cases, among institutionalized parties (see above). In terms of relations between the central and provincial governments, there are several characteristics of a "joint-decision trap" (Scharpf 1988), as are typical in a number of federal systems: intensive personnel interrelationships and interdependencies as well as complex collaborations among leading officials at different levels of the system; strong pressures to compromise and jointly resolve problems; and attempts to establish a vertical division of powers between the central government and the regions.

The fragility and precariousness of the informal rules for balancing central versus regional interests and for coordinating the division of labor in China became blatantly obvious after the appointment of the new president in 2013. Under Xi Jinping, there has been a clear trend toward conceptual and institutional recentralization. With the objective of creating a "unified market," both the party and the government are now committed to fighting "local protectionism" (地方保护主义). Simultaneously, the anti-corruption campaign drastically increased pressures on the lower levels to conform. In accordance with party headquarters, all of the provinces set up Leading Small Groups for Comprehensively Deepening Reforms under the leadership of the regional party secretaries and governors.

After 2012 Beijing made it clear that it intends that its reforms will be properly enforced, but at the same time it expects pragmatic regional solutions. Here the party leadership is treading a fine line: on the one hand, nationwide implementation of reform measures and the fight against regional networks of corruption are strongly supported by the general public as well as by foreign investors. On the other hand, the unilateral strengthening of the central party hierarchy and the political submission of the regions will jeopardize some of the essential factors driving China's development successes to date, namely, the decentralized initiatives and the willingness to experiment. Creating durable institutions for conflict management and a vertical division of powers between the central government and the regions remain unresolved challenges facing China's political system. As of yet, there have been no visible steps in the direction of establishing a formal federalist system.

2.6 Special Administrative Regions: Hong Kong and Macau

Sebastian Heilmann, Yi Zhu, and Johannes Buckow

The British colony of Hong Kong was returned to Chinese sovereignty in July 1997, followed by the former Portuguese colony of Macau in December 1999. However, neither territory was fully integrated into the Chinese administrative system. They each have the status of a SAR (特别行政区), with a supposed high degree of internal autonomy from the Chinese administrative hierarchy. "One country, two systems" (一国两制) is the constitutional principle formulated by the PRC government to describe this special arrangement.

A special *Central Coordinating Group for Hong Kong and Macau Affairs* (中央香港澳门工作协调小组) was established in Beijing in 2003. This body is responsible for coordinating the special political relations with the two SARs. There are central-government liaison offices (中央人民政府联络办公室, or for short: 中联办) both in Hong Kong and Macau. Although these representative bodies cannot issue binding instructions to the governments in Hong Kong and Macau, regular consultations with party and government headquarters have become indispensable for the ExCos in the SARs. The liaison offices therefore carry considerable political weight.

The Macau SAR (with a population of 577,900 and a GDP of USD 55.5 billion in 2014) is the only place in the PRC where casinos and gambling are legal (World Bank 2015). Between 2004 and 2013, Macau's growth in revenue from casinos accelerated rapidly, contributing to Macau widening its lead as the world's largest gambling hub. However, there has been a dip in its growth rate due to the 2012 anti-corruption campaign, which was directed at illegal capital transfers, money laundering, and credit-card fraud in Macau, among other things. Beginning in 2013, Macau's economy went through a period of economic restructuring and diversification, resulting in its establishment as a base for international tourism, shopping, and performances modeled after those in Las Vegas. In terms of Chinese foreign policy and trade, until now Macau has played only a minor role. With respect to domestic policy, the relationship between Macau's government, economy, and population and the central government in Beijing is a great deal less tense than the permanently conflict-ridden relations between Beijing and Hong Kong. In 2014, China's state media openly extolled Macau's "stability," contrasting it with the political unrest in Hong Kong.

Developments in the Hong Kong SAR (with a population of 7.24 million and a GDP of USD 290.9 billion in 2014) (World Bank 2015) are closely observed around the world due to Hong Kong's major role as an international financial and service center and because of the serious political tensions with regard to its electoral and democratization processes (Anderson 2005; Lo Shiu-Hing 2001; Martin 2007). Political and economic developments in the Hong Kong SAR are briefly outlined in the following sections.

2.6.1 Hong Kong's economic role

Hong Kong's economy is very closely linked to that of the PRC mainland. Economic integration between Hong Kong and the mainland, especially with Guangdong province which is located immediately to the north of Hong Kong, began at the end of the 1970s. Growth in the relocation of production facilities to the mainland created millions of new jobs in China and led to a "de-industrialization" in Hong Kong, where 93 percent of GDP was generated by the services sector in 2014 (World Bank 2015).

Economic relations intensified after the transfer of sovereignty in 1997. The Hong Kong government and its business community were strongly committed to creating a free trade zone with the mainland. Under the "Closer Economic Partnership Arrangement" (CEPA) of 2003, companies headquartered in Hong Kong (including non-Chinese transnational corporations) were granted preferential access to the mainland Chinese market. In June 2007, the scope of the CEPA was extended to include a number of services sectors. Hong Kong investments made a significant contribution to developing mainland China's export industry. By the end of 2015, with a share of 73.4 percent (Ministry of Commerce 2016), Hong Kong remained by far the primary source of inflows of direct investments on the Chinese mainland and also played a key role in the flotation of a number of Chinese companies on international stock markets.

In addition to its close links with the mainland, Hong Kong's economy has also been extensively integrated with international markets. Therefore, for a number of years Hong Kong functioned as the key intermediary between the PRC and the global economy; compared with the other financial and trade centers in East Asia, it provided numerous benefits to China. The extremely moderate government regulatory practices and tax rates and the independent judiciary that had been established under British rule have been traditionally seen as the advantages of Hong Kong. Since 1997, government departments in Beijing have made extensive use of Hong Kong's expertise on matters relating to the regulation of capital markets, the insurance sector, and foreign-exchange markets. Hong Kong also served as the first offshore financial center using Chinese currency for international trading. In the course of the 2010s, however, Hong Kong lost some of its traditional role as the primary interface between the PRC and the world economy due to strong competition from aspiring Chinese ports, services, and industrial sectors and, in particular, from Shanghai's rise as an increasingly international financial and services center.

2.6.2 Hong Kong's political trajectory

The general rules regarding the status of the Hong Kong SAR and its government system are stipulated in the Sino-British Joint Declaration of 1984, which is registered in the United Nations and satisfies the formal requirements of a treaty under international law. In 1990 the Chinese NPC in Beijing also drafted a basic law (基本法) for the Hong Kong SAR to legally substantiate and indemnify the agreements in the joint declaration. With the exception of foreign and defense policy, Hong Kong was granted a high level of autonomy and independent executive, legislative, and judicial powers that are not supposed to be bound by directives from Beijing.

The ExCo of Hong Kong is headed by a chief executive who is nominated by an electoral committee and elected for a term of five years. This electoral committee is made up of representatives of professional, social, and religious groups as well as political representatives from the Hong Kong districts. It is planned that in 2017 the chief executive will be elected by universal suffrage. A reform proposal, which was voted on in 2015, stipulates that the chief executive will be elected from a group of candidates nominated in a partially restrictive procedure by a 1,200-member committee made up of representatives of professional, social, and religious groups as well as political representatives of the Hong Kong districts. In August 2015, the reform proposal, in the face of sustained opposition from some sections of the legislature and the public, was rejected by the Legislative Council (LegCo). The outcome was widely considered to be a defeat for both Beijing and for the democracy movement, leaving the people of Hong Kong with less say in the selection of the chief executive than had the proposal been passed. However, the appointment of a chief executive who is sceptical of Beijing and who is in favor of greater autonomy and democracy in Hong Kong will be completely unacceptable to the central government and will face strong intervention from central-government headquarters. The political leadership in Beijing has regularly made it clear in no uncertain terms that the "patriotic" loyalty of the Hong Kong administration toward the central government shall never be jeopardized.

The LegCo passes, amends, and revokes bills, controls and approves the budget, taxation, and public spending, and monitors government performance. The procedures for electing members of the LegCo have been amended numerous times since 1997. By 2012, one-half of the seventy members of the LegCo were elected by geographical constituencies through direct elections, whereas the other half were nominated by functional constituencies made up of professional and special-interest groups.

After the transfer of sovereignty, calls from some sectors of the Hong Kong population for more extensive democratization have repeatedly triggered fierce debates and protests. The first mass protests took place in 2003 when the Hong Kong government attempted—without broad public consultation—to pass a National Security Bill proposed by Beijing, criminalizing subversion and secession against the national government. About 500,000 Hong Kong citizens demonstrated against this bill because it represented a deep intrusion into Hong Kong people's freedom of speech, freedom of the press, and freedom of association. The demonstrations resulted in withdrawal of the controversial bill by the SAR government.

The lack of democratic representation with regard to election procedures remains a hot topic of intense debate. The system of allocating seats in the LegCo works to the disadvantage of the anti-Beijing parties. The committee responsible for electing the chief executive is primarily made up of representatives from big business and pro-Beijing forces. Any reforms of the electoral system that might provide the possibility for more open and democratic competition have been consistently rejected or deferred by Beijing. In 2007 the NPC Standing Committee decided that the election of the chief executive of Hong Kong would take place at the earliest in 2017, and the election of the members of the LegCo would not take place before 2020.

Beijing's position with respect to Hong Kong policy hardened considerably in the mid-2010s. In a *White Paper* published in July 2014, the central government explains that the "one country, two systems" principle is intended to defend China's "sovereignty, security and development interests." The White Paper stipulates that Hong Kong is to develop within the framework of central-government guidelines (State Council 2014b) and that all civil servants and members of LegCo are required to remain loyal and patriotic to the state.

Many Hong Kong citizens perceived the directives from Beijing as a violation of the Sino-British Joint Declaration, thus leading to increased resistance from among the general public. In the fall of 2014 conflicts over the proposed framework for universal suffrage beginning in 2017 sparked weeks of mass protests. In an unofficial, Internet-led referendum, several hundred thousand Hong Kongers demanded liberalization of the nomination procedures for the 2017 election of the chief executive. Under the banner "Occupy Central with Love and Peace," thousands of protestors blocked the main traffic arteries in the financial district and other major shopping areas in order to present their political demands.

However, the protests revealed deep divisions among the Hong Kong population. Some sectors of the society, including a surprising number of students and younger Hong Kongers, abandoned their traditional political apathy and took to the streets despite the massive police presence and serious warnings from Beijing. The protests were initially staged with great self-discipline and in an almost carnival-like atmosphere. Western media extoled the emergence of a vibrant civil society, but their coverage often lacked journalistic distance and failed to look at the protests in a broader context. In response to the demonstrations, many Hong Kong residents—especially the older generations—kept a distance politically and voiced sharp criticism of the protestors. They feared the negative economic consequences and the

2 The Chinese Communist Party and state institutions

loss of income. Others considered the criticism of Beijing to be both excessive and unjustified, or completely futile. Intense shouting matches and fierce brawls broke out between protestors and counter-protestors, who included agents provocateurs from criminal organizations and secret-service circles. The public protests and street barricades ended after several heated weeks due to a major police crackdown and the sheer exhaustion of the protestors. But the underlying conflicts surrounding the democratization of Hong Kong's system of government and the difficult relationship with the central government remain unresolved.

2.6.3 Constraints on democratization

The establishment of an autonomous, democratic subsystem with open competitive elections is unrealistic given the PRC's nondemocratic state order. Under the "one country, two systems" principle, the state and party leaderships in Beijing have indeed accepted the continuation of the capitalist system and an independent administrative, legal, and social order in Hong Kong. However, this formula does not apply to democratization of the government system in Hong Kong in terms of installing a government that is critical of Beijing, even if it were to be supported by the majority in democratic elections. From Beijing's perspective, Hong Kong is similar to a foreign body within its political system, subject to alien rules and tolerated only because of its exceptional historical background and its position under international law.

The central government in Beijing has no intention of surrendering political control over Hong Kong. It is possible that the introduction of a more democratic system of government in Hong Kong might also lead to greater demands for political reform on the Chinese mainland. During the mass protests in Hong Kong in the fall of 2014, the supervisory bodies over the media and the Internet in the PRC took pains to block unfiltered reports about the democracy movement in Hong Kong. Instead, the Chinese state media presented their own version of the demonstrations, that is, irresponsible actions taken by naïve students or unpatriotic troublemakers and manipulated by the Western powers.

The Chinese leadership will never allow the Hong Kong chief executive to be elected by open competitive elections, nor will it be swayed by street protests. From Beijing's perspective, restrictive conditions with regard to the procedures for the nomination of candidates—in other words, controlled screening and pre-selection of acceptable candidates *prior to* the actual voting—represent a generous compromise. The scope for political bargaining with the central government, which is granted to both the official representatives as well as to the representatives of the opposition in Hong Kong, will narrow should Hong Kong's significance continue to decline in terms of China's position as a global economic power. The future political development of the Hong Kong SAR remains entirely in the hands of Beijing. The clamoring

98 | CHINA'S POLITICAL SYSTEM

by a large part of the Hong Kong's population for the right to universal suffrage is likely to remain a recurring challenge to Beijing and one that will not be resolved by unilateral measures.

2.7 Local governments at the county, township, and village levels

Dirk H. Schmidt and Sebastian Heilmann

For a more comprehensive understanding and evaluation of China's political system with all its capabilities/limitations and potential for development, it is necessary to understand not only the political institutions and processes at the national level, but also to look at the local governments at the county and township levels (see Figure 2.7) (see Ahlers 2014a; Ahlers 2014b; Ahlers/Schubert 2015; Heberer 2013). Since the 1980s, the local levels have been a key source of economic and social dynamism. Yet these levels have also been a source of some of the most pressing challenges and the most serious demands for reform of the political system facing the regime.

2.7.1 The functions of local government

In general, there is no system of local self-government in China. According to the PRC Constitution, only villages (in the rural areas) and neighborhoods (in the cities) are self-governing units, but they are not part of the formal government hierarchy. Decision-makers at the local levels are not directly elected by the people. They are not autonomous decision-makers with sole responsibility, nor do they merely mechanically carry out orders from higher levels. China's local governments are in a complicated position, sandwiched between orders from higher government levels and demands for greater political freedoms from local levels. Nevertheless, local governments play an important basic role in China's political system.

First, local governments have a laboratory function: local-government departments must respond actively and energetically to Beijing's political directives, which are often very general and must be aligned, substantiated, and refined for policy implementation at the local levels. In many policy areas, the central government intentionally focuses on practical experience and problem-solving approaches that have been gathered or developed at the local levels. Cities or counties try out a variety of

Figure 2.7

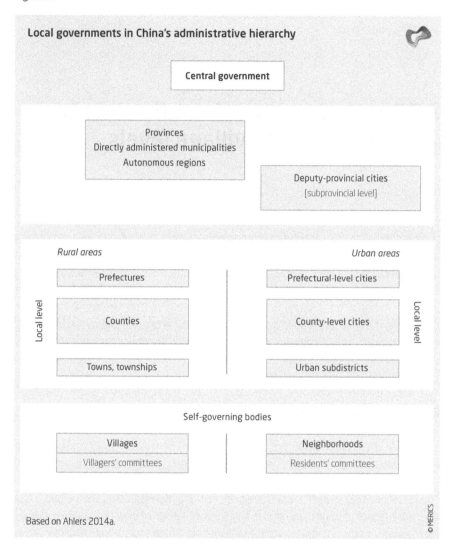

Local governments in China's administrative hierarchy

Central government

Provinces
Directly administered municipalities
Autonomous regions

Deputy-provincial cities
[subprovincial level]

Rural areas   *Urban areas*

Prefectures   Prefectural-level cities

Local level   Local level

Counties   County-level cities

Towns, townships   Urban subdistricts

Self-governing bodies

Villages   Neighborhoods

Villagers' committees   Residents' committees

Based on Ahlers 2014a.

© MERICS

political "experimental points" (试点) as pilot projects before the relevant legislation is formulated and implemented nationally. Local experiences with adapting and
refining new policy approaches—ranging from land administration and healthcare
to recycling—are keenly observed by political leaderships at higher administrative
levels. If local policy outcomes prove to be politically expedient and practical, they
are raised as "model experiences" (典型经验) and extended "from point to surface"
(由点到面), tested further, and ultimately applied universally. Some of the most

significant reforms in China in recent decades (in terms of agriculture, the fiscal system, and health insurance) have been the result of such local experiments.

Second, local governments have a hinge function: at the local levels, instructions are adapted to suit local conditions, funding is allocated, and implementation of political measures is coordinated. There are direct contacts and interactions at this level among the administrative bodies and the general public: this is where the general public can voice its specific needs and demands, where latent tensions and unresolved problems first come to light and administrative solutions and public services should be reached. As a result of the pluralization of society, an increasing awareness of people's rights, and the omnipresence of digital media, complaints and demands by the general public at the local levels are becoming increasingly vocal. In this sense, the local-government departments function as "seismometers" gauging public acceptance of legislative programs.

County governments play a particularly important role in China's administrative system. With an average population of over 400,000, about one-third of the county governments can look back to more than one thousand years of history. In comparison, the township level did not come into existence until 1954. The state constitution and the Law on Legislation assign county-level governments a broad range of tasks. In practice, their primary responsibilities include agricultural matters, especially promotion of the local economy and local employment as well as the steering of the urbanization process and the provision of an adequate public infrastructure. In comparison, governments at the township level have far fewer financial resources and competencies as well as less decision-making autonomy. Therefore, they predominantly function as an executive branch to implement measures devised by their counterparts at the county levels (Zhong Yang 2010). The extent to which township governments can turn requirements into reality depends not only on the availability of financial means and organizational abilities, but also on the feasibility and gravity of the instructions issued by the higher levels, to what extent there are conflicts of interest between the various administrative levels (in the area of land administration, for example), and how effectively the township governments are regulated by the county authorities.

2.7.2 Village self-governance and village elections

China's villages and rural regions began undergoing fundamental changes in the 1980s. Previously isolated villages were connected to road networks and numerous villages were absorbed into new urban settlements. Many young villagers left home as migrant workers in search of higher incomes in China's industrial centers. The left-behind elderly villagers often lived on extremely meager agricultural incomes and funds transferred by the migrants. Although government programs aimed at creating a "new socialist countryside" introduced the first forms of health and pension insurance in a number of rural regions, in many cases the former village structures were destroyed and the villagers were forced to resettle in newly built, state-planned settlements and residential structures. Thus, in many regions, rural China was replaced by a new urban way of life. Former village settlements were merged into new, larger urban administrative units. China's rural society was thus fundamentally transformed due to geographical mobility, demographic changes, new residential structures, and the vast urbanization program.

The spectrum of organizational forms found in China's rural administration is exceptionally diverse: village leadership structures range from party committees and party cells to seemingly archaic clans and elected village governments. Regional differences in terms of the level of economic development are usually decisive determinants of the types of political structures found in the rural areas.

To ensure the stability of the political framework in the rural regions, the Chinese government held direct elections for village committees and village committee chairmen on a trial basis in selected provinces in the mid-1980s. In November 1998, the NPC Standing Committee passed the Organic Law of the Villagers Committees of the PRC, establishing comprehensive rules and regulations regarding which Chinese villagers may govern their own villages as well as the terms and conditions for village elections. The law stipulates that all candidates should be directly nominated by the villagers, that the number of candidates should exceed the number of persons to be elected, and that the elections should be held by secret ballot every three years. The directly elected village committees are to assume executive functions regarding all village matters and are to be supervised by a villagers' assembly or by its representatives. The processes of drafting the Law of the Villagers Committees and holding the elections were supported both organizationally and financially by foreign advisers and foundations, since it was hoped that this would contribute to grassroots democratization. The Chinese government repeatedly praised the village elections in national and international media, referring to them as a grassroots democratic institution.

In view of the political expectations nurtured by many Westers advisers and foundations, assessments of the village elections more than fifteen years after the law was passed are largely disappointing (see Liu Yawei 2009; O'Brien/Han 2009; Schubert/Ahlers 2012). On the one hand, since 1998 hundreds of millions of villagers have taken part in several rounds of village elections. Elected village chairmen feel a stronger responsibility toward the villagers than the previously designated functionaries. On the other hand, however, the institutional shortcomings in the electoral process should not be overlooked. With regard to the voting procedures and the nomination process for candidates, there is considerable falsification and manipulation, and party representatives are able to intervene at any stage in the elections. From the outset, the village elections were designed by the

CCP primarily as an instrument to improve the functioning of the existing system. At no time did the party intend to establish new channels for independent interest articulation and co-determination outside the confines of the party-state. On the contrary, village self-governance was meant to ensure implementation of especially unpopular policies (such as family planning, tax collection, and maintenance of public security).

On the whole, the autonomous decision-making powers of the directly elected village representatives remain very limited. With the abolition of rural levies and taxes by order of the central government in the mid-2000s, the drying up of substantial sources of revenue has also affected village governance. Village chairmen are once again exclusively reliant on funding from higher levels in the hierarchy and on the goodwill or "guidance" of non-elected party and government functionaries in the township governments. In this context, village governments remain far more tightly integrated in the official administrative hierarchy than is suggested by the term "self-governance" (Alpermann 2001).

After Xi Jinping assumed office in 2012, as a result of the party leadership's centralization and discipline policies all election experiments beyond the village level ended on the grounds that they were "unconstitutional." "Democratization" and "juridification" at the lower administrative levels came to be seen only as a CCP means to increase administrative efficiency and to fight corruption. It was hoped that the new methods of e-government (online hotlines, discussion platforms, electronic complaint systems, etc.) would improve public services at lower administrative levels and would expose cases of official misconduct. On the whole, self-governing structures have proved to be either completely incompatible or only temporarily compatible with the hierarchical structure of the PRC party-state.

2.7.3 Recent developments and signs of crisis

Cities, counties, and towns/townships are expected, if possible, to fund their assigned public tasks from their own resources. This includes everything from infrastructure and education to healthcare. However, they are seldom in a position to do this effectively because they have no stable tax revenue. Many of the lower administrative units are chronically underfinanced and deeply in debt. To close the funding gaps, regional-government departments have resorted to a variety of different methods.

The first method is to sell or rent publicly-owned land to real-estate developers, generating substantial additional public revenue for a number of years. However, this approach has had negative social and political consequences. There have been numerous cases of local governments forcibly evicting residents from their land or homes without offering them acceptable financial compensation, thereby in some cases triggering years of protests by the residents. The general public's trust in party and government departments has been badly shaken, or even irreparably destroyed, by the obvious collusion and corruption between functionaries and re-al-estate developers for many major projects.

The second method involves funding from higher government levels that is intended to be invested to improve public services (building and maintaining schools and hospitals, for example). However, instead it has been misappropriated for real-estate and infrastructure projects. These construction projects provide lo-cal governments and functionaries with a number of direct financial benefits and income opportunities. The provision of public services has become loss-making ventures.

In the third method, because until 2014 Chinese local governments were for-bidden from borrowing outside capital (for example, by issuing municipal bonds), many city and county governments established local investment companies (com-mercial companies operating outside of the public budget). These companies enthu-siastically borrowed from the state banks, using public land as collateral. After the central government put a stop to this risky credit practice, the regional investment companies, in a quest for alternative funding sources, turned to high-interest loans in the shadow banking sector. The hidden financing and debt risks at the local levels thus increased rapidly by 2014.

Despite signs of administrative and fiscal crises in China's cities and counties, there is also a key feature of the regional debt crisis: state and party actors are generally involved on both the debtor and the creditor sides. These actors have multiple opportunities to roll over the debt or to apply disguised debt haircuts (for example, by shifting liability to the balance sheets of the state asset management companies). In 2014, the MOF launched a series of measures aimed at stabilizing the regional debt burdens and regional revenue by the year 2020 (see Section 2.8).

Moreover, additional steps have been taken to curtail the widespread public mistrust of local representatives of state power. Attempts have been made to more actively involve citizens in the preparation and evaluation of regional administrative measures by means of public hearings and consultations. Public complaints offices have been set up to encourage regional governments to be more service-orient-ed. These limited but workable mechanisms provide opportunities, at least tempo-rarily, for the local population to lobby and exert pressure (Ahlers 2014b). By the mid-2010s, however, local governments in a growing number of Chinese cities and counties were no longer able to govern without pressures from legally justified and publicly articulated interests, demands, and complaints. State organs were forced to consider the provision of public services, lawful administrative actions, and limited forms of control from the general public, in addition to stronger supervision and discipline by the party hierarchy, in order to avoid public protests, administrative tri-bunal proceedings, and interventions by higher levels of government.

2.8 Public finance

Sandra Heep

Since the 1980s, the Chinese government had been attempting to create an effective and sustainable fiscal system, focusing on institutional restructuring and the development of state taxation and budgetary systems, which had existed in only a very rudimentary form during the period of the former centrally planned economy. The necessity for fiscal reforms was exacerbated, as is the case in most government systems, by ongoing conflicts over the allocation of revenue and expenditures among various government levels and due to conflict-ridden negotiations regarding financial transfers and special allocations from the central government to the subnational governments. The rapid increase in indebtedness of provincial, city, and municipal governments (referred to below as the "subnational governments") became a serious challenge to China's economic stability during the 2010s.

2.8.1 Fiscal decentralization

During the period of the planned economy, China's fiscal revenue was primarily derived from the profits of the SOEs. Subnational governments collected this revenue and transferred it to the central government, which was solely responsible for making all expenditure decisions. Subnational governments, however, were responsible for providing and financing public services in areas such as education and health, for which they received funds allocated by the central government. Rather than the funds being allocated according to a single formula, they were based on individual negotiations between the subnational governments and the central government (Wong/Bird 2008).

Following the introduction of the reforms of the state-owned sector in the 1980s, profit transfers by the SOEs to the government began to decline. This is because the SOEs were independently allowed to use a substantial portion of their profits for investments. The easing of controls by the central government over the subnational governments also resulted in the transfer of less revenue to the central government (Wong/Bird 2008). As a result, by 1994 not only did fiscal revenue drop as a proportion of GDP, but central-government revenue also declined as a proportion of total state revenue (see Figure 2.8.A).

To remedy this situation, in 1994 Beijing approved a comprehensive reform of the taxation system that was aimed at making the allocation of public funding binding within the context of a revenue-sharing scheme. This new system distinguished between central, subnational, and collaborative (shared) types of taxes. Responsi-

Figure 2.8.A

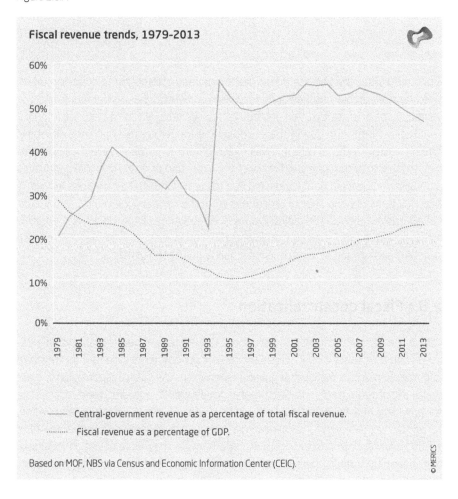

Fiscal revenue trends, 1979-2013

——— Central-government revenue as a percentage of total fiscal revenue.

·········· Fiscal revenue as a percentage of GDP.

Based on MOF, NBS via Census and Economic Information Center (CEIC).

bility for collecting central and shared taxes was handed over to new nationwide tax offices created by the central government. These new tax authorities were set up alongside the tax offices operated by the subnational levels of government (Lou Jiwei 2008). This reorganization allowed the central government to secure a large part of the tax revenue. The particularly lucrative value-added tax (VAT) was declared a shared tax, but three-quarters of it was allocated to the central government (see Figure 2.8.B). The central government also strengthened its position by centralizing the power to pass tax legislation.

Although it is true that these measures considerably improved the central-government's budgetary position, they also caused financial bottlenecks for the subnational governments because much less funding was available to them to finance

Figure 2.8.B

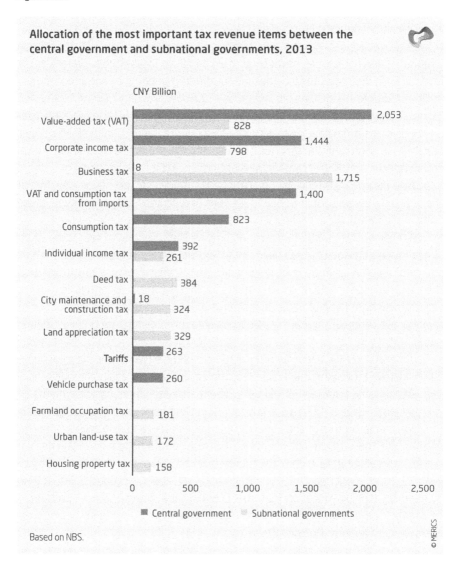

Allocation of the most important tax revenue items between the central government and subnational governments, 2013

CNY Billion

Value-added tax (VAT)	2,053 / 828
Corporate income tax	1,444 / 798
Business tax	8 / 1,715
VAT and consumption tax from imports	1,400
Consumption tax	823
Individual income tax	392 / 261
Deed tax	384
City maintenance and construction tax	18 / 324
Land appreciation tax	329
Tariffs	263
Vehicle purchase tax	260
Farmland occupation tax	181
Urban land-use tax	172
Housing property tax	158

0   500   1,000   1,500   2,000   2,500

■ Central government   Subnational governments

Based on NBS.

© MERICS

those areas for which they were still responsible. As a result, the central government had to introduce a system of transfer payments by which the central-government tax revenue was routed to the provincial governments. However, these transfers did not come close to ending the funding gaps in the budgets of the subnational governments. Furthermore, there were only limited compensation payments to the less well-developed interior regions (Wong 2010). Thus, no reliable financial compensation scheme existed between the central government and the regions, or even among the regions themselves.

China's subnational governments are responsible for providing essential public services (police services, schools, healthcare, road building, etc.). Depending on whether additional sources of revenue could be raised locally, the shortfalls in tax revenue encountered by the local authorities differed among the various authorities and therefore led to considerable variations in the overall quality of service provision (Hussain/Stern 2008). Subnational governments were forced to raise extra-budgetary funds to meet their many obligations. Consequently, revenue in the form of fees, penalties, or additional charges (for instance, for the direct sale of pharmaceutical products by local clinics) became increasingly important for the operation of schools, hospitals, and police stations (Wong 2013a, 2013b). Since the low-income sectors of the population were unable to pay these fees and additional costs, many of those living in the rural areas in particular had very limited access to public services.

To improve their budgetary position beyond the collection of fees, subnational governments also sold land-use rights. The real-estate sector became a major source of revenue as a result of the volatile urbanization progress, but it was also the most common source of social protests against the local authorities. In order to sell land-use rights at a profit, local residents were driven from their land or out of their homes, often without being paid a fair amount of compensation (see Section 5.8.2).

Under the Hu–Wen administration (2002–12), the situation for the rural population improved following the abolition of the agricultural tax and numerous special fees. At the same time, the central government increased its transfer payments by a wide margin, especially for rural education and the healthcare system, to enable the low-income sectors of the population to have better access to public services. All the same, these transfer payments were insufficient to close the funding gaps at the lower levels of government. Decisions about the allocation of fiscal funding to regional-government departments continued to be made by negotiation rather than by generally binding allocation formulae. Economically strong provinces possessed far greater bargaining power in these negotiations than provinces in the impoverished western regions (Dollar/Hofman 2008).

In the PRC's fiscal and investment system, subnational governments must either finance local infrastructure projects on their own or co-finance them, as in the case, for example, of national or provincial investment programs. In the main, however, local governments lack the funds for such investments. Until 2014, subnational governments were prohibited from taking out bank loans or issuing local-government bonds. Under these difficult circumstances, since the 1990s subnational governments set up investment and finance companies on a temporary basis to circumvent this regulation and to be able to borrow capital from banks. Although these funding vehicles were often officially registered as companies, in practice they acted as the investment departments of local governments. When, against the backdrop of the 2007–9 global financial crisis, Beijing required the subnational governments to expand their infrastructure investments within the context of the economic stimulus program, it became common practice that infrastructure projects would be financed through such companies. These opaque and unregulated financing mechanisms that were operating outside of central-government supervision resulted in a substantial, but largely hidden, increase in the indebtedness of the subnational governments. By the mid-2010s, this debt burden had become a serious risk not only to public finance but also to investors and companies (see Section 4.6 and Section 6.7).

Three decades of limiting fiscal-policy damage have been unable to eliminate the major problems, including the extreme lack of transparency, inadequate institutionalization, and unbalanced allocation of resources. The most serious consequence of these problems is that they reinforce social and regional disparities. At the same time, the lack of transparency in the use of extra-budgetary funding has opened the way for uncontrolled appropriations, corruption, and the accumulation of debt.

In 2013 the Xi–Li administration announced that reorganization of the fiscal system was a reform priority, and it appointed a renowned fiscal reformer as finance minister. A revised budget law setting out the major reforms was approved in September 2014. First, provincial governments would be permitted to raise capital via China's bond markets. Second, all levels of government were required to disclose all revenue and expenditures in the official budget. However, unavoidable yet highly controversial decisions about the reallocation of financial resources between the various levels of government were delayed. In China, as elsewhere, the state budgetary system is the subject of constant conflicts over funding allocations and negotiations.

2.8.2 Budgets and public debt

During the period of the planned economy, China's government did not accumulate large debts on either the domestic or the foreign side. It has only been since the beginning of the reform era that the government has recorded regular budget deficits. Initially, these deficits were mainly financed by borrowing from the central bank (Ma Jun 2013). It was only when this practice was abolished in 1994 that government bonds gained in importance. But budget deficits remained limited until the end of the 1990s. When the government approved an economic stimulus plan in reaction to the 1997–98 Asian financial crisis and introduced an expansive fiscal policy aimed at new areas of expenditure (including increased expenditures for social security), the deficit grew significantly (see Figure 2.8.C).

Nevertheless, official statistics provide a distorted view because they do not take into account expenditures that are financed outside of the official budget. In particular, many loans granted to the SOEs by state-owned banks in reality are state subsidies that are not reported on the government budget. If the SOEs cannot service their debt-service payments to the banks, these irrecoverable loans accumulate on the balance sheets of the state-owned banks. When a serious revenue crisis occurred in the state sector at the end of the 1990s, such irrecoverable loans in China's banking sector accounted for up to one-third of China's GDP (Naughton 2007). If these state-sector loans had been rep capital on the stock exchanges in China or abroad orted in the official government budget, the budget deficit would have been significantly higher.

Figure 2.8.C

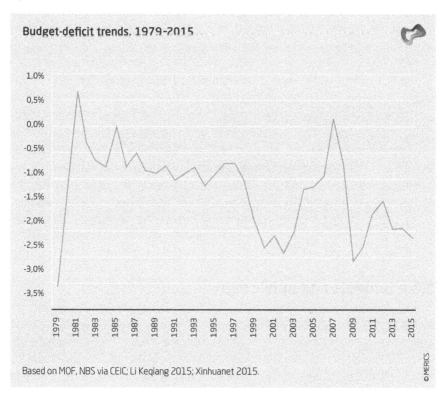

Budget-deficit trends, 1979-2015

Based on MOF, NBS via CEIC; Li Keqiang 2015; Xinhuanet 2015.

©MERICS

In the 2000s the official budgetary position eased due to the exceptionally strong economic growth and the rapidly increasing tax revenue. In 2007, for the first time since the beginning of the reform period, the government posted a budget surplus. At the same time, the number of state-controlled loans contracted as a result of the introduction of a stricter risk-management regime for the provision of bank loans. Nevertheless, quasi-fiscal loans continued to be provided on a large scale by state-owned banks well into the 2010s for the financing of infrastructure, in particular to construction companies and local-government financing vehicles.

When the central government approved a huge economic stimulus plan against the backdrop of the global financial crisis in 2007–9, the budgetary position once again worsened. Although the central-government deficit remained below the critical threshold of 3 percent of GDP (see Figure 2.8.C), the indebtedness of the subnational governments increased dramatically because they were required by the central government to finance numerous expensive infrastructure projects (see Section 6.7).

In mid-2013 the official debt of the central government amounted to only 17.3 percent of GDP (see Table 2.8). In addition, the central government was required to guarantee debts amounting to 4.5 percent of GDP. The majority of this guaranteed debt consisted of bonds issued on behalf of the China Railway Corporation (the successor organization to the former Ministry of Railways) for the further development of the national rail network.

A much more negative picture emerges when the local-government debt is taken into account. According to investigations by the NAO (2013), in mid-2013 local-government debt stood at 19.1 percent of GDP. Additionally, local-government contingent liabilities amounted to 12.3 percent of GDP. Nevertheless, there were significant differences in the level of debt among the various regions. Whereas the southwestern province of Guizhou posted a debt of more than 80 percent of provincial GDP, the indebtedness of the eastern province of Shandong was less than 20 percent of its GDP (*Economist* 2014). In the aggregate, by mid-2013 central and local-government debt, including guaranteed debt, amounted to total government debt of 53 percent of GDP. By international standards, such a moderate level of state debt is widely judged to be sustainable. Furthermore, the external government debt was also very small (2014: USD 55 billion).

However, given the opaque financing mechanisms at the lower levels of government (see Section 6.7), official statistics do not report the full extent of the indebtedness. These statistics also fail to take into account the irrecoverable state-owned bank loans. In the course of the economic stimulus program that was approved in 2008, state-owned banks (including commercial banks and state development banks, referred to as "policy banks") were required to vastly expand their lending without enforcing strict checks of creditworthiness. As a result of this relaxed credit policy, after 2008 the volume of irrecoverable loans increased significantly. In essence, this was due to the quasi-fiscal loans that were only partially reported in the government budgets. Furthermore, in the near future costs related to China's social-security system will place a much heavier burden on the government budget due to demographic changes and the rapidly increasing expenditures for pensions and the provision of healthcare.

Table 2.8

China's government debt, 2013

Type of debt	Percentage of GDP
Central-government debt	17.3
Debt guaranteed by the central government	4.5
Local-government debt	19.1
Debt guaranteed by local governments	12.3
Total	53.2

Based on NAO 2013.

The rapid growth in subnational government debt since the introduction of the economic stimulus plan and the infrastructure programs in 2008–9 was a source of concern to the Chinese government. Because the economically less-developed regions were heavily burdened with debt, quality differences in the provision of public services (such as education, healthcare, social security, and police services) increased. Therefore, between 2014 and 2020 the MOF plans to consolidate public finances at the lower levels of government by gradually reorganizing the budgetary and taxation systems.

2.8.3 Expenditure priorities in the national budget

The national budget reflects government priorities. General transfer payments and tax refunds to subnational governments represent the largest item in the central-government budget. Traditionally, the second-largest expenditure item has been defense (see Figure 2.8.D). Although the absolute increase in defense expenditures attracts much attention worldwide, in recent years the proportion of the total budget spent on defense has not changed significantly.

There were substantial shifts in the government's budgetary priorities under the Hu–Wen administration (2002–12). Against the backdrop of the global financial crisis, the leadership implemented social security, healthcare, and educational reforms that had long been planned and significantly increased financial resources in these areas. These measures were primarily aimed at closing the gap between urban and rural standards of living.

Figure 2.8.D

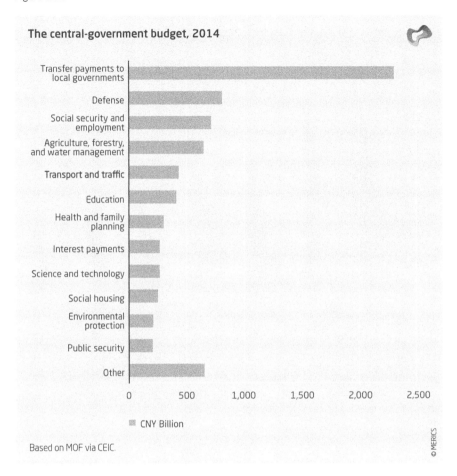

The central-government budget, 2014

Based on MOF via CEIC.

Whereas spending on social security, healthcare, and education accounted for less than 3 percent of the total national budget in 2007, it rose to almost 22 percent by 2014. The additional funding for these policy areas was reported in the central-government budget. Nevertheless, a large part of this funding was paid to the subnational governments in the form of earmarked transfer payments.

As a result of efforts to boost environmentally sustainable economic growth and to make productivity gains in agriculture, spending on farming, forestry, and water management as well as on environmental protection has increased markedly in recent years. Furthermore, funding to further develop the transport system has grown considerably, especially in the western regions (see Figure 2.8.E). However, the boom in state infrastructure investment, which began against the backdrop of the global financial crisis, was mainly financed by the local governments.

Figure 2.8.E

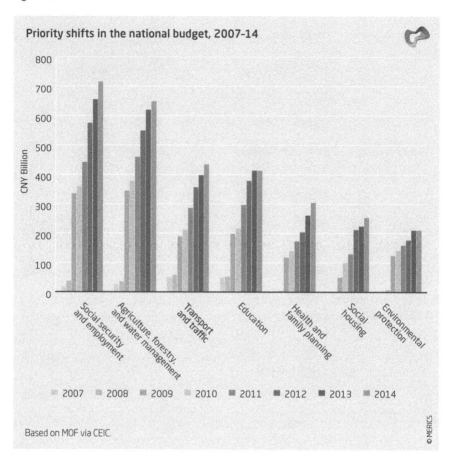

Priority shifts in the national budget, 2007-14

Based on MOF via CEIC.

© MERICS

2.9 The cadre system and public administration

Sebastian Heilmann, Lea Shih, and Matthias Stepan

In Chinese, the word "cadre" (干部) is used as a general designation for any leading officials appointed by the CCP to serve in the party, government, administration, judiciary, SOEs, public-service units, or other associations. The term also refers to military officers. Originally a French word, "cadre" was given a new, politicized meaning by the Russian Bolsheviks and was brought to China as a loan word from the

Japanese. Whereas in European languages "cadre" is used to refer to a group of leaders—i.e., the "executive level," in the sense of the elite or the avant-garde—the word in Chinese is a designation for individuals, whereby a "cadre" is a person appointed to a leadership position (Schurmann 1968).

2.9.1 The *nomenklatura* system for senior cadres

The right to appoint and remove top-ranking political and administrative personnel is an essential pillar of CCP power. To maintain such control, the CCP avails itself of the *nomenklatura* system (干部职务名单制), literally meaning the "system of lists designating cadre positions." Originally taken from the Soviets, the *nomenklatura* system was subsequently modified to meet Chinese requirements. The *nomenklatura* system defines the functions and job titles of leading party cadres. All functionaries from county leaders or division-chief levels and above are classified as leading party cadres. The leading party cadres, who are appointed by the leading organs of the party following the approval of the CCP organization departments, constitute the Chinese power elite who dominate and steer the political system. In 1997–98, there were about 500,000 such leading party cadres (see Tables 2.9.A and 2.9.B). According to unofficial figures, this figure is estimated to have risen to about 650,000 by 2015.

Table 2.9.A provides an overview of the number of cadres in the Chinese system. Such detailed data are only available until 1997. Since then, the Central Organization Department of the Communist Party has treated personnel statistics as a state secret because they provide insights into China's political hierarchies and power elite.

The CCP's *nomenklatura* system is based on the Leninist (Soviet) model. To this day, the CCP holds firm to the key Leninist principle according to which "the Communist Party controls the cadres" (党管干部). At the level of party headquarters, the *nomenklatura* system basically consists of three lists:

- a list of cadre positions to be filled and overseen directly by Communist Party headquarters (中央管理的干部职务名称表);
- a list of cadre positions to be filled by regional party offices but reported to party headquarters, meaning that the party leadership has the right to intervene if it has any objections to the appointments (向中央备案的干部职务名单);
- a "cadre reserve" list, which is a list of those persons suitable to fill the leadership positions in question (后备干部名单).

The organization departments at the various levels of the CCP hierarchy maintain their own lists. These are inaccessible either to the public or to party members.

Table 2.9.A

State and party cadres in the PRC, 1997

	Number	Percentage (%)
Total number of cadres	40,190,000	100
Leading party cadres	492,300	1.2
Lower-level cadres	39,697,700	98.8
CCP members among cadres	15,273,000	38.0
Non-CCP cadres	24,917,000	62.0
Members of the "United Front" parties among the cadres	224,000	0.6
Female cadres	13,838,000	34.4
Ethnic minority cadres	2,684,000	6.7
Cadres with academic degrees	17,730,000	44.1
Cadres younger than the age of 45	30,416,000	75.5
Cadres older than the age of 55	2,419,000	6.0
Total number of cadres as a percentage of the entire population	3.25%	
Leading party cadres as a percentage of the entire total population	0.04%	

Based on CCP CC Organization Department; Personnel Department 1999; Heilmann 2002. Most recent data unavailable.

© MERICS

The CCP CC Organization Department keeps a list of what in 2014 was an estimated 4,000 leadership positions that are directly filled and monitored by party headquarters. These positions are at the top China's pyramid of political power.

The criteria for selecting leading party cadres have changed since the 1980s in line with the changing priorities of the incumbent leadership. In the 1980s the criteria focused on rejuvenation and professionalization. Some 2.9 million older cadres—many of whom were veterans of the Chinese Revolution of 1949—retired and were gradually replaced by a new generation of younger, better-educated cadres. In the 1990s party headquarters established additional criteria for recruiting cadres, with greater weight placed on the applicants' personal political views, leadership qualities, and practical work experience in diverse areas, especially at the lower administrative levels ("grassroots experience").

Table 2.9.B

Hierarchy of leading party cadres, 1980-98*

	1980	1990	1998	
Total	167,650	344,785	508,025	100%
In central party or state organs	*17,498*	*29,274*	*41,689*	*8%*
Provincial leadership/ ministerial level and above	1,882	2,261	2,562	0.5%
Prefectural leadership/ bureau-head level	23,483	30,259	39,108	7.7%
County leadership/ division-head level	142,285	312,265	466,355	91.8%

Note: *Functionaries from the county leadership/division-head level and above in organs of the CCP, people's congresses, people's governments, CPPCC, judicial bodies, trade union federation, youth league, women's federation, and other para-state associations.
Based on CCP CC Organization Department 1999; Heilmann 2002.

© MERICS

In addition to establishing more stringent selection criteria, the process of recommending, nominating, and appointing leading party cadres has become more standardized since 1995. In 2002 and 2012, party headquarters issued modified regulations containing more specific instructions on the selection and deployment of leading party and government cadres. In light of the experience gained since the 1990s, however, it is questionable whether such formal requirements will be effective in limiting the personal power of party secretaries and patronage within the party if external-control mechanisms and open electoral processes are not introduced. Time and again, reports appear in the party and state media of the formal requirements for a career as a leading party cadre being circumvented, at least at the lower levels of government, based on patronage and "old boy networks" (including active bribery and the purchase of offices).

The *nomenklatura* authority of party headquarters has proven indispensable since the 1980s for the political enforcement of national programs and priorities, especially in policy areas in which there are ongoing conflicts of interest between the center and the regional governments. For example, measures such as those aimed at controlling inflation (1993–96), centralizing financial supervision (1997–99), reducing pollutants (since 2005), and fighting corruption (since 2013) have been enforced by means of the political pressures that party headquarters is able to exert on the provincial governments by virtue of its personnel authority and organizational power. Hence the *nomenklatura* system forms an indispensable, core element in the PRC's political system with regard to the hierarchy and integration of the power elite and the political authority of party headquarters.

2.9.2 Administrative reorganization

Due to the rapid economic, social, and technological transformations, entirely new administrative requirements have emerged in China. In this context, administrative reform has become an ongoing project. Some of the primary issues referred to in internal Chinese debates are overstaffing, especially at the lower administrative levels; insufficient or outdated skills on the part of personnel; unclear or overlapping areas of responsibility for government agencies; ineffective processes and unsatisfactory handling of administrative tasks; and new demands from the population regarding the provision of public services.

To manage personnel numbers and costs, both the party and the government use a system of staffing plans (编制) that list the number, rank, and pay grade of public-sector positions to be filled at state institutions. According to the National Bureau of Statistics (NBS), China had approximately 63 million urban public-sector employees in 2014, distributed among SOEs, the military, state organs, and public-service units (事业单位), such as educational and research institutes or hospitals. The Chinese government does not publish statistics on the distribution of personnel at various levels of government. However, there are well-established estimates regarding the distribution of such personnel in 2002 (Burns 2006).

Figure 2.9 shows that in 2002, almost one-half of all public-sector employees worked for SOEs. What is noteworthy with regard to the administrative personnel is that only a small proportion (50,000) worked in ministries or state bodies at the central-government level. The majority of the personnel were employed by regional administrative authorities or by public-service units.

Whereas the number of employees in SOEs has been declining since the end of the 1990s, the number of personnel in state and party organs has risen steadily and it surpassed the 40-million mark in 2008 (see Table 2.9.C). Between 1990 and 2000, the number of employees in the public sector increased by 68 percent. During the same period, the ratio of public-sector employees to the total population increased from 1:50 to 1:34. There has thus been a striking increase in the number of public-sector employees in China since the 1990s, despite the many reforms in the state economic sector and the numerous measures aimed at downsizing in terms of the bureaucracy and personnel.

The bureaucratic Leviathan embodied by China's huge state apparatus appears to be impervious to all political attempts to harness it or to trim it down. At most Chinese government agencies, staffing plans issued by upper hierarchical

Figure 2.9

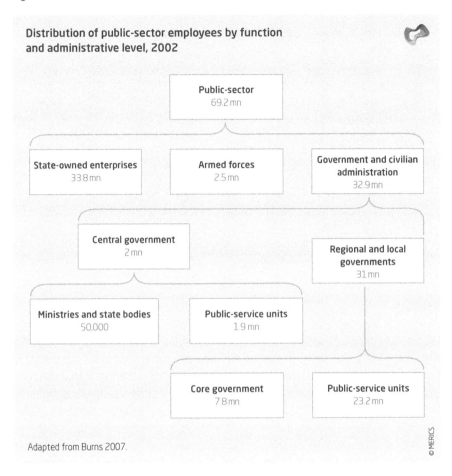

Distribution of public-sector employees by function and administrative level, 2002

Public-sector
69.2 mn

State-owned enterprises
33.8 mn

Armed forces
2.5 mn

Government and civilian administration
32.9 mn

Central government
2 mn

Regional and local governments
31 mn

Ministries and state bodies
50,000

Public-service units
1.9 mn

Core government
7.8 mn

Public-service units
23.2 mn

Adapted from Burns 2007.

© MERICS

levels have been exceeded as a matter of course ever since the 1980s—sometimes by more than 50 percent. The swelling bureaucracy has led to a dramatic rise in personnel costs. In some provinces, personnel costs amounted to up to 80 percent of public revenue in the mid-2000s (Burns 2007). In the 1990s and 2000s, the Chinese government repeatedly claimed to have successfully downsized after a number of ministries or other government agencies were shut down or merged. However, this was nothing but a repeating cycle of the same processes leading to the same outcomes. Other than those who directly retired, the majority of the laid-off personnel were outsourced to public-service units or state-run associations, which have experienced an especially high increase in staff levels since the end of the 1990s.

Table 2.9.C

Public-sector employees, 1995-2008									
	1995	2000	2001	2002	2003	2005	2006	2007	2008
State organs	9.4	10.2	10.2	9.8	10.6	11.2	11.7	11.9	12.3
Public-service units	24.1	25.6	25.5	25.1	25.1	25.9	27.1	27.4	27.9
Party organs	0.6	0.5	0.5	0.5	0.5	0.5	0.5	0.6	0.6
Total	34.1	36.3	36.2	35.4	36.1	37.6	39.3	39.9	40.8

Based on NBS, China Statistical Yearbook 1996; 2001–9. Figures in million (rounded).

© MERICS

Salaries

During the period between the introduction of the reform and opening policy and the early 1990s, civil servant salaries declined sharply in comparison to those of both white- and blue-collar workers. It was not until later in the 1990s that the central government implemented a series of substantial civil servant pay increases. In January 2015, the Ministry of Human Resources and Social Security (MOHRSS) and the MOF jointly announced a dramatic rise of up to 30 percent in basic pay levels. The stated objective was to make the public sector more meritocratic so that it would be more attractive to qualified candidates. At the same time, it was deemed illegal to earn additional income in the private sector. In the past, civil servants had significantly supplemented their incomes by taking on additional work for state agencies or by offering private consultancy services.

The salaries paid to public-sector employees comprise several components and can vary widely from one province or administrative department to another (Wu 2014a). Beginning in 2006, the central government took on the task of standardizing the pay system for public-sector employees based on a number of key indicators: administrative rank (级别), defined according to one's qualifications and experience, and the specific function and position (职务) within the state administration (Brødsgaard/Chen 2014). There are also pay supplements (补贴) based on local costs of living. In many places, these supplements actually exceed the basic salary, which means that there are considerable differences among the income levels of civil servants in various cities and provinces.

In addition to their pay, civil servants enjoy preferential treatment in terms of obtaining subsidized housing. They are also entitled to medical care with minimal deductibles as well as noncontributory pensions. In 2014 the privileges accorded to state-sector employees faced public criticism. Scholars close to the government proposed that state employees should make a greater contribution to the costs of their healthcare and pension schemes.

Job qualification requirements, recruiting, and further training

In the late 1980s the incumbent party leadership proclaimed the "separation of party and state." This sparked heated discussions regarding a possible loss of control by the party. Dozens of draft bills and directives that provided for making a distinction between political and professional career civil servants were defeated due to resistance from within the CCP leadership and the Central Organization Department. In 1993 the Provisional Regulations on Civil Servants were issued by the Ministry of Personnel, which was responsible for public-sector employees, in order to lay the groundwork for establishing a modern civil-service system in China.

These regulations represent a compromise. They set forth a series of detailed provisions to be put into effect in subsequent years with the objective of restructuring the state bureaucracy. The provisions include introducing open, competitive examinations to recruit personnel for the public sector, setting more stringent requirements for top-level appointments, and experimenting with performance reviews for leading officials. Regular rotations of officials in top positions were also introduced in order to prevent corruption and abuses of power.

The rapidly increasing educational levels (public-sector employees holding academic degrees) and the growing number of applicants for civil-service positions were signs that the reforms had been successful. In 2009 the number of applicants for civil-service positions exceeded the number of advertised positions by more than fiftyfold (see Table 2.9.D). Between 2004 and 2014 the number of participants in the annual civil-service exams held by the central government to fill open positions (国家公务员考试) rose from 140,000 to nearly 1.2 million. For those taking the selection exam, the chances of being considered for an open position were slim. In 2014 there was an average of 57 test participants for each open position.

By the mid-2010s, however, civil-service positions appeared to have once again diminished in popularity. The strict anti-corruption campaign meant that civil servants no longer had access to the additional income that had previously rendered their jobs financially lucrative. At the same time, many top civil servants complained of increased work responsibilities and pressures. In early 2015, the Chinese media reported that leading civil servants in cities and localities were leaving their jobs en masse.

Table 2.9.D

Popularity of the civil service: Applicants for open civil-service jobs, 2004-14

Year	Test participants (in thousands) (A)	Number of open positions (B)	Ratio of A : B
2004	140	7,572	19
2005	290	8,271	35
2006	536	10,282	52
2007	356	12,724	28
2008	637	13,787	46
2009	775	13,566	57
2010	928	15,526	60
2011	902	15,290	59
2012	960	17,941	54
2013	1,117	20,879	53
2014	1,119	19,538	57

Based on Civil Service Network (中央公务员考试网) 2013a, 2013b.

© MERICS

When recruiting personnel for positions in the central government, it became increasingly common to make use of multi-step evaluation and assessment procedures. The extensive selection process was intended not only to ensure that the applicants were suitably qualified, but also to prevent patronage and the purchase of positions. Education and training programs were implemented to increase professionalism and to enhance performance in the public sector, with nearly two-thirds of all civil servants taking part in such programs each year since 2010. In 2005 the NPC passed the National Public Service Act (公务员法). This new piece of legislation was the product of experience gained since the 1990s during the gradual restructuring of the civil service.

However, both party and government headquarters have made it clear that the Public Service Act is not intended to eliminate the cadre system of the Communist Party, nor does it seek to establish a politically neutral civil service. Rather, the government holds tight to the principles of loyalty to the Communist Party on the part of all public-sector employees, selecting personnel on the basis of ideological and moral criteria and making no distinction between political and professional civil servants.

Restructuring programs

Past attempts to streamline the administration usually resulted in merely superficial changes, such as state agencies being renamed and jobs being transferred to public enterprises, public-service units, or professional associations. It took a long time before any substantial organizational streamlining or performance improvements occurred.

In the mid-1990s, the central leadership began promoting measures to reduce the number of ministries and other government agencies under the State Council. The number of ministerial-level organs was reduced from 41 to 25 between 1994 and 2013. Sectoral and industrial ministries, which embodied the close relationship between government and the economy during the past era of the planned economy, were either shut down or downgraded to professional associations. By contrast, new types of government supervisory commissions with special administrative powers were established in order to establish market-based instruments for economic management.

Processes and working methods

Some of the most frequent areas of criticism from both the general public and industrial and service companies relate to the unclear division of responsibilities between the various government agencies as well as the lengthy and complicated administrative processes. Since the late 1990s, the Chinese government has made repeated attempts to reduce the bureaucracy and to simplify administration. One of the main thrusts of these efforts has been to expedite the process of obtaining administrative approvals. The Administrative Licensing Law (行政许可法), adopted in 2003, was designed to effect far-reaching administrative changes by promoting deregulation (see the case study on administrative modernization and economic deregulation described in Section 6.2 for more information).

2.9.3 New approaches in public administration

China's tradition of a state-controlled economy meant that a comprehensive reform of public administration was imperative if there was to be any chance of establishing the institutional requirements for a functioning system based on market mechanisms. For example, the established economic bureaucracy had proved to be incapable of controlling all aspects of the new private sector and of consistently imposing taxes. At times, twelve different government agencies competed to play a role in regulation of the private sector. Such bureaucratic confusion was essentially a political prerequisite—that initially went nearly unnoticed—in the extremely rapid growth of the private sector and in an administrative and economic system in which private enterprises were not treated as equal economic entities.

In the 1980s national leaders began discussing ways to modernize the administration. The intention was to create an efficient, lean administration in order to facilitate implementation of state policies, improve the economic environment, and regain legitimacy among the population. In 1987 Zhao Ziyang, then general secretary of the Communist Party, announced an ambitious "political structure reform" program intended to limit party control over state administration and thus to gradually depoliticize and professionalize the civil service. The reform met with massive resistance from some sectors of the party leadership and was silently laid to rest after Zhao was ousted in 1989. The political forces that prevailed between 1989 and 1991 supported strict party control over state administration and personnel. Very few of the intended administrative reforms were continued and only on a limited scale, often in the form of regional experiments.

It was not until the 1992 series of reforms that discussions on reform of the administration were resumed with fresh vigor. A number of party documents emphasized the necessity for a transition from direct administrative control over the economy to indirect regulation and macroeconomic control (宏观调控) and for measures to increase general administrative efficiency.

During the 2000s, and especially during the period from 2006 to 2010 when the 11th Five-Year Plan was in effect, new social concerns and demands were increasingly at the forefront of the administrative reforms. The focus was on forming a service-oriented administration that would provide reliable education and healthcare as well as effective consumer and environmental protection. A spate of scandals in the food industry, serious environmental degradation, and a lack of adequate public services (such as child care and care for the elderly) provoked criticisms about the lack of services provided by the state administration. Although the government increased the involvement of nongovernmental organizations (NGOs) to supply social services, such as healthcare, care for the elderly, and support for disabled persons, these measures had only minimal success. Moreover, critics from within the party warned of a potential loss of control and reputation if the state administration began delegating public responsibilities to NGOs.

In 2013 president and CCP general secretary Xi Jinping announced the goal of establishing a cleaner, more efficient government that is closer to the public. However, this goal will not be achievable without more extensive restructuring and liberalization of the administrative system. Until now, no effective regulatory or control mechanisms have been put in place in those areas that are regarded by the population as posing immediate risks—health, the environment, food, and pharmaceuticals—despite the fact that statutory and regulatory standards have already been established. Only active participation by citizens and the public, in combination with reliable administrative controls and sanctions, will result in improved government supervision in these key areas.

2.10 Legislation, the People's Congresses, and the Political Consultative Conferences

Sebastian Heilmann and Matthias Stepan

Until the end of the 1970s the Chinese party and state leaderships primarily made use of executive orders—internal party instructions and government decrees—to implement national political action programs. However, since 1979 the importance of formal legislation by the NPC, and particularly by its Standing Committee, has grown steadily. In addition, the expansion of the administrative staff of the people's congresses and the establishment of permanent committees, such as the budget committee, have enhanced the professionalization of legislative work. In spite of these developments, however, people's congresses still do not come close to having the capacities and competencies that are required for them to act as control entities or as counterweights to the dominance of the executive.

2.10.1 Regulation and law-making

Binding rules in the PRC may originate in various state or party organs (see Table 2.10.A). However, executive orders and provisions by the State Council and other government entities constitute the largest proportion of legal regulations. Economic law, in particular, has experienced extraordinarily dynamic development. Between 1978 and 1998 the NPC enacted 328 laws and decisions related to the economy, and the central government passed as many as 700 orders to regulate the economy. Furthermore, there were tens of thousands of decrees, ordinances, and implementation provisions issued by individual central ministries as well as thousands of local ordinances. Following the official commitment to build a "socialist market economy," drafts of economic legislation drew heavily and directly from foreign rules and regulations and from foreign advisers. Of all the sectors in the Chinese legal system, economic law most closely approximates international legal standards.

Table 2.10.A

Regulations of state and party organs

State/party organs	Instruments of regulation
NPC	General, basic laws (国法)
Standing Committee of the NPC	Laws and decisions
State Council (central government)	Legal orders (provisions [条例], regulations [规定], and measures [办法])
Ministries of the State Council	Implementing provisions for laws passed by the NPC, and administrative provisions related to a particular area or spanning multiple ministries
Central party organs (sometimes combined with government organs)	Political action programs and guidelines (for instance, on media control or to combat corruption); announced sometimes in internal party memoranda and sometimes in public documents
Party leadership organs at different levels	Guidelines and instructions, valid only within the scope of their power
Supreme People's Court	Instructions ("opinions") on applying laws or orders
Provincial people's congresses	Local legal provisions for solidifying central regulations or for filling existing legal gaps
State Council; Foreign Ministry; Ministry of Commerce, etc.	International agreements (ratified by the NPC Standing Committee)

Based on Heuser 2000.

© MERICS

As in most government systems, the majority of legislative proposals are introduced by the government. In China, however, groups of delegates to the NPC, the NPC special committees, and certain state organs (the CMC, the Supreme People's Court, and the Supreme People's Procuratorate) are also entitled to initiate legislation. The legislation introduced to the NPC is set forth in one-year or five-year plans. In addition to participation by special ministries, research institutes, and staff advisers, the Legal Office of the State Council (国务院法制办公室), the Legal Affairs Commission of the NPC (人大法律委员会), and the Legal Affairs Commission of the NPC Standing Committee (法工委) play key roles in drafting legislative proposals. Conflicts often arise within and among these participants, leading to extensive revisions of drafts and sometimes to delays that can drag on for years.

It took seven years of disputes over competencies on many levels before the Law on Legislation (立法法), which was intended to regulate legislative procedures, was passed in March 2000. This law (amended in 2015) stipulates that certain subjects (including national organization, criminal law, tax law, and other "basic" commercial law issues) can only be regulated by laws enacted by the NPC or its Standing Committee. The legislative authority of the government is restricted insofar as the executive bodies must now have specific authorization to issue legal orders. In addition, the NPC Standing Committee is authorized to rescind executive orders "that contradict the constitution or the law." Constraints on local-government regulations, which up until now have often run rampant, are intended to enhance the unity of the legal system and legal security. The Standing Committee of the NPC has the right to interpret the law and to perform judicial reviews (including in response to "proposals" by individual associations, businesses, or citizens). Furthermore, the law establishes a clear hierarchy of norms. Statutes enacted by the NPC and its Standing Committee have precedence over legal orders issued by the government.

2.10.2 The People's Congresses

The constitution of 1982 refers to the people's congresses as "organs through which the people exercise state power" and the NPC is referred to as the "highest organ of state power." In the tradition of the socialist system of soviets, the people's congresses are understood to be organs where the legislative, executive, and judicial functions converge. In other words, they practice a concentration of power instead of a separation of power as is commonly found in the liberal democracies. According to the constitution, governments at various administrative levels act as the executive organs of the respective people's congresses. Courts and procuratorates are deployed by the people's congresses.

However, in practice the people's congresses are subject to instructions and controls by the leadership organs of the CCP. In 2002, following efforts to consolidate personnel, the regional party secretaries were urged by the Central Organization Department to assume leadership positions in the regional people's congresses. The intention was to merge the party's political authority over instructions and controls with the formal constitutional authority of the people's congresses. In 2015, as part of a personnel merger, the party secretaries in most provinces, in their capacity as the "Number One Person" (一把手), also became the chairmen of the regional people's congresses. Exceptions to this rule were found only in the four directly administered municipalities, in the autonomous regions of Tibet and Xinjiang, and in Guangdong province.

In contrast to the Supreme Soviet of the former USSR, the NPC has only one chamber and convenes with almost 3,000 delegates once a year for one to two

Figure 2.10

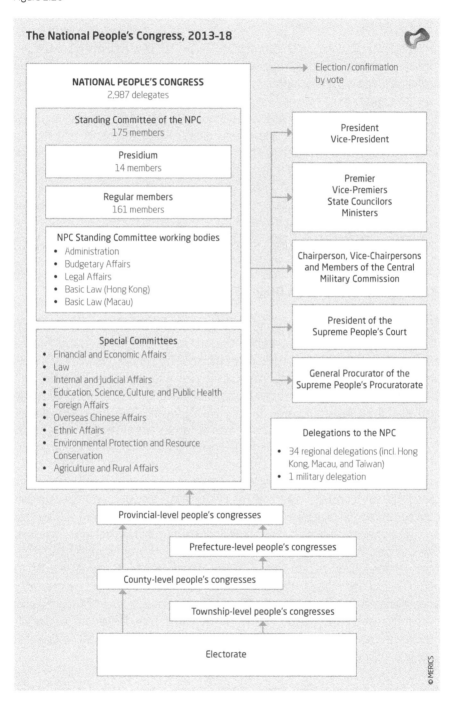

The National People's Congress, 2013-18

NATIONAL PEOPLE'S CONGRESS
2,987 delegates

⟶ Election / confirmation by vote

Standing Committee of the NPC
175 members

Presidium
14 members

Regular members
161 members

NPC Standing Committee working bodies
- Administration
- Budgetary Affairs
- Legal Affairs
- Basic Law (Hong Kong)
- Basic Law (Macau)

Special Committees
- Financial and Economic Affairs
- Law
- Internal and Judicial Affairs
- Education, Science, Culture, and Public Health
- Foreign Affairs
- Overseas Chinese Affairs
- Ethnic Affairs
- Environmental Protection and Resource Conservation
- Agriculture and Rural Affairs

President
Vice-President

Premier
Vice-Premiers
State Councilors
Ministers

Chairperson, Vice-Chairpersons and Members of the Central Military Commission

President of the Supreme People's Court

General Procurator of the Supreme People's Procuratorate

Delegations to the NPC
- 34 regional delegations (incl. Hong Kong, Macau, and Taiwan)
- 1 military delegation

Provincial-level people's congresses

Prefecture-level people's congresses

County-level people's congresses

Township-level people's congresses

Electorate

© MERICS

weeks, generally at the beginning or in the middle of March. Such a gargantuan assembly with such a brief duration is only capable of ratifying decisions made in advance, and it cannot introduce legislation or supervise the legislative process. For this reason, a major part of the legislative activity since the early 1980s has shifted to the Standing Committee of the NPC (see Figure 2.10). The Standing Committee is an assembly of full-time delegates that convenes approximately once every two months. The delegates are not allowed to occupy any other positions in the state or judicial systems. The members of the Standing Committee constitute only about six percent of the NPC delegates, but since the 1990s they have gained leverage in national policy making.

The constitution sets the legislative period at five years. This constitutional provision, however, was not strictly observed until 1978 (see Table 2.10.B). During the annual NPC sessions only several plenary sessions are held, in which reports on activities of the government and other organs are discussed and approved, important bills are passed, and personnel adjustments are made. The most important activity is participation in the group sessions of the thirty-five NPC delegations.

Table 2.10.B

National People's Congresses, 1954-2013

NPC	Inaugural Session	Chairman	Delegates, NPC plenum
1st	9/1954	Liu Shaoqi	1,226
2nd	4/1959	Zhu De	1,226
3rd	12/1964	Zhu De	3,040
4th	1/1975	Zhu De	2,885
5th	3/1978	Ye Jianying	3,497
6th	6/1983	Peng Zhen	2,978
7th	4/1988	Wan Li	2,970
8th	3/1993	Qiao Shi	2,978
9th	3/1998	Li Peng	2,979
10th	3/2003	Wu Bangguo	2,984
11th	3/2008	Wu Bangguo	2,987
12th	3/2013	Zhang Dejiang	2,987

Based on NBS 2015a; Heilmann 2002.

© MERICS

During these meetings, there are discussions on controversial topics and criticisms of the work of the government.

The military is highly overrepresented in the NPC. One military delegate generally represents about 10,000 military staff members, whereas the ratio for civilians is 1:400,000. For a long time there was also an imbalance between the representation of Chinese citizens living in the urban and those living in the rural areas. At the 10th NPC, one delegate from a rural region represented approximately 960,000 rural residents, whereas one delegate from an urban district represented only 240,000 urban residents. Not until 2010 did an amendment to the voting law put an end to this imbalance. At the 12th NPC, delegates from the rural and urban areas represented an equal number of eligible voters.

In the Standing Committee to the NPC, the economically more robust coastal provinces are more strongly represented than the poor inland regions. The regional proportions are important because provincial delegates, including retired provincial governors and other regional leading cadres, can pursue relatively open lobbying within the NPC in the interest of their home regions.

The total number of delegates to the people's congresses at various levels is substantial. In addition to the almost 3,000 delegates to the NPC, there are some 2.7 million delegates to the people's congresses at the lower governmental levels nationwide (provinces, prefectures, counties, and towns/townships). Delegates are directly elected only at the town/township and county levels. At the higher administrative levels they are elected indirectly by the people's congresses at the next lower level. This indirect, filtered voting procedure provides the CCP with considerable possibilities to control the personnel composition and to select delegates who are politically loyal.

Special attention is paid to achieving a visually pleasing, representative composition. This is demonstrated by a balanced mix of workers/peasants, functionaries, soldiers, and intellectuals, and by strong representation of ethnic minorities and women (see Table 2.10.C). The voting procedures and the exact numbers of the various representatives are announced at the closing session of the NPC.

Migrant workers, who make up almost one-fifth of the Chinese population, were granted their own representatives at the 2008 11th NPC (3 delegates) and at the 2013 12th NPC (31 delegates). With respect to political affiliations, more than two-thirds of the delegates to the NPC are put forward by the CCP. The remainder are allotted to members of the "United Front," consisting of representatives of the eight "democratic parties" and independents. The number of delegates representing China's extremely wealthy has increased: in 2013, 15 persons from among the 100 wealthiest Chinese were delegates to the 12th NPC.

A temporary party organization is established in the people's congress body for the duration of the annual meetings. CCP delegates are thus constantly reminded

Table 2.10.C

Delegates to the National People's Congress, 1954–2018 (percentages)

	1st NPC 1954–59	4th NPC 1975–78	6th NPC 1983–88	8th NPC 1993–98	9th NPC 1998–2003	10th NPC 2003–8	11th NPC 2008–13	12th NPC 2013–18
Political affiliations								
CCP members	54.5	76.8	62.5	68.4	71.5	72.9	70.3	72.2
"Democratic parties"	22.4	8.3	18.2	19.2	15.4	16	29.7	27.7
Independents	23,2							
Unavailable	0	14.9	19.3	12.4	13.1	11.1		
Social backgrounds								
Workers/peasants	13.3	51.1	26.6	20.6	18.8	18.5	n/a	13.4
Functionaries	n/a	11.2	21.4	28.3	33.2	32.4	n/a	34.9
Soldiers/officers	4.9	16.9	9.0	9.0	9.0	9.0	9.0	9.0
Intellectuals*	n/a	12.0	23.5	21.8	21.1	21.1	n/a	n/a
Gender and ethnic backgrounds								
Women	12.0	22.6	21.2	21.0	21.8	20.2	21.3	23.4
Ethnic minorities	14.4	9.4	13.6	14.7	14.4	13.9	13.8	13.7
Overseas Chinese	2.5	1.0	1.3	1.2	1.3	n/a	1.2	1.2
Educational backgrounds								
Academic degrees	n/a	n/a	44.5	69.0	81.2	92.5	n/a	n/a
Newly elected	n/a	n/a	76.5	71.0	74.1	70.1	n/a	n/a

Note: *Scientists, engineers, journalists, artists, etc.
Based on Heilmann 2002.

© MERICS

that party discipline requires staunch support of central party policies and rejection of "erroneous" initiatives from delegates who do not belong to the CCP.

Since the late 1980s, changes in the political role of the people's congresses have been manifested at all levels. To control and regulate economic change, the party leadership has made increasing use of legislation enacted by the NPC and its Standing Committee. At the same time, the people's congresses at lower administrative levels are expected to play a more effective role over regional government bodies to curb corruption and to control the budget. From the perspective of the party leadership, strengthening the people's congresses should not serve the purpose of establishing a parliamentary democratic opening up, but rather it should enhance the performance of the economic and administrative systems.

A prerequisite for the more active political role by the NPC and its Standing Committee was the organizational expansion of the special committees and working organs. Whereas the NPC had fewer than one dozen permanent employees at the end of the 1970s, during the 1980s this number grew to more than 2,000. These employees work on preparing for the sessions, attending to the delegates and the special committees, and participating in the legislative process. They create a markedly improved basis for working and obtaining information.

Voting behavior

Even though the Chinese people's congresses are not able to independently exercise genuine parliamentary rights (legislation, budget controls, appointing and removing governments, or representation of business interests), there are signs that a limited political life is emerging. Criticism is expressed by casting negative votes or abstentions on personnel decisions and on the work reports by the government and the national judicial organs. Since 1983 the NPC Standing Committee has occasionally blocked legislative proposals by the State Council. Still more important is the now substantial negotiating power of the NPC over government organs in the shaping of the legislative process, for there are now high-ranking "veteran" functionaries among the people's congress delegates who have developed a strong sense of self-esteem. The position of NPC chairman has been repeatedly filled by a high-ranking member of the Politburo.

Voting discipline has deteriorated since the late 1980s. In spite of the limited opportunities for action, delegates to the people's congresses occasionally demonstrate a remarkable obstinacy that is reflected in negative votes and abstentions against government proposals. For example, the Three Gorges Dam project on the Yangtze River, which was controversial due to financial, technical, and ecological reasons, met with stubborn resistance in the NPC. Following heated debates, one-third of the representatives voted against the project in 1992. In 1993 even the official media announced that the phenomenon of "unanimous consent" in voting was a thing of the past. Candidates for state leadership positions sometimes receive hundreds of opposition votes or abstentions. Since consensus rates of over 90 percent in the NPC unofficially count as a criterion for broad support, negative votes and abstentions accounting for more than 10 percent are considered to be a clear vote of disapproval. Under the Xi–Li administration (since 2012–13), however, voting discipline has been strengthened and the number of dissenting votes has declined (see Table 2.10.D).

Table 2.10.D

Selected voting results in the National People's Congress, 1995-2015

	Proportion of negative votes and abstentions
Votes on personnel matters	
Jiang Chunyun (Vice-Premier), 1995	37%
Jiang Zemin (Chairman, CMC), 2003	8%
Zeng Qinghong (Vice-President), 2003	13%
Xi Jinping (President), 2013	1%
Votes on legislative proposals /gov. programs	
Three Gorges Dam, 1992	29%
Central Bank Law, 1995	33%
Legislation Law (amendment), 2015	4%
Votes on work reports	
Government/Premier, 1995 / 2002 / 2015	3% / 3% / 1%
Supreme People's Procuratorate, 1998 / 2003 / 2015	44% / 27% / 12%
Ministry of Finance/budget report, 2002 / 2012 / 2015	20% / 20% / 14%

Based on Heilmann 2002.

© MERICS

The voting outcomes in the people's congresses at the subnational levels (provinces, prefectures, counties, and towns/townships) may occasionally offer real surprises. In the decade following 2000, official candidates appointed by the party center for the position of governor or vice-governor in isolated cases failed to win the required majority. Then, in the course of the necessary runoffs the candidates who were elected were nominated by groups of delegates. Typically, the names of the newly elected office-holders were not initially announced in order to await approval by the party center in Beijing, which occurred only after some hesitation since the party had been taken by surprise. Various research projects highlight a more active role for the local people's congresses in terms of government control of the lower administrative levels (Cho Young Nam 2009; Xia Ming 2008). However, depending on the local political context, significant differences and considerable fluctuations in the activity of the people's congresses have become apparent over the course of time. As of now, the party leadership has continued to compel "unity" and "discipline," as defined by the CCP, by exerting heavy pressure on the delegates in advance of the meetings of the people's congresses.

Controlling implementation of laws and the budget

Even though a large number of laws have been passed since 1979, it is the implementation of these laws that counts. Groups of people's congress delegates who are assigned to review the implementation of laws at irregular intervals will take inspection tours to supervise execution. Critical reports by these inspection teams can place considerable political pressures on state organs that are accused of inadequately enforcing legal provisions. For example, the following incident transpired in the spring of 2001, when the Standing Committee of the NPC sharply criticized the China Securities Regulatory Commission (CSRC) due to accusations of stock-market manipulation. However, the supervisory authority of the people's congresses always stops at the door of the party committee, which is exempt from control by the people's delegates. Therefore, as long as the autonomy of the party committees remains sacrosanct, tight constraints are placed on the control authority of the people's congresses.

Many people's congress delegates consider the limited inspections and control possibilities to be inadequate. Beginning in 1993, leading delegates to the regional people's congresses have repeatedly called for intensified democratic controls to curb corruption and abuses of power. They have argued that irregularities can only be controlled by creating a counterweight to the power of the administration. In individual provinces, regulations grant the local people's congresses greater control rights and require that the governments be accountable when responding to inquiries by delegates. In 2007 a national law went into effect in which the supervisory and control competencies of the standing committees of the people's congresses at all levels are to be strengthened relative to those of the government bodies (各级人民代表大会常务委员会监督法). This law had previously repeatedly failed in the face of objections by party and government bodies. The control rights contained in the version that was ultimately passed are significantly diluted and weakened.

Until now, the classic prerogatives of a parliament—approving taxation and controlling the budget—have had little meaning in the PRC. NPC activity in the field of budget policy primarily consists of ratifying the budget plan submitted by the MOF and issuing relatively mild admonishments to reduce the budget deficit in the following year. At least in theory, the party and state leaderships have recognized the importance of the people's congresses for budget control. Problems such as the misappropriation of state funds by local administrative bodies, the growing budget deficits, and the diminishing tax revenue collected by the central government should be kept under control by strengthening the local people's congresses.

An analogous situation existed with respect to the Budget Law, which went into effect at the beginning of 1995 (amended in 2014). In drafting, approving, implementing, and supervising public budgets there have been substantial irregularities due to a lack of legal regulations at all administrative levels. The law stipulates that a budget approved by a people's congress above the county level shall have binding force for the particular government and shall permit the standing committees of the people's congresses to carry out ongoing monitoring. In December 1998 the NPC Standing Committee took an important step by setting up a Budgetary Work Committee as a permanent working body. The purpose of establishing this working organ was to increase the possibility of continuously monitoring the government. The new Budgetary Work Committee works closely with the Financial and Economic Affairs Committee of the NPC and with the NAO.

In spite of these institutional innovations, the fiscal disciplinary effects that the legislators had been hoping for failed to materialize. Local indebtedness continued to skyrocket. Since in many cases the local governments acquired liquidity through finance companies and shadow banks, a thoroughly amended version of the Budget Law in 2014 stipulated that in the future every level of the government must disclose all income and expenditures in their budgets (see Section 2.8). Since the amended Budget Law is backed by the authority of the party leadership and by a concrete action plan of the MOF for the consolidation of local budgets from 2015 to 2020, it is likely that it will result in enhanced budget control.

The development potential of the people's congresses

In the Chinese political system decisive barriers to the development of strong legislative power persist unabated. These include, for example, delegates selected in a process that is manipulated by the party committees; the lack of an independent basis for legitimation through general elections; and, above all, the undiminished dominance of the party leadership and the state executive in policy making and legal regulation, thereby placing heavy constraints on the political leverage and the formal control authority of the people's congresses.

Until now, demands for structural reforms of the people's congress system (such as nationwide, free, and secret-ballot elections; election campaigns among several locally profiled candidates; longer and more frequent plenary sessions; and personnel choices in the election of the "people's governments") have remained unsuccessful. Party and government functionaries still regard the NPC as primarily an underling, not as an independent parliamentary control nor as an institutional counterweight to the state and party leaderships.

2.10.3 The Political Consultative Conferences

The CPPCC holds plenary sessions almost simultaneously with the annual NPC plenary meetings. This "United Front" came into existence even before the PRC was established in 1949 and before the NPC system was established in 1954 for the purpose of uniting all those parties and groups that were willing to cooperate under the leadership of the CCP. It is an advisory organ with no concrete authority to pass resolutions or to make decisions. Nevertheless, the state-run media prominently issue reports on the CPPCC to demonstrate the CCP's "multi-party cooperation" with the eight "democratic parties" and other social groups.

In 2013 the eight "democratic parties" that are represented in the CPPCC consisted of approximately 912,000 members (see Table 2.10.E). This is a clear gain over the membership figures in 2002 (580,000), 1997 (410,000), and 1985 (160,000). However, these numbers are infinitesimal when compared with CCP membership figures (close to 88 million at the end of 2014).

These are not parties in the true sense of the word that can compete with the CCP. Instead, they are organizations subordinate to the CCP that are intended to represent certain groups of people. Based on the initiative of the CCP leadership, since the mid-1990s these "parties" have been included in consultative processes on matters of economic policy and legislation. In its self-presentation, the CPPCC ascribes an important role to the All-China Federation of Industry and Commerce (中华全国工商业联合会). Since the early 1980s and during the build-up of the private economy, the political influence of this federation has grown. It primarily represents the interests of larger private companies.

The 2013 meeting of the 12th CPPCC (term from 2013 to 2018) was subdivided into thirty-four groups. Approximately 40 percent of the 2,237 delegates were members of the CCP. Unlike the NPC, where the CCP puts forward more than two-thirds of the delegates, CCP members in the CPPCC are in the minority. However, the chairman of the CPPCC is a member of the Standing Committee of the CCP Politburo (Yu Zhengsheng since 2013). Leading CCP functionaries are also strongly represented among the vice-chairmen (22 persons in 2013).

Table 2.10.E

Membership of the "United Front" parties, 2013

Party name	Number of members
Revolutionary Committee of the Chinese Guomindang (中国国民党革命委员会)	101,865
China Democratic League (中国民主同盟)	247,000
China Democratic Construction Association (中国民主建国会)	140,000
Taiwan Democratic Self-Government League (台湾民主自治同盟)	2,700
China Peasants and Workers' Democratic Party (中国农工民主党)	125,600
China Association for Promoting Democracy (中国民主促进会)	133,000
Jiusan Society (九三学社)	132,000
China Zhi Gong Dang (中国致公党)	30,000

Based on Yang Fengchun 2014.

Unlike in the NPC, CPPCC members do not form regional delegations; rather they are formed around functional criteria. The groups include the CCP, the eight "democratic parties," the eight mass organizations, associations, as well as groups from society at large, such as physicians, teachers, and peasants. The two largest single groups are made up of artists and actors, and of scientists and engineers. Additionally, approximately 150 representatives from Hong Kong and Macau belong to the CPPCC. There are also "specially invited personalities," including many prominent sports, film, and television stars. The CPPCC attracts more media attention due to its "VIP constituency" rather than due to its political functions.

The most important task of the CPPCC is to submit proposals to the party and state leaderships for political programs, particularly in the fields of economics, education, culture, and health policy as well as legal and administrative reform. However, because it does not participate in legislative decision-making and lacks a constitutionally guaranteed status, the CPPCC does not serve as a second parliamentary chamber.

2.11 The judiciary, police, and penal systems

Sebastian Heilmann, Lea Shih, and Moritz Rudolf

Under the traditional Chinese concept of law and order, law is regarded as an instrument for controlling crime and enforcing the power of the state. It was not until the beginning of the twentieth century that the idea of law as an instrument for defense against state intervention and protection of individual freedoms entered into discussions on the Chinese state and constitution. However, after the PRC was established, the Soviet view of jurisprudence prevailed and the concept of civil liberties, including the right to defend oneself against the state, faded into the background. The period of "legal nihilism" between 1957 and 1978 saw the courts, the offices of public prosecutors, and attorneys stripped of all authority and vilified as reactionary bourgeois institutions that were deemed to be incompatible with the political objectives of the revolution. During that time, the police and the state-security agencies received instructions only from the leading organs of the CCP.

After the Mao period, the party leadership turned its attention to restoring the judicial system as a key element in stabilizing the country's institutions. Moreover, as economic liberalization took hold, political interest grew with respect to improving the legal conditions for both the domestic economy and for foreign investors. For this reason, there were major advances in terms of establishing a system of justice in the area of economic law.

2.11.1 Party control over the judicial and police systems

Commissions for political and legal affairs（政法委员会）at various levels of the Communist Party hierarchy play a key role in the Chinese system of justice. They exercise political oversight over the police, the courts, and the offices of the public prosecutors. The commissions are regarded as "staff organs" of the party committees at the respective levels in the hierarchy, and they coordinate the work of the PRC's widespread network of police and judiciary organs, among which rivalries are common. The political weight of the commissions is evident in the fact that their leaders are usually high-ranking party functionaries at their respective administrative levels.

In the past it was common for local police presidents to head the commissions for political and legal affairs, thus giving them a higher position in the party hierarchy than the presidents of the courts and the public prosecutors. However, efforts by the Xi–Li administration to strengthen the judiciary as a control mechanism vis-à-vis the administrative and police apparatus means that since 2013 the constellation of traditional power began to shift in favor of jurists, at least at the provincial level. The provincial commissions for political and legal affairs are no longer headed by a police president but by a standing member of the provincial party committee; judges and public prosecutors are now in the majority. The party leadership did not intend that these measures would result in the judiciary becoming an independent actor in the sense of a constitutional division of powers. Rather, it was believed that an effective judicial apparatus to implement "rule by law" was an indispensable element of a modern state. The judicial reforms since 2013 do not mean that the CCP has in any way relinquished control of the constituent personnel of the judicial apparatus or of its political oversight of the judiciary.

2.11.2 The police

Although the Chinese police system is part of the state administration, it is run by CCP organs at various levels of the hierarchy. In their day-to-day administrative activities (with the exception of high-profile national security campaigns and man-hunts), the police organs are subject to decentralized controls by regional and local party committees. However, the central-government's supervision and control over local police organs is highly incomplete. For that reason, the repeated efforts by party and government headquarters to restructure the police system so as to reduce arbitrary proceedings, abuses of power, and corruption have had little impact (Tanner/Green 2007). The guidelines for police work are formulated by the local party committees at the various administrative levels in consultation with the leading police functionaries. Party committees exercise direct management and supervision over the police organs. Police officers are sworn in according to the following: First, they pledge allegiance to the Communist Party, then to the motherland, and then to the people. Upholding the law is only fourth on this list. Membership in the CCP is required of all mid-level or higher police positions. This is intended to guarantee the political loyalty of the police apparatus. The police are not permitted to investigate internal party processes, presiding party functionaries, or existing party organs. Only the disciplinary bodies of the CCP are authorized to conduct internal party investigations.

The police apparatus is composed of a number of organizations reporting to different state bodies:

- Most branches of the police are under the authority of the *Ministry of Public Security* (MPS). The most important of these are the public-order police, the criminal police, the patrol units, the border control, the Internet police, the traffic police, and the water police. At the end of 2007, some 1.6 million police officers reported to the Ministry of Public Security.

- Penitentiary staff (the prison police) are under the purview of the *Ministry of Justice*. This requires close coordination with the Ministry of Public Security.
- Each of the *People's Courts* and *People's Public Prosecutors' Offices* has its own judicial police force.
- According to official estimates, in 2013 the *People's Armed Police* (PAP) (人民 武装警察/武警) consisted of least 660,000 police officers, but unofficial estimates put this figure at closer to 1.5 million. The PAP was created in 1982 by combining existing military and police units tasked with similar functions. It is a special police force primarily responsible for controlling internal unrest and for providing security for government buildings and protection for high-ranking functionaries. Under the dual command structure of the PAP, the internal security forces (consisting of several hundred thousand men and women) as well as the border control forces, the fire departments, and the guard and logistics units are subject to both the CMC and the MPS. Such a dual structure is intended to facilitate cooperation between the PAP and the army with regard to both domestic operations (the police) and foreign deployments (the military). One of the PAP's primary missions is to combat unrest and terrorism in Xinjiang. In view of its size as well as its importance, since 1997 the PAP has sent its own delegations to the National Communist Party Congresses.
- In addition to the aforementioned police forces, the *Ministry of State Security* (MSS) has a separate command structure under which its local subordinate organs deal with subversive activities, foreign espionage, and counterintelligence. The MSS was established in 1983 from the intelligence services of the Ministry of Public Security. Since then, it has steadily built up a network of hidden operatives made up of both career agents and informal operatives all over China and throughout the world. The MSS maintains a number of front organizations operating internationally (companies, research institutes, NGOs, etc.) and expends a substantial portion of its intelligence resources on economic espionage.

2.11.3 Courts and judges

There are four categories of courts in the PRC, although the courts of appeals are limited to two levels. The state's highest judicial organ is the *Supreme People's Court*, which also oversees the courts of lower instance (see Figure 2.11.A).

Below the Supreme People's Court there are thirty-one *Higher People's Courts* at the level of the provinces, directly administered municipalities, and autonomous regions. Next in the hierarchy are the approximately 400 *Intermediate People's Courts* in major cities and the urban districts of the directly administered municipal-

Figure 2.11.A

Overview of the Chinese court system, 2014

Communist Party
Organization Departments

Communist Party Commissions for
Political and Legal Affairs

PARTY

Central Committee — Nomination of judges

Oversight — Central Committee

Provincial Committee — Provincial Committee

Prefectural Committee — Supreme People's Court — Prefectural Committee

County Committee — Higher People's Court (31) — County Committee

GOVERNMENT

National level — Intermediate People's Court (ca. 400) — State Council

Provincial level — Lower People's Court (ca. 3,000) — Provincial government

City level — City government

County level — Formal approval and assignment of judges — Budget planning — County government

People's Congresses

Executive

Based on Heilmann/Rudolf/Shih 2014.

© MERICS

ities. Approximately 3,000 *Lower People's Courts,* with some 9,900 *People's Tribunals* in towns and townships, make up the lower level of the Chinese court system. In total, China has 318,000 judges, assessors, and court officials (Zhu Jingwen 2013).

Chinese courts usually consist of at least four chambers for the hearing of criminal, civil, economic, and administrative cases. However, the judges do not enjoy autonomy in rendering their decisions. The majority of cases are decided by a collegiate body of judges (合议庭) composed of the presiding judge of the chamber and a judge selected by the presiding judge. Politically or economically sensitive cases are decided in advance by a judicial committee (审判委员会) in consultation with the party and administrative offices (Liebman 2015). The judicial committee is made up of the president of the court, the president's deputies, the presiding judge of the chamber, and other experienced judges. The judicial committee's decision-making process may be influenced by outside factors, which limits the ability of judges to issue independent rulings. Many Chinese jurists are highly critical of this practice.

Chinese judges are subject to oversight by the CCP. Membership in the Communist Party is a prerequisite to be appointed a "puisne judge" (普通法官). Presiding "chief justices" (大法官), for example the presidents of the Higher People's Courts, are elected by the people's congress at the respective administrative level after being nominated by party organs. Furthermore, the courts are dependent on the local governments for their financing. Judges' salaries are determined by functionaries at the same administrative level. As a result, Chinese judges do not enjoy any institutionally secure, professional, or personal independence (Bu Yuanshi 2009).

Beginning in 1978, the PRC began experiencing an extremely rapid rise in the number of court cases (see Figure 2.11.B). In 2012 more than 8 million cases were heard in the courts of first instance, most of them in civil proceedings. This upward trend illustrates the growing significance of adjudication in both economic and social life. Companies, institutions, and ordinary citizens are increasingly seeking recourse in the courts to assert their legal claims. What is remarkable is that the cases admitted for hearings often involve highly sensitive political issues, with citizens asserting their rights by contesting administrative decisions. However, the increase

Figure 2.11.B

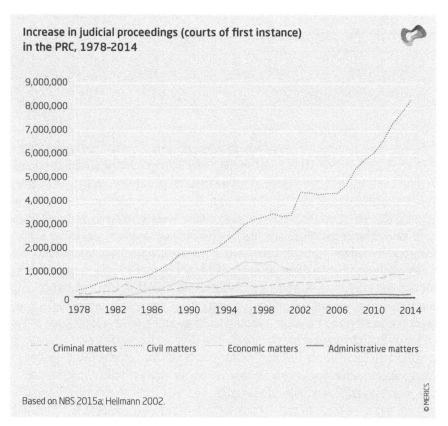

Increase in judicial proceedings (courts of first instance) in the PRC, 1978-2014

Criminal matters   Civil matters   Economic matters   Administrative matters

Based on NBS 2015a; Heilmann 2002.

© MERICS

in administrative proceedings is relatively minor when compared with the increase in civil and criminal proceedings. The courts continue to be extremely limited in their ability to protect the rights of citizens in the event of unlawful administrative acts.

2.11.4 Public prosecutors

The Chinese system of people's procuratorates consists of a four-level structure similar to that of the court system. The defects in the system are also similar to that of the court system and are due to the lack of political, institutional, and professional independence of the approximately 151,000 public prosecutors in 2011 (Zhu Jingwen 2013). The people's procuratorate generally plays a de facto subordinate role to the organs of the police with regard to the investigation of cases.

The mid-1990s saw the introduction of reforms to the judicial and penal systems designed to effect a more strict delineation between the functions of the police, the public prosecutors, and the courts. Since then, conflicts between the judiciary and the police organs have increased, and the people's procuratorates have been called upon by leading CCP organs to increase oversight of the police. In its work reports, the Supreme People's Procuratorate regularly accuses the police organs of abuses of power.

However, public prosecutors have also come under criticism. Since 2000, the Supreme People's Procuratorate has received the second-highest number of opposing votes with respect to its annual work report submitted to the NPC. Only the reports of the Supreme People's Court receive more opposing votes on a regular basis. These votes are a vehicle for China's elected delegates to express their mistrust of the effectiveness of the state judicial organs.

2.11.5 Attorneys

In line with the Soviet system, attorneys in the PRC were originally employees of the state judiciary. The first private law firm was not licensed until 1988. Creation of a private-cooperative system of advocacy was closely related to the government's interest in increasing the credibility of economic law among foreign investors. Enacted in 1996 and amended in 2001 and again in 2007, the Act on the Legal Profession defines attorneys as legal-services providers acting in the interests of their clients and, unlike in the past, not on the instructions of the state. Whereas in 1980 attorneys in China numbered about 1,000, there were approximately 232,000 full-time attorneys practicing law by the end of 2012 (Zhu Jingwen 2013).

Traditionally, Chinese attorneys tended to have deeper knowledge of the law than judges or public prosecutors owing to the highly demanding state aptitude test that they were required to pass. In 2002 the aptitude test for attorneys was expanded to include all of the legal professions, and its name was changed to the "state law examination." Since then, judges and public prosecutors are expected to demonstrate the same expertise as attorneys.

Chinese attorneys are still subject to monitoring by judicial bodies, from which they also receive instructions. It is common practice for attorneys who conflict with state agencies to have their licenses revoked. They may also risk severe reprisals, including possible imprisonment. If attorneys present evidence or witness statements that do not come from the police or the public prosecutor's office, they are suspected of manipulation. Thus it is rare for attorneys to be willing to appear before the courts as counsels for the defense. Even after the 2012 amendment to the Code of Criminal Procedure, only 30 percent of all defendants in criminal proceedings in 2014 had legal representation. Therefore, defendants have only very limited protection against the courts.

2.11.6 Criminal law and the penal system

According to official reports from both the Chinese government and international human-rights organizations, application of the Criminal Law and the Criminal Procedure Law in the PRC often involves arbitrary arrests, violent hearings, inadequate defense options, and a lack of transparency. Although the Penal Code was amended in 1996 and the Criminal Procedure Law was amended in 1997 and again in 2012—rendering confessions acquired under torture inadmissible and stipulating that defendants are assumed innocent unless proven guilty—the new provisions have not been successful in eliminating infringements in criminal proceedings.

The Chinese penal system continues to be characterized by excessive application of the death penalty. In 2013 China executed an estimated 2,400 prisoners—more than the rest of the world combined. This represented a drop of some 20 percent from the previous year. The decline can primarily be attributed to the 2007 requirement that all death sentences must be reviewed by the highest court, thus resulting in the lower courts exercising restraint in the issuance of death sentences (Duihua Foundation 2014). However, in the opinion of representatives of the Chinese judiciary, this trend is not indicative of a movement in the direction of abolishing the death penalty.

With regard to the administration of justice, which has been under the purview of the Ministry of Justice since 1983, official reports indicate that conditions in China's 680 prisons have gradually improved (Shao Lei 2014). Prison factories no longer use forced labor to create a "new Communist man." However, given that many prisons suffer from underfunding, the contribution of prisoners to production has gained in economic significance. The number of prisoners, and in particular the number of political prisoners, has decreased dramatically compared with the respective numbers during the Mao era. In mid-2014, some 2.3 million people were incarcerated in China's prisons. This rate is approximately only one-sixth that in the United States and one-third that in Russia (see Table 2.11).

Table 2.11

Number of prisoners, 2013-14

	Number of prisoners	Rate of incarceration*
PRC (mid-2014)	2,300,000	165
United States (end 2013)	2,217,424	698
Russia (end 2014)	644,237	446
Germany (2014)	61,872	76

Note: *Number of prisoners per 100,000 people.
Based on Institute for Criminal Policy Research 2015.

© MERICS

"Administrative detention" is an especially controversial practice to which, until recently, the Chinese judiciary has had recourse. Beginning in the 1950s, the police were authorized to impose sentences of several years without any judicial proceedings, i.e., "re-education through labor" (劳动教养, or for short: 劳教). Before 2014 when the *laojiao* system was finally abolished, approximately 260,000 persons were locked up in corrective facilities, most of whom (approximately 200,000) were drug addicts. The remainder consisted of members of prohibited religious movements or cults (in particular, the Falun Gong), prostitutes, and producers and distributors of pornography. After the abolition of such administrative detentions, these individuals were either released or turned over to drug rehabilitation centers (see the case study on the abolition of "re-education through labor" in Section 6.3).

2.11.7 Judicial reform

In 1999 the PRC Constitution was amended to include a commitment to "rule the country by law" and to build "a socialist country governed according to law." Judicial reform was supported by many members of the political leadership at the time, and the Supreme People's Court began regularly adopting five-year plans aimed at modernizing the court system. The plans were tenacious in terms of professionalizing the judiciary by placing higher requirements on judges and in terms of strengthening the institutional structure of the courts. However, many of these reforms were not implemented with any consistency.

Between 2008 and 2012, for example, the Central Political and Legal Affairs Commission of the CCP spoke out in favor of out-of-court arbitration proceedings and voiced explicit approval of law-enforcement populism, which stands in contradiction to rule of law. When rendering decisions in criminal proceedings, judges were instructed to take into account the moral sentiment among the population in order to ensure "social stability." This political line dealt a blow to previous efforts to reform the Chinese judiciary.

Following intense debates on the reforms prior to 2008, restructuring of the judicial system reappeared on the agenda of the party leadership when the Xi–Li administration came to power in 2012–13. Priority was placed on ending the spread of protectionism among local courts by removing court funding, judges' salaries, and court rulings from the influence of local governments. The objective was to reinforce the organizational structure of the courts in order to maintain better control over administrative and political institutions at the local levels and to link them to national regulations. Moreover, the quantitative targets (quotas and ratios) for arrests, convictions, and combating crime, which the Chinese judicial and police system had applied since the 1990s, were abolished by the Central Political and Legal Affairs Commission at the beginning of 2015.

The various reforms announced since 2013 nevertheless continue to conflict with the far-reaching CCP leadership ambitions, which require that any actions taken by the judicial branches with respect to proceedings or rulings of a politically, economically, or socially sensitive nature remain under the control of the party leadership. As Xi Jinping stated at a party meeting on the judiciary in early 2015 in reference to one of Mao Zedong's guiding principles: "The knife handle must remain firmly in the hands of the party and the people." The policy framework for judicial organs is no longer from the local party and government offices, but rather from the provincial levels or straight from the central government. As stated by the president of the Supreme People's Court in early 2015, in the Chinese system there is no "Western" notion of a separation of powers involving a "supposedly independent judiciary."

Even though court adjudication has become considerably more important since the 1980s, China's judicial bodies are still tightly interwoven with the political institutions so they are unable to contribute to overcoming the deficiencies in the legal system by virtue of their own efforts.

2.12 The military and politics

Johannes Buckow, Moritz Rudolf, and Nabil Alsabah

The PLA (中国人民解放军) was founded as the military arm of the CCP in 1927, twenty-two years before the establishment of the PRC. It is a product of the revolutionary war (1927–49) and the Communist consolidation of power (1949–53), achieved under challenging economic conditions and as a result of the merger between party and military organizations. The legacy of the revolutionary era continues to exist today and it is embedded in the PRC Constitution, the CCP Constitution, and the Law on National Defense. For example, Art.19 of the 1997 Law on National Defense states: "The armed forces of the People's Republic of China are subject to the leadership of the Communist Party of China." The PLA remains loyal to the CCP rather than to the constitution or to the NPC (theoretically, the "highest organ of state authority"). Therefore, unlike armies in democratic constitutional states, the PLA is not politically neutral. And unlike armies in many nondemocratic regimes that tend to operate like free-wheeling "states within a state," the Chinese PLA cannot eschew political controls and interference.

2.12.1 Party control over the military

CCP control over the PLA is guaranteed by a complex regime comprising party bodies and political-control structures at all levels of command. The CMC (中央军事委员会), as an organizationally integrated party and state institution (though with two official name plates: one for the party and one for the state), constitutes the highest military leadership body and thus is particularly important. The influence of the CMC is apparent in the way that all party chiefs, from Mao Zedong through to Deng Xiaoping, Jiang Zemin, Hu Jintao, and Xi Jinping, have insisted on assuming its chairmanship. However, unlike his two predecessors, Xi Jinping took over the chairmanship of the CMC simultaneously when he became CCP general secretary in 2012.

The Political Work Department (政治工作部), which was restructured in 2016 (see Section 2.12.3) serves as an organ of the CMC. It is responsible for exercising political control over the Chinese armed forces through a system of political commissars (政治委员) and political departments under its control at all levels of command. In the party hierarchy, the rank of the political commissars is above that of the commanders, contributing to rivalries between the two. In addition to the political commissar system and the party committee system, political control within the PLA is exercised by an internal discipline system. All three organizational structures are embedded in the military command structures down to the regiment level. The internal military security service is also an organ under the control of the Political Work Department. Party bodies are able to carry out continued supervision of military activities at the most crucial central and regional command levels of the PLA.

A number of serious regime crises since the founding of the state contributed to the formation of close links between the military and the CCP as well as to the continued importance of the PLA in intra-elite conflicts. In particular, the special significance of the PLA in terms of CCP authority was apparent during the Cultural Revolution and during the urban protest movement of 1989. The party organization was able to restore political control over the population during each of these crises only as a result of military intervention.

2.12.2 The political loyalty of the PLA

The loyalty of the PLA to the civilian leadership in the party and the state since 1989 appears to be assured and unchallenged, despite several changes in leadership. Political and ideological training courses continue to constitute a major part of the time spent in military training and in the everyday life of a soldier (Blasko 2012). The leadership of the PLA continues to be represented on leading party bodies, although no military officer has sat on the Standing Committee of the Politburo since 1997. Two generals (who are also vice-chairmen of the CMC) are represented on the 2012 Politburo. Nevertheless, the military, constituting somewhat more than one-sixth of the members, is highly represented on the CCP CC (including alternate members).

Even in the event of serious political crises, it seems unlikely that any sections of the Chinese officer corps would break ranks with the CCP. The fall of the powerful Soviet army after the collapse of the Soviet Communist Party is still viewed as a warning by many members of the Chinese military. In addition, the PLA is generously financed by the party leadership: military expenditures and military equipment have increased greatly (see Table 2.12). In addition, according to official statistics, defense spending grew fifteenfold during the 1994–2014 period. Therefore, the close links between the Chinese military and the CCP have been very advantageous to the PLA.

2.12.3 Defense policy and decision-making

Defense- and military-policy planning and policy making occur within party bodies under civilian leadership (see Figure 2.12.A). Whereas until the 1990s military and defense policies were highly personalized and formulated in consultation with informal bodies, defense-policy planning and policy making have since then become

Table 2.12

Chinese military expenditures:
Official statistics and unofficial estimates, 1994-2014

Year	PRC official statistics (CNY billion)	Annual growth compared to the previous year	SIPRI (CNY billion)	SIPRI (constant 2011 USD billion)	U.S. Dept. of Defense (USD billion)
1994	55	29.3%	87	22.4	no data available
1998	93	15.0%	150	29.9	no data available
2002	171	17.6%	262	52.8	45-65
2006	284	14.7%	452	84.0	70-105
2010	532	7.5%	835	136.2	>160
2011	601	12.6%	952	147.2	120-180
2012	670	11.2%	1071	161.4	135-215
2013	741	10.7%	1185	174.0	>145
2014	808	12.2%	1330	191.0	>165

Based on Heilmann/Schmidt 2014; MOF; Stockholm International Peace Research Institute (SIPRI); Military Expenditure Database; U.S. Department of Defense.

© MERICS

increasingly institutionalized. Representatives of all of China's service branches are now included in consultation processes at the highest levels. At no point have China's generals acted as an independent, coherent group vis-à-vis the political, civilian leadership (Li Nan 2010). Unprecedentedly, an air force commander was appointed a vice-chairman of the CMC under Xi Jinping.

The CMC is the highest military leadership organ. It is responsible for coordinating defense policy and for formulating official military doctrine. In times of war, it is the ultimate command organization. In organizational terms, it embodies the close relationship between the party and the PLA, acting as the key interface between the leadership of the PLA and the top party leadership. The CMC is a fairly small organization (comprising only several hundred officers and officials), with a general office that controls the flow of information among commission members and that

Figure 2.12.A

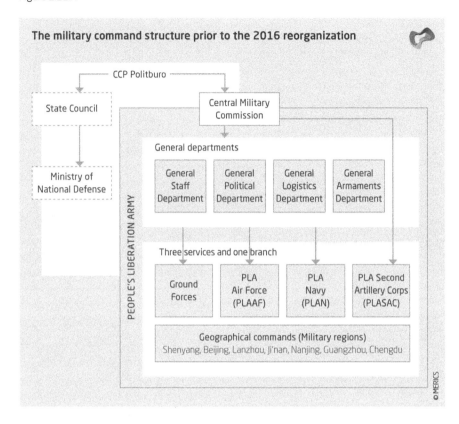

The military command structure prior to the 2016 reorganization

CCP Politburo

State Council

Central Military Commission

Ministry of National Defense

PEOPLE'S LIBERATION ARMY

General departments

| General Staff Department | General Political Department | General Logistics Department | General Armaments Department |

Three services and one branch

| Ground Forces | PLA Air Force (PLAAF) | PLA Navy (PLAN) | PLA Second Artillery Corps (PLASAC) |

Geographical commands (Military regions)
Shenyang, Beijing, Lanzhou, Ji'nan, Nanjing, Guangzhou, Chengdu

© MERICS

maintains links between party and State Council bodies. The routine work of the CMC takes place during weekly meetings and meetings of ad hoc committees and working groups.

The CCP Central Committee announced in November 2013 that the PLA will undergo a radical restructuring program by 2020. Implementation of this reform plan was heralded two years later by Xi Jinping, when, during the military parade to commemorate the 70th anniversary of Japan's defeat in World War II, Xi revealed a 300,000-troop cut to be completed within two years. In January 2016, the four traditional PLA General Departments were abolished. As successor organizations, fifteen departments, commissions, and offices were established within the CMC. The most important include:

• The *Joint Staff Department* (JSD) (联合参谋部) was established in 2016 to promote cross-service operations within the PLA (i.e., "jointness"). As such, it is the central interface for the flow of information and for the chain of command. It is

Figure 2.12.B

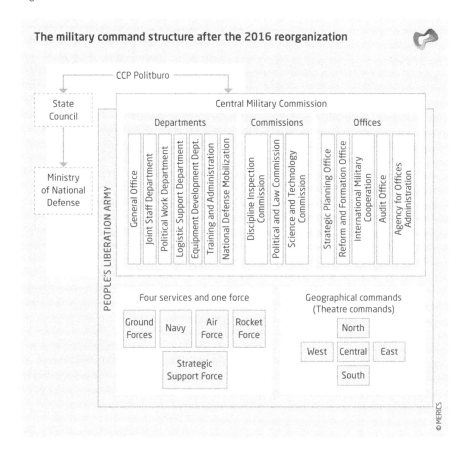

The military command structure after the 2016 reorganization

responsible for coordinating and planning military deployments in the event of conflicts. The JSD's predecessor, the General Staff Department, played a leading role in negotiations with the MOF regarding funding allocations for the defense budget. It remains unclear at the time of this writing (March 2016) whether the JSD will play this role in the post-2016 organizational setup.

- The *Political Work Department* (政治工作部) is responsible for party control over the PLA and for ideological training of the armed forces as well as supervision of the political officers (political commissars) who are assigned to be commanders of military units. Primarily confined to internal army supervisory and disciplinary functions, this department has only minimal influence on defense-policy decisions.
- The *Logistic Support Department* (后勤保障部) focuses on the maintenance of the independent infrastructure of the Chinese military (military supplies, communications, transport, military hospitals, etc.).

- The *Equipment Development Department* (装备发展部) is responsible for procuring weapons, conducting armaments research, and importing and exporting arms.

The *PLA armed services*—the ground forces, air force, navy, rocket force (formerly known as the second artillery corps), and the strategic support force—compete with one another for resources and for influence in military and armaments policy. For historical reasons, the ground forces have long enjoyed the greatest influence within the PLA. Since the late 1980s, however, shifts favoring the air force and the navy have become apparent. These two services are increasingly well represented on the top leadership bodies, though they still are not yet powerful enough to challenge the supremacy of the ground force generals.

Chinese territory is divided into geographical commands. Previously called military regions (军区), they have now been rebranded as theater commands (战区), and, within the context of Xi Jinping's extensive reorganization efforts, their number has been reduced from seven to five. More important than the name change, however, is the change in their mission statements. The command structure of the PLA was previously divided according to the service branches: The ground forces, the air force, and the navy each separately commanded their troops. In contrast, the service branches are now responsible for administrative tasks (for instance, equipping and manning the troops). Command authority rests with the theater commands. If implemented as intended, the new command structure will make jointness a reality, that is, interdisciplinary commanders leading cross-service units. But as Xi Jinping correctly recognizes, implementing the new system will require a radical change in the mindset of the armed forces.

In 2013, for the first time a CNSC was established to bring together representatives of all key bodies involved in internal and external security. This commission is designed to enable more effective coordination in matters of security strategy, especially in cases of serious security threats. Since its establishment, however, it has been impossible to assess the specific impact of this mysterious body (see also Section 2.3.4). In addition, the CMC has established a number of specialized Leading Small Groups within the PLA tasked with specific interdisciplinary responsibilities (for instance, combating corruption within the PLA and reorganizing military training).

The *Ministry of National Defense* holds very modest powers in the PRC, limited mainly to military diplomatic affairs, foreign military contacts, and the military attachés based in Chinese embassies abroad. It is excluded from the military command structure and, unlike defense ministries in most other countries, it possesses a limited amount of political and military influence.

3 Political leadership

Political decision-making in China is controlled by the leading organs and cadres of the Chinese Communist Party (CCP). The opportunities for active political participation are strictly limited, even for the vast majority of CCP members (the party boasted 87.793 million members at the end of 2014). The upper echelons of state decision-making bodies, such as the inner cabinet of the State Council, ministries, provincial or municipal governments, and the boards of state-owned enterprises, banks, and interest groups/mass organizations are almost exclusively headed by CCP "leading cadres" (领导干部), ranging from the division chief or county leadership levels upwards. The PRC had about 650,000 such functionaries in 2015. These party leading cadres tend to occupy senior positions not only in party bodies but also in state organs at the same administrative level. The CCP's monopoly on political power is protected across all the organizational areas of the state (the administration, police, military, state-owned enterprises, and mass organizations) by means of separate party structures that assume decision-making and supervisory functions parallel with the state and military hierarchies.

The preparatory stages in the decision-making procedures—everything from providing expert advice to incorporating special interests—and the process of policy implementation by administrative departments, security organs, enterprises, or mass organizations are influenced by a complex web of informal relationships. Opaque patronage networks (关系网) based on personal acquaintances and confidential exchanges rather than on any formal affiliation to a particular organization penetrate the party, the state, the military, and the economy. There are constant frictions between these informal networks and the formal rules as stipulated in the party constitution, the state constitution, and other organizational directives, even leading at times to permanent conflict if there is corruption at play. Informal networks in China are more opaque than they are in democratic political systems because media reporting and public criticism of elitist behavior are subject to tight restrictions. Information about the intricate web of political and economic relations and contacts will only be leaked to the public domain if there are ongoing corruption proceedings or cases of party expulsion. However, binding decisions of a routine nature remain the prerogative of the official leading bodies of the CCP and government at all levels of the political order.

3.1 The center of power

Sebastian Heilmann

China's center of power is composed of a small circle of select leaders. Currently, the highest political organ is the seven-person Politburo Standing Committee, which was reduced from nine members in 2012. This body is headed by the general secretary of the CCP (or simply the "party leader" for short). Additional members comprise the leading representatives of the party and state apparatus, including the premier. At the time of this writing (2016), the highest formal authority was held by Xi Jinping, who came to power in 2012–13 and holds the positions of CCP general secretary, president of the PRC, and chairman of the Central Military Commission (CMC).

3.1.1 Shifts in the decision-making system

Unlike during the Deng Xiaoping era that spanned from 1978 until 1993, when Deng was no longer able to participate in the decision-making process due to health reasons (he died in 1997), Jiang Zemin, general secretary of the CCP from 1989 to 2002, initiated a shift in the decision-making system away from a paramount party leader with almost absolute authority toward a system of collective leadership with an increasingly formalized code of practice. Under this system, General Secretary Jiang was accorded the role of "first among equals" *(primus inter pares)*, as was also his successor, Hu Jintao, who served as general secretary from 2002 to 2012.

Although up until the mid-1990s the Politburo Standing Committee constantly had to deal with ad hoc interference from forceful party veterans (who were no longer members of any official committees), governance later became more straightforward: the most powerful representatives of the generation that experienced the Cultural Revolution had died before the turn of the millennium or were no longer active in politics due to ill health. Since then, former top functionaries have regularly been invited to official party and state occasions merely as dignitaries. Generally, only the former CCP general secretaries remain actively involved, and they are consulted by their successors only if there are controversial decisions to be made concerning potentially conflict-prone policy and personnel issues, especially if there are any cases of imminent corruption and dismissal proceedings against top functionaries.

These consultations have been essential because of a number of spectacular corruption cases involving high-ranking officials who had been promoted during the tenures of former CCP general secretaries. Corruption proceedings of this kind can significantly damage the political reputation and legal unassailability of the former general secretaries. Relatives of top functionaries—the so-called "crown prince par-ty" (太子党) or "princelings" (高干子弟)—also regularly play a key role in corrup-tion investigations due to their patronage networks in the upper echelons of the party. The majority of senior cadres attempt to protect their family members from inquiries of this nature.

Details about decision-making within inner leadership circles regarding politi-cally sensitive issues (such as internal and external security) lack transparency and are treated as state secrets. A review of decision-making processes with respect to the reform policies since the 1990s points to some key features of politics at the center of power. Autobiographical memoirs and journal articles, as well as oral infor-mation passed on by members of the leadership and staff at party and government headquarters or family members, are additional sources of such information. These features do not coincide with the stereotypical image of Beijing's "palace politics" as portrayed in some Western media (see Table 3.1.A).

In light of the decision-making process at the political center of power since 1989, the image of a collection of narrow-minded "blockheads" is no longer justified, nor is the notion of a permanent power struggle between clearly distinct factions ("reformers" versus "hardliners," for instance). It is inaccurate to claim that members of the leadership generations who have dominated Chinese politics since the mid-1990s (see Section 3.2) are generally characterized by ideological inertia or political narrow-mindedness. On the contrary, they have demonstrated an often surprising degree of openness toward policy experimentation, at least with respect to eco-nomic, technological, administrative, and sociopolitical issues.

Table 3.1.A

Stereotypical representations of China's leadership in Western media

"Blockheads": China's leaders are politically narrow-minded, short-sighted, and do not embrace reform.

"Power struggle": Chinese politics is characterized by a permanent, ruthless power struggle between various individuals and groups.

"Hardliners": China's political actors can be assigned to dichotomous categories, such as "conservatives" versus "liberals," "hardliners" versus "reformers," or "radicals" versus "moderates."

"Westerners": Senior leaders from the younger generations who have been edu-cated or trained in the West representing a pro-Western force in Chinese politics.

Based on Heilmann 2002.

© MERICS

The dichotomous classification of China's leaders into "hardliners" and "liberals" is divorced from the reality of Chinese politics as it has developed since the 1990s. Instead, it is noteworthy that the positions held by individual politicians on issues concerning economic and administrative reforms have wavered significantly over time. Former premier Li Peng, frequently referred to as an adamant "hardliner," largely abandoned his resistance to market-oriented economic reforms following the collapse of the Soviet Union in 1991; Premier Zhu Rongji (1998–2003) and Premier Wen Jiabao (2003–13), who were often labeled by Western media as "liberal," did not show any obvious tolerance toward political opposition and political dissidents. With respect to the perpetuation of domestic stability and the inherent crackdown on opposition and protests, there is no evidence that consensus within the leadership on these matters has ever been in doubt since the events of 1989.

These examples show that assigning individual leaders to specific, unambiguous political mindsets is overly simplistic and it underestimates the dynamics of the political decision-making processes. Members of the Chinese leadership are characterized by a strong focus on tangible results. Until Xi Jinping assumed office in 2012–13, the party and state leaderships were characterized by individuals with a cautious, consensual political style, at least outwardly, aimed at avoiding conflicts within the leading party organs.

Although this style of leadership prevented public conflicts and visible divisions within the Politburo Standing Committee, it led to mounting tensions within the leadership of the Communist Party when General Secretary Hu Jintao held office (2002–12). These tensions were linked to the fight against corruption and the "crown prince party" as well as the trend toward autonomy within the national security apparatus. It was only when General Secretary Xi Jinping assumed power that the various conflicts culminated in a number of spectacular corruption proceedings, ending in the conviction of a former member of the Politburo (Bo Xilai, headstrong former party secretary of Chongqing and son of a prominent revolutionary veteran) as well as a former member of the Politburo Standing Committee (Zhou Yongkang, who had been responsible for China's domestic security apparatus under Hu Jintao) and former presidential aide to Hu Jintao, Ling Jihua. Corruption and abuses of power for personal gain were proven on both counts. The severity of the sentences, however, was due to the political provocations and damage to the coherence of the party leadership because of their personal ambition, lack of loyalty to fellow Politburo staff, blocking of the decision-making process, attempts at self-promotion, and clique-building within the party (拉帮结派) that are subject to a zero-tolerance policy.

The drastic violations of both the formal and informal organizational rules and codes of practice by members of the supreme party leadership under Hu Jintao gave reason to doubt the credibility of the closed façade of the ruling Politburo, even under Xi Jinping. In any event, it can be assumed that, as in all political organizations, personal ambitions and animosities, conflicts of jurisdiction and interest, as well as programmatic and ideological differences, will repeatedly give rise to tensions and clashes within the leadership. Although these tensions will generally remain latent, they will sporadically emerge in the public arena. In particular, the vehement anti-corruption campaign under Xi Jinping inevitably intensified intra-party tensions due to the fact that none of the senior politicians could rule out the possibility that they or members of their families might be the next targets of investigations.

An increasing number of China's political leaders have spent time in Western democracies, predominantly in the United States, either studying, training, or taking part in exchange programs. Contrary to the stereotype of the "Westerner"—which might seem intuitively plausible—it appears that a longer stay overseas is not necessarily conducive to a pro-Western or pro-America position. In fact, there are indications that many Chinese leaders returning from the United States harbor a pronounced distrust of America's China policy and are critical of the country. At the same time, they are aware that good relations with the United States and Europe are crucially important for China with respect to China's development opportunities and global role. This ambivalent attitude—a mixture of tolerance and admiration on the one hand, but a large element of suspicion and skepticism on the other—is widespread both among Chinese leaders and among the general public.

3.1.2 Capacity for policy innovation and imposition

To assess political leadership, special importance should be attached to creative political management and reform achievements. This refers to a willingness and capacity to respond to economic, social, technological, ecological, or international challenges with concerted political actions, even under difficult conditions.

Considering the constant demand for action and the need for adaptation, Chinese leaders are accountable for launching single measures or larger-scale programs to help overcome obstacles to development, to resolve current grievances or even acute crises, and to facilitate institutional modernization, thus opening up new development potentials for as many sectors of society as possible. Decision-makers in the national leadership—both in China and in other countries—play a significant role in initiating reform efforts and have a substantial impact on the likelihood of the success of the reforms, either by their personal commitment to new policy initiatives or by their attempts to block such initiatives.

At the beginning of the reform period, the Chinese leadership authorized a series of economic activities driven by local initiatives (household-based agricultural production and small private businesses). Although these initiatives initially resulted in a great deal of controversy, they vastly improved access to essential supplies, and their success provided an impetus for more extensive reform experiments. Thereafter, the leadership showed unprecedented openness—certainly for a Communist state—to learning and experimentation with respect to economic issues.

In particular, during intermittent periods of "extraordinary politics" (Balcerowicz 1995) when entrenched interest groups are undermined by political or economic upheavals, resolute political action has the potential to push through radical reforms. Such historically rare periods occurred in China following the failure of a program introduced by Chairman Hua Guofeng in 1978–79 aimed at recentralization and boosting investment, in 1992–93 in the wake of the collapse of the Eastern European socialist states, and in 1997–98 as a reaction to the Asian financial crisis. All three of these periods of "extraordinary politics" were exploited by reform-minded politicians to encourage rejection of the state-controlled economic order and to defy the resistance of interest groups affiliated with the former socialist system (Heilmann 2000).

However, the Chinese leadership's response to the global financial and economic crisis of 2007–9 was contentious. This was undoubtedly also a period of "extraordinary politics"—high-pressure crisis management aimed at averting an economic depression. One of the government's tactics was to launch very quickly in 2008 a huge economic stimulus program amounting to 13 percent of China's gross domestic product (GDP) that had a highly stimulating short-term effect not only on Chinese industry, infrastructure, and real estate but also on China's trading partners.

At the same time, the Chinese economy in the aftermath of the 2007–9 crisis was driven by a deluge of new credit and poorly audited investments. The medium- and long-term consequences resulting from the rapid increase in corporate and municipal debts, investment and speculation bubbles, and irrecoverable bank loans were not initially obvious. Between 2007 and 2009 the Chinese leadership reacted with great resolve and effectiveness in the interest of the national economic stimulus program. However, the needed structural changes that had already been introduced—with the particular objective of reducing the dependence of economic growth on investments and exports—were halted or blocked as a result of the stimulus program.

3.1.3 "Normal mode" and "crisis mode" in decision-making

Observers of contemporary Chinese affairs are continually faced with the conundrum that a previously "pragmatic," "moderate," and "reformist" Chinese leadership suddenly applies drastic measures of repression. For example, Deng Xiaoping—twice named "Person of the Year" by *Time* magazine— according to Western media was transformed into a "dictator" and "butcher" practically overnight, when pro-democracy protests were violently crushed by the military in June 1989. The leadership under Hu Jintao and Wen Jiabao, both of whom were initially rated favorably by the West for their commitment to social and environmental reforms, experienced a rapid negative swing in public opinion due to their suppression of unrest in Tibet in 2008. When he assumed the position of CCP general secretary in 2012, Xi Jinping took the West by surprise by introducing a combination of decidedly market-oriented reform programs and vehement anti-corruption measures, along with a tightening of ideological controls and domestic repression.

In order to understand these apparent contradictions, it is useful to differentiate between a "normal mode" and a "crisis mode" in Chinese politics (Heilmann 1996, 2004). Whereas decisions in times of "politics as usual" are reached after protracted processes of compromise, an exceptional mode of decision-making comes into force during acute crisis situations that are perceived as threats to stability. This mode is characterized by centralized ideological decision-making and rule by decree. The highest party leadership monopolizes all decision-making powers during such phases, and intra-party directives have top priority, severely constricting the latitude previously granted to subordinate state agencies and local governments. On the basis of China's contemporary political history, it is possible to identify certain events that are likely to trigger moves to a crisis mode (see Table 3.1.B).

During a normal and routine mode, decision-making at the center of power is typified by the following characteristics:

- Responsibilities and tasks are divided among the members of the Politburo Standing Committee or the members of the inner cabinet of the State Council according to their specific portfolios (such as the financial system, foreign trade, or domestic security).
- Coordinated, interdepartmental programs, with participation by relevant specialists, are implemented; internal and external expertise is enlisted from think-tanks and universities, and ad hoc task forces are set up to research decisions, negotiate compromises, and design a system of documentation.
- Consultative meetings to generate compromises are lengthy processes that require a high degree of coordination; top functionaries must act both as advocates and as mediators among the various state agencies.
- Top party leaders tend to exercise their authority only if they are under pressure to make decisions quickly (e.g., if there are timelines to pass multi-year programs or to implement international treaty obligations, or scandals that have attracted public attention).

Decision-making methods and longer-term political programs have changed whenever there has been a transition to a new generation of leaders—be it the veterans,

Table 3.1.B

Events that may trigger a crisis mode

Typical trigger factors	Examples since 1989
I Domestic security crises with a nationwide impact.	Urban protest movement of 1989; Falun Gong movement in 1999; protests in Tibet in 2008; Xinjiang unrest in 2009; terrorist attacks in Beijing and Kunming, 2013–14.
II Intra-party decision-making and organizational crises.	Loss of decision-making capacity in the Politburo in 1989; fight against intra-party corruption and the formation of cliques since 2012.
III Scandals that have repercussions for the national leadership.	Anti-smuggling campaign in 1998; combating the severe acute respiratory syndrome (SARS) epidemic after an initial cover-up in 2003; criminal proceedings against members of the Politburo since 2012.
IV Foreign policy and military tensions.	Taiwan Straits crisis in 1996; bombing of the Chinese Embassy in Belgrade in 1999; Sino-Japanese dispute, 2012–13.
V Acute threats to economic stability.	Inflation control, 1993–95; centralization of financial supervision, 1997–98; economic stimulus program, 2007–9.
VI Natural disasters.	Floods in 1998; earthquake in southwest China in 2008.
VII External shocks.	Collapse of the socialist states in Eastern Europe, 1989–91; Asian financial crisis of 1997–98, global financial crisis of 2007–9.

Based on Heilmann 1996, 2002.

© MERICS

the technocrats, or the cadres with more diversified qualifications who were appointed to the party leadership in 2007 and 2012 (see Section 3.5). Compared to the rule under Mao Zedong or Deng Xiaoping, the decision-making process under party leaders Jiang Zemin and Hu Jintao was considerably less centralized and personalized, at least during periods of routine politics when there was no acute sense of urgency. However, significant changes took place beginning in 2012 under Xi Jinping's leadership, with the general secretary holding an unusual concentration of decision-making authority across a vast number of various policies.

Table 3.1.C

Characteristics of the normal and crisis modes in Chinese politics

Normal mode	Crisis mode
• Party and government lead-ers set general guidelines and objectives for national policies. • Government departments negotiate with one anoth-er about the drafting of national regulations. • Local governments flexibly apply national laws and directives in accordance with local conditions. • The party center's capacity to enforce national rules vis-à-vis the local governments is limited.	• Abrupt centralization of the decision-making processes and central interventions across the party hierarchy. • Sense of urgency; limited willingness on the part of the central party headquarters to hold consultation meetings. • Personalization and increased emphasis on ideology in decision-making. • Recourse to militant mobilization rhetoric. • Political upgrading of the disciplinary and secu-rity organs. • If the party executive is united, their elite close ranks leading to a temporary increase in their capacity to enforce policies. • If the party executive is divided, then difficulties in implementing decisions and resultant con-flicts occur at all levels of the party-state.

Based on Heilmann 1996, 2002.

© MERICS

The changes to the decision mode under Xi Jinping fulfill all of the criteria listed in Table 3.1.C for a transition to a crisis mode of governance. Xi Jinping and his colleagues in the party leadership bodies had obviously sensed that the deci-sion-making and loyalty crises in the Politburo under General Secretary Hu Jintao (2002–12) and the corruption and organizational crises in the Communist Party had collectively reached a dangerous level that represented a threat to the system. Therefore, the best way to achieve institutional renewal and organizational stability within the party and state apparatus was through a concentration of political power and centralized decision-making, organizational and ideological discipline, extensive anti-corruption measures, and the prevention of any attempts to form factions or cliques within the party, coupled with a campaign against Western values and con-cepts.

In the crisis mode, decision-making procedures are abruptly centralized and dominated by the personalities of the top individual leaders. The familiar Mao-era ideology and militant rhetoric is reactivated. The central party leadership exerts an extraordinary sense of urgency in isolated policy areas, resorting to techniques used during the pre-1978 mobilization and campaign regimes. During such phases, China's political leadership is more assertive than leadership regimes in most other developing countries or emerging economies. The crisis mode represents the central leadership's ad hoc response to events that are deemed to be a threat to the stability of the national political system or a challenge to the authority and legitimacy of the national leadership. As soon as the acute threat has abated, Chinese politics tends to revert back to a *normal* mode.

3.1.4 How unified is the center of power?

In view of the great urgency of problems and the centrifugal forces at work in the economy, society, and the local administrations, the unity and decision-making capacities of party headquarters are fundamentally significant for the stability of CCP rule. Publicly displayed conflicts over power and policies, which previously had repeatedly paralyzed decision-making within the upper ranks of the CCP and the ability to work together effectively, became a thing of the past following the serious domestic crisis of 1989. The center of power in Beijing struggled for survival after 1989 due to the political shifts that were taking place both nationally and internationally. This strengthened cohesion within the party, or at least promoted a cautious approach to conflict management (mostly in the guise of internal anti-corruption investigations) that generally avoided public scrutiny.

Since the extensive reshuffling of the top members of the party leadership as a result of the 1989 crisis, there have been only a few, isolated personnel changes triggered by political conflicts, individualism, or disloyalty: the retirement of Yang Shangkun and Yang Baibing from the party leadership in 1992–93; the charges of corruption against Beijing Party Secretary Chen Xitong in 1995; the departure of Qiao Shi from the leading party organs in 1997; and the corruption proceedings against Shanghai Party Secretary Chen Liangyu in 2007 and against Chongqing Party Secretary Bo Xilai in 2013.

The comments and directives by leading representatives of party headquarters regarding urgently needed economic, social, ecological, and political actions suggest an unprecedented consensus with respect to fundamental political issues and practices after 1989. An outward show of cohesion and consensus has certainly been preserved under the system of collective leadership.

Whether this fundamental consensus—so meticulously staged by the state media—can be sustained under pressures of acute internal and external challenges remains to be seen. Official reports about serious violations of rules by members of the Politburo between 2012 and 2015 have revealed clear cracks in the carefully cultivated façade of unity and solidarity within the top party leadership.

3.2 Leadership generations: Revolutionaries, technocrats, and recent diversification

Lea Shih and Sebastian Heilmann

In simplified terms, the several generations of leaders in the history of the CCP can be distinguished by their differing experiences, educational backgrounds, and political orientations. Such a categorization of leaders into generations was first popularized in 1989 under Deng Xiaoping, who identified Mao Zedong as the key figure of the first generation, Deng as the core of the second generation, and Jiang Zemin as the leader of the third generation. This was a means to justify a collective transition in the party and leadership styles that varied over time. Such a concept of leadership generations is still common in studies of China (Li/White 2003; Miller 2008) (see Table 3.2). However, there are many overlaps in the biographies of the various generations, indicating that the boundaries are not always as clearly defined as suggested here.

The leaders of the Communist Revolution and the founders of the PRC, including Mao Zedong and Zhou Enlai, are classified as the first leadership generation. Representatives of this generation regarded the 1917 October Revolution in Russia and the political system of the Soviet Union as their dominant role models. They were the leading forces in the military struggle against the Japanese invasion (1937–45) and against the Nationalist government of the Republic of China under Chiang Kai-shek (1927–49).

The radical Maoists (the so-called "Gang of Four" led by Mao's wife, Jiang Qing), who, with Mao's support, were given a say at the center of power during the Cultural Revolution from 1966–76, and the Mao loyalists headed by Hua Guofeng, who played a leading role during the transitional phase from 1976–78, should actually be listed as a separate leadership generation due to their distinct political profiles (sanctioned by Mao they were party functionaries who clashed with the veterans of the revolution). However, the protagonists of this leadership generation, which ruled during the Chinese Cultural Revolution, were removed from their top positions following Mao's death in 1976 so their political roles can be considered no more than an intermezzo. The radical Maoists associated with the Cultural Revolution are officially ostracized in China today and they do not feature on lists of legitimate political leaders.

The dominant leader in the second generation is Deng Xiaoping. Deng temporarily occupied a key position at the party center during the Mao era, which gave him

Table 3.2

Leadership generations within the PRC

Leadership generation	Key representatives	Dominant politicians	Formative experiences	Political orientation, educational background
First generation (beginning in 1935)	Mao Zedong (*1893) Zhou Enlai (*1898)	Mao Zedong (1935-1976)	Civil war; war with Japan; the Long March; the Communist Revolution	Revolutionaries; influence of Soviet role models; close relationship between the party and the military
Second generation (beginning in 1978)	Deng Xiaoping (*1904) Chen Yun (*1905) Hu Yaobang (*1915) Zhao Ziyang (*1919)	Deng Xiaoping (1978-c.1992)	"Socialist construction"; loss of power during the Cultural Revolution (1966-76)	Economic reformers, to some extent more liberal politically; relatively high level of education
Third generation (beginning in 1989)	Jiang Zemin (*1926) Li Peng (*1928) Zhu Rongji (*1928)	Jiang Zemin (1992-2002)	Education in the Soviet Union; work experience in the state-owned enterprises or in the state bureaucracy	Technocrats (engineers); politics is regarded as an instrument of rapid economic growth
Fourth generation (beginning in 2002)	Hu Jintao (*1942) Wen Jiabao (*1942) Wu Bangguo (*1941)	Hu Jintao (2002-2012)	Education at elite Chinese universities; work experience in the provinces	Technocrats (engineers); complex modernization agenda (innovation, social security)
Fifth generation (beginning in 2012)	Xi Jinping (*1953) Li Keqiang (*1955) Wang Qishan (*1948)	Xi Jinping (since 2012)	Descendants of veterans of the Revolution, adolescent years shaped by the Cultural Revolution; political careers shaped by the reform and opening up policy	Law scholars, economists (heterogeneous career profiles); institutional restructuring and stabilization of the party-state and economy; global role of China

Based on Heilmann 2002.

© MERICS

experience in a number of fields of political-administrative work as well as an introduction to economic crisis management. In addition to Deng, CCP General Secretary Hu Yaobang (1980–87) and General Secretary Zhao Ziyang (1987–89) also belong to the second leadership generation. This generation witnessed recurring disputes over the acceptable extent of market-oriented economic reforms and political liberalization in a socialist system. The serious domestic crisis of 1989 heralded a shift to the next generation.

Deng Xiaoping initiated the transition to the third leadership generation, which centered around Jiang Zemin. Representatives of the third generation were considerably better educated than their predecessors, with the vast majority having studied engineering or having spent time in the Communist states of Eastern Europe during the 1950s. They had worked in state industries for a number of decades and had been involved in the PRC's initial phases of industrialization. The task assigned to the third generation by Deng Xiaoping was rapid economic expansion by any means ("economic growth is the only hard truth") and prevention of ideological conflicts about the nature of the economic reforms.

The dominance of engineers, typically with careers in state industry and the economic bureaucracy, is the reason why this generation is referred to as technocratic. Indeed, many of its representatives perceived political problem-solving as a technical challenge: the ruling administration was not propelled by visionary ideas as it had been during the Mao era but rather by the goal of optimizing administrative control mechanisms for the purpose of achieving economic modernization. The benchmark for political success was a high level of economic growth ("quadrupling China's GDP from 1980 to 2000"), albeit at the price of rapidly spreading social inequalities and enormous ecological damage.

The impetus for the shift to the fourth leadership generation led by Hu Jintao came with the 16th National Communist Party Congress held in November 2002. Most representatives of this generation also held degrees in science or technology. However, their political career paths were more heterogeneous than those of their predecessors: members ranged from the children of higher-level cadres to career officials and academics who developed an interest in politics later in life. This resulted in a political style based largely on consultation and compromise. No single representative of the fourth leadership generation had sufficient authority within the party to enforce programs or personnel decisions single-handedly. On the one hand, this was a form of protection against abrupt, radical policy changes. On the other, it hampered the process of reform implementation because it required the approval of all key decision-makers within the party leadership organs.

Some representatives of the fifth leadership generation, which has been in control since the 18th National Communist Party Congress in 2012, were promoted to central positions within leadership bodies as early as October 2007. In particular, the candidates for the posts of general secretary (Xi Jinping) and premier (Li Keqiang) spent five years on the Politburo Standing Committee and in deputy state executive positions before they assumed their top positions in 2012–13. Xi Jinping holds a PhD in law and Li Keqiang a PhD in economics. The share of politicians with backgrounds in engineering or science has decreased in favor of those with degrees in law or the

CHINA'S POLITICAL SYSTEM | **165**

social sciences. Members of the fifth leadership generation gained their practical work experience in a wide range of regional and provincial government and party positions during the economic boom years of the 1980s.

Unlike their predecessors, the fifth generation shows a stronger commitment to ideology-based and power-oriented problem solving, as opposed to favoring economic and technical solutions. General Secretary and President Xi Jinping has advocated revitalization and renewal (复兴) of the Chinese nation and its culture. China's rise to become a major power that is socially stable, highly developed culturally and technologically, and globally powerful (强国) has been extolled as part of a collective "China Dream." Based on programmatic statements by leading party leading bodies and specific media, cultural, and educational policies are directed toward creating an autonomous modern Chinese society—openly distanced from the guiding principles of the West—by combining socialist values and concepts of order with traditional Chinese values under the leadership of the CCP.

3.3 The division of labor within the party leadership

Sebastian Heilmann and Lea Shih

Inside the CCP Politburo, a balance is carefully maintained between major overlapping functional areas, *kou* (口), on the one hand, and bureaucratic sectors and hierarchies, *xitong* (系统), on the other. These must be supervised by and represented in the party leadership in order to link the most powerful functional and interest groups in the decision-making processes to the top party leaders.

In the Standing Committee of the Politburo, the division of responsibilities occurs in line with the organizational principles of the functional *kou* areas. The term *kou* refers to very broad overlapping areas that encompass a large number of specialized technical institutions from both the party and the state, whereas the term *xitong* is rather flexible and often imprecise: it can be applied to large functional areas (such as propaganda and media systems) as well as to more precisely defined administrative sectors and hierarchies (such as the financial and fiscal authorities).

Beginning in the 1950s, seven functional areas have been significant for CCP control. They are Party Organization, Ideology/Propaganda, Internal Security, Discipline Inspection, Finance and the Economy, Foreign Policy, and Defense. As a reflec-

Table 3.3

Responsibilities within central party and government offices, 2014

Cross-sectional functional areas	Responsible at the Politburo level	Responsible in the State Council "inner cabinet"
Party Organization	General Secretary/Member of the Standing Committee; Head of the Central Commission for Discipline Inspection (CCDI); Head of the Organization Department	[CCP prerogative]
Ideology and Propaganda	Member of the Standing Committee; Head of the Propaganda Department	[CCP prerogative]
Internal Security and Justice (Politics and Law)	Member of the Standing Committee; Head of the Political and Legal Affairs Commission	[CCP prerogative]
Discipline Inspection	Member of the Standing Committee; Head of the CCDI	[CCP prerogative]
Financial and Economic Affairs	General Secretary; two members of the Standing Committee; other Politburo members	Premier; various Vice-Premiers and State Councilors
Foreign Policy	General Secretary; other Politburo members	Premier; State Councilor
Defense	General Secretary (CMC Chairman); Politburo members from the military (two CMC Vice-Chairmen)	[CCP prerogative]
People's Congress and the Legislature	Member of the Standing Committee (also NPC Chairman)	Legislation mainly initiated by government organs
Cooperation with non-Communists (the "United Front")	Member of the Standing Committee (also CPPCC Chairman)	[CCP prerogative]

Based on Heilmann 2002.

© MERICS

tion of the political recognition of the National People's Congress (NPC) (as a legislative body) and of the Chinese People's Political Consultative Conference (CPPCC) (for consultation with non-Communist organizations), since the 1980s these two institutions have gained an improved standing in the party leadership. The top-level leaders of the NPC and the CPPCC represent their respective organizations on the Standing Committee of the Politburo.

Significant overlapping areas (Party Affairs, Ideology, Internal Security, Discipline Inspection, Defense, and the "United Front") are treated as CCP prerogatives to maintain control over the political system: top CCP cadres exercise direct leadership and supervision in these areas from the Politburo and the Central Leading Small Groups (LSGs). Government departments play only an executive role in these fields (see Table 3.3).

The two central functional areas of foreign and military affairs are classic responsibilities of the CCP general secretary. This person can, however, intervene at any time in other areas of responsibility to which other members of the Standing Committee are assigned (Yang Guangbin 2003). Inter-ministerial LSGs (中央领导小组) are regularly established to support the party leaders at the top of the relevant functional areas and to enable coordination among the relevant party, state, or military institutions (see Section 3.4).

Notwithstanding the division of responsibilities and delimitation of competencies among top-level CCP representatives, since the 1980s the collective leadership principle has applied to decision-making matters handed over to the Standing Committee of the Politburo, that is, instead of key decisions being made by a majority or by a decree of the CCP general secretary, they are settled on the basis of consensus. When controversial decisions are to be taken, the principle of collective leadership and the need for consensus can result in delays to important decisions and programs or to extreme cases of political stalemate, as occurred in May 1989 when the Standing Committee of the Politburo that confronted the mass demonstrations was unable to come to a common vote. Even during the later years of Hu Jintao's tenure as CCP general secretary (2002–12) obstructions and delayed decisions occurred increasingly in the Standing Committee of the Politburo regarding economic, foreign, and personnel policy, as well as in the struggle against corruption.

Experiencing these obstacles was crucial to empowering Xi Jinping's generation of leaders (those in office since 2012) and making them determined to strengthen the decision-making capacity of the central party headquarters. They did this by concentrating power in the position of the general secretary and establishing new LSGs under the direct leadership of the general secretary, thereby weakening the collective leadership in favor of the general secretary.

3.4 Central Leading Small Groups: Top-level decision-making under Xi Jinping

Sebastian Heilmann and Lea Shih

Beyond the official leadership bodies of the CCP and the central government, as established in the party and state constitutions described in Chapter 2, the Central Leading Small Groups (LSGs) are extremely important for regular consultations and for making decisions in overlapping areas, such as Ideology and Propaganda or Financial and Economic Affairs. LSGs at party headquarters are usually made up of at least one member of the Standing Committee of the Politburo and other relevant representatives of the government and party elite. They provide political coordination among several areas of responsibility, facilitating the formulation of overlapping and long-term programs. At the end of 2014, nearly twenty LSGs existed with different levels of importance and varying levels of activity.

Since 2013, Xi Jinping has actively used the reorganization and remodeling of the LSGs to implement his reform plans more effectively. Whereas his predecessor, Hu Jintao, generally headed only up to three LSGs, Xi Jinping has taken on the leading role in four newly established LSGs (implementation of the 2013 reform program; national security; military reform; and cyber security), as well as in the three already existing LSGs (Foreign Affairs; Taiwan Work; and Finance and Economy).

With the reorganization of these leading bodies, Xi Jinping assumed authority over decision-making and established for himself a clearly hierarchical, preeminent position, thus indirectly undermining the principle of consensus in the Standing Committee of the Politburo that had been established in the 1980s. Initially, the establishment of a "strong man" at the head of the party found clear broad support in the Politburo. Blockades of decisions and inertia, such as what occurred under CCP General Secretary Hu Jintao (2002–12), were thus avoided and Xi was able to expeditiously effect a strong concentration of power.

The premier and his inner cabinet were required to leave space for this new concentration of decision-making power in the hands of the general secretary. Since the 1980s, the premier has had jurisdiction over economic and reform policy, with party leaders taking a back seat. However, by establishing the LSG for "Comprehensively Deepening Reforms" in 2013, Xi Jinping also assumed control over economic and environmental policy, thus breaking the traditional division of labor between the head of the party and the head of the government. This concentration of the responsibilities of party leader and daily political activities changed how policies were formed and decisions were made at the center of power. CCP General Secretary Xi Jinping also assumed leadership of two newly created "super commissions" to deal with matters of national security and broad institutional reform. The following introduces some of the most important LSGs that are currently under the leadership of the general secretary.

Central National Security Commission (CNSC) (中央国家安全委员会)

The CNSC, set up in November 2013, is one of the largest LSGs. The designation "commission" is typical for coordinating bodies in the security field. However, in keeping with its structure and functions, the CNSC is classified as a LSG. It brings together all the relevant security institutions, including the military, under the leadership of the CCP general secretary. The CNSC is entrusted with planning and implementing internal and external national security strategy and it acts as the highest approval and coordination authority for the party and state leadership with respect to security matters. By establishing the CNSC, Xi Jinping succeeded in assuming control over security-related decision-making processes. This effort was initiated at the beginning of the 2000s, but it was deferred under his predecessor (for more on the CNSC, see Section 2.3.4).

Central Leading Small Group for Comprehensively Deepening Reforms (CDRLSG) (中央全面深化改革领导小组)

The CDRLSG is responsible for coordinating the program approved in November 2013 by the Central Committee (CC) to institutionally reorganize and modernize the economy, the party, the judiciary, and culture. With forty-three members, the CDRLSG is a "super commission" consisting of all relevant intra-party and state decision-makers under the personal leadership of the CCP general secretary. The CDRLSG oversees six subgroups that are charged with dealing with economic and environmental challenges, the legal system, cultural affairs, social issues, party building, and discipline inspection. The subgroup on the economy and the environment occupies a special place within the CDRLSG. It is responsible for almost two-thirds of the planned reforms (118 out of a total of 181). This subgroup is supported by the staff office of the Central Finance and Economy Leading Small Group (CFELSG) (see the following section). CDRLSG meetings are routinely arranged *before* meetings of the Standing Committee of the Politburo (or meetings of the entire Politburo) so that CDRLSG decisions can be promptly approved and confirmed by the body of top party officials. Although very little information about the work of the LSGs usually seeps out to the outside world, between 2013 and 2015 information about CDRLSG meetings and decisions was reported in unusual detail by the state media. This is because the CDRLSG has a clear public programmatic function to signal that implementation of the ambitious 2013 reform program is being systematically pursued with determination by the party leadership.

Central Finance and Economy Leading Small Group (CFELSG) (中央财经领导小组)

This LSG, which has existed—with some breaks—since the 1950s, is responsible for guidelines governing economic planning and economic policy. It relies on expertise support from a wide range of government bodies and research institutions. The CCP general secretary heads the CFELSG and all relevant authoritative decision-makers in economic and financial policy are members. The Office of the CFELSG (中央财经领导小组办公室, or for short: 中财办) represents the most important body for preparing decision-making regarding China's economic policy due to its direct access to the highest level of the party leadership and its formulation of national development strategies.

Central Leading Small Group for Cyber Security and Informatization (CSILSG) (中央网络安全和信息化领导小组)

This new LSG was established in the spring of 2014. The fact that party leader and head of state Xi Jinping has taken on the leadership of this seemingly technical LSG indicates the importance that China attaches to this subject area. In the past, China had not pursued a coherent cyber security strategy, and failure to pool decision-making powers had led to incoherent regulation and conflicting responsibilities among various ministries. This LSG is also charged with launching major initiatives in international Internet policy through promotion of regulatory norms and standards that are favored by the Chinese government and that stress the importance of national sovereignty in cyberspace (see Section 6.16 for more details).

Leading Small Group of the Central Military Commission for Deepening Reforms in National Defense and the Military (中央军委深化国防和军队改革领导小组)

This military policy LSG, under the CMC (not under the Politburo), was established in March 2014. However, the CCP general secretary, as chairman of both the party and the state CMC, also heads this LSG. It is entrusted with improving command structures, training standards, and discipline inspection (ideological education, loyalty to the CCP, and the fight against corruption) in China's military by taking organizational measures (for more details on military policy, see Section 2.12).

Consequences of the concentration of power

The drastically strengthened concentration of decision-making power at party headquarters under Xi Jinping is intended to enforce the authority of the party center with respect to ministerial, regional, and business special interests and to narrow the space for corrupt patronage networks within the political system. Since 1978 such a centralized and personalized decision-making process has only been implemented during very short periods of crisis.

The extent to which the concentration of power at CCP headquarters can be an effective remedy for enforcing a nationwide institutional reorganization over a period of up to ten years under Xi Jinping's leadership remains uncertain. In 2013 and 2014 widespread uncertainty was felt in many party and government bodies below the party center (hence in the ministries, regional/local administrations, and companies) regarding whether decentralized initiatives were desirable and could be pursued without political risk. This wait-and-see attitude put the brakes on implementation of many reforms that had been announced by party headquarters. As a consequence, party leadership organs have resolutely criticized such inactivity by local governments and officials. From 1978 to 2012 decentralized initiatives were crucial in creating an agile and adaptable political and economic system. Since 2013, however, the drastic measures undertaken by the party center to enforce hierarchical discipline and centralized authority have restricted the policy initiative and reform agility at the lower levels of China's state administration.

3.5 Top leaders

Kerstin Lohse-Friedrich and Sebastian Heilmann

In the following, we will briefly describe the members of the current Standing Committee of the Politburo, that is, China's most powerful leaders due to their rank in the party hierarchy. Beyond the Standing Committee of the Politburo, we will also introduce four of the most influential strategic advisers to Xi Jinping in his position as party leader and head of state. These "second-row strategists" play an important role in preparing decision-making agendas.

3.5.1 Members of the Politburo Standing Committee

CCP General Secretary and President (head of state) *Xi Jinping* (born in 1953, ranking first in the Politburo) comes from Shaanxi province. Like his predecessor, Hu Jintao, he is a graduate of Qinghua University in Beijing, where he was educated as a chemist and later earned a PhD in law. As the son of the late veteran of the Communist Revolution, Xi Zhongxun, Xi belongs to the group of party princelings. He spent his early political career in economic powerhouses along the eastern coast (2000–2: governor of Fujian province; 2002–7: governor and party secretary of the coastal province of Zhejiang, which is dominated by private enterprises, and; 2007: party secretary of Shanghai). Xi possesses broad economic experience, including regular interactions with foreign and Taiwan investors as well as with private firms. In 2007 he assumed leadership of the CCP Secretariat, serving as president of the Central Party School until 2012 and for five years in the position of vice-president preparing for a role as a diplomat on the international scene in expectation of eventually holding the highest party and state offices. In 2012 Xi became the party leader (CCP general secretary) and chairman of the CCP CC Military Commission. Then, in 2013—like his predecessor as general secretary—he also took on the important foreign policy role of president of the PRC. However, Xi Jinping has concentrated more power than his predecessor in the office of CCP general secretary. He achieved this by creating new LSGs and assuming a decidedly presidential political style that includes strong leadership coupled with effective public relations.

Premier *Li Keqiang* (born 1955, ranking second in the Politburo) comes from the family of a local official in Anhui province. His political career, after an education in law at Peking University (Beida) and a PhD in economics, began in the Communist Youth League (CYL) as a companion of Hu Jintao when Hu was its leader in the 1980s. Li Keqiang's career path followed in Hu Jintao's slipstream. In 1999 Li was appointed governor of Henan province and in 2004 he became party secretary of Liaoning province. As a result of his successful modernization policies in the "difficult" provinces of Henan and Liaoning, Li is highly regarded in terms of economic policy making. However, his work in Henan was overshadowed by a blood donation and AIDS scandal, infecting tens of thousands of people, that the local authorities sought to cover up for many years. From 2008 to 2012 Li served as vice-premier in preparation for assuming the position of premier, which he did in 2013. Li has been a member of the Politburo since 2007 and a member of its Standing Committee since 2012. He is regarded as knowledgeable, quick-witted, and humorous. As a result of the concentration of power—including economic policy making—under Xi Jinping personally between 2013 and 2015, Li Keqiang's actual decision-making powers declined compared to those enjoyed by his predecessor in the position of premier.

NPC Chairman *Zhang Dejiang* (born in 1946, ranking third in the Politburo) comes from Liaoning province and is a protégé of former party leader Jiang Zemin (1989–2002). Zhang studied economics in North Korea and served as party leader in Zhejiang, Jilin, and Guangdong provinces, among others. During the 2003 severe acute respiratory syndrome (SARS) crisis, as a leader in Guangdong province Zhang initially kept a lid on information about the extent of the outbreak. In 2012, at short notice, he was parachuted in immediately following the removal of Chongqing "party king" Bo Xilai to become party leader of Chongqing, a southwestern metropolis, to restore political order. He was elected chairman of the NPC in 2013 and has since served to ensure practically invisible legislative work.

Chairman of the CPPCC, *Yu Zhengsheng* (born in 1945, ranking fourth in the Politburo) is also considered to be a protégé of former party leader Jiang Zemin. Like Xi Jinping, Yu also belongs to the circle of party princelings. He has an extraordinary family background. His father was the ex-husband of Jiang Qing, who later married Mao Zedong. His brother, who had served as bureau chief in the Ministry of State Security, defected to the United States in the mid-1980s. He studied engineering at the Military Engineering Institute in Harbin and initially worked for some years in the Ministry of the Electronics Industry before becoming mayor of the port city of Qingdao. In 1998 Yu was appointed minister of construction. Beginning in 2001 he served as party secretary of Hubei province and then from 2007 to 2012 he served as party secretary of Shanghai. Yu has been a member of the Politburo since 2002 and a member of its Standing Committee since 2012. In March 2013 he took over the chairmanship of the CPPCC, which, in the context of the CCP's United Front with non-Communist organizations, has primarily symbolic and advisory functions.

Executive secretary of the CCP Secretariat, head of the Leading Small Group for Ideology and Propaganda, and president of the Central Party School, *Liu Yunshan* (born in 1947, ranking fifth in the Politburo) comes from Shanxi province. Liu studied at Jining Normal School in Inner Mongolia and then worked for two decades in Inner Mongolia, first as a teacher, then for the Xinhua News Agency and as a leading party cadre in the propaganda system. In 1993 he was called to Beijing to work in the CCP CC Propaganda Department where he eventually worked his way to the top. In 2002 Liu was promoted to the Politburo and to director of the CCP CC Propaganda Department. In the latter role, which he held until 2012, he was responsible for guiding and controlling the content of the traditional media and for regulating use of the rapidly expanding Internet. In 2012 Liu was promoted to the Standing Committee of the Politburo and assumed the chairmanship of the CCP Secretariat, director of the Leading Small Group for Ideology and Propaganda, and president of the Central Party School. He is one of China's most powerful political decision-makers based on the strength of his central roles in the party and propaganda apparatus. CCP strategy for modernizing its traditional propaganda system by linking it to new cyberspace communications and surveillance technologies bears his unmistakable imprint.

Chairman of the CCP CCDI, *Wang Qishan* (born in 1948, ranking sixth in the Politburo) comes from Shanxi province and is yet another of the party's "crown princes." Wang climbed up to the party "aristocracy" via his prominent father-in-law, Yao Yilin, a former Politburo member and vice- premier. In the 1980s Wang was committed to a group of young economic reformers with strong political contacts. (These contacts include the subsequent governor of the Central Bank, Zhou Xiaochuan.) This group achieved stellar careers in banking and government during the 1990s. At the beginning of the 1990s, Wang played an important role in authorizing the founding of the stock exchanges, for which, with support from his father-in-law, he successfully canvassed. During the 1990s Wang was governor of a major state-owned bank (China Construction Bank, 1994–97). He was also vice-governor of Guangdong province (1998–2000), responsible for economic and financial policy. From 2002 to 2003, he was party leader of the island province of Hainan and then from 2003 to 2007 he served as mayor of Beijing. His vigorous halting of the highly dangerous SARS epidemic in the capital city by means of an active information policy has been acknowledged not only by the population of the city and the central party leadership but also by the World Health Organization (WHO). In 2007 Wang was promoted to the Politburo, and in 2008 he also became a vice-premier. Since November 2012 he has been a member of the Politburo Standing Committee, entrusted with the thorniest problem in the highest echelons of the party, namely, the fight against corruption. With Xi Jinping's backing, Wang has pushed ahead very determinedly with the anti-corruption campaign and has succeeded in exposing a series of high-ranking officials for graft. Wang enjoys a good reputation as a crisis manager who has been able to make difficult decisions in the face of resistance from the CCP and the state. Among corrupt officials, since 2012 he has been regarded as the most hated person in the party leadership.

Executive Vice-Premier *Zhang Gaoli* (born in 1946, ranking seventh in the Politburo) comes from the southern Chinese province of Fujian. Zhang studied economics at Xiamen University and, after various positions, including in the oil industry, he worked in Guangdong and Shandong provinces. Between 2007 and 2012 he served as party leader of Tianjin municipality (located 120 km southeast of Beijing), a city under the direct jurisdiction of the central government. Under his leadership the city experienced rapid economic development. Zhang rose to the ranks of the Politburo in 2007 and to its Standing Committee in 2012. Since 2013, he has been one of the four vice-premiers, who is responsible for finance; development and reform; resources; environmental protection; and urban-rural development, among other fields.

3.5.2 Senior strategists and advisers

Several high-ranking officials, often referred to as "staff officers" (参谋), are members of the most trusted inner circle of party leaders. These officials serve the general secretary and his closest, high-ranking party leaders as strategy advisers on fundamental policy issues (Wang Huning); foreign policy (Yang Jiechi); the economy, technology, and the environment (Liu He); and intra-party coordination and security of the party leadership (Li Zhanshu). They have regular access to Xi Jinping and often accompany him on trips abroad.

Wang Huning (born in 1955 in Shandong province) is a graduate of Shanghai's Fudan University where he studied international politics. From 1989 to 1994 Wang lectured at his alma mater as a professor of international politics. In 1995 he was promoted to a leadership role in the CCP CC Policy Research Office (中央政策研究室). This organization advises the party leadership and writes speeches and draws up documents. Wang gained a seat on the CC in 2002 and on the Politburo in 2007. Uncommonly, he has served as a policy adviser to three consecutive party leaders (Jiang Zemin, Hu Jintao, and Xi Jinping). He was the *spiritus rector* behind several "government slogans," namely, the "Three Represents" under Jiang Zemin, "Harmonious Society" under Hu Jintao, and the "China Dream" under Xi Jinping. Since the 1990s, Wang has remained firmly in the background, avoiding public appearances, interviews, and socializing. He is a classic, almost untouchable, private strategy adviser, reserved in public and therefore, as far as the party leader is concerned, trustworthy, working quietly behind the scenes of high-level politics. Wang continues to hold his position close to the leadership as director of the Policy Research Office of the CCP CC, writing speeches for the party leader and head of state and accompanying him on trips abroad. The extent to which Wang is trusted by Xi Jinping became clear when Wang was appointed director of the Office of the CDRLSG (see above) to implement the 2013 reform program. Even in party circles, Wang is regarded as an éminence grise. He maintains no contacts with former college friends and colleagues in Shanghai, refrains from expressing any public opinions, and does not meet with any foreigners.

Liu He (born in 1952) is the director of the Office of the CFELSG and also deputy director of the National Development and Reform Commission (NDRC). In the 1990s Liu rose from the former State Planning Commission to become one of the leading industrial and technology policy strategists. He initially studied at People's University in Beijing, a university traditionally close to the government, where he also briefly taught and conducted research. After several years as an official in the State Planning Commission, Liu earned a Master's of Business Administration from Seton Hall University (in the United States) before earning a Master's of Public Administration degree at the Kennedy School of Government of Harvard University. He was instrumental in preparing a series of development planning and industrial policy programs in the 1990s and 2000s. In 2008 Liu worked closely with Premier Wen Jiabao in developing measures to lessen the impact of the global financial crisis on the Chinese economy. In 2012 he became a member of the 18th CCP CC and director of the office of the CFELSG. He is considered to be one of the masterminds behind the CCP CC's reform decision in November 2013.

Yang Jiechi (born in 1950 in Shanghai) has been state councilor for foreign affairs since 2013. An expert on the United States, Yang is often close at hand during Xi Jinping's trips abroad. He is regarded as a significant strategy adviser in terms of reorienting China's external relations and managing relations with the United States. He belongs to the small group of Chinese diplomats who were sent abroad during the Cultural Revolution. In the early 1970s Yang studied in Bath, England, and at the London School of Economics and Political Science. He received a PhD in history, and, in 1975, he began his career in the Chinese Ministry of Foreign Affairs. He was posted to the Chinese Embassy in Washington, DC for a total of thirteen years, including serving as ambassador from 2001 to 2005. Yang was vice–foreign minister between 1998 and 2001 and again from 2005 to 2007, and then became minister of foreign affairs until 2013. He has been a CCP CC member since 2008.

Li Zhanshu (born in 1950 in Hebei province) has been a close confidant of Xi Jinping's family for decades. In the 1980s Li and Xi worked in neighboring districts of Hebei province. For two decades, Li Zhanshu gained experience in the highest political positions in four provinces (Hebei, Shaanxi, Heilongjiang, and Guizhou). After 2012 he was appointed director of the General Office of the CCP CC where he is responsible for the information flow at party headquarters and for regular communications with regional party leaders. He is also in charge of the general secretary's security. Li Zhanshu serves as the closest confidant of the general secretary and is therefore Xi Jinping's most significant "gatekeeper" and troubleshooter at party headquarters.

3.6 The risks of political succession and Xi Jinping's presidential style

Sebastian Heilmann

Changes in leadership are more important in China than they are in most other political systems. The composition of the party and state leaderships is the result of many years of sounding out potential candidates, coming to agreements, and then trying them out within the top levels of the CCP. The media drama of democratic elections and majority decisions does not exist in Chinese politics. After they are appointed, China's political leaders govern for a period that can safely be said to be ten years (two five-year terms of office are standard). However, new priorities and leadership styles can lead to fundamental shifts in power and strategy.

Therefore, the arrival of a new party and government leadership in China may potentially be of greater long-term significance than it is in Western democracies. Although many policy announcements by newly appointed leaders build on programs initiated by the preceding administrations, crucial shifts in priorities are reflected in personnel decisions and organizational adjustments. Personnel changes and policy content are more tightly bound together than they are in liberal democracies because leadership positions in the Chinese system of government allow for more decision-making powers. Accordingly, political initiatives usually begin with executive regulations and action programs rather than with parliamentary legislative initiatives.

In the past, destabilizing conflicts within the CCP were frequently associated with transfers of power from one generation of leaders to the next; frequent leadership and succession crises in Communist systems kept researchers very busy (Holmes 1986). In brief, the factors having a crucial influence on power relations in the central leadership can be described by the formula "5P + X." While "X" denotes unforeseeable circumstances, such as unrest, financial crises, or international conflicts, "5P" refers to the factors listed in Table 3.6 that play a prominent role in determining power configurations in the political leadership. In the absence of reliable procedural rules, appointments to the ranks of the highest leadership within Communist parties must either be negotiated or fought over. Under these circumstances, the cultivation of power bases and alliances is the only way to guarantee political advancement.

In the history of the PRC, disputes over leadership succession have precipitated repeated political crises, such as those seen in the various failed succession arrangements under Mao Zedong or Deng Xiaoping. It was only with the appointment of Jiang Zemin as a compromise candidate within the context of the serious domestic crisis of 1989 that a smooth transition from the leadership system of the Deng era to today's system was achieved. Faced with the ongoing influence of formally retired party veterans, Jiang Zemin initially cautiously established himself up to the mid-1990s, then began to energetically consolidate his personal authority beginning in about 1994. That Deng Xiaoping until his death in 1997 retained the leadership unity without intervening in day-to-day politics proved to be decisive for Jiang Zemin.

The November 2002 personnel changes in the party leadership (from Jiang Zemin to Hu Jintao) represented the first change of party leadership in the history of the PRC that occurred without any crisis-laden conflicts (manipulative power strug-

Table 3.6

Crucial factors in leadership and succession conflicts

Personalities: Which members of the leadership have many years of experience in the ruling apparatus? Who has emerged, either as a result of political skills in previous crisis situations, dealings with colleagues, or sheer determination?

Positions: In the event of a conflict, which institutional positions of power can members of the political leadership draw upon to use as a power base?

Patronage: Have particular members of the leadership been able to cultivate far-reaching patronage networks and a large number of loyal protégés?

Political alliances: In the event of a conflict, do longstanding political or personnel policy alliances exist among various members of the leadership that could swing decisions?

Policies: Are there any clear differences in the political objectives of the candidates? How attractive is each political program to the political elite or to the population at large?

Based on Heilmann 2002.

© MERICS

gles or infighting in which internal party consensus-building processes were countermanded). This is often regarded as a sign of institutional consolidation by the CCP. However, the smooth transition of power was not the result of firmly established procedural rules. Instead, on the one hand, it was due to forward-looking personnel planning by Deng Xiaoping. Deng was already supporting Hu Jintao as a leading figure of the fourth leadership generation by the early 1990s—ten years before the latter assumed the position of general secretary. On the other hand, the smooth personnel changes can be attributed to the third leadership generation under Jiang Zemin who cautiously prepared and promoted this critical transfer of power.

Like other representatives of the fourth leadership generation, Hu Jintao did not possess the status, prestige, or power base on which the heroes of the Communist Revolution, Mao and Deng, were able to rely. Therefore, the transfer of power in 2012 was the first proper test of whether or not an institutionalized handover of office was possible within the CCP without an incontestable authority in the background to ensure stability. On his own, Hu Jintao was unable to determine his successor, but he was successful by consulting and reaching a compromise with former party leader Jiang Zemin.

The maneuvers, negotiations, and conflicts that occurred in the run-up to naming Xi Jinping general secretary cannot be reconstructed in detail due to the lack of reliable sources. Contradictory rumors and dramatized conspiracy theories are woven around the 2012 personnel decision-making processes. In any case, there were severe clashes within the party leadership regarding the Bo Xilai case (previously serving as party secretary of Chongqing), whose removal from power and subsequent prosecution jeopardized the future of other members of the leadership. Delays in decision-making occurred immediately before the 2012 party congress also because Xi Jinping insisted on not only becoming party leader and head of state but from the very outset becoming chairman of the CMC as well.

Xi Jinping aimed to achieve comprehensive authorization by the former party leadership to halt the CCP's organizational crisis by means of reorganization and concentration of power in the party leadership system. In the meantime, Xi Jinping disappeared from public view for several weeks, fueling rumors about an attempted putsch or—alternatively—threats to resign. The truth about these rumors can only be verified if and when the CCP's information and archives policies are relaxed. In any event, the change of leadership in 2012 was characterized by lengthy and conflict-ridden intra-party negotiations. However, Xi Jinping's demand for a clear mandate and a concentration of power was ultimately achieved between 2012 and 2014.

In addition to an exceptional concentration of power, a new communications and leadership style has also emerged under Xi Jinping. In the history of the PRC, modern political mass communications, using active external media branding and image stamping, have not played a significant role in the concentration of power after the personality cult surrounding Mao Zedong. But Xi Jinping's assumption of the positions of CCP general secretary and president of the PRC in 2012–13 marked a dramatic break with the past. Not only did Xi underscore the delivery of memorable photo opportunities that chimed with the people's lives (eating in a simple noodle kitchen, etc.), but he also endeavored to use a more lively way of speaking. Xi was the first Chinese party leader and head of state to initiate a New Year's speech on television, similar in style to the speeches given by Western leaders and heads of state, or even Russia's President Putin. Furthermore, he regularly appeared, especially on foreign trips, with his attractive wife, the well-known army folk singer Peng Liyuan, who is a popular figure. Overall, Xi Jinping introduced a media-savvy, presidential style that was new to Chinese politics, aimed not only at reinforcing his own preeminent political position but also eliciting broad, emotional support from the general population.

Traditional intra-party leadership selection processes and the exercise of power may experience changes due to new types of public relations and populist practices that have been introduced during Xi Jinping's term of office. Therefore, in the future the "wooden" apparatchiks will probably have less of a chance to assert themselves in the offices of party leader and head of state.

3.7 Informal methods of exercising power

Sebastian Heilmann

Informal methods of exercising power and taking political action that are contrary to the official rules in the party constitution, the state constitution, laws, and government decrees are fundamental features of governance in the PRC. In many cases, important decisions on principle are not made in the bodies intended for this purpose according to the state and party constitutions. The most dramatic case can be found in the decision that led to the Chinese military suppression of the urban protest movement in 1989: it was a vote passed by a number of veterans of the revolution who no longer belonged to any official decision-making body in the CCP or the government that provided the impetus for the military crackdown (Baum 1994).

Informal methods of exercising power have played a major role in Chinese politics for decades. The formal concentration of power that goes with the top positions in party and state bodies has been frequently circumvented by hidden hierarchies of influential people and decision-making processes. Political power is not only derived from people's positions and the organizations to which they belong but also to the personal prestige, the loyalty of one's protégés, and skillful behind-the-scenes political manipulation. The informal mode of consensus-building and exercise of power practiced under Mao Zedong and Deng Xiaoping created a high degree of political unpredictability. The internal party quarrels over the best way to handle the protest movement in 1989 made it clear how unreliable the mechanisms of conflict resolution were in China at the time. To this day, intra-party conflicts still have the potential to destabilize the entire political order.

3.7.1 Formal versus informal rules

The members of the third and fourth leadership generations consequently advocated strengthening the formal decision-making processes that already existed, acting in their own interests as well as in the interests of the party. The reason for this was that they no longer possessed such a high degree of personal authority as was held by the veterans of the Chinese Revolution, and therefore they sought to reinforce their own power through formal institutions.

These efforts to achieve political institutionalization were not only hindered by the continued existence of informal decision-making rules and personal considerations but also by new developments beginning in the 1980s. Specific steps to bring about deregulation and privatization in the business sector created opportunities to take advantage of political "rents," with constant interventions by state departments and party officials: top officials (or members of their families) and their closest colleagues discovered additional sources of personal income by exploiting their ability to access information and to influence decision-making. This has been demonstrated in a wide variety of cases involving corruption in politics and the administrative sector, which have had an erosive effect on the official institutions of the party-state. Informal political rules of the game thus evolved, often in blatant contradiction to the existing formal institutions (see Table 3.7).

Table 3.7

Tensions between formal and informal rules in Chinese politics

Formal rules	Widespread informal rules
Formalized system of cadre recruitment	Party patronage networks and the sale of political positions
Bureaucratic hierarchy and the establishment of universal rules	Domestic lobbies and clientele-based economic regulation
State property rights	Informal privatization and uncontrolled draining of state assets
Equality before the law	Manipulation of the judicial system to benefit party officials and their relatives
Fiscal system with binding allocations of revenue	Revenue retained by local governments and continual negotiations over the division of revenue

Based on Heilmann 2002.

© MERICS

When having recourse to informal methods of pursuing interests and exercising power becomes the rule, the effectiveness of a country's formal institutions are obviously undermined. Brie (1996) writes that such a weakening of state institutions is one of the most influential aspects of the socialist legacy. However, reverting to informal methods provides the relevant people with more flexibility than they ever would have had in a rigid Leninist institutional framework (Shirk 1993). Seen from this perspective, the informal modes of exchange that have evolved among party officials and key players in the Chinese economy can also be regarded as an essential political precondition for the party's successes in the course of its economic reforms:

if the political representatives in China had merely followed the official rules of the Leninist institutional order, then the economic liberalization and structural reforms that the country has experienced may never have been introduced in the first place (Heilmann 2000).

3.7.2 The Beidaihe conferences and the role of retired leaders

The annual party conferences held in July and August of each year in the colonial villas of the small seaside resort of Beidaihe, 200 kilometers (125 miles) east of Beijing, have taken place ever since 1958 and have been an opportunity to discuss important decisions and policies at the highest levels of the political system. The meetings staged far from Beijing's bureaucratic apparatus enable high-ranking members of the party to informally exchange views, sound out matters, and prepare key decisions by involving former general secretaries and members of the Politburo who are officially in retirement. In particular, the Beidaihe meetings are intended to prepare for the meetings of the CC (which take place annually) or for the National Communist Party Congresses (held once every five years). Those attending the party conferences in the autumn vote on policy and personnel decisions that have been prepared beforehand at Beidaihe.

In the summer of 2003, however, Hu Jintao, who had just become the new general secretary, made an unexpected decision, announcing that the meetings in Beidaihe would not take place. Ostensibly, the reason was said to be the outbreak of the SARS epidemic the previous spring, but Hu Jintao's actual intention was to limit meddling in current decision-making by retired top officials. Not surprisingly, the former officials were not very pleased with this. Thereafter, Hu Jintao's plans met with reservations and mistrust on the part of his predecessors. For instance, Jiang Zemin (general secretary of the CCP from 1989 to 2002) still attended the summer get-togethers in Beidaihe, meeting informally with current and former party and government officials. The Beidaihe meetings were resumed in 2005, albeit in a shortened form. In fact, the backing that former top officials provided turned out to be indispensable for the incumbent party leaders when it came to making controversial decisions and compromises, particularly concerning personnel issues.

Jiang Zemin's shadow was still noticeable when Xi Jinping—his successor's successor—took office. Xi was obliged to obtain Jiang Zemin's approval before initiating an investigation into charges of corruption against a former member of the Politburo Standing Committee. Without Jiang's approval, the investigation might have been regarded as the onset of a broader attack on former top officials and their families, an act that would have met with strong resistance from influential retired cadres and consequently might have weakened Xi Jinping's position.

The incumbent party leaders have an understandable interest to limit consultations with their predecessors and to prevent retired politicians from exerting undue influence on current policy making as they seek to be able to make their own decisions. But even a power-conscious politician such as Xi Jinping cannot solely rely on the authority that comes with formal bodies and positions. Rather, he must constantly keep in mind the informal sources of influence and networks upon which his predecessors can still rely to obstruct his course of action.

3.7.3 Informal rules of leadership selection and patronage networks

The formation of internal factions (集团, 帮派) within the CCP is not permitted. Membership in any associations that are not officially recognized (e.g., for university alumni, military cadets, etc.), or any informal regional clubs (e.g., for party functionaries who come from the same home area) is prohibited by internal party regulations. Members of the CCP are only permitted to join associations whose establishment expressly meets with official government approval.

In contrast, forming and expanding patronage networks is encouraged by the official cadre system. Anyone who wishes to pursue a career in Chinese politics needs to win the support of a top cadre who is willing to pave the way for him/her and who expects absolute loyalty in return. Becoming part of such a web of interpersonal relations is of decisive importance if one wishes to climb the political ladder or to have an influence on political decision-making. The majority of top Chinese officials have spent many years working as personal secretaries (秘书) to older officials in leading positions. Work of this kind provides broad experience as well as contacts at high levels. Sudden, rocket-like promotions are only possible due to personal relations with older officials in key positions.

Graduates from Qinghua University in Beijing attract the attention of politicians because this university is regarded as the cradle for technocrats. As a result, its graduates have often been able to rise to high positions. For example, Zhu Rongji, who was prime minister until 2003, and Hu Jintao and Xi Jinping, who were each appointed to the position of general secretary of the CCP, all graduated from Qinghua. Dozens of ministers and governors, hundreds of mayors and county party secretaries, and thousands of other high-ranking officials working in the administration or the business sector once passed through the gates of this university. The growth of a network on such a scale is due to conscious efforts by Qinghua's former dean, Jiang Nanxiang, who in the 1950s already began to build up an elite group of politically and academically minded talented students in order to recruit capable people for leading positions in the CCP.

The network of former officials in the CYL is also widely seen as playing an influential role. Hu Jintao was regarded as a leader of this network when he held the position of general secretary (2002-12). As it so happened, a large number of former CYL officials assumed leading political positions when Hu Jintao was in power, including Li Keqiang, who was appointed a vice-premier in 2008 and became premier in 2013. Unlike many of the previous top officials, who were often rather colorless and not very media-oriented, many of the politicians who had been members of the CYL pay attention to the impression they make on the general public: at least, they make it seem as if they lead modest private lives and work in a unassuming way, paying frequent visits to poorer segments of the population and avoiding making public appearances in the company of nouveau riche representatives in the real-estate or entertainment sectors.

However, such a one-dimensional linkage of particular leaders to specific networks is problematic: graduates from Qinghua University and top officials who rose from the ranks of the CYL have now become so numerous and hold so many top positions that it has become increasingly doubtful whether these broad networks still produce a demonstrably strong sense of cohesion among those who now sit on political decision-making bodies. Personal loyalties are generally much looser and casual in groups of this kind than in patron–client networks based on connections to a top functionary, as in the case of Jiang Zemin's former patron–client network known as the "Shanghai Gang."

Between 2013 and 2015, the CCP's CCDI uncovered specific cases of creating contemporary cliques within the party. Charges of corruption were raised not only against a former member of the Politburo Standing Committee (Zhou Yongkang), but the investigations also caused a host of former staff members of this political patron, who had worked in the oil industry, in Sichuan province, or in the state-security sector, to lose their jobs. Revelations concerning the case of Ling Jihua, a former director of the CC's General Office, were equally spectacular. He is said to have formed a network of prominent politicians and businesspeople (the so-called "Xishan Society") who regularly met in the mountains west of Beijing to secretly negotiate about the allocation of political offices and the placing of lucrative economic orders. (He was sentenced to life in prison in July 2016.) In view of such evidence indicating that the CCP was in danger of collapsing, the party media and Xi Jinping himself announced that the formation of political cliques for the purpose of personal enrichment (结党营私) would absolutely no longer be tolerated and would be dealt with the utmost severity.

Children and other relatives of former or current party and army cadres also play a prominent role in politics, the armed forces, and the economy. These cadre "princelings" receive privileged educations at elite Chinese schools and foreign colleges and universities. Furthermore, because of their special family backgrounds, at an early age they become familiar with the networks of relations and with the "rules of the game" that apply to power politics and personnel policies within the CCP. Beginning in the 1990s, many such princelings managed to obtain top political and economic positions in China's prosperous coastal regions. Their share of high-ranking officers in the Chinese army is even larger than their share of top civilian positions.

Princelings of the CCP can act as the heads of politically and economically active "clans" that combine the leading positions in the state apparatus with entrepreneurial pursuits of profit for private gain. The princelings are not only unpopular with the general public but also with many members of the party because they are always suspected of having obtained their positions because of their family backgrounds rather than because of their own hard work and ability. As a result, they are often thought to be involved in organized corruption and capital flight—and there is indeed ample evidence of such activities.

Resistance to the princelings' rapid climb up the political ladder took on a more concrete form at the end of the 1990s. Prominent "crown princes" faced a hard time when votes were taken on personnel issues at party congresses and people's congresses. The organization and discipline departments of the CCP imposed restrictions on the involvement of cadre children in business activities (e.g., in management consultancies and stock trading due to insider offenses). When Hu Jintao became general secretary, many people thought he was more credible and possessed more integrity than his predecessors because he did not come from a princeling background. Nevertheless, Hu had to cope without any broad networks of contacts created by his family and without being able to draw on the self-confidence so typical of the party's princelings.

Many of the princelings believe they are a kind of "red nobility" that can base its legitimacy and standing on the work of their parents during the Communist Revolution. Some of the princelings who assumed an air of self-importance, such as former Chongqing party secretary Bo Xilai, who was imprisoned in 2013 on charges of abusing his position and corruption, felt that party leader Hu Jintao was not one of them and thus they attempted to discredit him, claiming he was an upstart who had not gained his position by any legitimate means.

An astonishing number of princelings were elected to leading organs of the CCP during the 2007 and 2012 party congresses; the results of the voting indicate that there was no longer any evidence of resistance to their rise to power. For example, in 2012 Xi Jinping and Wang Qishan both obtained key positions due to their princeling backgrounds—their previous posts had provided them with a wealth of practical experience working at every level of the political system, a great deal of self-confidence, and a large network of personal relations. In Xi Jinping's case, in particular, his acquaintances with a number of high-ranking army officers during his teen-age years gave him a degree of support among military leaders that his predecessor Hu Jintao lacked. Unlike the corrupt reputation of the "red nobility," the group of princelings surrounding Xi Jinping and Wang Qishan was vehement in its call to fight corruption in the CCP and the army, to end wastefulness, and to lead modest private family lives little influenced by materialism. They attempted to establish a link to the Chinese Revolution's ideals of simplicity and equality. At the same time, however, it is noteworthy that Xi and Wang did not squarely attack organized economic crime among other princelings within the CCP, even though many of them had previously played key roles in privatization operations and initial public offerings (IPOs) that have been linked to corruption as well as in transnational takeovers and investments.

There is no doubt that the princelings in the CCP enjoy a privileged position in Chinese politics, the armed forces, and business and trade. However, they definitely do not constitute a uniform group with identical political orientations and economic interests. Furthermore, their special positions do not seem to be safe with respect to future generations of leaders, as accusations of nepotism and unfair privileges may be raised against this "revolutionary nobility" at any time.

3.7.4 Vested interests in flux

If one considers what issues, goals, and power bases the most influential interest groups have had in the course of CCP history, then a number of striking power shifts and changes in constellations that have had considerable consequences become apparent. Between 1927 and about 1953, the poorer tiers of the rural population constituted the most important social base for the CCP as it fought the Communist Revolution and consolidated power. The party and army largely recruited members from the poorest villages in the country. The interests of the rural population were at the very heart of the comprehensive land reform and the partly violent redistribution of land in the years before and after the PRC was established.

The political goals and forces at play within the party leadership changed when the sweeping programs of nationalization and industrialization were introduced in the mid-1950s as part of the socialist transformation. During the period from 1953 to 1997, players in the state-controlled economy, i.e., state-owned enterprises along with their management committees and workforces, became the most successful interest group in the struggle to secure state investments and privileges. Forced industrialization and financial support for large state-owned enterprises were pursued at the expense of the rural population. Even after the reform policy began in 1978–79, China's state-owned industry continued to enjoy a special, unassailable position and was coddled by preferential subsidies and loans, despite the fact that many companies wasted resources and manufactured products for which there was little demand. As the party leadership became increasingly urbanized, the state's industrial bureaucracy became the most powerful interest group. Much like the So-viet model, this group mainly consisted of those ministries responsible for particular industries and large state-owned companies.

Toward the end of the 1990s, the lobbies for the state-owned economy faced difficulties when it became clear that artificially sustaining state-owned enterpris-es that were constantly operating at a loss was an unbearable financial burden on the government. Zhu Rongji's tenure as premier (1998–2003) marked the beginning of a new phase. As plans were made for the PRC to join the World Trade Organi-zation (WTO) in 2001, state-owned enterprises were restructured, placed under fi-nancial pressures, and many smaller companies were shut down or merged. Tens of thousands of small and medium-sized state-owned businesses that were in the red disappeared from Chinese economic statistics within a matter of several years as a result of takeovers, partial privatizations, or bankruptcies. The winners in the government's restructuring program were the large state-controlled corporations that had been transformed into holding or joint-stock companies. They were able to benefit from having a monopoly or oligopoly position and from rapid growth in their captive markets (e.g., energy, commodities, and banking). Over the past two decades, these businesses have been reaping rapidly growing profits and have been highly successful at raising capital at home and abroad.

At the same time, however, these government-linked corporations have re-mained parts of domestic lobbies and negotiating mechanisms that, in political terms, follow the basic logic of the original socialist system. The chairmen of the boards of the restructured companies continue to be given top positions in the CCP's cadre system, corresponding to the positions of ministers or vice-ministers. Due to their direct contacts with the political decision-makers, these top representatives of the Chinese economy are able to influence decisions about industrial policy, com-mercial legislation, the allocation of resources, business investments, and access to capital. Many examples of this kind of influence can be seen—often to the detriment of more open competition or to the disadvantage of foreign or private competitors (Naughton 2008; Walter/Howie 2006). These are all cases of lobbying within the state itself, or, rather, among the elite who rule the state—lobbying that cannot be conducted in the same way by representatives of competing interests (particularly foreign and nonstate actors).

Despite these organizational disadvantages, since the mid-1990s transnation-al interest groups (i.e., international companies active in the Chinese market togeth-er with their partners in China) have become more influential in shaping Chinese economic policy. This influence became apparent in a series of steps to liberalize and open up the market as a result of China's efforts to join the WTO. Foreign lobbyists attempted to get a foothold in parts of the central government, particularly in the ministries that control access to lucrative domestic markets. They tried to influence the regulation of the Chinese economy and the issuance of licenses and contracts by the Chinese authorities, albeit with varying degrees of success. In fact, since 2010 such attempts have proven to be increasingly ineffective.

Transnational business groups have spent considerable amounts of money on advertising and lobbying in a bid to facilitate access to and expansion in the Chinese market. This has often included special, one-off payments to well-networked go-betweens, contacts, and people closely connected to Chinese decision-makers. Thousands of professional Chinese and foreign mediators and lobbyists work for foreign businesses in Beijing and Shanghai—they generally call themselves "communications specialists" or "investment consultants"—with the mission of currying favor with state decision-makers.

3.7.5 Informal lobbying, consultations, and think-tanks

Officially, political lobbying by interest groups was not desired in China's Leninist order, nor was it regulated by law. In view of the new economic and social plurality that has characterized the PRC since the 1990s, the political leadership has partially accepted modern-day realities and has attempted to channel in a manageable direction those unavoidable activities in which interest groups have been engaged. However, instead of allowing unrestricted pluralistic competition and hidden lobbying, regular consultations on potential new legislation and other political issues that require regulation are held in an effort to "formulate policies scientifically." The government or the NPC regularly invites various representatives—from state bodies, research institutes, business, society, and authorized professional associations—to attend these meetings (see Section 5.5).

Consultations with social and economic organizations and groups that are directly affected by state regulations or changes in legislation have been mandatory since 2004. Foreign companies, business associations, and chambers of commerce have all become involved in discussions and are invited to express their opinions on draft regulations and legislative bills related to state regulation of the economy.

Formal political consultations largely focus on discussions and revisions of draft regulations and laws whose wording has already been completed. The influence that interest groups have at the earliest stage of policy making (agenda-setting) and on policy implementation once the state's new rules have been introduced (administrative implementation provisions and how they are handled in practice) usually occurs in a more informal way. Special interests are fed into processes of policy implementation or policy revisions by way of informal and personal contacts among lobbyists and administrators. Such exchanges are not regulated in any way and are highly prone to corruption.

Think-tanks also play a very important role in Chinese politics because they provide practical research and advice for the party and government. Their work focuses on the preparation of decisions, government programs, and regulatory documents. Think-tanks exist in a number of areas: as sub-units of the Chinese State Council and ministries (portfolio research), as university research institutes with a practical focus, or as private consultancies. Many of the researchers from these organizations have access to decision-makers and are regularly involved in the task forces that are set up to formulate new government programs or regulatory documents. Consequently, researchers at important Chinese think-tanks are popular targets for Chinese and foreign lobbyists who are attempting to include their interests in Chinese government policy.

In the 1990s, large foreign companies and private Chinese firms, particularly those active in the high-tech fields that enjoy political support, gained a say in economic regulatory matters and legislation in China. However, the system of lobbying and negotiating that existed within the state and that developed around the stock corporations close to the government was the dominant factor in Chinese economic policy making and still had a strong influence on it when Xi Jinping took office.

The special political position that large businesses close to the government enjoy is partly due to the fact that company directors are included in the CCP's *nomenklatura*, with direct access to decision-makers at the highest levels. At the same time, state-owned enterprises remain extremely important for the national budget (tax revenue plus dividends from state shares in companies), for raising capital, and for economic expansion abroad (safeguarding future access to markets and resources). The anti-corruption campaign initiated by Xi Jinping in 2012 is explicitly aimed at combating economic crime and networks of corruption as well as vested interests (既得利益) in state-owned industries. But it does not seem likely that economic-structural reforms will be able to dismantle the oligopolies that large state-owned companies enjoy and thereby to provide assistance to private or international competitors.

3.8 Between fragmented authoritarianism and a re-concentration of power

Sebastian Heilmann

The current political system in the PRC is sometimes still characterized as totalitarian. However, this claim is not tenable if the assessment is based on the criteria developed by Linz (1975) and Linz and Krämer (2000). According to Linz, a system is said to be totalitarian if it has the following characteristics: it possesses a monistic power center capable of freely imposing its will and eliminating its opponents; it has a militantly propagated revolutionary ideology that seeks to radically transform the political order; there is a permanent mobilization of the masses; and a strict political code of conduct and constant declarations of political loyalty are imposed on the daily life of the citizens.

In contrast, Linz states that an authoritarian system has the following characteristics: a plurality of decision-makers, organizations, and interest groups that are regularly involved in political decision-making; militant forms of ideology and mass mobilization are not employed, and instead political apathy and passivity are promoted.

In light of these criteria, the PRC clearly can be classified as an authoritarian regime in the context of the normal mode of political decision-making, as described above. However, it exhibits totalitarian characteristics during exceptional phases in the context of the crisis mode, particularly with respect to the degree of centralization and the role of ideology in decision-making as well as the severity of political repression. The centralization, repression, and campaign politics that distinguish the crisis mode have characterized the first several years of Xi Jinping's tenure as general secretary. The rapid development of state-regulated technologies used in ICT, the media, databases, and censorship may offer new possibilities of totalitarian control that are terrifying from the perspective of any democratic society. Thus the risks associated with the practices of totalitarian governments continue to exist. During the twenty-first century, driven by the new technologies these are likely to make themselves felt in novel ways.

Nevertheless, despite the political concentration of power under Xi Jinping, the Chinese party-state cannot be regarded as a self-contained, monolithic entity. In fact, it is a conglomeration of organizations and regions, each of which has its own specific traditions, interests, internal rules, and links with the business community, society, and international partners. Enforced political conformity does not seem practical in this tense, continental political system—unless some major leaps are taken in the development of surveillance technology to monitor the administration, the business sector, and society.

Whether or not the PRC's decision-making system can continue to be characterized as "fragmented authoritarianism," which is the term generally used by China scholars since the work by Lieberthal/Oksenberg in 1988 and Lieberthal/Lampton in 1992 (see also Mertha 2009), will depend on actual developments during Xi Jinping's tenure. After Xi became CCP general secretary in 2012, top CCP leaders amassed comprehensive decision-making powers, with Xi Jinping acting as the ultimate hub. Power to make decisions is now concentrated in newly created or reorganized LSGs. Xi Jinping has acquired a considerable amount of personal power and the media have created a personality cult around him such that has not been enjoyed by any other leader since Mao Zedong. In this regard, Xi Jinping is clearly departing from the trajectory established by Deng Xiaoping who consistently and vehemently rejected the emergence of a personality cult.

4 Governing China's economy

China's economy is a challenge to basic assumptions in comparative political economy. Despite supposedly dysfunctional political and economic institutions, between 1980 and 2014 China's economic policy sustained rapid economic growth, at an average annual rate of about 10 percent. Although many sectors of the Chinese economy are driven by intense market competition and are tightly integrated into the world economy, the economic process remains firmly in the grip of government bodies that have a strong presence and are granted broad scope for intervention.

4.1 China's economic transformation

Mikko Huotari

Although Chinese economic statistics continue to be unreliable (see Section 4.2), the general trend is indisputable: with an average per capita annual income of about USD 7,924.7 in 2015, China has been promoted to the "high to medium income" group of countries. This increase in income has enabled the PRC to reduce the proportion of the population living in absolute poverty. However, the country has been left wrestling with the partially catastrophic environmental impact of its rapid economic growth as well as its controversial social consequences.

Taking the economic system as a whole, China had already become the largest national economy in the world by 2014 in terms of purchasing power parity. Based on the prevailing annual exchange rate, according to the International Monetary Fund (IMF) in 2014 the PRC had the second largest gross domestic product (GDP) in the world, at approximately USD 10,356 billion, second only to that of the United States (USD 17,348 billion) and ahead of that of Japan (USD 4,602 billion). China's GDP was actually larger than the combined GDPs of Germany, France, and the UK. Figure 4.1 indicates growth in GDP since 1953.

There are at least four economic factors that explain the rapid mobilization of capital, labor, and productivity since the 1980s:

(1) The previously centrally planned command economy and system of collectivized agriculture were gradually replaced by an economic system that today is largely determined by market forces, intense competition, and private-sector entrepreneurs.

Figure 4.1

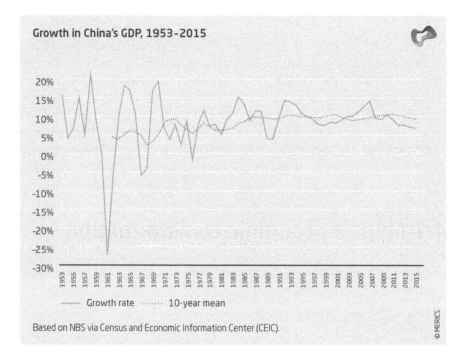

Growth in China's GDP, 1953–2015

Growth rate ······ 10-year mean

Based on NBS via Census and Economic Information Center (CEIC).

©MERICS

(2) The introduction of market mechanisms was accompanied by an opening up to the global economy, primarily through the expansion of trade and foreign direct investments (FDI). Today China is a trading nation and world export champion, involved in worldwide production networks and also increasingly involved in global financial flows (see Section 4.7). Along with investments, technology, and management expertise brought in from abroad, the special economic zones facilitated a process of accelerated industrialization that mainly began in the coastal regions.

(3) The mobilization of hundreds of millions of agricultural workers to engage in industrial production was a key prerequisite for the following decades of extensive growth. The migration of laborers into the metropolitan areas served to reduce underemployment in the rural economy. Up until the early 2010s, China's economic-growth clusters could count on a constant influx of cheap labor. Jobs were created in the industrial, construction, and service sectors of the economy, leading to greater productivity and higher incomes than were possible in the agricultural sector. Since 2012, however, the influx of underemployed laborers from agricultural or underdeveloped regions in central and western China has been curtailed due to the improved employment opportunities in those regions

that originally experienced net outward migration. In addition, the next generation of migrant workers is smaller than the older cohorts of migrants due to
demographic changes. This means that migrant workers are scarcer and hence
more expensive. Unit labor costs in Chinese industry increased during the 2010s
by up to 20 percent per year.

(4) China's growth was also driven by state-led investments, which reached an extremely high level in relation to China's GDP and other international benchmarks.
Since the end of the 1990s, government investments have primarily been flowing into infrastructure projects and the construction of new urban housing. Expansionary investment activities were facilitated by financial repression: interest-rate levels were kept low by the Chinese state, enabling vast deposits held
by private savers to be diverted into state investments at negligible costs (see
Section 4.6).

Specific political and economic conditions are key to explaining how this induced
"catch-up growth" was driven forward for decades without any lasting negative
economic or political setbacks. China's economic reforms were gradually introduced
during the several initial phases and could easily be reversed. This prudent approach
avoided potential destabilization of CCP rule. Such step-by-step implementation of
complementary economic reforms and the gradual build-up of a regulatory framework remain characteristic features of China's economic modernization. At the same
time, multi-year government programs determined the basic course of economic
policy and the main focus of investment activities.

Chinese economic policy has proved to be remarkably flexible and adaptable
over many decades. On the operational side, the drivers of economic growth are
found in the countless decentralized initiatives and experiments aimed at promoting
the economy and supporting businesses in China's cities, counties, townships, and
villages. Unlike in the collapsed Soviet Union, China's socialist economy was already
organized in a highly decentralized way before the introduction of the reform and
opening policy. After the central government gave the go-ahead for economic reforms and for the creation of new regional markets, strong incentives were provided to promote regional competition (see Section 4.3). These special circumstances
and approaches allowed China to transform its socialist command economy through
market mechanisms and to overcome obstacles to economic growth without the
collapse of the political order.

However, since 2000 the structural conditions for economic growth have
changed fundamentally. Many of the instruments and institutions that previously
served to promote growth, such as government investments, an export orientation,
interregional competition, regulatory flexibility, and informal political and economic
networks, began to block the economic system from expanding further in terms of
productivity and innovation. The downsides of the growth model—environmental

Table 4.1

China's economic growth and reform coalitions

1977-1988	Introduction of market mechanisms and opening up to the world economy	**"Reform without losers"**: "dual-track" reforms; new structures develop alongside old structures; growing out of planned economy structures.
1989-1991	↓	Setback for the market-oriented reforms due to the domestic political crisis.
1992-2001	Economic liberalization ("socialist market economy" [SMEc])	**"Reform with losers," but with a strong coalition of winners** in the functionary and the new entrepreneurial classes; further development of market-economy characteristics; restructuring of large state-owned enterprises; partial privatization of smaller state-owned enterprises; strong position for large-scale foreign investors.
2002-2012	↓	Reforms in line with conditions set by the World Trade Organization (WTO); "going-global" strategy; **active social policy aimed at social stability;** active innovation policy; boom in state investments in the aftermath of the global economic crisis.
2013	Adjustment of the growth model and restructuring	Program aimed at economic restructuring; "new growth model" based on domestic consumption, innovation, deregulation, and growth of the private sector; acceptance of lower growth rates; **disciplining of interest groups operating within the state** (functionary classes, the state sector); **limitations on the influence of foreign investors;** fostering of the private sector.

Based on Perkins 2013; Pettis 2014; Naughton 2004, 2011; Garnaut et al. 2013.

© MERICS

pollution, unequal distribution of wealth and income, legal uncertainties, and so on—increased pressures on the government to take political action. In 2007 incumbent premier Wen Jiabao warned of "unstable, unbalanced, uncoordinated, and unsustainable growth." In 2012 a study by the World Bank, in collaboration with the Development Research Center (DRC) (国务院发展研究中心), presented a firmly market-oriented plan without a breakdown of the political order to overcome the structural deficits—distortions in competition and price formation, and government interventions serving as an obstacle to entrepreneurship and technological innovation—and to stimulate new drivers powering China's economic expansion. Key features of this reform agenda were approved by the Chinese Communist Party Central Committee (CCP CC) in November 2013 with the objective of fundamentally updating the structure of the economy, the growth model, and government involvement in economic activities.

Table 4.1 provides an overview of China's economic growth and reform coalitions since the beginning of the reform period. In the course of the successive reform phases, the top party leadership has repeatedly succeeded in forging broad coalitions of support among party functionaries and the population and in promoting new business activities. As a result of regulatory reforms, a more extensive opening up of the economy, the dynamism of the private sector, and a targeted industrial policy, the Chinese economy has developed in many sectors, changing from the "workbench" of the world into a global competitor in high-end, technologically intensive markets (machines, electronics, etc.). However, strong pressures have emerged to make adjustments that will allow for sustained growth and will anticipate any sharp economic downturns in the future. In light of deep-seated contradictions and uncertain prospects for the future, it continues to be difficult to summarize China's economic system as a whole in a few words. There is no prospect of long-term stability and equilibrium, and the economic challenges facing the political leadership remain enormous.

4.2 Economic growth: Official data and alternative indicators

Sandra Heep, Mikko Huotari, and Marc Szepan

Over the past three decades China has achieved economic growth unparalleled by international standards. The country's rise is not only reflected in a wide range of socioeconomic indicators, but can also be seen indirectly in the significant improvement in living standards. Although there is no doubt about the rapid economic growth achieved during the reform period, accurately measuring the size of the Chinese economy is a huge statistical challenge. A number of economists have expressed doubts about the reliability of Chinese official GDP statistics. As the growth rates achieved since 1978 have played a key role in China's global political and economic roles, it is necessary to examine the quality of the official growth statistics more closely.

Strong criticism of official statistics began in 1998 when it became evident that local governments had deliberately manipulated the statistics to cover up the economic slump triggered by the Asian financial crisis. Since then, both Chinese and Western economists have been using alternative methods to calculate China's GDP and have obtained results that often differ considerably from the official figures (see Figure 4.2).

Official statistics also reveal internal discrepancies. For example, adding up the data provided by individual provinces regarding their respective economic strength suggests a substantially larger national GDP than the figure calculated on the basis of aggregate national data (Crabbe 2014). The relatively large discrepancy in international standards between the results obtained using different methods for calculating GDP (the income approach and the expenditure approach) is also problematic.

Figure 4.2

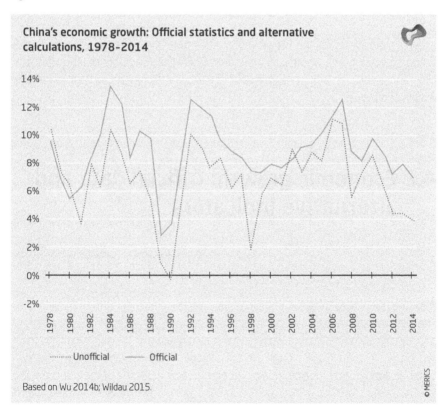

China's economic growth: Official statistics and alternative calculations, 1978-2014

Based on Wu 2014b; Wildau 2015.

The inaccuracy of the official statistics can be attributed to various technical and institutional factors. First, the National Bureau of Statistics (NBS) has not yet achieved the level of technical competence commonly found in Western government agencies (Koch-Weser 2013). Although the precise methods the NBS uses to calculate GDP cannot be examined in detail due to a lack of transparency, economists have nevertheless criticized the practice of adjusting inflation figures as part of the revision of GDP statistics (Holz 2014). Furthermore, the planned-economy tradition of focusing on large-scale industrial production is problematic because it leads to inadequate reporting of the added value contributed by small private companies and the services sector (Wu 2014b). In addition, the relative importance—by international standards—of the shadow economy in China leads to a distortion of the official data since this sector is not included in the statistics.

The NBS improved the quality of data at the beginning of the new millennium by making continuous adjustments and refinements to its statistical methods. China conducted a macroeconomic census in 2004 and subsequently revised its GDP statistics. Since then, the discrepancy between provisional and revised GDP data has steadily decreased.

Nevertheless, the NBS continues to suffer from a lack of political independence, bureaucratic authority, and adequate resources. Political incentive mechanisms complicate the work of the NBS, since career paths within China's government and party apparatuses are essentially determined by economic growth–focused assessment criteria. Therefore, inaccuracies in the official GDP statistics are due less to a deliberate falsification of the records by the NBS at the national level than to a combination of technical inadequacies and powerful incentives to "dress-up" the statistics at the local levels (Holz 2014).

In view of these difficulties, numerous observers have resorted to alternative indicators that are intended to contribute to making a more realistic assessment of China's economic strength. Data related to production and consumption of electricity, construction activity, transportation, and the development of consumer prices are often used for this purpose. In this context, the so-called "Li Keqiang index" is particularly noteworthy. During his term as party secretary of Liaoning province, the future premier tracked provincial economic growth on the basis of data related to rail freight transport, energy consumption, and bank lending. However, many of the conventional alternative indicators are of limited value to assess the growth of the national economy because they focus on heavy industry, despite the fact that growth in China is increasingly dependent on the services sector and the consumer goods industry.

After the party and state leadership under Xi Jinping began to pursue comprehensive structural reforms of the economy, there has been a rethinking of growth indicators. The quality and sustainability of economic growth are now taking center stage, replacing the previous exclusive focus on quantitative GDP growth. In 2014 the NBS announced the development of an indicator system intended to facilitate measurement of qualitative criteria, such as economic stability, innovation, the environment, and living conditions. To this end, the indicator system will combine GDP data with information on the ratio of tax revenue to government debt, private consumption, and expenditures on research and development (Zhongguo xinxi bao 2014).

4.3 Prerequisites for Chinese economic reform

Sebastian Heilmann

A brief comparative or differentiated analysis of the typical characteristics of conventional socialist state-controlled economies governed by Communist parties can serve to highlight the extent to which China has distanced itself from other socialist state-controlled economies.

Before 1989 (that is, before the collapse of the Soviet Union and the system of alliances among the Eastern European socialist states), the socialist economic systems were characterized by the following: centralized administrative planning and allocations of raw materials, investment funds, and goods; the dominance of state and collective ownership; a lack of hard budget constraints on companies; preferential political treatment for heavy industry and the arms industry; and a highly centralized foreign-trade system (Kornai 1995). As opposed to market coordination, which depends on prices, demand, and competition indicators, bureaucratic coordination, price setting, and allocations governed economic life. Resources were allocated according to political priorities. This led to an enormous waste of resources and permanent bottlenecks in the supply chain.

There were many differences between the various Communist political and economic systems, despite their shared key characteristics, in terms of specific practices and effects of administrative planning and allocations. These differences created very different preconditions for the implementation of structural changes and market competition in the national economies.

A systematic comparison of the way in which economic transformation occurred in the former Soviet Union and China highlights just how strongly these differences influenced reform opportunities and the outcomes of the reform in the two countries (Heilmann 2000). There are several strikingly distinctive features of

Table 4.3

Preconditions for the introduction of market-oriented reforms in China

Economy	Comparatively small state-owned industrial sector; low degree of interregional division of labor, consequently less vulnerability to the dismantling of central planning and space for decentralized personal initiatives; macroeconomic stability during the initial period of the reform policy (low inflation rates, low budget and current account deficits).
Administration	Unlike the Soviet model, under Mao China put considerably more emphasis on regional autarky and a decentralized planned economy.
Politics	Lower political and bureaucratic resistance to reforms because the central planning bureaucracies were weakened organizationally during the Cultural Revolution (1966–76).
Society	A tradition of family businesses; forced collectivization of agriculture for just over twenty years.
International context	Dynamic Asian-Pacific environment; investments by overseas Chinese; close economic ties, initially with Hong Kong and since the 1990s also with Taiwan.

Based on Heilmann 2002.

© MERICS

the Chinese state-controlled economic system that proved to be favorable for initiating structural reforms. These special conditions are summarized in Table 4.3.

Many typical structural distortions of the state economy could also be found in China at the end of the Mao era, such as government investments without feasibility studies, prices set by the administration, monopolistic setups and a lack of competition, overemployment in the state-owned industrial sector, and isolation from competition in international markets. Nevertheless, China displayed major differences compared to the other state-controlled economies in terms of the degree of industrialization, regional specialization, and macroeconomic instability.

There is one significant feature of the PRC's state-controlled economic structure prior to 1979 that set it apart from the systems operating under the Soviet model: control over the economy was far less centralized and institutionalized in China than it was in the Soviet Union. This was due to several factors, such as the Maoist vision of regional economic autarky, the successive waves of decentralization that occurred in the course of the various political campaigns beginning in the 1950s, and the inadequate administrative and technical capabilities of the central economic bureaucracy. After China's early departure from the Soviet development model in the second half of the 1950s, local governments were granted extensive authority with respect to planning and managing the economy. The majority of state-owned enterprises were subject to decentralized controls at the provincial, prefecture, city, or county levels. As a consequence, a complex network of state-ownership rights, ranked by administrative hierarchy, developed. This network was subject to centralized control and planning only in certain subsectors (Herrmann-Pillath 1990; Naughton 1995). China also differed fundamentally from the former Soviet Union in terms of the extent of planned centralization, industrialization, regional specialization, and macroeconomic instability, thus inheriting a significantly lighter burden in these respects.

After the initial steps toward liberalizing the market, social factors helped to create a broad range of entrepreneurial initiatives in China. Despite just over twenty years of forced collectivization, the experience of family businesses was still present in the minds of the Chinese population, at least in the countryside. In addition, from the outset the active involvement of Hong Kong and overseas Chinese promoted the transfer of entrepreneurial knowledge, as did China's integration into the dynamic economic environment of the Asia-Pacific region.

4.4 The political initiation and implementation of economic reform

Sebastian Heilmann and Sandra Heep

However, it is not only country-specific preconditions that determine economic-reform trajectories and strategies. The key to understanding the dynamics of the Chinese reforms is the shifting configuration of political forces and the changing mobilizational capacities of the reformist leadership as well as the specific implementation approaches and procedures.

Unlike the situation in the former Soviet Union, despite political upsets and social unrest, over a number of decades the political authority of the Chinese Communist Party (CCP) and the state government proved to be sufficiently robust to avoid a breakdown in public order. At the same time, key economic powers were entrusted to local governments. The central government gradually accepted, at least sporadically, a loss of control in the face of reform initiatives and informal avoidance strategies at the regional levels.

The course taken by the economic reforms is a prime example of how a policy that promotes decentralized institutional experiments, innovation, and learning can create particularly favorable prerequisites for the successful introduction of structural reforms. The precarious balance between central-government authority and decentralized reform initiatives constituted the political basis for China's path to reform, which was driven forward in a series of individual steps during the first two decades after 1978. Table 4.4.A indicates the core elements of China's reform practices between 1978 and 1998.

Table 4.4.A

Distinctive policy features of Chinese reform practices, 1978-98

Dual-track reforms (new structures develop alongside the old structures, but do not initially replace them; instead, the new structures grow faster, leaving the old structures to become obsolete).

Political enforcement of painful reforms during periods of crisis (1979, 1992, and 1998).

Tolerance and selective promotion of decentralized reform initiatives and local experiments.

Regional competition for investment funds, economic growth, and revenue growth.

Willingness to learn from foreign institutional models.

Authority of party headquarters is sufficiently strong to prevent political disintegration despite the economic decentralization.

Greater flexibility through decentralized reform initiatives and informal avoidance tactics at the regional and local levels.

"Cadre capitalism" and "systemic corruption" among party and government officials.

Based on Heilmann 2002.

© MERICS

During this period, China's economic reforms were not driven by a coherent, preconceived strategy; and economic change was not prompted by a search for optimal economic efficiency. Instead, China's economic reformers faced all kinds of resistance to the restructuring of the state-controlled economic system from party cadres, the state bureaucracy, and state-owned enterprises. The strong ideological resistance and the pressures for compromise are reflected in the official wordings used to characterize the PRC's economic system (see Table 4.4.B).

The dual-track reforms were a distinctive feature of the economic-structural changes during the initial stages. These enabled the coexistence of a planned and a market economy, with a gradual shift away from the planned component—"growing out of the plan," as noted by Naughton (1995). China's reform practices avoided political resistance for almost two decades because the socialist state sector (the "old track") was not initially included in the restructuring. At the outset, the Chinese government authorized a nonstate economy only outside of the plan as an add-on (a "new track").

However, by the second half of the 1990s the dynamic growth of the economy outside of the plan placed the state sector under increasing competitive pressures and ultimately forced unprofitable state-owned enterprises to undergo restructuring. This incremental transition enabled a gradual process of realignment and learning in which there was room for competing reform experiments and for corrections to individual reform measures.

The dual-track reforms have considerable advantages in terms of political enforceability. On the one hand, they minimize opposition due to the fact that interest groups in the old system do not have to bear any initial costs. If the reform measures are successful, however, new interest groups will emerge to defend the new developments and to promote expansion of the experiments. In fact, the Chinese approach to reform has led to a comprehensive reorganization of interest groups in the political and economic systems (see Section 2.5.2).

It is only under exceptional circumstances—usually immediately after a change in government or a sharp economic downturn—that there are opportunities to push through radical structural reforms. During such "periods of exceptional politics," as Polish economist and finance minister Leszek Balcerowicz (1995) aptly calls them, there is a temporary greater acceptance of painful reforms. Periods like these occurred in China after the collapse in 1978–79 of the program of administrative recentralization under Chairman Hua Guofeng, in the aftermath of the collapse of the Eastern European socialist states in 1989–91, and in the context of the financial crisis in a number of East and Southeast Asian states in 1997–98 (the "Asian financial crisis"). They were also a reaction to the crisis surrounding the export- and investment-driven growth model in 2013–14. These opportunities were seized upon by reform-minded Chinese politicians to move forward resolutely with economic-structural changes and to overcome political resistance within the party leadership, the state administration, and the large state-owned enterprises.

The global financial crisis between 2007 and 2009 triggered a crisis response that was not based on structural changes but rather on comprehensive stimulus measures and "revitalization programs" (振兴规划). The Chinese government launched the world's largest economic stimulus plan, amounting to about 13 per-

Table 4.4.B

Developmental phases and reform measures since 1979

	Official terminology used to characterize the economic system	Economic reform measures
1979–1984	"Planned economy, supplemented by market elements"	Agricultural decollectivization and expansion of small-scale agricultural industries; authorization of small private companies; establishment of special economic zones.
1984–1988	"Planned commodity economy"	Incremental reforms in urban industry; greater decision-making powers for company managers; opening up to foreign trade in the coastal regions.
1988–1991	"The state regulates the market, and the market regulates companies"; "integration of the planned economy and market regulation"	Slowdown of economic liberalization; attempts to recentralize economic regulation; economic stabilization through administrative controls.
1992–1997	"SMEc with the dominance of public ownership"	Fight against inflation; accelerated economic liberalization, decentralization, and opening up to foreign trade; reorganization of the financial and fiscal systems.
1998–2002	SMEc with the "coexistence of various forms of ownership" and "integration into world trade" (WTO)	Reorganization/partial privatization of state-owned enterprises; reorganization of economic administration; strengthening of the private sector; accession to the WTO; greater integration into world markets.
2003–2007	SMEc realigned by "going global" and "indigenous innovation"	Global investments by Chinese companies; stock market flotations by state-owned enterprises; easing of capital controls; very active technology and social policies.
2008–2012	SMEc in "revitalization phase"	Large-scale government economic stimulus plan and lending and investment programs; active approach to industrial policy.
since 2013	SMEc with a "key role for the market"	Preparation for fundamental institutional reforms, including the financial/fiscal systems and the legal system; deregulation.

© MERICS

cent of GDP (based on GDP in 2008) by gradually flooding the economy with loans and investments without any form of beforehand credit assessments. These comprehensive stimulus measures, which were introduced extremely rapidly by international standards, reversed the earlier structural adjustments and investment controls. This crisis policy worsened risk management in bank-lending practices, in the approval process for public-sector investments, as well as in the budget processes of subnational governments (see Section 6.6 and Section 6.7).

As a result, the economic stimulus plan reinforced a trend that had existed since the mid-2000s, namely, state infrastructural investments as the driving force for sustaining the high Chinese growth rates. Early on, however, even critics within the Chinese government pointed out that the exorbitant levels of indebtedness resulting from the stimulus measures could not provide a basis for sustainable and stable economic growth over the long term.

The Chinese government had to enforce structural reforms in the investment, financial, and public budget systems in order to facilitate the changeover to the strong consumption and innovation-driven growth that has been much heralded since the 1990s (see Section 2.8 and Section 4.6). These structural reforms met with significant opposition from functionaries, managers, and entrepreneurs because the various approval rights and opportunities to skim off money ("rent-seeking") ceased to apply to politically well-connected regulators and market participants and they were replaced by a more transparent, rule-based system (see Section 4.8). For these reasons, the new party and state leaders appointed in 2012–13 championed Xi Jinping's campaign to curb the influence and rent-seeking behavior of privileged political and economic actors (especially in the functionary classes and in state-owned enterprises) in order to open up possibilities for enforcing the painful structural reforms.

In retrospect, it can be said that the Chinese path to reform thus far has challenged the assumption commonly found among political scientists and economists that a market-oriented transformation is impossible under Communist rule. Furthermore, the belief held by many economists that radical structural reforms are preferable to a gradual approach, even if they incur high social costs, has been put into perspective by the Chinese experience.

To understand the Chinese path to reform, it is essential to realize that the necessary adaptability was not generated by official institutions but rather by a widespread practice of avoidance. Key political and economic actors flexibly used the opportunities provided by the economic liberalization. Many local governments continued to circumvent guidelines issued by Beijing and so as to follow their own paths. However, the party leadership perpetuated the authority and unity of the central government without being able to fully control the way in which national policy was actually implemented on the ground.

The "winning formula" for enforcing economic-structural reforms in China after 1978 was achieved by making the rigid Communist system more flexible through decentralized initiatives that did not trigger any collapse of the political order. This was always a risky balancing act, however, since the expansion of the informal exchange networks and the corruption in the Chinese economy (see Section 4.8) not only led, for example, to considerable distortions with regard to investment activities and income distribution but also to a legitimacy and organizational political crisis. The party leadership under Xi Jinping therefore pursued an aggressive reform policy of "top-level design" (顶层设计), with the aim of suppressing established interest groups, networks of corrupt individuals, and decentralized avoidance mechanisms by capitalizing on the authority of the party and pursuing a rigorous anti-graft campaign. Looking back from the current perspective (in 2016), it is doubtful whether the party will be successful in enforcing the diverse and far-reaching structural reforms announced in the fall of 2013.

4.5 Government involvement in the Chinese economy

Marc Szepan

Our perception of China's real economy—industry, technology, raw materials, and food production, as opposed to the financial sector—is shaped by highly contradictory observations and characterizations. On the one hand, China describes its economic and social systems as "socialism with Chinese characteristics" (中国特色社会主义). On the other hand, however, active market participants—investors, managers, and employees—in a number of sectors leave the impression of a merciless form of "bare-knuckled capitalism."

China's current economic system can be described as a mixed system in which unorthodox features of a state capitalist economy are combined with a market economy; on no account can the real economy still be defined as a socialist planned economy. The share of China's economic output generated within the framework of binding government plans and/or price controls has drastically decreased during recent decades. Many sectors of the economy in China today are characterized by intense competition among Chinese companies, or between Chinese companies and foreign enterprises. At the same time, political pressures and interventions continue to be omnipresent.

Ever since the beginning of the reform period in 1978–79, the Chinese economy has been undergoing a process of profound sectoral changes. Activities in the

Figure 4.5

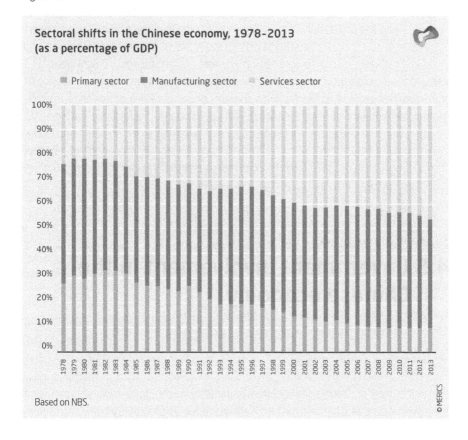

Sectoral shifts in the Chinese economy, 1978-2013 (as a percentage of GDP)

■ Primary sector   ■ Manufacturing sector   ■ Services sector

Based on NBS.

© MERICS

primary sector (agriculture, forestry, and fishing) declined from almost one-third of national economic output in the early 1980s to only about 10 percent of GDP in 2013, as shown in Figure 4.5. Consequently, the discussion below focuses on the types of companies found in the secondary and tertiary sectors.

4.5.1 Diverse types of ownership and corporate governance

China's real economy has grown exceptionally rapidly during the last several decades (see Section 4.1). This expansion has led to the emergence of state-owned and privately owned enterprises that compete with foreign investors in the Chinese market, and many of these enterprises have become firmly established in global product and capital markets. In 2014, the annual *Fortune Global 500* ranked China as having the

Table 4.5.A

Basic types of Chinese companies under state and private control, 2014

		Main rights of ownership and control	
		State ownership	Private ownership
Position relative to the state and/or markets	State-proximate and state-supported	*Type 1* China Petroleum & Chemical Corporation (Sinopec); China National Offshore Oil Corporation (CNOOC); Aviation Industry Corporation of China (AVIC); State Grid; China Telecom	*Type 3* Huawei; ZTE
	Market-based and competition-oriented	*Type 2* Shandong Heavy Industry Group; Shanghai Automotive Industry Corporation (SAIC)	*Type 4* Alibaba; Geely; Sany; Fosun; Xiaomi

© MERICS

second-highest number of Global 500 companies, with the United States occupying first place (Fortune 2015). China's real economy is characterized by the coexistence of and intense competition among state-owned enterprises and private companies. These businesses can be grouped in four basic types, as shown in Table 4.5.A.

- *Type 1:* Strategically important industries from the perspective of the Chinese state (such as oil and gas, or aerospace) are dominated by large state-owned enterprises (for instance, Sinopec or AVIC), which in turn are controlled by the Chinese central government. These industries are mainly characterized by oligopolistic or even monopolistic structures. The same applies to core infrastructure industries, such as electricity and telecommunications networks (State Grid and China Telecom respectively).
- *Type 2:* A second group of state-owned enterprises—often medium-sized businesses—consists of competitive, market-oriented companies that are often owned or controlled by local governments. These companies mainly operate in nonstrategic sectors, such as the automotive industry (Shandong Heavy Industry Group [SAIC]), and face intense competition from both Chinese and foreign companies.
- *Type 3:* The third group comprises companies under private ownership that predominantly operate as private-sector or entrepreneurial businesses. They can be considered companies with close government links (such as Huawei or ZTE)

due to the strategic importance of their products and the importance of their maintaining good relations with state bodies (for sales). However, these firms are not simply an extended arm of the Chinese government. Instead, they navigate a complex negotiation process with state bodies which—depending on the industry, context, and market risks—can result in differing managerial leeway.

- *Type 4:* The fourth group consists of companies under private ownership that openly compete in nonstrategic markets. Some of these firms have attained a considerable size in the domestic market and also operate successfully in global markets (Alibaba or Sany as examples). However, this group only includes a handful of large companies with global equity interests.

Overall, it is important to note that the share of state-owned enterprises in China's economic output has declined rapidly. Between 1978 and 2014, the proportion of total industrial employment in China made up of state-owned enterprises fell from 78 percent to 16 percent. From 1998 to 2014 the number of state-owned enterprises fell from 65,000 to 19,000.

4.5.2 Party and government interference in business

Government bodies in China continue to wield significant direct and indirect influence on businesses. The methods employed, however, have evolved from direct administrative interventions to more subtle regulatory or industrial-policy control mechanisms (Heilmann 2011). State bodies exert an influence on companies through the use of six typical mechanisms, as shown in Table 4.5.B.

The state as the owner: Both the central and local governments hold ownership rights to state-owned enterprises. Shares in a company owned by the central government are held by an asset management commission subordinate to the State Council (see Section 2.4.1). In 2014 the State-owned Assets Supervision and Administration Commission (SASAC) was responsible for strategic control of more than 100 of the largest Chinese state-owned enterprises. SASAC is officially responsible for appointments to top management positions, the strategic development of each company, and dividend management. Comparable institutions exist at local levels and manage the shares in companies held by local governments.

The CCP cadre system: SASAC is officially responsible for making appointments to top managerial positions within the state-owned enterprises under its supervision. De facto, even senior leadership positions in big publicly listed companies in which state bodies have majority shareholdings are filled by formal state shareholders in close consultation with the Organization Department of the CCP. Ultimately, the CCP has power over all major personnel matters in companies with government links (McGregor 2010). Also, there is a regular exchange of personnel between gov-

Table 4.5.B

State mechanisms for influencing and intervening in business

Influence and intervention mechanisms	Form of company ownership	
	State ownership (types 1 + 2)	Private ownership (types 3 + 4)
The state as the owner (profit transfers)	✓	
The cadre system (managers)	✓	
Financing (lending by banks)	✓	✓
Industrial policy (funding programs)	✓	✓
Regulation (approvals, etc.)	✓	✓
The state as the key customer (public procurements)	✓	✓

ernment and CCP bodies on the one hand and state-linked companies and state organizations on the other. It is not unusual for the CEO of a state-owned enterprise managed by SASAC to take on governmental tasks at the ministerial level for a period, but to return to the corporate sector at a later point. In fact, the CEOs of the largest state-controlled enterprises simultaneously hold a vice-ministerial rank (and in some cases even a ministerial rank) within the CCP cadre system. The CCP also has the power to exert its influence with regard to internal personnel decisions below the top-management level, as upper and even middle management positions in firms with government links are generally given only to CCP members.

Financing: The two mechanisms outlined above formally only apply to state-owned enterprises. In contrast, government bodies in China wield significant influence over state-owned and privately owned companies by means of capital allocations. Both the equity and debt markets in China are managed by the state via a range of formal or informal approval processes. Without the goodwill of the appropriate government bodies, it is exceedingly difficult to finance working capital and investments. As a result, even private companies depend on government bodies with regard to business investment decisions.

Industrial policy: The Chinese state pursues an active sector-specific industrial policy. Central and subnational governments define industrial priorities and related support measures in multi-year programs. The issuance of licenses and state-directed mergers and restructurings offer the government a broad range of options to influence the strategies and day-to-day operations of private companies.

Regulation: Since the 1990s the Chinese government has established a series of regulatory and supervisory bodies in an attempt to minimize direct administrative interventions in economic activities and instead to create indirect legal forms of neutral regulation. These bodies are designed to act as arbitrators to ensure fair market access and market competition. In reality, however, interventions by these new regulators are often politically motivated. Approvals to raise capital on the stock exchanges in China or abroad continue to be determined by policy guidelines and negotiations. Even implementation of China's Anti-Monopoly Law demonstrates the risks of unpredictable state interventions. Anti-monopoly regulation in China is divided among three different agencies (the National Development and Reform Commission [NDRC], the State Administration for Industry and Commerce [SAIC], and the Ministry of Commerce [MOFCOM]; see Section 2.4). This has given rise to a wide range of options for interventions by agencies that sometimes appear to be characterized by inter-agency rivalries and sometimes are initiated on their own authority against domestic and foreign companies (Slaughter and May 2015).

The state as the key customer: The Chinese state is the "largest customer" in the Chinese market, both directly by way of its procurement and investment measures and indirectly through the procurement policy of state-owned enterprises. By choosing particular Chinese or foreign suppliers, government bodies possess considerable leverage to support individual companies, industries, technologies, products, or technical standards. Government procurement decisions thus exert a significant influence in terms of which companies or technologies become firmly established in a given market.

In summary, it can be argued that China's economic system combines state capitalist control mechanisms with free market competition mechanisms. State interventions in both companies with government links and private enterprises remain a significant force.

4.6 The role of government in the banking and financial systems

Sandra Heep

To scrutinize the policy processes that are driving the Chinese economic reforms, it is essential to understand developments in the financial system through which capital is allocated. Since the financial system is subject to tight state controls in China, the government can steer the course of economic development in a very proactive and straightforward way. For this reason, China's party and state leaderships have restricted their power over the financial system very hesitantly and with great caution. Political control of the financial system is based on several crucial factors:

- First, the financial system is dominated by state-owned banks whose managerial staff is drawn from the ranks of the CCP cadre system (see Section 2.9). This enables the party and government leaderships to exert an influence over bank lending.
- Second, the state used to ensure that state-owned enterprises obtain favorable loans for their investments by the administrative setting of interest-rate levels. This occured at the expense of Chinese savers: interest rates on savings deposits used to be comparatively low, thereby subsidizing bank lending and investments in the state-preferred parts of the economy.
- At the same time, the Chinese government has curtailed the growth of capital markets to prevent savings from flowing out of the banking industry. Even China's equity and bond markets primarily satisfy the financing requirements of state institutions and state-owned companies.
- In addition, this state-controlled financial system has been supported by strict exchange-rate management and capital controls that are designed to prevent outflows of savings abroad (see Section 4.7).

As a result, China's financial system has long been a prime example of a system of financial repression (Heep 2014; McKinnon 1973), whereby capital resources are specifically mobilized to promote economic growth at the expense of savers. The following sections will provide an overview of the way in which individual parts of this system have developed during the reform period.

At the time of the planned economy, China's financial system consisted of a single, state-controlled bank (a "monobank"), which mainly fulfilled a passive function as the state's treasury for the administration and transfer of state funds. Because all investments were financed from the national budget, the monobank merely provided the infrastructure for the transfers. It was only during the reform period that a conventional banking system, which conveyed savings from households to investing companies ("financial intermediation"), came into existence. This development began in the 1980s when the monobank was divided into a central bank (the People's Bank of China [PBOC], 中国人民银行, or for short: 人行 or 央行) and four large, state-owned commercial banks (the Industrial and Commercial Bank of China [ICBC], 中国工商银行, the China Construction Bank [CCB], 中国建设银行, the Bank of China [BOC], 中国银行, and the Agricultural Bank of China

[ABC], 中国农业银行) (Naughton 2007). These institutions dominate the banking system to this day.

However, commercial banks were by no means free of political influence. On the contrary, they were given by various levels of government the task of providing loans to state-owned enterprises, regardless of their creditworthiness. This use of the banking system to support the state sector was also motivated by dwindling fiscal revenues (see Section 2.8). The close cooperation between the state-owned banks and the state-owned industrial sector fulfilled some very important political functions. First, it prevented the sudden collapse of large and unprofitable state-owned companies. Second, the restructuring of the state economy could be spread out over a longer period of time. Third, it minimized resistance from the state sector to the introduction of market competition and to an opening up to foreign trade by not initially exposing the state-owned enterprises to a full blast of competition (see Section 4.4). The cost of this policy was reflected in the steadily growing volume of bad loans in the state sector, which in turn jeopardized the medium- and long-term stability of the banking system.

In the 1990s the government took its first steps toward strengthening the independence of banks. For example, the Beijing headquarters of the commercial banks were strengthened in order to weaken the influence of local governments in terms of bank lending. In addition, three state-run development banks were established with an explicit political mandate ("policy banks"): the China Development Bank, 国家开发银行, the Export-Import Bank of China, 中国进出口银行, and the Agricultural Development Bank of China, 中国农业发展银行. These policy banks were designed to free the state-owned commercial banks from the burden of politically controlled loans (Naughton 2007).

Critical steps toward stabilizing the banking system occurred against the backdrop of the 1997–98 Asian financial crisis. The bad loans of the commercial banks were transferred to independent asset management companies that were specifically set up for this purpose. A second round of reforms began in 2004 when banks were recapitalized with the help of China's currency reserves. Strategic investors were recruited and new capital was raised through the stock markets in Shanghai and Hong Kong. These steps resulted in a radical reorganization of the state-owned commercial banks in terms of their capitalization, management, and risk controls.

Nevertheless, the party and state leaderships continue to exert a significant influence over China's commercial banks, especially during times of crisis (Schlichting 2008). This became apparent during the 2007–9 global financial crisis when banks granted a veritable flood of loans to local governments and state-owned enterprises at the behest of the party and state leaderships without appropriate credit assessments (see the case studies on the impact of the Asian financial crisis and the local-government financing platforms in Section 6.6 and Section 6.7). Therefore, since 2009 the volume of bad loans in the banking system has again increased sharply. Figure 4.6.A indicates the asset structure of China's banking sector in 2013.

Figure 4.6.A

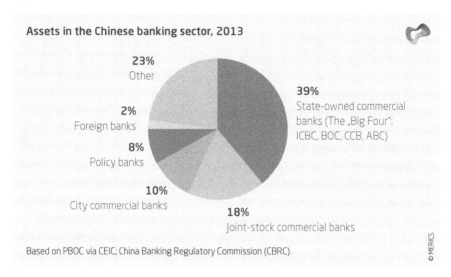

Assets in the Chinese banking sector, 2013

23% Other

2% Foreign banks

8% Policy banks

10% City commercial banks

18% Joint-stock commercial banks

39% State-owned commercial banks (The „Big Four": ICBC, BOC, CCB, ABC)

Based on PBOC via CEIC; China Banking Regulatory Commission (CBRC).

© MERICS

In addition to the banking system, the Chinese government gradually introduced capital markets. The initiative to establish stock markets came from the local governments in Shanghai and Shenzhen, which competed with one another in the late 1980s to establish stock exchanges. Both stock exchanges were officially opened in the early 1990s, initially for a test experimental period. These stock exchanges were primarily designed to raise capital for publicly listed subsidiaries of state-owned groups, and hence to tap into additional sources of funding for the state sector. To insure its control over listed state-owned enterprises, the state retained the majority of shares and excluded these shares from being traded on the market (Naughton 2007).

The original decision to use stock exchanges primarily for the financing and restructuring of state-owned enterprises has remained a characteristic function of China's stock markets to this day. Although since the mid-2000s an increasing number of privately owned companies have been listed on the stock exchanges, particularly in Shenzhen, China's stock markets continue to be dominated by state-owned enterprises. Share prices are influenced more by government regulatory interventions and signals than by specific successes or failures of individual companies ("policy-driven markets") (Heilmann 2002). This has resulted in a high degree of volatility, heightened by the dominance of private investors with a propensity to speculation.

The growth in bond markets also began in the 1980s when the central government reported its first budget deficits (see Section 2.8.2). The Ministry of Finance issued its first government bonds in 1981. Initially, state-owned enterprises bought these bonds, followed increasingly by private households. The Ministry of Finance put an end to this development in the 1990s, however, when it required state-owned commercial banks to purchase government bonds in order to finance the government's budget deficit at a low cost (Walter/Howie 2011). The bond markets were particularly important for the PBOC during the 2000s. In fact, during the period between 2003 and 2010, the PBOC dominated the bond markets by issuing central bank bills. The China Development Bank, which was responsible for financing infrastructure projects, also became a significant issuer of bonds. Both institutions profited from the requirement that China's state-owned commercial banks purchase bonds issued by the central bank and the policy banks.

Beginning in the mid-2000s, the market for corporate bonds has also grown significantly. The PBOC has served as the driving force behind this growth in an attempt to shift the risks from the banking system to the capital markets. Companies with government links have become important issuers. Not only state-owned financial institutions but also nonstate investors (including foreign banks) have purchased these bonds (Walter/Howie 2011). Figure 4.6.B illustrates the growth of the Chinese bond market.

In addition to government controls over the banking system and the steering of the development of the capital markets, the administrative setting of interest rates has also played a key role in China's financial system. The central bank ensured that state-owned enterprises were able to receive financing at favorable rates by placing a ceiling on deposit rates and a floor on lending rates. At the same time, the spread between these two interest rates set by the administration guaranteed a stable source of income for the banks. However, against the backdrop of a de facto liberalization of interest rates in the growing shadow banking sector, the ceiling on deposit rates was abolished in 2015. The floor on lending rates had already been eliminated in 2013.

China's system of financial repression has supported the country's former growth model with its focus on investments and exports. However, the necessary reorientation toward a growth model based on domestic consumption, innovation, and productivity will require a fundamental restructuring of the financial system. More flexible interest rates will contribute to a strengthening of household purchasing power and, as a consequence, to growth in domestic demand. At the same time, the preferential treatment of state-owned enterprises in terms of bank lending must give way to a stronger focus on lending risks. The financing of profitable privately owned companies and innovative startup companies must take priority over

Figure 4.6.B

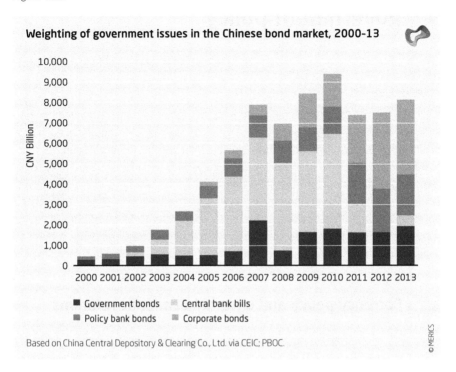

Weighting of government issues in the Chinese bond market, 2000-13

CNY Billion

Government bonds   Central bank bills
Policy bank bonds   Corporate bonds

Based on China Central Depository & Clearing Co., Ltd. via CEIC; PBOC.

© MERICS

the hidden subsidies to loss-making state-owned enterprises. Any such restructuring of the financial system will certainly have far-reaching consequences in terms of the scope to control and steer policy in China's economic system, since the ability to steer policy is vested in the state-owned enterprises and financial institutions, which are tightly linked to the CCP and the government through their managerial staff and ownership rights.

China's political leadership approved a wide-ranging reform agenda in 2013, a central pillar of which is intended to introduce a reorganization and increased flexibility of the financial system. Financial-system reforms gained pace in 2015 (Heep 2015), yet they nevertheless remained contested. The reasons for this are obvious. A loss of control over the financial system weakens the party-state's ability to manage the economy. In addition, since 2008 the risks of a financial crisis in China have grown as a result of the rapidly increasing indebtedness of the state-owned companies and the local governments as well as the increasing significance of the shadow banking sector. In the context of an already fragile financial system, financial liberalization measures may easily trigger a financial crisis.

4.7 Economic globalization and government policy

Mikko Huotari, Dirk H. Schmidt, and Sebastian Heilmann

Well into the 1970s the PRC remained isolated from international flows of goods and capital. The Chinese economy was largely decoupled from the global economy, in which it played no significant role. However, during the three decades after liberalization was initiated in 1978–79, China grew with remarkable speed to become the world's most important export economy as well as a key recipient of international capital flows. Government policy making, particularly with respect to currency policy and foreign trade, played a crucial role in this trend—albeit one that is quite controversial from the perspective of China's trading partners and is the subject of recurring criticism.

4.7.1 Currency policy and external economic relations

Whereas Chinese trade accounted for only a fraction of global trade in 1980, by 2009 China had surpassed Germany as the world's biggest exporter of goods. Today the PRC is the world's second-largest importer after the United States and is already by far the most important market for many products, especially commodities. It became the world's largest trading power in 2012, holding more than a 13 percent share of total global trade in 2015. However, foreign-trade data for China as a whole give no indication of the drastic regional differences existing within the country in terms of global trade integration—differences that are of major significance with regard to the political processes and power structures within the government. At the time of this writing (2016), for instance, some three-quarters of Chinese foreign trade can be attributed to just four coastal provinces (Guangdong, Zhejiang, Jiangsu, and Shandong) and the cities of Beijing and Shanghai. These administrative units have played a major role in shaping Chinese foreign-trade policies.

In its rise to become a leader in global trade, China has benefited from a number of economic and political factors. These include an acceleration of trade, investment, and capital flows since the 1980s; a world trade regime that did not prevent China from becoming a member, but rather enabled a dismantling of its trade barriers (accession to the World Trade Organization [WTO] in 2001); close integration of China into the rapidly growing transnational production networks; the extremely high-growth momentum of the neighboring Asian-Pacific countries; and the establishment of exchange-rate policies that supported growth of Chinese exports.

As a central instrument in China's external economic relations, the exchange-rate regime has undergone a number of fundamental changes since 1978. Until the end of the 1970s, Chinese currency (the renminbi, CNY) was fixed at a significantly overvalued rate to facilitate the acquisition of foreign currency. Between 1979 and 1994, the rigid exchange-rate regime was gradually reformed in a series of measures and local experiments, and in 1994 a uniform exchange rate was introduced. The subsequent relative undervaluation of the Chinese currency became a basic requirement for expanding the export sector. In an environment of turbulent exchange rates during the Asian financial crisis of 1997–98, the Chinese authorities pegged the CNY to the U.S. dollar (USD) and the exchange rate remained by and large stable until July 2005.

Figure 4.7.A shows the appreciation of the CNY against the USD since 2005. This long-term trend has been accompanied by ongoing intervention by the Chinese central bank to stabilize and control the currency. China actively implements exchange-rate control mechanisms to support its political objectives, which, however, are subject to constant change. Under the new exchange-rate regime introduced in 2005, the CNY was allowed to fluctuate against the USD within a given daily range. In the context of the global financial crisis, however, in 2008 China again

Figure 4.7.A

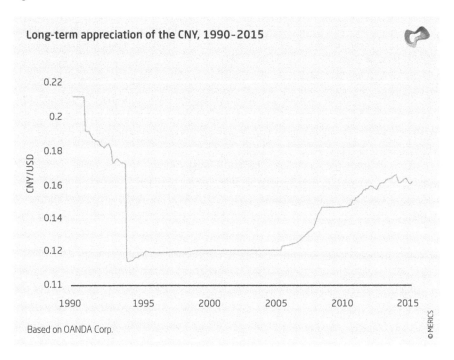

Long-term appreciation of the CNY, 1990–2015

Based on OANDA Corp.

© MERICS

pegged the CNY to the USD for two additional years. Not until June of 2010 did it return to the crawling peg system. Since then, the tolerated range of fluctuation has been expanded. The upward revaluation of the CNY by nearly 40 percent in real terms between 2005 and 2014 resulted in the Chinese export sector becoming less competitive in terms of exchange rates and prices. The Chinese central bank and the government have both accepted this situation, given that a stronger Chinese currency is perceived as a prerequisite for transitioning to a new growth model fueled by domestic demand and purchasing power within China.

The catalyzing effect of China's accession to the WTO in 2001 was a key factor in integrating China into the global economy and in promoting competition and deregulation in the domestic economy. The necessary adjustments to the domestic economy went far beyond the reduction of import restrictions that had already been implemented prior to its accession to the WTO. The political leadership at the time took advantage of the required changes in state regulation of the economy to promote market reforms in spite of domestic resistance.

With regard to his negotiating policy, at the time Premier Zhu Rongji took a classic two-level approach (Putnam 1988). At home, he used the necessity of making changes for the purpose of meeting the WTO requirements in order to overcome domestic resistance. In his diplomatic negotiations aimed at WTO membership, he used references to internal resistance and opposition within China to gain concessions from the other parties to the WTO negotiations.

Although China's position in international trade was further reinforced by the country's accession to the WTO and the resultant domestic economic adjustments and gains in competitiveness, China's violations of the rules have repeatedly been the subject of WTO arbitration proceedings. The infringements have typically involved accusations of subsidizing Chinese exporters and discriminating against foreign competitors. After a delay of several years, however, the Chinese government began utilizing WTO instruments to take actions against contractual breaches in its export markets. Table 4.7 shows the impact of the dismantling of customs barriers and the move in the direction of an export economy.

With a trade openness ratio of more than 60 percent (i.e., the ratio of foreign trade to GDP, from 2001 to 2008), China rose to become one of the most open national economies in the world. However, by 2014 the trade openness ratio had dropped to only 43 percent. China's current capital account and trade surpluses continue to be the subject of international criticism. The country's major trading partners, especially the United States, often denounce China's "mercantilist" currency and foreign-trade policies. The Chinese government continues to be accused of holding Chinese currency at an artificially low level to gain export benefits for Chinese enterprises. Furthermore, the government is criticized for practicing protectionism in key sectors of the Chinese economy, discriminating against non-Chinese

Table 4.7

China's foreign trade, 1980-2014

	1980	1990	2000	2004	2008	2010	2012	2013	2014
Trade (USD billion)	38	115	474	1,155	2,563	2,974	3,867	4,159	4,305
Share of global trade (%)	0.9	1.6	3.6	6.1	7.8	9.7	10.4	11.0	11.5
Balance of trade (USD billion)	-1.9	8.8	24.1	32.1	298.1	181.5	230.3	259	380
Trade openness ratio (ratio of foreign trade to GDP, %)	no data	26.7	44.2	65.5	62.3	55.0	51.8	50.2	42.9
Current account surplus (as a percentage of GDP)	0.1	3.1	1.7	3.6	9.3	4.0	2.6	2.6	3.8

Note: The absolute figures for trade, exports, and imports have been rounded up or down to the next billion.
Based on NBS via CEIC.

© MERICS

companies with regard to market access, and subsidizing the global expansion of Chinese businesses by granting them cheap loans from state banks.

However, according to all standard criteria—including imports as a percentage of GDP and customs revenue as a percentage of imports—China cannot by any means be called a closed "mercantilist" economy. In addition, at the time of the writing of this chapter (2016), the exchange rate between the USD and the CNY had reached an acceptable level, even in the view of former critics, as a result of the gradual appreciation of the Chinese currency. However, China's persistent current account surplus will continue to be a source of international tensions.

Opening its economy to FDI has been a key part of China's reform policy since 1979. Both foreign enterprises and Chinese-international joint ventures have played a major role in gaining access to advanced technology, transforming the industrial structure, and expanding foreign trade. After 1992, foreign-invested companies were provided access to many new sectors in the Chinese market (beyond the previously opened special economic zones and individual sectors). In fact, the Chinese government has attempted to promote the development of specific sectors and technologies and to direct investments in certain regions by means of binding investment catalogs and additional instruments.

Figure 4.7.B

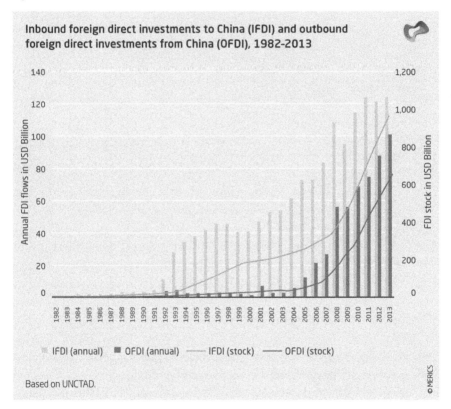

Inbound foreign direct investments to China (IFDI) and outbound foreign direct investments from China (OFDI), 1982-2013

IFDI (annual)   OFDI (annual)   IFDI (stock)   OFDI (stock)

Based on UNCTAD.

© MERICS

Foreign investors and foreign enterprises play an indispensable role in China's economy—a role that is also acknowledged by the Chinese government. Currently, approximately half a million companies with foreign shareholders operate in the PRC. According to official figures, these companies accounted for about 45 percent of China's foreign trade in 2013 and created millions of jobs (55 million in the urban economy alone, accounting for approximately one-sixth of all urban employees). Since the year 2000, 8–9 percent of all global direct investments have gone to China. A more recent phenomenon has been the active promotion of outbound foreign direct investments from China (OFDI). Figure 4.7.B shows the rapid rise in the flows and stocks of inbound foreign direct investments to China (IFDI) as well as the flows and stocks of OFDI from China to foreign markets (after a delay of approximately ten years).

Media reports in the West have a tendency to attribute political objectives rather than business acumen to the foreign expansion of Chinese enterprises. Contrary to this assumption, however, it is evident that the foreign engagements of Chinese companies and investors have been driven primarily by commercial interests, such as tapping into sales markets or acquiring advanced technologies. Nevertheless, the objectives and interventions by the Chinese state can be clearly seen in Chinese efforts to gain long-term access to sources of energy and raw materials, especially in Africa and Latin America. Even though private Chinese OFDI has increased sharply, by about 2015 it was still primarily Chinese state-owned companies that were expanding globally. The Chinese government has provided strong support to expansion of its "national champions" in foreign markets so as to enable them to compete with leading conglomerates in world markets. The complicated administrative procedures for approving and supervising major Chinese investments abroad, involving many different government offices, have been increasingly liberalized (Sauvant/Chen 2014).

4.7.2 Capital account controls

Unlike FDI, short-term portfolio investments and loans from foreign banks played almost no role in the Chinese economy until the mid-2000s. Experience gained from the Asian financial crisis between 1997 and 1998 reinforced concerns among party and state leaders about the convertibility of the currency and the free movement of capital, as China maintained its capital controls in order to reduce the economically and politically destabilizing effects of volatile capital movements. Restrictions on the flows of capital were only gradually eased in controlled steps and in selected market segments starting in about 2000. The resulting distance from international financial markets during the global financial crisis that we saw after 2007 ensured that the Chinese economy was not directly impacted via world financial markets. However, its real economy was hit hard, albeit indirectly and after some delay, with exports and industrial production collapsing in 2008 and 2009.

In line with the reforms of the financial system (see Section 4.6), cautious steps to selectively permit portfolio investments and to allow foreign banks to operate in the domestic market have been taken since 2003, despite concerns in parts of the Chinese government. The agreement governing China's membership in the

WTO stipulates that the Chinese banking and securities market would be further liberalized starting in 2006. One important step toward selective financial internationalization was the establishment of a bond market denominated in Chinese currency. Moreover, "qualified," i.e., specially licensed, financial service-providers were permitted to invest capital in Chinese financial products on the basis of strict quotas. The Chinese government has stated that its long-term objective is to make Shanghai a dominant international financial hub in East Asia.

Beginning in 2008, cautious steps were taken to internationalize the Chinese currency. The government is seeking to gradually create conditions for increased use of the CNY in global trade, in international foreign-exchange markets, and in the International Monetary Fund. The Chinese central bank has signed a series of agreements in order to build up a global infrastructure capable of supporting the growing role of the CNY in the global financial system (currency swap agreements and agreements on both direct currency trading and designated clearing banks).

Although the Chinese government only began relaxing its capital controls very cautiously and in small steps as of 2008, the country has nonetheless seen a substantial increase in speculative capital flows due to ingenious methods aimed at thwarting the usual restrictions, including forged import-export invoices and money laundering in Macau and offshore financial centers. China has also experienced a significant increase in the foreign debt of its domestic enterprises, ranging from land developers and shipyards to IT startups. Reservations on the part of the Chinese government and its hesitant liberalization of capital movements have proven increasingly less effective in safeguarding the economy against the risks of financial crises in China and abroad.

Key Chinese state actors in international financial markets include the State Administration of Foreign Exchange (SAFE) (国家外汇管理局) and the China Investment Corporation (CIC) (中国投资有限责任公司). The SAFE operates under the purview of the Chinese central bank and is responsible for investing China's currency reserves, which totaled USD 3.3 trillion at the end of 2015. The SAFE has typically made conservative investments, for example in U.S. and European government bonds. In the 2000s, however, it began investing a small portion of the rapidly growing currency reserves in riskier instruments such as equities. The investments were transacted by the SAFE Investment Company, a subsidiary of the SAFE in Hong Kong.

The CIC was established in 2007 for the purpose of investing a portion of China's currency reserves in higher-risk, higher-yield instruments. Upon its establishment, the CIC took over Central Huijin, the holding company via which the state held its shares in Chinese banks. In 2011 the CIC moved its international investment activities to CIC International, a newly formed subsidiary. For the most part, CIC International holds relatively small stakes in the companies in which it invests. However, it has also acquired strategic shareholdings of more than 10 percent, particularly in enterprises in the commodities and energy sectors. In 2014 the CIC managed assets totaling USD 746 billion.

The National Social Security Fund (NSSF) (全国社会保障基金) also operates in international financial markets. The NSSF was established in 2000 as a strategic reserve fund intended to bolster the social-security system. The reserve fund is managed by the National Council for Social Security Fund, a ministerial-level body. The NSSF is primarily financed by tax proceeds and shares transferred from state-owned enterprises. In 2014 the fund managed assets totaling CNY 1.5 trillion. Its articles of incorporation limit foreign investments to 20 percent of the portfolio.

The SAFE, the CIC, and the NSSF compete with one another to invest the foreign-exchange assets they manage as profitably as possible. In the case of the SAFE and the CIC, competitive pressures have repeatedly led to risky investments that have resulted in high losses and garnered sharp criticism from the general public.

4.7.3 The political impact of economic globalization

China's integration into the world economy has led to a growing presence of international actors in China and to Chinese enterprises, along with the interest groups behind them, taking an increasingly global stance. The deepening of trade and investment liberalization and China's partial integration into global financial and currency markets mean that Chinese economic actors are extremely dependent on global exchanges with respect to production networks, commodities, technologies, capital, and sales markets. International economic trends affect decisions on economic policy and programs within China. Thus the global integration of the Chinese economy heavily impacts the balancing of interests, decisions, and actions by the Chinese party and government.

Moreover, China's inclusion in transnational trade and capital flows has resulted in shifts of power, new learning processes, and changes in the political landscape, not all of which were foreseen or intended by the Chinese leadership. New corporate forms, such as those permitting foreign companies to hold stakes in Chinese companies, have triggered immense pressures for changes in the state economic sector. The integration of China's coastal economy into transnational production networks has altered the central-government's position and authority in the political system, given that the decentralized networks between local governments and functionaries, as well as those between non-Chinese companies and investors, do not necessarily pursue the same interests as the Chinese central government.

Most state authorities are now in regular, and sometimes quite close, contact with international organizations and globally operating conglomerates. A substantial amount of China's new economic legislation was drafted with the assistance of foreign legal consultants. In addition, the increasing need for administrative cooperation that has ensued from China's integration into foreign-trade networks has brought changes to the internal organization of Chinese state organs. The restructuring of the patent system and the customs office, for example, have been supported by programs promoting cooperation with international partner organizations. The central bank and MOFCOM have often spoken out in favor of furthering collaboration with international partner organizations, and many local-government offices are intertwined in close symbiotic relationships with foreign investors. Within China, these forms of cooperation have resulted in new transnational interest groups and new groupings of traditional interests whose fates are closely tied to integration in world markets.

It is erroneous to assume that there is an automatic correlation between opening an economy to foreign trade and political liberalization (or destabilization of the existing political system, for that matter). The challenge for China's foreign economic policies is that opposing objectives—some more liberal and some more mercantile—that are supported by heterogeneous interest groups need to be brought in line with one another. China's export industries are calling for liberalization and global market integration. The major state industries, however, are demanding political protection from overpowering foreign competition. Such tensions within China mean that the pace and the direction of internationalization are subject to repeated political corrections.

In essence, the main issue is the extent to which China's political leadership will tolerate the transformation of the economic and administrative structures through international competition and integration in world markets. Should the party leadership feel its political control is threatened by adaptive and competitive pressures, it will likely return to protectionist measures rather than accept social and political disintegration.

4.8 "Cadre capitalism" and corruption

Sebastian Heilmann

When China's economic reforms were first introduced in 1978–79, the basic organization of the party-state remained essentially unchanged. However, the behavior of the involved political actors changed dramatically: networks of political and economic players who belonged to the tier of officials employed by the CCP in the state sector and who were keen to improve their own situations began to undermine the official order to an extent that no one would ever have dreamed of under Mao's leadership. In many respects, the Chinese party-state became a kind of administrative market in which political power was systematically exchanged for economic benefits. Such "cadre capitalism" became the most obvious expression of the organizational decay of the CCP. Consequently, the party leadership regards the containment of corruption in China as a "fight to the death" for the CCP (Cai Yongshun 2015). (The term "corruption" is defined here in broader terms than in Western societies, covering not only political corruption, misappropriation of public funds, and illegal acquisition of state property but also moral and personal transgressions.)

4.8.1 Assessing the extent of corruption

In the social sciences, researchers find it difficult to measure the level of corruption in various countries on a comparative perspective. However, figures based on surveys of internationally operating businesspeople, researchers, and management consultancies regarding the way they view corruption provide some useful pointers. According to Transparency International's periodically updated *Corruption Perception Index,* in 2013 the PRC was ranked 80th among a total of 175 countries and was one of a number of countries with an average susceptibility to corruption. Tunisia and El Salvador were gauged at a similar level, ranking 77th and 83rd respectively. China was regarded as less influenced by corruption than countries like India, which ranked 94th, or Russia, which ranked 127th (TI [Transparency International] 2013 and 2014).

The Central Commission for Discipline Inspection (CCDI) (中央纪律检查委员会), which is the CCP body charged with combating corruption nationally (see Section 2.3.2), provides detailed information about the outcomes of current investigations and corruption scandals as part of its regular disciplinary campaigns (especially when a new premier has assumed office). This official information is selected on the basis of political criteria and is not exhaustive, but nevertheless it allows us to reach some conclusions about patterns of activity and the structure of corrupt networks in China.

Investigations into corruption within the CCP were stepped up after 2012 when General Secretary Xi Jinping and head of the CCDI Wang Qishan took office. In 2014, more than 282,000 members of the party and hundreds of leading cadres were subject to internal investigations, including ninety top officials. Among the majority of cases to date, the CCP's disciplinary bodies have imposed a variety of internal sanctions, ranging from warnings and fines to demotions; however, 82,000 party members have faced severe punishments. In particularly serious cases in which the party feels it must demonstrate its ability to remain clean, the accused are initially expelled from the party. The results of investigations by the disciplinary bodies within the party are then turned over to the public prosecutors to conduct criminal investigations and to undertake legal proceedings.

The transfer of capital assets to foreign accounts (that is, the "flight of capital") is a rough quantitative indication of the extent of national corruption. A comparison of Chinese and non-Chinese trade and customs statistics provides a particularly clear indication of the scope of illegal movements of capital, as such Chinese transfers are often achieved by false declarations on import and export bills. Moreover, during the first half of this decade investigative journalists conducting careful research managed to furnish detailed proof that the families of many of China's top government officials and other prominent Chinese had accumulated an extraordinary amount of offshore assets (Barboza 2012; International Consortium of Investigative Journalists 2014). Capital flight not only reflects movements of "hot" "corrupt" capital, but it is also a general indicator of political stability, of expectations about economic growth and returns, and of what kinds of risks investors face within China compared with foreign markets. A pronounced rise in the outflow of capital became apparent prior to 2012 when China's political and economic stability was called into doubt, even by the country's top leaders. The tendency to send capital abroad grew less pronounced for a while after Xi Jinping took office, but it grew stronger again in 2014–15 when it was facilitated by the loosening of capital controls.

Beginning in 2000, Chinese officials often attempted to obtain foreign citizenship for their children or sent members of their families to Western countries for long-term stays. Foreign investments and sending family members abroad are regarded as safeguards from the risks to stability and security within China. In this way, China's most powerful political, business, and military clans set themselves up "transnationally" to protect themselves from possible future setbacks in China.

4.8.2 Informal rules in China's "administrative market"

During its policy of reform and opening, the CCP generally renounced what had previously been extremely influential disciplinary measures, such as recurrent campaigns to combat political opponents, "self-cleansing" activities, and daily ideological indoctrination. Economic incentives and rewards gradually became increasingly important factors influencing conduct in public office, even among high-ranking party officials.

In connection with the rapid progress in the transition to a market-driven economy, the Chinese state became an enormous illicit trading floor: company directors, party secretaries, and heads of authorities diverted the means of production and funding from the state's economic sector to supply newly created markets; leading political positions and official approvals were exchanged for shares of profits in lucrative private transactions; and individual, high-ranking officials began acting as patrons to those involved in the rapidly growing underworld, particularly in the commodities, real-estate, and construction sectors. Because party officials still occupied key positions in administrative organs, the police force, and many other institutions, those seeking to set up businesses could not get past them without political connections.

Thus a hidden market for exchanging services developed within the state—a veritable "administrative market" (Heilmann 2000; Naishul' 1991). Under these circumstances, the CCP became an organizational "shell" for a range of completely unrelated activities. The members of the functionary class continued to operate within the various state hierarchies, but the behavior of a growing number of them was shaped by very different rules of conduct, that is, by "transactions" conducted in the "administrative market."

The power party officials held over businesses was no longer due to direct political and ideological controls but rather to the comprehensive rights of disposal held by the economic administration. Party and state cadres had a decisive influence on which entrepreneurs received cheap loans, who was given certain plots of land or buildings to develop or to use, who was permitted to enter into favorable contractual agreements, who had to pay how much tax, and who was able to enjoy political protection. Consequently, Chinese entrepreneurs had no choice but to continue to work as closely as possible with party offices and government departments. However, this dependence was mutual: the cadres' private income and the revenue obtained from local authorities were based on the revenue gained from profitable businesses.

This move away from a socialist command economy leveled the way for a form of capitalism characterized by the omnipresence of cadres involved in business. Major and minor holders of power at every level of the party, administration, and the armed forces enriched themselves by taking advantage of the opportunities provided by the still imperfect market and legal order. The close intermingling of the established power elites and the new economic elites shaped the relationship between the party-state, the economy, and society. Those CCP power elites and the new business elites, who came from a range of different organizations, were linked by a symbiotic network of personal relations of mutual benefit that flourished below the surface of the established system. It was in these networks of party cadres, administrative officials, bank officials, financial managers, and entrepreneurs that the exchange and negotiation processes, which were the drivers behind economic life in many parts of China, took place.

The informal links that existed on the borderlines between politics and business were largely responsible for the loosening of the command system of the central and unitary state governed by the CCP. In some ways, the administrative and government bodies established at the lower levels of the state system faced a conflict of loyalties between central-government policies and economic demands expressed locally through informal networks. At the county, township, and village levels local officials and top company executives were united in an alliance of interests that worked to act as autonomously as possible vis-à-vis the central government. Political power was transformed into personal wealth as many officials began enriching themselves and their personal entourages. The political elite of the Communist regime thereby effectively adapted to the changed economic environment.

4.8.3 Various forms of corruption

In general, a high level of corruption has been found to have a dampening effect on investment behavior and economic growth. This is because political manipulation and distortion of economic regulation means that there are few incentives for structural changes or productive activities. How can China's high economic growth be explained in view of the high level of corruption? For this purpose, it is useful to distinguish between different types of political corruption that have very different effects on the economy (Wedeman 2012). In the Chinese context, three basic kinds of political corruption can be identified, as listed in Table 4.8.

Although the effectiveness and impact of predatory corruption and organized crime are well known, "dividend collection" requires further explanation, as this type of corruption has played a key role during the twenty-first century in the successful export-oriented regions of China. Dividend collection is a byproduct of economic policies promoting growth, allowing political individuals at higher levels to claim part of the profits earned by prosperous private companies. It permits political and administrative rules and regulations, measures, and services that enable a share of the profits of nonstate-owned firms to be exchanged with political individuals. The claiming of dividends in this way creates strong incentives for political actors to pursue a form of economic regulation that encourages productive activities and entrepreneurial expansion. The compensation of corrupt politicians is thus coupled with the development of corporate profits. Seen in this light, company transfer payments to political patrons in the state and the bureaucracies can be understood as a form of profit-sharing and dividend payouts.

The dominance of dividend collections in relation to other kinds of corruption is characteristic of societies that simultaneously experience high economic growth and extensive corruption. (For many decades, South Korea was also in this class.) Corruption can have a positive impact on economic growth only if the financial and capital assets that have been diverted are re-invested in productive sectors and enterprises, but this is likely to occur only under exceptional political and economic circumstances, as the corrupt individuals must hold safe positions and be in office for long tenures if they are not to be tempted by predatory motives due to the desire to amass personal wealth within a short period of time. In addition, domestic

Table 4.8

Basic kinds of political corruption in the PRC

Form	Characteristics	Effect on economic growth
"Predatory" corruption	Systematic theft of public and private assets; consumption or export of misappropriated assets (capital flight).	Highly damaging to growth
"Dividend collection"	Political actors regularly demand a share of company profits in exchange for growth- and stability-enhancing administrative services; the involved companies often grow quickly for a period of time.	Temporarily growth-supporting
Organized crime	Occurs both as "predatory" corruption and as "dividend collection." Regularized exchange relationships among political and criminal individuals, sometimes leading to wholesale "privatization" of state authority.	Mostly damaging to growth

Based on Heilmann 2002.

© MERICS

investments must be more profitable than they are abroad if one wishes to avoid the large-scale export of illegally acquired capital.

Corrupt members of the *nomenklatura* in China obviously regarded domestic investments as rewarding, as "hot" capital acquired by private means was re-invested in China after being laundered abroad. Should other targets for investments prove to be more profitable in the future, this cycle might be interrupted.

Levels and types of corruption are strongly affected by the sectoral and export structure of an economy (Wedeman 2012). If a broad range of industrial goods (whose production can only be maintained by constant investments) is exported, as in the case of China, unrestricted predatory behavior will lead to a decline in investments and thereby will destroy the foundation for industrial production. The associated drying up of sources of income is contrary to the interests of officials and managers who benefit from a stable arrangement for their rent-seeking.

The numerous indications that the kind of corruption found in organized crime seems to be spreading rapidly in China and infecting party and government offices, even in large cities, are worrying. Beginning in the 1990s, many large networks of people involved in organized economic crime have been discovered in the PRC, each of which included senior party and government officials who were operating in sectors such as commodities, financial services, and real estate or who were involved in smuggling. The problem of party and government officials protecting criminal organizations has been raised by representatives of the judiciary at a number of the annual meetings of the NPC. If this kind of political corruption continues to spread, it will undermine the state's monopoly of power, the organizational unity of the CCP, and the potential for economic growth much more than the "dividend collection" that for two decades has ensured mutually lucrative government-business exchanges and economic growth in the coastal regions.

The reputation of party headquarters as the defender of a modernization strategy that will benefit all Chinese in the long term has taken a severe beating by a series of public scandals involving high-ranking officials since 2012. Revelations about power abuses by a member of the Politburo (Bo Xilai) and his entourage in the city of Chongqing and reports about the incredible amount of personal wealth amassed by the family of former premier Wen Jiabao damaged the image that party headquarters had built (Barboza 2012). In 2014 and 2015, criminal investigations into the political activities of Zhou Yongkang, who once oversaw China's security apparatus and law enforcement institutions, revealed some extremely serious offenses and corrupt activities while he was a member of the Politburo Standing Committee. The real-estate, stock-exchange, foreign-trade, and investment businesses conducted by the spouses and children of members of the Politburo are proof of the immense personal enrichment among party officials. Many families possess offshore assets in the order of several hundred million dollars, or even billions of dollars (Barboza/LaFraniere 2012). When this came to light, an extremely valuable aspect of the CCP legitimacy was destroyed, namely the widespread belief that the majority of officials who have a say in matters at party headquarters are highly responsible cadres who always behave with integrity.

Since the 1980s, the informal power and exchange networks of Chinese functionaries have been held together not only by the CCP's monopoly on political power but also by their exclusive access to the most lucrative assets in the Chinese economy. This arrangement will remain attractive and stable as long as the state economy provides sufficient distributional gains for every clan and interest group associated with the political elite. But if the country's economic dynamism is to decline for a long period of time and ominous cracks are to appear in the façade of the political leadership, many insiders might be tempted to abandon their loyalty to the CCP and, along with their families, leave the country. Provided the leading officials grouped around Xi Jinping are able to maintain citizen trust in long-term political stability and in China's economic attractiveness, this propensity to leave China might be kept under control. Nonetheless, the way in which corruption and capital flight have grown since 2010 is a clear warning of how unstable support for the CCP leadership is likely to become among the country's political and economic elite if an acute crisis is to develop.

4.8.4 Resistance to combating corruption

The "deep structure" of China's political economy (as opposed to the "surface structure" of official economic and political institutions) is characterized by informal exchange networks among those who are politically well-connected and thus enjoy access to the discretionary approval and allocation powers of the party-state decision-makers. These underlying informal structures prevent the emergence of a more open form of economic and political competition and they also undermine the efficacy and credibility of the official laws and regulations. Major political and economic players move confidently within gray areas of mutually beneficial exchanges, leaving no doubt that unconventional ways of achieving one's own interests are much more effective than legal means. The informal rules of politics, business, and commerce work in parallel with the official rules, either by changing them, canceling them, or supplementing them. In order to comprehend how Chinese business has managed to bypass the restrictive official policies and how the extensive corruption networks have taken shape, it is essential to understand the patterns of the hidden interactions and double standards that result from the tensions between the formal and informal rules of the game.

So far, the vehement but generally short-lived campaigns to fight corruption within the CCP and the government have been only modestly successful. The reasons are obvious: many of the prominent party officials and their family members are part of the widespread networks of corruption and are not interested in uncovering such links. Consequently, the fight against corruption has met with stubborn resistance and obstruction from party officials in many parts of the country. Even the investigations into the cases of the graft of top officials since 1995 have done little to change the situation, despite having led to a series of prominent figures, including members of the Politburo, losing their positions and facing imprisonment.

One of the goals of Xi Jinping's leadership is to fight corruption at the very highest levels, which include the Politburo Standing Committee and the Central Military Commission. 68 party officials in top positions, such as vice-ministers or higher, were sentenced to imprisonment in 2014. It should be noted, however, that China's government consists of over 5,000 functionaries who work at these hierarchical levels (Li/McElveen 2014).

The lack of a clear distinction between political and economic rights of disposal in China's state-dominated economy has prepared the way for rampant corruption. Opaque market competition distorted by political interference creates a host of opportunities to personally gain from the situation through corruption. Without a drastic restriction of rights of disposal, competencies, and opportunities for intervention by the authorities vis-à-vis companies, and without sweeping institutional reforms at the heart of the political system, namely an independent judiciary and a mass media critical of the government, the problem of corruption is not likely to be curbed. Because reforms of this kind would restrict the monopoly of power enjoyed by the CCP, resistance to the creation of independent supervisory bodies is insurmountable.

4.9 Decentralized economic policies and regional disparities

Sandra Heep and Sebastian Heilmann

The control that subnational governments exercise over the economy is a defining characteristic of the Chinese economic order. In the latter part of the 1950s China began turning away from the Soviet model of development, thus leading to local governments being accorded extensive rights of control over economic administration. The majority of state enterprises were placed under the decentralized control of the provinces, prefectures, cities, and counties. As a result, a complex network of state property rights spanning various territorial levels developed, with only parts of the network subject to central controls and planning (Lyons 1987).

In the 1980s, in a bid to stimulate more local initiatives, China's central government improved the incentives for regional leaders to promote economic growth in their administrative areas (Shirk 1993). Most markets and enterprises, both state-owned and private, ended up under decentralized control. Even today, the Chinese economy continues to display features of a decentralized state economy characterized by competition among regional administrative bodies (provinces, cities, and counties) as well as among the businesses under their authority. Not only does the intertwining of local-government offices and enterprises have a major impact on the conduct of political actors, but it also affects the relations among local governments and the various economic regions.

4.9.1 The diversity of the regional economies

Over the course of the reform period, considerable differences emerged in the growth models of the various regions due to the country's vast size, its decentralized administration, and local experiments with economic policy. For that reason, Zhang and Peck (2016) argue that China should be regarded less as a homogeneous economic entity and more as a laboratory for developing and testing different regional varieties of capitalism. To illustrate this idea, they analyze a range of local varieties of capitalism that can be found in Guangdong, Sunan, and Zhongguancun.

Among the local variants of capitalism, the southern province of Guangdong conforms most closely to common perceptions of the Chinese developmental model. In the late 1970s, Guangdong became a test area for experimenting with opening to world markets. The province attracted many Hong Kong and Taiwan investors who transformed the region into an enormous workshop for the export of consumer goods and electronics. However, productivity growth and innovation were slow to materialize because regional economic policy makers and enterprises continued to focus on labor-intensive production. By 2010, numerous regional export industries were experiencing hardships due to Chinese wage increases.

Less frequently mentioned in Western discussions has been the economic development in Sunan, the southern part of Jiangsu province. Many profitable "collective enterprises" came into being in Sunan in the 1980s due to the region's strong tradition of skilled trades, an underground economy in existence since the Mao era, and competition among municipal governments. Initially, these enterprises remained the formal property of the local municipal administrations. They were managed, however, as profit-oriented companies in the competitive regional environment. Over the course of the 1990s, many of these businesses were privatized—frequently by way of management buyouts—and were rapidly integrated into transnational production networks incorporating increasingly high levels of technology. At the same time, the municipal governments were successful in using financial incentives to bring international electronics and IT firms to local industrial zones. Thus research and development played a much more significant role in the Sunan model of development than it did in Guangdong. The weakness of the Sunan model, however, was due to the fact that mainly foreign companies were driving the development of the advanced technologies, whereas domestic innovative capabilities remained in their infancy (Zhang/Peck 2016).

The shape of local capitalism was quite different in Zhongguancun, a technology hub built in the northwestern part of central Beijing in the 1980s. This industrial center produced many of China's high-tech pioneers who benefited from access to both research facilities and graduates of the leading national universities as well as the excellent opportunities for networking in the capital city. Transnational networks of researchers, startup companies, and private equity investors resulted in vigorous exchanges of information with innovation centers abroad. High state subsidies in conjunction with private investments, both domestic and international, enabled companies based in Zhongguancun to focus on research, design, and marketing in the high-tech sector. In the 2010s, a number of these companies were on the brink of making the leap to international stock exchanges (Zhang/Peck 2016).

Thus the conflictual idea of an authoritarian government that allows free market competition among businesses is handled by a variety of models and with varying results. The different regions of China act as dynamic laboratories for many variations of political and economic institutions and processes.

4.9.2 Divergent levels of economic development

The various economic models that emerged during the period of reform led to great differences in terms of how the regions of China developed (see Figure 4.9). By affording foreign-trade privileges to the coastal regions, for example, the central government effectively promoted conditions for unequal development, leading to a gap between the coastal areas and the inland provinces. The resulting differences in economic development resulted in the financial strength and growth potential of

Figure 4.9

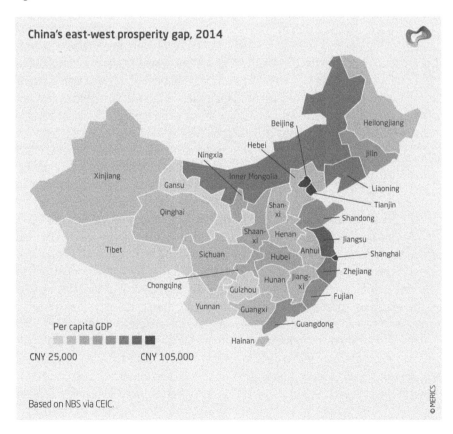

China's east-west prosperity gap, 2014

Per capita GDP

CNY 25,000   CNY 105,000

Based on NBS via CEIC.

© MERICS

the coastal provinces developing much more rapidly than that in the other provinces. In addition, regions with smaller state sectors generally developed more quickly than those with a preponderance of the older socialist industries. In terms of financial strength, the disparities in development between the richest and poorest regions grew particularly rapidly following the 1992 wave of reforms (Wang/Hu 2001).

To counteract the social and political consequences of these imbalances, the central government began revising its regional policies in the mid-1990s. Thereafter, programs to combat poverty and to foster economic cooperation between the interior provinces and the coastal provinces have been vigorously advocated, and the inland provinces have been accorded additional privileges with regard to opening up to foreign trade.

In 2000 a large-scale development program was initiated for western China (西部大开发). Huge investments were made to improve the infrastructure of the western regions in order to connect them with the markets of the coastal regions. The program also sought to tap into the commodities and energy resources found in western China, particularly natural gas and hydropower, in order to promote growth in those regions while at the same time to secure the supply of energy that the coastal provinces required. Moreover, the program sought to establish the western regions as attractive locations for FDI and to integrate them with international trade. The program was funded by central-government and local-government budgets as well as by loans from the policy banks.

In 2007 the central government approved an additional regional development program, known as the "plan for revitalizing the northeast of China" (东北地区振兴规划). During the era of the planned economy, northeast China had been a center for heavy industry. However, the restructuring of the state economic sector initiated in the 1990s resulted in serious unemployment in the region. The development plan was geared toward fundamentally realigning the industrial base in this part of the country (Heilmann/Melton 2013).

Since the mid-2000s, development has been more balanced due to the greater momentum in the western regions. This trend had been reinforced by the effects of the global financial crisis that led to a collapse in the growth of exports from the coastal provinces and hence to a slowdown in the economic growth in these regions. The growth rates in some of China's western regions have now begun to surpass those of the coastal regions. Additionally, the flow of FDI has started reaching regions that previously had been neglected. The relocation of production facilities to western regions has also accelerated due to the much lower wages prevailing in those areas compared to those in the coastal regions, in combination with the equally strong rise in demand for capital and consumer goods in the western regions. The development program for the west has led to a significant rise in growth rates, even in the autonomous regions of Tibet and Xinjiang, which are home to various ethnic minorities. It should be noted, however, that Han Chinese have tended

Table 4.9

Regional economic disparities, 2014			
	Jiangsu	Shanxi	Guizhou
Population (million)	79.6	36.5	35.1
Per-capita GDP (CNY)	81,874	35,064	26,393
GDP growth (%, official statistics)	8.7	4.9	10.8
Share of national GDP (%)	10.2	2.0	1.5
Exports (USD billion)	350.6	11.6	3.6
Realized FDI (USD billion, 2013)	33.3	2.8	1.5

Based on NBS; MOFCOM; General Administration of Customs via CEIC.

© MERICS

to benefit from this trend to a greater extent than Tibetans or persons of Uyghur descent, resulting in intensified social and political tensions in these regions (see Section 5.7.2).

Despite the increase in economic momentum in western China, the fundamental disparities between the country's developing regions and the more prosperous coastal areas have remained substantial. In 2014, Jiangsu, the wealthiest province, had a per-capita GDP that was more than triple that of Guizhou, the poorest province (see Table 4.9). Furthermore, inequalities between the urban and rural populations within the various regions began to increase in the 2000s (World Bank 2009). These differences have been exacerbated by a public budget system that does not provide for sufficient transfer payments (see Section 2.8).

4.10 The dynamics of a developmental state

Mikko Huotari, Sandra Heep, and Sebastian Heilmann

Regardless of the internal contradictions and regional disparities, it is still useful to attempt to obtain a view of the political and economic system as a dynamic whole. As illustrated in the previous sections, however, simple dichotomies, such as "planned economy vs. market economy" or "state vs. private," do not adequately describe the forces driving the political economy of China. Although we find many features that are generally associated with modern capitalism, China's political order and economic system are undergoing an accelerated and compressed evolution that defies categorization on the basis of static models.

Neither the manner in which the system functions as a whole nor its capacity to resolve problems can be described by institutional constants, such as CCP one-party rule or the special position enjoyed by the state sector. Even though on the surface the individual components of the political economy may be comparable to traditional or other current institutional systems, efforts to shape the Chinese political landscape and the political-economic transformation have been driven time and again by unconventional instruments and processes as well as by independent institutional innovations. The evolution of China's political economy must therefore be viewed as a highly contradictory process that is historically unprecedented, inevitably surprising, and open in terms of its eventual outcome.

Moreover, it is of little use to attempt to comprehend the special prerequisites, dynamics, and risks associated with China's developmental path by discussing a possible "Chinese model" (frequently referred to as the "Beijing consensus"). This is particularly the case because such a debate portrays the Chinese experience as a clearly defined alternative to other systems, which likewise exist only in theory as uniform, fixed models of liberal or neo-liberal development.

On the surface, the Chinese combination of an authoritarian regime with capitalistic tendencies may appeal to many authoritarian leaders. However, the prerequisites, practices, and dynamics associated with China's political economy are so unusual when compared with other societies, both past and present, that it is impossible to take the Chinese model as a simple solution that can be usefully applied to other contexts. China's unconventional combination of traditional and modern political and economic methods, instruments, and institutions may well serve as an inspiration for independent, context-specific, and experimental development efforts in other countries. Nonetheless, the Chinese experience is by no means a ready-made model appropriate for transfer to other societies.

The basic pattern of political and economic interactions has remained constant in China in spite of its momentum in terms of economic development and the many institutional changes: the task of the Chinese government is to create and guide the development of the economy and society and to intervene massively in day-to-day economic operations. The leadership role of the Communist Party and its all-encompassing controls are inherent in China's official designation as a "socialist market economy" (SMEc).

It is of little use to refer to a static, unifying model to explain the exceptional dynamics of change that are at work in China's political economy. At a general level and with important country-specific qualifications, China can be characterized as a perpetually evolving developmental state which, during certain phases of advancement, assumes functions similar to those that existed during the phases of major industrial growth and transformation in Japan, South Korea, Taiwan, and Singapore, for example. The term "developmental state" not only refers to economic regulation, but also describes a state that systematically intervenes in economic processes in order to foster catch-up development by mobilizing production factors (via industrial policy as well as by targeted investments and lending). To be sure, market mechanisms have been gaining in significance in the Chinese developmental state. However, all investors and enterprises in the Chinese economy still operate under the shadow of the state hierarchy, with the state intervening in nearly all economic sectors and processes. State activities even extend to efforts to prevent the dominance of foreign investors and technologies in areas considered to be of key future significance, such as the strategic industries and the new technologies.

It should be noted that a developmental state is not a static system, but rather it is subject to constant transformation in response to changing economic, social, technological, and international opportunities and limitations. Following three and a half decades of breakneck industrialization and rising prosperity, the developmental state of China must now deal with numerous instances of crisis because the country has reached a stage of development requiring a fundamental realignment of the economic model; the former strategies of economic development—mobilization of the working population and expansion of the capital base to enable rapid growth fueled by exports and investments—have reached their limits. No longer are cheap labor, state investments, and global exports sufficient to drive economic momentum. To generate further growth, higher domestic consumption and a stronger service industry within China, as well as increases in the productivity of Chinese enterprises, will be required. Only if the forces of private enterprises are incentivized in all economic sectors will China be able to prevent an even greater loss of momentum than has already occurred.

This undeniable need to adapt will have extensive political consequences for the developmental state of China, as evidenced by the minimum steps that will be required for such a far-reaching restructuring of the economy, namely (1) implementing measures to liberalize the private sector and the financial system; (2) ensuring legal certainty and equal treatment for all forms of enterprises; (3) restructuring and in some cases privatizing state-owned enterprises; and (4) drastically reducing state interventions in the economy. In November 2013 the Chinese leadership adopted a reform agenda that is largely consistent with these requirements. Such an agenda, however, will lessen the power of the party-state considerably and will conflict with the interests of the established political forces and the ties to the state of the economic elite. In addition, it will not solve the basic contradiction of how any such comprehensive program of liberalization can be brought into line with the needs of the Communist Party for unfettered leadership and control. Therefore, it cannot be ruled out that the 2013 economic deregulation and liberalization measures will not be implemented until the economy has declined to a level considered by the Communist Party leadership to threaten the country's political stability.

5 Governing China's society

Beginning in the 1980s, the party leadership began to reduce the extent of its control over society and over the private lives of the Chinese population. Opportunities for international exchanges were gradually expanded with the objective of promoting economic growth. People enjoyed greater flexibility in their lifestyle choices and buying habits, and the previously homogeneous value system began to break down as new technologies and social media brought new ways of accessing and sharing information and forming opinions. What sort of political backlash ensued from these changes in Chinese society? How did they challenge the authority of the party and state?

5.1 Political control and "social management"

Kristin Shi-Kupfer and Sebastian Heilmann

The PRC employs special methods to maintain political and administrative control over its people. These include restrictive policies with respect to registering places of residence, birth control measures that only recently have been relaxed, and IT-based surveillance of the population in public spaces through camera systems with face-recognition technology and comprehensive online monitoring and data evaluation. Since the 1990s, the traditional means of control, such as work units (*danwei*) (单位) and urban residents' committees (居民委员会), have become less effective as their functions have been redefined by the government or they have been replaced by new structures. In the 2000s China's political leadership began to pursue active, preventive "social management" (社会管理). Public services were expanded, restructured, or outsourced, and the manner in which social tensions were handled at lower administrative levels was professionalized in order to resolve conflicts as early as possible. At the same time, however, the state-security and monitoring apparatus rapidly ballooned to cover those instances in which the government believed that preventive "social management" would not suffice to ensure social and political stability.

5.1.1 Changing mechanisms of control

Until the end of the 1970s, two of the characteristic instruments of power utilized by the Communist Party were the "mass line" and "class struggle." In a continuing series of political campaigns, the party mobilized the "popular masses" to carry out its revolutionary objectives. This served to exact a high degree of political conformity. Driven by the "struggle against class enemies," which involved regular denunciations and acts of violence, the mass political campaigns reached a pinnacle during the 1966–76 Great Proletarian Cultural Revolution.

Following the turmoil of the Cultural Revolution and the death of Mao Zedong in 1976, the Chinese leadership under Deng Xiaoping at the end of the 1970s began to support a path of administrative and economic consolidation. From that point onward, mass campaigns were launched only occasionally, for example to combat crime or to contain religious groups. In 2012, however, party leader Xi Jinping began advocating a revival of the "mass line" as an instrument of control. The idea was for party cadres to once again emphasize their proximity to the masses by taking on work assignments in poor, rural regions. Leading party cadres had to disclose their mistakes in the form of written or verbal "self-criticisms" at internal party meetings. The Chinese Communist Party (CCP) Central Commission for Discipline Inspection (CCDI) employed aggressive propaganda, public displays of selected cadres suspected of corruption, and denunciations (mostly via the Internet) in a vehement anti-corruption campaign. All undesirable political voices in society—particularly bloggers critical of the government, journalists, and attorneys—were decried as politically disloyal, ideologically Westernized, unpatriotic, or agitators, and they were often forced to appear on television for public displays of self-incrimination ("self-criticisms").

In the 1950s Chinese cities had tight networks of "work units" that had been established at companies, government agencies, and schools as well as in neighborhood districts. The units were supervised by the Communist Party, and each citizen was allocated to a work unit at his or her place of employment, educational or training institution, or residence. These *danwei* (literally "units") assumed a key role in daily life—from obtaining housing to marriage counseling—and thus enabled an effective system of nearly complete control over society. However, the work units lost much of their effectiveness with the advent of the market economy in the 1980s. The emergence of the private economic sector created alternatives with regard to finding employment and housing. For many Chinese, the emergence of the market economy brought new freedoms and greater opportunities to pursue personal interests. The downside was an increase in life risks due to the demise of the social integration and security that had existed in the work units (Liu Tianbao/Chai Yanwei 2013; Lü Xiaobo/Perry 1997).

In response to the diminishing role of the *danwei* and the rapid urban influx of migrant workers beginning in the 1990s, the central government established self-governing residents' committees (社区居民委员会) in the major urban residential districts. These committees incorporated many of the neighborhood committees that had been in existence since the 1950s, and they acted as a neighborhood watch and point of contact for residential concerns. At first, predominantly older residents, appointed by the state, were active in the self-governing committees. In 1999, however, the government launched an initiative to boost acceptance of the committees and to strengthen their sense of responsibility by initiating direct elections (Kojima/Kokubun 2002). The committees were generally responsible for residential districts of between 1,000 and 3,000 households. They played an important role in allocating social benefits, which was intended to ease the burden on higher-ranking government bodies. The self-governing committees in the residential districts also recruited "security volunteers" (治安志愿者) to act as informal monitors to supply information on crimes and other incidents relevant to security, especially in the context of major events such as the 2008 Olympic Games or the Asia-Pacific Economic Cooperation (APEC) summit in 2014. Tensions resulting from the changed urban landscape with respect to housing, ownership structures, and administrative organizations manifested themselves in conflicts between the self-governing committees, commercial property-management companies, and the newly created self-organized homeowners' committees.

5.1.2 Birth control

Due to the far-reaching economic and social consequences of the growing population in China, one of the greatest challenges for the political leadership has been to control the rapidly rising birth rate. Under Mao's leadership, the Chinese population exploded so quickly that despite the high economic growth rates registered during certain periods, living standards did not improve for much of the rural population. The optimum population for the territory of the PRC, after taking into account economic and ecological factors, has been defined by government scientists as 700 million people. The actual population was nearly 1.36 billion in 2014 and is expected to peak at 1.7 billion by 2030 (Banister et al. 2010; UN Department of Economic and Social Affairs 2015). Table 5.1 provides an overview of population trends since the 1950s.

The population control measures initiated by the state at the end of the 1970s were highly controversial not only in the West but in China as well. The new restrictions, mandating one child per couple, were especially unpopular among the rural population. Education campaigns, bolstered by threats of fines, were initiated to encourage cooperation. The penalties imposed by many rural administrations were

Table 5.1

Population growth in the PRC, 1953-2014

	Total popula- tion (million)	Urban/Rural (million)		Degree of urbaniza- tion (%)	Popu- lation growth rate* (%)	Age breakdown** (%)			Number of persons per family (Ø)
1953	594	77	505	15	No data available	36	59	4	4.33
1964	695	127	567	18	No data available	41	56	4	4.43
1982	1,008	211	797	21	1.57	34	62	5	4.41
1990	1,134	300	834	26	1.44	28	67	6	3.96
2000	1,265	458	807	36	0.80	23	70	7	3.44
2010	1,341	670	671	50	0.48	17	75	9	3.10
2014	1,368	749	618	55	0.5	17	73	10	2.97

Notes: Due to rounding differences, the totals may differ from the individual sums. *Natural growth rate (in %) during the respective years. ** Three age categories: 0-14, 15-64, and 65+.
Based on National Bureau of Statistics (NBS) 2014a; NBS Department of Population and Employment Statistics 2015; World Bank 2016.

© MERICS

extremely strict, extending to forced sterilizations and abortions even in the later stages of pregnancy (Greenhalgh 2008). However, certain rural areas benefited from special regulations permitting families to have a second child if the first one was female. Ethnic minorities were also allowed to have more than one child.

The Chinese government prides itself on the fact that state population controls prevented some 400 million births between the beginning of the 1980s and the turn of the century. However, opinions among Chinese scientists vary as to the extent to which state policies impacted this decline in the number of births. Based on experience in other developing nations and emerging economies, it can be assumed that population growth in China would have slowed down regardless of the state intervention as families tend to have fewer children when there is greater prosperity and better access to education and birth control (Feng Wang, Cai Yong, and Gu Baochang 2013).

Chinese population control policies resulted in the number of people aged 60 and older increasing four times as rapidly as the rest of the population between

2010 and the time of this writing (2016). The 60+ age demographic is expected to exceed 30 percent of the population by the year 2050 (Banister et al. 2010). This trend will necessitate an extremely efficient social-security system (see Section 6.5).

China has seen a massive shift in the ratio of male to female births as a consequence of the traditional preference for males, especially in the rural areas where abortions of female fetuses and infanticide are not uncommon. According to the official 2010 census, there were 118 male births for every 100 female births. Although this imbalance appears to have lessened somewhat since 2010, the considerable surplus of males means that by the middle of the twenty-first century approximately one-fifth of Chinese men will not find a marriage partner from among the available pool of Chinese women (Jiang Quanbo, Ying Li, and Sánchez-Barricarte 2013).

To counteract the consequences of an aging society, the government began to gradually relax its birth control measures in 2009. At first, married couples in cities could apply to have a second child if they both had been only children. Beginning in November 2013, it was sufficient if only one of the spouses provided evidence of having no siblings. However, the easing of these restrictions did not lead to changes in the birth rate as anticipated by the government. Many young married couples have indicated a hesitation about having additional children due to a lack of time and finances as well as career considerations. According to the National Family Planning Commission, by the end of May 2015 only approximately 1.45 million, or 13 percent of those entitled, had applied for permission to have a second child.

5.1.3 Household registration

Established in 1958, the system of household registration, the *hukou* system (户口 登记制度), remains of central importance to state control of the population. The registration system entailed making a strict distinction between urban and rural households in order to halt the uncontrolled migration to Chinese cities in the 1950s. Moreover, the *hukou* system has been used to control access to education, healthcare, urban dwellings, and, until the 1990s, the right to food rations and other state benefits. Before the introduction of market economy mechanisms in the 1990s, the urban population was at a distinct advantage over the rural population in terms of supplies (including rationed food) and other state benefits (such as free healthcare). Additionally, household registration was intended to enable better control over unstable social elements, such as migrant workers, criminals, political dissidents, and ethnic or religious minorities.

By enforcing strict control over household registration, China has managed to avoid a common situation in developing nations, i.e., massive slums forming on the outskirts of cities due to uncontrolled migration from the rural areas. Since the 1980s, however, economic growth has led to fundamental changes in the movement of the Chinese population due to the extremely high demand for workers in China's booming coastal regions. As a result, beginning in the early 1990s rural job seekers have been permitted to take up temporary employment in the cities. In small to medium-sized cities, the household registration requirements have been gradually relaxed.

In July 2014 the State Council published a document calling for comprehensive reform of the household registration system. The document announced the abolition of the traditional distinction between "rural" and "nonrural" households in connection with establishing a uniform national registration system to be in place by 2020. However, the distinction between permanent and temporary household registrations was maintained. Hence the new provisions do not allow for people to voluntarily select their primary place of residence or to enjoy free access to public services in Chinese cities. Depending on the size of the city, local governments are still able to make the allocation of local residences dependent on various conditions, such as the duration of the stay, income level, amount of taxes paid, home ownership, and educational background (Goodburn 2014).

5.1.4 Society: The focus of active government management

The party leadership's objective of sustaining control over politics and society is in fundamental conflict with economic and technological progress, which requires a society that is dynamic, cosmopolitan, diverse, innovative, and entrepreneurial. Those demands on society conflict with the traditional paternalistic view of a Communist Party that acts as an elite avant-garde guiding the broad masses.

After the crackdown on the Tiananmen Square protesters in 1989, the Communist Party leadership moved to depoliticize the population by channeling all of society's energy into economic development, career advancement, and private consumption, thus bringing a halt to political activism; at first indication, any attempts to organize an opposition were suppressed.

However, as economic prosperity grew and people became more educated, the population's growing expectations led to greater demands on the government. People were becoming more diverse and setting higher standards. The CCP reacted to this new situation in 1998 by developing the concept of active "social management." No longer are state agencies to act primarily as arms of control and allocation in the government hierarchy. Rather, they are to form new relationships with society and to restore CCP legitimacy by taking a service-based approach to governance and self-governance.

The concept of "social management" also involves establishing transparent professional standards for administrative work. The initial cover-up of the out-break of the lethal severe acute respiratory syndrome (SARS) virus in 2003 led to increased demands for a government that is more strongly focused on the needs of its citizens and the general public, both in terms of social perceptions and among parts of the new party leadership. Social tensions, injustices, and protests, as well as unforeseen natural disasters (such as the 2008 earthquake in Sichuan) and eco-nomic crises (such as the 2007–9 global financial crisis) are to be contained and dealt with by means of a forward-looking state management employing modern methods, some of which are imported from abroad and then adapted to fit the Chinese context.

In 2012–13, the party leadership introduced the concept of "social governance" (社会治理) in public documents. Based on international discussions on gover-nance, the concept of social governance is intended to imply an interactive, cooper-ative relationship between government actors and society (Novaretti 2014). How-ever, the trend toward greater hierarchical state control and oversight over actors in the society (nongovernmental organizations [NGOs] and charitable organizations, for example) has been intensifying since 2012–13 (see Section 5.5.3).

5.2 Political controls and popular demands for civil rights

Sebastian Heilmann and Yi Zhu

5.2.1 Changing concepts of human rights

Traditional Chinese ideas of statehood leave little room for the concept of human rights in the sense of individual, inalienable rights independent of the state. For the most part, law has been traditionally applied as an instrument for controlling crime and enforcing the power of the elite. After the establishment of the PRC, all party-designated "class enemies" were denied both human and civil rights, as dictat-ed by the "revolutionary class struggle" and the "dictatorship of the proletariat." At least ten million people, including several million political prisoners, were interred in forced labor camps at any given time prior to the introduction of the policy of reform and opening in 1978–79. Although it is true that there were never any death camps in the People's Republic of China (PRC), nonetheless abuses, epidemics, and famines led to above-average death rates in the labor camps (Domenach 1995).

After 1979, the Communist Party leadership downgraded the significance of "class struggle." The wording of the extensive catalog of basic rights contained in the 1982 state constitution shows many similarities with Western concepts. In 2004 the constitution was amended to also include "safeguarding human rights." However, the addition of basic rights has had very little effect thus far because the lack of a division of powers and of judicial protections means that no rights can be asserted that are contrary to the political objectives of the state.

In 1982 China became a member of the UN Human Rights Commission (UN-CHR) and by 2013 it had signed a total of twenty-six human-rights conventions. In 2001 the National People's Congress (NPC) ratified the International Covenant on Economic, Social and Cultural Rights (ICESCR). Although the Chinese government also signed the International Covenant on Civil and Political Rights (ICCPR) in 1998, it never ratified it. Any credible implementation of the ICCPR in the PRC would require a number of changes to the Chinese Constitution as well as to its laws and judicial organizations, which the country's political leadership thus far has been unwilling to undertake.

Since the beginning of the 1990s, the Chinese government has been attempting to formulate its own position in the debate on human rights. This began in response to severe Western criticism of the political repression in China, especially after the violent suppression of the Tiananmen Square protests in 1989. The Chinese government continues to prioritize collective, unenforceable human rights (such as the right to development, and social and economic rights), which are based on a modernized socialist and culturalist interpretation (see Figure 5.2).

A new awareness of rights has been developing in Chinese society due to the establishment of judicial institutions, the rising level of education, and the increase in private ownership. More citizens are demanding the right to defend themselves against state interventions. Public debates have led to some improvements in the field of human rights. One example is the 2012 amendment to the Code of Criminal Procedure, which for the first time anchors the "protection of human rights" in criminal law. The abolition of the decades-old *laojiao* system ("re-education through labor," or forced labor ordered by the police without a trial; see Section 6.3) can also be regarded as a significant advance.

In an international comparison, human-rights organizations such as Amnesty International and Human Rights Watch continue to assess the situation in China as extremely negative. Their key points of criticism are arrests of political dissidents, civil rights attorneys, and NGO activists, as well as general repression of freedom of opinion and freedom of organization.

Figure 5.2

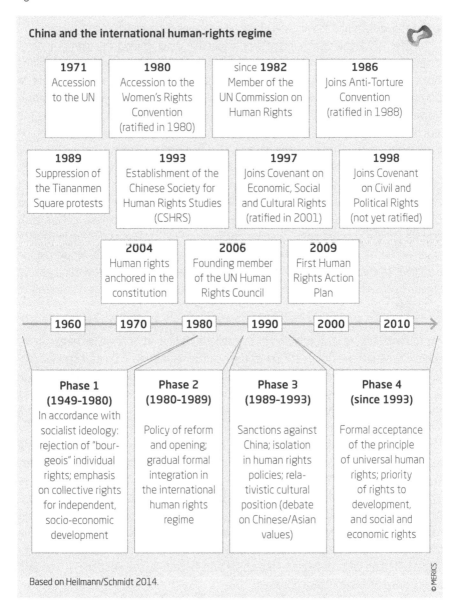

China and the international human-rights regime

1971	1980	since 1982	1986
Accession to the UN	Accession to the Women's Rights Convention (ratified in 1980)	Member of the UN Commission on Human Rights	Joins Anti-Torture Convention (ratified in 1988)

1989	1993	1997	1998
Suppression of the Tiananmen Square protests	Establishment of the Chinese Society for Human Rights Studies (CSHRS)	Joins Covenant on Economic, Social and Cultural Rights (ratified in 2001)	Joins Covenant on Civil and Political Rights (not yet ratified)

2004	2006	2009
Human rights anchored in the constitution	Founding member of the UN Human Rights Council	First Human Rights Action Plan

1960 — 1970 — 1980 — 1990 — 2000 — 2010 →

Phase 1 (1949-1980)	Phase 2 (1980-1989)	Phase 3 (1989-1993)	Phase 4 (since 1993)
In accordance with socialist ideology: rejection of "bourgeois" individual rights; emphasis on collective rights for independent, socio-economic development	Policy of reform and opening; gradual formal integration in the international human rights regime	Sanctions against China; isolation in human rights policies; relativistic cultural position (debate on Chinese/Asian values)	Formal acceptance of the principle of universal human rights; priority of rights to development, and social and economic rights

Based on Heilmann/Schmidt 2014.

© MERICS

5.2.2 Political opposition and protest movements

Since the 1950s the Communist regime has suppressed all manner of organized political opposition. Numerous intellectuals and party critics took advantage of brief
phases of liberalization, occurring in 1957 (the Hundred Flowers Campaign) and in
1976 (the April Fifth Movement, commemorating the death of Premier Zhou Enlai)
to protest against practices by the Communist Party. Beginning with the Democracy
Wall Movement of 1978–79, there have been periodic demands for the regime to
honor human and civil rights on a broad scale.

During the urban protests of 1989, the terms "democracy" and "human rights"
became associated with political solutions that expressed the population's rejection
of political despotism and longing for greater freedoms. The protests began with
Beijing students, whose demonstrations and hunger strikes in Tiananmen Square
succeeded in mobilizing as many as two million citizens to oppose inflation, corruption, and abuses of power. In the night of June 4, 1989, the Chinese military moved
in with guns and tanks to crack down on the protesters. Although approximations
of the total death toll vary, it is estimated that between 500 and 1,500 people were
killed in Tiananmen Square. Across the nation as a whole, tens of thousands of dem-
onstrators were arrested. Thousands were jailed and dozens sentenced to death
(Brook 1998; Schier, Cremerius, and Fischer 1993).

The suppression of the Tiananmen Square protesters marked a turning point in
Chinese political development. As a consequence of the shock resulting from the violent manner in which the protests were quelled, political apathy became prevalent
in Chinese society. In the aftermath of the protests, policy makers made specific attempts to depoliticize the people by channeling all of society's energy into economic
development. The political idealism that had been widespread among the younger
generation in the 1980s was replaced by a focus on economic growth and consumption, energetically promoted by the Communist Party. Grassroots political activism
no longer found any resonance in China. Although a few underground organizations
came into being in some of China's major cities in the 1990s, these organizations
generally had no more than several dozen members. In 1998, several hundred dissidents in various parts of the country combined forces to form the China Democracy
Party. The security forces took rigorous measures to prevent this party from becoming a major political organization.

At the same time, however, the number of local protests has increased apace
(see Section 5.8). The protests usually focus on specific objectives, such as eliminating local abuses of power (including, for example, refusals to pay outstanding wages
or to pay compensation to residents for the demolition of their residences or to halt
the spread of environmental degradation). Although the protesters do not directly
approach the Communist Party leadership with their demands, they do put those in

power under pressure because the legitimacy of the Communist Party leadership rests on the promise of prosperity for the people and a stable society.

Due to the rapid proliferation of new communications technologies and social media in China, activists and critics, who had formerly acted in isolation, have been able to connect with a far greater share of the population. Rather than calling for a general transformation of the political system, they voice specific demands. One example is the rights-protection attorneys who support "safeguarding the legal rights" (维权) of protesting farmers or workers. Another is journalists who use the Internet to monitor corruption and power abuses by local cadres. Other activists have cooperated with local NGOs or have supported "independent candidates" (独立参选人) in direct elections to the people's congresses at the county levels. New ways of connecting and launching campaigns have come into being due to the new technologies.

However, party organs and security forces have regarded the new methods of linking up previously isolated elements of society as a serious political challenge and in 2008 they began stepping up their repressive measures. On International Human Rights Day in December 2008, 300 intellectuals published on the Internet a citizens' rights manifesto, known as Charter '08, and called for additional supporters to sign. Before the government shut down the website in January 2009, more than 8,000 people from entirely different strata of society had come out in support of the call to action. As a result, writer and human-rights activist Liu Xiaobo—one of the initiators of Charter '08—was eventually sentenced to eleven years in prison. In 2010, while still incarcerated in China, he was awarded the Nobel Peace Prize.

When vague references to a "Jasmine Revolution" in China (named after the Jasmine Revolution in Tunisia that brought down the government) began making the rounds on the Internet in 2011, China's security forces preemptively began rounding up political activists in several cities and either imprisoning them or placing them under house arrest. However, there was no visible organization or concept behind the Chinese "jasmine" rallies. The harsh official reaction reflected a deep-rooted uncertainty regarding the future stability of the regime and its support in society. Government expenditures for "maintaining stability" as well as the size of the security forces have been rising sharply since 2008, and the new leadership that took power in 2012 has increased pressure on human-rights activists. Beijing attorney Xu Zhiyong, who had attempted to establish a New Citizens' Movement (新公民运动) as a national network, was sentenced to four years in prison for having "disrupted public order." Other human-rights activists have been either imprisoned or placed under house arrest.

Since 2008 the Communist Party leadership has left no doubt that it intends to nip in the bud any and all form of cross-regional political activism. This approach to maintaining stability is expected to increase due to the intensification of conflicts of interest and the quick proliferation of information, including information that the government wishes to keep suppressed.

5.3 Rural society

Matthias Stepan and Sebastian Heilmann

Since the introduction of the reform and opening policy, the structure of China's rural society has undergone a fundamental transformation. The disintegration of rural communities in the 1980s and the gradual liberalization of the household registration system since the mid-1990s (see Section 5.1.3) have had a major impact on the living conditions and employment opportunities for residents in rural regions of the country. Furthermore, considerable disparities continue to exist between the levels of development in rural and urban areas. However, it is difficult to make sweeping generalizations about China's "rural society" and its development potential because of the vast and glaring discrepancies between the impoverished regions in the west and the economically advantaged coastal areas, and between the barren mountainous regions and the fertile loess regions. The following sections therefore focus on major trends.

5.3.1 Social change in rural areas

China's rural society has changed dramatically since the 1980s. According to official National Bureau of Statistics (NBS) data, the proportion of the population classified as rural residents in 2014 was about 45 percent. In contrast, in 1990 almost three-quarters of the total population lived in rural areas. Furthermore, the number of workers in rural regions has been declining since 1997: from a workforce of around 490 million in 1997 (constituting approximately 70 percent of the total working population then) to under 387 million in 2013 (almost exactly 50 percent of the total working population). Of these 387 million people, more than one-half were migrant workers pursuing employment in metropolitan regions, either permanently or on a seasonal basis.

The labor market in the rural regions is extremely heterogeneous and there are considerable regional variations. In 2011, about two-thirds of the rural workforce was still employed in the agricultural and forestry sectors. This is a sharp drop in comparison to the 80 percent in the early 1990s. One of the reasons for this fluctuation is the introduction of new cultivation techniques, which increase productivity while requiring less manpower.

This transformation was initially sparked by the agricultural and rural development policies of the 1980s. Nationwide implementation of the household (or contract) responsibility system (家庭承包责任制) allowed rural households to sell their surplus produce on free markets at unregulated prices. After the gradual elimination of the rural collective economy (the "people's communes"), private-sector businesses gradually began to emerge in the rural areas. Today many different kinds of endeavors, ranging from profitable specialist agricultural enterprises to wealthy private households to farmers struggling for survival on modest incomes exist in the rural areas. The emergence in the 1980s of township and village enterprises (TVEs) (乡镇企业), which were increasingly operated as private companies, provided new employment opportunities outside the agricultural sector.

In spite of these changes, rural society has benefited less than the urban population from the enormous growth of the Chinese economy. The income gap between urban and rural households has been increasing since the early 1990s. In 2014 the average annual income of rural households was about one-third of that in urban areas (see Table 5.3.A). In some cases, despite rising income levels, the overall supply situation in the rural areas has actually deteriorated. The dissolution of the collective economy and the people's communes was followed by bottlenecks with regard to the provision of public services, particularly in terms of health and education. To close this gap and create alternatives, in the 1990s the Chinese government experimented with market-based solutions. Rural residents were forced to accept the high costs for schooling and healthcare, for example, while the revenue generat-

Table 5.3.A

Rural household incomes and urban-rural income gaps, 1990–2014

	1990	1995	2000	2005	2010	2011	2012	2013	2014
Average annual rural income (in CNY)	686	1,578	2,253	3,255	5,919	6,977	7,917	8,896	9,892
As a percentage of the annual income of urban households	45%	37%	36%	31%	31%	32%	32%	33%	33%

Based on NBS 2013a, 2015a.

© MERICS

ed from agricultural products declined (Shue/Wong 2007). In addition, in many areas the rural population was burdened by an extremely confusing array of taxes, special levies, and fees, often charged at random by local governments.

5.3.2 Rural poverty and rural development policies

Up until the mid-1970s many Chinese provinces were hit by periodic famines and repeated supply bottlenecks in a number of rural regions. Rural poverty was the subject of heated debates in the Politburo in 1975, when, in the face of those advocating ideological collectivist campaigns, Deng Xiaoping pushed for increased individual material incentives to expand the agricultural economy. Deng's efforts initially failed, but following Mao's death, he tenaciously enforced a review of the collectivist social policy in the rural areas.

Since 1986, coordination of China's fight against poverty at the national level has been the responsibility of a central Leading Small Group under the State Council. Governments at the provincial, and especially at the county, level are responsible for implementing alleviation measures. In terms of the content and partial funding of the poverty reduction programs, international organizations—in particular, the United Nations Development Programme (UNDP), the Asian Development Bank (ADB), and the World Bank—and national development agencies, such as the Deutsche Gesellschaft für internationale Zusammenarbeit (German Corporation for International Cooperation, or GIZ for short) have played an active supporting role. However, the decades of more or less continuously high rates of economic growth and the associated new income opportunities, which, admittedly, are distributed extremely unevenly, have been the decisive factors in rapidly reducing the amount of absolute poverty in China.

According to official government statistics, based on the 2010 rural poverty alleviation standard, the proportion of the rural population living below the official poverty level decreased from 17.2 percent (165 million people) in 2010 to 7.2 percent (70.2 million people) in 2014 (NBS 2015a). Based on the World Bank's higher poverty threshold, there were still over 84 million Chinese living in poverty in 2010—around 11.18 percent of the total population—in *both* the urban and rural areas (World Bank 2014). The official poverty level established by the Chinese government at the end of 2011 was set at an extremely low annual per capita income of the equivalent of USD 1.00 per day), whereas the threshold defined by the World Bank in 2014 was USD 1.90 per day (at 2011 purchasing power parity [PPP]). Despite the different assessment criteria, no international organization has questioned the PRC's exceptional progress in alleviating poverty. These advances rank among the major humanitarian successes of the Chinese economic reform policies (UNDP 1997, 1999, 2001, 2008).

The substantial decrease in poverty in the 1980s was a consequence of measures taken to liberalize agricultural markets (see Section 5.3.1): the introduction of market incentives was sufficient to trigger a strong increase in productivity without major government investments. In the 1990s, government initiatives aimed at combating poverty in economically isolated and underdeveloped regions made slow progress, despite an ambitious program and generous international aid. In 1998 the CCP Central Committee passed a decision aimed at modernizing the rural areas. However, structural deficits were not openly addressed until after 2000 by the so-called "three rural issues" formula (三农问题): the social predicament of Chinese farmers (农民), the outdated agricultural structure (农业), and the lack of administrative capacity in Chinese villages (农村) (Ahlers 2014c).

Since the early 1990s, Chinese government departments—supported by experts from the World Bank and other international organizations—have been working on plans for extensive modernization of the rural areas (Nyberg/Rozelle 1999). Repeated initiatives were introduced to reduce the fiscal burdens on China's farmers, but for years the measures remained patchy and ineffective. In 2000 the CCP leadership announced a nationwide reform of rural taxes and administrative fees (农村税费改革), with the previous array of fees and taxes to be pooled in a general agriculture tax amounting to no more than 7 percent of the total farming income. However, this plan did not have the desired effect. The fiscal burden was reduced only marginally, while in many rural regions the provision of public goods (health and education) deteriorated due to the reduced budget revenue generated in counties and townships. Periods of sharply falling prices for agricultural products also increased the need for action with regard to economic and social policy in the rural areas. Underemployment and a lack of employment prospects in rural society sparked a series of violent protests (Bernstein/Lü Xiaobo 2003) (see Section 5.8).

Following the 2002 and 2003 changes in party and state leadership, a change in policy with respect to rural development was introduced. The focus of the political agenda of the Hu Jintao and Wen Jiabao leadership was to improve rural livelihoods. In March 2003 new legal regulations on land-leasing contracts and land-use rights entered into effect. Under the new regulations, China's rural population is allowed to sell future land-use rights on a voluntary and legal basis, and farmers are to receive adequate compensation for transfers of land-use rights. Farmers' rights have thus been strengthened against random local-government actions, and they are better protected from land grabs by real-estate developers. At the same time, the central government pursued its economic objectives by establishing larger business operations, managed by entrepreneurs, in the rural areas. The government also introduced a new urbanization strategy (with a focus on developing small and medium-sized cities) in order to provide unemployed farmers and impoverished rural populations with new employment opportunities (see Section 5.3.3). The Hu–Wen administration also took a new course with respect to expanding the social-security system in the rural areas. Several pilot projects were initiated in 2003, including the rural minimum living standard security system (农村低保) and rural health insurance, both of which were supported by extensive state subsidies.

A comprehensive program aimed at structural reforms in the rural areas and the building of a "new socialist countryside" (社会主义新农村建设) took shape during the 11th Five-Year Plan (2006–10) period. Part of this program involved the central-government's official abolition in 2006 of the various local agricultural taxes and special fees. This meant, however, a sudden substantial loss of local fiscal revenue. But due to the increase in tax revenue generated at the national level, the government was able to increase transfer payments to local administrative levels. As a result, fiscal and social stability in the rural areas in the decade following 2006 became increasingly dependent on the transfer of funds from higher administrative levels (see Section 6.7).

5.3.3 Migrant workers and urban–rural integration

The impact of migration on the urban economy is an obvious indication of the fundamental social changes that have been taking place in Chinese society since the 1980s. According to official surveys, about 298 million Chinese—almost one-fifth of the total population—were classified as migrant workers (农民工) in 2014 (NBS 2015a, 2015c). Regarding patterns of geographical mobility, more than two-thirds of these migrant workers have left their home counties. However, only about one-third have migrated across provincial borders in search of higher wages. The majority of construction workers, domestic help, and food services staff employed in the cities comes from the rural areas. In many cities, the migrant population is concentrated in certain neighborhoods where they organize into groups based on kinship or ethnicity and establish their own social infrastructure (kindergartens, schools, health counseling, etc.) because they are usually excluded from municipal facilities.

In principle, the Hu–Wen administration supported gradually achieving equal treatment of urban citizens and rural migrant workers. In many places, however, migrant workers remained second-class citizens without access to public services or fixed housing. Urban governments regarded migrant workers primarily as a cheap, replaceable source of labor. Although the rural workforce made an essential contribution to economic growth and to improvements in the provision of services in the cities, its concentration in certain neighborhoods and its tendency to stay for longer periods led to migrant workers being deemed a risk group by many cities in terms of increasing the potential for crime and social unrest.

In the 1980s local governments attempted to restrict the influx of migrants and to send "illegal" immigrants home. Since the mid-1990s, however, the central government has been attempting to improve the administrative coordination of migration movements. New nationwide registration regulations were introduced in 1995, requiring that migrant workers receive permission to migrate from the relevant rural authority and obtain a temporary residence permit from the city authorities. Some local governments formalized the process of allocating residence permits. The city of Guangzhou, for example, introduced a point system whereby a migrant's educational background or financial position to purchase an apartment plays a significant role.

Discrimination against rural migrants in Chinese cities is no longer passively accepted by the second generation of migrant workers, who are better educated, have often grown up in the cities, and have no desire to return to their rural origins. There has been a significant rise in the number of individual and collective protests, particularly among industrial workers. China's young generation of migrant workers has stood up for equal treatment both as citizens and as employees, revealing much more assertiveness than the extremely acquiescent agricultural generation to which their parents belonged.

In 2014 the central government passed a national plan to expand small and medium-sized cities. The program for "new forms of urbanization" (新型城镇化规划) included restricting the influx of migrant workers to Beijing, Shanghai, and Tianjin as well as to selected provincial capitals. Previously, only thirty cities, absorbing one-third of all China's migrants, were deemed to be especially attractive destinations for migrants. As a result, urban infrastructure and urban public services were increasingly stretched to their limits (see Table 5.3.B). The government therefore decided to regulate and support the previously largely uncontrolled process through an extremely costly new urbanization program. It also sought to open up new economic growth potentials in the urban centers (see Section 6.15).

Table 5.3.B

Top destinations of Chinese migrant workers, 2014

Total	Directly administered municipalities		Provincial capitals		Cities		Small towns		Other(s)	
No. (million)	No. (million)	Percentage	No. (million)	Percentage	No. (million)	Percentage	No. (million)	Percentage	No. (million)	Percentage
168	13.6	8.1	37.7	22.4	57.5	34.2	58.6	34.9	0.7	0.4

Based on NBS 2015c.

© MERICS

5.4 Urban society and new social forces

Kristin Shi-Kupfer and Sebastian Heilmann

After the CCP came to power in 1949, there was a radical transformation of China's traditional social structure. The social classes that had previously dominated (such as landlords and merchants) were suppressed. Ownership rights were changed fundamentally due to radical redistributive measures (land reform, collectivization of agriculture, and nationalization of key industries).

New fluid social structures have been developing in Chinese cities since the 1980s as a result of the differentiation of income structures, professional groups, and consumption and communications patterns. Thus far, the political consequences of these changes in the social structure have been deeply contradictory and may turn out to be different than those suggested by the experiences of other societies (where the wealthy, educated middle classes demanded political rights and thus accelerated the transition to democracy) in the nineteenth and twentieth centuries.

5.4.1 Income differentiation and social mobility

Up until 1978, Chinese society was characterized by a de facto egalitarian distribution of income and an extremely low level of wealth. Due to the privileged treatment of the urban population with public services, however, there was a clear gap between urban and rural society in terms of the provision of food and housing as well as education and health; this gap is not properly reflected by conventional statistics on income distribution. The diverse benefits enjoyed by functionaries (government apartments, domestic staff, government cars, etc.) are not conveyed in official income statistics, nor is the "gray income" generated in the shadow or alternative economy.

Various calculations of the Gini coefficient (a measure of income distribution between 0 [perfect equality] and 1 [maximal inequality]) come to the unanimous conclusion that the current unequal distribution of wealth in the PRC is most pronounced among all East Asian countries. According to official sources, the coefficient reached an all-time high of 0.49 in 2008, and in spite of government measures aimed at redistributing wealth it remained at 0.47 in 2012. According to official statistics, the Gini coefficient in 1978 was 0.21 in the rural areas and 0.16 in the urban regions.

The economic reforms that began in 1978–79 helped many urban households achieve a rapid leap in their living standards and consumption levels. The benefits of this increase are extremely unevenly distributed among the various regions (see Table 5.4.A). Nevertheless, according to official statistics, the previously widening gap between urban and rural income levels has been narrowing since 2006 (Lü Qingzhe 2013).

Table 5.4.A

Annual income and consumption by region, 2013						
Administrative division		Per capita net annual income (CNY, rounded)	Number of household devices per 100 households			
			Personal computers	Washing machines	Cell phones	Air conditioners
Shanghai	Urban	43,900	144	101	240	207
	Rural	19,600	49	90	200	136
Henan	Urban	22,400	74	100	200	138
	Rural	8,500	20	93	194	37
Guizhou	Urban	20,700	71	100	215	22
	Rural	5,400	5	70	173	0,8
Tibet	Urban	20,000	63	88	187	15
	Rural	6,600	0.5	8	132	0.2

Based on NBS 2013b, 2014b.

© MERICS

Comprehensive studies by the Chinese Academy of Social Sciences (CASS) (中国社会科学院) (Lu Xueyi 2002, 2010) divide contemporary Chinese society into ten professional and financial categories based on income, status, access to opportunities, and qualifications and position within or outside of state-affiliated structures (see Table 5.4.B). A popular model based on these studies, defining a demarcation criterion for each class, is a regular feature of academic blogs on the Internet.

Surveys suggest that the majority of Chinese people regard their social mobility as extremely restricted. Lower and lower-middle-class Chinese do not perceive an improvement in their social status in comparison to that of their parents, observing a fixed class affiliation over at least two generations (Goodman 2014). In the 2010s, popular designations for social identities have mirrored this perception: terms such as "second generation of government officials" (官二代) or "rich second generation" (富二代) have been frequently used by state media. Many of those

Table 5.4.B

Social classes based on opportunities for social participation*

1.	Leading party cadres (Politburo level)	Involved in decision-making at the national level	
2.	Cadres at the ministerial level; CEOs of "national champions"	Access to decision-making at the national level	Upper class
3.	Cadres at the vice-ministerial level; provincial-level cadres; managers of large enterprises	Involved in some political and economic decision-making	
4.	Leading local cadres; prominent advisers and professors; media stars	Selective access to the upper classes	
5.	Mid-level cadres; small entrepreneurs; professors; regional stars	Possibility of advancing to the upper middle classes	Middle class
6.	Civil servants; white-collar workers; teachers; freelancers; engineers	Limited opportunities for advancement	
7.	Clerks; skilled workers; well-off farmers	Regular, but modest incomes	
8.	Factory workers; migrant workers; farmers in wealthier regions	Living at the subsistence level	Lower class
9.	Unemployed workforce in the urban areas; farmers in impoverished regions	Living below the subsistence level	

Note: *A popular class model found in a number of different variations in China's social media. Based on Baidu tieba 2013; Tianya shequ 2013; Zhihu 2013; Zhonghua luntan 2013.

© MERICS

questioned consider a person's family background to be the main criterion for their social status and their likelihood of success in life (see Figure 5.4).

5.4.2 China's new middle classes: Professionals and private entrepreneurs

One of the most frequently discussed social changes in China is the emergence of a new urban middle class, characterized, among other things, by a comparatively

Figure 5.4

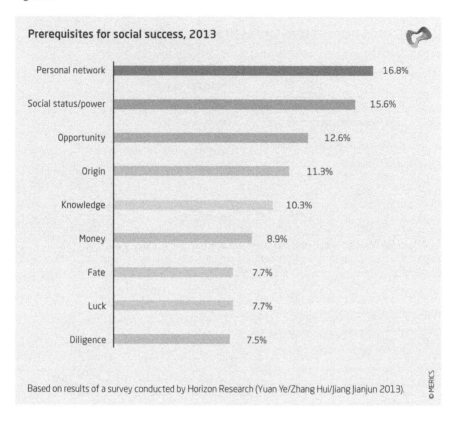

Prerequisites for social success, 2013

Personal network	16.8%
Social status/power	15.6%
Opportunity	12.6%
Origin	11.3%
Knowledge	10.3%
Money	8.9%
Fate	7.7%
Luck	7.7%
Diligence	7.5%

Based on results of a survey conducted by Horizon Research (Yuan Ye/Zhang Hui/Jiang Jianjun 2013).

© MERICS

high level of education, a stable household income, and an increasing level of private wealth. The members of this class belong to a variety of different professional groups, including managers of state-owned enterprises, architects, and administrative employees who advanced into the middle classes as a consequence of the economic reforms. Other professions such as entrepreneurs, attorneys, realtors, and IT specialists also developed in the context of China's economic growth. Although national averages should be treated with considerable caution, social scientist Lu Xueyi has noted that the middle class constituted about 23 percent of China's total population in 2008 (Xinhuanet 2009). Based on an annual income of between USD 10,000 and USD 100,000, China's middle classes comprised about 300 million people in 2013, some 22 percent of the total population (Credit Suisse 2014).

The so-called professionals (职业人) have become an important group among the middle classes. These include attorneys, journalists, IT specialists, doctors, engineers, and academics who have developed particular professional standards and who make specific demands regarding their quality of life as a consequence of their educational levels and social statuses. Many professionals have spent time studying abroad and have returned to China—often lured by government assistance schemes—as "overseas returnees" (海归, a homonym of 海龟, meaning "turtles") with globalized mindsets and a wealth of international experience. The professionalism of these returning academics, attorneys, and journalists are therefore based on global standards, often leading to tensions and disappointments with regard to government attempts to exert political and ideological controls. With respect to how professionals perceive themselves and how they are regarded by the media and in public discussions, the concept of personal "quality" (素质), in terms of educational levels and cultivated behavior, is often used as a criterion to distinguish professionals (who consider themselves to have high "qualities" and qualifications) from private entrepreneurs (who are not always credited with such personal "qualities").

Due to the extremely heterogeneous social backgrounds of private entrepreneurs (ranging from college graduates to self-made men without high-school diplomas) and their considerable variations in economic status—larger private enterprises carry considerable weight with the authorities in their capacity as significant sources of tax revenue and without a need to form alliances to represent their interests—private entrepreneurs tend not to have a strongly developed group identity. Relations between private businesses and local governments vary considerably, depending on their level of influence. In regions with a high percentage of private entrepreneurs (in Zhejiang or Fujian provinces, for example) local authorities

Table 5.4.C

China's super rich and their wealth, 1999-2015

Year	Number of rich persons on the Hurun list	Wealth threshold for a listing in the "Top 50" (million USD)	Number of billionaires (USD)
1999	50	6	1
2002	100	145	0
2005	400	320	7
2008	1,000	1,500	101
2011	1,000	2,700	271
2014	1,271	3,300	354
2015	1,738	4,700	556

Based on Hurun Report 1999-2015.

have often attempted to shield the interests of the business community from central-government interventions and restrictions.

According to official figures, the number of private entrepreneurs increased sevenfold from about two million in 2001 to approximately 14 million by the end of 2014. Private companies of all sizes (from local small businesses to listed corporations such as Alibaba) have generated as much as two-thirds of China's gross domestic product (GDP). Given the continuing preferential political treatment of state-owned enterprises, however, private entrepreneurs still see themselves confronted by numerous forms of discrimination in terms of legal security and access to loans. Nonetheless, China's private entrepreneurs have been successful in accruing astronomical levels of private individual wealth (see Table 5.4.C).

Surveys have repeatedly revealed that many Chinese people look up to the super rich as role models. Debates on class envy or violent attacks on millionaires and billionaires are extremely rare, despite the fact that the legitimacy of the wealth of China's nouveaux riches (暴发户) is often strongly contested and there have been calls for a greater degree of social responsibility.

5.4.3 Patterns of consumption and political attitudes

At the end of the 1980s, China's urban population began to have access to an increasingly diverse and attractive range of products and services, not to mention ideas and values. Products and thinkers from Western industrialized countries became icons of progress and freedom. Following the crackdown on the urban protest movement in 1989, the CCP leadership attempted to overcome the misgivings of the elite by loosening constraints on market dynamics. Large sections of urban society accepted the promises of prosperity and growing consumption as the basis for the legitimacy of the Chinese leadership. China's middle classes remained politically silent, seeking an identity and values primarily in commerce and consumerism. The pursuit of status and security also defined the consumption patterns of the urban population. Buying a car, which represented personal mobility, became one of the key indicators of upper- or middle-class status in the late 1990s (see Table 5.4.D).

The extensive move in the direction of consumerism was intended to be in the interests of the party leadership, acting as a substitute for a lack of political participation, and this objective was indeed achieved. With the exception of sporadic protest movements at the local levels, the CCP's vision of a social contract in post-1989 China proved to be surprisingly viable. Although the government promised an increase in material prosperity and authoritarian stability both internally and externally, the overwhelming majority of the population stagnated in political docility and passivity.

Table 5.4.D

Per capita annual cash living expenditures of urban households, 2012

	Lowest income house-holds (10% of all house-holds)	Low-income house-holds (10%)	Lower middle income house-holds (20%)	Middle income house-holds (20%)	Upper middle income house-holds (20%)	High-income house-holds (10%)	High-est income house-holds (10%)
Share of consumer spending for specific goods (in %, rounded)							
Food	45	43	41	39	36	33	27
Clothing	10	11	11	11	11	11	10
Housing	11	10	9	9	9	8	8
House-hold goods	6	6	6	6	7	7	7
Trans-portation and commu-nications	8	10	11	13	15	17	21
Edu-cation; culture; recrea-tion	10	11	11	11	12	13	14
Health-care and medical services	8	7	7	7	6	6	5
Other	2	3	3	3	4	5	6

Note: Distribution of household expenditures per decile (ten equal parts).
Based on NBS 2013b.

© MERICS

Even among China's consumer-oriented urban middle classes, defense of their newly acquired property has led to only sporadic political involvement: apartment owners began to organize owners' meetings to defend the value of their real estate vis-à-vis developers, real-estate managers, or local-government authorities (in the event of a chemical factory or a waste-incineration facility being built in the vicinity of their property, for example). However, this type of self-organization remained focused on the material interests of the involved individuals. It was manifested in the form of "NIMBY" activities ("not in my backyard!") that were extremely limited in terms of content and geographical location and that rarely had an impact beyond the affected neighborhood.

Official surveys of the political views of China's population reflect widespread apathy. Experience has shown that surveys on politically sensitive topics in China are subject to a high degree of distortion, however: respondents tend to be cautious and to give the answers they think the authorities want to hear. Nevertheless, researchers based at the CASS (Comprehensive Survey Team on the Chinese Social Situation 2013) came to the conclusion that the majority of respondents had never been involved in legal institutionalized forms of participation (such as voting for local people's congress candidates) or in unofficial political activities (owners' demonstrations or online protests), nor did they harbor any aspirations for future involvement. Among those questioned, 40 percent were satisfied with the opportunities for political participation promoted and regulated by the government, such as residents' committees or village elections. A desire for noninvolvement or even explicit disinterest in such forms of involvement prevailed among the respondents.

In contrast, surveys on specific social issues show signs of an emerging political consciousness with regard to the distribution of wealth and social equality. In a 2013 survey, 34 percent of those questioned rated the social order as basically unjust. Among the respondents, 30 percent had expressed the same opinion as in an identical survey in 2006. In terms of questions related to "applicable political rights of citizens," there was a particularly marked rise in discontent. Surveys carried out among students (who are generally less cautious in their responses than the average adult citizen) reveal that almost two-thirds of those questioned considered CCP cadres to be cool and calculating, motivated primarily by their own best interests and lacking any real empathy for the concerns of the general public (Zhao Lianfei/Tian Feng 2013).

5.4.4 Indications of a nascent civil society

Historically, well-educated and wealthy urban populations have repeatedly proven to be a political force capable of successfully pressing the state for fundamental political rights. In other East Asian states, particularly Taiwan and South Korea, the new urban middle classes played a significant role in democratization efforts as part of a politically active civil society. The question of whether there are signs of an emerging civil society in China has been a source of heated discussions ever since 1989 (Brook/Frolic 1997; Teets 2014; Zheng/Fewsmith 2008). The debates revolve around issues that are familiar throughout the history of democracy: the problems of self-organization in society, community spirit, the foundations of social pluralism, and the differentiation of the state, the economy, and the political public.

To date, the majority of China's urban population has remained first and foremost interested in climbing the social ladder—by attaining higher levels of income and amassing personal wealth—and in political stability. Private entrepreneurs have profited from the economic reforms and fostered close contacts with political and administrative elites in order to safeguard their business activities. They have not become an autonomous sociopolitical force vis-à-vis the state due to the fact that their economic success rests on the protection provided by party and government functionaries (Chen Jie/Dickson 2010; Dickson 2008).

Beyond the open articulation of interests and self-organization, however, there have also been signs of a greater sensitivity toward political and social inconsistencies in some sectors of urban society due to the rising levels of education and wealth. The rapid spread of the Internet has fostered a pluralism of information and a general suspicion of political and economic elites, but these are rarely expressed openly.

Open political activities are banned in the cities. However, a growing number of city dwellers are involved in volunteer work and donate money for charitable purposes (Shi-Kupfer/Zhu Yi 2014). Cases of failure to render assistance at accident scenes in everyday life have sparked profoundly self-critical public debates on the reasons for the emergence of a ruthless and immoral society. Shortcomings in the political and economic systems are not the only factors cited as possible causes for the moral decay and decline in trust within society. Controversial media and online debates also criticize the urban middle classes for being jointly responsible.

These debates clearly indicate that there is a critical public emerging in Chinese urban society that is not constrained by state media or government attempts to manipulate opinion. If present tendencies continue—despite widespread efforts by the government to actively steer public opinion in cyberspace and social media—China's future political, economic, and social development will no longer be shaped primarily by authoritarian decisions, but rather it will likely be characterized by a much wider range of interests and values.

One social group that has rapidly gained prestige and influence during the course of the 2010s is the so-called "geeks" (极客). This is the term used in China to refer to entrepreneurs who have successfully set up their own companies in IT-based sectors, mobile communications, or e-commerce. IT entrepreneurs in China are not at all derided as being unworldly "nerds"; rather, they are hailed as trendsetters and role models. Many young entrepreneurs in the IT sector display a remarkable level of self-confidence and sense of mission. Bolstered by the opportunities provided by social media, they have pushed themselves into the public eye and have attracted a huge online following. Instead of following state careers, hierarchies, plans, or the ideological appeals of the party leadership, China's IT startup generation is exploiting technological innovations and entrepreneurial expansions to work toward a sweeping transformation of social communications and lifestyles without directly challenging the political authority of the CCP, at least for the time being.

The popularity of China's IT entrepreneurs embodies a profound shift in values, future expectations, and behavioral patterns, especially among the younger generations. These changing expectations are bound to have an impact on the political system in the long term (unless drastic restrictions are placed on the private IT sector). The current exclusive methods of interest aggregation, authoritarian administrative actions, and lack of responsiveness to societal demands are likely to become increasingly incompatible with China's aspiring information and communications society in the future.

5.5 Social organizations and trade unions

Lea Shih, Yi Zhu, Matthias Stepan, and Sebastian Heilmann

The emergence of a public and civil society in China is closely linked to the question of whether it is possible to form social organizations, since such organizations, acting as mediators between state and society, would be in a position to articulate and aggregate group interests. There was nothing resembling a system of associations in China immediately before the policy of reform and opening was initiated. Special interests were represented solely within and among the organs of the party-state. This included the "mass organizations" established by the party, particularly the All-China Federation of Trade Unions (see Section 5.5.2).

Against this background, it is all the more remarkable that a system of social associations has developed as rapidly and become as strongly diversified as it has since 1978–79. A wide variety of new forms of social organizations appeared during the 1980s and 1990s, especially in China's urban areas. After 2004, with the advent of the government's program to create a "new socialist countryside," the number of organizations dedicated to agricultural and rural development also grew dramatically.

At the end of 2014, there was a total of approximately 310,000 officially registered social organizations in China. In addition, there were about 292,000 registered noncommercial, nonprofit organizations (foundations, charities, etc.; see Table 5.5.A). They dealt with social challenges in fields as varied as healthcare, vocational training and higher education, poverty alleviation, or environmental protection—areas in which the government was granting social organizations increasing scope for action.

Table 5.5.A

The development of social organizations in the PRC, 2004-14

	2004	2006	2008	2010	2012	2014
Social organizations	153,359	191,946	229,681	245,256	271,131	309,736
Nonprofit organizations	135,181	161,303	182,382	198,175	225,108	292,195
Foundations	892	1,144	1,597	2,200	3,029	4,117

Based on MOCA 2013; NBS 2015a.

© MERICS

5.5.1 State regulation of social organizations

Regulation of associations is one of the most politically sensitive matters in the PRC. After 1989, state policy with respect to social organizations was characterized by a dual strategy: suppression of organizations that could pose a potential threat to the CCP's power monopoly on the one hand, and efforts to create a tightly knit corporatist integration of new social forces on the other.

The corporatist integration strategy has been undergoing modification since the mid-2000s, when the government announced a cautious functional classification and division of labor between government and society (政社分开) and encouraged new forms of social self-organization in politically nonsensitive areas. At subnational levels, frequently competing organizations were allowed in several fields of work or economic sectors. Up to that point, government-affiliated organizations had exercised a monopoly of representation in specific sectors. In 2013, the previously very restrictive barriers for official registration were relaxed: new organizations were no longer required to submit proof of state surety and sponsorship in order to register. However, the looser rules explicitly excluded human-rights and religious organizations as well as transnational NGOs. Organizations of this nature remained subject to restrictive approval constraints. The ban on establishing political organizations, even only potentially party-like organizations, remained intact.

The intention behind allowing competing organizations in the economic sphere was to improve representation of private-sector interests. Public lobbying is not allowed according to the principles of the socialist system. Thus, economic and industrial associations, in the sense of pressure groups of a sharply defined clientele, are not mentioned in government documents. However, in practice lobbying is a standard part of everyday life for Chinese business associations (see Table 5.5.B). The article on the protection of private property that was added to the constitution in 2004, for example, was the outcome of a quietly persistent campaign waged for years by the national umbrella organization of private entrepreneurs, the All-China Federation of Industry and Commerce (ACFIC) (中华全国工商业联合会). With this article, private property was given constitutional protection on a par with public property (see Heilmann/Schulte-Kulkmann/Shih 2004).

National industrial-sector federations frequently originate from state-sector administrations and they maintain extremely close ties with both the government

Table 5.5.B

Selected associations active in national economic policy making

Association	Members represented
China Enterprise Directors' Association, CEDA	Umbrella organization of employers' associations
China Group Companies Association, CGCA	Major state-owned enterprises ("national champions")
China Association of Automobile Manufacturers, CAAM	Automobile manufacturers
China Association for Science and Technology, CAST	Industrial enterprises
Securities Association of China, SAC	Securities firms
All-China Federation of Industry and Commerce, ACFIC	Larger private enterprises

© MERICS

and major corporations. Therefore, they primarily represent the interests of state-owned companies and can actively influence national industrial policy and funding programs (Shih 2015).

5.5.2 Party-controlled trade unions

Contrary to the growing importance of business associations, representation of employees' interests by trade unions is coming under increasing pressures. Irrespective of the economic and social changes, the CCP continues to perceive of itself as the "vanguard of the working class" (CCP Constitution 2012). Therefore, the All-China Federation of Trade Unions (ACFTU), which comprised 288 million registered members at the end of 2014 and thus represented 36 percent of the total Chinese workforce, is under the direct supervision of party organs.

The ACFTU is the umbrella organization of 34 regional subdivisions, 12 trade union federations, and approximately 31,000 local union organizations. The full-time functionaries in these organizations belong to the cadre system and are appointed by the organization departments of the CCP (see Section 2.9.1). In addition, as of 2014 there were 2.78 million grassroots organizations, with leaders who are elected by their members under the Trade Union Law and who are responsible for representing the interests of the rank-and-file employees in companies, institutions, and government agencies. In reality, however, free elections are more often the exception than the rule. For the most part, the leaders of the grassroots trade unions are nominated by the party and the trade-union organs responsible for supervision. As a result, the ACFTU has been unable to shed its image as a subsidiary of the CCP.

The Trade Union Law of 1992 (amended in 2001), the Labor Law of 1995, and the Labor Contract Law of 2008 all demand a precarious balancing act on the part of trade unions. Not only are they supposed to represent workers' interests, they are also expected to cooperate harmoniously with company managers and state agencies to promote rapid economic development. As a result of this dual role, trade unions often side with management and local governments in the event of conflicts, instead of standing up for the interests of the workforce. Employee demands for higher wages and social benefits, which are increasingly expressed by strikes and other forms of protest, have the potential to frighten off investors and pose a threat to social stability. Trade unions in China thus seldom take a confrontational approach to representing workers' interests, unlike the case in many Western industrialized nations (Schlinger/Schucher 2014).

Moreover, the setting up of independent trade unions is prohibited. Therefore, workers have no alternative organization to collectively consolidate and assert their own interests. Under these circumstances, they resort to spontaneous strikes or protests to defend themselves against violations of rights or other injustices. As a consequence, the number of unorganized strikes has increased significantly since the 2000s. According to the *China Labour Bulletin* published in Hong Kong, the number of documented strikes rose from 182 in 2011 to 1,379 in 2014. The CCP leadership has reacted with regional experiments to create "harmonious" labor relations through regulated collective bargaining in companies. However, waiving the claim to political control over trade unions or separating union functionaries from the cadre system are not open to debate. Moreover, the reform plans of the CCP leadership under Xi Jinping do not include any provisions to grant official approval for competing worker representation, which would signify abandonment of the representational monopoly of the official trade unions.

5.5.3 Foreign foundations and international NGOs

After the PRC was established, all international nongovernmental organizations (INGOs) were required to terminate their activities in China and to leave the country. After the policy of opening began at the end of the 1970s, the World Wide Fund for Nature (WWF), the Ford Foundation, and Oxfam were among the first INGOs to return to China. At the time, the Chinese government was attempting to modernize with the aid of funding and technical expertise from abroad.

The number of INGOs active in China remained modest into the 1990s, not rising significantly until after the 1995 World Conference on Women in Beijing. As part of this UN event, over 30,000 people from all over the world took part in an NGO forum at which many participating organizations were able to forge contacts with Chinese partners.

There are no authoritative quantitative figures on the widespread presence and activity of INGOs in China. Due to difficult legal and political conditions, most INGOs have been unable to register officially and have persevered with a precarious legal status due to a lack of specific, reliable government regulations. In practice, government bodies have applied a two-step administrative procedure with considerable scope for making and rescinding case-by-case decisions. Based on this procedure, every foreign organization first must find a state-run institution as a guarantor in order to apply for registration with the civil affairs authorities (Yin Deyong 2009). In reality, this has resulted in vast organizational diversity: many INGOs opened permanent representative offices or worked on a project-by-project basis with Chinese partners. Others registered as companies. Under these circumstances, contractual employment of Chinese personnel and visa applications for foreign representatives were characterized by provisional measures with the potential to abruptly jeopardize the entire undertaking if subjected to a strict legal review or in the event of a political conflict.

For this reason, the majority of foreign NGOs active in China sought forms of cooperation with official partners. For instance, a number of German political foundations worked closely with the Central Party School or CASS. Chinese party and government bodies have benefited from such cooperation. A study on NGOs in the United States estimates that between 2002 and 2009 86 percent of the expertise and funds transferred to China went to state institutions (universities, research institutes, government organs, etc.). Chinese nongovernmental organizations (by strict definition, organizations that are not run or financed by the state) received less than one-tenth of the payments for support and cooperation (Peng Jianmei/Liu Youping 2012).

INGOs in China are involved in diverse fields of activity, including the classic sectors of development cooperation, combating poverty, disaster relief, environmental protection, and nature conservation. Since 2000, these fields have expanded to include politically sensitive areas, such as labor rights, gender equality, and administrative and judicial reform. However, the leeway allowed for INGOs to deal with politically delicate topics declined sharply during the initial years of Xi Jinping's leadership.

The Chinese government has demonstrated a deeply ambivalent attitude toward INGOs that has fluctuated over time. In a political system where the state endeavors to guide and control society by applying authoritarian methods, the concept of a self-managed civil society is alien and therefore subject to suspicion. The government regularly alleges that Western INGOs acted as destabilizing and infiltrating political forces in overthrowing the regimes in Eastern Europe and North Africa. In the government's opinion, if covert political activities in the interests of foreign governments lead to INGOs becoming "enemy forces" (敌对势力) aiming to bring about change to the Chinese system, they will no longer be tolerated.

The division between politically sensitive or even hostile activities and desirable development-related fields of activity has always been fluid. When Chinese environmental NGOs protested in 2005 against a large dam construction project on the Nujiang River in Yunnan province, the Chinese government investigated their connections to international environmental organizations. For the next three years, it was close to impossible for any new INGOs to gain a foothold in China. Not until 2008, when international disaster relief poured into China after a major earthquake in Sichuan, did the Chinese government temporarily relax its controls over INGOs (Lin Dechang 2010).

INGOs that deal with issues that are even potentially politically charged—or can suddenly turn explosive in certain contexts—have to deal with official warnings and bans at very short notice or with termination of cooperation with their Chinese guarantors and partner organizations. In 2014 and 2015, inspections of INGOs active in China were again conducted by government authorities and Chinese partner organizations. The CCP leadership intensified the struggle against "infiltration by hostile foreign forces" in society, the media, and the education system. INGOs were classified as potential risks to "state security" in the broad sense and subjected to stricter controls. In the spring of 2015, the draft of a new law on the activities of

INGOs was published. This draft is designed to transfer supervision of the INGOs to the Ministry of Public Security (the police ministry) and to place clear constraints on their activities in China.

5.5.4 Prospects for more open interest intermediation

The number of registered social organizations in China has more than doubled since the turn of the millennium, but this development has not provided the impetus for stronger pluralism in terms of political representation of interests. These seemingly contradictory developments are the result of an attitude of lasting distrust of civic organizations on the part of party and government bodies. The activities of nongovernmental players are rated positively by the government when they take the burden off public bodies with regard to providing public and social services (education, healthcare, care for the elderly and disabled, etc.). However, the authorities remain extremely distrustful of all activities that might spark new political movements in the medium to long term. State-controlled mass organizations such as the ACFTU are behind the times when it comes to mediating between the interests of public bodies and an increasingly pluralistic society that is aware of its own best interests. In the social-services sector, the division of labor between the authorities and NGOs is already changing significantly due to the growing importance of associations and foundations in the public-service sectors. The burgeoning division of labor in this field requires new mechanisms for representation of interests as well as (new) contractual models for the delivery of public goods and services by nonstate bodies. The German corporatist model, and specifically German charitable organizations, is attracting the interest of Chinese government representatives who are seeking more stable forms of balancing the interests of state and society. However, the rights to self-organization and political participation, which are part and parcel of the German corporatist system, continue to be banned by the Chinese.

5.6 The media and public opinion

Yi Zhu

China's media system was altered significantly in the course of the economic reforms. The financially profitable commercialization of the media industry was not, however, accompanied by any sort of political liberalization in the direction of freedom of the press. Despite continuing restrictive media controls, the variety of media content and the number of media makers in pursuit of a freer flow of information and quality journalism have grown. In particular, the rapid spread of the Internet and interactive social media has facilitated public discussions on a greater number of critical issues. Consequently, signs of an energetic, politically active general public have emerged as an accompaniment to official propaganda.

5.6.1 The commercialization of China's media

Ever since its establishment, the CCP has always placed great importance on media policy. Following the Soviet example, the CCP leadership assigned the press the role of the party's "mouthpiece" and "ideological weapon" (Xu Guangchun 2011). The Chinese media were used for political indoctrination from the 1950s through to the end of the Cultural Revolution. After the introduction of the reform and opening policy, advertising was authorized in newspapers, on the radio, and on television. At the time, the political leadership attempted to modernize and commercialize the media system without however surrendering the CCP's control of public opinion. Media institutions underwent a series of structural reforms. They maintained their status as "public-service units" (事业单位), yet at the same time they were supposed to be run as profit-making enterprises.

The state withdrew its subsidies to the majority of China's media outlets during the 1990s. The resultant funding gaps could only be filled by achieving success among consumers and generating revenue from advertising. The various media companies hence engaged in competition with one another, and there was a trend toward consolidation into larger groups covering a wide range of areas. In the 2000s, the propaganda authorities cautiously relaxed rules on the raising of capital: media group branches, with the exception of those with the core tasks of news reporting and propaganda, were allowed to borrow capital through stock-market flotations. Annual turnover in the media industry almost quadrupled between 2004 and 2013 (Cui Baoguo 2009, 2015). As a consequence, the media industry reported significantly higher growth than that of Chinese GDP during the same period.

5.6.2. Media firms and entrepreneurs

The extremely dynamic growth of the media industry reflects the pent-up demands in Chinese society. After decades of biased propaganda, Chinese media users longed for more attractive media services and greater access to information. In the 1980s newspapers began publishing weekend or evening editions in order to provide reader-oriented content as well as to carry out their function as the mouthpiece of the

CCP. The *Southern Weekly* (南方周末), a weekly newspaper founded in Guangzhou in 1984, with critical news reporting and controversial supplements, has become one of the most influential and powerful media outlets in China.

In view of the growing prosperity of the population and the rapid expansion of infrastructure, television became the most popular media sector in the 1990s (by 2009, 97 percent of the total population had access to television). Advertising revenue generated by the national broadcasting company, China Central Television (CCTV), increased from CNY 100 million in 1990 to CNY 14.26 billion in 2011. This was partly due to its monopoly privileges: CCTV is classified as a "unit with vice-ministerial rank" and comes under the mandate of the Central Propaganda Department (中宣部). All Chinese broadcasters at the provincial level are required to transmit CCTV's main evening news program, including its subsequent advertisements, as a joint broadcast. The other factor behind the jump in advertising revenue is that CCTV has sufficient resources to produce a wide range of programs and enjoys long broadcasting hours. CCTV has been broadcasting "Focus Report" (焦点访谈) since 1994, a program that has made investigative reporting socially acceptable in China. "Focus" reports have criticized individual cases of misconduct by local cadres and have exposed selected local problems. Such critical reporting, which targets individual cases without questioning the workings of the political system, acts as a release valve and is popular with the general public.

New Internet-based media have been challenging China's traditional media since the turn of the millennium. By virtue of their status as private companies, online news portals such as Sina, Sohu, or NetEase do not hold a state license for their own news reporting. They do offer commentary and communications platforms, however, that accommodate the interactive media preferences of many users. The rapid growth of the IT sector has made Internet-based media attractive to many experienced journalists and editors. Since the 2010s, some have founded their own media startup companies, known as "WeMedia" (自媒体).

Chinese journalists are often described as "dancers with shackles" (Shirk 2011). In the 1980s, as members of the intellectual elite, they were involved in debates about reform. In 1989 a number of journalists openly sympathized with the student protests and became targets of the security authorities after the crackdown. Many previously prominent journalists were forced to give up their professions, voluntarily changing to other jobs or moving overseas.

Present-day journalists have usually undergone training underpinned by ideological indoctrination, but at the same time they have been influenced by international exchanges and new professional standards (Wu Fei 2009). The notion of the media as an indispensable instrument of control is consistent with their mouthpiece functions as ascribed by the CCP. Surveys clearly indicate that journalists have a significant motivation "to uncover societal problems." China's media makers must constantly be aware of the risks they are taking when they test their space for maneuver by criticizing social problems and those in power. A specific genre has emerged since the 2000s, under the remit of journalistic professionalism. Finance and economics magazines, such as *Caijing* (财经) and *Caixin* (财新), both of which were founded by the pioneering journalist Hu Shuli, began to discover inefficiencies and corruption in companies and regulatory authorities based on substantiated, investigative news reporting. The result has been the development of new criteria for critical and serious quality journalism in the Chinese media industry.

Nevertheless, it should be stressed that China's media industry still generally falls far short in terms of professional journalistic standards as well as in terms of a binding code of ethics. Extremely stiff competition for advertising revenue, a lack of separation between editorial work and management tasks, and a lack of self-control have all led to the spread of corruption in China's media companies. Even the media group that publishes *Southern Weekly*, previously regarded as the spearhead of quality journalism, was the subject of investigations into corruption in 2014, leading to a temporary shutdown. It is common practice for business firms to make special payments to journalists to secure more favorable reports, either with respect to financial statements and general annual meetings or prior to flotations on the stock market. On several occasions, cases of blackmail have been discovered in the editorial departments of both state and commercial media outlets, with journalists demanding special payments from companies to counter negative publicity.

5.6.3 Media control and "guidance" of public opinion

China's media system contradicts the view that market-oriented media are incompatible with an authoritarian system over the longer term. Indeed, several researchers support the theory that the commercialization of the Chinese media may even have strengthened the CCP's authoritarian regime (Stockmann 2013). It is important in this context to note that the commercialization of the media is also controlled by the state in China. As the principal owner of the majority of media companies, government agencies benefit from the profits while also continuing to maintain media controls in especially sensitive policy areas (Zhao Yuezhi 1998).

The CCP's Central Propaganda Department continues to be responsible for monitoring the media, with the assistance of a powerful, bureaucratic apparatus including the State Administration of Radio, Film and Television (SARFT) (国家新闻出版广电总局). Controls may be applied using the following mechanisms (Abels 2006; Shambaugh 2007):

- Formal regulation: the granting of licenses; approving and initiating reorganizations and changes to the ownership structure; press accreditations; training (including political and ideological training).

- Content supervision: checking and censoring specific content; setting binding rules for the content being disseminated; ad hoc interventions by propaganda and supervisory authorities in the work of the editorial departments.
- Psychological discipline: the media and journalists are forced to impose self-censorship as a result of intimidation. Senior members of media companies are subject to supervision by the propaganda apparatus. Critical reporting can be criminalized as defamation, treason, or appeals to overthrow the regime. INGOs such as Freedom House or Reporters Without Borders classify China as among the countries with the least press freedom in the world. In 2014 the Committee to Protect Journalists identified forty-four Chinese journalists who at the time were in prison for their work.
- Technological monitoring: Internet monitoring on an extensive scale and the blocking of online information and discussions.

In addition to the restrictive media controls, since the Hu–Wen administration the CCP has attempted to bolster a proactive variant of propaganda, referred to as "media guidance" (舆论引导). This is aimed at controlling the interpretation of events in sensitive public debates "in advance" (Ren Xianliang 2010) or influencing from the outset the terms and connections desired by the CCP in critical debates.

In 2009 China's political leadership embarked on an extremely costly "foreign propaganda strategy," setting up several foreign-language press companies and TV channels to promote a more positive global image of China and China's global "soft power." Whenever there were unforeseen events that could reflect badly on China, Chinese propaganda authorities sought to provide an official, ideologically compatible interpretation as timely as possible in order to avoid facing pressures from independent sources of public opinion. When an anti-Beijing protest movement erupted in Hong Kong ("Occupy Central") in 2014, the protesters from the outset were portrayed in the Chinese media as unpatriotic forces that were being manipulated by the West. Information and discussions that varied from the party line were strictly prohibited. After Xi Jinping assumed office, he asked the media to spread "positive energy" (正能量) in harmony with the CCP's plans for modernization. Between 2012 and 2016 public space for a more pluralistic media system was increasingly cut back and party control over the official media was strictly enforced.

5.6.4 The Internet and political communications

The tightening of media controls and the enforcement of active "media guidance" indicate that the diversity of information and opinion on the Internet has profoundly unsettled China's political leadership (Lorentzen 2014). Paradoxically, the rapid growth of the Chinese Internet has been facilitated by massive state subsidies.

Since 1994, the government has invested substantial sums to set up an Internet infrastructure. At the time, the leadership regarded the Internet as a key technology which would promote China's economic growth and strengthen its international competitiveness. Since 2008, China has had the most Internet users in the world. At the end of 2014, 641 million Chinese were using the Internet on a regular basis, representing growth of 4 percent since the last year (see Figure 5.6). The majority use it to communicate (by instant messaging), to access information (search engines, online news), for entertainment (online music, videos, and games), and for online shopping.

China's netizens are constantly rediscovering their virtual individuality and identity in the space between commercialization and state control. The user-generated communications of the Internet offer them an opportunity to express their opinions. But the fast and volatile flow of information on the Internet represents a challenge to the state's censorship tools. Corruption and misconduct by local cadres are often first exposed online. Protests against large-scale projects with unknown environmental risks (chemical factories, waste incineration plants, etc.) have been

Figure 5.6

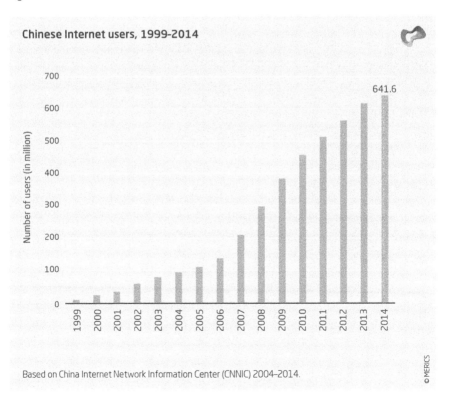

Chinese Internet users, 1999-2014

641.6

Number of users (in million)

Based on China Internet Network Information Center (CNNIC) 2004–2014.

© MERICS

organized via discussion forums and social media. A number of protest demonstrations organized online have succeeded in mobilizing thousands of participants.

Since the 2000s, prominent bloggers in their roles as opinion leaders and public intellectuals (including film and music stars but also some prominent business people) have used the Internet as a virtual arena to shape debates on social issues. Having gained several million "followers" on social media, by the mid-2010s prominent opinion-makers had a significantly wider reach than many national newspapers. Net activists in China originally hoped that the new Internet technologies would lead to political liberalization and democratization. However, China's Internet public is extremely fragmented and for the most part politically uninterested. Censorship authorities have intermittently allowed discussion of certain critical subjects as long as they do not directly attack the CCP or the political system (King/Pan/Roberts 2013). However, the online content of politically active associations or movements is consistently censored.

Sina Weibo, which had been the most popular social media platform, suffered a major setback when the government started a campaign against prominent opinion leaders in 2013 (Shi-Kupfer/Zhu Yi 2013). At the same time, the government began implementing a comprehensive strategy to guarantee cyber security aimed at the total elimination of politically undesirable content from the Internet, deploying significant personnel and financial resources and continually improving Internet monitoring software (Gierow 2014a).

Time and again, the Internet has challenged China's political ambitions to control the general public and the media. In March 2015, for instance, video documentation about the causes and consequences of urban air pollution went viral within hours and was viewed on the Chinese Internet about 200 million times. Initially, state censorship had not prevented dissemination of the video, since the fight against air pollution is also on the government's agenda. However, when its widespread distribution gave rise to commentaries that were critical of the government, China's Internet watchdogs intervened and immediately blocked access to the video.

Interactions between the Internet-based public and the state's ambitions to control the Internet continued to take some unexpected turns in the mid-2010s. The rapid development of new monitoring, censorship, and blocking software—accompanied by the vigorous expansion of a centralized "cyberspace administration" under the direct control of the party leadership (see Section 6.16)—suggest that by no means will there be linear growth in the freedom of expression on the Internet. On the contrary, there are indications that the propaganda apparatus is beginning to actively use the new opportunities presented by the Internet to monitor the dissemination of information and to restrict opinion to the interests of the party. From the perspective of the CCP, propaganda work within the technological context of the twenty-first century must make proactive use of the Internet and social media in order to further optimize selective disclosure of information that is in the interests of the political leadership.

5.7 Ethnic and religious groups

Kristin Shi-Kupfer and Sebastian Heilmann

Ethnic minorities and religious groups in China represent a considerable challenge to the absolute control by the CCP from both an administrative and ideological perspective. In comparison to the former Soviet Union or modern-day India, the PRC is a largely homogeneous state: in 2010, Han Chinese (the official name for the Chinese ethnic group) accounted for 91.65 percent of the total population in China. Although the fifty-five officially recognized ethnic minority groups, referred to as "minority nationalities" (少数民族), make up just 8.35 percent of the total population, they inhabit a huge amount of territory along the border regions, which are rich in resources and significant in terms of geostrategy (Mackerras 2011; NBS 2014a).

5.7.1 Ethnic minorities and autonomous regions

Ever since the PRC was established, these various minority nationalities have posed a challenge to China's Communist government in terms of safeguarding territorial integrity and establishing a unifying national identity. The First National Population Census of the PRC, which took place in 1953, revealed the party leadership was confronted with no less than 400 self-designations reported by ethnic minorities, beyond the five historically recognized "peoples" (Han, Manchus, Mongols, Tibetans, and Hui). Based on the model of the USSR, the CCP went on to classify a final total of fifty-five "minority nationalities" as officially recognized ethnic groups and awarded them a special administrative status (Hao Shiyuan 2012) (see Table 5.7.A).

After decades of oppression within the framework of the Maoist campaigns, the Law of the People's Republic of China on Regional National Autonomy (for short, the "Regional Ethnic Autonomy Law") was passed in 1984. Amended in 2001, the law gives minority nationalities living in concentrated communities the right to set up organs of self-government and guarantees them the freedom to use and develop their own languages and to preserve their own ways and customs. The Regional Ethnic Autonomy Law also makes it clear that safeguarding the unity of the PRC remains the primary goal of China's nationalities policy, and all nationalities and

Table 5.7.A

Distribution and population of the "minority nationalities," 2010

Name	Areas inhabited	Population (million)	Percentage of the total population
Zhuang	*Guangxi*, Yunnan, Guangdong	16.9	1.3
Manchu	Six northern and northeastern provinces	10.4	0.8
Hui	*Ningxia* and eighteen other provinces	10.6	0.8
Miao	Seven southwestern and central Chinese provinces	9.4	0.7
Uyghurs	*Xinjiang*	10.1	0.8
Tujia	Hunan, Hubei, Guizhou, Chongqing	8.4	0.6
Yi	Yunnan, Sichuan, Guizhou	8.7	0.7
Mongols	*Inner Mongolia* and five other northern provinces	6.0	0.5
Tibetans	*Tibet*, Sichuan, Qinghai, Gansu, Yunnan	6.3	0.5

Note: The areas in italics refer to the autonomous homeland regions of the minority nationalities. Based on NBS 2010.

© MERICS

autonomous regions come under the leadership of the CCP. The dual political and administrative structure of party and state organs in the PRC (see Section 2.3 and Section 2.4) has proved to be particularly problematic when it comes to how regional autonomy functions on a daily basis. Local powers of self-government are inevitably limited given that CCP organs that steer decision-making processes are dominated by Han Chinese and are integrated into a centralized party hierarchy.

At an administrative level, the autonomous powers granted to the ethnic minorities are in fact extremely limited. As a result of their economic underde-velopment, most ethnic minorities are completely dependent on grants from the central government, and key local political and business positions are assigned by high-ranking CCP organs according to political loyalty. The police force, judiciary, and military are dominated by Han Chinese and are particularly ready to crack down on political "differences," "separatist" movements, and "terrorist" activities in areas with large populations of minority nationalities. The right to local self-government, guaranteed by the state, specifically excludes the right to secession from the Chinese state. It is only in areas such as language, culture, education, and local economic development that the ethnic minorities can be said to enjoy any real rights of autonomy. Constraints on the free practice of religion, coupled with the gradual spread of Chinese as the language of instruction in schools since the end of the 1990s, are seen by Tibetans and Uyghurs as threats to their cultural heritages.

Members of ethnic minorities do enjoy certain privileges, however. For example, they are allowed special admission quotas for college entrance and they were exempt from the one-child policy. The tensions arising from the state drive for integration and assimilation on the one hand and the special privileges and quota systems on the other have contributed considerably to the politicization of the relationship between Han Chinese and ethnic minorities (Ma Rong 2010).

5.7.2 Conflicts in Tibet and Xinjiang

The serious ethnic tensions in Tibet and Xinjiang result from a complex web of factors. The central government takes aggressive steps as soon as there are any signs that the country's territorial integrity may be endangered. At the same time, there is a continuous backdrop of heightened political tensions resulting from the self-determination of the Tibetans and Uyghurs in cultural and religious matters. In addition, both Tibet and Xinjiang have been put into the spotlight as a result of the economic modernization and the extraction of raw materials forced upon them by the central government, mainly via state-owned enterprises. This background of conflict has repeatedly led to violent public protests and terrorist attacks in both regions. Such protests and acts of violence are mainly directed against Chinese domination and migration, but also against religious suppression and discrimination of the indigenous ethnic populations (for more on Tibet, see Sautman/Dreyer 2006; Shi-Kupfer 2014a; Tsering 1999; for more on Xinjiang, see Dillon 2004; Mackerras/Clarke 2009; Shi-Kupfer 2014b).

Adjustments of selective political measures by the central government are unlikely to be sufficient to mitigate the conflicts in Tibet and Xinjiang on a permanent basis; peace will depend on changes in the national political system of China—possibly even a transition to a federal system that offers better institutional protection of the autonomous rights granted to the ethnic minorities. As the last several decades have revealed, increased repression, Han Chinese in-migration, and stricter central-government decrees are unlikely to stem the tensions in these regions.

The political situation in Tibet

The Chinese government justifies its claim to sovereignty over Tibet due to the fact that the region has been an inseparable part of China since its integration into the Yuan dynasty during the middle of the thirteenth century. This is rebuked by the Tibetan government in exile, which is headed by the Dalai Lama, as throughout its history Tibet enjoyed long periods of complete autonomy. The violent methods used by the Chinese government to exert leadership over the region resulted in the Dalai Lama taking up exile in Dharamsala, India at the end of the 1950s. The central government claims these methods represent the "liberation" of Tibet from the "feudal serfdom" under which, to all intents and purposes, 95 percent of Tibetans lived as slaves. However, not only Tibetans opposed to Chinese rule were victims of this harsh "liberation." A large part of Tibet's cultural heritage was destroyed as well. Monks and nuns who cannot come to terms with the Dalai Lama's exile and the political interference in their faith and monastic life are subjected to especially harsh surveillance and repression. At the same time, the infrastructural and economic improvements by the Chinese state have resulted in a substantial improvement in terms of living standards and the availability of resources in the region. However, Han Chinese migrants are often given priority over Tibetans when it comes to job allocations and business licenses, with the result that the local population fears a total "Sinicization" of the region through Han in-migration.

The Chinese government insists that the path to formal negotiations on a return of the Dalai Lama is completely open, provided that he officially recognizes Tibet as an integral part of Chinese territory. The Dalai Lama in turn has stated that his aim is not to establish Tibet as an independent state, but that he wants genuine, guaranteed autonomy for all historically Tibetan settlements within the PRC (which make up a considerably larger area than the current Tibet Autonomous Region).

The Chinese party leadership (represented by cadres from the United Front Work Department at the ministerial or vice-ministerial levels) and representatives of the Dalai Lama held a series of informal talks between 2002 and 2010 (most were held in Beijing, although some also took place in provincial capitals). At these negotiations, the Tibetan side put forward proposals to guarantee more extensive autonomy for Tibetan settlements. However, the Chinese ultimately rejected all of the proposals made by the Dalai Lama's representatives and the talks ended in 2010 without any tangible results.

The central-government's current policy appears to be to wait for the death of the 14th Dalai Lama, who has become a popular international figure, in order to resolve the Tibet issue. However, it cannot be ruled out that his death may actually provide a greater level of radicalism in the Tibetan exile community and within Tibet itself, something that would definitely not be in Beijing's best interests.

The political situation in Xinjiang

In the predominantly Muslim area of Xinjiang (translated as "New Frontier") growing numbers of the Uyghur minority have begun to oppose Chinese rule. Since the 1990s, the region of Xinjiang has seen increasing numbers of attacks and violent unrest, particularly in the city of Kashgar and in the southwestern border regions. Between 2008 and 2014, there were at least 900 deaths in the region resulting from politically motivated riots, assassinations, or terrorist attacks, and between 2013 and 2014 the frequency of such violent incidents rose significantly (Collins 2015).

According to the Chinese government, resistance fighters in the region have links to radical Islamic groups in Central Asia, with training, financial and logistical support, and weapons all supposedly supplied for years by the Taliban in Afghanistan and Pakistan and the terrorist network built up by Osama bin Laden. China made use of international efforts against terrorist activity after 9/11 to tighten criminal law clauses against terrorist activities and to use them against groups and individual activists in Xinjiang as a pretext for mass arrests—people whom the security forces accuse of carrying out subversive or terrorist actions "under the guise of religion." Beginning in 2013, a sporadic spate of attacks also occurred outside of Xinjiang in Han Chinese cities. Allegedly carried out by Uyghur or Islamist terrorists, these attacks, directed at innocent civilians, aimed at attracting international attention. Local and central authorities classify very diverse kinds of violence as terrorist attacks in a rather sweeping manner—anything from social unrest involving violent demonstrations and attacks on police stations to bombings and knife attacks. Evidence provided by the Chinese government attesting to active transnational Islamist terrorist networks in Xinjiang has been, at best, piecemeal (Rodríguez-Merino 2013).

Unlike in Tibet, so far there have been no political dialogues regarding the Xinjiang problem. The World Uyghur Congress, which is based in Munich, Germany, and claims to represent the collective interests of the Uyghur people both in China and abroad, calls for an independent "East Turkestan." Among other things, the Chinese government has accused the organization of planning the violent riots in 2009 in Urumqi, the capital of the Xinjiang region, which resulted in at least 200 deaths and over 1,700 injuries. German investigating authorities found no evidence that the World Uyghur Congress had been involved in any acts of terrorism. Due to the lack of political mechanisms for negotiations and therefore the absence of any real chance of a solution to the issue, Xinjiang, particularly the southwestern areas of the region, remains stuck in a cycle of open ethnic resentments and recurring violent unrest.

5.7.3 Religious organizations and groups

Religious communities in the PRC are subject to varying degrees of state restrictions. After its consolidation of power in the early 1950s, the CCP launched a radical campaign against "feudal superstitions" and "reactionary" religious groups. These groups were persecuted from the 1950s to the 1970s, reaching a peak during the Cultural Revolution (1966–76) when numerous religious sites were destroyed or reclaimed, and a large number of spiritual leaders and believers were rounded up, tortured, or even killed. To this day, belonging to a religious community is officially incompatible with CCP membership, although there are a considerable number of party members who maintain regular links to religious communities and practices.

The protection of "regular religious activities" has been firmly anchored in the Chinese Constitution and state legislation since 1978, but only within the boundaries of the five religions that are officially recognized by the state (see Table 5.7.B). The founding of new religious communities, the training of clergy, and general religious practices and worship are all subject to approval and supervision by the state religious affairs authorities. Any religious activity that endangers public order or national security, harms the physical health of citizens, or compromises the public education system is strictly prohibited. Additionally, religious communities in China are not permitted to make use of support from organizations outside the country. This presents a dilemma for Chinese Catholics, who are forced either to sever ties with the Vatican (which the official state-recognized Catholic Church in China has done) or to engage in illegal underground activities. Foreign religious communities and organizations are prohibited from carrying out missionary work in China, although a number of religious charity organizations have been present since the 1980s. However, they do not ostensibly engage in missionary activities; rather, they are involved in charitable work and are active in poverty-stricken regions, in healthcare, and in providing care for the elderly and disabled.

Since the 1990s, religious (mainly Protestant) communities have seen their membership figures swell, with sections of the well-educated urban middle classes joining their ranks in ever-increasing numbers. Active Protestant communities in China offer a wide range of religious orientations and a variety of different types of worship. Protestantism is deemed to be a religion that is in touch with reality and compatible with the pursuit of material wealth. It is also internationally respected and therefore perceived by many Chinese to be modern and fashionable. Unofficial estimates differ widely, with citations of figures of between 30 and 80 million Protestants and 6 to 13 million Catholics in the mid-2010s, depending on the degree of affiliation. The number of active Protestant "house churches" and underground Catholic congregations cannot be reliably estimated because they are not registered, meaning that the figures can only represent approximate estimations. Depending on the level of regional and national political tensions, some Christian house and underground congregations are tolerated by the authorities, whereas others become targets of political repression. Large religious groups that have a significant level of visibility and might be considered political risks, or have somehow fallen prey to a political religious agenda on a regional or national level, are particularly vulnerable.

Table 5.7.B

Participation in religious activities in the PRC, 1949-2010

		1949	1978	2010
Buddhism		No figures	No figures	150–200 million
Daoism		No figures	No figures	50–100 million
Protestantism	Registered congregations	1–7 million	At least 3 million	23 million
	Nonregistered congregations (estimated)	No figures	No figures	45–60 million
Catholicism	Registered congregations	Approx. 3 million	2–3 million	6 million
	Nonregistered congregations (estimated)	No figures	No figures	5–7 million
Islam (ethnic Muslim minorities)		No figures	No figures	22 million

Based on China Center in Sankt Augustin, Germany; CASS.

© MERICS

In addition to Christians, according to state censuses and nonofficial surveys conducted in the mid-2010s there were also up to 250 million loosely associated Buddhists and Daoists. Most of these participate in religious practices ("popular beliefs") only occasionally, without officially belonging to any religious community. Many people practice both Buddhist and Daoist activities, meaning that some of the figures may overlap. The total number of Chinese belonging to Muslim ethnic minorities in 2014 was about 22 million, with the majority living in China's northwestern regions (Wenzel-Teuber 2015).

The Chinese government has attempted to co-opt religions in the country, particularly the "indigenous religions" (本土宗教) of Buddhism and Daoism, to take on a more charitable role. Since the turn of the century, the charitable functions and stabilizing effects of religious communities on society have been recognized by state religious policy—as long as their activities take place under strict government control. Even though party members are not officially allowed to practice any religion, media reports suggest that Chinese folk religion practices (fortune-telling and worshiping different deities based on who can help most in a specific situation) and personal consultations with Buddhist and Lamaist masters are particularly popular among party cadres.

The end of the 1990s saw a rise in popularity of the Buddhist-inspired Falun Gong movement, the "Law Wheel Practice" (法轮功). The movement, which practices traditional regulated breathing methods, *qigong* (气功) and at times has had several million followers, has grown to represent a challenge to the CCP. Falun Gong founder Li Hongzhi (who emigrated to the United States in 1996) has mobilized believers from all levels of society—including party members and military personnel—to participate in its explicitly anti-modernist moral teachings, collective practice groups, and mass-healing events. A sit-in demonstration by Falun Gong members around the Zhongnanhai party and government compound in Beijing in 1999 and the movement's strong transnational financial stability resulted in a strict ban by the CCP leadership that continues to this day with rigorous repression of all Falun Gong practitioners and activities.

As part of the ban on Falun Gong, the CCP initiated an "anti-heterodoxy" campaign (反邪教) against other spiritual groups and movements, with the security services claiming that these groups are led by charlatans who abuse their members both financially and sexually. The leaders of such groups have regularly been sentenced to long prison sentences or, in exceptional cases, even death. Some Christian-inspired groups (such as Eastern Lightning—also known as the Church of Almighty God—and the Three Class Servants Church) have mobilized well-organized transregional networks of activists and followers who have even been evangelizing among existing Christian congregations. An important part of the sometimes very elaborate doctrines of salvation among these groups is resistance against state repression, which is often portrayed as a "fight against evil."

The CCP leadership fosters a profound mistrust of foreign associations and religious beliefs that might potentially represent a threat to state order. The proliferation of underground religious or spiritual movements, despite the government ban and the massive reprisals from the security forces, poses a challenge to the CCP and is closely associated with a growing potential for social unrest.

5.8 The potential for social unrest

Kristin Shi-Kupfer and Sebastian Heilmann

Social unrest is seen as a threat to the stability of the political order and is therefore considered by the CCP leadership as one of its most sensitive challenges. Unrest not only questions both party and state legitimacy and monopoly on the use of force, but also results in growing administrative and financial costs.

According to the Ministry of Public Security (China's principal police authority), the number of "unexpected incidents involving mass participation" (群体性突发事件), such as public crowds, protests, or riots, increased from 10,000 in 1993 to 60,000 in 2003. To date, the ministry has not published more recent figures, but Chinese protest researchers report around 180,000 such "incidents" in 2010 (Lü Li 2013).

All figures on protest numbers should be treated with caution as they include many different causes, motives, events, participants, and numbers (see Table 5.8.A). China's security agencies have an institutional self-interest in dramatizing the extent of social unrest. At the same time, rising levels of protest might also be a sign of a changing, more flexible—possibly even more tolerant—approach to social complaints and demands on the part of the Chinese leadership. If taken seriously, social protests resulting from actual grievances can be a valuable learning experience for

Table 5.8.A

Social protests in the PRC

Reason for protest	Typical causes	Participants	Nationwide political impacts
Labor disputes	Unpaid salaries; salary negotiations; working conditions; insurance contributions	Industrial workers	Medium to high (to date localized but persistent; potential for nationwide networking)
Environmental damage	Fear of environmental damage; environmental scandals (water contamination); building of chemicals factories, waste incineration plants, etc.	Rural and urban inhabitants in the affected areas	Medium (to date localized and short-lived; potential for nationwide solidarity)
Official prohibitions and directives	Mistrust of government; lack of explanations or arbitrariness of decisions; corruption	Entire urban and rural populations	Low to medium (potential for solidarity generally limited to local regions)
Real-estate projects	Forced expropriation and demolitions; lack of transparency in amounts of compensation	Affected rural and city residents	Low (limited numbers of people affected; short-lived protests)

© MERICS

the government and can serve as a corrective mechanism, thereby resulting in long-term political stability. It is therefore not useful to draw sweeping conclusions about an increasing social and political destabilization of China based solely on the rising number of often very minor protests.

5.8.1 Labor protests

The restructuring of the often heavily indebted state-owned enterprises in the late 1990s resulting in a huge number of layoffs—about 36 million people lost their jobs—was a socially explosive issue for the CCP. It resulted in walk-outs and mass protests (especially in 2001–2 in the northeast of China—which was the most heavily-affected area—and in 2004 in Sichuan and Hebei provinces). One of the recurring demands by the workers was the right to set up independent trade unions (see Section 5.5.2). Regional governments often yielded to individual demands from the workers, meaning that there was only sporadic use of violent repression (Chan 2001). Beginning in 2004, workers in the state sector were generally much calmer, as most of the state-owned enterprises that had undergone huge restructurings between 1997 and 2003 were profiting from rapid growth, generous financing from state banks, and monopolistic advantages in protected economic sectors.

Nationwide protests in the private sector in the 2000s and 2010s have mainly been organized by workers at large companies run by foreign investors from Hong Kong, Taiwan, or South Korea. The first generation of migrant workers in transnational companies were content with low wages and very modest working conditions, whereas the more self-confident and better-educated second generation began to insist on their legally guaranteed rights (the new Labor Contract Law in 2008 represents a significant milestone in this respect). This generation demanded higher wages, improved opportunities for training and promotion, and better representation of their interests by elected workers' councils. The wave of strikes that took place in southern China in 2010 at manufacturing plants belonging to Foxconn (a Taiwanese investor manufacturing iPhones and other electronic goods) and Honda (a Japanese investor) made it clear that activists were becoming better networked in order to coordinate their strategies, demands, and nationwide public relations activities. This type of networking represents a particularly challenging political risk for the Chinese government (Chan/Ngai 2009). Local-government representatives have actively tried to mediate between workers and company managers in order to prevent strikes and escalating tensions. Since the official company unions are often seen by the workers as little more than management stooges, intervention by the local authorities, at least in the 2010s in the southern province of Guangdong, facilitated a handful of tentatively "more open" collective- bargaining negotiations between elected workers' representatives and company management boards.

On the whole, surveys and field studies carried out in the mid-2010s in China's largest industrial manufacturing facilities indicate that tensions in labor relations and the frequency of walk-outs and protracted collective negotiations have increased. Due to improved lobbying and diminishing numbers of migrant workers in China, industrial laborers were able to negotiate considerable wage increases for several successive years. This increase in labor costs in turn put pressures on investors and managers to increase productivity through automation (robots) or to relocate their production facilities to locations outside of China where average unit labor costs are lower.

At the same time, students and university graduates came under increased scrutiny from state supervisory bodies in the mid-2010s because prior to 1989 they had often been at the forefront of the social protests that took place in China. Despite a huge increase in student numbers, China's universities became a haven of political stability after 1989 due to the tightening of internal supervision, high academic standards, and good career and salary prospects. However, government departments have recently begun to express concerns about the increasing number of graduates that has led to a decrease in the availability of suitable, adequately paid jobs for the coming generations—in 2014, just over one-half of all students had signed work contracts by the time of graduation. Entry-level salaries for the majority of graduates, who mainly go into the public or service sectors, are only marginally higher than factory workers' salaries. Skilled industrial workers are highly sought after in many places as the influx of migrant workers from the rural areas dropped off considerably in the mid-2010s.

5.8.2 Urbanization and land grabs

The second leading cause of social protests after worker protests are conflicts involving land-use rights. The main reason behind this is the enormous urbanization process that the Chinese government has been promoting during the last two decades (see Section 6.15). According to a report written by the Agriculture and Rural Affairs Committee of the NPC in 2011, China has lost about one-tenth of its agricultural land as a result of real-estate and infrastructure projects. Sales of land to real-estate developers have become one of the leading sources of income for local governments.

Laws and regulations regarding the transfer of land-ownership rights contain many ambiguities and contradictions (see Section 5.3). Government agencies have the right to confiscate land from farmers in the name of the "public interest." The level of compensation awarded to those affected is generally set by the relevant local authority. Since the 2000s, there have been increasing numbers of localized, sometimes violent, protests against forced land expropriations and insufficient or

arbitrary compensation. However, it is seldom possible to mobilize and organize local protest groups on any sort of sustainable basis. Local county and city governments make widespread use of different incentives and pressures to remove land
from its owners (such as financial supplements, emotional pressures from relatives
or friends, use of third parties as mediators, or infiltration by agents provocateurs to
discredit and divide protesters) (Lee Ching Kwan/Zhang Yonghong 2013).

Urban areas have also witnessed their fair share of protests against expropriations and court-ordered forced evictions and demolitions. Again, the disputes focus
primarily on irregularities at the project-inception stages with regard to calculating compensation payments. Photos of so-called "nail houses" (钉子户), that is,
homes belonging to people who refuse to make room for real-estate development,
whereby an enormous building project is surrounded by one "hold-out," and even
desperate homeowners setting fire to themselves have shocked both Chinese and
outsiders. Since 2011, the central government has passed a series of laws with strict
guidelines for the land and real-estate markets, but these have had little impact on
reducing the general mistrust or on quelling the embittered protests against the
widespread collusion between local-government authorities and real-estate developers at the expense of the urban population. However, because nearly all of these
incidents have been confined to local levels, their impact on the national political
system remain very limited.

5.8.3 Environmental protests

Ecological issues are also a leading cause of complaints to the authorities. Between
1995 and 2006, the number of pollution-related petitions submitted to the authorities increased tenfold. Demonstrations against waste incineration plants or production sites that are opposed on environmental grounds have often made national
news due to social media, putting the local authorities under pressure to act, or at
least to justify their decisions.

Most environmental protests in China are so-called "NIMBY" protests, and dem-
onstrators in rural areas often use the ecology card to voice other demands (such as
issues of land ownership). The ability to mobilize large sections of the population in
the rural areas to participate in ecological protests depends greatly on the extent of
their economic dependence on the companies accused of harming the environment.
Farmers whose fields are contaminated take a very different stance from employees
who work for the companies involved in the conflicts (Deng Yanhua/Yang Guobin
2013).

Since the mid-2000s, several large cities have seen protests against planned
factory complexes and waste incineration plants. These protests, which have generally been peaceful (with only a few violent exceptions) cannot be fully explained

only by NIMBYism. Large numbers of urban middle-class citizens have become increasingly dissatisfied with the state's environmental policy, with a 2007 survey by CASS showing that 46 percent of the respondents described themselves as either "not really satisfied" or "not satisfied at all" with the government's environmental policies. Knowledge of and insistence on applying existing environmental laws, a certain level of political risk-taking, and novel methods of protest (such as "collective walks," referring to demonstrations organized on the Internet) all point to a new form of civil activism in support of the environment. These protests have often resulted in local authorities either ending the projects completely or moving them to different sites.

5.8.4 Arbitrary authorities, rampages, and self-administered justice

In 2009 there were seventeen mass incidents sparked by seemingly insignificant conflicts. The following example gives an account of one such incident: a street vendor was reprimanded by a municipal police officer. When the street vendor refused to pay a fine, the disagreement turned into a verbal attack. Witnesses and passers-by sided with the street vendor and the officer called for backup. The additional forces were still unable to put an end to the dispute or to lead away the street vendor. The situation escalated out of control within a matter of minutes, developing into a violent street battle between the spontaneous crowd of several thousand protestors that had gathered and the hastily summoned security forces. The combination of an underlying distrust of local authorities and an "us down here against them up there" mentality quickly turn such insignificant incidents into a collective frenzy of violence, often with no discernible leadership, organization, or concrete demands. Against this backdrop, such street fights become a valve for those involved to vent frustrations and dissatisfaction.

Beginning in the mid-2000s, hospitals also became an outlet for social frustrations. According to official figures from the Ministry of Health, over 17,000 violent attacks on the staff of healthcare facilities were recorded in 2010, and several fatal attacks on doctors were documented in 2012. There was a rise in the number of organized "hospital rioters" (医闹) who offer their "services" to patients who have been, or believe they have been, the subject of medical malpractice in order to demand compensation payments or purely to settle the score (Hesketh et al. 2012). Opaque costs for treatment, "special payments" to hospital staff to secure care, and the patients' high expectations coupled with their general distrust of doctors all contributed to the increase in such violent incidents. The signs of widespread loss of confidence among the public and the deep frustration with state authorities and public services were impossible to ignore by the 2010s.

5.8.5 Crime

The sharp rise in criminality since the beginning of the 1990s is also indicative of a general destabilization of the social fabric. Based on comparative studies carried out in other countries, criminality is a relative minor issue in the PRC (see Table 5.8.B). As in other emerging economies (such as India or Indonesia), however, there are large numbers of unrecorded or unreported cases of murder and rape that are not included in the official figures, so the statistics alone only tell part of the story.

Figures reveal that there has been a considerable rise in crime since the 1990s, with the rate of recorded crimes per 100,000 citizens increasing from 4.7 percent in 1997 to 7.4 percent in 2007. The highest figures are found in the major Chinese cities of Beijing, Shanghai, and Chongqing as well as in the eastern provinces. Rapid social changes, a decline in traditional lifestyles, growing inequalities, and an inadequate judicial system are all perceived as the primary causes of this development (Cheong Tsun Se/Wu Yanrui 2013).

According to police statistics, during the same period criminal gang activity has also increased dramatically. The spread to the mainland of gangs that historically were only active in Taiwan or Hong Kong and the rising political criminal "red–black" nexus (Communist-mafia) are often quoted as part of the reason for the increased prevalence of criminal networks (Wang Peng 2013a). Although the vast majority of criminal gangs are small and only active at the local levels, there has been a rise in

Table 5.8.B

Crime rates in the PRC: An international comparison, 2008-15

	Prison population (per 100,000 inhabitants)	Recorded murders in % of population (per 100,000 inhabitants)	Recorded rapes in population (per 100,000 inhabitants)
China	165 (2014)	1.1 (2008)	2.8 (2010)
USA	698 (2013)	5.0 (2009)	27.3 (2010)
Germany	76 (2015)	0.8 (2010)	9.4 (2010)
India	33 (2014)	3.4 (2009)	1.8 (2010)
Indonesia	567 (2015)	8.1 (2008)	0.7 (2013)

Based on Institute for Criminal Policy Research 2015; NationMaster 2010; UNODC 2011; Walmsley 2011.

© MERICS

larger criminal organizations operating across provincial borders or even transnationally. These gangs are particularly active in the regions bordering Myanmar and Vietnam as well as Pakistan and Central Asia. They are primarily involved in drug smuggling and human trafficking, but they have also been found to trade illegally in wild animals, electronic scrap, and wood. In a number of places, they have been able to infiltrate the local authorities, the CCP, customs offices, businesses, and banks. Chinese gangs are also involved in human trafficking and money laundering both in the United States and Europe.

Since the 1990s, the authorities have repeatedly launched new regional and national "strike hard" (严打) campaigns against criminality. In the latest campaign against organized crime, conducted between spring 2006 and fall 2009, about 13,000 gangs were broken up, 870,000 suspects were arrested, and 89,000 charges were filed. These campaigns are an official admission of the extent of the problem that criminal organizations pose to the security services. However, the spread of organized crime has partly been the result of gangs being protected by corrupt businesspeople and government officials, particularly those working for the public-security apparatus. A campaign against organized crime launched in June 2009 by Bo Xilai, who at the time was party chief of Chongqing, initially specifically targeted party and government cadres as well as businesspeople. The so-called Chongqing model exposed previously unprecedented levels of infiltration by a "red mafia" comprised of leading party officials and prominent businesspeople (Wang Peng 2013b). The zealous nationwide anti-corruption campaign launched in 2013 has uncovered further cases of tight-knit criminal exchange networks between mafia-like business communities and government officials in a vast number of counties, cities, and provinces. Due to a lack of independent judicial and supervisory bodies, it seems unlikely that these well-established and lucrative shadow business practices will be eliminated by political campaigns any time soon (see Section 4.8).

5.9 The political consequences of social change

Sebastian Heilmann

The nationwide potential for unrest, which can only be gleaned from the generally fragmented data and available information, seems at first sight to be considerable. Explosive social and political issues that have built up as a result of the economic reforms potentially could represent a threat to the political regime, but only if the impetus arises simultaneously in numerous regions.

Warnings from the central government of a deterioration in public order in parts of the country have arisen partly as the result of a deep concern regarding the gradual erosion of political and social control over the general public. However, government appeals often serve to discipline regional authorities and to justify repression of all forms of organized opposition: the slogan "ensuring stability" is used to gloss over political repression in the name of holding on to power.

There are currently no real signs of attempts to mobilize the population to overturn the existing order, with the exception of underground movements in Xinjiang and isolated radical religious organizations. There is no segment of the population that seems intrinsically capable of organizing a broad social movement sufficiently strong to bring down the Communist regime. However, the situation may be more serious with respect to industrial workers due to their repeated attempts to set up autonomous workers' councils. Faced with the state's instruments of repression in a constant state of alert, the possibilities of forming transregional or even national labor movements only appear to be possible under very extreme circumstances (in the event of a deep economic crisis with massive layoffs in China's industrial heartlands, for example).

Through a combination of repression and political concessions, the Chinese leadership has so far been able to limit social unrest to the local levels without such disturbances becoming a threat to the national political system. As long as the protesters focus their demands on specific issues, most authorities have been willing to listen to what the affected population groups have to say. In this respect, social protest has contributed to a change in how state bodies and social groups in China interact, but always against a backdrop of a lack of legal certainties and the possibility of violent backlashes.

It is unclear whether the current social tensions in China will have a long-term impact or whether they are a transitory phenomenon: social upheaval is an almost inevitable result of the extensive structural changes currently taking place in China. In the context of present circumstances, social instability need not necessarily be a sign of the impending downfall of the political system but might actually represent a painful, but ultimately better-balanced process of adaptation.

The economic and social changes sparked by China's policy of reform and opening are more of a gradual transformation than a sudden reduction of state interventions in social and economic life. To date, the authority of the central government and the vigor of the security apparatus have proven to be irresistible forces when challenged by any kind of conflict.

The despotic power of the Chinese state, which reached its apogee under the leadership of Mao Zedong with almost unlimited political power over the economy and society, has in the meantime encountered substantial restrictions. The simplified assumption that there are perpetual confrontations between the state and the people cannot possibly reflect all of the complex networks that characterize state–society relations in China.

Many urban middle- and upper-class Chinese are professionally involved in state organizations or state-owned enterprises. Others enjoy links with functionaries through private acquaintances, regular communications, or informal exchange networks in China's "administrative market" (see Chapter 4). A large proportion of the population tolerates the directives and interventions from state bodies as an inescapable fact of public life in an ingrained political system, with very few people actually rebelling against the government partly due to the fact that they can avoid dealings with officials and that they are generally left to get on with both their private and professional lives.

In China's aspiring information and communications society, state authorities and social powers have begun to find new ways to coexist. There are signs of profound changes in the values, future expectations, and behavioral patterns of the younger generations of "digital natives." Social forces that might be intrinsically capable of securing rights of political co-determination and institutional innovations have thus far been hesitant to do so. As long as there is no overt organizational crisis within the CCP with a loss of control over the security forces, media, and society, the scope for autonomous political activity is likely to remain extremely limited and subject to strict repression.

6 Policy making: Processes and outcomes

Traditional models of political systems primarily concentrate on classifying types of regimes on a spectrum that ranges from democracy to dictatorship (Gandhi 2008; Smolik 2012; Teorell 2010), with a gray area of hybrid or fragile systems (Diamond 2002; Levitsky/Way 2010; Naude et al. 2011). The outcomes of state activity (understood in this volume to refer to the continuous formulation, implementation, and readjustment of policy action programs) are often derived in a generalized way from the classification of the institutional system (democratic, open, and inclusive versus dictatorial, closed, and extractive) (for highly influential publications on the subject, see Acemoglu/Robinson 2006, 2012).

Because of the experiences of the collapsed socialist systems in Eastern and Central Europe, political systems in which Communist parties maintain a monopoly of power are credited with only a marginal ability, if any at all, to adapt. Communist one-party systems not only show fundamental political defects (a lack of power control, suppressed pluralism of opinion, and systematic human-rights violations), but historically, they have also been extremely inflexible in terms of adjusting their institutions, policy goals, policy-making processes, and administrative practices. The standard literature on socialist systems therefore disputes their ability to make improvements with respect to administrative organization, economic coordination, and technological innovation, and to compete on an international stage (Brown 2009; Bunce 1999).

However, this systemic, institutional classification and explanatory perspective is not helpful to understand the dynamics of the system of government in the People's Republic of China (PRC), a system which is unexpectedly adaptable and versatile in many policy areas, particularly with regard to economic and technology policy. The experiences of the collapsed Eastern European Communist systems do not help to understand developments in the PRC. The observation that many official institutions in the PRC are similar to those in the former USSR or the German Democratic Republic (GDR) does not contribute to an understanding of their completely different achievements or the outcomes of state activity. For a better understanding of China's development dynamics, analytical perspectives that go beyond preconceived institutional and regime typologies are needed.

To examine China's development dynamics with fewer preconceived assumptions, and consequently a more open and unbiased mindset, this chapter uses analytical approaches drawn from policy studies (process, interaction, and problem-solving studies in concrete policy areas). The case studies focus on the manner in which new policy programs in China's government system can be developed, formulated, implemented, adjusted, and revised. Key to this are the political and administrative methodologies as well as the capacity to deal with both existing and emerging challenges, the correction mechanisms when things go wrong and conflicts arise, and the adaptability to a constantly changing economic or international context.

Such process-, interaction-, and results-based studies of the dynamics of state activity over time go beyond abstract, generalized, systemic, and institutional perspectives. This chapter therefore is not focussed on the "hardware" of the political system (constitutional bodies, leading party organs, bureaucratic organizations, etc.), nor does it examine the major variables on their own (the concentration of power, hierarchical controls, inclusive versus extractive institutions, etc.). Instead, the focus is on the "software" of Chinese politics with which action requirements and policy programs are processed. The chapter deals with the processes of policy making that bring otherwise cumbersome bureaucracies and static constitutional rules to life. The analysis centers on observable patterns of interactions, methods for dealing with problems, adaptive capacities, as well as outcomes and the potential for future development in specific policy areas.

A key advantage of this kind of policy analysis is that it provides an *open perspective:* when new action requirements emerge (and in their wake, new definitions of problems, interests, programs, and conflicts), policy formulation and the decision-making processes can be analyzed in a straightforward manner. However, preconceived regime and institutional analyses tend to blind us to new and divergent observations and developments that do not fit into predefined analytical frameworks. Social-science research that is fixated from a teleological point of view on the search for signs of a "real" market economy or a "real" democracy in China shuts its eyes to surprising observations and unexpected features and capacities as well as to unorthodox methods and mechanisms that influence political decision-making and problem-solving processes in China. Therefore, in this chapter policy making is regarded as an action process with an uncertain outcome, driven by interests, interactions, results, conflict, and continuous feedback. Thus, policy making is not predetermined by history, regime type, or institutions in a straightforward manner.

The case studies in this chapter are designed to demonstrate the wide variety of requirements, programs, instruments, and procedures that are specific to a policy area. Concrete observable practices and processes represent the starting point. Because of the emphasis on concrete actors and processes, these studies will also offer a great deal of important information and knowledge to practitioners in areas of diplomacy, business, nongovernmental organizations (NGOs), and the media who have regular dealings with Chinese government departments.

The case studies focus on policies that are especially significant for China's current and future development and they cover a broad range of different types of state activity. They all follow the same pattern: an analysis of the actors and interests is followed by that of the decision-making and conflicts, implementation, policy outcomes and adjustments. This structured comparison allows us to identify not only commonalities and basic patterns across policy areas but also significant variations and distinctive features. The studies clearly indicate the wide variety and dynamics of state activity in the PRC.

The following section begins by explaining the distinctive features of policy making and state activity in China: the normal mode and crisis mode; development planning and mega projects; experimental programs and policy innovation; adjustment of priorities by means of target setting in the cadre system; policy implementation through highly focused CCP-led mobilization campaigns; advice and consultations from within the state on government policy; external inputs into political decision-making (lobbying, nongovernmental initiatives, and surveys); e-government; and cyber control and active state guidance of public opinion. These distinctive features of the policy processes highlight strengths and weaknesses of the Chinese approach to governance.

6.1 Distinctive features of the policy process

Sebastian Heilmann

Policy making and state activity in China are characterized by procedures, methods, and instruments, that are markedly different from those in democratic constitutional states (or other large emerging countries such as India, Brazil, or Mexico) and they produce different opportunities for action or limitations on action as well as different outcomes. Other distinctive features of the policy process (for instance, development planning, campaigns, propaganda, etc.) are derived from the institutional peculiarities of the authoritarian party-state. Yet it should be noted how these seemingly conventional and well-known instruments were realigned to completely new state-action requirements during the reform and opening period and were therefore able to produce unexpected outcomes.

The normal mode versus the crisis mode: Between fragmentation and a concentration of power

Even in democratic political systems, a crisis mode is deemed to be an exceptional political context during which far-reaching legislative decisions—regarding the use of budgetary funds or security forces, for instance—can be made and implemented much more quickly than during normal times. Indeed, in China the "crisis, war, and mobilization" mode (see Section 3.1.3) is not implemented within the context of constitutional rules; instead, it essentially causes the decision-making and leadership systems to shift to a different framework for political action and interactions.

In sharp contrast to the political and administrative fragmentation that is typical during normal times, China's leadership system assumes a completely different nature in times of crisis. It is transformed from a lethargic and fragmented bureaucratic system into a centralized, autocratic mobilization system with a high concentration of personalized power. Triggers for a shift into a crisis mode can be events such as natural disasters, terrorist attacks, or financial crises (as is the case in other political systems as well), but political unrest or leadership conflicts and organizational crises within the Chinese Communist Party (CCP) may also cause such changes.

During phases when it has been in a crisis mode, until now the Chinese political leadership has been more assertive than leaderships in any other developing or emerging countries. On the one hand, the traditional characteristics of a party dictatorship are evident during these phases, namely, crisis and conflict management is based on massive ad hoc mobilization and repressive measures that have no legal foundation, and dissident voices within the CCP and external critics are suppressed. On the other hand, new approaches and noteworthy capabilities to learn become more visible, for instance in disaster relief (with comprehensive preventive planning for emergencies and coordination of civilian/military relief operations), in adopting internationally accepted "best practices" to stem financial crises, or in combining bureaucratic and legal approaches with the mobilization techniques of the Mao era to fight epidemics or corruption.

In the following case studies, the basic patterns of the crisis mode can be seen in China's management of the global financial crisis (Section 6.6) and state budgetary policy (Section 6.7). The disaster relief following the devastating earthquake in Sichuan in 2008 (Section 6.13) provides an additional case study, but other policy areas also demonstrate a centralization of decision-making powers that is typical of the crisis mode, especially during the conflict-ridden stages of policy corrections, for example when redefining maritime interests (Section 6.14) or reorganizing cyber controls (Section 6.16).

Development planning, macro programs, and mega projects

The Chinese leadership regards the opportunity to set long-term development priorities and to "concentrate forces" (集中力量) on large, national projects as one of the greatest strengths of the PRC political system. In contrast, it regards one of the greatest weaknesses of democratic political systems to be unable to pursue long-term development targets and programs due to the frequency of election campaigns and changes in government.

In fact, medium- and long-term development planning (中长期发展规划) play a key role in the PRC in coordinating and directing state activity across various policy areas. The most visible features of this development planning continue to be the national five-year plans in which the CCP and the government establish their priorities. In administrative practice, national long-term planning consists of contradictory packages of thousands of specific action programs at various administrative levels. Such a web of programs continues to evolve before, during, and even after the official term of the national five-year plan, hence over staggered and uncoordinated periods. Multi-year plans in present-day China do not consist of a single, standardized planning period for all policy areas and administrative levels, but rather a variable and continuous cycle of coordination and evaluation. Since the year 2000, China's development plans have included complex lists of indicative targets (预测性指标), that is, targets that are desired by the government, but that are also flexible, and strictly binding targets (约束性指标) that simultaneously serve as administrative benchmarks and are useful for cadre assessments.

Meanwhile, the functions, procedures, and instruments of development planning diverge substantially from the traditional socialist economic planning that the Chinese Communists originally borrowed from the Soviet Union. Since the 1990s, China's development plans have explicitly targeted planning for and with national and international markets to open up new growth potentials for the economy and to redirect economic organization and social and environmental development over the long term. Development planning represents the political leadership's aspirations to perpetuate "macroeconomic control" (宏观调控) through the CCP and the government. The processes of drawing up, evaluating, and adjusting development plans have included many more government departments and scientific advisers, as well as corporate and social interests, than was the case in previous decades. Even foreign economic and environmental experts and organizations (such as the World Bank) take part in regular consultations to formulate and evaluate the Chinese government's multi-year programs.

China's medium- and long-term development planning is a state activity designed to exceed separate work in individual policy areas. It focuses on the following core functions:

- *Strategic policy coordination* in the sense of prioritizing and coordinating state action programs in many policy areas from an anticipatory, long-term perspective.
- *Resource mobilization* in the sense of mobilizing and pooling limited resources with the aim of bringing about structural changes that are identified by the government as necessary to achieve sustainable and lasting economic, social, or environmental development.
- *Macroeconomic control* in the sense of controlling the level of, and changes in, key economic variables, with the aim of achieving set priority development targets, preventing serious economic downturns, and mitigating the effects of external shocks that may be driven by the global trading and financial systems.

However, the effectiveness of development planning is subject to dispute in China. Although there is substantial evidence of efficient planning implementation with respect to infrastructure development, the fight against poverty, or technology policy, for example, there are also cases of planning failures, particularly regarding efforts to introduce a new growth model that is not investment- and export-led. Due to this significant variation in the efficiency of state development planning in China, it is difficult to make general judgments about the planning system (for instance, "China's state planning is effective and up-to-date" or it is "ineffective and obsolete") and instead one must differentiate according to different policy areas based on the different outcomes over time.

The processes and effects of long-term programs can be seen in a number of the following case studies, but especially clearly in infrastructure policy (Section 6.8), industrial policy (Section 6.9), and education policy (Section 6.17). An exceptional variation in international comparisons of long-term planning is found in China's "centennial projects," such as the South–North Water Transfer Project (Section 6.18). The case study on environmental policy (Section 6.11) again illustrates the considerable tensions between long-term developmental priorities and short-term economic growth.

Experimental programs and policy innovation

Decentralized reform initiatives and local reform experiments capable of becoming nationwide political programs have been of utmost importance for China's economic development since 1978. They are part of a special methodology for policy experimentation (政策试验) that is able to open up a wide range of unexpected opportunities for action in a cumbersome, bureaucratic, and authoritarian system of government.

This special methodology, which also finds expression in the rather idiosyncratic Chinese terminology used to describe it, essentially consists of three steps. First, local "experimentation points" (试点) or "experimentation zones" (试验区) are established. Second, from these pilot projects successful "model experiments" (典型试验) are identified and expanded "from point to surface" (由点到面 or 以点带面) to test the extent to which the new policy options can be generalized or require modification. Third, the policies are not implemented in national legislation until they have been thoroughly tried and tested in a real-life administrative environment, a process that usually takes a number of years. As an example, it took a total of twenty-three years from 1984 when the first experiments with the insolvency of state-owned enterprises (SOEs) occurred until 2007 when a national bankruptcy law entered into force, during which time many experimental regulations were tested in this controversial policy area—initially in individual cities, industries, and companies.

The best-known variants of this experimentation internationally are China's special economic zones (SEZs) (经济特区), which were explicitly set up as experimental areas open to the outside world and governed by modern, economic regulations. Almost without exception, the most important policy reform measures— ranging from rural decollectivization and management reforms in the SOEs and the setting up of stock markets to reforms in the rural healthcare system—originated from decentralized experiments that always remained subject to selective interventions from high-level party and government leaders. The essential interplay between decentralized and centralized initiatives promotes experimental policy making: some phases of the experimentation process are strongly decentralized (the initiation of local experiments and the carrying out of official experimental programs), whereas other phases (the identification of successful, local "model experiments" and the initiative to expand "from point to surface") are centralized. Overarching policy targets are established centrally, but policy instruments are developed and tested locally before they are applied nationwide.

In practice, the experimental approach allows new solutions, which continue to emerge in a permanent search process, to be identified for adaptation. This approach of step-by-step policy making was a critical prerequisite for China to be able to carry out such comprehensive political and institutional changes since the 1980s—despite the inertia of many institutional, policy, and ideological forces—without the party-state collapsing as a result.

The Chinese approach to developing reform and innovation measures is unconventional, since testing of new action programs routinely occurs ahead of national legislation. In contrast, in the democratic constitutional states, a new law or regulation generally kicks off policy implementation, and administrative activity is bound by statute as a matter of principle. However, China's experimental activity is incompatible with the strict legal standards for administrative action. The testing of reforms *before* enacting legislation is key to understanding the Chinese government's ability since 1978 to adapt and innovate in many policy areas —not only with respect to economic and technology policy, but also in terms of expanding its social-security systems.

The following case studies clearly highlight the distinctive features of policy experimentation, driven essentially by the dynamics of local experimentation zones and pilot projects, for example, the introduction of state pensions for China's rural population (Section 6.5), China's innovation policy (Section 6.10), and urbanization strategy (Section 6.15).

Adjusting priorities by means of target setting in the cadre system

In most political systems, the overarching lists of targets and priorities set by governments and parliaments are framed in vague and selective terms (often only immediately after a new government has come to power) or for narrowly defined policy areas based on consensus (environment and technology policy, for instance). In everyday governance, however, the original list of goals is usually transferred only in part or incrementally to national legislation, as the process tends to be diverted and thwarted by the constraints of domestic compromise or by a constant stream of urgent new action requirements (crisis management).

Governments and the parliamentary majorities that support them very rarely define the quantitative performance targets against which government activity can subsequently be periodically measured in legislation. In fact, legislators usually avoid committing to quantitative performance targets in transparent and verifiable ways. Plausible reasons are given to justify this reasoning, for instance, governments are unable to control or influence many economic and social development variables in an open market economy. At the same time, there is a strong political interest to not allow government performance to be measurable via quantitative guidelines because this would leave the government open to political attack in the event of negative developments.

In administrative practice, this procedure means that the vaguely defined goals in established laws are unable to provide any effective guidance. The administrative systems of many industrial and emerging countries are organized according to principles and practices of corporate management ("New Public Management"), whereby quantitative performance targets play a crucial role to steer administrative action within departmental bureaucracies. These performance targets generally refer only to narrow bureaucratic departmental guidelines (in line with their remit for fiscal or environmental administration, for example) and do not refer to key political goals, such as providing comprehensive support for an economic-structural change, maintaining social stability, or supporting technological investments.

Governments and administrations in China operate quite differently from most political systems. They try to channel the activities of leading cadres (领导干部) within party and state bodies based on a broad spectrum of quantitative targets (干部指标). These goals are not restricted to the specific responsibilities of individual departmental administrations ("mission-based targets"); they also include overarching national and political objectives ("nonmission-based targets"; Gao Jie 2010) that are determined by high levels in the party and government leaderships. These range from advancing the organization of the CCP and the fight against corruption to orienting the economy and administration toward innovation, and finally to the maintenance of social stability.

Targets and performance goals for leading cadres are designed to guarantee enforcement of national policies at lower levels of government. Consequently, administrative action in China is guided by people and party-based (cadre-based) responsibility and accountability. An assessment of administrative performance is primarily based on political specifications and interventions by means of the CCP cadre system, not on state statutory or bureaucratic rules.

The system of cadre evaluation that is based on political priorities and target setting is the central mechanism for carrying out the national political leadership's priorities that are partly adjusted in the medium and long term and partly adjusted in the short term. Promotions, demotions, and dismissals of state-sector employees are formally dependent on regular (mostly annual) assessments of cadre performance (干部考核). In addition, promotions and recommendations by high-ranking inner-party patrons are essential for careers as leading party cadres. Since the 1990s, the CCP organization departments responsible for cadre administration have continuously adjusted the lists of goals and assessment processes in line with the priorities of the party leadership. However, quantitative performance benchmarks are very susceptible to manipulation of the results and of the reporting of data (for instance, those containing economic, social, or environmental statistics), which can be used to systematically distort or gloss over actual evaluation results.

It is evident that government and administrative activities in the PRC are driven by completely different mechanisms, criteria, incentives, and sanctions than they are in other industrial and emerging economies. Policy priorities set over the long term, or added at short notice and predetermined by the party leadership, take precedence over legal and departmental criteria. The CCP's action priorities are indicated in the performance targets of the leading cadres. Compared with international benchmarks, this administrative management practice produces special opportunities for action and creates unique outcomes.

On the one hand, work priorities can be clearly indicated and adjusted at short notice by means of the cadre performance targets. Since the 1990s the national party leadership has been setting quantitative targets to require all government authorities to actively attract foreign investors, force the expansion of China's physical infrastructure, introduce new environmental standards in industry, and abolish special rural levies. On the other hand, hard quantitative targets give rise to state interventions that do not show any consideration for the interests and rights of the affected societal groups and individuals. For example, quantitative targets for birth control (strict upper limits for domestic birth rates) or for the fight against crime (arrest quotas and conviction rates) regularly lead to excessively violent law enforcement that is accompanied by serious violations of civil rights. This indicates that the legacy of authoritarian planning and the campaign regime is incompatible with law-based administrative practices and judicial review. Ultimately, China's administration continues to be unaccountable either to the law or to the general public; it is only accountable to the top level of the CCP hierarchy.

In all of the following case studies, the incentive and sanction mechanisms for cadre evaluations play a key role in the dynamics and outcomes of state activity. Governance via performance targets is particularly important in the areas of infrastructure policy (Section 6.8), industrial policy (Section 6.9), innovation policy (Section 6.10), and environmental policy (Section 6.11), for which binding, indisputable performance targets are set by national or subnational party leaderships.

Policy implementation by means of campaigns

Policy action programs are implemented by the state authorities in all government systems in the form of laws and regulations. Political communication skills and public relations campaigns may facilitate the acceptance of action programs among the administration and the population, thereby expediting implementation. However, with respect to the instruments available to implement and carry out policies, the methods in democratically elected governments are limited to lawful administrative authorities and courts or to legally authorized central banks and state development banks.

With respect to its revolutionary origins, the PRC's political system is a mobilization and campaign regime that until now has not relied only on bureaucratic methods of policy implementation: mobilization campaigns led by the CCP can serve to push urgent action requirements and crisis responses past the bureaucracy. If the party leadership is unhappy with the state administration's implementation of priority policy programs or seeks to achieve accelerated implementation of crisis measures, for example, it regularly falls back on direct mobilization via the party hierarchy, state media, and grassroots organizations. Strikingly, this campaign mode emerged in the recent past in the fight against the deadly severe acute respiratory syndrome (SARS) epidemic of 2003 and in the national relief measures for the catastrophic earthquake of 2008, and even in the anti-corruption campaign of 2013–15. In all these cases, conventional bureaucratic, organizational instruments were combined with political pressures, ideology and media campaigns, inspection teams sent from party headquarters, and ad hoc disciplinary measures. In its campaign mode, the Communist Party has at its disposal the opportunity to push through its political will even when it faces lethargic, reluctant, or corrupt administrative departments at lower levels of government.

The typical sequence of events for each campaign is the following: (1) The higher echelons of the CCP reach a consensus about which action requirements have highest priority; (2) The CCP headquarters sets the campaign targets; (3) Enormous pressures for implementation are applied to the lower levels of the CCP via the party hierarchy and cadre system by means of deadlines, quotas, and propaganda; (4) Administrative work routines are allowed to lapse in an almost military combat and mobilization atmosphere; party secretaries take over direct supervision of the key authorities; (5) The higher levels of the CCP and government demonstrate their power to crack down on local departments by establishing new, on-the-spot command headquarters or by dispatching high-ranking special inspection teams from party headquarters; (6) Communist Party discipline inspection commissions remove incompetent or recalcitrant officials from office in summary trials; CCP organization departments reorganize leading party organs; and (7) the state media broadcasts news of successes, praises campaign models, and warns about the consequences of misconduct or lack of discipline based on real examples.

The direct, military mobilization variety of policy implementation has repeatedly proven to be effective in the fight against serious wrongdoings and crises (for instance, in the fight against smuggling in 1998; the containment of SARS in 2003; and the investment program to counter the effects of the global financial crisis in 2007–9). Ineffective campaigns seek to improve implementation of ongoing administrative and legal tasks (for example, combating counterfeiting; insuring the safety of pharmaceutical drugs; or improving healthcare in the rural areas).

Policy campaigns can be understood as a type of "reserve capacity" that allows party headquarters to exert extreme nationwide pressures in order to implement policies selectively and for a limited period. These mobilization methods are a mainstay of the Chinese central state authority and capacity for action, and are in no way consistent with a constitutional or regulatory state based on a lawful administration.

The importance of the campaign methodology for state activity in China is particularly striking in the following case studies on disaster management (DM) (Section 6.13), the countermeasures against the global financial crisis in 2007–9 (Section 6.6), and media policy and perception management (Section 6.4). The limits of the effectiveness of campaigns to resolve ongoing administrative and legal tasks can clearly be seen in the area of food safety (Section 6.12).

Inputs from within the state: Policy advice and consultation on government policy

CCP headquarters and the State Council have jurisdiction over the setting of strategic guidelines and national programs. At the preparatory stages of the decision-making process during normal times (that is, when the government is not in a crisis or mobilization mode), the political leadership is supported by an "army" of technocrats, think-tanks, and experts who have considerable influence over the formulation of state action programs and long-term planning. Since the 2000s, the working rules of the State Council have explicitly insisted on including scientific advice in policy preparation.

One striking example of the importance and scale of consultations was the preparation of the long-term national plan for technological development for the 2006–20 period. Between 2003 and 2006, more than 2,000 scientists, engineers, and representatives of the business world were consulted on this strategic project to identify challenges and ways to overcome them. These discussions occasionally gave rise to fierce arguments over priorities, organizational models, and the use of funds. The balance between "indigenous innovation" (自主创新) and international cooperation provoked controversial discussions. The party leadership ultimately decided that indigenous innovation should take priority in order to limit the dominance of foreign-technology companies over the medium and long term.

With respect to national policy formulation, China has become a considerable expertocracy: the political leadership routinely farms out the protracted processes for internal consultations and for reaching compromises to dedicated task forces assembled from a mix of top officials and a large number of experts in the relevant fields, some with and some without links to the government. The offices of the Leading Small Groups (LSGs) serve as a linchpin by taking on the role of preparing and formulating the national long-term restructuring programs (see Section 2.3.4 and Section 3.4). The heads of the task forces are usually former scientists now conducting background work for the CCP Politburo, and additional external experts and scientists recruited to work for limited periods of time on the task forces that are set up for specific projects.

In the field of policy advice provided by think-tanks (Zhu Xufeng 2012), the following actors can be identified: (1) Ministerial research and advisory institutes that carry out studies for state departments, but these studies are limited by ministerial interests; (2) State think-tanks that are not under the control of any particular ministry and therefore enjoy more latitude in terms of their areas of research (this also includes the State Council Development Research Center (DRC), which can initiate research programs independently); and (3) Nongovernmental think-tanks that are financed by state, private, or international sources and thus enjoy greater independence from the government, even though they sometimes are suspected of falling victim to the interests of lobbies. It is not the institutional classification that is crucial in terms of the influence of the think-tanks, but the access and trust that the leading researchers and advisers enjoy among high-ranking policy makers. China's highest-ranking decision-makers are placing increasing weight on expertise that comes from outside the state apparatus instead of being filtered by ministerial interests.

In all the policy areas examined in the following case studies, scientific policy advice and consultation play an important role in policy preparation, evaluations, and revisions, no matter whether they are drawn from within the state, from academia, or from abroad.

External inputs: Lobbying, policy entrepreneurs, nongovernmental initiatives, and surveys

Policy formulation and policy revisions in China are still primarily dominated by actors within the state. Nevertheless, there are various informal channels through which economic and societal interests may be fed into official policy making.

Political lobbying by interest groups is not officially acceptable within the PRC. Instead, regular consultations about legislative initiatives are held, to which the government may invite selected representatives from the relevant branches of industry and society. Opinions on draft laws and regulations may also be sought from foreign companies and organizations. In many cases, the objections and recommendations from those consulted will lead to modifications or corrections, and in exceptional cases they will lead to substantial changes, even to the extent of resulting in the withdrawal of the proposals. The influence of interest groups in policy formulation and implementation occurs in informal ways beyond the formal consultation procedures. Special interests become part of the policy process via informal and personal contacts between the lobbying actors (including many "princelings" and think-tank researchers) and the administrative policy decision-makers (see Section 3.7.4).

Beyond the predominantly economic lobbying, it is worth noting that sometimes very effective activities will be carried out by individual policy entrepreneurs who seek to put particular topics and concerns on the policy agenda, such as environmental protection, judicial reforms, protection of private companies, or disability rights. The chances that such policy entrepreneurship will be successful depend on a range of typical preconditions: nonconfrontational "framing" and careful timing of the initiatives with a view to the possibility that they are included on the current policy agenda; scientific or entrepreneurial prestige, media prominence, and active multimedia public relations work; building the largest possible following on social media; and personal access to insiders within the CCP and government headquarters.

Nongovernmental initiatives that are successfully incorporated into domestic policies are often closely connected to individual policy entrepreneurs. In the context of large-scale state projects (such as dam building) or major accidents (water contamination by chemical plants, for instance), some environmental initiatives have been successful in changing the location, adjusting the plan, or even abandoning the projects (Mertha 2008). The Xi–Li administration, however, has restricted the room for maneuver for those initiatives that include extensive dialogues with foreign NGOs and that are supported by foreign funding (see Section 5.5.3).

At present, opinion polls are the most systematic external inputs in domestic, especially local, policy making. With increasing frequency, opinion poll studies are assigned by government departments at local levels to test the response to government measures and administrative actions (for instance, with respect to the environment, education, or transportation). Yet most such surveys are not published. They merely serve as feedback and as an early warning mechanism, aimed at helping the government identify areas of dissatisfaction or social unrest as early as possible (*Economist* 2015). Used in this way, surveys may indeed contribute to increased levels of responsiveness within the government system. Such state surveys focus on recording the collective, "objective," ascertainable will of the "masses," rather than particular preferences, pluralistic competitions, or even criticisms of the political system. Therefore, surveys do not generate political participation and responsibility. But they are useful for providing concrete administrative adjustments under the control of the party bodies. The impacts of such surveys are limited to the subnational levels that provide most public services.

Particularly active involvement by lobbies, policy entrepreneurs, and nongovernmental initiatives can be seen in the following case studies in the fields of industrial policy (Section 6.9) and environmental policy (Section 6.11). A striking example of a struggle by various interest groups is provided by the case study on the abolition of administrative detention ("re-education through labor") (Section 6.3). An example of the way in which the government has dealt with unwanted external inputs can be seen in the case study on mega projects (Section 6.18).

Governance based on ICT: E-government and public services

Since 2002, the Chinese government has approved extensive programs aimed at using information and communications technologies (ICT) to modernize state activity, that is, to establish a stronger service-oriented administration and new forms of interaction among the citizenry and the administration. However, there is no single, standardized, efficient e-government platform. Rather, there is a patchwork of local initiatives with completely different functions and services. Due to ICT, there were huge leaps forward in fiscal administration with regard to registration and revenue, but social-security systems still remain a huge challenge due to fragmented administrative and ICT infrastructures.

Access to government documents for citizens and companies has improved significantly because of the rise in the number of comprehensive institutional websites (Liou 2007). Yet China's state authorities are still a long way from their stated aim of promoting transparent and open administrative processes (政务公开). Online platforms have gained increasing importance in terms of accepting reports and complaints from the general public in the event of abuse of office and corruption. The purpose of setting up complaints bureaus, however, is to tighten monitoring of individual authorities and officials within the state administration (Göbel 2016).

At the time of this writing (2016), it is striking how actively many Chinese authorities use online messaging services to keep the general public informed in the event of disasters, to coordinate relief efforts, or to organize searches for missing persons, for instance. The police in many cities routinely use social media for traffic information or even for launching appeals to trace wanted persons.

Many areas of state activity in China are increasingly characterized by ICT. It is foreseeable that by the beginning of the 2020s, China's state administration will rank among the world's most advanced innovators in e-government. In parallel, supervisory and service functions for the new technologies will develop and likely will be performed on increasingly integrated technological platforms.

Propaganda and cyber control: Controlling public opinion

Pluralist political systems begin from the assumption that public opinion is formed by different positions competing with one another, but it cannot and should not be predetermined, channeled, or manipulated by the state. However, the CCP has a completely different perception that governs its views of the Internet and social media. According to CCP propaganda experts, public opinion is malleable and can be actively shaped through selective information and political guidance. The general public—including cyberspace—is defined as a "battleground" that must be dominated and controlled by the CCP in order to root out "incorrect," "unpatriotic," and politically inflammatory positions.

The "propaganda work" (宣传工作) of the CCP has been fundamentally transformed and updated in the age of the Internet and social media. Although the CCP propaganda specialists initially viewed the new interactive media as a threat to CCP hegemony, they have now begun to use the new technology to implement comprehensive control and censorship measures and to actively regulate cyberspace.

Traditionally, political conformity within the PRC was ensured by strict regulation of public language. Politically binding standard phrases (提法)—such as "Harmonious Society," the "Scientific Outlook on Development," the "China Dream," or the "Four Comprehensives" (see Section 2.1.2)—function as a loyalty ritual built into the language. As a consequence, conformity becomes audible and the political hierarchy is reinforced, since only party headquarters, with the CCP general secretary at the helm, is allowed to coin such standard phrases. The political effects of this are far-reaching: the public language used by the Chinese leadership is homogenized. Public speech remains separate from private social discourse. The dilemma for the CCP is that any official regulation of language usually produces only ritual lip-service and empty, tactical, and clichéd phrases. The divide between public and private language encourages cynicism and constant psychological tensions, even among the political elites who are supposed to support the political system.

Since the 1980s, the state media has no longer been able to reach the bulk of the population with its standard phrases, with the result that in the era of cyberspace officials in charge of ideology and propaganda have been trying to develop new ways to reach the general public. Party departments use popular formats, such as social media, messaging services, short message services (SMS), and cartoons, to broadcast their official communications to previously unreachable "netizens." Hence, control of public opinion by party authorities has adapted to the new technologies (Tai Zixue 2006). Internet-based technologies are deliberately encouraged by the Chinese government and they are protected from politically unreliable foreign competition. At the same time, one of the world's most effective supervisory and censoring systems has been developed (often referred to as the "Great Firewall") to maintain CCP control over public opinion in cyberspace.

By 2015, party and government bodies had made great strides in extending the new institutional technology to manage public opinion in cyberspace. In 2015 the party leadership demanded that all party and government organs actively engage in the new "battleground of public opinion," i.e., cyberspace, to propagate and popularize government positions. Heavily clichéd official language remained the domain of the traditional print and television formats. In social media, however, government opinions are spread via concise and casual WeChat styles, with simply expressed colorful graphics and cartoons. The state media continue to define official positions and messages, but more recently such communications have been reformatted and popularized through social media.

The political instruments for channeling public opinion in China are undergoing a complete reorganization driven by the new communications technologies. Many cadres in the propaganda system regard social media as an extremely flexible and effective new tool. The case studies on managing social media (Section 6.4) and Internet security (Section 6.16) reveal the importance of control over public opinion and the battle over cyberspace.

6.2 Administrative modernization and economic deregulation

Matthias Stepan

Since the 1980s, restrictions on state interventions in economic life have been a key element of administrative reforms aimed at strengthening economic growth in many states. Reducing the bureaucracy and deregulating economic administration are potentially capable of being much more effective in China than they are in liberal market economies, since the legacy of the planned economy in China allows state authorities ample scope for intervention. Until now, the extent of state economic management in many sectors in China is far greater than it is in liberal market economies.

Reducing the bureaucracy primarily means reducing the bureaucratic costs for the state and for companies, with the objective of making processes more efficient and more transparent. The declared goals of deregulation are to simplify and reduce the applicable regulations—those assessed as being obsolete or redundant, such as the administrative requirements for starting a company. At the same time, the Chinese government must adopt new regulations aimed at promoting investment activities and market competition by establishing legal and regulatory treatments that are the same for all market participants (especially nondiscrimination of private and foreign companies).

Administrative modernization in China is facing difficult barriers, and there is no sign that the political and social controls will be surrendered. In fact, there are even plans to concentrate and strengthen state supervision in sensitive areas. This is not a question of "liberalization" per se, but rather a case of strictly controlling market deregulation through simultaneous reorganizitation and streamlining, and therefore making the state supervisory authorities potentially more effective.

Since the start of this century, the system of administrative examinations and approvals (行政审批制度) has been at the center of debates about administrative modernization. Examination and approval items are a central part of Chinese administration. By virtue of the large number of involved authorities, the unclear jurisdictions, high fees, and long waiting times, these procedures have long been irritants for entrepreneurs.

Key actors and interests

The State Commission Office for Public Sector Reform (SCOPSR) (中央机构编制委员会办公室, or for short: 中编办) has been a central actor with regard to reforms to reduce the bureaucracy and to deregulate economic administration. As a commission under the direct leadership of the premier, the SCOPSR has a special influence on organizational and departmental reforms as well as on the administrative areas of authority of Chinese government bodies.

Although the SCOPSR has extensive powers within the state administration, other authorities are still able to oppose reform initiatives in a covert manner. For instance, they may delay reorganization instructions or use evasive strategies during implementation of such initiatives to postpone staff cuts or to limit the scope of authority. It is the task of the Ministry of Supervision (MOS) (监察部) to prevent such evasive strategies. Given that state supervision and sanctions were often in-

Table 6.2.A

Actors involved in deregulation programs

Actors	Tasks and interests
State Commission Office for Public Sector Reform (SCOPSR)	Planning administrative reforms; distributing tasks among state bodies; determining departmental plans and public-sector salaries; increasing the efficiency of state authorities
Ministry of Supervision	Supervising the work of the ministries and individual officials; ensuring that central-government instructions are followed
Office of the State Council Leading Small Group for Reform of the Administrative Approval System	Coordinating inter-ministerial collaboration to reform the system of administrative examinations and approvals; supervision over implementation
Companies	Interest in clearly regulating areas of authority, procedures, and administrative costs; reducing bureaucratic obstacles and compliance costs
General public	Interest in clearly regulating areas of authority, procedures, and administrative costs; reducing the number of authorities
WTO; Foreign chambers of commerce in China	Reducing bureaucratic obstacles and costs for market access, investments, and entrepreneurial activity in China
Subnational governments	Retaining approval items to ensure control over the economy and society; administrative fees as a source of income

© MERICS

effective, during the 1990s the central government opened its first channels for economic actors to voice their demands. Interest groups from Chinese industry, foreign chambers of commerce, and the World Trade Organization (WTO) have since intensified calls for reducing the bureaucracy and deregulation (see Table 6.2.A).

Decision-making and conflicts

In 1998, during the negotiations in the run-up to WTO accession, former Premier Zhu Rongji who supported deregulation used the WTO requirements to overcome resistance within the economic bureaucracy. The work on draft laws began with the involvement of academic experts and led eventually to passage by the National People's Congress (NPC) of the Administrative Licensing Law (行政许可法) in August 2003. By 2001, the State Council had established a LSG, with an administrative office in the MOS, that was designed to coordinate and supervise the work of the various ministries in their work on reducing the administrative examination and approval items.

Although administrative examination and approval items may entail high costs for both individuals and companies, economic interests were central to the debate. Experts discussed not only ways of simplifying and reducing the items, but also reviewed the advantages and disadvantages for foreign and domestic companies. Many central-government actors supported a nationwide standardization of items. But subnational governments feared losing both influence and income. At the end of 2002, not long after China's entry into the WTO, the State Council abolished almost 800 such approval items. The Administrative Licensing Law contained additional new measures designed to reduce the number and types of items and to make the entire process more transparent. However, the law provided no guidance about how these goals were to be achieved.

Implementation

After the law was passed, the State Council pushed ahead with rapid implementation. In September 2003, senior state and party representatives approved further training programs for government staff at all levels. At the end of December, the State Council published a notice about the implementation provisions: during the first phase, extending to the end of March 2004, authorities were to verify the necessity of the examination and approval items within their respective areas of responsibility; during the second phase, until the end of May, all items deemed unnecessary were to be abolished.

The LSG responsible for the draft bill had already identified a widespread circumvention strategy. To avoid losing their decision-making powers as well as their income, the authorities utilized a number of loopholes to bypass the items. Because the law only covered administrative actions, the number of items classified as non-administrative approval items (非行政审批) increased.

The state attempted to prevent this avoidance strategy. Two documents released by the State Council Legal Office in 2004, with the goal of clarifying "relevant issues regarding the Administrative Licensing Law," attempted to define the scope of the law (Bath 2008). Three main criteria for administrative approvals were established: (1) Activities were to be financial or societal in nature; (2) Administrative approvals were to relate to activities that took place outside the territory of the authorities; and (3) Administrative approvals were to refer to decisions taken by the authorities that occurred at the request of a citizen or a legal entity, after verification of the factual circumstances.

In January 2004, the premier stressed the significance of the law in terms of administrative modernization. By mid-2004, the State Council decided to streamline or completely abolish almost one-half of all approval items that fell within the authority of the central government. In the summer of 2004, the State Council guaranteed the continued existence of 600 items that required state supervision or confidentiality.

Policy outcomes and policy adjustments

Implementation of the Administrative Licensing Law initially led to large-scale inventories, documentation, and verifications of the various examination and approval items. The reforms improved the procedures and responsibilities involved in granting approvals. Nevertheless, this did not lead to a fundamental rethinking of the role of the state in supervising and regulating economic activities. Today, there are still no nationwide procedural standards due to the influence of subnational governments. Companies therefore have complained that the reforms did not go far enough. In fact, even though the number of required approval items has declined, the number of criteria they must meet has stayed about the same. The lack of transparency with regard to the responsibilities of the various authorities, as well as the requisite high fees, have been repeatedly criticized in media reports. In 2007 the State Council responded by approving a document designed to increase transparency and to simplify open access to government documents (State Council 2007).

At regular intervals—in 2007, 2010, and 2012—the State Council called for additional reductions in the number of approval items. By the beginning of Li Keqiang's tenure as premier in March 2013, the number of items for which central-government authorities were responsible stood at about 1,700. Li promised either to abolish about one-third of these items or to delegate them to lower levels of government (Song Shiming 2013).

Organizationally, the office of the State Council LSG for Reform of the Administrative Approval System was transferred from the MOS to the SCOPSR, which was headed by Premier Li Keqiang. Between March 2013 and September 2014, six rounds of deregulation and decentralization took place. Efforts by the central government to deregulate the bureaucracy accelerated considerably compared to the efforts undertaken during the previous administrations (see Table 6.2.B).

In 2014 the State Council ordered systematic disclosures of all existing examination and approval items. The central-government authorities subsequently published detailed lists of examination and approval items under their respective jurisdictions. Within the government, there were discussions as to which items could be abolished or delegated to other departments without relinquishing control and supervision over important areas. Unlike under his predecessors, administrative powers of approval under Premier Li Keqiang were no longer transferred to business associations and other government-sponsored organizations. Instead, almost all examination and approval powers were delegated to subnational governments, even though these authorities had very little experience in processing such items that involved very complex materials and huge investments. Implementation of the

Table 6.2.B

Deregulation: Reducing central-government approval items, 2002-14

	Zhu Rongji's government (2002-3)	Wen Jiabao's government I (2003-8)	Wen Jiabao's government II (2008-13)	Li Keqiang's government (2013-14)
Rounds of reforms	2	2	2	6
Items abolished	1,195	537	284	333
Delegation of items to non-state institutions (business interest groups, for example)	82	39	0	1
Delegation of items to local authorities (decentralization)	0	76	188	106

Sources: 2002-2012: Reform Magazine: Thematic Research 2013; 2013-2014: State Council Decisions.

new push toward deregulation involves two basic risks: delays due to a lack of the requisite expertise in local procedures, and growing uncertainties on the part of companies with regard to the increasingly varied procedures and standards.

6.3 Internal security and justice: Abolition of "re-education through labor"

Yi Zhu

In November 2013 China's party leadership announced abolition of the system of administrative detentions, "re-education through labor" (*laojiao*) (劳动教养, or for short: 劳教). International organizations and the media praised this decision as an important step in legal reform, which would have a positive impact on protecting fundamental human rights, especially in terms of arbitrary detentions. Like many other changes in the Chinese judicial and penal systems, abolition of this system could only be achieved after many years of sometimes internal and sometimes public controversies. The key steps involved in bringing about the elimination of "re-education through labor" created new problems.

Key actors and interests

Since the 1950s, the police have been allowed to detain people without trials for *laojiao* in labor camps or prisons for up to four years and to force them to work in industry, construction projects, or agriculture. This system of administrative detention proved to be extraordinarily susceptible to arbitrariness and abuse by the police authorities: without judicial interventions, many Chinese citizens were condemned to years of forced labor for minor offenses or for arbitrarily determined moral or political misdemeanors. Efforts to change or abolish this iron-handed form of punishment began in the 1990s, with legal scholars and public intellectuals playing a leading role. In specialist publications and internal reform papers, jurists and attorneys, along with members and advisers to the Legal Affairs Commission of the NPC and judicial organizations, called for a new law governing "re-education through labor." Prominent "public intellectuals" then used their access to the market-oriented media and their prominence in social media to mobilize wider attention to the grievances and to the need to reform the *laojiao* system (see Table 6.3).

Table 6.3

Actors and interests involved in reforming the penal system

Actors	Tasks and interests
National: CCP Central Committee's Political and Legal Affairs Commission and the MPS	To use the *laojiao* system as a flexible instrument for suppressing unwanted political behavior and for "maintaining social stability"; to generate profits from forced labor
Local governments and police authorities	To use the *laojiao* system as a flexible instrument for suppressing resistance against the local authorities and investors; to generate profits from forced labor
NPC (Legal Affairs Commission); Ministry of Justice (MOJ); courts	To strengthen the legislature with respect to administrative orders; to strengthen judicial organizations with respect to the police
Legal experts outside the state administration	To support rule of law and human rights
Attorneys	To improve labor conditions in criminal proceedings
Social campaigners (including former detainees)	To abolish arbitrary detentions
Market-oriented media	To increase users through reports and debates with wide appeal

© MERICS

Decision-making and conflicts

The principle of "re-education through labor" follows the ideological and practical example of the USSR model. After the victory of the Chinese Revolution and the founding of the state in 1949, China's new Communist government carried out a full-scale "purge" of the society, the economy, and the administration, and set up a comprehensive labor camp system. Political rivals and suspects were arrested as "counterrevolutionaries" and sent to penal camps for "re-education." Waves of arrests were carried out in successive political campaigns and by tribunals of party and security bodies rather than through criminal proceedings bound by regulations. In 1957 China's central government adopted a formal regulation that served as the basis for the further development of the *laojiao* system.

Following the end of the Mao era, the *laojiao* system was transformed from an instrument for ideological supervision and indoctrination into an instrument to maintain stability and to combat unwanted and new forms of divergent social behavior. Beginning in 1982, the Ministry of Public Security defined a list of offenses that merited "re-education through labor," as opposed to criminal or legal prosecution. The list included, among others, prostitution, drug use, and the unapproved submission of petitions (mostly complaints against local authorities). New offenses were continually added to the list. Official statistics about the number of people sent to *laojiao* have never been published. But in 2013 the Chinese media reported that there were more than 300 detention centers throughout the country, with a total of about 260,000 inmates (Xinhuanet 2013).

The *laojiao* system produced complex social and political conflicts. Chinese attorneys criticized the illegality of administrative detention because the Chinese Constitution only allows detention with the permission of the district attorney or the courts. The Legislation Law states that only the NPC and the NPC Standing Committee can pass regulations to sentence people to imprisonment. Irregularities in the practice of *laojiao* attracted intense public criticism because the local police authorities had sole responsibility for making decisions about detention and the length of sentences. Detainees labored under very harsh conditions. Cases have been documented of physical abuse, torture, and even death during periods of administrative detention. The use of income generated from the forced labor generally remained unknown, but because the scope for creating additional income was under cover, it was very much in the interests of the security authorities to retain the system. Attorneys criticized these various difficulties by providing legal representation to those held in *laojiao*. However, unlike in judicial proceedings, no reliable remedial actions could be taken against police decisions regarding *laojiao* procedures.

Implementation

Beginning in the 1990s, reorganization of the *laojiao* system was supported by many Chinese legal scholars as well as individual members of the party and government. Nevertheless, the process of implementing the reforms proved to be extremely difficult. To begin with, experts in the Ministry of Justice (MOJ) and the Legal Affairs Commission of the NPC Standing Committee sought to create a standardized statutory basis for administrative detentions. The relevant legislative procedures found their way into a number of official NPC legislative plans. The project was put on hold, however, in 1999 when the government cracked down on the nationwide activities and protests by the Falun Gong movement, which was perceived to be a dangerous cult that had to be suppressed. Supported by the security services, the *laojiao* system proved to be a quick and flexible instrument for sending large numbers of Falun Gong supporters to forced labor without trials. Because the government prohibited any criticism of its repression of Falun Gong, preparations for the reorganization of "re-education through labor" failed to make any progress.

Subsequently, individual demands for reform appeared in the form of academic papers, open letters, and motions during NPC meetings. The line of reasoning was usually based on legal issues and it failed to attract wide attention in society. In 2005 the NPC Standing Committee enacted a law on the "correction of unlawful conduct" (违法行为矫治法), which was designed to replace the traditional *laojiao* system. However, as a result of massive resistance by police authorities and local governments, this initiative never took hold.

In addition to these internal state clashes, a new kind of public media was simultaneously growing (see Section 5.6). Due to the rapid development of social media in particular, prominent opinion-makers were increasingly able to raise and popularize topics in public debates that previously had been limited to opinions expressed internally within the state. Social scientist Yu Jianrong was influential in the formation of opinion regarding the reorganization of administrative detention. To circumvent the political red line that had been drawn regarding the repression of Falun Gong, Yu Jianrong focused on studies of less highly charged cases, in which Chinese citizens had been punished with *laojiao* because they had submitted petitions or complaints about local authorities. Together with journalists, attorneys, and artists, Yu distributed these personal and tragic stories in a media-friendly format via his own personal microblog. A decisive breakthrough occurred in 2010: the taboos on discussions about "re-education through labor" were removed and it became a popular topic in the extremely active media of the time.

Public debate alone could not have produced a political breakthrough—not without tapping into intra-party decision-making. However, favorable circumstances occurred in 2011: an intra-party power struggle between Bo Xilai (party secretary of Chongqing municipality at the time) on the one hand and party headquarters led by CCP General Secretary Hu Jintao on the other. In the area controlled by Bo Xilai, the police imposed *laojiao* on a number of citizens who had expressed on the Internet criticism of Bo's policies. When Bo Xilai was removed from office in 2012, these critics were released and once again were free to speak out. China's traditional and social media then presented their tragic stories as examples of the arbitrariness and susceptibility to abuse of the *laojiao* system, and demanded that it be abolished. In short, a serious intra-party conflict, combined with an increasingly lively public debate, ensured the creation of favorable circumstances for a reorganization of the *laojiao* system.

Policy outcomes and policy adjustments

The new party leadership that came to power under Xi Jinping in 2012 decided to abolish "re-education through labor" not on legal grounds but rather on political grounds. On the one hand, it could blame grievances about the penal system on intra-party opponents (in 2015, Zhou Yongkang, the former head of security and judicial services, was sentenced to life imprisonment for corruption and abuse of office). On the other hand, the new party leadership could present a progressive image both to the general public and to the international media. In this way, supervision of the security services and the strengthening of the court system appeared on the political agenda of the new party leadership as a counterweight to the power of the police.

This development can be perceived as a political success for legal scholars, public intellectuals, journalists, and attorneys. Although these actors stood at the margins of the political center of power, in this case they were able to successfully encourage the general public to talk about a politically sensitive subject as well as to put it on the political agenda of the party leadership.

Yet the real effects of abolishing administrative detention and the progress made in terms of police work and the penal system were regarded with skepticism by many Chinese legal experts, even after 2013. The draft of a new law on the correction of unlawful conduct was not made available to the public. There are still ongoing conflicts over the distribution of decision-making powers between the police and the judicial system. In addition, other—de facto administrative—detention systems continue to exist, such as "detention for education institutions" (收容教育), for prostitutes, or for being committed to psychiatric facilities (安康医院) by the police authorities. New forms of repression for politically undesirable conduct emerged: since 2013 a number of critics of the legal system, including influential opinion-makers in China's social media, such as human-rights attorney Pu Zhiqiang, who earlier had been awarded a media prize for his efforts to abolish the *laojiao* system, have been sentenced to imprisonment for "creating public disturbances" (寻衅滋事罪).

6.4 Media policy: Controlling social media

Kristin Shi-Kupfer

The Chinese government initially paid little attention to social media. In 2007, only a small group of civil rights campaigners, academics, and journalists were using freely accessible American platforms, such as Facebook and Twitter, or their Chinese offshoots. But this changed in the spring of 2009 when users of Chinese microblogging services throughout the country rapidly disseminated online photos and commentaries ridiculing a fire at the controversial new CCTV building in Beijing. During unrest in the autonomous region of Xinjiang in July 2009 (see Section 5.7), eyewitnesses sent independent information from the capital city of Urumqi around the world via Twitter. This was a shock to the government in Beijing. Therefore, in August 2009, the government ordered the closing of all microblogging platforms and the blocking of access to Twitter and Facebook; since then, online messaging services have been the main focus of control of social media (see Table 6.4).

Table 6.4

Actors, tasks, and interests involved in media control

Actors	Tasks	Interests
LSGs for Propaganda and Ideology, and for Cyber Security and Informatization	Formulating national guidelines for media work and Internet regulation	Ideological guidance, controlling information, and retaining the prerogative of interpretation
State Council Internet Information Office (since March 2011)	Carrying out the directives of the LSGs	Powers to intervene; authority to provide instructions regarding the budget and staffing
National ministries and subnational state and party bodies (propaganda, the police, the IT industry)	Specifying national standards in concrete terms for media reporting, propaganda work, crisis communications, etc.	Social media as a source of information and a "mood barometer"; to prevent civil society from mobilizing via the Internet
IT companies	Developing IT products; implementing state provisions (censorship)	Corporate profits; innovative products; legal certainties
Informal IT sector ("Internet Water Army")	Paid public relations work for companies and authorities	Corporate profits; covert influence
Prominent Internet figures	Self-marketing; image-building	Shaping of topics; public influence; increasing revenue
Civil society activists	Criticizing injustices; commitment to disadvantaged people and legal reforms, among other things	Shaping of topics; pluralism of information and opinions; mobilization of citizens

© MERICS

Decision-making and conflicts

After the summer of 2009, it became clear to the Chinese authorities that with the help of microblogging platforms citizens were capable of breaking the CCP monopoly over information. Even so, Beijing still wanted to promote the development of social media. In addition to its economic potential, the Chinese government saw an opportunity to monitor and shape "public opinion on the Internet" (网络舆论) via the new communications channels. In a joint venture with established private IT companies, the CCP leadership sought to build a microblogging sector that it could control. To this end, Beijing prohibited potential foreign competition from the market by means of censorship. In return, domestic Internet companies were supposed to filter "damaging content," that is, content that was politically sensitive. The largest company to profit from this was Sina.com, which already had a fully developed microblogging service, and Sina Weibo, which was able to launch its services only several days after all other platforms had been banned. It took other Chinese IT companies and the state media (China Central Television [CCTV] and the *People's Daily*) several months to catch up. Through careful marketing, such as targeted recruitment of prominent celebrities, economists, and journalists, Sina.com was able to quickly establish itself as a market leader (Wang Tong 2012).

However, the co-opting of microblogs by the government using IT companies did not work as planned: the "V people" attracted by Sina.com ("V" initially stood for "VIP," but later it came to refer to "verified users") quickly gained several million "fans" or followers. They used the platform to disseminate information and to discuss topics that the state media either did not broach at all or only broached in accordance with official propaganda regulations (see Section 5.6). This "counter-media" displayed the official propaganda in its true colors and forced the state authorities to correct their behavior (for example, regarding the train accident in Wenzhou in July 2011). Netizens also increasingly used microblogs to organize protests, such as the demonstrations against a chemical plant in Dalian in August 2011 (Shi-Kupfer/Zhu Yi 2013).

The mobilization potential of microblogs alarmed the top leaders: the former head of the national security apparatus, Zhou Yongkang, and the newly founded Cyberspace Administration of China (CAC) (国家互联网信息办公室) urged IT companies to tighten their control. One month later, Beijing municipality published the first specific conditions for regulating microblogging services: registration under one's real name was compulsory within three months and forbidden content was specified (including "rumors and information that disrupt social order"). Guangdong province imposed its own more liberal conditions that were applied to Tencent, an IT company with headquarters in Guangdong: in this case, registration under one's real name was required only for new users. Concerned that they would lose users, companies implemented the new regulations half-heartedly (Lagerkvist 2012). After microbloggers posted rumors of a military putsch in Beijing as the popular Chongqing party secretary, Bo Xilai, was being removed from office in mid-March 2012, the CAC sent out a clear warning to all microblogging services: sixteen news platforms were closed down and six microbloggers were arrested. Microblogging services Sina.com and Tencent were forced to shut down their comment functions for three days in order to "clean up their information."

Implementation

It clearly surprised the Chinese government that microblogs could develop so quickly into an independent communications and mobilization platform. State authorities initially delegated control to companies that in turn protected them from foreign competition. However, China's leadership underestimated the entrepreneurial interests of the IT companies: the firms felt that excessive regulation blocked the provision of information in an attractive and professional manner and in effect alienated users.

As a result of resistance by the Internet companies, since 2013 the Chinese leadership has been targeting the criminalization of microbloggers. After an ideological policy document on taboo subjects appeared in public debate, the CAC began a campaign on May 2, 2013, against the spreading of "rumors." It deliberately resisted precisely defining "rumors" so as to encourage bloggers to engage in self-censorship. The authorities often classify sensitive information or political statements as "rumors." By the end of August 2013, the security authorities had arrested several hundred microbloggers for "spreading rumors."

The CCP leadership accompanied the wave of arrests with Maoist-style policy instruments: ideological articles in key media, the politicization of real or fabricated moral misdemeanors by prominent microbloggers, and staged "confessions" by suspects held in pretrial custody for violations of the Code of Criminal Procedure. To establish a criminal foundation for such detentions, the government expanded existing laws through the use of legally binding statements issued by the judicial system. In this way, the security services were able to circumvent the formal legislative and appeal processes of the NPC.

Policy outcomes and policy adjustments

The CCP dampened the economic and political momentum of the market leader, Sina Weibo, due to the wave of arrests of opinion-makers (意见领袖). According to a study by East China Normal University (华东师范大学) commissioned by the British newspaper *The Telegraph*, the number of active microbloggers (writing forty posts or more per day) dropped by 79 percent between August and December 2013

(Moore 2014). Since then, Sina Weibo has placed increasing emphasis on the professionalization of infotainment content and on additional commercial functionalities for corporate accounts.

The central leadership also intensified pressures on microblog operators: in October 2014 the Supreme People's Court adopted a judicial "declaration" whereby operators may face civil liability suits for privacy violations committed by their users. Supporters report that user rights have been strengthened, whereas critics regard this as a step toward creating the potential for abuse by the state. The declaration is the first to regard the paid writing of posts by companies working in the previously unregulated informal public-relations sector as illegal (these ghostwriters are known as the "Internet Water Army," 水军).

The instant messaging platform WeChat (微信), which was established in 2011 by the IT company Tencent, has experienced very strong economic growth (see Figure 6.4). Scared off by the state restrictions against Sina Weibo, China's netizens started disseminating potentially sensitive information via closed "friendship circles" (personal contact groups of up to 100 people), which were very difficult for the state censors to filter.

In reaction to this development, in August 2014 the CAC banned private media-makers (自媒体), that is, users not registered as media institutions, from redistributing the "latest news." At the end of April 2015, the authorities published new guidelines on regular inspections of IT information service-providers: if IT service-providers do not consistently implement the state censorship requirements, they will face fines or the cancellation of their licenses. Earlier, the authorities had publicly criticized Sina.com and Netease for inadequate implementation of censorship regulations with respect to pornography, violence, and "rumors that disrupt the social order." This hinted at the silent resistance and delays in implementing intensified state interventions on the part of the important IT companies.

After 2010, state and party institutions increasingly integrated social media into their own propaganda and communications networks. According to official statistics, about 180,000 institutional and 75,000 personal state and party microblog accounts existed at the end of 2013—twice the number in 2012. Police authorities alone operated about one-third of these accounts. They are increasingly using these platforms in the fight against crime as well as for traffic and security bulletins (China Academy of Governance 2014).

Along with the necessary training of cadres in collaboration with IT companies, the CCP Propaganda Department has pushed ahead with a restructuring of the media industry. The idea behind this restructuring is that the state media should use the successful social media platforms and develop their own media apps and online information channels. In addition, the CCP leadership should disseminate official political positions to younger audiences in shorter, more lighthearted formats through the use of cartoons and entertaining infographics.

Figure 6.4

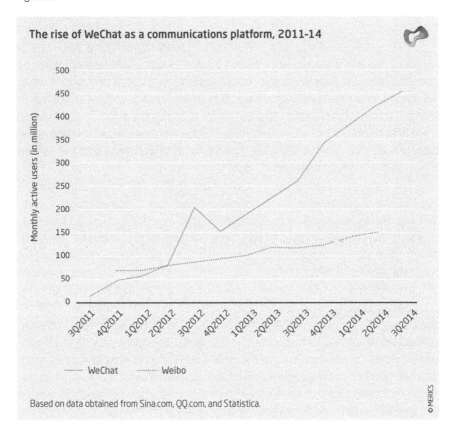

The rise of WeChat as a communications platform, 2011-14

Based on data obtained from Sina.com, QQ.com, and Statistica.

© MERICS

6.5 Social security: State pensions for the rural population

Matthias Stepan

The establishment of state welfare programs and social insurance schemes in cases of illness, unemployment, or incapacity to work is a development that began basically after World War II. China is no exception in this respect. Up to the mid-2000s, however, state social services were primarily the privilege of a minority of state employees and urban workers.

After the establishment of the PRC in 1949, following the Soviet Union's example the CCP focused on setting up a social-security system in the cities. In the rural areas, providing old-age support was entrusted to families and village communities. This led to a two-tier system. In the cities, social security was organized via membership in a work unit (*danwei*) (单位). According to the labor insurance regulations (劳动保险条例), after 1951 companies were responsible for providing for their workers and their families. Administrative units and the military performed similar functions for their respective staff. They ran hospitals, nursery schools, and homes for the elderly, and also provided pension payments. In contrast, in the rural areas the family remained the principal source of social security (Dixon 1981).

Structural reforms since the 1980s have undermined both subsystems. In the cities, existing labor insurance rules could not be transferred to the new, highly staffed private companies without some adaptations. Much of the labor force in private companies and in the informal urban sectors—tens of millions of people— were initially left without any social security. In the rural economically underdeveloped regions, the elderly in particular suffered from the consequences of the rural out-migration by the young workforce. This younger generation no longer provided support for the elderly, or if it did, it was only to a limited extent. At the beginning of the 1990s the central government finally began to take measures to counteract this development with an active state social policy. Compared to the situation in other emerging economies, the expansion of social-security provisions—especially in the areas of health insurance and pensions—to include nearly all Chinese citizens by the end of the tenures of President Hu Jintao and Premier Wen Jiabao in 2013 represented great progress.

Key actors and interests

China's system of social security is characterized by the dominance of state actors, with social welfare groups and labor unions playing minor roles. Two ministries compete for influence with different programs in the field of public social policies, which also include pensions. The Ministry of Human Resources and Social Security (MOHRSS) (人力资源和社会保障部), which from 1998 to 2008 was called the Ministry of Labor and Social Security (MOLSS) (劳动和社会保障部), is built on the principle of social insurance financed by contributions. In contrast, the Ministry of Civil Affairs (MOCA) (民政部) favors benefits financed by taxation. Local governments at both the city and county levels are entrusted with actual implementation of the measures. State think-tanks, such as the DRC (国务院发展研究中心), which is subordinate to the State Council, support the government in identifying and testing new solutions. The Ministry of Finance (MOF) decides on the allocation of funds. Since the 1990s, international organizations such as the Asian Development

Table 6.5

Key actors involved in China's pension policy

Actors	Tasks and interests
MOHRSS	Formulating and expanding the state social insurance program; strengthening budgetary funds, staff, and areas of authority
MOCA	Administering social policy programs (basic social services and the fight against poverty) beyond the scope of the social insurance systems
MOF	Budgeting; deficit control; financial transfers to other state authorities
Provincial governments	Negotiating with the central government about financial transfers; implementing central-government programs; preserving regional autonomy to make decisions; securing regional economic momentum and social stability
County governments	Negotiating provincial financial transfers; implementing provincial decisions; providing social benefits and safeguarding social stability at the local levels
International organizations (such as the United Nations Development Programme [UNDP], and the World Bank)	Fighting rural poverty; sharing expertise and "best practices" and providing aid; influencing pilot projects and legislation

© MERICS

Bank (ADB), the World Bank, and foreign governments have served as project partners. They have primarily contributed technical expertise and financial resources to various pilot projects (see Table 6.5).

Decision-making and conflicts

The introduction of a state pension program for the rural population is part of the state's active social policy. The initial initiatives between 1991 and 1998 failed due to the limited number of persons insured, the low level of pensions, and the high administrative costs (Gong Sen 2003). Consequently, in 1998 responsibility for rural pensions was transferred from the MOCA to the MOLSS. However, this ministry did not have much visibility until it began planning its own initiatives in 2003.

The social and economic situations worsened in many rural areas at the beginning of the twenty-first century, and, as a result, the number of rural protests increased. This was the trigger for the Chinese leadership under Hu Jintao and Wen Jiabao to focus on improvements in the situation for farmers as one of the main objectives of its policy program beginning in 2003. In addition to economic programs, the program sought to expand state welfare. The MOLSS and the MOCA focused on the growing problem of poverty among the elderly. Independently of one another, they carried out experimental pilot programs in individual counties and they sought dialogues with international organizations and foreign governments. Among other organizations, the ADB and the World Bank participated in implementing and evaluating the local experiments.

With the passage of time, various ideological and programmatic preferences began to emerge inside the state and party leaderships. Traditionalists were of the opinion that families in the rural areas continued to be in a position to provide for the elderly and that state interventions were incompatible with Chinese culture. In contrast, modernizers supported the establishment of a system oriented toward the Western model of a welfare state. Two fundamentally different financing models were under discussion at the program level. The proposal put forward by the MOLSS was oriented toward a pension program for urban laborers in companies. This consisted of two components: one was social insurance financed by contributions, and the other was a funded personal account. To distinguish this program from the failed initiative of the 1990s, it was referred to as the "New Rural Pension Scheme" (新型农村社会养老保险). The other alternative under debate took the form of a basic pension financed by taxes.

The central leadership's announcement of its "building a new socialist countryside" campaign in 2006 gave subnational governments an additional impetus to make progress in terms of testing a rural pension scheme. In the end, a formula was agreed upon in which it was stated that rural pensions from the state should only support the existing system. In terms of building a new program, the contributions-based model was pushed through due to its popularity.

By the end of 2007, more than two-thirds of the 3,000 Chinese county governments had already begun to prepare pilot programs for the introduction of contributions-based pensions. It was another two years, however, before the State Council published guidelines on implementation of the pilot programs (State Council 2009). The MOF and the provincial governments struggled for a long time to apportion the costs of the state subsidies and to balance the deficits in the pension scheme fund. Provincial governments feared that the central government might leave them to bear the costs on their own. The guidelines stipulated that the state would guarantee a basic pension and pay a lower per-capita subsidy into the pension scheme fund each year. The apportionment of costs between the central government and the provinces was based on economic growth. The central government agreed to pay the entire amount in the western provinces, but only 50 percent in the central provinces. In contrast, the wealthy coastal provinces were supposed to cover the costs based on their own income.

Implementation

In 2009 the State Council set up a LSG to liaise among government departments as they implemented pilot programs for rural pension schemes. This LSG operated under the leadership of a vice-premier. Within several months, the provincial governments had translated the standards for implementation of the New Rural Pension Scheme into local administrative regulations (Stepan 2015). However, regional differences in implementation remained in terms of how the program was administered and financed. In some provinces, the local MOHRSS offices took on the role of administration, whereas in other regions this role fell to the taxation offices. The amount of the pension scheme contributions and the apportionment between the provincial and local governments revealed striking differences.

Policy outcomes and policy adjustments

The introduction of the new pension program has primarily been a success in terms of the number of people involved. During the period from 2009 to 2012, the number of contributors grew from 71 million to 353 million, whereas the number of recipients over the same period increased from 15 million to 130 million (see Figure 6.5). Nevertheless, fundamental problems continued to exist because in many provinces the amount of the pension was below the minimum subsistence level as defined by the state. Moreover, the system was closely linked to a person's geographical location: pension recipients could lose a substantial portion of their pension entitlements by moving from a rural to an urban location or to another province.

To combat poverty among the elderly, in 2014 the State Council raised the minimum pension amount to CNY 75 per month. However, the extent of implementation usually depended on the financial means of the relevant governments. With respect to urban–rural mobility, the central government pushed ahead with consolidating the New Rural Pension Scheme with a pension scheme for nonworking urban residents (城镇居民社会养老保险). Most provinces quickly implemented this new regulation, so for the first time Chinese citizens with either an urban or a rural household registration were able to enjoy the same access to a state social program (城乡居民社会养老保险).

Figure 6.5

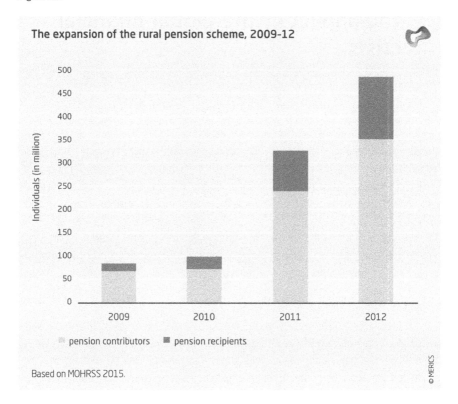

The expansion of the rural pension scheme, 2009-12

Individuals (in million)

■ pension contributors   ■ pension recipients

Based on MOHRSS 2015.

© MERICS

The Chinese government achieved a historic milestone by opening up social insurance schemes to almost the entire population. This helped the government gain legitimacy, especially among the poorer strata of the population. Even so, the social insurance system still faces challenges, especially with respect to the financial sustainability of the aging population. In this context, the significant factors are the ratio between the number of active pension contributors and the number of benefit recipients as well as the accumulation of financial reserves. Apart from the demographic trends, the effects of which will be apparent beginning in 2030, the regions that are already excessively burdened are the places of origin of most of the young migrant workers. A standard nationwide pool for pensions and health insurance might have been the solution, but provincial governments vigorously opposed this idea since they feared losing their right to levy and administer social-security contributions. It remains to be seen to what extent the deposits in the National Social Security Fund (NSSF), which was set up in 2000, are sufficient to cushion the impact of the costs of the social-security benefits.

6.6 Macroeconomic control: Managing the impact of the global financial crisis

Dirk H. Schmidt

China's management of the global financial crisis between 2007 and 2009 went significantly beyond standard Western notions of stabilization policy. This can be attributed to a specific Chinese understanding of macroeconomic control (宏观调控): the Chinese leadership seeks to use macroeconomic control to combat serious cyclical fluctuations in the economy as well as the consequences of external shocks by using monetary and fiscal policy interventions—not only on an ad hoc basis, but also to preemptively prevent them. Key macroeconomic variables (growth, inflation, fiscal deficits, lending volumes, capital and current accounts, and exchange rates) should not be given free rein over volatile market forces; instead they should remain subject to state control (Heilmann/Melton 2013).

In the views of leading CCP economic policy makers (Liu He 2014), state interventions in the workings of the Chinese economy—in contrast to those in the Western market-economy democracies—have not been subject to populist pressures oriented toward short-term measures in times of crisis, nor have they been captured by organized interest groups. Representatives of the Chinese government—and leaders of some foreign states and corporations—highlight the ability of the Chinese political system to implement the necessary long-term structural reforms and to concentrate state resources on priority areas (集中力量) as a particular strength of the system.

In the normal mode of Chinese politics, however (see Section 3.1.3), this demand for far-sighted national leadership and priority-setting regularly collides with the decidedly special interests of regional governments as well as those of state and private companies. The latter are primarily oriented toward short-term economic growth and immediate improvements in revenue and earnings rather than toward structural changes (fiscal reforms, strengthening competition, etc.) approved by the central government, which are risky both politically and entrepreneurially (see Table 6.6).

Decision-making and conflicts

The global financial crisis did not hit China directly by way of the banking and securities sector because China's financial system was protected from the worst

Table 6.6

Key actors and interests involved in macroeconomic control

Actors	Tasks	Interests
Party and state leaderships	Macroeconomic and political stability	Continual economic growth; national stability and security
National Development and Reform Commission (NDRC)	Macroeconomic stability; long-term planning; coordination of state investment programs	Special status as a coordination center for all government activities
MOF	Limiting the deficit; fiscal reforms; economic stimulus measures	Strengthening centralized budgetary power
Central Bank	Stability of the financial and monetary systems; monetary policy; economic stimulus measures through the use of monetary policy instruments	Serving as a central body for economic policy (in line with the model of independent central banks)
China Banking Regulatory Commission (CBRC)	Supervision and risk management in the banking system	Expansion and internationalization of the banking system
Ministry of Commerce (MOFCOM)	Organizing China's integration into global markets	Supporting the export sector
State-owned Assets Supervision and Administration Commission (SASAC)	Supervising state-owned companies; promoting "national champions"	Protecting markets for state-owned companies
Local governments	Acquisition of investments (real estate, industry, or infrastructure)	Supporting the local economy; tax revenue; social stability

© MERICS

turbulence in global financial markets by strict capital controls. Instead, the global crisis exerted strong downward pressures on the country through real economy trade channels: Chinese exports fell dramatically as a result of the abrupt decline in demand in the United States and Europe. China's economic growth fell rapidly to less than 7 percent during the last quarter of 2008. This precarious situation was viewed by the leadership as a serious danger to social stability and triggered a crisis mode in Chinese politics, resulting in centralized and accelerated decision-making. Within several weeks, the central government announced a preliminary economic stimulus package of about 13 percent of the gross domestic product (GDP). The party leadership required all levels of government to achieve economic growth of at least 8 percent in order to prevent massive lay-offs in the export sector. At the same time, the central government pursued long-term targets using generous financing schemes, for instance developing the western and central Chinese provinces, reforming the health insurance system, building new social housing, and supporting the industries of the future.

Reverting to planning and investment methods taken from the previous command economy, which had been greatly reduced during the 1990s, was of particular significance for the Chinese government's crisis management. When the central government and the National Development and Reform Commission (NDRC) encouraged lower levels of government to immediately submit realistic proposals for expanding the infrastructure, local governments presented a long list of projects on their wish-lists. These projects had been part of local investment plans for years, but they had not been approved by higher levels of government due to their high costs or minimal benefits.

This time, project proposals were collected within four weeks in the amount of about 70 percent of GDP in 2007. Although only a fraction of the projects were actually approved by the NDRC, local governments gained substantial autonomy due to the need to act quickly and due to the authorities' reduced risk and cost controls. In many cases China's huge economic stimulus plan was characterized by wastes of funding and corruption.

Conflicts of interest erupted within the state in the second half of 2009 when it appeared that economic stabilization had been achieved, thus ending the crisis mode. The central bank and the China Banking Regulatory Commission (CBRC) wanted to return to a tighter monetary policy in view of the dangers to the financial system (inflation, gluts in lending, and asset price bubbles). But the Ministry of Commerce and the local governments fought to uphold the support measures for the export sector. It was only at the beginning of 2010 when the macroeconomic risks had grown and the restrictive position of the central bank was justified that the economic stimulus measures were gradually cut back.

Implementation

Compared to the Western measures, the content and implementation of the Chinese economic stimulus program have been characterized by several unusual features (Langhammer/Heilmann 2010; Lardy 2012; Wong 2011):

(1) *The dominance of administrative tools:* PRC monetary and fiscal policy measures were only in part based on standard market-economy tools. In the case of monetary policy, price-based tools played merely a supporting role (lowering key interest rates, reducing reserve ratios, and open market operations). Instead, volume-driven or administrative interventions dominated, such as indicative lending schemes or binding quotas that determined bank lending practices down to the level of the individual banks. In the case of fiscal policy, the Chinese leadership primarily focused on the expenditure side. Consequently, substantial funding went to expanding transportation and energy infrastructure as well as to stimulating private consumption in the rural areas. In terms of foreign trade and payments, the Chinese currency was once again tightly pegged to the US dollar. Exporters were aided by tax rebates and domestic companies received preferential treatment, to the disadvantage of their foreign competitors, when making bids for state tenders.

(2) *The creation of new financing tools at local-government levels:* Whereas the stimulus measures in the West were usually financed from the state budget, the Chinese central government made directly available only 25 percent of the necessary budgetary funds. The remainder of the financing was provided via local governments that established their own investment companies as financing vehicles to enable large-scale loans from state-owned banks (at that time, local governments were denied access to other ways of raising capital; see Section 6.7). This newly created huge scale of liquidity was channeled into the infrastructure and industrial sectors according to political instructions without adequate risk assessments and so—in contrast to the situation in the West—it rapidly and directly reached the real economy.

(3) *Campaign style:* To accelerate implementation and overcome administrative resistance and delays, government authorities reverted to the campaign rhetoric and methodology of the Mao era (the fight against the economic crisis was presented as a patriotic duty, inspection teams led by senior figures were sent to apply pressure on lower levels, etc.).

Policy outcomes and policy adjustments

The stabilizing effects of China's economic crisis management was very impressive over the short term: growth jumped to 11 percent by the fourth quarter of 2009, that is, to approximately the same level as that before the crisis. Furthermore, social policy makers in the central government were able to promote several large projects—in particular, expansion of the health insurance system—that previously had come to a halt because of internal concerns and cost risks.

At the same time, however, the economic stimulus package produced a number of negative side-effects: China's high rate of investment, which was already unique by international standards, increased yet again. This resulted in considerable mis-allocations and excess capacity, especially in the steel, cement, and construction industries. Measures that existed prior to the financial crisis to improve investment and risk management in state-owned companies, banks, and national budgets were all delayed. Above all, institutions that had powers to manage investments, such as the NDRC, the Ministry of Railways, and the Ministry of Industry and Information Technology (MIIT), benefited from the state crisis management — at the expense of the supervisory and regulatory authorities.

In official statements by government representatives, Chinese crisis management between 2007 and 2009 is presented as evidence of the success of the government's brand of macroeconomic control. In internal and scientific discussions, however, there have been harsh criticisms that indicate the medium- and long-term costs and risks resulting from the economic stimulus plan and the investment program. As China's economic momentum slowed down markedly in 2014–15, the government initially responded with targeted and limited stimulus measures. Calls for comprehensive central state programs to combat the deflationary pressures— in the style of the expansive U.S. and European central bank policy known as "quantitative easing"—became increasingly vocal in China.

6.7 Public budgets: The role of local-government financing platforms

Sandra Heep

China's budgetary policy is characterized by an imbalance in the allocations of public funds between the central government on the one hand and subnational governments on the other. Because local governments do not receive sufficient tax revenue for their costly tasks, they depend on extra-budgetary financing mechanisms (see Section 2.8). Consequently, they raise capital for infrastructural investments via local-government financing platforms (地方政府融资平台). These platforms played a central role in implementing the economic stimulus program during the global financial crisis. Their investments facilitated a rapid economic recovery, but simultaneously they also led to an increasing indebtedness of local governments.

Key actors and interests

The responsibility of local governments for infrastructural investments led to funding problems as early as the 1990s. Not only were they granted insufficient tax revenue, but also the Budget Law prohibited them from falling into debt. To circumvent this ban, they set up financing platforms that were registered as companies but that functioned as de facto investment departments. The local governments provided these platforms with capital, mostly by the transfer of tax revenue and land-use rights. In turn, the platforms deposited the assets with the state-owned banks as collateral and in return they received loans to expand the local infrastructure.

Since the central government was unwilling to allocate a greater proportion of tax revenue to local governments, it tacitly tolerated this funding mechanism until the outbreak of the global financial crisis in 2007. It was only after it approved a comprehensive economic stimulus plan of about 13 percent of total GDP in 2008 (see Section 6.6) that it began to actively support local-government financing platforms. This was intended to allow local governments to finance three-quarters of the stimulus program. Such a course of action was beneficial to the central government because it produced an effective economic stimulus while also protecting the central-government budget (see Table 6.7).

Decision-making and conflicts

The sharp downturn in economic growth at the end of 2008 triggered a crisis mode in Chinese politics. This was accompanied by a corresponding centralization of the decision-making process (see Section 3.1.3). As the top CCP leaders declared that stabilizing the growth rate was their highest priority, all involved actors sought to expand the funding options for local governments. The local-government financing platforms were intended to receive almost unlimited support from the banks.

No conflicts arose until the economy recovered in mid-2009 and the political system returned to a normal mode of operation. Concerned about the stability of the financial system, the CBRC, the PBOC, and the MOF were among the first to point to the high default risks of the financing platforms, and hence they implemented measures to halt bank lending to these platforms. Since 2010, they have been supported by the NDRC, which sees the growing local government levels of indebtedness endangering economic stability.

As these governments did not have access to alternative sources of funding for their infrastructure projects, they still relied on bank lending. They received support from state-owned banks that profited from the strong demand for loans by these financing platforms. Because the banks assumed that these loans were guar-

Table 6.7

Key actors and interests involved in budget policy

Actors	Tasks	Interests
Local governments	Implementing and financing investment projects	Economic growth; the closing of financing gaps
Central government	Regulating local-government financing platforms	Economic stability
NDRC	Investment planning; approval of projects	Economic stability
MOF	Rule-making for state budgets at the lower levels of government	Securing central-government income and reducing the deficit; minimizing financial transfers to lower levels of government
People's Bank of China (PBOC)	Monetary policy	Financial stability; developing sovereign bond markets for lower levels of government
CBRC	Drawing up bank-lending guidelines	Stability of the banking sector
National Audit Office (NAO)	Supervising the national budget at all levels of government	Identifying wastes of funding and fiscal risks
State-owned commercial and development banks	Subsidizing investment projects by granting loans on favorable terms	Preferential granting of loans to state-owned borrowers and to those with government links

© MERICS

anteed implicitly by the central government, they did not note any appreciable risks associated with such transactions.

Implementation

In a joint March 2009 document, the PBOC and the CBRC explicitly requested that local governments establish financing platforms. They simultaneously mandated that banks finance the local-government investment projects (PBOC/CBRC 2009). These governments immediately implemented this mandate because it offered them an opportunity to carry out already-planned projects, thus enabling them to contribute to the economic growth of their respective regions. At the same time, the personal motives of local cadres played a key role because regional growth rates made a crucial difference to their careers. By the end of 2010, the number of platforms had increased to more than 10,000 equal to an increase of 25 percent within two years (PBOC 2014). After the introduction of the economic stimulus plan, these platforms became one of the major recipients of bank loans. It has been estimated that they held 18.5 percent of all outstanding loans by the end of 2009 (Bateson 2010).

At the end of 2009 when the risks resulting from the financing platforms had become apparent, the CBRC instructed the banks not to provide the platforms with any more than 30 percent of the funding needed for any individual investment project. After Premier Wen Jiabao came out firmly in favor of strengthening central-government control of the platforms, the State Council in June 2010 approved a range of respective instructions, which would later be specified in a joint document issued by the MOF, NDRC, PBOC, and the CBRC (Ma Jun 2013). First, the new rules aimed to classify financing platforms according to their financial dependence on local governments. Consequently, the debts were no longer guaranteed by local governments if they could be serviced from the platforms' current income. Second, local governments were forbidden from financing infrastructure projects that did not generate income via their platforms. Third, banks were encouraged to provide loans to local-government platforms only after conducting strict risk assessments (MOF et al. 2010; State Council 2010).

Policy outcomes and policy adjustments

The expansion of funding options for local governments achieved the desired results within a very short time: the massive raising of capital via financing platforms allowed them to stimulate the economy by means of numerous infrastructure projects. However, this success was achieved at the cost of the enormous indebtedness of the local governments. According to a report issued by the National Audit Office (NAO), by mid-2013 local-government debts amounted to 31 percent of GDP. More than one-third of these debts were allotted to the financing platforms (NAO 2013).

Such indebtedness endangered China's economic stability because it took place in a gray area where there were no established procedures for risk or debt management. Most long-term infrastructure projects were financed via bank loans with relatively short loan periods. As a result, maturity mismatches were aggravated and the risks of default increased. Indeed, the central government and the supervisory authorities attempted to stem these risks through increased supervision and restrictive regulations. Yet they failed to close the financing gaps at the local levels. Since the platforms no longer had access to the formal financial sector, their financing shifted to the shadow banking sector where lending took place beyond the supervision of the authorities.

At the same time, however, the central government did attempt to establish low-risk financing mechanisms for the subnational governments. The first pilot projects began to issue bonds through selected provincial-level governments in 2009. These pilots led to a reform of the Budget Law, and since 2015, provincial-level governments have been allowed financing via bond markets up to a limit set by the central government. This is a step in the right direction because it increases transparency and lowers the funding costs for provincial-level governments. However, if the central government does not close the funding gaps at the local levels, local cadres will have every incentive to circumvent the new rules and to develop new opaque financing mechanisms that threaten financial stability.

6.8 Infrastructure policy and the high-speed rail network

Mirjam Meissner

Since the beginning of the 1990s, China has invested an enormous amount of time and money to repair and rebuild its infrastructure, for example by building highways and airports. In the rail industry, between 1997 and 2007 China upgraded 22,000 km of existing railway infrastructure as part of an "acceleration campaign," thus enabling maximum speeds of up to 250 kmh (155 mph). Beginning in 2006, the focus has been on building a high-speed rail network for passengers, with possible speeds of up to 350 kmh (217 mph) under the Medium- to Long-term Railway Network Scheme (中长期铁路网规划). By the end of 2014, this network already stretched for more than 16,000 km, and another 8,000 km were under construction. The rail network was designed not only to link urban centers throughout the country, but also to enable faster passenger transportation. Additionally, it was intended to create greater capacity for freight transport on expanded conventional rail networks as the government sought to push ahead with the economic development and political integration of the western parts of the country.

Key actors and interests

Until 2013, the former Ministry of Railways (铁道部) was at the same time the regulatory authority, the investor, and the developer of construction projects, as well as the rail network operator and service-provider for passenger transportation. This concentration of decision-making power became a breeding ground for corruption and allowed for a cover-up of rail network safety issues. After the Ministry of Railways was disbanded in March 2013, the Ministry of Transport (MOT) (交通运输部) became one of the key actors in policy making for all sectors of nationwide transportation infrastructure, including railway infrastructure. The other two influential bodies were the NDRC and the State Council. Within the MOT, the Railway Bureau (铁路局) is responsible for the rail industry. Operation of the railway network is the responsibility of the China Railway Corporation (CRC) (中国铁路总公司). In nearly all instances, construction projects are allocated to one of several major state-owned corporations. These carry immense political weight as a result of their close links with the government authorities. As in other state infrastructure sectors, there is no strict separation of political and economic actors in the rail industry. Consequently, infrastructure projects remain susceptible to corruption and inadequate quality controls (see Table 6.8).

Decision-making and conflicts

Fundamental decisions about medium- to long-term targets for expansion and investment volumes are made at the central-government level, along with the selection of technologies for inter-state infrastructural expansion. Whereas the NDRC is responsible for nationwide, cross-sectoral development programs, the MOT formulates policy programs and plans for the transportation sector and the rail industry. The inner cabinet of the State Council has the final say regarding MOT proposals. This decision-making process can involve lengthy coordination and negotiation procedures with the concerned SOEs as well as with scientific advisers. The Medium- to Long-term Railway Network Scheme was the result of a decision-making process that commenced in 1998, was approved by the inner cabinet of the State Council in 2006, and then was revised by the NDRC in 2008. There were two basic decisions to be made: first, the selection of the train technology (i.e., magnetic levitation trains or conventional trains). In 1998 Premier Zhu Rongji had initially supported the use of magnetic levitation (maglev) technology. Since 2006, however, China has opted for conventional train technology—with the exception of the Shanghai Transrapid pilot line—due in part to the high costs of the German maglev technology.

The second fundamental decision was related to the rail network. It took a long time for the involved actors to reach agreement as to whether to extend the

Table 6.8

Key actors and interests involved in railway policy

Actors	Tasks and interests
Inner cabinet of the State Council	Authority to issue guidelines; decision-making powers regarding infrastructure development plans; issuance of development plans
NDRC	Formulating cross-sectoral development and infrastructural plans; approval of infrastructure projects
Railway Bureau (under the MOT)	Formulating infrastructure plans for the rail industry; quality assurance
China Railway Corporation (CRC)	Operations; planning and ultimate supervision of construction projects
Major Chinese state-owned corporations (train manufacturers: China South Locomotive and Rolling Stock Corporation [CSR], China North Locomotive and Rolling Stock Corporation [CNR]; construction groups: China Railway Engineering Corporation [CREC], China Railway Construction Corporation [CRCC])	Carrying out construction projects; building trains
State-owned commercial banks and the China Development Bank (CDB)	Providing favorable loans for infrastructure projects
Provincial and local governments	Planning and financing infrastructure projects with the CRC
Ministry of Environmental Protection (MEP)	Assessing environmental impact; authorization to end construction work
Scientific institutions	Advisory functions
General public; media; the Internet; online public media	Influence through protests, reports, analyses, and petitions

© MERICS

existing network or to build a new, independent high-speed network specifically designed for passenger transportation. The issue of how cost-efficient it would be to build an independent high-speed network was particularly contentious, although ultimately this solution was accepted. In 2008 the NDRC used the expansion of the high-speed rail network to counteract the economic impact of the global financial crisis. The 2006 investment targets were increased on an ad hoc basis, thereby considerably accelerating the expansion.

Implementation

Approvals for large, inter-state infrastructure projects are granted by the NDRC. The CRC proposes construction projects together with the affected provincial governments. Financing for the projects is shared between local governments, the CRC, and the central government. The share of funding provided by the central government dropped from an average of 45 percent in 2008 to about 20 percent in 2015. Furthermore, China is increasingly opening up infrastructure projects in the rail industry to private and foreign investors. After approving a construction project, the CRC then issues an invitation to tender for the project and to provide trains and signal technology.

In 2013 and 2014 foreign companies were basically excluded from the tender process due to the regulations. Therefore, the only bidders were large Chinese state-owned construction companies, such as China Railway Engineering Corporation (CREC) and China Railway Construction Corporation (CRCC), and train manufacturers, such as China South Locomotive and Rolling Stock Corporation (CSR) and China North Locomotive and Rolling Stock Corporation (CNR) and their subsidiaries. After the Ministry of Railways was disbanded, quality assurance for construction projects became the responsibility of the MOT's railway authorities.

Policy outcomes and policy adjustments

Quality issues and corruption in the rail industry resulted from the long-term linkages between policy regulation, administration, and network operations. The immense political pressures to rapidly expand the network aggravated this situation considerably, and by the beginning of 2011, former Minister of Railways Liu Zhijun was removed from office after a corruption scandal and abuse of his power. (In July 2013 he was convicted and received a death sentence with reprieve.) Shortly thereafter, in July 2011, there was a train crash near the city of Wenzhou, resulting in forty deaths. According to a government report, the accident was caused by a defect in the signaling equipment and inadequate safety management. After the disaster, the Chinese government temporarily suspended approval of additional lines and in March 2013, the NPC decided to disband the Ministry of Railways. To this day, however, there are still close links between the political administrators and the railway operators, which is why the effectiveness and impartiality of railway quality controls remain questionable.

China has managed to catch up with the Western countries in terms of technology by expanding its high-speed lines. Initially, Chinese train manufacturers were dependent on collaborations with foreign bidders to develop its high-speed trains, although the political objective from the outset was to develop China's own high-speed trains by means of technology transfers. This was achieved in 2010—a step that strengthened the dominance of Chinese state-owned corporations in the infrastructure sector. Supported by the government, Chinese companies have been increasingly involved in infrastructure projects abroad and have also been exporters of signal and train technology. As a result of foreign bidders' disadvantages in public tenders, their future prospects in the Chinese market will be limited to supplying components.

The expansion of the high-speed rail network also led to considerable state debt at the central- and local-government levels. Having assumed the debts of the former Ministry of Railways, the CRC carries a debt burden of about 5 percent of Chinese GDP. If there are payment defaults, the central government will step in as guarantor (see Section 6.7 on state debt). This is a particularly precarious situation, as the operation of the lines has so far proved to be unprofitable, partly due to high ticket prices—the prices fail to reflect actual operating costs and are still too expensive for the majority of Chinese citizens to represent a real alternative to slower trains and buses. Supporters of the rapid expansion nevertheless point to its long-term contribution to stable economic growth and its positive impact on the labor market. Until now, the central government has left no room for doubt that it will continue to pursue expansion of the high-speed network, despite the financial risks and the unresolved issues concerning quality management.

6.9 Industrial policy and investment catalogs in the automotive sector

Mirjam Meissner

The objective of China's industrial policy is to produce efficient and internationally competitive Chinese companies as well as technological innovations, and by so doing to create sustained growth. The government aims to strengthen selected industries and technologies and to restructure sectors of the economy through state interventions. With the help of mechanisms such as public procurements and investment catalogs, which steer investments toward specific industries, the Chinese government is attempting to achieve this goal.

Key actors and interests

Responsible for formulating industrial plans and programs, the NDRC is the dominant state actor in Chinese industrial policy. Ultimate decision-making powers with regard to industrial policy programs are mainly held by the inner cabinet of the State Council. Other ministries, particularly the MIIT, but also specialist ministries such as the Ministry of Science and Technology (MOST) and the MOF, along with companies and their industry associations, exert an influence on the formulation of industrial policy programs and are key actors with respect to policy implementation.

The importance and influence of these individual actors vary considerably from industry to industry. In the automotive industry, the MIIT competes with the NDRC in terms of formulating regulatory policies. On the company side, three large state-owned corporations (First Automotive Works [FAW], Shanghai Automotive Industry Corporation [SAIC], and Dongfeng), along with the associated industry association, the China Association of Automobile Manufacturers (CAAM) (中国企业工业协会), wield a great deal of political influence. Private companies, such as the automobile manufacturer BYD, are increasingly broadening their influence and gradually changing the established power structure. Foreign companies and boards of trade, for instance the EU Chamber of Commerce, also wield some influence. Additionally, a group of high-ranking government bureaucrats and leaders of state research institutions has been assigned to serve as a policy community for the formulation of industrial policy programs (Heilmann/Shih 2013) (see Table 6.9.A).

Decision-making and conflicts

Decision-making with respect to industrial programs focuses on selecting which industries and technologies to support as well as their quantitative targets. The initiative for formulating a new program can come from central-government state bodies, from industry associations, or from the recommendation of government-linked research institutions. The first draft of an industrial policy is drawn up by the NDRC, the MIIT, or, on occasion, by several ministries jointly. Beginning from the drawing up of the first draft to the approval of a new policy program, a process of negotiation and coordination occurs among the relevant actors. Of course, the sheer number of

Table 6.9.A

Key actors and interests involved in the formulation of automobile policy

Actors	Tasks and interests
Inner cabinet	Approving and publishing industrial programs
NDRC	Formulating cross-sectoral industrial programs; publishing sectoral industrial plans and investment catalogs
MIIT	Formulating and publishing industrial programs; key actor in implementation
MOF	Coordinating and implementing financial and fiscal measures
Other ministries and authorities	Participating in the formulation of policies according to specialty; responsible for implementation in specific areas (for example, the Ministry of Science and Technology [MOST] is involved in issues related to technology policy)
Top officials; industrial policy experts	Providing momentum and knowledge to influence industrial policy decision-making processes; acting as a coordinator
SOEs; SASAC	Representing interests vis-à-vis policy-makers; investing in technology and products in the state framework plans
Industry associations (such as CAAM)	Advisory function in terms of formulating industrial policy programs and framework plans
Private companies	Lobbying on behalf of their own interests, sometimes via the business associations
Provinces and municipalities	Formulating local industrial programs; implementing central-government framework plans/measures at the local-government levels; promoting the local economy through decentralized experiments, among other measures
Customers; drivers	Deciding on a car brand, for example based on market-economy criteria such as price, quality, and prestige

© MERICS

influential actors creates coordination challenges. In such cases, the policy community for industrial policy takes part in the coordination. Its members contribute to the decision-making process by supporting the construction of formal and informal platforms via their wide networks and hence promoting regular discussions among decision-makers and opinion-makers.

After approving an industrial plan, the individual ministries—the MIIT or the MOF for the automobile industry—draw up specific funding measures for implementation. The extent of intervention by the state in shaping the market is the fundamental source of contention in industrial policy. The main clash occurs between those in favor of greater competition based on free-market principles and those in favor of focusing industrial policy on SOEs. Large corporations, such as the three "national champions" in the automobile industry (FAW, SAIC, and Dongfeng), attempt to oppose measures that strengthen competition by using the political clout that they have accumulated over many years (see Table 6.9.B).

Implementation

China's industrial policy continues to be characterized by state control over investments in specific technologies or branches of industry. This occurs in the form of investment catalogs that establish those industries in which investment is either encouraged or limited. For example, the catalogs issued by the NDRC specify that foreign investments in the automobile industry may only be made in the form of joint ventures with Chinese automobile manufacturers.

In addition, a powerful tool in Chinese industrial policy is the ability to influence demand through public procurement. Due to the size of the state sector, by using cars made by Chinese manufacturers in the fleet of state vehicles, for example, the state has an important lever with which to increase demand for Chinese-built automobiles. Non-Chinese companies only have equal access to public tenders in a few instances and therefore have long pushed for China to become a member of the WTO's Government Procurement Agreement. Other Chinese industrial policy tools include the unlimited or preferential awarding of loans, tax concessions, and price subsidies for products and services, such as linking electric car subsidies to the range of the cars.

The typical effect of these measures is that large state corporations are given preference over small and private companies, and national companies are favored over international companies. However, industrial policy is challenged by negligible monitoring by provincial and municipal governments and by companies to make sure that the policy is actually being implemented. Numerous political and economic actors, from the central-state level down to the provincial and municipal levels, are involved in implementation. Programs often do not stipulate a review of the im-

Table 6.9.B

Major industrial policy programs, 2004–14

cross-sectoral programs	2005	Adapting industrial setups	State Council
	2007	Accelerating development of the service sector	State Council
	2009	Industrial technology policy	MIIT
	2010	Accelerated development of "strategic emerging industries"	State Council
	2011	Industrial transformation and upgrading, 2011–15	State Council
		12th Five-Year Plan for industrial technological innovations	MIIT
	2012	12th Five-Year Plan for "strategic emerging industries"	State Council
		International cooperation and competition	NDRC, among others
	2013	Reducing excess capacity	State Council
sectoral programs	2004	Automotive industry	NDRC
	2006	Mechanical engineering	State Council
	2009	E-commerce	State Council
		„Revitalization programs" for ten industries	State Council
		The arts and media	State Council
	2011	A total of twenty-one sectoral five-year plans	Various ministries
		Rare earth	State Council
	2012	New energy vehicles	State Council
		Civil aviation	State Council
		Biotechnology	State Council
	2013	Semiconductor industry	State Council
		Internet of Things	State Council
		Information technology	MIIT, NDRC
		Solar industry	State Council
		Energy and environmental protection	State Council
		Satellite navigation	State Council
	2014	Tourism	State Council
		Shipping	State Council
		Logistics	State Council
		R&D services	State Council
		Insurance	State Council

Updated and modified table based on Heilmann/Shih 2013.

© MERICS

plementation process or even impose a penalty for breach of central-government guidelines. State-owned companies, in particular, whose investments should be closely geared to the policy provisions, cannot be prosecuted by central-government bodies for irregular conduct.

Policy outcomes and policy adjustments

With only several exceptions, China's industrial policy so far has not led to the politically desired competitiveness of Chinese companies. In particular, this applies to industries like the automotive sector in which a few large, state-owned corporations exert a significant influence over policy decisions, thereby preventing successful competition in the Chinese market. Indeed, the state-owned corporations have benefited from numerous state subsidies and high levels of income through joint ventures with foreign partners, but they are hardly in a position to develop competitive products on their own. Accordingly, foreign car manufacturers continue to hold about 60 percent of the market share in the Chinese automobile market. One of the reasons for this is that the influence of the state on demand is weaker in the automobile industry than it is in industries in which China's industrial policy can show clear results, for instance high-speed trains or renewable energy.

Other examples of the success of Chinese industrial policy can be seen in some new and rapidly expanding sectors, such as the Internet. This is due to the fact that these sectors are not dominated by state-owned corporations, hence more favorable conditions exist for the expansion of innovative private companies. China's industrial policy supports this by protecting newly emerging companies from both foreign competition and foreign takeovers, and in so doing it favors the emergence of its own internationally competitive companies, such as Huawei and Alibaba.

During the past several decades, China has reorganized its industrial policy at regular intervals. This has been accompanied by shifts in power among key actors. In the case of the automotive sector, policy adjustments began in 2013–14. The NDRC, MIIT, MOST, and MOF drafted new pilot projects for electro-mobility, adjusted the levels and duration of subsidies, and established new targets for public procurement of electric cars. At the same time, the Chinese government placed foreign car manufacturers and Chinese corporations under increasing pressure through anti-trust proceedings and measures against corruption, among others.

This indicates that supporters of more competition succeeded by simultaneously protecting the domestic industry from excessively strong competition from foreign car manufacturers. However, shifts in the balance of power among the involved actors are capable of changing this trend at any time. What is certain here is that the Chinese government is convinced that industrial policy has a positive impact on the development of domestic industry. In the future, the Chinese government is likely to use industrial policy to strengthen the domestic economy and to steer it in politically desirable directions.

6.10 Innovation policy: Promoting the Internet of Things

Jost Wübbeke

An innovative capacity is essential for China's future economic development. Since cheap labor, mass production, and exports can no longer guarantee high growth rates over the long term, the Chinese government is focusing on "indigenous innovation" (自主创新) in order to catch up with, or even surpass, the leading industrialized nations in the field of technology. The Internet of Things, or "IoT" for short (物联网), is one of the new technologies that China intends to incorporate into key future economic sectors. The Internet of Things embeds "smart" networks of objects, or "things," with new capabilities in order to establish interactive infrastructures, ranging from smart refrigerators that decide when food stocks need to be replenished to connected cars that exchange traffic data.

Key actors and interests

IoT is illustrative of some typical features of China's innovation system. The MOST, which is the main body involved in drafting science and technology policies, is generally responsible for China's national research programs. It has gradually lost influence, however, due to other agencies claiming increasingly large sums of the allocated funds. After the State Council placed IoT on the research agenda in 2009, it was not the MOST but rather the NDRC and the MIIT that were entrusted with devising a clear policy framework and for coordinating the relevant ministries.

There are two additional actors that have become increasingly involved in IoT. First, the local governments have proven to be important catalysts for innovation. They contribute the bulk of public funding for research and development (R&D) and they have been ahead of the central government in terms of setting up innovation centers and technology parks to foster IoT. Second, although the Chinese Academy of Science (CAS), state research institutes, and elite universities are still at the forefront of IoT research, many successful innovations are emerging in companies that

Table 6.10

Key actors and interests involved in the "Internet of Things" policy

Actors	Tasks and interests
State Council LSG for Science, Technology, and Education	Devising national guidelines for science and innovation policies
MOST	Developing medium- and long-term programs for promoting innovation
NDRC	Inter-sectoral coordination; patronage of traditional industries
MIIT	Patronage of new IT industries
MOF	Allocating funds for national priority programs
National Science Foundation of China (NSFC)	Conducting basic research in compliance with state directives
CAS	Conducting basic research in compliance with state directives
Provinces; cities; technology zones	Local growth; utilization of funding programs; marketing of innovation locations; scope for independent creativity
Companies; interest groups	Profits and expansion into new business areas such as IoT; acquisition of state funding
Universities; state research units	Conducting basic and applied research in compliance with state directives; funding; patents; reputation

© MERICS

are sometimes part of transnational research networks (CCID Consulting 2013; Sun Yutao/Cao Cong 2014) (see Table 6.10).

Decision-making and conflicts

China's innovation system, which traditionally was subject to strict state controls, has now opened up to decentralized decision-making. Local experimentation and central state decision-making power exist in tandem.

Research priorities are defined by the "National Medium- and Long-Term Plan for the Development of Science and Technology (2006–2020)." More than in any other field of technology, the NDRC and the MIIT have been playing leading roles with regard to the strategic alignment of innovation policies affecting IoT. Both have a major influence with respect to the setting of national R&D priorities, and innovation policy is very much shaped by the focus on industrial policy. In addition to fostering technological progress, the objective of these ministries is to build companies that are capable of competing on an international stage. The emphasis on industrial policy is due to the fact that IoT is based on integrating existing technologies: for example, connected cars interlink sensors, on-board computers, data-transfer technologies, and software platforms. In this context, the demonstration, commercialization, and development of new business models are the main focal points. All of these tasks come under the remit of the NDRC and the MIIT (NDRC 2013).

The key aspects of the regional innovation systems are also incorporated into innovation policy at the central-government level. For example, the intelligent sensor technology cluster in the city of Wuxi served as a role model for the national "Sensing China" strategy in 2009, which sought to foster innovation in the sensor industry. On the one hand, local experimentation enhances China's potential for innovation considerably. However, on the other hand, competition among local players leads to unnecessary duplication and a lack of coordination (ETIRI 2013; Heilmann, Shih, and Hofem 2013).

Implementation

The state has intensified its support for innovation activities through a notable increase in R&D spending. At 2.1 percent in 2013, gross domestic expenditures for R&D ("GERD") as a percentage of GDP were higher than the average in Europe and it is forecast to reach 2.5 percent by 2020. Hierarchical instruments, such as the research agendas of the "863 Program" that was launched in 1986 and the "976 Program" that was launched in 1997, are key elements of research policy.

The state plays a significant role with regard to effective commercialization of innovations. This is especially true in the case of IoT, since the market is not yet fully developed. Using demonstration projects and catalogs for public procurement, the state generates demand in various application areas, such as smart city, smart grid, and smart manufacturing (Industry 4.0). China's commitment to "autonomous innovation" in the field of public procurement led to the temporary exclusion of foreign technology. However, in the wake of heavy criticism from abroad, the central government has since repealed these regulations. Industrial policy funding mechanisms, such as subsidies for IoT technology companies, are also an integral part of innovation policy. Since technology standards have a substantial impact on a company's competitive position, the government attempts to actively influence international standard-setting processes (ETIRI 2013; Zhao Bo/Zhang Zhihua 2013).

In addition to these state-propelled mechanisms, in 2006 the government began to increase its focus on company innovation. Because IoT requires a variety of different technologies, a particularly strong focus has been directed to "collaborative innovations" (协同创新) among companies and research institutions. The IoT technology parks, such as the one in Wuxi, attract networks of universities, research institutes, and companies with investment funds.

Policy outcomes and policy adjustments

Despite its huge investments in R&D, China's capacity for innovation continues to lag in a number of sectors in comparison with the leading industrialized nations. Although key output indicators show a considerable increase in the number of patents issued, these applications are often low in quality, resulting in a glut of weak patents. Although China has catapulted to the forefront of worldwide research in specific technological fields, such as mobile communications, it has not been able to keep pace with the level of technological developments in the industrialized nations in a broad range of areas. With respect to the essential IoT components, such as the sophisticated sensors, for example, China is dependent on imports (Pan Ying/Lu Zhangping 2012).

There are a host of factors hindering effective deployment of R&D funds and successful commercialization of inventions. The funding allocation system remains opaque and is based on patronage networks, the project evaluation system is rudimentary, and there is widespread corruption and misappropriation of funds. The innovation system is shaped by industrial policy, which supports large SOEs that offer few incentives for innovation. A large majority of companies invests too little in R&D and instead specializes in simple products. To a certain extent, government subsidies stifle high-risk innovations and instead sustain loss-making companies, such as in the IoT technology park in Wuxi. Thus far, Chinese collaboration with foreign companies has not resulted in a lasting spillover effect in innovative capabilities (CATR 2014; OECD 2008; Shi Yigong/Rao Yi 2010).

Spurred on by these shortcomings, the government has plans for a radical reform of its innovation system. The LSG for State Scientific and Technological Reform and Innovation System Construction (国家科技体制改革和创新体系建设领导小组), which was established by the State Council in 2012, aims to improve the funding opportunities for innovative small and medium-sized companies and to further strengthen collaborative ties among education, research, and science. Innovative partnerships between industry and science in the IoT sector represent an initial step in this direction. A further goal is to assign responsibility for the allocation of funds and for the evaluation process to two separate institutions. The government is also experimenting with reforms in education, including the National Higher Education Entrance Examination and the dual vocational training system. In spite of initial implementation difficulties, protection of intellectual property rights has also intensified (State Council General Office 2013).

Despite these obvious deficiencies, it is likely that China's national innovative capacity will continue to expand. Although it is not yet a technology leader, it is important to bear in mind that the country has succeeded in steadily narrowing the technology gap and replacing foreign products with domestic technologies. The reforms that are currently in place may help China to overcome the current weaknesses in the system and to produce considerably more groundbreaking innovations in the future. If current plans are successful, China is in a good position to make a substantial contribution to the continuing development of future technologies.

6.11 Environmental policy: Curtailing urban air pollution

Björn Conrad

The yellow-brown clouds of smog that encase China's major cities are the most visible sign of the country's current dramatic environmental situation. Poisoned rivers, contaminated soil, and polluted air cause several hundred thousand premature deaths each year. This destruction of the environment is the price China is paying for decades of unchecked growth, propelled by industrialization and coal-fired power. Parallel to the environmental crisis, the previous guarantors of economic success, such as cheap labor, mass production, and exports, are becoming less important. The goal of radically transforming the Chinese economic growth model to realize added value and to reduce resource consumption unites economic and ecological interests. In the meantime, the central government intentionally uses environmental policy as a catalyst to promote economic reforms, even against internal opposition and in the face of powerful special interests that repeatedly subvert Chinese environmental policy.

Key actors and interests

The clash between short-term economic interests and long-term environmental protection divides the key actors into two principal interest groups. One side comprises the industrial players, primarily the large SOEs in the highly polluting sectors that naturally have an interest in limiting pro-environmental interventions. At the central state level, the MIIT (工业和信息化部) is an important patron of industrial interests. Dense webs of shared interests also exist between local governments and industrial companies.

The other side is primarily made up of the Ministry of Environmental Protection (MEP) (环境保护部). In order to strengthen its position, on the one hand the MEP has sought alliances with line ministries such as the State Forestry Administration (SFA). On the other hand, it has skillfully used public discontent and the numerous protests by pro-environment groups to extend its influence. The MEP is now firmly established as the people's advocate for environmental issues, thereby expanding its field for political action (Geall 2013).

The past focus on economic development meant that when it came to the contradictory objectives of rapid industrialization and environmental protection, there was a strong political bias in favor of industrialization. Since the long-term economic agenda has become increasingly compatible with ecological objectives, however, this situation has changed. Greater environmental protection is also driving the reform of China's economic model. Against the backdrop of efforts to transform the economy, it is in the interest of the party leadership to shift the balance more clearly in the direction of environmental protection. At the same time, the central government does not want to risk curbing the economic momentum over the short term due to overly drastic environmental directives. Managing this complex balancing act is primarily the task of the NDRC, with the inner cabinet of the State Council occasionally stepping in. The NDRC makes use of its dominant role to formulate long-term objectives. Furthermore, the party and government leaderships have a direct influence on the balance of power among the actors in the two main interest groups. The most obvious example is the extended jurisdiction of the MEP. Beginning as an environmental agency with virtually no influence, by 2008 it had evolved into a full-fledged ministry with five regional inspection centers and a network of local environmental protection bureaus (see Table 6.11).

Decision-making and conflicts

Conscious of the challenges involved in enforcing stronger environmental protection measures against the interests of a powerful alliance comprising SOEs, national ministries, and local-government departments, the Chinese leadership realized that the environmental objectives had to be firmly entrenched in the country's long-term development plans. For the first time, the 10th Five-Year Plan (2001–2005) defined detailed targets with regard to air and water quality. This signal from the party and government placed environmental protection high on

Table 6.11

Actors and interests involved in environmental policy

Actors	Tasks and interests
NDRC	Formulation of long-term national objectives and targets; coordination of environmental policies in the state executive
NPC	Preparation of legislative proposals by the Environmental and Resources Conservation Committee of the NPC
Inner cabinet of the State Council	Targeted action programs; alignment of national environmental protection targets
MEP	Implementation of environmental regulations; the level of authority over other state actors is often unclear
Local environmental protection agencies	Ambivalent function with respect to monitoring environmental regulations as part of both the respective local government and a decentralized element of the MEP
Regional centers of the MEP	Support for monitoring and implementation of environmental regulations
Line ministries	Involved in negotiating environmental measures
MOST	Patronage of environmental technologies; interface between environmental and innovation policies
Local governments	Responsible for formulating and implementing local environmental targets in compliance with national standards; linking interests with local industry
Companies	Bound to implementing environmental regulations; actors in the negotiation process; sometimes obstruct practical implementation and sometimes benefit from environmental incentive systems
Scientific institutions	Policy consultation on environmental targets, regulation, and incentive systems
NGOs	Pressure groups; provide expertise; advice from international environmental NGOs
General public	Discontent and pro-environment protests are a driving force behind environmental protection measures

© MERICS

the political agenda. The importance of environmental protection was consolidated in the subsequent five-year plans as well as in other national medium- to long-term programs.

However, the setting of environmental targets did not resolve the fundamental conflicts that exist between environmental protection and short-term economic interests. What it did achieve was to ensure that such conflicts are rarely conducted openly. The national environmental standards were smoothly and efficiently integrated into local development plans by government organs at all administrative levels. This led to the emergence of a comprehensive system of environmental legislation and standards as well as to appropriate regulatory measures—all within several years. Efforts have been especially strong with respect to urban air pollution. The smog-plagued Chinese cities have virtually outdone each other with their lists of environmental measures, ranging from the closing down of municipal coal-fired power plants and companies that increase pollution levels to stringently limiting the use of private cars by the general public.

The numerous municipal activities aimed at improving air quality veils the gap that still exists between the long-term ecological aspirations of the central government and what appears to be achievable at the local levels given the economic costs. Figure 6.11 indicates the local targets for particulate matter concentration (PM2.5) to be reached by 2017 in fifteen highly polluted Chinese cities. In each of these cities, the target remains well below national guidelines that will apply by 2016 (35 µg/m³). The gap between national requirements and local realities is even more apparent with regard to the implementation of the environmental protection guidelines.

Implementation

The major weaknesses of China's environmental policy are revealed when it comes to actual implementation. The MEP, even after expansion of its capacity, is unable, either from a technical perspective or in terms of personnel, to ensure effective monitoring of environmental standards. In addition, the MEP's supervisory function is undermined by the ambiguous role of the local environmental protection bureaus. These organizations, responsible for environmental monitoring at the local levels, are under the authority of local-government departments rather than the MEP. Until recently (see below, *Policy outcomes and policy adjustments*), the position of the MEP was further diminished because it could only impose minor penalties for any environmental offenses that it exposed. Alliances among companies and local governments systematically exploit MEP flaws to avoid having to implement the environmental protection measures (Economy 2004; Kostka/Hobbs 2013).

Figure 6.11

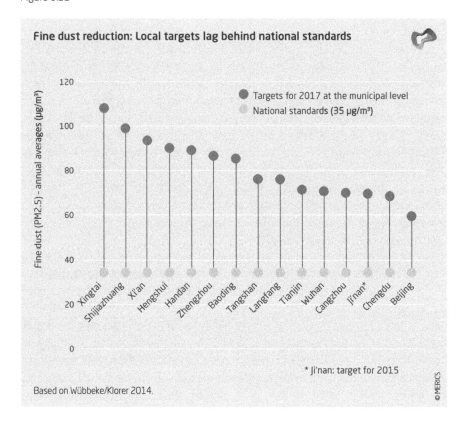

Fine dust reduction: Local targets lag behind national standards

● Targets for 2017 at the municipal level
National standards (35 µg/m³)

Fine dust (PM2.5) – annual averages (µg/m³)

Xingtai · Shijiazhuang · Xi'an · Hengshui · Handan · Zhengzhou · Baoding · Tangshan · Langfang · Tianjin · Wuhan · Cangzhou · Ji'nan* · Chengdu · Beijing

* Ji'nan: target for 2015

Based on Wübbeke/Klorer 2014.

© MERICS

For a long time, the central government tolerated the obvious shortcomings in the implementation of the system and thus accepted the breach of environmental standards. It was not until the beginning of the 2010s that the government began to actively strengthen the supervisory system. The long absence of a strong commitment can be explained by the fact that the weak implementation system compensated for the consequences of overambitious regulations. Environmental targets at the national level are difficult to balance and are always linked to the danger of overstepping the mark and unwittingly placing severe limitations on economic growth. A weak implementation system provides local-government departments with alternatives, thus serving as a safety valve.

There is an additional problem with respect to implementation: the majority of environmental issues arises due to the fundamental nature of the Chinese economic model and ultimately this can only be resolved by transforming the system. The smog problem is a prime example: the emissions from coal combustion are one of the main causes of the air pollution. The Chinese government is making considerable efforts to slash coal consumption by promoting energy efficiency and renewable energy. However, it will not be possible to cut its dependence on cheap coal power over the medium term. Even if the cities take rigorous steps to tackle urban smog and use the measures at their disposal, over the short term this is not likely to have a significant impact on what is deemed to be one of the leading causes of the problem.

Policy outcomes and policy adjustments

Environmental protection is now a firmly established political priority of the Chinese government. Relatively quickly, a statutory and regulatory framework has emerged to provide a stable basis for effective environmental policies. However, these parameters are not fulfilled in terms of successful implementation. The tangible achievements of China's environmental policy are still a long way from resolving its environmental problems.

The weaknesses of China's environmental policy stem from a combination of strong vested interests at the local levels and deficits in the monitoring system. Responding to both of these weaknesses, the government has devised new political instruments. On the one hand, the aim is to curb special interests with new incentive systems. Politically, this includes incorporating environmental criteria into the cadre evaluation system. It is hoped that entrepreneurial interests will be shifted through market-based mechanisms, such as emissions trading. On the other hand, measures have been taken to strengthen the regulatory role of the MEP. The new Environmental Protection Law (in effect since January 2015) is set to play an important role in this regard (Wübbeke 2014), since it will allow the MEP to impose significantly higher penalties for environmental offenses. The "carrots" of environmental incentives and subsidies will now be supplemented by the "sticks" of strict environmental fines.

The sincerity of Chinese environmental policy is incontestable, particularly at the central level. The "war on pollution" (向污染宣战), as declared by Premier Li Keqiang, is more than mere rhetoric. However, securing long-term economic growth still remains the primary goal. Accordingly, the government has so far not been willing to risk any interventions that might radically impede its economic dynamism. The central-government's attempt to strike the right balance has prevented it from cracking down more strongly at the local levels (Ran Ran 2009). Instead, the leadership supports a gradual transition to a new economic model to resolve the environmental problems. Even in a best-case scenario, this is likely to take many years. In the meanwhile, the quality of China's air, water, and soil is likely to remain unsatisfactory.

6.12 Food safety: Preventing health risks

Jost Wübbeke

In recent decades, food contamination in China and its consequences for public health have reached an alarming level. The numerous food safety scandals, such as the incident of melamine-contaminated milk, have left the public distrusting the entire food industry. The state regulatory system that has developed since the 1980s is not properly enforced and it is ineffective with respect to imposing penalties on those responsible for food contamination. Recent revelations regarding the use of contaminated cooking oil illustrate yet again the impotence of the state in this regard. In 2010 it came to light that about 10 percent of the cooking oil in China is recycled from sources such as food slop and garbage. The recycled waste oil is also known as "gutter oil" (地沟油) since it is produced from food waste collected illegally from drains and gutters near restaurants (Peng Liu 2010).

Key actors and interests

The state has repeatedly reacted to the widespread problem of food contamination with regulatory and institutional reforms. After the State Council realized that the lack of cooperation among the various ministries was a major obstacle to better controls, the number of ministries with direct responsibility for food safety was significantly reduced (see Table 6.12). The leading agency for food control since 2013 has been the China Food and Drug Administration (CFDA) (国家食品药品监督管理总局). Taking over the planning side from the Food Safety Commission, it is responsible for supervision along the entire value chain.

The National Health and Family Planning Commission (NHFPC) (国家卫生和计划生育委员会) took over the duties of the former Ministry of Health with regard to defining food standards and devising food safety risk-assessment systems. Other ministries are involved as well, such as the Ministry of Agriculture (MOA) (Jia/Jukes 2013).

China's gutter oil is manufactured by highly professional production rings. Numerous players, scooping out the food waste from restaurant gutters, reprocessing the oil, and reselling it on the market, are involved in this illegal value chain. It has become extremely lucrative for some producers to reclaim the cheap oil and to sell it back to food vendors as expensive cooking oil. The actors involved in the manufacturing rings range from small-time criminals to interprovincial illegal networks.

Table 6.12

Key actors involved in food safety

Actors	Tasks and interests
NHFPC	Risk assessments; definition of food standards
CFDA	Planning of food safety control systems; investigations and licensing along the entire food value chain
MOA	Quality of agricultural products (certifications)
General Administration of Quality Supervision, Inspection and Quarantine (AQSIQ)	Monitoring of food imports and exports
State Administration for Industry and Commerce (SAIC)	Official investigations and raids; closure of production plants
State Administration of Grain (SAG)	Quality standards for the sale of cooking oils
Ministry of Public Security (MPS)	Prosecution
Supreme Court	Interpretation of laws and jurisdiction orders
Local authorities	Implementation of national policy; waste management; local regulations; limited allocation of funds for food safety control and waste management
Food industry	Food production and sales; profits, partly by illicit means
Consumers	Consumption; healthy food

© MERICS

Although gutter oil is often sold as a mixture with pure cooking oil, there are no regulatory incentives for wholesalers and retailers who purchase the oil from the producers to screen the suspect oil.

The substances and additives contained in gutter oil are harmful to consumers and may even be carcinogenic. However, there are no independent interest groups in China to represent consumer interests or to coordinate effective, civil measures for food control. Although many consumers may be willing to spend more on safe foodstuffs, others feel that they are not provided with sufficient information or food labeling to help them identify variations in quality. Both the traditional media and social media played an important role in bringing the gutter oil scandal to light (Liu Shan et al. 2013; Yang Guobin 2013).

Decision-making and conflicts

Up until 2009 no standard statutory framework was in place for food safety, and each of the various responsible ministries relied on different laws. This meant that the Ministry of Health, the Ministry of Agriculture (MOA), and the General Admin- istration of Quality Supervision, Inspection and Quarantine (AQSIQ) issued varying and often contradictory food standards. The government has been working on a Food Safety Law since 2004 (食品安全法). However, a number of ministries have blocked this process in order to avoid a loss of authority. After the melamine milk scandal in 2008, the State Council and the Law Committee of the NPC changed to crisis mode and assumed responsibility for the legislative process. The first compre- hensive Food Safety Law entered into effect in 2009 (Balzano 2012).

This initial Food Safety Law made a clear differentiation among the roles of the various ministries. It established the Commission on Food Safety of the State Council (国务院食品安全委员会) as the unit responsible for planning and coordi- nation. However, the institutional reform was unable to resolve intragovernmental disputes over respective areas of jurisdiction. Disagreements between the Food Safety Commission and the former Ministry of Health over planning and execution caused intermittent tensions, with the result that the Ministry of Health was forced to give up its management role.

Implementation

The authorities at the municipal and county levels are responsible for carrying out food hygiene and safety inspections. In practice, this monitoring system has proved to be inadequate with regard to containing the problem of food contamination. First, the fragmented nature of the food industry as well as the insufficient technical ca- pacity and lack of personnel render systematic supervision impossible. The majority of local laboratories are not adequately equipped to carry out reliable screening of gutter oil and there is a dearth of independent or private test laboratories. Inad- equate practices with regard to municipal waste disposal mean that it is easy for criminals to dredge food waste from restaurants on a large scale. Whenever new scandals expose the failure of the system, central and local governments respond with large-scale raids, such as those in 2011 and 2012, aimed at seizing the gutter oil, but these tend to be short-lived and do not improve the long-term situation (Lu Fangqi/Wu Xuli 2014).

Second, the shared mandate for certain parts of the value chain hampers the process of exposing gutter oil production networks. Each ministry focuses on its own field of competency and denies all further responsibility. Third, the NHFPC has not yet succeeded in devising authoritative standards for the testing and identifying of gutter oil; screening is currently based on the existing standards for cooking oil. Producers of gutter oil have found ways of complying with these standards by adding chemical substances to the oil (Jia/Jukes 2013).

Policy outcomes and policy adjustments

The state measures taken thus far have led to an improvement in the legal regulations. However, the same cannot be said about the effectiveness of the food safety control system. The government still has much to do before the widespread problem of food contamination is finally brought under control. Public distrust is greater than ever, and there are still frequent media reports about diseases and deaths caused by contaminated food. Criminals continue to peddle gutter oil on the food market. In 2014 the government focused on raids aimed at breaking the gutter oil supply chain. Such sporadic actions, however, clearly demonstrate the failure of systematic administrative food safety inspection measures.

The Food Safety Law introduced a number of new elements with respect to food safety control. The NHFPC began by setting up a system for risk assessments. The National Center for Food Safety Risk Assessment (卫生部食品安全风险评估中心) is responsible for monitoring food-borne diseases and for analyzing their potential dangers. In April 2015, the NPC passed an amendment to the Food Safety Law; the major changes include harsher penalties for food contamination, a more comprehensive consumer-protection framework, and new rules for online sales. The amendment also includes much stricter regulations regarding the production of baby food.

Following the exposure of gutter oil production as an industrial operation, the government significantly increased the penalties for the production and trading of contaminated cooking oil. According to new sentencing guidelines under the Food Safety Law, in especially serious cases peddlers of gutter oil may face the death penalty (Lu Fangqi/Wu Xuli 2014). In addition, the NDRC has initiated a pilot program designed to improve municipal food waste disposal. Moreover, the different areas of jurisdiction along the food value chain are no longer allocated to separate ministries. Food production and imports were previously overseen by the AQSIQ, monitoring food consumption in the hotel and restaurant industry was under the purview of the CFDA, and food sales came under the State Administration for Industry and Commerce (SAIC). Since 2013, these functions have been pooled under the remit of the CFDA.

The reforms that are now in place show that the government is devoting considerable attention to food safety issues. However, in the face of the current challenges, the reforms are unlikely to provide a speedy solution. The legal process will remain ineffective as long as food control measures are not rigorously linked with the issuance of penalties to producers and sellers of gutter oil and other contaminated food. Nevertheless, a growing awareness among consumers and a strengthening of consumer organizations may help to improve the food control systems over the long term.

6.13 Disaster management: Contingency planning and rescue programs

Johannes Buckow

Many millions of people in China are affected each year by natural disasters, such as floods, droughts, and earthquakes, or by industrial, ecological, and meteorological disasters. The Chinese government has been working on a permanent integrated DM program since the early 2000s. However, the institutional development of this system remains incomplete.

When the county of Wenchuan in Sichuan province was struck by an earthquake measuring 8.0 on the Richter scale in May 2008, many of the disaster response mechanisms had only recently been put in place; the majority of the contingency plans had been finalized during the previous several months. Thus far, the Wenchuan earthquake has been the worst natural disaster to hit China since the turn of the millennium. According to official sources, it claimed 69,000 lives and injured 374,000. Another 18,000 people were listed as missing (UNESCAP 2008).

In addition to the difficult terrain and tough weather conditions, coordinating the rescue response, providing medical care to civilians, rebuilding the damaged infrastructure, and cleaning up the disaster zone were an acid test for the recently installed DM system.

Key actors and interests

According to the Emergency Response Law of 2007 (突发事件应对法), the State Council, i.e., the central government, has ultimate authority for China's DM. During noncrisis periods, inter-ministerial steering committees within the central government have decision-making powers with regard to the structure of the DM system—how tasks are distributed and how resources are allocated. In the event of a disaster, however, the inner cabinet, headed by the premier, takes charge of managing "particularly serious" crises. If the impact of a disaster is limited to a local area, primary responsibility for action rests at the county or provincial levels.

Responsibility for crisis prevention, for preparing contingency plans, and for disaster research and monitoring are spread across a number of government departments that answer either to the State Council directly or that are incorporated into the various ministries (e.g., the MOCA). The China Earthquake Administration (CEA) (中国地震局) plays an especially important role with regard to earthquake protection and mitigation as well as to the establishment of national emergency responses in regions affected by destructive earthquakes.

A first step toward pooling competencies for more streamlined DM was taken in 2005 when the State Council set up a permanent DM task force, the State Council Emergency Management Office (EMO) (国务院应急管理办公室), which was allocated its own personnel and budget. The idea was that the EMO should serve as a central information interface for the State Council and should coordinate cooperation among the relevant ministries, public agencies, programs, and other organizations. A number of specialized commissions for the different types of disasters are attached to the EMO. In crisis situations, these commissions are responsible for collaborating with the EMO to coordinate relief efforts across the various ministries and government levels. The responsible commission in cases of natural disasters is the National Commission for Disaster Reduction (NCDR) (国家减灾委员会).

Because the Chinese armed forces are substantially involved in China's DM system, coordination between civilian and military decision-makers plays a crucial role during crisis situations. According to the Emergency Response Law, the People's Liberation Army (PLA), the People's Armed Police (PAP), and the militia may be deployed to participate in disaster relief and rescue missions under the command of both the State Council and the Central Military Commission (CMC). In the event of disasters, Chinese NGOs and international aid organizations play an important role with respect to mobilizing supplies and raising relief funds (see Table 6.13).

Decision-making and conflicts

The structure of the Chinese DM system is highly centralized: during noncrisis periods, the premier assigns responsibilities in consultation with the various ministries and central party organs. In the event of actual disasters, the state leadership assumes all decision-making powers in the crisis zone and sets up local command structures.

Table 6.13

Key actors involved in disaster management

Actors	Tasks and interests
State Council, Premier	Coordination and management of disaster responses in very serious cases
EMO	Expertise and coordination of DM; proactive development of emergency programs
Specialized state organs: • National Commission for Disaster Reduction (NCDR), under the Ministry of Civil Affairs • State Supervisory Authority for Production Safety (SSAPS), in DM only under the Ministry of Civil Affairs • Patriotic Health Campaign Committee (PHCC), under the Chinese Center for Disease Control and Prevention • Central Commission for Comprehensive Management of Public Security (CCCMPS), under the MPS	Monitoring and forecasting; disaster prevention; drafting of contingency plans; adviser to the State Council on disaster responses • NCDR: natural disasters • SSAPS: industrial accidents • PHCC: epidemics • CCCMPS: terrorism
National ministries	Ad-hoc: provision of additional resources
Specialized organizations: • China Earthquake Administration (CEA) • State Forestry Administration (SFA) • State Oceanic Administration (SOA) • Office of State Flood Control and Drought Relief	Preventive measures and contingency plans; special expertise for disaster protection
Heads of provincial and county government departments	Management of isolated, local disaster situations; establishment of infrastructure for local emergencies
Provincial and county EMOs	Consultancy services for provincial and county government departments; cooperation with the national EMO
PLA and PAP (in the event of disasters, under the dual command of the CMC and the State Council)	Implementation of emergency procedures and rescue measures; maintaining social order
NGOs, aid organizations	Mobilization of donations and relief supplies

© MERICS

Below the State Council level, however, the areas of competency of the involved organs in disaster prevention and DM tend to overlap: with regard to earthquake protection, the CEA, and the NCDR each have their own seismic monitoring infrastructure. The CEA, the NCDR, and the EMO each vie for positions as central advisers to the premier and the ministers involved in DM. All three agencies have separate earthquake prevention programs.

National contingency plans drafted by the EMO define the chain of command for mobilizing relief and rescue efforts in the event of a crisis. However, the EMO is only partially able to fulfill its original remit as the central point of coordination for all DM measures because the relevant ministries and government departments tend to coordinate activities among themselves (Lü Xiaoli/Zhong Kaibin 2012).

Since the PLA often reaches the scene of a disaster before any civil decision-makers and is subsequently responsible for planning and implementing its own rescue and aid measures, the army's command setup on the ground is crucial to the disaster response (Li Nan 2010). The communications channels and the distribution of tasks between the military and the state bureaucracy are not always clearly defined. In 2008, this led to problems coordinating the response to the earthquake in Sichuan province (Li Nan 2010).

Implementation

When Wenchuan was hit by an exceptionally powerful earthquake in May 2008, evacuation efforts by rescue teams were hampered by the mountainous terrain, falling rocks, landslides, collapsed roads, burst dams, as well as by heavy rain and dense fog.

Headed by the premier, the inner cabinet immediately raised the disaster alert to the highest level and set in motion its contingency plans for earthquakes and other natural disasters. The premier took control of the disaster response and assumed all decision-making powers at the local level. At the same time, the Organization Department of the CCP strengthened hierarchical discipline and control mechanisms, and increased political pressures for rapid, coordinated mobilization of leading party cadres and party members in government and military organs at all levels (Xiao Yuefan 2013).

Within minutes of the earthquake, the PLA dispatched the first military rescue teams to the disaster zone. It set up an ad hoc command force and attempted to reach the devastated areas. When the premier arrived on the scene, he set up a provisional civil command center with nine task forces, including participation by the NCDR, the CEA, and other disaster relief organizations.

Coordination of cooperation among the civil and military decision-makers and the rescue workers proved to be difficult, especially during the initial days of the operation. Collaborations between civil agencies and PLA rescue units were complicated because they were anchored in different command chains. Not all of the State Council's directives could be implemented by the PLA—sending in parachutists over destroyed towns, for example—due to persistent thunderstorms, poor visibility, and unsafe terrain. As a result of tensions between government departments and army units, in mid-May CCP General Secretary Hu Jintao stepped in to lead the disaster response and to amalgamate the civil and military task forces for better coordination of the aid measures (Li Nan 2010; Mulvenon 2008).

After some initial hesitation, unlike during previous disasters nonstate media were officially allowed to provide comprehensive coverage of the disaster and the ensuing rescue efforts. However, the state was back in control after only several days (Xiao Yuefan 2013). In the wake of the disaster, volunteers and representatives of NGOs arrived en masse to provide humanitarian aid and help with the reconstruction efforts. This was the first time that foreign and international search and rescue units took part in a Chinese disaster recovery operation.

Policy outcomes and policy adjustments

In comparison to the somewhat chaotic efforts during previous crises, the 2008 emergency response, including the prompt evacuation of over 200,000 people, the securing of water, basic food supplies, and medical care for nearly 400,000 casualties, and the restoration of key traffic and transport routes in the almost impassible disaster region were a remarkable achievement by China's newly installed DM system (UNESCAP 2008). The rapid centralization of decision-making powers facilitated large-scale mobilization of state and military resources. At the same time, however, coordination problems between the government and the army revealed significant weaknesses in the response and impeded rescue operations, at least during the crucial initial days after the earthquake.

Weaknesses also came to light with regard to crisis prevention. Although the contingency plans facilitated a rapid response in the areas affected by the earthquake, the equipment and training provided to the civil and military rescue teams were inadequate. In addition, despite the known risks, many of the buildings in the disaster zone had not been constructed to withstand earthquakes. Because the majority of the nearly 70,000 fatalities was caused by collapsed buildings, a host of scandals erupted about the safety of public buildings. The quality of school buildings came under particular scrutiny since a large number of schools collapsed, leaving hundreds of children buried.

The state and party leaderships applied the lessons learned from the 2008 earthquake disaster to critically review and refine the DM system. In the wake of the disaster, provincial and county governments set up their own EMOs and DM infrastructures. The CMC devised guidelines for collaboration between the PLA and the civil agencies. To optimize its crisis management and prevention skills, the PLA set up emergency rescue units consisting of a total of 50,000 soldiers, providing them with specialized equipment and training for conducting rescue and humanitarian aid operations (Suttmeier 2012).

6.14 Foreign and security policies: Maritime rights and interests

Mikko Huotari

China's maritime interests are much more far-reaching than merely territorial claims or the commercial use of oceans. Chinese foreign policy in this area must therefore be viewed as an integral part of the country's security and embedded in its economic interests. International observers often interpret China's maritime activities as a kind of willful, orchestrated, top-down assertiveness. However, for a long time they were characterized by a rather weak level of coordination between a host of state and military actors which, for the most part, pursued conflicting interests and activities (ICG 2012; Schmidt 2012). When Xi Jinping assumed power in 2012, the leadership attempted to cluster the regulatory capacities in the area of maritime policy with the objective of establishing China as a major maritime power. This centralization of decision-making powers was a key prerequisite for the realignment of foreign policy under Xi Jinping.

Key actors and interests

A variety of different civilian and military authorities, ranging from the Ministry of Land and Resources to government departments in the coastal provinces, right up to the People's Liberation Army Navy (PLAN), are actively involved in China's maritime policies. Before 2013, there were five different regulatory agencies including, among others, the Fisheries Law Enforcement Command (FLEC), the General Administration of Customs (GAC), and the China Coast Guard, that pursued their own interests with regard to coastal and ocean management. Local governments, economic and military actors in the coastal provinces, and state-owned oil companies with offshore activities all looked after their own coastal and maritime interests, which were not necessarily compatible with the priorities set by the government and military headquarters. In addition, there were tensions between the civil bureaucracies and the military authorities. For instance, when the PLAN was pressing for an extension of its authority and action, the Ministry of Foreign Affairs (MOFA) was in favor of a neighborhood policy aimed at diplomatic dialogue (see Table 6.14).

Table 6.14

Actors and interests involved in Chinese maritime policy

Actors	Tasks and interests
Central LSG for the Protection of Maritime Interests	Centralized, inter-ministerial authority; guidelines; coordination; strict enforcement of central directives
CMC; PLAN	Expansion of maritime power; modernization of the PLAN and extension of its radius for action
MOFA	Diplomatic mediation for regional policy; little say about issues related to economic and military maritime powers
State Oceanic Administration (SOA), including the Coast Guard	Clustering of skills to enforce maritime rights and interests; civil-military coordination
SOEs (energy, raw materials)	Increase exploitation of maritime resources by setting up offshore locations
Government departments in the coastal provinces	Establishment of coastal marine development zones

© MERICS

Decision-making and conflicts

As early as the 1990s, government advisers had already called for an administrative reorganization to merge the various maritime regulatory bodies. Under the Hu-Wen administration (2002–12), some agencies were amalgamated in order to test the scheme at the provincial levels. The 12th Five-Year Plan (2011–15) emphasized the importance of developing the maritime economy, something that was also openly promoted by China's leading politicians in charge of foreign policy and military affairs. The rapid expansion of maritime activities and ambitions was resolutely continued by the Xi–Li administration beginning in 2012. To develop comprehensive maritime powers, the political leadership handles economic and security interests within the common conceptual and programmatic framework of China's "maritime rights and interests" (海洋权益).

The increasingly centralized coordination of China's maritime foreign policy resulted after years of internal controversies. Reorganization of the maritime regulatory bodies was accompanied by extensive, fiercely contested domestic restructuring, personnel redeployments, and shifts in power. The decision-making process was eclipsed by internal maneuvers as part of the leadership changes at the end of 2012. Before his appointment as party leader Xi Jinping had been designated leader of a newly established Central LSG for the Protection of Maritime Interests (中央海洋权益工作领导小组). In the context of China's dispute with Japan over the Senkaku Islands (known as the Diaoyu Islands in Chinese), Xi took over leadership of what was a particularly contentious policy area. The growing number of maritime conflicts in the East and South China Seas had an accelerating effect on the reorganization of China's maritime institutions.

Implementation

China's rise as a maritime power is taking place at a number of different levels. The country's diplomatic apparatus has been increasingly focused on asserting China's maritime interests. At the end of 2013, the state leadership and the MOFA began a charm offensive to woo China's neighboring states. Proposals were introduced for a "Maritime Silk Road" (combining trade routes, ports, and logistics centers from China's south coast through South and Southeast Asia to the Middle East and Africa) to fuse economic ties with diplomatic interests. An active "neighborhood policy" (周边外交工作), especially for South and Southeast Asia, was confirmed by Xi Jinping at an October 2013 high-level conference, attended by all leading officials in foreign affairs work and China's overseas ambassadors.

At party headquarters—in close proximity to China's party leader and head of state Xi Jinping—the office of the LSG for the Protection of Maritime Interests plays a key role in planning and coordination. It is also involved in the decision-preparation phase regarding the disputed maritime zones and other contentious topics. An additional government steering committee for maritime issues, the State Oceanic Administration (SOA) (国家海洋委员会) has been established to improve coordination among ministries with regard to implementation of civil maritime programs.

The restructuring and consolidation of China's maritime agencies at the intermediate governmental level that began in 2013 were similarly extensive. Administratively, the SOA remains subordinate to the Ministry of Land and Resources. From an operational perspective, a vice-minister from the Ministry of Public Security in the SOA is responsible for "integrated ocean management." The China Coast Guard (中国海警局), pooling the resources of the previously five separate maritime regulatory organs, is now a national agency within the SOA (Zhou Hang 2014).

The economic ambitions associated with expanding China's maritime activities and presence are set out in a five-year plan, published by the State Council in January 2013, for the maritime economy. The objective is to rapidly increase the added value created by the maritime economy, for example by systematically promoting the maritime development zones that have been emerging along the coastal regions since 2011.

Policy outcomes and policy adjustments

The process of consolidating China's maritime interests is not yet complete. Diplomatic initiatives for engagement with neighboring states tend to meet with concern and resistance. There is still uncertainty at party and government headquarters regarding the status of the newly created decision-making, coordination, and leading organs for maritime issues vis-à-vis the traditional hierarchies of foreign policy, foreign trade, and security. The division of competencies and power among the various state organs remains contested.

However, the sweeping institutional reforms have provided the party leadership with an opportunity to implement new priorities and programs in a policy area that is vitally important in terms of foreign policy, security policy, and foreign trade. Civil–military coordination between national maritime agencies and the PLAN has been facilitated and the China Coast Guard and the PLAN have recently begun to conduct joint maneuvers. Maritime economic activities in the coastal provinces have grown substantially, along with massive land reclamation activities and offshore and deep-sea exploration.

Due to years of commitment to an active maritime strategy and the institutional reorganization, China's prospects of enforcing its economic and security interests as a major maritime power in the twenty-first century have increased considerably. For its neighbors in the region, reform of Chinese maritime policy has resulted in ambivalent consequences: on the one hand, there is less of a danger of uncoordinated escalations of activity due to the centralization of decision-making and improved coordination on the Chinese side. On the other hand, the Chinese leadership now has more clearly defined targets and stronger mechanisms at its disposal to more effectively pursue its interests in the South and East China Seas.

6.15 Urbanization policy: Experimental urban concepts

Elena Klorer

Urbanization is regarded by the Chinese government as a powerful engine for achieving sustained economic growth and for restructuring the economy, as cities provide an ideal location for promoting technological progress, expanding the services sector, and enhancing domestic demand. Therefore, the government is seeking to actively control the urbanization processes and to deploy them as instruments of economic, social, and technological change. However, the urbanization processes create enormous challenges for the government. These challenges include reorganization of the residence registration system (the *hukou* system), redistribution of tax revenue among central and local governments (see Section 2.8), and dealing with land-use rights and the ecological impacts of forced urbanization.

For many years, the Chinese government has established pilot projects to experiment with various urban concepts in order to come up with solutions to these manifold challenges. Existing models focus on opportunities for sustainable development that save resources and protect the environment. Such opportunities can be better explored at urban levels, resulting in more specific practical findings than in large, heterogeneous provinces. In addition to the emphasis on the environmental aspects of "eco-cities" or "low-carbon cities," the spectrum of existing urban concepts is steadily expanding into other fields, such as cities with pilot projects for electro-mobility or smart grids.

Key actors and interests

Party and government headquarters are the determinants of the essential direction of China's urbanization policy and are the driving forces behind a new model for lasting growth. Policy is shaped and coordinated through national urbanization plans under the auspices of the NDRC. Various government ministries (MEP, the Ministry of Housing and Urban-Rural Development [MOHURD], MIIT, and MOST) and the NDRC compete with one another to develop and promote individual urban concepts at the national level. This is the reason why support for certain ideas is closely linked to the interests and powers of the individual ministries, e.g., the MEP promotes the eco-city model, whereas the MIIT supports smart-city models. The ministries attempt to exploit certain urban concepts to expand their own range of influence in competition with other ministries.

City and county governments are responsible for implementing their respective urban concepts. They are keenly interested in being assigned pilot projects—not only for image reasons, but also for financial reasons—because such projects are generally accompanied by generous grants. Due to this financial aid, public and private businesses (including investors, construction firms, and real-estate companies) have also become involved in initiating and establishing pilot projects.

Some pilot projects, such as the Wuxi Sino–Swedish Low-Carbon Eco-City, have been created in conjunction with international partners. At the scientific level, urban-planning policy is influenced by government-affiliated research institutes (the China Academy of Urban Planning and Design [CAUPD], the DRC, and the China Society for Urban Studies [CSUS]). In addition, national and international NGOs often act in advisory capacities to assist in the development and promotion of sustainable urban concepts (see Table 6.15.A).

Decision-making and conflicts

The introduction of pilot projects for sustainable urbanization began in the 1990s. The number of comprehensive urban projects has increased dramatically since 2000 due to support from the central government, local initiatives, and international partners. China is currently one of the world's most active nations in the field of experimental projects with respect to sustainable urban development (Liu Hongling et al. 2014).

The relevant ministries decide upon which urban concepts will be supported, but such decisions are not coordinated at a high level. As a result, there are often several parallel initiatives supporting similar urban concepts. Participating provinces, cities, and local authorities are selected at the national level by the responsible ministries. The cities are chosen in accordance with criteria such as whether or not plans and financing for the concept already exist. Such cities can then apply to establish pilot projects.

Not only political interests but also economic incentives play an important role in the choice of pilot cities. Pilot-project status is financially beneficial to the cities: once these projects are assigned, the respective cities can apply for grants from the central government and may also profit from the increase in the price of land for construction. In addition, pilot projects may be used to attract investors and to stimulate the local economy. This provides an important incentive for local cadres and municipalities that are still judged primarily by their contribution to economic performance. However, conflicting political and economic interests can distort the intended objectives of the model cities and obstruct successful implementation (see Table 6.15.B).

Table 6.15.A

Actors and interests involved in urbanization policy

Actors	Tasks and interests
Party/central government	Macro-management to achieve growth, innovation, and protection of the environment
NDRC	Planning authority; national coordination
MEP	Upgrading of environmental protection in economic administration
MOHURD	Development of national standards
MIIT	ICT policy
MOST	Innovation policy
MOF	Urban development that is feasible from a fiscal perspective; the MOF served as an advisory partner to the World Bank report on "Urban China"
MOT	Infrastructure for transportation and traffic engineering
CAUPD	Research institute under MOHURD, supports the Urban Planning Society of China (UPSC)
CSUS	Research and consultations on sustainable urban development
DRC	Consultation and scientific reporting
NGOs	Support for pilot projects (such as the World Wide Fund Low-Carbon City Initiative)
International actors	Bilateral pilot projects (such as the Sino-Singapore Tianjin Eco-City)
Provincial governments	To increase resources; lobbying on behalf of provincial cities
Municipal governments	Project implementation; urban financing; urban marketing
Citizens	Rural migration; protests against resettlement; compensation
Companies; investors	Public contracts/grants; lucrative investments

© MERICS

Table 6.15.B

Selected designations and government ministries that support urban projects

	Name	Year	Ministry	No. of cities
ECO	Eco-garden City	2004	MOHURD	12
	Eco-county; eco-city; eco-province	2003	MEP	38
	Environmental Protection Model Cities/districts	1997	MEP	84
LOW-CARBON	Low-carbon Provinces and Cities	2010	NDRC	8
	Low-carbon Eco-city	2009	MOHURD; CSUS	13
SMART	EU–China Smart and Green City Cooperation	2014	EU; MIIT	30 (including 15 EU/China)
	Smart City Pilot Project	2013	MIIT	2
	Smart City Pilot	2013	MOHURD	171
	863 Smart City Project	2013	MOST	2

© MERICS

Implementation

Pilot projects are assigned on the basis of existing projects or plans. On the one hand, this procedure encourages cities to take an initiative by rewarding successful projects. On the other hand, it also encourages the setting of exaggerated goals in order to improve the chances of being assigned a pilot project.

Such conflicting incentives repeatedly result in projects that have no basis in reality, as revealed by the example of the Dongtan eco-city project. Dongtan was supposed to be built 25 km outside of Shanghai as Asia's first carbon-neutral eco-city. However, this prestigious project launched by Shanghai's mayor ground to a halt when he was prosecuted for corruption and it was determined that the land slated for construction was located in the immediate vicinity of an environmentally protected area (Yu Li 2014). The case clearly illustrates that city governments and investors are often more interested in maximizing their own profits than in successfully implementing ecological urban concepts (Chien Shiuh-Shen 2013). For local cadres, winning the assignment of a pilot project provides an opportunity to attract foreign and domestic investments and thus also to advance their own careers. The risks of this intense coupling of local economic and individual political interests result in that the pilot projects may fail to adequately take into account the actual needs of the general public.

Another factor that prevents implementation of sustainable urban concepts is that many cities have little experience with experimental urban concepts. As a consequence, in the process of planning they tend to focus on national objectives rather than on local needs. Currently, there are no market-based mechanisms to identify local needs (Wang Can et al. 2014). Only in exceptional cases does the development of urban projects include consultations with the general public, and even when projects have already been implemented, they can still end in failure due to a lack of practicality or inadequate public awareness, as illustrated by the example of the Sino-Singapore Tianjin Eco-City. The majority of the population did not understand the purpose or the usefulness of the energy-efficient systems in their homes, so they did not use them (Yu Li 2014).

Policy outcomes and policy adjustments

Urbanization policy is a broad field involving numerous actors, as indicated by the steadily growing number of pilot projects. There is no central control or organizing authority. As a result, experiments with urban concepts are conducted independently of one another and are geared toward different indicators depending on the particular project (Zhou Nan, Gang He, and Williams 2012). This makes it difficult to measure and compare the success of the various pilot projects.

Nonetheless, in light of the continued increase in urbanization and the resultant huge environmental problems, there is an urgent need for development and promotion of alternative sustainable urban concepts. The Chinese government is actively addressing this issue, as illustrated by the example of the National New-Type Urbanization Plan (2014–20) (State Council 2014a). This plan presents urbanization as the key factor responsible for stable, long-term economic growth. However, it is also explicitly linked to the demand for ecologically sustainable urbanization. The government has set specific political goals to improve the urban environmental situation, such as expansion of local public transportation; prices for electricity, water, and gas that are adjusted to meet consumption needs; achieving international air standards; and introducing tradable emissions rights.

China's urban pilot projects, based on such guidelines, test new instruments and procedures. In spite of the difficulties with their practical implementation, some of these experiments are a source of innovative solutions to urgent problems. However, in order to come up with a fundamental solution to these problems, promising approaches must be effectively implemented in many more cities beyond the scope of local pilot projects.

6.16 Internet security: National IT independence and China's cyber policy

Hauke Gierow

"[There is] no national security without cyber security" (没有网络安全就没有国家安全). This April 2014 statement by President Xi Jinping has since become a programmatic guideline for all government work (Xinhuanet 2014). In fact, Internet security has now become a political priority of the Chinese leadership. However, the Chinese government's definition of cyber security differs from that of Western countries. Beijing claims the right to control information, networks, and technologies as comprehensively as possible. It follows that Internet censorship is an essential component of China's cyber-security policy. In practice, this leads to conflicts within the government as well as with private-sector businesses.

Western technologies and software are regarded as security risks. Therefore, the development of China's own technologies and security standards, with the aim of becoming largely self-sufficient, lies at the heart of Chinese cyber-security policy. Chinese policy oscillates between economic interests and actual security concerns. In this regard, security issues also serve as a means to justify protectionist measures.

Key actors and interests

The guidelines for China's cyber-security policy were established by the Central Leading Small Group for Cyber Security and Informatization (CSILSG), established in April 2014. This LSG, directed by President Xi Jinping, is made up of high-ranking decision-makers from various ministries and the CCP. It is closely linked to the Cyberspace Administration of China (CAC) (国家互联网信息办公室). The latter body was expanded to become a key component in Internet policy, combining the diverse interests of the decision-making entities.

Everyday cyber-policy power primarily resides in the security bodies: the Ministry of Public Security (公安部); the Central Commission for State Secrets (中央

保密委员会), identical with the National Bureau for State Secrets (国家保密局); the Central Encryption LSG (中央密码工作领导小组), which is the same as the National Encryption Office (国家秘码管理局), and the cyber units of the PLA's General Staff Department. The civilian MIIT is also involved in cyber-security policy (see Figure 6.16).

In the early 2000s cyber security had not yet become a focal point of government work. Various ministries exploited the unclear responsibilities in this rapidly growing sector to enhance their own influence over Internet supervision. Long-standing disputes about responsibilities extended beyond bureaucratic rivalries to include differences of opinion regarding content, including the methods and scope of Internet censorship. Companies and economic administrative bodies believed that tighter controls and stricter censorship would inhibit economic growth. However, these critics did not prevail over the comprehensive surveillance interests of party and government headquarters.

Decision-making and conflicts

China's party headquarters drafted its first cyber-security strategy in 2003 (CCP CC General Office 2003). This strategy paper was written by a group of political leaders who now occupy the highest offices, including Premier Li Keqiang. However, this strategy was not consistently enforced until President Xi Jinping assumed office.

The regulatory security requirements for Chinese IT products increased steadily in the 2010s. On the one hand, this was due to the increased global integration of China and the growing importance of the Internet for economic development. On the other hand, Edward Snowden's revelations about Western surveillance activities accelerated Chinese political decision-making in the field of cyber policy (Williams 2014). The government extensively intensified its claim to comprehensive control of all information: in addition to censorship of undesirable content, control over all relevant IT technologies was included in the state's cyber strategy.

Under President Xi, the Chinese leadership reacted to previous gaps and shortcomings in the field of Internet control by assigning various executive responsibilities to the CAC. For President Xi Jinping, cyber security is a political priority, thereby unprecedentedly involving the interests of the ministries, party bodies, surveillance services, and the military. This has had far-reaching effects: since 2013 China has become increasingly self-confident regarding matters of Internet diplomacy and has exerted growing Internet pressures on other countries. Large American IT companies have felt the consequences of this self-protective mindset, as some of their products are now excluded from Chinese purchases and others are subject to comprehensive security checks by Chinese authorities.

Figure 6.16

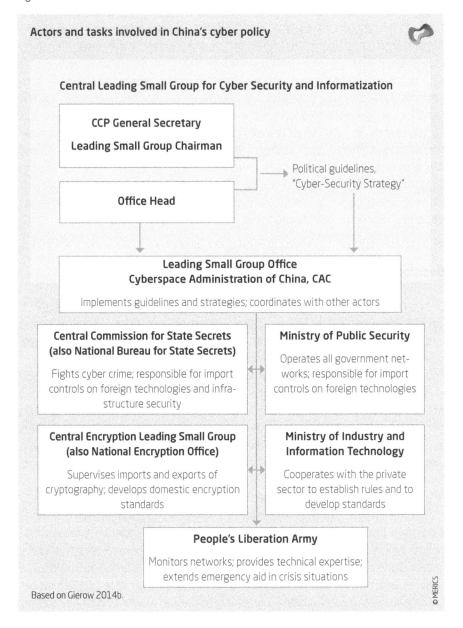

Actors and tasks involved in China's cyber policy

Central Leading Small Group for Cyber Security and Informatization

CCP General Secretary

Leading Small Group Chairman

→ Political guidelines, "Cyber-Security Strategy"

Office Head

Leading Small Group Office
Cyberspace Administration of China, CAC

Implements guidelines and strategies; coordinates with other actors

Central Commission for State Secrets (also National Bureau for State Secrets)

Fights cyber crime; responsible for import controls on foreign technologies and infrastructure security

Ministry of Public Security

Operates all government networks; responsible for import controls on foreign technologies

Central Encryption Leading Small Group (also National Encryption Office)

Supervises imports and exports of cryptography; develops domestic encryption standards

Ministry of Industry and Information Technology

Cooperates with the private sector to establish rules and to develop standards

People's Liberation Army

Monitors networks; provides technical expertise; extends emergency aid in crisis situations

Based on Gierow 2014b.

© MERICS

Implementation

Sketchy implementation, at least until 2013–14, was manifested in the contradictory measures taken by the various ministries. These ministries often attempted to promote differing security standards for IT products. This created problems for small and medium-sized IT companies that are required to undergo complex certification procedures if they wish to sell to public entities. Many companies therefore waived their right to enter the lucrative IT market in the Chinese public sector (Goodrich 2012).

In order to promote security and growth in equal measure, in 2007 the Chinese government developed what is known as the Multi-Level Protection Scheme, or the "Regulations on the Classified Protection of Information Security" (信息安全等级保护管理办法) (see Table 6.16). Based on these regulations, public authorities and businesses in areas critical to security are no longer allowed to purchase certain products from foreign manufacturers. For example, virus scanners made by Kaspersky or Norton have been affected by this development, as has Microsoft's Windows 8 operating system. The Chinese government has issued detailed lists indicating what products may be purchased. The purchase of foreign encryption technology is also strictly controlled: Chinese companies are only permitted to use products made by foreign manufacturers if they can prove that they are necessary for communications with external business partners.

A persistent problem for many companies has been that adequate, high-performance Chinese alternatives to foreign products are not always available. The Chinese leadership has accepted the high costs of adaptation and the weaker economic performance in order to promote its political and technological security interests.

Many Western economists see a contradiction between strong state control of the market and the innovative power of an economy. In spite of these conventional assumptions, international publicly listed, highly profitable, and strongly innovative IT corporations have emerged in China (Ernst/Naughton 2008). Since 2010 China has attempted to promote its own IT standards throughout the world. However, technologies supported by the Chinese government in the field of mobile communications have been unsuccessful outside of China's borders: for example, mobile networks using the Chinese standard, TD-SCMA, are only used in Nicaragua and Zimbabwe. However, China is at the forefront of developing 5G mobile technology and can be expected to dominate international markets in the future.

Policy outcomes and policy adjustments

The Chinese government uses the international cyber-security debate to promote its own concepts of national Internet sovereignty and censorship. The priority on

Table 6.16

China's Multi-Level Protection Scheme for IT security

Level	Affected entities	Consequences of an IT failure	Security requirements	Affected foreign software (examples)
1 + 2	Private users; small and medium-sized companies	Individual damage; no direct risk to society	Self-protection by users and companies, for instance through firewalls and virus scanners	No requirements
3	Businesses in the energy, finance, transportation, and infrastructure sectors	A threat to social order and the public interest; possible damage to national security	Requirements for access and use of the systems; information for the responsible authorities concerning tests and security risks; annual security checks	Foreign antivirus and business software
4	Public authorities	Particularly serious damage to the public interest; damage to national security	Clearly defined protective levels and access authorizations; expanded security tests; "trusted computing" hardware; security checks every six months	Windows operating system
5	Public authorities with heightened security requirements	Especially serious damage to national security	Mandatory access controls; minimal system complexity; continuous security checks	Windows operating system

Based on Gierow 2014b.

© MERICS

cyber-security policy under Xi Jinping sent an emphatic signal: "Internet Minister" Lu Wei became a key player in matters of network regulation and he actively promoted the position of the Chinese government at international events. But if the Chinese government is to continue on its path of isolating the Chinese IT market, then Western IT corporations will find it increasingly difficult to gain a foothold in the Chinese market.

However, it remains to be seen whether isolation and IT self-sufficiency do, in fact, represent a security gain. Chinese and Western experts (Maurer/Morgus/Skierka 2014; Zhang Yu 2014) stress that the origin of an IT product is not a reliable indication of its security. China's cyber-security policy focuses on government defenses against domestic and foreign dangers. Until now, the protection of network users from hackers and data manipulation has not been a key component of government policy (Kovacs/Hawtin 2013). However, one of the main objectives of Chinese cyber policy is clear: China intends to become entirely independent of foreign IT technologies.

6.17 Education policy: Popularization and improvements in vocational training

Elena Klorer

The Chinese government regards education as a key factor for strengthening China's human resources (人力资源) and a prerequisite for increasing economic- and technology-sourced productivity, innovation, and competitiveness. A high priority is attached to education in Chinese society. Obtaining a university degree is regularly mentioned in opinion polls as being essential for a successful career, material wealth, and personal happiness. Since 2010, however, a growing number of graduates have encountered difficulties in securing well-paid jobs that meet their expectations and that build on their training.

Despite active state promotion of educational institutions and the constant updating of the subject matter covered in courses, the skills that Chinese school-leavers and university graduates obtain often fail to match the requirements of the job market and the expectations of employers. The main reasons are the strong emphasis in the educational system on examinations (reproducing standardized knowledge that can be tested rather than fostering creative thinking) and the complete lack of emphasis on relating theoretical knowledge to practical experience.

Due to the realignment of the Chinese economy with a view to developing and manufacturing technologically advanced products and sophisticated system-based solutions, demand has been growing for skilled workers and technicians who have acquired modern qualifications that have a practical focus. These professionally trained people are perfectly capable of making a major contribution to productivity and innovation in modern industrial economies without university degrees. Therefore, since 2010 the Chinese government has been promoting occupational training courses related to the production industries.

Key actors and interests

The State Council LSG for Science, Technology, and Education decides on national strategies and research programs and it coordinates them with national research policy. The Ministry of Education (MOE) is responsible for shaping the primary, secondary, and tertiary education systems as well as for determining what is taught. In addition, the MOE is tasked with supervising implementation of national and vocational education policies. Implementation is undertaken by the respective education authorities at the provincial, city, and county levels. In contrast, the MOHRSS is responsible for labor-market policies. It has a say in vocational education policy insofar as it formulates standards for occupational skills and issues appropriate certificates when such standards are met. The MOF assigns funds for national education programs to the subnational governments, which are then responsible for the educational institutions within their respective jurisdictions.

Overall, various government agencies are involved in shaping vocational education, some of which have widely differing interests (see Table 6.17). This considerable variety of bodies and interests is also reflected in the organizations operating the vocational colleges, which are either private or state authorities and thus ultimately have either commercial or nonprofit interests. Numerous international organizations—educational institutions from other countries, foundations, NGOs, and foreign companies—also play a role in the Chinese education system. In the vocational training sector, the Chinese government is particularly interested in obtaining expert knowledge based on foreign models, such as the German system of dual vocational education that combines theory and practice. Foreign organizations also play an active role in serving as professional partners on projects designed to improve the quality of existing vocational training institutions. International companies operating in the PRC are very interested in recruiting well-trained Chinese staff. Therefore, completely on their own initiative, they often invest in job-related training at their respective production sites.

Table 6.17

Actors and interests involved in education policy

Actors	Tasks and interests
State Council LSG for Science, Technology, and Education	Formulation/coordination of national strategies and programs
MOE	General responsibility for the institutional framework and for the subject matter taught in the school system
MOHRSS	Labor-market policies; standards for vocational education
MOST	Support for technology and innovation programs
MOF	Assignment of funding for national education programs
China Institute for Vocational and Technical Education (CIVTE)	Research institute affiliated with the MOE; provides expertise to the MOE and to educational establishments
China Society of Vocational Education and Training (CVET)	Forum for exchanging information on international cooperation between Chinese and foreign vocational training institutions
Subnational governments	Institutional funding for educational establishments; distribution of resources from national programs
NGOs; foundations	Promotion of educational projects and educational equity
International organizations	Bilateral educational cooperation; internationalization
Companies	Cooperation with vocational colleges and universities
Citizens	Demand for and funding of educational courses

© MERICS

Decision-making and conflicts

Initiatives for Chinese vocational education come from academic and professional elites rather than from industrial federations, chambers of commerce, or specific trades (Schucher 2012). This explains the various structural problems that China faces with respect to implementation of job-related education policies. After introduction of the government's policy of reform and opening in 1978–79, there was a high demand for workers with technical qualifications, making vocational training an increasingly important component of education policy. Initially, the government primarily focused on expanding and internationalizing the existing system of tertiary education. The Vocational Training Act that is in place today was passed in 1996, and since then the number of vocational colleges has boomed (Yang Po 2014). The Hu–Wen administration (2002–12) promoted an expansion of vocational training at the same time that it enhanced the country's system of general education. However, funding and restructuring measures have lagged well behind what has actually been promised.

The reason for the policy-implementation problems is a lack of coordination among the wide range of responsibilities that rest with different authorities and administrative departments. This has resulted in a patchwork system consisting of various kinds of schools, colleges, and certification bodies, thus rendering the vocational education system rather ineffective due to the lack of binding and uniform quality standards (Hansen/Woronov 2013).

Additionally, the position of vocational training in society is undermined by the fact that (due to the *hukou* registration system) the students' educational achievements are directly linked to where they are registered as residents. For example, until 2013 schoolchildren were required to take the general secondary-school entrance examination (中考) in the location where they were registered residents. This meant that many examinees from rural areas were prevented from attending better schools in the urban areas. This problem crops up again when taking the university entrance exams (高考). A reform of these restrictive rules was introduced in 2013, but it has not been implemented single-mindedly and so far it has failed to change the nationwide situation (Schulte 2014). If students are unsuccessful in the general education system, they often have no choice but to attend a vocational training institute. Consequently, such educational establishments have gained a reputation for being a "catch-all" for weak students who have performed poorly on examinations that would have qualified them for a university education.

Implementation

Strengthening vocational education in China is not only constrained by a lack of funding but also by weaknesses in terms of implementation coupled with a lack of social acceptance. Chinese businesses show little interest in supporting student training at vocational schools; trainees at firms are primarily regarded as financial burdens whose loyalty to the company is constantly in doubt because of the high staff turnover. This is why firms instead tend to invest in the continuing professional development of their own employees (Schulte 2014). The amount of work experience included in vocational training courses is generally limited to classroom simulations and internships that last only several weeks.

In many cases, the subject matter covered in vocational secondary schools is simply a smaller amount of what is taught at the general secondary schools. But the absence of binding quality standards and comparable training programs is a major problem. Additionally, qualified teachers who also have practical experience in their subjects are often lacking, schools and colleges do not have appropriate or sufficient equipment for teaching purposes, and links between vocational colleges and the manufacturing industries are few and far between. Obviously, only a small number of practical qualifications that meet the needs of the job market can be acquired in this way. The fact that vocational colleges focus on full-time students is also problematic; other potential target groups, such as part-time workers, migrant workers, and the unemployed, are unable to take advantage of such programs (Shi Weiping 2013).

Policy outcomes and policy adjustments

As an industrial society in the twenty-first century, China requires a large number of highly qualified specialists, including technicians and engineers, if it is to avoid the "middle-income trap," that is, the productivity and innovation trap into which emerging economies, such as Brazil and Thailand, have already fallen. However, thus far China has not managed to achieve its true potential in terms of vocational training (Stewart 2015). Admittedly, the number of students enrolled in vocational courses has been growing steadily, but vocational colleges still suffer from the stigma of being catch-all institutions for poor achievers. To make matters worse, it is practically impossible for students from vocational colleges to find their way back into the general education system.

The Chinese government has introduced a series of measures to improve the vocational training sector. The National Plan for Medium- and Long-term Education Reform and Development (教育改革和发展规划), introduced for the period from 2010 to 2020, explicitly addresses weaknesses in the country's vocational training system. Since 2011, pilot projects have been conducted in fifty-six cities in order to strengthen the links between businesses and vocational colleges (Hao Yan 2012).

A plan to modernize vocational education during the period from 2014 to 2020 (Plan to Construct a Modern Vocational Educational System, 现代职业教育体系建

设规划) and the introduction of a new law on vocational training are intended to help overcome structural problems. One of the main goals is to remove the artificial barriers that have been erected between general education and vocational education. Local universities are expected to gain a boost in prestige by becoming "universities of applied sciences" and by working more extensively with local businesses, thereby enabling local industries to meet their demands for manpower. A university entrance exam with more emphasis on specialist, practical, and occupational knowledge is expected to provide an alternative to the general university entrance exam. Financing of the vocational training system will be boosted by new funding models and greater involvement by companies. In fact, businesses in the future will be expected to work with the vocational colleges to shape the subject matter covered in courses and the ways in which such programs are organized. Considerable doubts exist among Chinese educational researchers as to the degree to which these goals can be achieved in practice in view of the scant acceptance of vocational education in society and in the business world.

6.18 Mega-projects: China's South-to-North Water Transfer Project

Björn Conrad

China has carried out a considerable number of mega projects during the previous two decades. Rivers have been dammed and diverted, mountains have been moved or tunnels have been built through them, bridges have been constructed across entire mountain ranges and gorges, urban conurbations have been extended and redesigned, and regions that were previously inaccessible have been linked to national logistics networks and markets. The most ambitious of these huge ventures is known as the South-to-North Water Transfer Project (SNWTP), one of the biggest and most technically complex infrastructure projects ever undertaken. Once it is completed, this project will enable 45 billion cubic meters of water per year to be transported from the wet south to the dry plains of the north via three canals spanning a total length of 1,553 miles (almost 2,500 km). The amount of water to be transported is roughly equivalent to one-half the volume of water flowing down the Nile River each year. The Chinese government estimates that the cost of the total project will be more than USD 60 billion, or more than twice that required for the Three Gorges Dam. The SNWTP is a particularly striking example of how the Chinese administration is able to implement mega construction projects despite strong technological, ecological, social, or political reservations (see Figure 6.18).

Key actors and interests

Infrastructure projects on the scale of the SNWTP are subject to control by the highest levels of the government. The Politburo Standing Committee and the inner cabinet of the State Council formulated the central directives for this project. In addition, all related important decisions must be approved by the NDRC, the national planning authority. The Ministry of Water Resources (MWR) (水利部) has the most influence in terms of technical management of the planning and implementation

Figure 6.18

A huge undertaking: China's South-to-North Water Transfer Project

1 The eastern canal (operating in test mode since 2013)

2 The central canal (operating in test mode since 2014)

3 The western canal (currently being planned)

Based on Moore 2013.

© MERICS

of large water infrastructure projects, such as constructing irrigation systems, diverting rivers, and dam-building. The MWR bases its work on seven regional water authorities, each of which reports directly to the ministry and is responsible for one of the large rivers. The MWR coordinates the line ministries involved in water infrastructure, which include the MEP (water quality), the MOFCOM (shipping), and the MOA (irrigation infrastructure).

As the key Chinese legislative body, the NPC generally only serves to grant formal approval; it does not have any influence regarding which water infrastructure projects are carried out or their scope. However, the Three Gorges Dam was an exception; it was approved only after controversial debates, some taking place within the NPC. When a ballot was held on the issue in 1992, almost one-third of the NPC delegates voted against the State Council's proposal. In contrast, the NPC has not played any major role in the SNWTP.

The range of bodies and organizations involved in initiating, planning, and implementing water infrastructure projects has grown over the years. Civil society organizations and the mass media (both traditional and digital) have been playing an increasingly important role in the controversies over such large-scale projects. However, the SNWTP is a special case in this respect: there has been very little civil resistance (see below, *Decision-making and conflicts*).

The effects of large-scale water infrastructure projects can be felt well beyond provincial boundaries. The involved provincial and local governments often have widely differing, or even conflicting, interests, which they attempt to promote during the course of the planning and construction work. In the case of the SNWTP, for example, there has been a fundamental clash of interests between the northern provinces on the one hand, which will benefit from the project, and the southern provinces on the other hand, which will suffer from having less water at their disposal (see Table 6.18).

Decision-making and conflicts

Ultimately, the idea behind the water transportation project can be attributed to Mao Zedong, who made a suggestion in 1952 that seemed particularly bold at the time: the government would simply "borrow" water from the wet south and use it to irrigate the fields in the dry north. In its initial form, the SNWTP was approved by party leaders as early as 1958, but it was not implemented until several decades later. China's planning bureaucracies proposed a new initiative to develop more viable plans when financial and technical possibilities became more realistic in the 1990s. The planning process, characterized by centralized decision-making at the highest governmental levels, was driven by a technocratic, authoritarian approach to problem-solving. Among Chinese leaders at this time, there was a great amount of trust

Table 6.18

Actors and interests involved in mega projects concerning water infrastructure

Actors	Tasks and interests
Politburo Standing Committee	Directives and decisions on mega projects at the highest levels
Inner cabinet of the State Council	Decision-making/supervision regarding implementation of mega projects
NDRC	Planning supervision; approval of individual decisions
MWR	Leadership of and responsibility for project implementation
Regional water authorities	Units that report directly to the MWR; checking on implementation; coordinating among administrative units
SNWTP Company	State-owned company established explicitly to serve as the "command center" for mega projects; control over water-utilization rights
Line ministries	Consultations: Ministry of Environmental Protection (MEP) on water quality, Ministry of Commerce (MOFCOM) on shipping, and Ministry of Agriculture (MOA) on irrigation infrastructure
NPC	Under normal circumstance: approval, but without being able to exert any influence
Subnational governments	Position depends on the pros and cons of the project; interest in compensation for damages from the central government
Civil society organizations; the media	Public debates, criticism, monitoring; level of activity depends on whether or not consensus can be reached

© MERICS

in the possibilities of modern hydro-engineering and this was reflected in the decision-making process. Construction of the canals actually began in 2002. Two of the three canals—the eastern canal and the central canal—have been pilot-tested since 2013 and 2014 respectively.

Conflicts of interest among the provinces that will be affected by the mega project in different ways became clearly apparent during the initial decision-making process. Provinces such as Sichuan, which was not only concerned about the water withdrawal but also feared an increased risk of earthquakes due to the construction work, openly opposed the SNWTP. In the course of the decision-making process, however, the central government managed to put a damper on resistance at the provincial and local levels. It achieved this with the aid of decrees, police operations, and units of construction workers who suddenly appeared on the scene. Local resistance along the route of the SNWTP was broken up by a combination of methods, which went far beyond merely applying pressure. A huge media campaign promoted the mega project as a challenge to the entire nation, which admittedly entailed making sacrifices but could be overcome if the population showed sufficient patriotism. At the same time, the central government paid a considerable amount in compensation to those localities and individuals who were negatively affected by the construction work. In fact, the state created opportunities to allow citizens to lodge complaints or to make demands in a carefully controlled manner by way of official "consultation procedures." Ultimately, however, those people affected by the project had no choice but to accept the national plans and to attempt to receive as much as possible in the way of financial compensation (Moore 2014). In return, the local governments generally ended their resistance. In addition, civil society generated surprisingly little resistance to the huge water-diversion project during the decision-making process and the implementation stage. This was despite the fact that there were actually numerous reasons to oppose the government's monumental scheme: wide-scale forced resettlement in the affected regions, destruction of religious buildings on the Qinghai–Tibetan plateau, and enormous environmental damage caused by the construction work and the diversion of water to other areas.

Implementation

A state-owned company was set up specifically to carry out the SNWTP. In this way, the government was following its former organizational model from the era of state planning: ever since the 1950s "command centers" (司令部), with extensive decision-making powers, financial means, and rights to utilize land and water, had been established to facilitate major projects that were planned by the Chinese state. The government generally ruled out any funding or implementation involvement by private companies due to the strategic importance of the project.

Construction work initially focused on the eastern and central canals. The former uses the existing facilities along the historic Grand Canal, for which construction began in the sixth century. As a result, construction work along this route was less extensive. The entire eastern canal was filled with water by the end of 2013. In December 2014, the central canal was opened for testing along a stretch from Hubei province to Beijing. This meant that progress on the construction project was not far behind the original schedule.

The biggest problems in the course of implementation occurred along the eastern route. This canal passes through densely populated areas and plots of land that have been developed for industrial use. The upshot is that water flowing through the canal on its way north became much more polluted than originally anticipated by the planners. Initially, water that was ultimately intended for use in northern Jiangsu and Shandong provinces became useless as it was transferred to its final destination. The government reacted by installing a water treatment system on a scale well beyond what had originally been planned—a total of 426 treatment plants were eventually built along that section of the route to ensure that water quality would be maintained when it reached its final destination.

Policy outcomes and policy adjustments

Mega projects are used by the Chinese central government to demonstrate its political, financial, and technological competence as well as its ability to assert its authority. According to the central government, the SNWTP has been a success: resistance and conflicts of interest were eliminated at an early stage, construction work has made rapid progress, and technical problems have quickly been solved.

However, experts in the field of water engineering have their doubts about whether the SNWTP will really be able to solve China's main water problem—the fact that resources are not evenly distributed across the country. Considerable skepticism exists among both international and Chinese scientists. The various arguments against the SNWTP include the following: much water will be wasted as a result of evaporation; environmental damage along the central canal will incur very high costs; and the cost–benefit ratio will be lower than that for less expensive alternatives (more economical and more efficient use of water; higher costs for water consumption; a greater capacity for treating water). The real contribution that the SNWTP will make to alleviate the shortage of water in northern China will only be ascertained with certainty after many years. Until then, the venture will continue to serve its purpose as a political showcase for the central government.

6.19 Strengths, weaknesses, and special characteristics of Chinese policy making

Sebastian Heilmann

Central mechanisms in political communications (propaganda), the setting and adjusting of political priorities (development planning; targets set in the cadre system), policy innovation and policy evaluation (experimental state activity), and implementation (crisis modes; campaigns) are all based on the CCP's special organizational and mobilization experiences. From a comparative international perspective, this has resulted in a host of unconventional forms of state activity, some of which have led to unexpected outcomes.

The "rhythm" of Chinese politics is completely different from that of most other political systems. It is not characterized by election cycles or sudden changes in government—its government remains in power for long periods and its programs span long terms (such as the five-year plans). Its patterns of behavior in terms of crisis management (centralization; campaigns) also tend to differ widely in comparison with crisis programs in other countries, even though it has experienced comparable shocks and events, such as those related to the 2007–9 global financial crisis.

In brief, the Chinese political system works according to processes that differ significantly from the government systems in Europe or the United States. The Chinese approach to policy making is rather unorthodox: action programs are frequently initiated as experiments—without appropriate legislation and regulation in place beforehand—and only subsequently with the passage of time are they developed further (during the implementation, adaptation, and re-implementation phases). Approved multi-year plans are subject to ongoing adjustments and policies are repeatedly revised in terms of administrative practices. As a result, the processes and the results of policy making are less predictable and they are characterized by many more legal uncertainties than those in constitutional democracies.

There is one main characteristic of the Chinese reform policy-making process: key political goals are centrally defined; the policy instruments, however, are regularly developed and tested locally and are only applied later on a national scale. A policy-making process driven by constant experiments and feedback in a country as heterogeneous as China gives rise to a broad range of policy instruments and organizational patterns. Such a process has allowed the government to resort to a host of alternative policy options in order to respond to changing conditions and needs for action. The interplay between centralized power and the political hierarchy on the one hand and local initiatives, experiments, and deviations from the norm on the other (even going so far as organized corruption) is part and parcel of the Chinese political system. Such central-local interactions are neither rigid nor ossified—in fact, they are flexible and fragile at the same time.

In sum, political decisions and policy programs in China cannot be regarded as clearly demarcated events or actions. Rather, they are part of a chain of official statements, documents, implementation experiments, feedback loops, and ongoing modifications. Such policy making is driven by interactions and feedback in practice rather than by legal rules or standards of accountability. This can lead to an authoritarian type of flexibility, adaptability, and assertiveness. At the same time, however, it is also the basis for discretionary government actions, a lack of political accountability, and inadequate checks on power.

Seen from a historical perspective, China's policy-making process, which promotes the learning of lessons, is unusual for a one-party regime. The learning process takes place within narrow constraints, however, remaining strictly instrumental, problem-related, reversible, and under tight control. It is by no means a capacity for learning that might lead to changes in the system of party leadership, or even to a new constitution in the sense of constitutional learning. The major defects in the Chinese system of government—a lack of control over power and a lack of legal security—can only be compensated for in part and cannot be alleviated by an unexpectedly productive policy-making process.

7 Perspectives on China's political development

Sebastian Heilmann

The final section of this book returns to some of the basic trends in China's development and key observations referred to in the previous chapters. It begins by looking at China's path toward transformation and the idiosyncrasies of change in China as well as the power bases and underlying fragilities in the current political system. Based on this assessment, a series of medium-term scenarios is presented with respect to how the political scene in China might develop and the chances of democratic evolution. To conclude, the focus turns to the consequences of these factors for international cooperation. Future interactions with China will likely be characterized by intensified systemic competition, recurring tensions and even open conflicts while opportunities for constructive collaboration will have to be constantly sought and reshaped.

7.1 Erosion of the party-state and restorative efforts

China's transformation since the historic swing to a "socialist market economy" in 1992–93 is deliberately referred to here in terms of an intertwined system of political and economic coordination (political economy) and it is presented according to the self-perception of the party leadership (see Figure 7.1). Western assessments of China's political development tend to focus on a progressive transition to a more liberal political order and the conflicts that arise between state authority and an emerging civil society in this process. From the perspective of the Chinese party-state, however, it is the progressive deterioration of the organizational hold and internal discipline of the Chinese Communist Party since the 1980s that must be seen as the decisive change and catalyst for transformation of the political system in the PRC. Economic transformation followed a hesitant, selective, and restricted process of opening, deregulation, and liberalization that continued despite recurring, yet mostly short-lived, efforts by the central party leadership to enforce organizational discipline.

Although official political institutions have appeared sclerotic, since the 1980s decision-making powers in many economic and administrative fields have been delegated to lower levels of government. In addition, informal modes of exchange between political and economic players have undermined the formal CCP command structure, resulting in the emergence of a shadow system of endemic corruption that has eluded control by party headquarters. China's political order has changed considerably from the totalitarianism of the Mao era (when CCP functionaries and party organs enjoyed practically limitless control over economic and social life) to a "fragmented authoritarianism" in which centralized intervention by the party only takes place during exceptional periods of "crisis mode" governance (see Chapter 3). Toward the end of the Hu–Wen administration (2002–12), China appeared to be entering a "post-socialist" political system—one in which changes in the official political institutions lagged far behind the rapid developments in the economy, society, technology, and, indeed, the global environment.

The Xi–Li administration (since 2012-13) initiated a pronounced change of direction in terms of China's political development: the party leadership revealed an extraordinary determination to combat the previously unstoppable erosion of the party's internal organization by launching an extensive anti-corruption and discipline campaign and it began to reinforce the party-state hierarchy by concentrating decision-powers at party headquarters, even in those policy areas that previously had been delegated to government organs or subnational authorities. General Secretary Xi Jinping made it clear that only the CCP was capable of steering the country through the twenty-first century and that the party would fight vehemently against any attempts to undermine its leadership or to drive the country in the direction of a Western-style democratic system. For the new party leadership, this was a case of reconfiguring the entire party-state in order to achieve a national "China Dream." In order to rapidly increase "comprehensive national strength," there was a need to create the right political and economic conditions. Hence, in 2013 the party leadership launched a structural-reform program that was designed to avoid the much-feared "middle-income trap" and to transform China into one of the world's most advanced and innovative economic and technological powers. The program promised to allow market forces to play a "decisive role" in the future development of the economy, meaning liberalization of the private sector and the financial system, legal security and equal treatment for all types of businesses, reorganization and partial privatization of state-owned enterprises, and a drastic reduction in state interference in the economy as a whole.

Rigorous application of this reform agenda would indeed have drastic political consequences for China's developmental state. A comprehensive program of economic liberalization would greatly curtail the party-state's capacity to intervene and would come into direct conflict with the interests of the established party- and

Figure 7.1

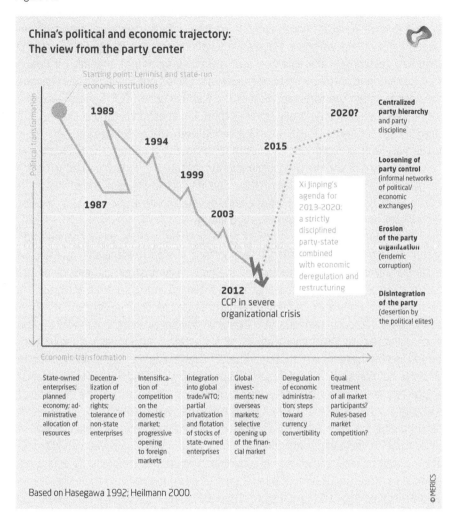

China's political and economic trajectory:
The view from the party center

Based on Hasegawa 1992; Heilmann 2000.

© MERICS

government-backed economic elite. As it turned out, however, by 2016 the 2013 economic liberalization measures were being implemented inconsistently and selectively. Only piecemeal or marginal restructuring was undertaken in crucial yet politically sensitive areas, such as deregulation of state-sector oligopolies, more transparency in debt management of the fiscal and banking systems, establishment of a level playing field for nonstate market participants, and improved market access for foreign investors.

The strengthening of centralized party control over the political and economic system clearly was the prerogative of Xi Jinping who was situated at the helm of power. There was a chance for a boost in economic liberalization only if the party leadership felt it was politically safe to loosen controls or if a decline in economic growth posed an immediate threat to CCP rule. During the first several years of Xi Jinping's tenure, political objectives, such as enforcing domestic discipline and pursuing "great power" diplomacy in combination with military modernization, took precedence over economic restructuring.

7.2 Foundations of Communist Party rule

The fact that the Chinese government appears to be more stable and to enjoy greater authority than governments in most developing nations and emerging markets tends to attract many foreign investors. First and foremost, foreign investors appreciate the country's predictable political environment and their only interest is how the government formulates policies and if its policies will have a detrimental effect on economic regulation and business operations. But how robust and resilient is the political-power foundation upon which the CCP leadership relies?

The most important factors supporting the CCP leadership are the following:

- the considerable improvement in material living standards for large sections of the overall population and for the political elite (CCP leading cadres and their family and patronage networks) since 1979;
- the loyalty to the current regime by a large part of the new economic elite and the new upper and middle classes;
- the outward appearance of unity among the party's top leadership: in previous decades (up until 1989), open divisions and organizational collapse at the center of decision-making repeatedly destabilized the political system; such incidents of an open breakdown among the leaders have been avoided since 1989, even though intra-elite conflict has not disappeared;
- the maintenance of civilian control over the military by the party leadership;
- the uncompromising defense of the party's monopoly on power through an extensive and proliferating surveillance and police system;
- the widely shared patriotic or nationalistic sentiments among both officials and the general public, allowing the party to portray itself as the guardian of China's national dignity in the face of external challenges or diplomatic conflicts.

From a more fundamental perspective, political power can be dissected into several central components that shed light on whether power can be exercised effectively (based on Mann [1984] and Göbel [2013]). In China's case, the symbolic, despotic, infrastructural, and communicative-discursive components of power are particularly important.

The symbolic component of power is epitomized by the Chinese leadership behind the walls of Zhongnanhai (the party's central headquarters and the government offices located to the west of the Forbidden City), with its impenetrable, mystical aura of a detached and inaccessible command center. In many Western systems, the government's focus on the media and the inclusion of politics in general media entertainment have led to a trivialization of the political processes and functions, whereas the sense of mystery surrounding the center of political power in China remains largely intact. This is demonstrated by the tens of thousands of Chinese citizens who regularly make their way to Beijing to petition party headquarters (the general secretary, the premier, the Politburo, etc.), as they believe that the leadership will offer them help if it realizes the extent of the abuses and scandals taking place in the provinces. This semblance of power is used by the Chinese party and government as a symbolic source of its own authority, giving it the right to demand respect and allegiance from the population at large. In addition, Xi Jinping has introduced an unprecedented style of media-savvy "presidential behavior," making public broadcasts from his office, using livelier public language, and involving his popular cosmopolitan wife, particularly on the diplomatic stage. With this new style of political representation, Xi is attempting to solicit emotional support from the general population.

China's state institutions still have a veritable arsenal of despotic components of power at their disposal, which are only partially limited and still are insufficiently monitored: an entire array of dictatorial tools, ranging from a comprehensive network of informants and various forms of informal detention to arbitrary use of violence and highly sophisticated electronic surveillance systems to monitor people's activities. The campaign terror that seemed to come out of nowhere during the Mao era is nothing but a distant memory for most Chinese (with the notable exception among the ethnic and religious minority groups). China's rulers today carefully use dictatorial means of repression to target specific groups or individuals rather than large segments or entire classes of the population as they did in the past. Western discussions of Chinese politics often revert to familiar narratives, such as "the oppressors versus the oppressed" or "the party-state versus civil society." These narratives, however, explain only a small part of Chinese political dynamics today.

What is much more important for the day-to-day running of the country and its social life is the infrastructural component of power. This refers to state functions and services that are implanted in society and accepted by most citizens as essential benefits, including particularly the state's provision of material and non-material goods: from healthcare to security and national pride and to careers in the civil service or employment in state-owned enterprises. Chinese society is receptive to state influence and government goals due to spending programs that combine associated benefits with rules of expected behavior. This results in patterns of co-operation, or a kind of symbiosis between state and society that is achieved through public benefits rather than through coercive despotic measures.

Perhaps the greatest challenge to the Chinese party-state is the communicative-discursive component of power in today's digital society. Despite the country's tight rein on what citizens can access on the Web, interactive digital media are a potentially disruptive libertarian force that can challenge state institutions and influence public opinion. The "demystification" of politics by revealing the ordinariness or corruption among those in power, particularly at the lower levels of government, is something that has been revealed by social media in China. Interactive digital media thus represent a fundamental challenge to Communist rule in China, and the government has taken active steps to control the modern media and to exploit the Internet to present its own agenda. Actually, this policy approach is no different from traditional CCP approaches that are geared to "create a favorable public opinion" regarding the goals and actions of the party (see Chapter 5)—only this time with the help of digital media.

In summarizing the various components of power in China, it can be said that the traditional, symbolic, despotic, and, first and foremost, infrastructural levers of power employed by the Chinese government are still much more effective than those in most other countries. However, the communicative-discursive power of the CCP is now being challenged to a greater extent than before as a result of the IT revolution.

7.3 The underlying fragility of the Chinese political order

The foundations upon which the CCP leadership is built are facing daunting tasks, entailing huge risks that will test the party's political leadership in the near future (see Table 7.3.A).

One analytical model derived from the specific crises that took place at the beginning of the twenty-first century focuses on the conditions required for the robustness and resilience (i.e., "anti-fragility") of a political system when faced with unexpected internal or external shocks. According to this model, the resilience of a political system is not determined by outwardly stable and powerful institutions; rather, it is derived from its capability to absorb shocks and to avoid functional collapse in the event of an acute crisis and to actually reorganize and strengthen per-

Table 7.3.A

Prerequisites for China's future political development

Strengths and capabilities	Weaknesses and risks
Comparatively strong administrative capacity to implement political measures	Weakening of this capacity due to corruption and local private interests
Among political and economic leaders, a remarkable willingness to learn	Rigid Leninist official institutions in the political system
Permanent institutional adjustments and corrections (administration, legislation, etc.)	Political legitimacy of the CCP dependent on economic successes
Highly dynamic private entrepreneurship; growing capacity for innovation	Loss-making, partially reformed state sector; state interventions in economic affairs
High domestic savings rate; high levels of investments in infrastructure and education	Unstable financial system; high levels of debt in companies and local governments
Indispensability as an international market	High potential for conflict in foreign policy and trade
First-rate infrastructure	Disparities in regional development; serious environmental issues
Growing middle classes; ambitious and energetic population that is willing to learn	Social inequalities and tensions; rapid demographic changes
Wide range of instruments for steering and controlling public opinion	Unofficial information and rumors via social media; mistrust of government communications during periods of crisis

Based on Heilmann 2002.

© MERICS

formance during periods when recovering from crises (Taleb/Treverton 2015). Based on the criteria of this model, China's political system scores higher under previous administrations than it does under Xi Jinping's more centralized, personalized, and rigid decision-making system (see Table 7.3.B).

One of China's greatest sources of resilience is its diversified economic structure, especially in comparison to other historically authoritarian states (particularly the Communist party-states). China is not dependent solely on specialized indus-

Table 7.3.B

A stable exterior with underlying fragilities:
How resilient is China's political order to unexpected shocks?

	Prerequisites for a resilient political system	Jiang-Zhu administration (1998-2002)	Hu-Wen administration (2002–12)	Xi-Li administration (2012–present)
1	Diversified economic structure	+	+	+
2	Decentralized policy initiatives	+	~	–
3	Moderate levels of state debt	+	–	–
4	Political variability and diversity	–	–	–
5	Experience in dealing with systemic crises	+	+	~

+ resilient   ~ not very resilient   – fragile

Modifi ed and applied to the China case based on the general model of Taleb/Treverton (2015).

© MERICS

tries or on the export of raw materials—its economy has exhibited a limited, yet arguably growing innovative capacity and it is able to fall back on a huge domestic market that will allow it to expand further in the future, even if export markets shrink. This economic diversification is a huge advantage in terms of the resilience of the political system: if drastic contractions occur in some parts of the economy, national social and political stability will not necessarily be disrupted because other parts of the economy that remain dynamic will serve to buffer the shocks and will provide resources to compensate for those individual sectors or regions that have been affected by crises.

In other areas, however, in comparison to previous decades, the resilience of China's political economy is now in danger of weakening as a result of both economic-structural changes and heavy-handed political interventions. This applies in particular to the level of state and corporate debt in relation to GDP and GDP growth and the resultant negative effects on the fiscal and financial systems. The extremely rapid increase in national debt since the massive post-2007 stimulus package will seriously limit the government's ability to act in the event of an acute economic or political crisis. The Xi–Li administration can no longer rely on the rapidly growing and abundant tax revenue that the Chinese government commanded after the turn of the millennium to implement an expansionary fiscal and financial policy over an extended period of time.

The results in other areas that affect resilience are inconclusive, but again the overall trend points toward a weakening. In times of political or economic stress, decentralized policy making by effective local authorities helps to compensate for blockades, political errors, or failed reforms on the part of the central government. Yet Xi Jinping's centralization of policy initiative is weakening this all-important buffer against crises and limiting the Chinese government's adaptive and innovative capacities. In effect, overcentralized decision-making abolishes the advantages of the system of distributed intelligence and local initiative that Deng Xiaoping had purposively crafted in the 1980s and 1990s.

It remains unclear whether China's historical experiences in dealing with earlier systemic crises are still present in the minds of the Xi–Li administration (particularly the 1989 crisis). All of the current members of the Chinese leadership do have experience as political decision-makers in the wake of the 2007–9 global financial and economic crisis. However, they do not have any experience in making decisions during large-scale political crises. Judged by the wording of public speeches and internal communiqués, Xi Jinping and party headquarters are fixated on the "lessons" learned from the downfall of the former Soviet Union and the "failure" of the political regime under Gorbachev. But external analyses cannot determine the extent to which such lessons have resulted in a more repressive political program rather than any sort of willingness on the part of the Chinese leadership to respond flexibly and creatively when confronted with political destabilization.

The greatest systemic weakness in terms of the resilience of China's government system is its lack of political variability and diversity. Political competition and peaceful change in the ruling party are not possible in the Chinese political system. Open debates on the underlying shortcomings of the political system are rare and are only allowed within strict confines. Critical political views, and those who spell them out, are much less likely to be tolerated today in the inner policy-making circle of the Xi–Li administration than they were during previous governments. These restrictions make it more difficult to notice any early signs of impending crises that might threaten the system and to be able to respond to them in a timely manner with measures to reinforce stability.

The political "top-level design" introduced with great fanfare under Xi Jinping contains systemic risks that cannot even be discussed in domestic policy circles. The new system involves a substantial hardening and narrowing of previously much more flexible and exploratory policy processes, as described in many of the cases examined in Chapter 6. In effect, decision-making powers with respect to the institutional restructuring of the state and the economy have been concentrated in Central Leading Small Groups located in party headquarters. Xi Jinping has acquired a considerable amount of personal power within a short period of time. Around him a personality cult has been created by the media such that no other party leader enjoyed since the Mao era (see Chapter 3).

As a result, political decision-making under Xi Jinping is much more "top-down." Experiences and initiatives put forward by various regions tend to be ignored by the centralized, personality-based decision-making system. This leads to typical policy failures. In the 2014-16 period, centrally imposed policies on fiscal reform, stock market regulation, and IT security faced immediate and heavy criticism by regional governments and market participants respectively, resulting in their eventually being withdrawn and revised. The decision-makers and their advisers at party and government headquarters apparently had been unable to realistically assess and anticipate the consequences of the new regulations.

Xi Jinping prefers centralized decision-making by a small circle of top leaders and trusted advisory staff. Such decision-making (top-down "decisionism") contrasts markedly with the type of policy making (bottom-up "implementationism") promoted by Deng Xiaoping and later continued by Jiang Zemin. For decades, China's reform policy had been the result of exploratory leadership based on decentralized reform experiments and the specific lessons learned from implementation of such experimentation.

The CCP leadership styles shaped by Deng Xiaoping and Jiang Zemin, which explicitly included initiatives and innovations by local authorities on how best to implement policies, were very different from the "top-level design" preferred by Xi Jinping. As a self-assured political leader with the mission to achieve a national "China Dream," Xi relies much less than his predecessors on consultation, exploration, and reflection in making decisions. This more impulsive or even aggressive style of decision-making has become apparent in China's foreign and security policies, for example, with respect to the territorial disputes in the South China Sea.

It is an open question whether the changes to the decision-making system under Xi Jinping will endure. In cases of serial policy failures and deepening economic problems, it may well turn out to be only a temporary centralization and rigidity. A return to a more exploratory leadership may take on an urgency should implementation of the 2013–2020 structural-reform program reach a deadlock.

However, if China moves further in the direction of top-down policy making, the fragility of the political system will increase and the ability to learn from and to correct policy mistakes will decrease, rendering the system both rigid and inflexible. Should there be irrefutable failures of central policy or should Xi Jinping for some reason become incapacitated, there will be no reserve central-government legitimacy in the provinces if the regional authorities are not allowed to take legitimate independent actions to compensate for those of the central government.

7.4 Scenarios for political development

So what does the future hold for the CCP and the political system it so dominates given the assortment of both favorable and unfavorable conditions outlined above? The following scenarios are to be understood as heuristic instruments and analytical constructs; they are designed to look at the scope of alternative development options by deliberately exaggerating current trends and projecting them into the future. The scenarios only apply to the medium term, that is, the next three to ten years.

This period is set to witness a number of significant milestones:

- 2017 will see the endorsement of the incumbent general secretary for another five years and the integration of the next generation of leaders into the highest echelons of the party and government.
- 2020 is when the economic-structural reforms presented in 2013 are set to be implemented in order to achieve the "moderately prosperous society" that is part of the 13th Five-Year Plan (2016–20).
- 2022 will see the installment of a new party leadership and a new CCP general secretary according to current organizational rules.

Figure 7.4 illustrates the various scenarios, with the vertical axis showing the degree of decentralization and the flexibility of policy making in three broad steps: from the return to strictly centralized policy initiative under Xi Jinping's "top-level design" (顶层设计) to central–local interactions that were typical of Deng Xiaoping and Jiang Zemin's reform methods ("experimentation in the shadow of the party hierarchy"), all the way down to centrifugal independence—"the mountains are high and the Emperor is far away" (山高皇帝远) and "the higher authorities have policies, the localities have countermeasures" (上有政策，下有对策).

The horizontal axis shows the changing economic conditions for the political leadership over time, grouped in three phases: the very favorable political conditions from 1992 to 2007 when economic growth was rapid and there was greater room to maneuver in fiscal terms; the government-driven fiscal stimulus and industrial program between 2008 and 2012 that created huge levels of debt; and the considerably more difficult conditions faced by the Xi–Li administration today. This government is faced with a slowdown in economic growth and a rise in state and corporate debt, coupled with increased spending on foreign, domestic, and social security. Four potential scenarios are outlined, covering the full range of possibilities from centripetal to centrifugal political development.

Figure 7.4

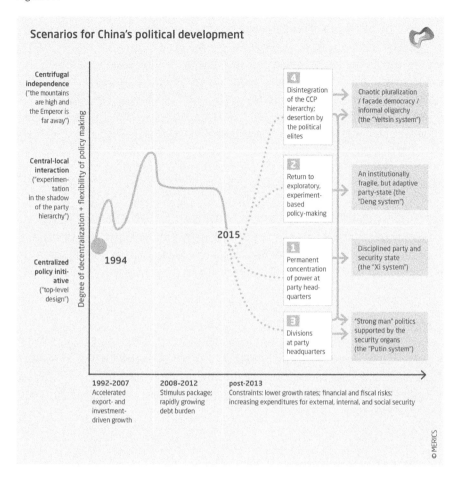

Scenarios for China's political development

Scenario 1 – Permanent concentration of power at party headquarters → Disciplined party and security state (the "Xi system")

Scenario 2 – Return to exploratory, experiment-based policy-making → An institutionally fragile, but adaptive party-state (the "Deng system")

Scenario 3 – Divisions at party headquarters → "Strong man" politics supported by the security organs (the "Putin system")

Scenario 4 – Disintegration of the CCP hierarchy; desertion by the political elites → Chaotic pluralization / façade democracy / informal oligarchy (the "Yeltsin system")

© MERICS

Scenario 1: A centralized and disciplined party and security state (the "Xi Jinping system")

Domestic politics:

- Permanent concentration of power at party headquarters
- Effective crackdown on corruption and abuses of power
- Increased efficiency of state administration; expansion of e-government at all levels
- Repression of ethnic and religious minorities in Xinjiang and Tibet

Society:

- Expansion of a state-controlled corporatist system of interest mediation involving cooperation among social and economic groups
- Strict ban on the further development of independent NGOs and civil society
- A more equitable society based on effective redistributive policies in line with the vision of a "moderately prosperous society for all" (小康社会，共同富裕)
- Re-ideologization in the media and the education system: amalgam of nationalism, selected traditions, and "socialism with Chinese characteristics"

Cyberspace:

- Comprehensive IT-based surveillance of digital media and urban public space
- Evaluation of the "social credibility" (社会信用) of producers, consumers, and citizens based on transactional, behavioral, communication, and mobility data
- Formation of an ICT-based party dictatorship with the potential for totalitarian rule

Economy:

- Sustained economic growth; overcoming of the structural defects in the economy; self-supporting market growth within the country
- Aggressive national industrial policy; decreasing foreign investments; recurring trade conflicts

Foreign and security policies:

- Rapid military expansionism; open claim to regional hegemony in the Asia-Pacific area; superpower rivalry with the United States and increasing international tensions; intensified cyber conflicts; risks of military confrontations in the Asia-Pacific region or with the United States
- Global diplomatic activities in conjunction with exports, investments, and financing initiatives; expansion of China-based, multilateral institutions to compete with established U.S.–dominated institutions; increased Chinese influence on multilateral standard-setting
- Expansion of China's global market and regulatory power in cyberspace with the aid of Chinese IT companies and diplomacy; dismantling of U.S. dominance in Web technologies and infrastructure; anchoring the principle of national cyber sovereignty in multilateral rules and regulations

Scenario 2: A decentralized, institutionally fragile, but adaptive and flexible party-state (the "Deng Xiaoping system")

Domestic politics:

- Return to an exploratory, experiment-based governance and reform process
- Unconsolidated government and legal system; powerful and corrupt political, economic, and military networks as a backdrop to the official party organization
- Progressive decentralization of the system of government, with widely differing regional development models
- Willingness to compromise on the issues of Xinjiang, Tibet, and Hong Kong; however, these regions still marked by recurring protests and episodes of unrest

Society:

- Continued development of social self-organization and a pluralistic civil society
- Growing social, regional, and ethnic disparities; ineffective redistribution policy
- Nationalism openly becomes the dominant ideology in the media and the education system

Cyberspace:

- Increasing loss of control over interactive digital media; more open debates about politically sensitive topics; short-lived media and censorship campaigns
- Fragmented electronic surveillance systems

Economy:

- Moderate economic growth, with recurring slumps; state interventions in the economy increasingly ineffective
- Openness to foreign investments; further integration of China into the global economy

Foreign and security policies:

- Fluctuations in international cooperation; overall willingness to cooperate in the Asia-Pacific region and with the United States
- Deceleration of military expansionism due to high costs; loss of civil control over the military; growing risks of accidental military confrontations
- Declining global exports, investments, and financing initiatives from China; no further expansion of China-based, multilateral institutions; integration as a global partner for cooperation, with recurring tensions and setbacks

Scenario 3: "Strong man" politics supported by the security organs and nationalism (the "Putin system")

Domestic politics:

- Divisions at party headquarters; concentration of power in a single leadership figure
- Authority of the leadership figure supported primarily by the security and military apparatuses
- Formal party organization remains in place; however, decisions are negotiated among informal oligarchies and networks; informal strengthening of the regions, and only loose coordination with party headquarters
- No reorganization or modernization of state administration, hence institutional stagnation
- Harsh domestic repression; a high percentage of the government budget is devoted to security

Society:

- Strict ban on the further development of civil society and a political opposition; however, political control over society remains patchy
- Rapid increase in social, regional, and ethnic disparities; increased unemployment; rural exodus; high pressures to emigrate
- Recurring social and ethnic unrest; revival of religious movements
- Weak political and economic order reinforced by nationalism and populism

Cyberspace:

- Intense surveillance of digital media; focused on most politically sensitive issues, yet limited by financial and organizational bottlenecks

Economy:

- Low economic growth; reduction in domestic and international investments
- Flight abroad of capital and entrepreneurship

Foreign and security policies:

- Rivalry with a superior United States and growing international tensions; intensified cyber conflicts; risks of military adventurism to distract from domestic tensions

Scenario 4: Chaotic pluralization, a façade of democratic institutions, and informal oligarchies (the "Yeltsin system")

Domestic politics:

- Divisions and a power vacuum at party headquarters; CCP disintegrates into feuding groups at all organizational levels; ordinary CCP members spontaneously abandon the party; the CCP collapses
- "Centralized" power is only symbolic; strong centrifugal forces
- Regional and national elections held without a run-up period and without democratic rules or competition from other parties; extreme political polarization; acts of political violence and terror
- Rushed constitutional reforms; broad powers granted to the provinces in exchange for their support of party headquarters; concessions to Xinjiang, Tibet, and Hong Kong
- Independence for provincial political and military cliques; no opening up to democracy despite regional elections

- Alliances between the old power elite and the new economic elite that exclude the majority of the population; endemic corruption and organized crime firmly ingrained at all levels of society
- Pattern of development similar to that during the first ten years of post-Communist Russia under Yeltsin

Society:

- Boom in social self-organization; chaotic political pluralization
- Uncontrolled intensification of social, regional, and ethnic disparities; rapid rise in unemployment; rural exodus; emergence of slums in metropolitan areas
- Recurring social and ethnic unrest; revival of religious movements
- Uncontrolled mass emigration and exodus to neighboring countries or elsewhere

Cyberspace:

- Social media provide a crucial arena for political debates; manipulation; conspiracy theories; mud-slinging; polarization

Economy:

- Drastic slump in economic performance; flight abroad of capital and entrepreneurship
- Withdrawal of foreign investors; serious global economic backlash, with extremely negative short- and medium-term consequences for all of China's trade partners

Foreign and security policies:

- Unpredictable foreign and security policies; total loss of government control over the military; military units act on their own; serious risks of nuclear proliferation

The results of an informal survey carried out in 2015 among the associates and fellows at the Mercator Institute for China Studies reveal that a clear majority thought the first of the four scenarios (the "Xi system") was the most plausible for the short term (2015 to 2018). For the medium term (2018 to 2025), just over one-half of those questioned thought that the "Xi system" eventually would have to grant significant economic-policy concessions to subnational governments as a result of a failure to implement the promised economic-structural reforms and/or due to a sustained deceleration in the growth rate.

The "Xi system" is likely to retain its centralized character with respect to political control, public security, technical surveillance systems, and foreign, security, and military policies. Because the lessons from the exploratory and flexible reform methods under the "Deng system" from 1978 to 2008 (at least in the field of economic regulation) reveal that overly centralized control of economic policy results in a decline of regional initiative, these ideas are probably once again gaining traction and may moderate the overly rigid "Xi system." In order to boost the momentum for growth, China's political leaders will have to begin to accommodate the interests of private and foreign investors to a much greater extent than they did during the period from 2013 to 2016.

Only a small minority of those who took part in the survey thought that there was any chance of a clear split occurring within the party leadership or of the CCP disintegrating (Scenarios 3 or 4). As the editor of this book and author of this chapter, I am more skeptical in this respect. The fundamental risk of systemic collapse is higher in China's party-state than it is in systems that are characterized by regularized and democratic government turnover. Authoritarian systems of government (such as that in China) that base their legitimacy primarily on economic success are particularly vulnerable to abrupt political disintegration in the event of a slump: economic crises will quickly reveal the fragile foundations on which political legitimacy is based, the unreliable support for the current regime among the political and economic elite and the general public, and especially the lack of regular mechanisms to appoint a new legitimate government.

The medium-term future of the political system will very much depend on the extent to which the party leadership under Xi Jinping is able to reverse the internal symptoms of decline within the CCP and to consolidate a continuation of the current polity. Attempts to bring about an economic rebalancing must not be allowed to fail if long-term political decay is to be avoided. The Chinese party leadership will need a great deal of skill to implement its economic policy and also a certain amount of luck regarding the international economic environment so that any external shocks that might hit the country will not be too debilitating while it is still in the midst of its restructuring process. If Xi Jinping's agenda to revitalize party rule and to restructure the economy by 2020 should visibly fail and social and political tensions become exacerbated, the risk of a collapse of the entire system will be a definite possibility.

Should the party hierarchy fall apart, the state's ability to continue operating will greatly depend on how long its organizations are able to maintain a self-supporting system based on the constitution and the law rather than on party directives. Past experience suggests that a transformation from a one-party dictatorship to a constitutional state can very rarely be achieved without a temporary collapse of the political and social order. If the CCP collapses, the PRC is thus likely to pass through a deep valley of political destruction and reconstruction. However, as the economic-structural changes are much further advanced in China than they were in the Eastern European states in 1989, economic decline in China is unlikely to be quite so drastic during any such systemic transition. China's energetic and ambitious population is likely to show great entrepreneurial dynamism, even under volatile political conditions.

Whatever scenario ultimately plays out, the Soviet experience of a total collapse of the state is not directly applicable in the Chinese context. Unlike the former Soviet Union that had a large non-Russian ethnic minority population of almost 50 percent, China is rather homogeneous, with a minority population of less than 10 percent. The vision of a unified nation-state is strongly anchored in Chinese society and among the political elite, and the country's unity is supported by an extremely strong nationalistic undercurrent. The situation in areas where ethnic minorities live, such as Tibet and Xinjiang, is very different: a weakening of central-government power in these regions could well give rise to far more widespread separatist movements than we have seen so far. It is, however, very unlikely that secessionist aspirations in those remote regions will spill over into the central Chinese heartland.

7.5 The potential for gradual democratic evolution

Due to its international importance, China's political development is considered by leading political scientists as key for a global democratic breakthrough (Diamond 1999, 2012). However, is the Western model of a democratic constitutional state a realistic possibility in a future China?

Economic development coupled with a better-educated population have resulted in a differentiated society that is now more aware of its rights and has produced diverse forms of social self-organization. As a consequence, some observers even see buds of "creeping democratization" (Pei Minxin 1997) that may eventually take root on the Chinese mainland, just as has already occurred in Taiwan. There are, however, major objections to these optimistic perspectives.

According to comparativist research on the functional requirements for a viable democracy (Schmidt 2000), the PRC meets several promising criteria for democracy: broad ethnic homogeneity (its ethnic minorities are largely concentrated along the western periphery), high economic growth coupled with moderate levels of inflation, hitherto very positive experiences in joining global markets, and growing technological and cultural ties with democratic societies. China's per capita GDP surpassed an average of USD 7,000 in 2014. Historically, such favorable conditions have led to continued social pluralization and political liberalization. China's most developed regions have seen the formation of a middle class (albeit very heterogeneous), numbering several hundred million people. These citizens may become the driving force behind democracy due to their income and educational levels and also based on how well informed they are regarding political issues.

As it is virtually impossible to carry out valid representative surveys on the extremely sensitive issue of political-system change in China, the information we do have as to whether there is any interest among the urban middle classes regarding democratic elections and competition is very limited and patchy (beyond the small number of political activists who have come into conflict with the government). It is these urban middle and upper classes who have benefited the most from the economic changes over the past several decades. According to the limited fieldwork and survey research that we can draw on, many members of the Chinese middle classes appear primarily interested in political stability to ensure that their new-found prosperity and wealth will remain protected. State media channels have also made use of assiduously selected reporting on social injustices in democratic systems (such as the violence and discrimination in the United States and India, or the brawls in parliament in Taiwan and South Korea) to sow seeds of mistrust of democratic competition among large swathes of the middle classes. Additionally, any criticism of the CCP from the West is portrayed in the state media and in educational institutions as direct attacks on national sovereignty and the dignity of the Chinese people: any negative comments from abroad tend to result in patriotic responses and solidarity with the party and state. Furthermore, state power is considered so overpowering that many people believe that any advocacy of systemic change is simply hopeless. As long as people feel that the government is leaving them alone to get on with their professional and private lives, is not interfering arbitrarily, and state interference and excessive regulation can be avoided, the vast majority of the middle classes prefer to stay away from political activities.

In addition to the passive political behavior of the middle classes, there are many other constraints when it comes to China becoming a more democratic nation. Social and regional disparities throughout the country will be detrimental in the long term. Another major constraint is that civic engagement in social organizations continues to be stifled and underdeveloped, and the legal and judicial systems still largely bow to CCP instructions rather than behave as an institutional counterweight to the power held by CCP organs and cadres.

The core features of China's political culture are not conducive to supporting democratic checks and balances: there is a broad lack of powerful liberal and constitutional traditions and positive historical experience with political competition and peaceful political conflict resolution, as well as a total absence of a minimal consensus with regard to civil rights and limits to the power of the state. The potential contribution of the media and the Internet to form more pluralistic opinions and to provide the public oversight that is necessary for democratic change must be viewed with skepticism at present (see Chapter 5).

The greatest obstacle to a substantial, and not just formal, democratization of China is that the country's economic and political power resources are currently concentrated among an extremely small section of the population. Generally, economic liberalization is much less advanced than suggested by official policy statements. Many Chinese economists and entrepreneurs believe that the actual degree of economic freedom in the country is substantially more limited than the tough competition in domestic markets suggests: Chinese businesspeople are so dependent on informal political and economic relationships that it is not really possible to talk of entrepreneurial freedom or property or contractual security (see Chapter 4).

All of the above offer a simple explanation as to why democratic checks on power are not making headway: the political class is inextricably linked to informal economic-exchange networks and the leading economic players are subordinate to myriad political dependencies. In many locations, the CCP, particularly at its lower organizational levels, is used to acting as a mafia-like group (at least until the start of Xi Jinping's discipline campaign): party functionaries skim profits off of both legal and illegal companies and fight any resistance to such practices with the help of the state's monopoly on the legitimate use of physical force. The predominance of informal exchange networks that operate not only within the world of corruption, but also as a flourishing part of China's legal economy is often understood by Western scholars and businesspeople as a manifestation of a flexible "network capitalism" (Wang Hongying 2001). In fact, informal networks in economies characterized by heavy political interference often have the advantage that they can help overcome counterproductive state restrictions and can keep entrepreneurial dynamics alive. The drawbacks, however, are clearly manifested in rampant corruption, in a plundering of the financial assets of the state sector, in manipulation of the financial system, and in political cynicism and growing social inequalities.

The entire Chinese economic and political system operates in two very different worlds simultaneously: on the one hand, there is the layer of officially praised economic growth and restructuring under the leadership of the CCP, and on the other, there is an underlying, dynamic shadow economy involving many members of the functionary class who are primarily interested in securing their own vested interests—a secondary marketplace where political power is systematically traded for economic influence and material gain. Underestimating or misconstruing this ambiguous, yet very powerful, political component of economic life occurs when the Chinese economy is subject to narrow technical analyses that attempt to shut out the effects of continual political interference and government-business exchanges.

According to the results of historical and quantitative studies of democratization (Vanhanen 1997), the marked unequal distribution of economic, social, and political power resources in China does just as little to build democratic institutions as the ingrained informal networks among political and economic players who will likely manage to benefit materially from any destabilization or even collapse of the current political system. As a result, the best that can probably be hoped for in China is the establishment of a formal "façade democracy," characterized by very strong social and regional disparities, limited political and economic competition, and oligarchic power structures —somewhat similar to the situation in Brazil or Russia today.

Who would be capable of promoting democratization in China? There is currently no leading political or social group in China that is capable of representing democratic values and ideals and that has the resources to accelerate China's transition to democracy. The urban middle classes and the private entrepreneurs are too closely linked to government bodies and the functionary class, so any push in the direction of democratization will have to come from the latter. The problem is that up until now the functionaries have been very resistant to any institutional reforms that will be crucial for a political and economic regeneration—withdrawal of the state from the economy, credible protection of private property and contractual rights, and the establishment of independent political and judicial control bodies—which would also undermine the special position they currently occupy.

The evolutionary perspective of a peaceful, controlled, and negotiated transition from CCP rule to a pluralistic democracy currently does not enjoy any support whatsoever. The political leadership under Xi Jinping has consistently shown to be interested only in strengthening and modernizing the party-state. Under no circumstances is it interested in starting down a path toward democratization in the Western sense of the word—a separation of powers, competition among opposing parties, and free elections. Even many of the inner-party reforms tentatively introduced since the 1990s (such as competition among candidates for leading party bodies) have been abandoned (Fewsmith 2013). Social tensions are considered to be reduced through a combination of improved public services ("social management") and more effective police work, and not through any political reform or self-organization of civil society. Hence, there is no chance of the party-state developing into a liberal competitive democracy under the current political leadership.

7.6 Is China a possible developmental model for other countries?

The rapid global economic rise of the PRC has resulted in extensive debates as to whether a "Chinese model" is evolving that can be followed by other developing nations and emerging markets that combine market-based economic development and an authoritarian leadership. The controversy centers around very different ideas about the different characteristics of an East Asian "developmental state" (Heilmann 2006; Johnson 1982; Woo-Cumings 1999), the emergence of an authoritarian economic "Beijing consensus" in contrast to the liberal "Washington consensus" (Halper 2010; Ramo 2004), novel "state capitalist" systems (Bremmer 2010), an economically and technology-driven boost in output in certain authoritarian systems of government ("authoritarian upgrading") (Heilmann 2010), historically based, self-reliant, ideological beliefs and legitimacy (Jacques 2012), or the benefits of a meritocratic form of government when recruiting political leaders and legitimizing power in the twenty-first century (Bell 2015). Table 7.6 summarizes the most important characteristics and methods attributed to a potential "Chinese development model."

Even within China there have been lively debates regarding the main features of a high-performance "Chinese model" (中国模式) (see Pan Wei 2009) or even a "new type of superpower" (新型超级大国) (Hu Angang 2012; Hu Angang et al. 2014). Such discussions have been popularized in a series of publications written mainly by prominent social scientists (many of whom come from party or government backgrounds) and with some contributions from retired party cadres (Chen Jinhua et al. 2012). However, arguments in favor of a distinct "Chinese model" have also encountered strong criticism within China (Ding Xueliang 2011; Zheng Yongnian 2010b).

It is noteworthy that the Chinese government has never attempted to portray its political and economic system as an exemplary model for other states to follow. In fact, Chinese diplomats are insistent that their partner countries in Asia, Africa, and Latin America should follow independent national development strategies in accordance with their local circumstances. Chinese diplomats and commentators criticize cooperative Western development programs for imposing conditions on the beneficiaries and offering one-size-fits-all solutions. In contrast, they hold that China avoids setting any standardized conditions that do not match the specific national and regional contexts.

International discussions of the "Chinese model" did not attract much attention until the global financial and economic crisis of 2007–9. In the West, public and social-science discussions were dominated by the logic of the "interdependence of orders" that maintains that political and economic freedoms and competition are mutually dependent, and that wealth and growth can only be guaranteed over the long term in a democracy with a market-based economy. However, this explanatory model does not offer any plausible explanation for economic and political developments in China after 1989. The contrasts to the experiences of the Eastern European Communist party-states with regard to economic and institutional flexibility as well as to the competitiveness within the global economy are obvious.

Table 7.6

Characteristics and methods attributed to a "Chinese development model"

Domestic and legal policies	Authoritarian, developmental, economically agile, and adaptive government; prohibition against political competition; suppression of political opposition; recruitment of local political and administrative leaders according to their experience, qualifications, and performance ("meritocracy"); compartmentalized administrative reforms in reaction to economic pressures; neither constitutional reform nor political liberalization; legitimization based on economic performance and nationalism; consultations with important lobbies ("consultative authoritarianism"); an extensive system of laws and regulations; lack of an independent judiciary
Social and welfare policies	Suppression of political self-organization in NGOs, instead promotion of state-controlled, government-organized non-governmental organizations (GONGOs); prevention of unrest through preventive "social management" (surveillance, complaints offices, social services, with police repression always a possibility); strict residence and birth controls; high investments in the education system, with a focus on mathematics, informatics, natural and technical sciences; extension of social security; official aim is "prosperity for all"
Labor relations	State-guided official unions; prohibition against strikes and collective-bargaining across companies; close alliances between government and big business
Domestic economy	Long-term development planning; high willingness to learn from international experience; strictly pragmatic (aimed at specific problem-solving) non-ideological economic policy and a willingness to try out new options; growth at any price; massive state investments in industry and infrastructure; protection of government-linked companies; state control of the banking system
Financial markets	State financial repression (low interest rates on deposit accounts with limited alternatives for savings and investments); channeling of private savings into investments for state-approved industries and infrastructure; state-controlled sovereign wealth funds investing internationally; capital controls; active currency management and limited currency convertibility
Foreign policy	Global diplomatic presence; blend of diplomacy with foreign-trade policy and financial diplomacy ("checkbook diplomacy"); strict defense of national sovereignty and territorial claims; insistence on national sovereignty in all political issues (including human rights) as well as in cyberspace; massive military build-up
Foreign trade	Orientation toward global markets and exports; government-sponsored programs aimed at import substitution; selective protectionism for domestic infant industries; targeted promotion and control of foreign investments; preference for global market share over short-term revenue; special funding for overseas involvement by Chinese companies; support for geopolitical goals via foreign-trade policy
Industrial policy	Targeted state promotion of "strategic emerging industries"; state interference in sectoral industrial structure; maintenance of state control in "strategic" industries
Energy/environmental policies	Extensive use of resources with serious environmental consequences; technology-driven efforts to move to a more resource-conserving energy and environmental policy
Technology policy	Acquisition of advanced foreign technology through targeted regulations and incentives; access to the market in exchange for investment and technology; long-term programs for building a globally competitive national innovation system
Media and general public	Active steering of media and shaping of public opinion; commercialization and de-politicization of the media sector; enlargement of electronic surveillance systems on the Internet
Domestic security	Expansion of the security apparatus (including in cyberspace); comprehensive IT surveillance systems

© MERICS

Investors and companies operating in China believe that one of the greatest strengths of the Chinese political system is that the government places much greater emphasis on long-term development priorities and large-scale projects than do governments operating in short-winded, reactive, and seemingly volatile democratic systems. Leading proponents of the "Chinese model" view China as one of the few remaining systems that is capable of implementing strategic, long-term policies. The chances of pursuing long-term priorities, ranging from infrastructure and education to technology planning in China, are, however, inseparable from authoritarian rule and executive continuity—including the absence of democratic elections and checks on executive power.

Does China really offer a model for an efficient, technocratic state characterized by cooperation among political, economic, and technological players and resources, long-term development goals, and greater assertiveness against lobbies and vested interests?

When discussing these issues, nothing is as plausible or sustainable as it first appears when one looks in more detail beyond the simplified descriptions. Remarkably, even the traditional hierarchical foundations of state power in China tend to crumble when scrutinized under a microscope. In addition, state capacity to actively shape and control key development issues (such as the financial system, income distribution, the environment, and demography) also appears to be rather limited, and the push toward greater centralization under Xi Jinping has not done much to change that. All in all, the widespread perception of China as a centralized autocracy explains only a small part of the overall political and social dynamics. These dynamics are driven much more strongly by decentralized, uncontrollable forces than by all-or-none thinking in terms of different types of systems (autocracy versus democracy) would suggest (see Chapters 4–6).

With regard to the influence that Chinese experiences and practices may have on other developing nations and emerging markets, there is no suggestion that they should be directly implemented in the same way in other countries. In fact, China's economic approach is seen as a more flexible, more selective, alternative frame of reference that may provide productive ideas, methodologies, justifications, and legitimization beyond the so far predominant Western models and influences. In particular, authoritarian or "illiberal" polities, and the political elite in them, can refer to China's success story as a source of legitimacy for authoritarian methods of leadership and national development under a "strong state."

The Chinese government has not yet approached its own foreign economic, financial, and development policy with missionary zeal: rather than publicizing its development experience as a self-contained model, the experience is promoted as a suggestion about how to advance independent, national "catch-up" development. However, even without active propagation, the combination of an authoritarian state and rapid economic development has obvious demonstration effects and strong appeal to authoritarian and illiberal governments, such as in Russia, Hungary, Venezuela, Ecuador, Iran, Ethiopia, Zimbabwe, Thailand, and Cambodia. Even if the political elite and societies in countries with diplomatic and economic links to China are suspicious of Chinese influence, the Chinese approach to politics and economic development is still hugely attractive to their ruling classes. China's global economic and investment activities encourage the spread of Chinese approaches to governance and the legitimation of a "strong state."

Is a form of modern Chinese statehood that might challenge or even reject the Western model of market-based democracy currently in the making? The leading Western democracies and market economies of the United States, Europe, and Japan have experienced a significant loss of reputation and credibility among the developing nations and emerging markets, particularly since the global financial and economic crisis of 2007–9—something that China has seized upon to promote its own global agenda. Current Chinese geopolitical initiatives are based on the assumption that the United States and Europe are in a state of decline and that China is the only nation currently capable of filling the gap. This weakening of the established market-based democracies that formerly held strong appeal as a model has become a key to China's improved prestige and attraction.

Under certain circumstances, this new configuration may result in veritable competition between the two different models: should Xi Jinping's agenda (increased political discipline and centralization combined with economic deregulation and restructuring) be successful before the year 2020—without the respective economic and technological performance and ability to take political action in the United States and the European Union being revived—the much stronger authoritarian Chinese party-state will doubtlessly represent formidable systemic competition and a permanent yardstick for comparison with the market-based democracies. In the crisis-prone twenty-first century, discussions will focus on whether China has succeeded in developing a more efficient, flexible system of government with a more stable core. The greater global presence and activities of Chinese diplomats and investors are bound to foster methods of rule in partner and target countries that tend to correspond with Chinese practices. One of the leading fields for this type of convergence will be the continued rollout of comprehensive and effective state surveillance systems based on new IT and communications technologies. Commercial interests will drive this development globally, as China exports its increasingly powerful security and surveillance technologies.

In the context of a volatile, crisis-ridden twenty-first century, one specific feature of China's approach to governance might substantially challenge the Western democracies: its capability to react and to adapt in a flexible and agile manner to recurrent acute crises and to novel demands on government activity.

This important quality of political systems has been played down and neglected for decades in both Western Europe and the United States based on the simplified argument that democratic competition automatically results in the development of an adaptive and innovative political system. However, as a result of the recent failings of democratic systems to correct serious structural and regulatory short-comings, both before and even after the global financial crisis and the euro crisis, such assumptions are risky and no longer tenable. Complacency and psychological barriers with regard to renovating traditional political institutions and approaches to governance may ultimately result in their downfall. Today's political systems must respond to novel requirements for managing recurrent economic and se-curity crises, reducing risks in capital markets, regulating cyberspace, countering growing social inequities, and incorporating social media–driven public opinion in the policy process. Traditional political and legal systems are lagging in terms of dealing with these urgent contemporary challenges. The use of the organizational and administrative models of the nineteenth and twentieth centuries, persistent institutional and political inertia, and the resultant lack of drive to renew approach-es to governance are all central weaknesses of many governmental systems. All political and legal systems will inevitably need to undertake huge adjustments in the radically changing economic, technological, and communications environment of the twenty-first century while avoiding breakdowns of political systems and economic depressions.

China's authoritarian party-state is unacceptable and unsuitable as a model for democratic societies. Rule of law, limited state power, and guaranteed individual civil liberties remain the most attractive form of government, especially for large sections of Chinese society. A very visible indication of this is the large number of people among China's political and economic elite who send their children and assets abroad so as to prepare for an exit option and to have access to alterna-tive lifestyles. China's "system insiders" do not appear to have much confidence in the sustainability of the current regime, thereby undermining the public façade of self-confidence and loyalty that has been cultivated by official government state-ments.

Despite these profound weaknesses, the apparent recent success of the Chi-nese system of government has resulted in a debate on the international stage that has cast doubt on the decades of undisputed institutional and economic su-periority of the market-based democracies. The era when the West was the ob-vious or the only model to follow is most definitely over. Competition in terms of economic and technological efficiencies, as well as in terms of state capacity and credibility, is intensifying. In the face of a rising China, Western liberal models of governance are currently facing growing pressures to perform better and to reas-sert their legitimacy.

7.7 Implications for international interactions with China

The Chinese approach to foreign policy has changed since the 2000s, and dramatically so since Xi Jinping took over the reins of power. China is no longer content with the international intergovernmental order that, from the Chinese perspective, has been shaped by American predominance since the end of the Cold War. Chinese diplomacy has been trying to reshape the rules of the game that were primarily established by the West and to contribute to institution-building and rule-making based on its own interests and those of other non-Western countries. Long-established forms of cooperation between the West and China—for example based on NGOs and foundations that support civic, charitable, or legal-aid projects within China—are now regarded with suspicion and as potential sources of infiltration by "hostile forces" that might undermine the Chinese political system.

At the same time, China is also changing its foreign-policy methods and ambitions: backed by massive diplomatic and financial resources, the leadership under Xi Jinping is pursuing new international priorities and new geostrategic projects. In particular, it is focusing on building up economic corridors ("silk roads") involving China's neighbors through the construction of infrastructure, reduction of trade barriers, and security-related cooperation. Additionally, "south-to-south" cooperation is becoming increasingly important: Beijing has been expanding its economic and diplomatic links with developing nations and emerging markets. Rivalries between China and the United States over the rebalancing of power and dominance in the Asian region have become increasingly overt. These will likely intensify in the coming years, thereby altering on-the-ground conditions for all regional players, including their European trade partners.

The causes of this shift include decisions by the Chinese leadership as well as domestic political, social, and economic signs of crisis: China's economy is entering a new stage of development characterized by much lower growth rates. As a result, sectors of the Chinese economy that have thus far been very lucrative for foreign companies will become less attractive. At the same time, the Chinese economy will remain irreplaceable due to its sheer size and its continued growth of demand. Western policies toward China will have to find creative solutions to what will become a "gravitational dilemma": even if businesses make efforts to diversify away from China, they will not be able to do so in the foreseeable future.

European and American policies with respect to China must be adjusted according to this new framework and their traditional aims and priorities must be readjusted. Until now, their main goals have been as follows: First, to gradually promote a more liberal China—"change through trade" and "change through dialogue"; second, to incorporate China into international rules and organizations as established under Western leadership: "change through international law" and binding multilateral regulations; and third, to safeguard economic interests in the Chinese market (often the principal goal of bilateral relations), including diplomatically supported advances in access for foreign companies and protection of their intellectual property.

If we look at these three traditional goals during the decades when business with China was growing rapidly, there is one unavoidable and sobering conclusion: neither rapid economic and technological growth nor the extensive involvement of China in the global economy have led to domestic liberalization or international political integration of China based on Western ideals.

So perhaps the time has come to discard these goals? Definitely not. Both Europeans and Americans need to hold fast to established mechanisms of cooperation and dialogue and in fact to promote them further, even if the current environment may appear to be unfavorable. Dealings with China must be seen from a long-term perspective; we must continue to persevere: the construction of a legal system with an efficient, independent judiciary and a law-abiding, reliable administration will take many decades to be realized and it will be plagued by various setbacks—as Western states know only too well from their own experiences.

Any demand or hope in America or Europe to guide China in the direction of Western-style democracy from the outside is unrealistic and should be removed from the agenda—targeted manipulation of Chinese political development and outright democracy promotion would be even more complicated today than it was in previous decades. External pressures, such as the threat of sanctions, lead to nationalistic displays of solidarity within China and actually tend to strengthen the authority of the Chinese political leadership rather than to result in local demands for greater liberalization.

Democratization in China must be led by the Chinese themselves, in their own way and based on their own very different experiences and institutions. Americans and Europeans will not be able to supply any one-size-fits-all recipes for political regeneration in China. At the same time, the attraction and performance of the Western market-based democracies need to be improved in order to renew the appeal of Western models. In view of the competition among the different models of political and economic order in the developing nations and emerging markets, Europeans and Americans should not surrender to China's very active diplomacy and foreign-trade policy.

There is one central area where cooperation with China is likely to become more constructive due to shared interests. Although China is increasingly challenging the status quo of an U.S.-led world order, an unstable international environment plagued by military conflict, contested borders, civil wars, and terrorism is as little in Beijing's interest as it is in that of Washington, Berlin, London, or Paris. This common perspective is likely to offer numerous opportunities for cooperation in the future.

Because Western domination of international institutions appears to be declining, the Western powers must make concerted efforts to allow China to become more involved in adjustments to the rules governing the global economy and world politics. Close cooperation with China is essential to tackle the greatest challenges of the twenty-first century: from managing new threats to security and environmental risks, to regulating trade and financial markets, and to developing a multilateral regime for cyberspace.

If China's rapid rise in the global economy and on the world stage continues, it will no doubt lead to increased tensions and acute conflicts that will require preventive management. Trade disputes, diplomatic confrontations, and, in extreme cases, even limited military skirmishes should not be considered unlikely. The belief that China has not yet reached the zenith of its national power is firmly anchored among Chinese policy-makers and in domestic public opinion. China's neighbors, the United States, and Europe will be forced to face a fundamental challenge—a world order that China will accept and help sustain does not yet exist. Such an order, which will involve a protracted and conflict-ridden process, must be designed with active involvement and collaboration by China.

8 Glossary

English	Acronym	Chinese
All-China Federation of Industry and Commerce	ACFIC	中华全国工商业联合会 （工商联）
All-China Federation of Literary and Art Circles	ACFLAC	中国文学艺术界联合会
All-China Federation of Trade Unions	ACFTU	中华全国总工会
All-China Journalists Association	ACJA	中华全国新闻工作协会
All-China Women's Federation	ACWF	中华全国妇女联合会
CCP CC Central Security Bureau		中共中央警卫局
CCP CC Documents Research Office		中共中央文献研究室
CCP CC General Office		中共中央办公厅
CCP CC International (Liaison) Department		中共中央对外联系部 （中联部）
CCP CC Organization Department	COD	中共中央组织部 （中组部）
CCP CC Party History Research Center		中共中央党史研究室
CCP CC Policy Research Office		中共中央政策研究室
CCP CC Politburo		中共中央政治局
CCP CC Politburo Standing Committee	PSC	中共中央政治局常务委员会

CCP CC Propaganda Department   中共中央宣传部

CCP CC Secretariat   中共中央书记处

CCP CC United Front Work
Department   中共中央统一战线工作部
（统战部）

CCP Central Committee CCP CC 中国共产党中央委员会
（中共中央）

CCP National Congress   中共全国代表大会

Central Commission for CCCMPS 中央社会治安综合治理委
Comprehensive Management of 员会
Public Security

Central Commission for Discipline CCDI 中央纪律检查委员会
Inspection

Central Commission for State   中央保密委员会
Secrets

Central Coordinating Group for   中央香港澳门工作协调小组
Hong Kong and Macau Affairs

Central Encryption Leading Small   中央密码工作领导小组
Group

Central Finance and Economy CFELSG 中央财经领导小组
Leading Small Group

Central Foreign Affairs Work CFALSG 中央外事工作领导小组
Leading Small Group

Central Institutional Organization SCOPSR 中央机构编制委员会 （中
Commission (also called: State 编委）
Commission Office for Public Sector
Reform)

Central Leading Small Group for Comprehensively Deepening Reforms	CDRLSG	中央全面深化改革领导小组
Central Leading Small Group for Cyber Security and Informatization	CSILSG	中央网络安全和信息化领导小组
Central Leading Small Group for Propaganda and Ideology		中央宣传思想工作领导小组
Central Leading Small Group for Rural Work		中央农村工作领导小组
Central Leading Small Group for the Protection of Maritime Interests		中央海洋权益工作领导小组
Central Military Commission	CMC	中央军事委员会
Central National Security Commission (also called: National Security Council)	CNSC	中央国家安全委员会
Central Party School		中央党校
Central Party-Building Leading Small Group		中央党的建设工作领导小组
Central Political and Legal Affairs Commission		中央政法委员会 （政法委）
Central Taiwan Work Leading Small Group		中央对台工作领导小组
China Association for Science and Technology	CAST	中国科学技术协会
China Banking Regulatory Commission	CBRC	中国银行业监督管理委员会
China Earthquake Administration	CEA	中国地震局

China Food and Drug Administration	CFDA	国家食品药品监督管理总局
China Insurance Regulatory Commission	CIRC	中国保险监督管理委员会
China Investment Corporation	CIC	中国投资有限责任公司
China Securities Regulatory Commission	CSRC	中国证券监督管理委员会
Chinese Academy of Engineering	CAE	中国工程院
Chinese Academy of Sciences	CAS	中国科学院
Chinese Academy of Social Sciences	CASS	中国社会科学院
Chinese Communist Party	CCP	中国共产党（中共）
Chinese People's Political Consultative Conference	CPPCC	中国人民政治协商会议
Commission for Comprehensive Governance of Social Management		社会管理综合治理委员会
Commission on Food Safety of the State Council		国务院食品安全委员会
Communist Youth League	CYL	共产主义青年团
Cyberspace Administration of China	CAC	国家互联网信息办公室
Development Research Center of the State Council	DRC	国务院发展研究中心
Equipment Development Department (of the Central Military Commission)		（中央军事委员会）装备发展部
General Administration of Customs		海关总署

General Administration of Quality Supervision, Inspection and Quarantine	AQSIQ	国家质量监督检验检疫总局
General Office of the State Council		国务院办公厅
Joint Staff Department (of the Central Military Commission)	JSD	（中央军事委员会）联合参谋部
Leading Small Group	LSG	领导小组
Leading Small Group of the Central Military Commission for Deepening Reforms in National Defense and the Military		中央军委深化国防和军队改革领导小组
Logistic Support Department (of the Central Military Commission)		（中央军事委员会）后勤保障部
Ministry of Agriculture	MOA	农业部
Ministry of Civil Affairs	MOCA	民政部
Ministry of Commerce	MOFCOM	商务部
Ministry of Culture	MOC	文化部
Ministry of Defense	MOD	国防部
Ministry of Education	MOE	教育部
Ministry of Environmental Protection	MEP	环境保护部
Ministry of Finance	MOF	财政部
Ministry of Foreign Affairs	MOFA	外交部
Ministry of Housing and Urban-Rural Development	MOHURD	住房和城乡建设部

Ministry of Human Resources and Social Security	MOHRSS	人力资源和社会保障部
Ministry of Industry and Information Technology	MIIT	工业和信息化部
Ministry of Justice	MOJ	司法部
Ministry of Labor and Social Security	MOLSS	劳动和社会保障部
Ministry of Land and Resources	MLR	国土资源部
Ministry of Public Security (Police Ministry)	MPS	公安部
Ministry of Railways	MOR	铁道部
Ministry of Science and Technology	MOST	科学技术部
Ministry of State Security	MSS	国家安全部
Ministry of Supervision	MOS	监察部
Ministry of Transport	MOT	交通运输部
Ministry of Water Resources	MWR	水利部
National Audit Office	NAO	审计署
National Bureau for State Secrets		国家保密局
National Bureau of Statistics	NBS	国家统计局
National Commission for Disaster Reduction	NCDR	国家减灾委员会（减灾委）
National Development and Reform Commission	NDRC	国家发展和改革委员会（发改委）

National Encryption Office		国家秘码管理局
National Energy Commission	NEC	国家能源委员会
National Health and Family Planning Commission	NHFPC	国家卫生和计划生育委员会（卫计委）
National People's Congress	NPC	全国人民代表大会
National People's Congress Standing Committee	NPCSC	全国人民代表大会常务委员会
National Social Security Fund	NSSF	全国社会保障基金
Party Committee	PC	党委
Party Group		党组
Patriotic Health Campaign Committee	PHCC	爱国卫生运动委员会
People's Bank of China	PBOC	中国人民银行
People's Liberation Army	PLA	人民解放军
People's Liberation Army Navy	PLAN	人民解放军海军
People's Republic of China	PRC	中华人民共和国
Politburo		政治局
Politburo Standing Committee	PSC	政治局常务委员会
Political Work Department (of the Central Military Commission)		（中央军事委员会）政治工作部
Provincial Party Committee		省党委

Provincial People's Congress		省人民代表大会
State Administration for Industry and Commerce	SAIC	国家工商行政管理总局
State Administration of Foreign Exchange	SAFE	国家外汇管理局
State Administration of Grain	SAG	国家粮食局
State Administration of Radio, Film and Television	SARFT	国家新闻出版广电总局
State Council		国务院
State Council Emergency Management Office	EMO	国务院应急管理办公室
State Ethnic Affairs Commission	SEAC	国家民族事务委员会
State Oceanic Administration	SOA	国家海洋局
State Supervisory Authority for Production Safety	SSAPS	国家安全生产监督管理总局
State-owned Assets Supervision and Administration Commission	SASAC	国务院国有资产监督管理委员会

9 References and sources

9.1 Reference works

Bartke, Wolfgang (1997). *Who Was Who in the People's Republic of China.* Munich: K.G. Saur.

Benewick, Robert and Stephanie Hemelryk Donald (2009). *The State of China Atlas: Mapping the World's Fastest-Growing Economy.* Rvsd. Berkeley: University of California Press.

Fischer, Doris and Michael Lackner (eds.) (2014). *Länderbericht China.* Schriftenreihe Bd. 351. Bonn: Bundeszentrale für politische Bildung.

Goodman, David S.G. (ed.) (2015). *Handbook of the Politics of China.* Cheltenham, UK: Edward Elgar.

He, Henry Yuhuai (ed.) (2001). *Dictionary of the Political Thought of the People's Republic of China.* Armonk, NY: M.E. Sharpe.

Mackerras, Colin (2001). *The New Cambridge Handbook of Contemporary China.* Cambridge, UK: Cambridge University Press.

Mackerras, Colin, with Donald H. McMillen and Andrew Watson (1998). *Dictionary of the Politics of the People's Republic of China.* London: Routledge.

National School of Administration 国家行政学院 (ed.) (2000).中华人民共和国政府机构五十年, *1949–1999* (50 years of governmental bodies in the People Republic of China, 1949–1999). Beijing: Dangjian duwu chubanshe.

NBS [National Bureau of Statistics] 中华人民共和国国家统计局 (annual). *China Statistical Yearbook/Zhongguo tongji nianjian* 中国统计年鉴 (bilingual). Beijing: Zhongguo tongji chubanshe/China Statistical Press. http://www.stats.gov.cn/tjsj/ndsj/. Accessed: January 15, 2016.

Ogden, Chris (ed.) (2013). *Handbook of China's Governance and Domestic Politics.* London: Routledge.

Radiopress (ed.) (2014). *China Directory 2015* 中国组织别人名簿 (bilingual). Tokyo: JPM Corp., Ltd.

Sullivan, Lawrence R. (ed.) (2007). *Historical Dictionary of the People's Republic of China*. 2nd ed. Lanham, MD: Scarecrow Press.

9.2 Internet sources

Economy and the environment

http://english.caixin.com/ (English, Chinese). Economic information and analyses.
http://finance.ifeng.com/ (Chinese). Economic information and analyses.
https://www.chinadialogue.net/ (English, Chinese). Bilingual website of China Dialogue, London/Beijing, NGO, focusing on environmental issues.
http://www.chinaeconomicreview.com/ (English). Greater China economic analyses.
http://www.ft.com/intl/world/asia-pacific/china (English). *Financial Times* China coverage.
http://www.gtai.de/GTAI/Navigation/DE/Trade/Weltkarte/Asien/china.html (German). GTAI China information, with recent China news reports.
http://www.merics.org (German, English). Research programs focusing on economic and environmental issues.
http://www.worldbank.org/en/country/china (English). Website of the World Bank, with recent economic data and studies.

Foreign policy

http://eeas.europa.eu/china/index_en.htm (English). Information about EU–China relations.
http://www.auswaertiges-amt.de/DE/Aussenpolitik/Laender/Laenderinfos/01-Nodes_Uebersichtsseiten/China_node.html (German). Information about German–Chinese relations with respect to politics, the economy, and culture.
http://www.fmprc.gov.cn (Chinese, English). Official website of the Ministry of Foreign Affairs.
http://www.merics.org/en/programmes/foreign-relations.html (German, English). Research program of the Mercator Institute for China Studies, with recent analyses.

http://www.state.gov/p/eap/ (English). Bureau of East Asian and Pacific Affairs of the U.S. State Department.

Government and politics

http://carnegietsinghua.org/ (English, Chinese). Background analyses of recent politics.
http://cpc.people.com.cn/gbzl/index.html (Chinese). Official biographical information.
http://www.chinapolitik.de (German, English). Academic analyses of domestic and economic policy.
http://www.chinavitae.com/ (English). U.S. database, with biographical information on leading Chinese cadres.
http://www.gov.cn (Chinese, English). Official website, with government information and links to the provincial governments.
http://www.gov.cn/guowuyuan/ (Chinese). Website of the State Council; government activities (also single ministries), including recent documents, meeting reports, and speeches.
http://www.hoover.org/publications/china-leadership-monitor (English). Academic analyses of recent political, economic, and military developments.
http://www.jamestown.org/chinabrief/ (English). Brief analyses of recent political developments.
http://www.merics.org/ (German, English, Chinese). Analyses and updates by the Mercator Institute for China Studies in Berlin.
http://www.npc.gov.cn/ (Chinese, English). Internet presence of the National People's Congress; information about recent legislative processes.
http://www.peopledaily.com.cn/zcxx/zcbw_home.html (Chinese). Recent information from PRC ministries and the CCP.

Legal system and human rights

http://chinalawtranslate.com/ (English, Chinese). Website run by students at the Yale China Law Center; translation of legislative texts.
http://hermes.gwu.edu/archives/chinalaw.html (English). CHINALAW; electronic discussion platform on PRC, Hong Kong, and Taiwan law.
https://www.amnesty.org/en/countries/asia-and-the-pacific/china/ (English). China reports by Amnesty International human rights organization.
http://www.chinacourt.org/index.shtml (Chinese, English). News on Chinese courts, with links to local courts.
http://www.chinalawinfo.com/ (Chinese, English). Website run by law students at Peking University; legislative texts, legal advice.

http://www.hrichina.org (Chinese, English). Human rights organization established by Chinese academics living in the United States.

http://www.humanrights-china.org (Chinese, English). Government documents on human rights policy.

http://www.lawinfochina.com/ (English, Chinese). Largest database of Chinese legislative texts and verdicts, with English translations.

http://www.legalinfo.gov.cn/ (Chinese, English). Website of the Ministry of Justice; database of legislative texts, with search function (Chinese).

Military

http://mil.news.sina.com.cn/ (Chinese). Information about recent developments in the PLA; basic information.

http://military.people.com.cn/ (Chinese). Official news on military and security policy as well as defense issues.

http://www.comw.org/cmp/ (English). Online resources about the Chinese military by the Commonwealth Institute.

http://www.mod.gov.cn/ (Chinese). Official website of the Ministry of Defense.

News websites

http://blogs.wsj.com/chinarealtime/ (English). China Real Time; *Wall Street Journal* articles.

http://chinadigitaltimes.net/ (English, Chinese). U.S. website run by students at the University of California, Berkeley, with news summaries and many links.

http://english.caixin.com/ (English, Chinese). Website of an influential mainland Chinese news magazine.

http://foreignpolicy.com/channel/tea-leaf-nation/ (English). China coverage of the U.S. news magazine.

http://thediplomat.com/ (English). *The Diplomat Magazine;* Online news magazine, with reports and analyses focusing on Chinese foreign policy and international relations.

http://www.21ccom.net/ (Chinese). Website of mainland Chinese Consensus Media Group, with analyses and essays.

http://www.chinablaetter.info/ (German, English, Chinese). Private website, with many links to German-, English-, and Chinese-language news reports on China.

http://www.chinafile.com/ (English). Online magazine of the Asia Society (U.S.), on recent trends and developments in China and in the field of China research.

http://www.economist.com/sections/china (English). *Economist* China coverage.

http://www.ft.com/intl/world/asia-pacific/china (English). *Financial Times* China coverage.

http://www.omnitalk.com/ (Chinese). Private website, with many links to overseas Chinese news platforms and Chinese discussion forums.

http://www.peopledaily.com.cn (Chinese, English). Internet platform of the official newspaper of the CCP, *Renmin ribao/People's Daily.*

http://www.scmp.com (English). *South China Morning Post;* Hong Kong daily newspaper, with extensive China coverage.

http://www.xinhuanet.com/ (Chinese, English, German). Internet presence of the official press agency of the PRC (Xinhua News Agency).

http://www.zonaeuropa.com/weblog.htm (English, Chinese). Website of the Hong Kong–based blogger Roland Soong, with selected news and analyses.

Society, Internet, media, and technology

https://chinacopyrightandmedia.wordpress.com/ (English). Translations and analyses of new legislative initiatives in China, with a special focus on Internet regulation.

http://chinadevelopmentbrief.cn/ (English, Chinese). Information about social and sociopolitical issues; NGO database.

http://cmp.hku.hk/ (English). China Media Project of the University of Hong Kong.

http://technode.com/ (English). Leading tech blog on start-up entrepreneurs, investors, large companies, and industry trends in China and Asia.

http://www.cac.gov.cn/ (Chinese). Website of the Cyberspace Administration of China and the Office of the Central Leading Group for Cyber Security and Informatization.

http://www.chinahightech.com/ (Chinese). Portal of the high-technology zones in China.

http://www.clb.org.hk/en/ (English, Chinese). Website of the Hong Kong–based *China Labour Bulletin.*

https://www.techinasia.com/tag/china/ (English). IT and startups.

Statistics

http://data.worldbank.org/country/china (English). World Bank statistics and collections of data.

http://dc.xinhua08.com/ Website of the official news agency, with recent statistics.

https://www.cia.gov/library/publications/the-world-factbook/geos/ch.html (English). *CIA World Factbook;* PRC data and facts.

http://www.stats.gov.cn/ (English, Chinese). Website of the National Bureau of Statistics.

9.3 Periodicals

Asian Survey (University of California, Berkeley)
Asien (Deutsche Gesellschaft für Asienkunde, Hamburg)
Caijing (Stock Exchange Executive Council, Beijing)
China: An International Journal (National University of Singapore, Singapore)
China & World Economy (Chinese Academy of Social Sciences, Beijing)
China Journal, The (Australian National University, Canberra)
China Leadership Monitor (Hoover Institution, Stanford University)
China Perspectives (French Centre for Research on Contemporary China, Hong Kong)
China Quarterly, The (School of Oriental and African Studies, London)
China Review: An Interdisciplinary Journal on Greater China (Chinese University of Hong Kong, Hong Kong)
Chinese Journal of International Politics, The (Tsinghua University, Beijing)
Journal of Chinese Political Science (San Francisco State University, San Francisco)
Journal of Contemporary China (Center for China–U.S. Cooperation, University of Denver, Denver)
Journal of Current Chinese Affairs (GIGA Institute of Asian Studies, Hamburg)
Modern China (University of California, Los Angeles)
Twentieth-Century China: Official Journal of the Historical Society for Twentieth-Century China (SUNY, Buffalo)
Zeitschrift für Chinesisches Recht (Deutsch–Chinesische Juristenvereinigung, Bonn)

9.4 Further readings for individual chapters

1.1 Historical foundations:

Heilmann, Sebastian and Elizabeth J. Perry (eds.) (2011). *Mao's Invisible Hand: The Political Foundations of Adaptive Governance in China.* Harvard Contemporary China Series 17. Cambridge, MA: Harvard University Asia Center.
Womack, Brantly (ed.) (2010). *China's Rise in Historical Perspective.* Lanham, MD: Rowman & Littlefield.

1.2 How China is portrayed in Western media

Cao, Qing (2012). "Modernity and Media Portrayals of China." *Journal of Asian Pacific Communication* 22 (1): 1–21.

Richter, Carola and Sebastian Gebauer (2010). "Die China-Berichterstattung in den deutschen Medien." Berlin: Heinrich-Böll-Stiftung. November 6. https://www.boell.de/sites/default/files/Endf_Studie_China-Berichterstattung.pdf. Accessed: January 10, 2016.

1.4 Utilizing information and data from China

Crabbe, Matthew (2014). *Myth-Busting China's Numbers: Understanding and Using China's Statistics.* London: Palgrave Macmillan.

Orlik, Tom (2012). *Understanding China's Economic Indicators: Translating the Data into Investment Opportunities.* Upper Saddle River, NJ: FT Press.

2.1 Socialist organizational and ideological features

Deng, Xiaoping (1987) [1994]. "To Uphold Socialism We Must Eliminate Poverty," April 26. In: Xiaoping Deng. *Selected Works of Deng Xiaoping: Vol. III (1982–1992),* 221–223. Beijing: Foreign Languages Press.

Heilmann, Sebastian (2000). *Die Politik der Wirtschaftsreformen in China und Russland.* Mitteilungen des Instituts für Asienkunde Hamburg 317. Hamburg: Institut für Asienkunde.

Holbig, Heike (2009). "Regime Legitimacy in Contemporary China: Challenges in the Post-Jiang Era." In: Thomas Heberer and Gunter Schubert (eds.). *Regime Legitimacy in Contemporary China: Institutional Change and Stability,* 13–34. London: Routledge.

Mao, Zedong (1937) [1961]. "On Guerrilla Warfare." In: *On Guerrilla Warfare,* trans. by Samuel B. Griffith. New York: Praeger.

2.2 The constitution of the party-state

Balme, Stéphanie and Michael W. Dowdle (eds.) (2009). *Building Constitutionalism in China.* The Sciences Po Series in International Relations and Political Economy. London: Palgrave Macmillan.

Zhang, Qianfan (2012). *The Constitution of China: A Contextual Analysis.* Constitutional Systems of the World. Oxford, UK: Hart Publishing.

2.3 The Chinese Communist Party

McGregor, Richard (2010). *The Party: The Secret World of China's Communist Rulers.* New York: Harper.

Shambaugh, David L. (2008). *China's Communist Party: Atrophy and Adaptation.* Washington, DC: Woodrow Wilson Center Press; Berkeley: University of California Press.

2.4 The central government

Lieberthal, Kenneth (2003). *Governing China: From Revolution through Reform.* 2nd ed. New York: W.W. Norton.

Saich, Anthony (2015). *Governance and Politics of China.* 4th ed. Comparative Government and Politics. London: Palgrave Macmillan.

2.5 Provincial- and municipal-level governments

Donaldson, John (2010). "Provinces: Paradoxical Politics, Problematic Partners." In: Jae Ho Chung and Tao-Chiu Lam (eds.). *China's Local Administration: Traditions and Changes in the Sub-National Hierarchy,* 14–38. London: Routledge.

Zheng, Yongnian (2010a). "Central-Local Relations: The Power to Dominate." In: Joseph Fewsmith (ed.). *China Today, China Tomorrow: Domestic Politics, Economy, and Society,* 193–222. Lanham, MD: Rowman & Littlefield.

2.6 Special Administrative Regions: Hong Kong and Macau

Lam, Wai-man (2012). "Political Context." In: Wai-man Lam, Percy Luen-tim Lui, and Wilson Wai-ho Wong (eds.). *Contemporary Hong Kong Government and Politics,* 1–21. 2nd exp. ed. Hong Kong: Hong Kong University Press.

Schubert, Gunter (2013). "Das politische System Hongkongs." In: Claudia Derichs and Thomas Heberer (eds.). *Die Politischen Systeme Ostasiens: Eine Einführung,* 233–253. Wiesbaden: Springer VS.

2.7 Local governments at the county, township, and village levels

Lam, Tao-Chiu (2010). "The County System and County Governance." In: Jae Ho Chung and Tao-Chiu Lam (eds.). *China's Local Administration: Traditions and Changes in the Sub-National Hierarchy,* 149–173. London: Routledge.

Zhong, Yang (2010). "Chinese Township Government: Between a Rock and a Hard Place." In: Jae Ho Chung and Tao-Chiu Lam (eds.). *China's Local Administration: Traditions and Changes in the Sub-National Hierarchy,* 174–195. London: Routledge.

2.8 Public finance

Ma, Jun (2013). "Hidden Fiscal Risks in Local China." *Australian Journal of Public Administration* 72(3): 278–292.

Wong, Christine and Richard M. Bird (2008). "China's Fiscal System: A Work in Progress." In: Loren Brandt and Thomas G. Rawski (eds.). *China's Great Economic Transformation,* 429–466. Cambridge, UK: Cambridge University Press.

2.9 The cadre system and public administration

Brødsgaard, Kjeld Erik (ed.) (2014). *Globalization and Public Sector Reform in China.* Routledge Contemporary China Series 118. London: Routledge.

Brødsgaard, Kjeld Erik and Yongnian Zheng (eds.) (2006). *The Chinese Communist Party in Reform.* Routledge Studies on the Chinese Economy 21. London: Routledge.

2.10 Legislation, the People's Congresses, and the People's Political Consultative Conferences

Cho, Young Nam (2009). *Local People's Congresses in China: Development and Transition.* Cambridge, UK: Cambridge University Press.

Xia, Ming (2008). *The People's Congresses and Governance in China: Toward a Network Mode of Governance.* Library of Legislative Studies 22. London: Routledge.

2.11 The judiciary, police, and penal systems

Clarke, Donald C. (ed.) (2008). *China's Legal System: New Developments, New Challenges.* China Quarterly Special Issues, New Series 8. Cambridge, UK: Cambridge University Press.

Potter, Pitman B. (2013). *China's Legal System.* Cambridge, UK: Polity Press.

2.12 The military and politics

Blasko, Dennis J. (2012). *The Chinese Army Today: Tradition and Transformation for the 21st Century*. 2nd ed. London: Routledge.
Guo, Xuezhi (2012). *China's Security State: Philosophy, Evolution, and Politics*. Cambridge, UK: Cambridge University Press.

3.1 The center of power

Fewsmith, Joseph (2008). *China Since Tiananmen: From Deng Xiaoping to Hu Jintao*. 2nd ed. Cambridge Modern China Series. Cambridge, UK: Cambridge University Press.
McGregor, Richard (2010). *The Party: The Secret World of China's Communist Rulers*. New York: Harper.

3.2 Leadership generations: Revolutionaries, technocrats, and recent diversification

Li, Cheng (2013). "The Rise of the Legal Profession in the Chinese Leadership." *China Leadership Monitor* (42). http://www.hoover.org/research/rise-legal-profession-chinese-leadership. Accessed: January 10, 2016.
Shih, Lea and Moritz Rudolf (2014). "Machtzentralisierung im Eiltempo: Die Zentrale Reform-Führungsgruppe und die Neuorganisation der Entscheidungszentrale unter Xi Jinping." *MERICS China Monitor* (13). July 4. http://www.merics.org/fileadmin/templates/download/china-monitor/China_Monitor_No_13.pdf. Accessed: July 30, 2015.

3.3 The division of labor within the party leadership

Lieberthal, Kenneth (2003). *Governing China: From Revolution through Reform*. 2nd ed. New York: W.W. Norton.
Miller, Alice (2013). "The Work System of the Xi Jinping Leadership." *China Leadership Monitor* (41). http://media.hoover.org/sites/default/files/documents/CLM41AM.pdf. Accessed: January 10, 2016.

3.4 Central Leading Small Groups: Top-level decision-making under Xi Jinping

Miller, Alice (2014). "More Already on the Central Committee's Leading Small Groups." *China Leadership Monitor* (44). http://www.hoover.org/sites/default/files/research/docs/clm44am.pdf. Accessed: January 10, 2016.
Naughton, Barry (2014). "'Deepening Reform': The Organization and the Emerging Strategy." *China Leadership Monitor* (44). http://www.hoover.org/sites/default/files/research/docs/clm44bn.pdf. Accessed: June 22, 2015.

3.6 The risks of political succession and Xi Jinping's presidential style

Lieberthal, Kenneth, Cheng Li, and Keping Yu (eds.) (2014). *China's Political Development: Chinese and American Perspectives*. Washington, DC: Brookings Institution Press.
Xi, Jinping (2014). *The Governance of China*. Beijing: Foreign Languages Press.

3.7 Informal methods of exercising power

Brown, Kerry (2014). *The New Emperors: Power and the Princelings in China*. London: I.B. Tauris.
Unger, Jonathan (ed.) (2002). *The Nature of Chinese Politics: From Mao to Jiang*. Armonk, NY: M.E. Sharpe.

3.8 Between fragmented authoritarianism and a re-concentration of power

Lampton, David M. (2013). *Following the Leader: Ruling China, From Deng Xiaoping to Xi Jinping*. Berkeley: University of California Press.
Lieberthal, Kenneth G. and David M. Lampton (eds.) (1992). *Bureaucracy, Politics, and Decision Making in Post-Mao China*. Studies on China 14. Berkeley: University of California Press.

4.1 China's economic transformation

Naughton, Barry (2007). *The Chinese Economy: Transitions and Growth*. Cambridge, MA: MIT Press.

Perkins, Dwight H. (2013). *East Asian Development: Foundations and Strategies.* The Edwin O. Reischauer Lectures. Cambridge, MA: Harvard University Press.

4.2 Economic growth: Official data and alternative indicators

Crabbe, Matthew (2014). *Myth-Busting China's Numbers: Understanding and Using China's Statistics.* London: Palgrave Macmillan.
Fernald, John, Israel Malkin, and Mark Spiegel (2013). "On the Reliability of Chinese Output Figures." FRBSF Economic Letter. March 25. http://www.frbsf.org/economic-research/publications/economic-letter/2013/march/reliability-chinese-output-figures/. Accessed: July 15, 2015.

4.3 Prerequisites for Chinese economic reform

Brandt, Loren, Debin Ma, and Thomas G. Rawski (2012). *From Divergence to Convergence: Re-evaluating the History behind China's Economic Boom.* London: Department of Economic History, London School of Economics.
Naughton, Barry (2007). *The Chinese Economy: Transitions and Growth.* Cambridge, MA: MIT Press.

4.4 The political initiation and implementation of economic reform

Fan, Gang (1994). "Incremental Changes and Dual-Track Transition: Understanding the Case of China." *Economic Policy* 9(19): 99–122.
Naughton, Barry (1995). *Growing Out of the Plan: Chinese Economic Reform, 1978–1993.* Cambridge, UK: Cambridge University Press.

4.5 Government involvement in the Chinese economy

Lardy, Nicholas R. (2012). *Sustaining China's Economic Growth after the Global Financial Crisis.* Washington, DC: Peterson Institute for International Economics.
Naughton, Barry (2007). *The Chinese Economy: Transitions and Growth.* Cambridge, MA: MIT Press.

4.6 The role of government in the banking and financial systems

Allen, Franklin, Jun "JQ" Qian, Chenying Zhang, and Mengxin Zhao (2012). "China's Financial System: Opportunities and Challenges." In: Joseph P.H. Fan and Randall Morck (eds.). *Capitalizing China*, 63–143. Chicago: University of Chicago Press.

Walter, Carl E. and Fraser J. T. Howie (2011). *Red Capitalism: The Fragile Financial Foundation of China's Extraordinary Rise*. Singapore; Hoboken, NJ: John Wiley & Sons.

4.7 Economic globalization and government policy

Breslin, Shaun (2012). "Government-Industry Relations in China: A Review of the Art of the State." In: Andrew Walter and Xiaoke Zhang (eds.). *East Asian Capitalism: Diversity, Continuity, and Change*, 29–45. Oxford, UK: Oxford University Press.

Pearson, Margaret M. (2014). "China's Foreign Economic Relations and Policies." In: Saadia M. Pekkanen, John Ravenhill, and Rosemary Foot (eds.). *Oxford Handbook of the International Relations of Asia*, 160–178. Oxford, UK: Oxford University Press.

4.8 "Cadre capitalism" and corruption

Cai, Yongshun (2015). *State and Agents in China: Disciplining Government Officials*. Stanford, CA: Stanford University Press.

Wedeman, Andrew (2012). *Double Paradox: Rapid Growth and Rising Corruption in China*. Ithaca, NY: Cornell University Press.

4.9 Decentralized economic policies and regional disparities

Fan, Shenggen, Ravi Kanbur, and Xiaobo Zhang (eds.) (2009). *Regional Inequality in China: Trends, Explanations and Policy Responses*. Routledge Studies in the Modern World Economy 77. London: Routledge.

Zhang, Jun and Jamie Peck (2016). "Variegated Capitalism, Chinese Style: Regional Models, Multi-Scalar Constructions." *Regional Studies* 50(1): 52–78.

4.10 The dynamics of a developmental state

Kennedy, Scott (ed.) (2011). *Beyond the Middle Kingdom: Comparative Perspectives on China's Capitalist Transformation*. Stanford, CA: Stanford University Press.

Walter, Andrew and Xiaoke Zhang (eds.) (2012). *East Asian Capitalism: Diversity, Continuity, and Change.* Oxford, UK: Oxford University Press.

5.1 Political control and "social management"

Greenhalgh, Susan (2008). *Just One Child: Science and Policy in Deng's China.* Berkeley: University of California Press.
Wang, Mark Y., Pookong Kee, and Jia Gao (eds.) (2014). *Transforming Chinese Cities.* Routledge Contemporary China Series 116. London: Routledge.

5.2 Political controls and popular demands for civil rights

Schubert, Gunter and Anna L. Ahlers (2012). *Participation and Empowerment at the Grassroots: Chinese Village Elections in Perspective.* Challenges Facing Chinese Political Development. Lanham, MD: Lexington Books.
Shi-Kupfer, Kristin (2014c). "Menschenrechte in der Volksrepublik China: Fortschritte, Defizite, Herausforderungen." In: Doris Fischer and Michael Lackner (eds.). *Länderbericht China,* 327–350. Schriftenreihe Bd. 351. Bonn: Bundeszentrale für politische Bildung.
Svensson, Marina (2002). *Debating Human Rights in China: A Conceptual and Political History.* Lanham, MD: Rowman & Littlefield.

5.3 Rural society

Ahlers, Anna L. (2014). *Rural Policy Implementation in Contemporary China: New Socialist Countryside.* Routledge Studies on China in Transition 47. London: Routledge.
Heberer, Thomas and Wolfgang Taubmann (1998). *Chinas ländliche Gesellschaft im Umbruch: Urbanisierung und sozio-ökonomischer Wandel auf dem Lande.* Opladen; Wiesbaden: Westdeutscher Verlag.

5.4 Urban society and new social forces

Li, Peilin (ed.) (2012). *Chinese Society: Change and Transformation.* China Policy Series 24. London: Routledge.
Shi-Kupfer, Kristin and Yi Zhu (2014). "Chinesische Träume: Wohin führt die Suche nach Werteorientierungen in der Volksrepublik?" *MERICS China Monitor* (5). February 28. http://www.merics.org/fileadmin/templates/download/china-monitor/China_Monitor_No_5_gesamt.pdf. Accessed: July 10, 2015.

5.5 Social organizations and trade unions

Asche, Josephine (2008). "Vereinsrecht in der Volksrepublik China – Eine Einführung." *Zeitschrift für Chinesisches Recht* 15(3): 233–243.

Fulda, Andreas (ed.) (2015). *Civil Society Contributions to Policy Innovation in the PR China: Environment, Social Development and International Cooperation.* London: Palgrave Macmillan.

5.6 The media and public opinion

Brady, Anne-Marie (2008). *Marketing Dictatorship: Propaganda and Thought Work in Contemporary China.* Asia/Pacific/perspectives. Lanham, MD: Rowman & Littlefield.

Shirk, Susan L. (ed.) (2011). *Changing Media, Changing China.* Oxford, UK: Oxford University Press.

5.7 Ethnic and religious groups

Goossaert, Vincent and David A. Palmer (2011). *The Religious Question in Modern China.* Chicago: University of Chicago Press.

Mackerras, Colin (ed.) (2011). *Ethnic Minorities in Modern China: Critical Concepts in Asian Studies.* London: Routledge.

5.8 The potential for social unrest

Cai, Yongshun (2010). *Collective Resistance in China: Why Popular Protests Succeed or Fail.* Studies of the Walter H. Shorenstein Asia-Pacific Research Center. Stanford, CA: Stanford University Press.

Tong, Yanqi and Shaohua Lei (2014). *Social Protest in Contemporary China, 2003–2010: Transitional Pains and Regime Legitimacy.* China Policy Series 35. London: Routledge.

5.9 Political consequences of social change

Fulda, Andreas (ed.) (2015). *Civil Society Contributions to Policy Innovation in the PR China: Environment, Social Development and International Cooperation.* London: Palgrave Macmillan.

Goodman, David S.G. and Minglü Chen (eds.) (2013). *Middle Class China: Identity and Behaviour*. Cheltenham, UK: Edward Elgar.
Whyte, Martin King (2010). *Myth of the Social Volcano: Perceptions of Inequality and Distributive Injustice in Contemporary China*. Stanford, CA: Stanford University Press.

6.1 Distinctive features of the policy process

Heilmann, Sebastian (2008). "Policy Experimentation in China's Economic Rise." *Studies in Comparative International Development* 43(1): 1–26.
Heilmann, Sebastian and Oliver Melton (2013). "The Reinvention of Development Planning in China, 1993–2012." *Modern China* 39(6): 580–628.
Mok, Ka-Ho and Ray Forrest (2009). *Changing Governance and Public Policy in East Asia*. London: Routledge.

6.2 Administrative modernization and economic deregulation

Bath, Vivienne (2008). "Reducing the Role of Government: The Chinese Experiment." *Asian Journal of Comparative Law* 3(1): 9-1–9-37.
Brødsgaard, Kjeld Erik (ed.) (2014). *Globalization and Public Sector Reform in China*. Routledge Contemporary China Series 118. London: Routledge.

6.3 Internal security and justice: Abolition of "re-education through labor"

Wilson, Scott (2015). *Tigers Without Teeth: The Pursuit of Justice in Contemporary China*. Lanham, MD: Rowman & Littlefield.

6.4 Media policy: Controlling social media

Schlaeger, Jesper and Min Jiang (2014). "Official Microblogging and Social Management by Local Governments in China." *China Information* 28(2): 189–213.
Shi-Kupfer, Kristin and Yi Zhu (2013). "'V-Leute' im Rampenlicht–Chinas virtuelle Meinungsmacht und ihre Macher." *MERICS China Monitor* (1). November 11. http://www.merics.org/fileadmin/templates/download/china-monitor/2013-11-18/china-monitor-v-leute.pdf. Accessed: July 10, 2015.

6.5 Social security: State pensions for the rural population

Chan, Chak Kwan, Jinglun Yue, and David Phillips (2008). *Social Policy in China: Development and Well-Being.* Bristol, UK: Policy Press.

Stepan, Matthias (2015). "Towards State Guaranteed Old-Age Income for All: The Transformation of the Pension System in China." Dissertation. Vrije University (Amsterdam).

6.6 Macroeconomic control: Managing the impact of the global financial crisis

Langhammer, Rolf J. and Sebastian Heilmann (2010). "Managing the Crisis: A Comparative Assessment." In: Bertelsmann Stiftung (ed.). *Managing the Crisis: A Comparative Assessment of Economic Governance in 14 Countries,* 9–30. Gütersloh: Verlag Bertelsmann Stiftung.

Wong, Christine (2011). "The Fiscal Stimulus Program and Public Governance Issues in China." *OECD Journal on Budgeting* 11(3): 1–22. http://www.oecd-ilibrary. org/governance/the-fiscal-stimulus-programme-and-public-governance-issues-in-china_budget-11-5kg3nhljqrjl. Accessed: June 11, 2015.

6.7 Public budgets: The role of local-government financing platforms

Lu, Yinqiu and Tao Sun (2013). "Local Government Financing Platforms in China: A Fortune or Misfortune?" IMF Working Papers (13/243). Washington, DC: International Monetary Fund.

Ma, Jun (2013). "Hidden Fiscal Risks in Local China." *Australian Journal of Public Administration* 72(3): 278–292.

6.8 Infrastructure policy and the high-speed rail network

KPMG (2013). "Infrastructure in China: Sustaining Quality Growth." http://www.kpmg. com/CN/en/IssuesAndInsights/ArticlesPublications/documents/Infrastructure-in-China-201302.pdf. Accessed: July 5, 2015.

Swiss Rail Industry Association (2011). *China Railway Market Study: Final Report.* Zurich: Osec Business Network.

6.9 Industrial policy and investment catalogs in the automotive sector

Ahrens, Nathaniel (2013). "China's Industrial Policy Making Process." Washington, DC: CSIS Center for Strategic & International Studies. http://csis.org/files/publication/130124_Ahrens_ChinaPolicymaking_Web.pdf. Accessed: January 10, 2016.

Shih, Lea (2015). *Chinas Industriepolitik von 1978–2013: Programme, Prozesse und Beschränkungen*. Wiesbaden: Springer Fachmedien.

6.10 Innovation policy: Promoting the Internet of Things

Liu, Xielin (2009). "National Innovation Systems in Developing Countries: The Chinese National Innovation System in Transition." In: Bengt-Ake Lundvall, K.J. Joseph, Cristina Chaminade, and Jan Vang (eds.). *Handbook of Innovation Systems in Developing Countries: Building Domestic Capabilities in a Global Setting*, 119–139. Cheltenham, UK: Edward Elgar.

Mu, Rongping and Qu Wan (2008). "The Development of Science and Technology in China: A Comparison with India and the United States." *Technology in Society* 30(3–4): 319–329.

6.11 Environmental policy: Curtailing urban air pollution

Economy, Elizabeth C. (2004). *The River Runs Black: The Environmental Challenge to China's Future*. Ithaca, NY: Cornell University Press.

Shapiro, Judith (2012). *China's Environmental Challenges*. Cambridge, UK: Polity Press.

6.12 Food safety: Preventing health risks

Jia, Chenhao and David Jukes (2013). "The National Food Safety Control System of China: A Systematic Review." *Food Control* 32(1): 236–245.

Peng, Liu (2010). "Tracing and Periodizing China's Food Safety Regulation: A Study on China's Food Safety Regime Change." *Regulation and Governance* 4(2): 244–260.

6.13 Disaster management: Contingency planning and rescue programs

Chung, Jae Ho (ed.) (2012). *China's Crisis Management*. China Policy Series 20. London: Routledge.

Xue, Lan and Kaibin Zhong (2010). "Turning Danger (危) to Opportunities (机): Re-constructing China's National System for Emergency Management after 2003." In: Howard Kunreuther and Michael Useem (eds.). *Learning from Catastrophes: Strategies for Reaction and Response*, 190–210. Upper Saddle River, NJ: Pearson Education.

6.14 Foreign and security policies: Maritime rights and interests

Jakobson, Linda (2014). "China's Unpredictable Maritime Security." Lowy Institute for International Policy. December. http://www.lowyinstitute.org/files/chinas-unpredictable-maritime-security-actors_1.pdf. Accessed: July 11, 2015.
Yahuda, Michael (2013). "China's New Assertiveness in the South China Sea." *Journal of Contemporary China* 22(81): 446–459.

6.15 Urbanization policy: Experimental urban concepts

Baeumler, Axel, Ede Ijjasz-Vasquez, Shomik Mehndiratta (eds.) (2012). *Sustainable Low-Carbon City Development in China*. Washington, DC: International Bank for Reconstruction and Development.
Wu, Weiping and Piper Rae Gaubatz (2013). *The Chinese City*. London: Routledge.

6.16 Internet security: National IT independence and China's cyber policy

Chang, Amy (2014). "Warring State: China's Cybersecurity Strategy." Center for a New American Security. http://www.cnas.org/sites/default/files/publications-pdf/CNAS_WarringState_Chang_report_010615.pdf. Accessed: June 28, 2015.
Lindsay, Jon R., Tai Ming Cheung, and Derek S. Reverson (eds.) (2015). *China and Cybersecurity: Espionage, Strategy, and Politics in the Digital Domain*. Oxford, UK: Oxford University Press.

6.17 Education policy: Popularization and improvements in vocational training

Guo, Zhenyi and Stephen Lamb (2010). *International Comparisons of China's Technical and Vocational Education and Training System*. UNESCO-UNEVOC Book Series 12. Dordrecht: Springer.

Yu, Kai et al. (2012). *Tertiary Education at a Glance: China*. Global Perspectives on Higher Education 24. Rotterdam; Boston: Sense Publishers.

6.18 Mega-projects: China's South-to-North Water Transfer Project

Heggelund, Gørild (2003). *Environment and Resettlement Politics in China: The Three Gorges Project*. King's SOAS Studies in Development Geography. Aldershot, Hants, UK; Burlington, VT: Ashgate.
Moore, Scott M. (2014). "Modernisation, Authoritarianism, and the Environment: The Politics of China's South–North Water Transfer Project." *Environmental Politics* 23(6): 947–964.

6.19 Strengths, weaknesses, and special characteristics of Chinese policy making

Fewsmith, Joseph (2013). *The Logic and Limits of Political Reform in China*. Cambridge, UK: Cambridge University Press.
Heilmann, Sebastian (2010). "Economic Governance: Authoritarian Upgrading and Innovative Potential." In: Joseph Fewsmith (ed.). *China Today, China Tomorrow: Domestic Politics, Economy, and Society*, 109–126. Lanham, MD: Rowman & Littlefield.

7.1 Erosion of the party-state and restorative efforts

Lieberthal, Kenneth, Cheng Li, and Keping Yu (eds.) (2014). *China's Political Development: Chinese and American Perspectives*. Washington, DC: Brookings Institution Press.
Shambaugh, David L. (2008). *China's Communist Party: Atrophy and Adaptation*. Washington, DC: Woodrow Wilson Center Press; Berkeley: University of California Press.

7.2 Foundations of Communist Party rule

Göbel, Christian (2013). "The Innovation Dilemma and the Consolidation of Autocratic Regimes." *SSRN Journal (SSRN Electronic Journal)*. January 30. http://papers.ssrn.com/sol3/papers.cfm?abstract_id=2287539. Accessed: January 10, 2016.

Heilmann, Sebastian (2010). "Economic Governance: Authoritarian Upgrading and Innovative Potential." In: Joseph Fewsmith (ed.). *China Today, China Tomorrow: Domestic Politics, Economy, and Society*, 109–126. Lanham, MD: Rowman & Littlefield.

7.3 The underlying fragility of the Chinese political order

Fewsmith, Joseph (2013). *The Logic and Limits of Political Reform in China.* Cambridge, UK: Cambridge University Press.
Taleb, Nassim N. and Gregory F. Treverton (2015). "The Calm Before the Storm: Why Volatility Signals Stability, and Vice Versa." *Foreign Affairs* 94(1): 86–95.

7.4 Scenarios for political development

Lynch, Daniel C. (2015). *China's Futures: PRC Elites Debate Economics, Politics, and Foreign Policy.* Stanford, CA: Stanford University Press.

7.5 The potential for gradual democratic evolution

Nathan, Andrew J., Larry Diamond, and Marc F. Plattner (eds.) (2013). *Will China Democratize?* Baltimore: Johns Hopkins University Press.

7.6 Is China a possible developmental model for other countries?

Halper, Stefan (2010). *The Beijing Consensus: How China's Authoritarian Model Will Dominate the Twenty-First Century.* New York: Basic Books.
Jacques, Martin (2012). *When China Rules the World: The End of the Western World and the Birth of a New Global Order.* 2nd ed. London: Penguin.

7.7 Implications for international interactions with China

Heilmann, Sebastian and Dirk H. Schmidt (2014). *China's Foreign Political and Economic Relations: An Unconventional Global Power.* Lanham, MD: Rowman & Littlefield.

9.5 Bibliography

Abels, Sigrun (2006). "Medien, Markt und politische Kontrolle in der Volksrepublik China: Eine Untersuchung zur Rolle der Medien seit Beginn der Reformära (1979–2005) unter besonderer Berücksichtigung des Hörfunks." Dissertation. Ruhr-Universität (Bochum). http://www-brs.ub.ruhr-uni-bochum.de/netahtml/HSS/Diss/AbelsSigrun/diss.pdf. Accessed: January 10, 2016.

Acemoglu, Daron and James A. Robinson (2006). *Economic Origins of Dictatorship and Democracy.* Cambridge, UK: Cambridge University Press.

Acemoglu, Daron and James A. Robinson (2012). *Why Nations Fail: The Origins of Power, Prosperity and Poverty.* New York: Crown.

Ahlers, Anna L. (2014a). "Kommunalpolitik in China: Warum wir chinesische Politik erst verstehen, wenn wir auch die lokale Ebene in den Blick nehmen." *MERICS China Monitor* (10). June 18. http://www.merics.org/fileadmin/templates/download/china-monitor/China_Monitor_No_10.pdf. Accessed: June 6, 2015.

Ahlers, Anna L. (2014b). "Lokales Regieren und administrative Interessenvermittlung in China." In: Hubert Heinelt (ed.). *Modernes Regieren in China,* 89–115. Baden-Baden: Nomos.

Ahlers, Anna L. (2014c). *Rural Policy Implementation in Contemporary China: New Socialist Countryside.* Routledge Studies on China in Transition 47. London: Routledge.

Ahlers, Anna L. and Gunter Schubert (2015). "Effective Policy Implementation in China's Local State." *Modern China* 41(4): 372–405.

Ahrens, Nathaniel (2013). "China's Industrial Policy Making Process." Washington, DC: CSIS Center for Strategic & International Studies. http://csis.org/files/publication/130124_Ahrens_ChinaPolicymaking_Web.pdf. Accessed: January 10, 2016.

Allen, Franklin, Jun "QJ" Qian, Chenying Zhang, and Mengxin Zhao (2012). "China's Financial System: Opportunities and Challenge." In: Joseph P.H. Fan and Randall Morck (eds.). *Capitalizing China,* 63–143. Chicago: University of Chicago Press.

Alpermann, Björn (2001). *Der Staat im Dorf: Dörfliche Selbstverwaltung in China*. Mitteilungen des Instituts für Asienkunde Hamburg 341. Hamburg: Institut für Asienkunde.

Anderson, Severn (2005). *Hong Kong 2005: Changes in Leadership and Issues for Congress*. July 15. Washington, DC: Congressional Research Service. http://fpc.state. gov/documents/organization/57790.pdf. Accessed: January 10, 2016.

Asche, Josephine (2008). "Vereinsrecht in der Volksrepublik China–Eine Einführung." *Zeitschrift für Chinesisches Recht* 15(3): 233–243.

Baeumler, Axel, Ede Ijjasz-Vasquez, Shomik Mehndiratta (eds.) (2012). *Sustainable Low-Carbon City Development in China*. Washington, DC: International Bank for Reconstruction and Development.

Baidu Tieba 百度贴吧 (2013). "最近网络上出了一个最新中国社会的阶层划分模型, 很有意思" (A new class module for Chinese society now to be found on the Internet...very interesting). November 23. http://tieba.baidu.com/p/2720663675. Accessed: April 27, 2015.

Balcerowicz, Leszek (1995). "Understanding Postcommunist Transitions." In: Larry Diamond and Marc Plattner (eds.). *Economic Reform and Democracy*, 86–100. Baltimore: Johns Hopkins University Press.

Balme, Stéphanie and Michael W. Dowdle (eds.) (2009). *Building Constitutionalism in China*. The Sciences Po Series in International Relations and Political Economy. London: Palgrave Macmillan.

Balzano, John (2012). "China's Food Safety Law: Administrative Innovation and Institutional Design in Comparative Perspective." *Asian-Pacific Law & Policy Journal* 13(2): 23–80.

Banister, Judith, David E. Bloom, and Larry Rosenberg (2010). "Population Aging and Economic Growth in China." Program on the Global Demography of Aging Working Paper 53. http://www.hsph.harvard.edu/program-on-the-global-demography-of-aging/WorkingPapers/2010/PGDA_WP_53.pdf. Accessed: July 31, 2015.

Barboza, David (2012). "Billions in Hidden Riches for Family of Chinese Leader." *The New York Times*. October 25. http://www.nytimes.com/2012/10/26/business/global/family-of-wen-jiabao-holds-a-hidden-fortune-in-china.html. Accessed: July 28, 2015.

Barboza, David and Sharon LaFraniere (2012). "'Princelings' in China Use Family Ties to Gain Riches." *The New York Times*. May 17. http://www.nytimes.com/2012/05/18/world/asia/china-princelings-using-family-ties-to-gain-riches.html. Accessed: July 28, 2015.

Bateson, Andrew (2010). "A Window onto Local Government Debt in Tianjin." *The Wall Street Journal*. China Realtime. June 9. http://blogs.wsj.com/chinarealtime/2010/06/09/a-window-onto-local-government-debt-in-tianjin/. Accessed: July 30, 2015.

Bath, Vivienne (2008). "Reducing the Role of Government: The Chinese Experiment." *Asian Journal of Comparative Law* 3(1): 9-1–9-37.

Baum, Richard (1994). *Burying Mao: Chinese Politics in the Age of Deng Xiaoping*. Princeton, NJ: Princeton University Press.

Bell, Daniel A. (2008). *China's New Confucianism: Politics and Everyday Life in a Changing Society*. Princeton, NJ: Princeton University Press.

Bell, Daniel A. (2015). *The China Model: Political Meritocracy and the Limits of Democracy*. Princeton, NJ: Princeton University Press.

Bernstein, Thomas P. and Xiaobo Lü (2003). *Taxation without Representation in Contemporary Rural China*. Cambridge Modern China Series. Cambridge, UK: Cambridge University Press.

Billioud, Sébastien (2007). "Confucianism, 'Cultural Tradition,' and Official Discourses in China at the Start of the New Century." *China Perspectives* (3): 50–64, 161.

Blasko, Dennis J. (2012). *The Chinese Army Today: Tradition and Transformation for the 21st Century*. 2nd ed. London: Routledge.

Blechinger-Talcott, Verena, Christiane Frantz, and Mark Thompson (eds.) (2006). *Politik in Japan: System, Reformprozesse und Aussenpolitik im internationalen Vergleich*. Frankfurt am Main: Campus.

Bo, Zhiyue (2010). *China's Elite Politics: Governance and Democratization*. Series on Contemporary China 19. Singapore: World Scientific.

Brady, Anne-Marie (2008). *Marketing Dictatorship: Propaganda and Thought Work in Contemporary China*. Asia/Pacific/perspectives. Lanham, MD: Rowman & Littlefield.

Brandt, Loren, Debin Ma, and Thomas G. Rawski (2012). *From Divergence to Convergence: Re-evaluating the History behind China's Economic Boom.* London: Department of Economic History, London School of Economics.

Brandt, Loren and Thomas G. Rawski (eds.) (2008). *China's Great Economic Transformation.* Cambridge, UK: Cambridge University Press.

Bremmer, Ian (2010). *The End of the Free Market: Who Wins the War between States and Corporations?* New York: Portfolio.

Breslin, Shaun (2012). "Government-Industry Relations in China: A Review of the Art of the State." In: Andrew Walter and Xiaoke Zhang (eds.). *East Asian Capitalism: Diversity, Continuity, and Change,* 29–45. Oxford, UK: Oxford University Press.

Brie, Michael (1996). *Transformationsgesellschaften zwischen Institutionenbildung und Wandel des Informellen.* Arbeitspapier AGTRAP 96/8. Max-Planck-Gesellschaft. Arbeitsgruppe Transformationsprozesse. Berlin: Humboldt-Universität.

Brødsgaard, Kjeld Erik (ed.) (2014). *Globalization and Public Sector Reform in China.* Routledge Contemporary China Series 118. London: Routledge.

Brødsgaard, Kjeld Erik and Gang Chen (2014). "Public Sector Reform in China: Who is Losing Out?" In: Kjeld Erik Brødsgaard (ed.). *Globalization and Public Sector Reform in China,* 77–99. London: Routledge.

Brødsgaard, Kjeld Erik and Yongnian Zheng (eds.) (2006). *The Chinese Communist Party in Reform.* Routledge Studies on the Chinese Economy 21. London: Routledge.

Brook, Timothy (1998). *Quelling the People: The Military Suppression of the Beijing Democracy Movement.* Stanford, CA: Stanford University Press.

Brook, Timothy and B. Michael Frolic (1997). *Civil Society in China.* Studies on Contemporary China. Armonk, NY: M.E. Sharpe.

Brown, Archie (2009). *The Rise and Fall of Communism.* London: Bodley Head.

Brown, Kerry (2014). *The New Emperors: Power and the Princelings in China.* London: I.B. Tauris.

Bu, Yuanshi (2009). *Einführung in das Recht Chinas.* Juristische Schulung/Schriftenreihe 191. Munich: Beck.

Bunce, Valerie (1999). *Subversive Institutions: The Design and the Destruction of Socialism and the State*. Cambridge Studies in Comparative Politics. Cambridge, UK: Cambridge University Press.

Burns, John P. (2006). "The Chinese Communist Party's Nomenklatura System as a Leadership Selection Mechanism: An Evaluation." In: Kjeld Erik Brødsgaard and Yong-nian Zheng (eds.). *The Chinese Communist Party in Reform,* 33–58. London: Routledge.

Burns, John P. (2007). "Civil Service Reform in China." *OECD Journal on Budgeting* 7(1): 1–25.

Cai, Yongshun (2010). *Collective Resistance in China: Why Popular Protests Succeed or Fail*. Studies of the Walter H. Shorenstein Asia-Pacific Research Center. Stanford, CA: Stanford University Press.

Cai, Yongshun (2015). *State and Agents in China: Disciplining Government Officials*. Stanford, CA: Stanford University Press.

Cao, Qing (2012). "Modernity and Media Portrayals of China." *Journal of Asian Pacific Communication* 22(1): 1–21.

CATR [China Academy of Telecommunication Research] 工业和信息信化部电信研究院 (2014). 物联网白皮书(2014年) (White paper on Internet of Things [2014]). Beijing: CATR. May. http://www.miit.gov.cn/n11293472/n11293832/n15214847/n15218338/n16046559.files/n16046558.pdf. Accessed: January 10, 2016.

CCID Consulting 赛迪顾问股份有限公司 (2013). 物联网产业发展及应用实践 (Development and practical use of the Internet of Things industry). Beijing: Dianzi gongye chubanshe.

CCP 中国共产党 (2012). "中国共产党章程" (Constitution of the CCP). November 14. http://www.gov.cn/jrzg/2012-11/18/content_2269219.htm. Accessed: July 4, 2015.

CCP CC General Office 中共中央办公厅 (2003). "关于加强信息安全保障工作的意见" (Opinions on strengthening work on information security). Zhongbanfa [2003] 27 hao. http://www.360doc.com/content/14/0423/10/93013_371341672.shtml. Accessed: July 14, 2015.

CCP CC General Office 中共中央办公厅 (2013a). "Communiqué on the Current State of the Ideological Sphere: A Notice from the Central Committee of the Communist Party of China's General Office." April 23. http://www.chinafile.com/document-9-chinafile-translation. Accessed: June 9, 2015.

CCP CC General Office 中共中央办公厅 (ed.) (2013b). "关于培育和践行社会主义核心价值观的意见" (Opinions on the cultivation and practice of socialist core values). December 23. http://www.gov.cn/jrzg/2013-12/23/content_2553019.htm. Accessed: June 6, 2015.

CCP CC Organization Department 中共中央组织部 (1999). 党政领导干部统计资料汇编1954–1998 (Collection of statistical data on party and government leading cadres 1954–1998). Beijing: Dangjian duwu chubanshe.

CCP CC Organization Department 中共中央组织部 (2004). 中国共产党历届中央委员大辞典, 1921–2003 (Dictionary of previous members of the Chinese Communist Party Central Committee, 1921–2003). Beijing: Zhonggong dangshi chubanshe.

CCP CC Organization Department, Personnel Department 中共中央组织部人事部 (ed.) (1999). 中国干部统计五十年: 1949–1998年干部统计资料汇编 (Fifty years of statistical materials on cadres: 1949–1998 collection of statistical materials on cadres). Beijing: Dangjian duwu chubanshe.

Chan, Anita (2001). *China's Workers under Assault: The Exploitation of Labor in a Globalizing Economy*. Asia and the Pacific. Armonk, NY: M.E. Sharpe.

Chan, Chak Kwan, Jinglun Yue, and David Phillips (2008). *Social Policy in China: Development and Well-Being*. Bristol, UK: Policy Press.

Chan, Chris King-chi and Pun Ngai (2009). "The Making of a New Working Class? A Study of Collective Actions of Migrant Workers in South China." *The China Quarterly* (198): 287–303.

Chang, Amy (2014). "Warring State: China's Cybersecurity Strategy." Center for a New American Security. http://www.cnas.org/sites/default/files/publications-pdf/CNAS_WarringState_Chang_report_010615.pdf. Accessed: June 28, 2015.

Chen, Jie and Bruce J. Dickson (2010). *Allies of the State: China's Private Entrepreneurs and Democratic Change*. Cambridge, MA: Harvard University Press.

Chen, Jinhua 陈锦华 et al. (eds.) (2012). 中国模式与中国制度 (The China model and the Chinese system). Beijing: Renmin chubanshe.

Cheong, Tsun Se and Yanrui Wu (2013). "Inequality and Crime Rates in China." University of Western Australia. Discussion Paper (13.11). http://www.business.uwa.edu.au/__data/assets/pdf_file/0005/2275763/13-11-Inequality-and-Crime-Rates-in-China.pdf. Accessed: July 10, 2015.

Chien, Shiuh-Shen (2013). "Chinese Eco-Cities: A Perspective of Land-Speculation-Oriented Local Entrepreneurialism." *China Information* 27(2): 173–196.

China Academy of Governance 国家行政学院电子政务研究中心 (2014). "2013年中国政务微博客评估报告" (Evaluation report of the Chinese government on micro blogging accounts, 2013). April. http://www.egovernment.gov.cn/art/2014/4/5/art_477_722.html. Accessed: July 31, 2015.

Cho, Young Nam (2009). *Local People's Congresses in China: Development and Transition.* Cambridge, UK: Cambridge University Press.

Chung, Jae Ho (2000). *Central Control and Local Discretion in China: Leadership and Implementation During Post-Mao Decollectivization.* Studies on Contemporary China. Oxford, UK: Oxford University Press.

Chung, Jae Ho (2010). "The Evolving Hierarchy of China's Local Administration: Tradition and Change." In: Jae Ho Chung and Tao-Chiu Lam (eds.). *China's Local Administration: Traditions and Changes in the Sub-National Hierarchy,* 1–13. China Policy Series 122. London: Routledge.

Chung, Jae Ho (ed.) (2012). *China's Crisis Management.* China Policy Series 20. London: Routledge.

Chung, Jae Ho and Tao-Chiu Lam (eds.) (2010). *China's Local Administration: Traditions and Changes in the Sub-National Hierarchy.* China Policy Series 122. London: Routledge.

Civil Service Network 中央公务员考试网 (2013a). "2014年国家公务员考试参考人数110万余人40万人弃考" (National civil-service exam 2014: Participants 1.1 million, 400,000 did not attend). November 11. http://www.chinagwyw.org/zhongyang/gkzx/248407.html. Accessed: April 30, 2015.

Civil Service Network 中央公务员考试网 (2013b). "2003–2013年国家公务员考试考情汇总" (Overview of the national civil-service exams 2003–2013). March 7. http://www.chinagwyw.org/zhongyang/gkzx/4929.html. Accessed: April 30, 2015.

Clarke, Donald C. (2008). *China's Legal System: New Developments, New Challenges.* China Quarterly Special Issues, New Series 8. Cambridge, UK: Cambridge University Press.

Collins, Gabe (2015). "Beijing's Xinjiang Policy: Striking Too Hard?" *The Diplomat.* January 23. http://thediplomat.com/2015/01/beijings-xinjiang-policy-striking-too-hard/. Accessed: June 19, 2015.

Comprehensive Survey Team on the Chinese Social Situation中国社会状况综合调查项目组 (2013). "中国梦是每个中国人的梦：2013 年中国社会状况调查报告" (The China dream is the dream of every Chinese: China social survey report 2013). In: Li Peilin 李培林, Chen Guangjin 陈光金, and Zhang Yi 张翼 (eds.). 2014 年中国社会形势分析与预测 (Analysis and forecast of China's society 2014), 106–129. 社会蓝皮书 (Blue book on Chinese society). Beijing: Shehui kexue wenxian chubanshe.

Crabbe, Matthew (2014). *Myth-Busting China's Numbers: Understanding and Using China's Statistics.* London: Palgrave Macmillan.

Credit Suisse (2014). "Global Wealth Report 2014." https://publications.credit-suisse.com/tasks/render/file/?fileID=60931FDE-A2D2-F568-B041B58C5EA591A4. Accessed: July 10, 2015.

Cui, Baoguo 崔保国 (ed.) (2009). 2009 中国传媒产业发展报告 (Report on the development of China's media industry 2009).传媒蓝皮书 (Blue book on China's media). Beijing: Shehui kexue wenxian chubanshe.

Cui, Baoguo 崔保国 (ed.) (2015). 2015 中国传媒产业发展报告 (Report on the development of China's media industry 2015).传媒蓝皮书 (Blue book on China's media). Beijing: Shehui kexue wenxian chubanshe.

deLisle, Jacques and Avery Goldstein (eds.) (2014). *China's Challenges.* Philadelphia: University of Pennsylvania Press.

Deng, Xiaoping (1987) [1994]. "To Uphold Socialism We Must Eliminate Poverty." April 26. In: Xiaoping Deng. *Selected Works of Deng Xiaoping: Vol. III (1982–1992)*, 221–223. Beijing: Foreign Languages Press.

Deng, Yanhua and Guobin Yang (2013). "Pollution and Protest in China: Environmental Mobilization in Context." *The China Quarterly* (214): 321–336.

Derichs, Claudia and Thomas Heberer (eds.) (2003). *Einführung in die politischen Systeme Ostasiens: VR China, Hongkong, Japan, Nordkorea, Süd Korea, Taiwan.* Opladen: Leske + Budrich.

Derichs, Claudia and Thomas Heberer (eds.) (2013). *Die Politischen Systeme Ostasiens: Eine Einführung.* 3rd ed. Wiesbaden: Springer VS.

Diamond, Larry (1999). *Developing Democracy: Toward Consolidation.* Baltimore: Johns Hopkins University Press.

Diamond, Larry (2002). "Thinking About Hybrid Regimes." *Journal of Democracy* 13(2): 21–35.

Diamond, Larry (2012). "China and East Asian Democracy: The Coming Wave." *Journal of Democracy* 23(1): 5–13.

Diamond, Larry and Marc F. Plattner (eds.) (1995). *Economic Reform and Democracy.* Journal of Democracy Book. Baltimore: Johns Hopkins University Press.

Diamond, Larry et al. (eds.) (1997). *Consolidating the Third Wave Democracies: Regional Challenges.* Journal of Democracy Book. Baltimore: Johns Hopkins University Press.

Dickson, Bruce J. (2003). *Red Capitalists in China: The Party, Private Entrepreneurs, and Prospects for Political Change.* Cambridge Modern China Series. Cambridge, UK: Cambridge University Press.

Dickson, Bruce J. (2008). *Wealth into Power: The Communist Party's Embrace of China's Private Sector.* Cambridge, UK: Cambridge University Press.

Dikötter, Frank (2010). *Mao's Great Famine: The History of China's Most Devastating Catastrophe, 1958–62.* London: Bloomsbury.

Dillon, Michael (2004). *Xinjiang: China's Muslim Far Northwest.* Durham East-Asia Series. London: RoutledgeCurzon.

Ding, Xueliang 丁学良 (ed.) (2011). 中国模式: 赞成与反对 (The "Chinese model": Pros and cons). Hong Kong: Oxford University Press.

Dixon, John (1981). *The Chinese Welfare System, 1949–1979*. New York: Praeger.

Dollar, David and Bert Hofman (2008). "Intergovernmental Fiscal Reforms, Expenditure Assignment, and Governance." In: Jiwei Lou and Shuilin Wang (eds.). *Public Finance in China: Reform and Growth for a Harmonious Society,* 39–51. Washington, DC: World Bank.

Domenach, Jean-Luc (1995). *Der vergessene Archipel: Gefängnisse und Lager in der Volksrepublik China*. Hamburg: Hamburger Edition.

Donaldson, John (2010). "Provinces: Paradoxical Politics, Problematic Partners." In: Jae Ho Chung and Tao-Chiu Lam (eds.). *China's Local Administration: Traditions and Changes in the Sub-National Hierarchy,* 14–38. London: Routledge.

Duckett, Jane (2003). "Bureaucratic Institutions and Interests in the Making of China's Social Policy." *Public Administration Quarterly* 27(1/2): 210–237.

Duihua Foundation (2014). "China Executed 2,400 People in 2013." http://duihua. org/wp/?page_id=9270. Accessed: January 28, 2016.

Eberhard, Wolfram (1980). *Geschichte Chinas*. 3rd ed. Stuttgart: Alfred Kröner.

Economist, The (2014). "Bridging the Fiscal Chasm: Fancy Infrastructure is One Example of Local-Government Largesse. Which Province is Deepest in Debt as a Result?" February 22. http://www.economist.com/news/china/21596991-fancy-infrastructure-one-example-local-government-largesse-which-province-deepest-debt. Accessed: November 27, 2014.

Economist, The (2015). "The Critical Masses: Officials Increasingly Ask People a Once Taboo Question: What They Think." April 11. http://www.economist.com/news/china/21648053-officials-increasingly-ask-people-once-taboo-question-what-they-think-critical-masses. Accessed: January 10, 2016.

Economy, Elizabeth C. (2004). *The River Runs Black: The Environmental Challenge to China's Future*. A Council on Foreign Relations Book. Ithaca, NY: Cornell University Press.

Emergency Response Law of the PRC 中华人民共和国突发事件应对法 (2007). August 30. http://www.gov.cn/flfg/2007-08/30/content_732593.htm. Accessed: July 9, 2015.

Ernst, Dieter and Barry Naughton (2008). "China's Emerging Industrial Economy: Insights from the IT Industry." In: Christopher A. McNally (ed.). *China's Emergent Political Economy: Capitalism in the Dragon's Lair,* 39–59. London: Routledge.

ETIRI [Electronic Technology Information Research Institute] 工业和信息化部电子科学技术情报研究所 (2013). 2013 中国物联网发展报告 (Report on the development of China's Internet of Things 2013). Beijing: ETIRI. http://cac.gov.cn/files/pdf/2013zgwlwfzbg.pdf. Accessed: January 10, 2016.

Fan, Gang (1994). "Incremental Changes and Dual-Track Transition: Understanding the Case of China." *Economic Policy* 9(19): 99–122.

Fan, Shenggen, Ravi Kanbur, and Xiaobo Zhang (eds.) (2009). *Regional Inequality in China: Trends, Explanations and Policy Responses.* Routledge Studies in the Modern World Economy 77. London: Routledge.

Feng, Wang, Yong Cai, and Baochang Gu (2013). "Population, Policy, and Politics: How Will History Judge China's One-Child Policy?" *Population and Development Review* 38(S1): 115–129.

Fernald, John, Israel Malkin, and Mark Spiegel (2013). "On the Reliability of Chinese Output Figures." FRBSF Economic Letter. March 25. http://www.frbsf.org/economic-research/publications/economic-letter/2013/march/reliability-chinese-output-figures/. Accessed: July 15, 2015.

Fewsmith, Joseph (2008). *China Since Tiananmen: From Deng Xiaoping to Hu Jintao.* 2nd ed. Cambridge Modern China Series. Cambridge, UK: Cambridge University Press.

Fewsmith, Joseph (ed.) (2010). *China Today, China Tomorrow: Domestic Politics, Economy, and Society.* Lanham, MD: Rowman & Littlefield.

Fewsmith, Joseph (2013). *The Logic and Limits of Political Reform in China.* Cambridge, UK: Cambridge University Press.

Fischer, Doris and Michael Lackner (eds.) (2014). *Länderbericht China.* Schriftenreihe Bd. 351. Bonn: Bundeszentrale für politische Bildung.

Fortune (2015). "Fortune Global 500 2015." http://fortune.com/global500/. Accessed: January 10, 2016.

Fulda, Andreas (ed.) (2015). *Civil Society Contributions to Policy Innovation in the PR China: Environment, Social Development and International Cooperation*. London: Palgrave Macmillan.

Gandhi, Jennifer (2008). *Political Institutions under Dictatorship*. Cambridge, UK: Cambridge University Press.

Gao, Jie (2010). "Hitting the Target but Missing the Point: The Rise of Non-Mission-Based Targets in Performance Measurement of Chinese Local Governments." *Administration & Society* 42(1): S56–S76.

Garnaut, Ross, Cai Fang, and Ligang Song (2013). "China's New Strategy for Long-Term Growth and Development: Imperatives and Implications." In: Ross Garnaut, Cai Fang, and Ligang Song (eds.). *China: A New Model for Growth and Development*. Canberra: ANU E Press.

Geall, Sam (ed.) (2013). *China and the Environment: The Green Revolution*. London; New York: Zed Books.

Gernet, Jacques (1996). *A History of Chinese Civilization*. 2nd ed. Cambridge, UK: Cambridge University Press.

Gierow, Hauke Johannes (2014a). "Chinas Cyber Security (I): Divergenzen hinsichtlich Informationskontrolle, Sicherheitsstandards und Industriepolitik als Herausforderungen für das deutsche China-Engagement." *MERICS China Monitor* (19). October 8. http://www.merics.org/fileadmin/templates/download/china-monitor/China_Monitor_No_19.pdf. Accessed: January 10, 2016.

Gierow, Hauke Johannes (2014b). "Cyber Security in China: New Political Leadership Focuses on Boosting National Security." *MERICS China Monitor* (20). December. http://www.merics.org/fileadmin/templates/download/china-monitor/China_Monitor_No_20.pdf. Accessed: January 10, 2016.

Gill, Graeme (1994). *The Collapse of a Single-Party System: The Disintegration of the CPSU*. Cambridge Russian, Soviet and Post-Soviet Studies 94. Cambridge, UK: Cambridge University Press.

Göbel, Christian (2013). "The Innovation Dilemma and the Consolidation of Autocratic Regimes." June 30. University of Vienna and Lund University.

Göbel, Christian (2016). "Accountable Autocrats? E-Government, Empowerment and Control in China." Work in Progress.

Godement, François (2012). *Que veut la Chine? De Mao au Capitalisme.* Paris: Odile Jacob.

Godement, François (2014). "China on Asia's Mind." European Council on Foreign Relations. September 18. http://www.ecfr.eu/page/-/ECFR112_ASIA_BRIEF.pdf. Accessed: January 10, 2016.

Gong, Sen (2003). "The State and Pension Policy Instability in the People's Republic of China." Dissertation. University of Sheffield (UK).

Goodburn, Charlotte (2014). "The End of the Hukou System? Not Yet." China Policy Institute Policy Paper 2. http://www.nottingham.ac.uk/cpi/documents/policy-papers/cpi-policy-paper-2014-no-2-goodburn.pdf. Accessed: July 15, 2015.

Goodman, David S.G. (2014). *Class in Contemporary China.* China Today Series. Cambridge, UK: Polity Press.

Goodman, David S.G. and Minglü Chen (eds.) (2013). *Middle Class China: Identity and Behaviour.* Cheltenham, UK: Edward Elgar.

Goodrich, Jimmy (2012). "Chinese Civilian Cybersecurity: Stakeholders, Strategies, and Policy." In: Jon R. Lindsay (ed.). *China and Cybersecurity: Political, Economic, and Strategic Dimensions,* 5–7. Report from Workshops held at the University of California, San Diego. April. https://www.usnwc.edu/Academics/Faculty/Derek-Reveron/Documents/China-and-Cybersecurity-Workshop-Report-final.aspx. Accessed: January 10, 2016.

Goossaert, Vincent and David A. Palmer (2011). *The Religious Question in Modern China.* Chicago: University of Chicago Press.

Greenhalgh, Susan (2008). *Just One Child: Science and Policy in Deng's China.* Berkeley: University of California Press.

Greenstein, Fred I. and Nelson W. Polsby (eds.) (1975). *Handbook of Political Science, Vol. 3: Macro-political Theory.* Reading, MA: Addison-Wesley.

Guo, Xuezhi (2012). *China's Security State: Philosophy, Evolution, and Politics.* Cambridge, UK: Cambridge University Press.

Guo, Zhenyi and Stephen Lamb (2010). *International Comparisons of China's Technical and Vocational Education and Training System*. UNESCO-UNEVOC Book Series 12. Dordrecht: Springer.

Halper, Stefan A. (2010). *The Beijing Consensus: How China's Authoritarian Model Will Dominate the Twenty-First Century*. New York: Basic Books.

Hanitzsch, Thomas et al. (2011). "Mapping Journalism Across Nations: A Comparative Study of 18 Countries." *Journalism Studies* 12(3): 273–293.

Hansen, Mette Halskov and T. E. Woronov (2013). "Demanding and Resisting Vocational Education: A Comparative Study of Schools in Rural and Urban China." *Comparative Education* 49(2): 242–259.

Hao, Shiyuan (2012). "Ethnicities and Ethnic Relations." In: Peilin Li (ed.). *Chinese Society: Change and Transformation,* 86–107. China Policy Series 25. London: Routledge.

Hao, Yan (2012). "The Reform and Modernization of Vocational Education and Training in China." Discussion Paper (SP III 2012-304). Berlin: Wissenschaftszentrum Berlin für Sozialforschung. February. http://bibliothek.wzb.eu/pdf/2012/iii12-304.pdf. Accessed: May 28, 2015.

Hasegawa, Tsuyoshi (1992). "The Connection Between Political and Economic Reform in Communist Regimes." In: Gilbert Rozman, with Seizaburō Satō and Gerald Segal (eds.). *Dismantling Communism: Common Causes and Regional Variations,* 59–117. Washington, DC: Woodrow Wilson Center Press; Baltimore: Johns Hopkins University Press.

He, Baogang, Brian Galligan, and Takeshi Inogushi (eds.) (2007). *Federalism in Asia*. Cheltenham, UK: Edward Elgar.

Heberer, Thomas (2003). "Das politische System der VR China im Prozess des Wandels." In: Claudia Derichs and Thomas Heberer (eds.). *Einführung in die politischen Systeme Ostasiens,* 19–121. Opladen: Leske + Budrich.

Heberer, Thomas (2013). "Das politische System der VR China im Prozess des Wandels." In: Claudia Derichs and Thomas Heberer (eds.). *Die Politischen Systeme Ostasiens: Eine Einführung,* 39–231. Wiesbaden: Springer VS.

Heberer, Thomas and Wolfgang Taubmann (1998). *Chinas ländliche Gesellschaft im Umbruch: Urbanisierung und sozio-ökonomischer Wandel auf dem Lande.* Opladen; Wiesbaden: Westdeutscher Verlag.

Heep, Sandra (2014). *China in Global Finance: Domestic Financial Repression and International Financial Power.* Cham: Springer International Publishing.

Heep, Sandra (2015). "Marketisation under the Party's Command: An Interim Balance of the Economic Reforms since the Third Plenum." *MERICS China Monitor* (27). http://www.merics.org/fileadmin/user_upload/downloads/China-Monitor/China_Monitor_No_27_Reform_Progress_Economy.pdf. Accessed: January 10, 2016.

Heggelund, Gørild (2004). *Environment and Resettlement Politics in China: The Three Gorges Project.* King's SOAS Studies in Development Geography. Aldershot, Hants, UK; Burlington, VT: Ashgate.

Heilmann, Sebastian (1996). *Das politische System der VR China im Wandel.* Mitteilungen des Instituts für Asienkunde Hamburg 265. Hamburg: Institut für Asienkunde.

Heilmann, Sebastian (2000). *Die Politik der Wirtschaftsreformen in China und Russland.* Mitteilungen des Instituts für Asienkunde Hamburg 317. Hamburg: Institut für Asienkunde.

Heilmann, Sebastian (2002). *Das politische System der Volksrepublik China.* Wiesbaden: Westdeutscher Verlag.

Heilmann, Sebastian (2004). *Das politische System der Volksrepublik China.* 2nd rvsd. ed. Wiesbaden: VS Verlag für Sozialwissenschaften.

Heilmann, Sebastian (2006). "Das Modell des ostasiatischen Entwicklungsstaates in der Revision." In: Verena Blechinger-Talcott, Christiane Frantz, and Mark R. Thompson (eds.). *Politik in Japan: System, Reformprozesse und Aussenpolitik im internationalen Vergleich,* 103–116. Frankfurt am Main: Campus.

Heilmann, Sebastian (2008). "Policy Experimentation in China's Economic Rise." *Studies in Comparative International Development* 43(1): 1–26.

Heilmann, Sebastian (2010). "Economic Governance: Authoritarian Upgrading and Innovative Potential." In: Joseph Fewsmith (ed.). *China Today, China Tomorrow: Domestic Politics, Economy, and Society,* 109–126. Lanham, MD: Rowman & Littlefield.

Heilmann, Sebastian (2011). "Making Plans for Markets: Policies for the Long-Term in China." *Harvard Asia Quarterly* 13(2): 33–40.

Heilmann, Sebastian and Oliver Melton (2013). "The Reinvention of Development Planning in China, 1993–2012." *Modern China* 39(6): 580–628.

Heilmann, Sebastian and Elizabeth J. Perry (eds.) (2011). *Mao's Invisible Hand: The Political Foundations of Adaptive Governance in China.* Harvard Contemporary China Series 17. Cambridge, MA: Harvard University Asia Center.

Heilmann, Sebastian, Moritz Rudolf, and Lea Shih (2014). "Chinas Justizreformen nehmen Gestalt an: Gerichte der unteren Ebenen erhalten größere Eigenständigkeit im politischen Machtgefüge." *MERICS China Monitor* (7). May. Berlin: MERICS. http://www.merics.org/fileadmin/templates/download/china-monitor/China_Monitor_No_7.pdf. Accessed: May 5, 2015.

Heilmann, Sebastian and Dirk H. Schmidt (2014). *China's Foreign Political and Economic Relations: An Unconventional Global Power.* Lanham, MD: Rowman & Littlefield.

Heilmann, Sebastian, Nicole Schulte-Kulkmann, and Lea Shih (2004). "Die Farbe der Macht hat sich geändert: Kontroversen um die Verfassungsreform in der VR China." China Analysis 31. Trier: Center for East Asian and Pacific Studies. Trier University. February. http://www.chinapolitik.de/studien/china_analysis/no_31.pdf. Accessed: July 4, 2015.

Heilmann, Sebastian and Lea Shih (2013). "The Rise of Industrial Policy in China, 1978–2012." Harvard-Yenching Working Paper Series. http://www.harvard-yenching.org/sites/harvard-yenching.org/files/featurefiles/Sebastian%20Heilmann%20and%20Lea%20Shih_The%20Rise%20of%20Industrial%20Policy%20in%20China%201978-2012.pdf. Accessed: July 5, 2015.

Heilmann, Sebastian, Lea Shih, and Andreas Hofem (2013). "National Planning and Local Technology Zones: Experimental Governance in China's Torch Programme." *The China Quarterly* (216): 896–919. Heinelt, Hubert (ed.) (2014). *Modernes Regieren in China.* Baden-Baden: Nomos.

Herrmann-Pillath, Carsten (1990). "Struktur und Prozeß in der chinesischen Wirtschaftspolitik, oder: Warum China doch anders ist." *Politik und Zeitgeschichte* (B 48): 18–30.

Hesketh, Therese, Dan Wu, Linan Mao, and Nan Ma (2012). "Violence Against Doctors in China." *British Medical Journal (Clinical Research Ed.)* 345(5730): 1–5. DOI: 10.1136/bmj.e5750.

Heuser, Robert (2000). "Das chinesische Gesetzgebungsgesetz vom 15.3.2000." *China aktuell* 29(8): 937–949.

Ho, Peter and Richard Louis Edmonds (eds.) (2008). *China's Embedded Activism: Opportunities and Constraints of a Social Movement.* Routledge Studies on China in Transition 30. London: Routledge.

Holbig, Heike (2009). "Regime Legitimacy in Contemporary China: Challenges in the Post-Jiang Era." In: Thomas Heberer and Gunter Schubert (eds.). *Regime Legitimacy in Contemporary China: Institutional Change and Stability,* 13–34. London: Routledge.

Holbig, Heike and Bruce Gilley (2010). "Reclaiming Legitimacy in China." *Politics and Policy* 38(3): 395–422.

Holmes, Leslie (1986). *Politics in the Communist World.* Oxford, UK: Clarendon.

Holz, Carsten A. (2014). "The Quality of China's GDP Statistics." *China Economic Review* 30(3): 309–388.

Hu, Angang 胡鞍钢, (2012). 中国2020: 一个新型超级大国 (China in 2020: A new type of superpower). Hangzhou: Zhejiang renmin chubanshe.

Hu, Angang 胡鞍钢, Tang Xiao唐啸, Yang Zhusong杨竺松, and Yan Yilong鄢一龙 (eds.) (2014). 中国国家治理现代化 (Modernization of Chinese national governance). Beijing: Zhongguo renmin daxue chubanshe.

Huntington, Samuel P. (1993). *The Third Wave: Democratization in the Late Twentieth Century.* The Julian J. Rothbaum Distinguished Lecture Series 4. Norman: University of Oklahoma Press.

Hurun Report (2015). "China Rich List." www.hurun.net/en/HUList.aspx. Accessed: January 28, 2016.

Hussain, Athar and Nicholas Stern (2008). "Public Finances, the Role of the State, and Economic Transformation, 1978–2020." In: Jiwei Lou and Shuilin Wang (eds.). *Public Finance in China: Reform and Growth for a Harmonious Society,* 13–38. Washington, DC: World Bank.

ICG [International Crisis Group] (2012). "Stirring Up the South China Sea." ICG Asia Report 223. April 23. http://www.crisisgroup.org/~/media/Files/asia/north-east-asia/223-stirring-up-the-south-china-sea-i.pdf. Accessed: June 15, 2015.

Institute for Criminal Policy Research (2015). "World Prison Brief." http://www.prison-studies.org/world-prison-brief. Accessed: January 28, 2016.

International Consortium of Investigative Journalists (2014). "Leaked Records Reveal Offshore Holdings of China's Elite." January 21. http://www.icij.org/offshore/leaked-records-reveal-offshore-holdings-chinas-elite#. Accessed: July 28, 2015.

Jacques, Martin (2012). *When China Rules the World: The Rise of the Middle Kingdom and the End of the Western World.* 2nd ed. London: Penguin.

Jakobson, Linda (2014). "China's Unpredictable Maritime Security." Lowy Institute for International Policy. December. http://www.lowyinstitute.org/files/chinas-unpre-dictable-maritime-security-actors_1.pdf. Accessed: July 11, 2015.

Jenner, W.J.F. (1992). *The Tyranny of History: The Roots of China's Crisis.* London: Allen Lane.

Jia, Chenhao and David Jukes (2013). "The National Food Safety Control System of China: A Systematic Review." *Food Control* 32(1): 236–245.

Jiang, Quanbao, Ying Li, and Jésus J. Sánchez-Barricarte (2013). "Trafficking of Women from Neighboring Countries into China for Marriage within the Context of Gender Imbalance." https://mecon.nomadit.co.uk/pub/conference_epaper_download.php5?-PaperID=8111&MIMEType=application/pdf. Accessed: July 10, 2015.

Johnson, Chalmers (1982). *MITI and the Japanese Miracle: The Growth of Industrial Policy, 1925–1975.* Stanford, CA: Stanford University Press.

Joseph, William A. (ed.) (2014). *Politics in China: An Introduction.* 2nd ed. Oxford, UK: Oxford University Press.

Kennedy, John J. (2014). "Rural China: Reform and Resistance." In: William A. Joseph (ed.). *Politics in China: An Introduction,* 293–319. 2nd ed. Oxford, UK: Oxford University Press.

Kennedy, Scott (ed.) (2011). *Beyond the Middle Kingdom: Comparative Perspectives on China's Capitalist Transformation.* Stanford, CA: Stanford University Press.

King, Gary, Jennifer Pan, and Margaret E. Roberts (2013). "How Censorship in China Allows Government Criticism but Silences Collective Expression." *American Political Science Review* 107(2): 326–343.

Klein, Thoralf (2007). *Geschichte Chinas: Von 1800 bis zur Gegenwart.* Paderborn: F. Schöningh.

Koch-Weser, Iacob N. (2013). "The Reliability of China's Economic Data: An Analysis of National Output." U.S.-China Economic and Security Review Commission Research Report. January 28. http://www.uscc.gov/sites/default/files/Research/TheReliabilityofChina%27sEconomicData.pdf. Accessed: July 9, 2015.

Kojima, Kazuko and Ryosei Kokubun (2002). "The 'Shequ Construction' Programme and the Chinese Communist Party." *The Copenhagen Journal of Asian Studies* 16: 86–105. http://rauli.cbs.dk/index.php/cjas/article/viewFile/6/6. Accessed: January 10, 2016.

Kornai, János (1995). *Das sozialistische System: Die politische Ökonomie des Kommunismus.* Baden-Baden: Nomos.

Kostka, Genia and William Hobbs (2013). "Embedded Interests and the Managerial Local State: The Political Economy of Methanol Fuel-Switching in China." *Journal of Contemporary China* 22(80): 204–218.

Kovacs, Anja and Dixie Hawtin (2013). "Cyber Security, Surveillance and Online Human Rights." May 22. http://www.gp-digital.org/publication/second-pub/. Accessed: January 10, 2016.

KPMG (2013). "Infrastructure in China: Sustaining Quality Growth." http://www.kpmg.com/CN/en/IssuesAndInsights/ArticlesPublications/documents/Infrastructure-in-China-201302.pdf. Accessed: July 5, 2015.

Kuhn, Philip A. (2001). *Origins of the Modern Chinese State.* Stanford, CA: Stanford University Press.

Lagerkvist, Johan (2012). "Principal-Agent Dilemma in China's Social Media Sector? The Party-State and Industry Real-Name Registration Waltz." *International Journal of Communication* (6): 2628–2646.

Lam, Tao-Chiu (2010). "The County System and County Governance." In: Jae-Ho Chung and Tao-Chiu Lam (eds.). *China's Local Administration: Traditions and Changes in the Sub-National Hierarchy,* 149–173. London: Routledge.

Lam, Wai-man (2012). "Political Context." In: Wai-man Lam, Percy Luen-tim Lui, and Wilson Wong (eds.). *Contemporary Hong Kong Government and Politics,* 1–21. 2nd exp. ed. Hong Kong: Hong Kong University Press.

Lampton, David M. (2013). *Following the Leader: Ruling China, From Deng Xiaoping to Xi Jinping.* Berkeley: University of California Press.

Langhammer, Rolf J. and Sebastian Heilmann (2010). "Managing the Crisis: A Comparative Assessment." In: Bertelsmann Stiftung (ed.). *Managing the Crisis: A Comparative Assessment of Economic Governance in 14 Countries,* 9–30. Gütersloh: Verlag Bertelsmann Stiftung.

Lardy, Nicholas R. (2012). *Sustaining China's Economic Growth after the Global Financial Crisis.* Washington, DC: Peterson Institute for International Economics.

Lee, Ching Kwan and Yonghong Zhang (2013). "The Power of Instability: Unraveling the Microfoundations of Bargained Authoritarianism in China." *American Journal of Sociology* 118(6): 1475–1508.

Levitsky, Steven and Lucan Way (2010). *Competitive Authoritarianism: Hybrid Regimes after the Cold War.* Cambridge, UK: Cambridge University Press.

Li, Cheng (2013). "The Rise of the Legal Profession in the Chinese Leadership." *China Leadership Monitor* (42). http://www.hoover.org/research/rise-legal-profession-chinese-leadership. Accessed: January 10, 2016.

Li, Cheng and Ryan McElveen (2014). "Debunking Misconceptions About Xi Jinping's Anti-Corruption Campaign." China US Focus. July 17. http://www.chinausfocus.com/political-social-development/debunking-misconceptions-about-xi-jinpings-anti-corruption-campaign/. Accessed: July 28, 2015.

Li, Cheng and Lynn White (2003). "The Sixteenth Central Committee of the Chinese Communist Party: Hu Gets What?" *Asian Survey* 43(4): 553–597.

Li, Hongtao and Chin-Chuan Lee (2013). "Remembering Tiananmen and the Berlin Wall: The Elite U.S. Press's Anniversary Journalism, 1990–2009." *Media, Culture & Society* 35(7): 830–846.

Li, Keqiang (2015). "Report on the Work of the Government." March 5. http://news. xinhuanet.com/english/china/2015-03/16/c_134071473.htm. Accessed: February 12, 2016.

Li, Nan (2010). "Chinese Civil-Military Relations in the Post-Deng Era: Implications for Crisis Management and Naval Modernization." *U.S. Naval War College China Maritime Studies* (4). http://www.dtic.mil/dtic/tr/fulltext/u2/a519026.pdf. Accessed: July 10, 2015.

Li, Peilin (ed.) (2012). *Chinese Society: Change and Transformation*. China Policy Series 25. London: Routledge.

Li, Peilin 李培林, Chen Guangjin 陈光金, and Zhang Yi 张翼 (eds.) (2013). 2014 年中国社会形势分析与预测 (Analysis and forecast of China's society 2014). 社会蓝皮书 (Blue book on Chinese society). Beijing: Shehui kexue wenxian chubanshe.

Lieberthal, Kenneth (2003). *Governing China: From Revolution through Reform*. 2nd ed. New York: W.W. Norton.

Lieberthal, Kenneth and David M. Lampton (1992). *Bureaucracy, Politics, and Decision Making in Post-Mao China*. Studies on China 14. Berkeley: University of California Press.

Lieberthal, Kenneth, Cheng Li, and Keping Yu (eds.) (2014). *China's Political Development: Chinese and American Perspectives*. Washington, DC: Brookings Institution Press.

Lieberthal, Kenneth and Michel Oksenberg (1988). *Policy Making in China: Leaders, Structures, and Processes*. Princeton, NJ: Princeton University Press.

Liebman, Benjamin L. (2015). "China's Law and Stability Paradox." In: Jacques deLisle and Avery Goldstein (eds.). *China's Challenges,* 157–176. Philadelphia: University of Pennsylvania Press.

Lin, Dechang 林德昌 (2010). "全球公民社會對國際非政府組織在中國大陸發展的影響" (The impact of global civil society on the development of international NGOs in China). *Soochow Journal of Political Science* 東吳政治學報 28(4): 93–146.

Lindsay, Jon R., Tai Ming Cheung, and Derek S. Reveron (eds.) (2015). *China and Cybersecurity: Espionage, Strategy, and Politics in the Digital Domain*. Oxford, UK: Oxford University Press.

Linz, Juan J. (1975). "Totalitarian and Authoritarian Regimes." In: Fred I. Greenstein and Nelson W. Polsby (eds.). *Handbook of Political Science, Vol. 3: Macro-political Theory*, 175–411. Reading, MA: Addison-Wesley.

Linz, Juan J. and Raimund Krämer (eds.) (2000). *Totalitäre und autoritäre Regime*. Berlin: Berliner Debatte Wissenschaftsverlag.

Liou, Kuotsai Tom (2007). "E-Government Development and China's Administrative Reform." *International Journal of Public Administration* 31(1): 76–95.

Liu, He (2014). "Overcoming the Great Recession: Lessons from China." Paper. Cambridge, MA: Belfer Center for Science and International Affairs and Mossavar-Rahmani Center for Business and Government, Harvard Kennedy School. http://belfer-center.ksg.harvard.edu/files/Comparative%20Crises%20final%202.pdf. Accessed: January 21, 2016.

Liu, Hongling, Guanghong Zhou, Ronald Wennersten, and Björn Frostell (2014). "Analysis of Sustainable Urban Development Approaches in China." *Habitat International* 41: 24–32.

Liu, Shan, Zhimei Xie, Weiwei Zhang, Xiao Cao, and Xiaofang Pei (2013). "Risk Assessment in Chinese Food Safety." *Food Control* 30(1): 162–167.

Liu, Tianbao 刘天宝 and Chai Yanwei 柴彦威 (2013). "中国城市单位制研究进展" (Research progress on the urban work-unit system in China). *Areal Research and Development* (地域研究与开发) 32(5): 13–21.

Liu, Xielin (2009). "National Innovation Systems in Developing Countries: The Chinese National Innovation System in Transition." In: Bengt-Ake Lundvall, K.J. Joseph, Cristina Chaminade, and Jan Vang (eds.). *Handbook of Innovation Systems in Developing Countries: Building Capacities in a Global Setting*, 119–139. Cheltenham, UK: Edward Elgar.

Liu, Yawei (2009). "Are Village Elections Leading to Democracy?" *China Elections and Governance Review* (1) (February): 1–4. https://www.cartercenter.org/resources/pdfs/peace/china/CEG-review-issue1.pdf. Accessed: January 11, 2016.

Lo, Shiu-Hing (2001). *Governing Hong Kong: Legitimacy, Communication and Political Decay*. Huntington, NY: Nova Science.

Lorentzen, Peter (2014). "China's Strategic Censorship." *American Journal of Political Science* 58(2): 402–414.

Lou, Jiwei (2008). "The Reform of Intergovernmental Fiscal Relations in China: Lessons Learned." In: Jiwei Lou and Shuilin Wang (eds.). *Public Finance in China: Reform and Growth for a Harmonious Society,* 155–169. Washington, DC: World Bank.

Lou, Jiwei and Shuilin Wang (eds.) (2008). *Public Finance in China: Reform and Growth for a Harmonious Society.* Washington, DC: World Bank.

Lu, Fangqi and Xuli Wu (2014). "China Food Safety Hits the 'Gutter.'" *Food Control* 41(1): 134–138.

Lu, Xueyi 陆学艺 (ed.) (2002). 当代中国阶层研究报告 (Research report on social classes in contemporary Chinese society). Beijing: Shehui kexue wenxian chubanshe.

Lu, Xueyi 陆学艺 (ed.) (2010). 当代中国社会结构 (Social structure of contemporary China). Beijing: Shehui kexue wenxian chubanshe.

Lu, Yinqiu and Tao Sun (2013). "Local Government Financing Platforms in China: A Fortune or Misfortune?" IMF Working Paper 13/243. Washington, DC: International Monetary Fund.

Lü, Li 吕莉 (2013). "网络群体性事件的成因与传播模式" (Origins and distribution modes of online mass events). *Xinwenshijie* (7). http://mall.cnki.net/magazine/Article/PXWS201307093.htm. Accessed: July 7, 2015.

Lü, Qingzhe 吕庆喆 (2013). "2013 年中国城乡居民收入和消费状况" (China's urban and rural residents' income and consumption in 2013). In: Li Peilin 李培林, Chen Guangjin 陈光金, and Zhang Yi 张翼 (eds.). 2014 年中国社会形势分析与预测 (Analysis and forecast of China's society 2014), 13–28. 社会蓝皮书 (Blue book on Chinese society). Beijing: Shehui kexue wenxian chubanshe.

Lü, Xiaobo and Elizabeth J. Perry (eds.) (1997). *Danwei: The Changing Chinese Workplace in Historical and Comparative Perspective.* Socialism and Social Movements. Armonk, NY: M.E. Sharpe.

Lü, Xiaoli and Kaibin Zhong (2012). "The Chinese Emergency Management System." *Crisis Response Journal* 8(4): 54–55.

Lynch, Daniel C. (2015). *China's Futures: PRC Elites Debate Economics, Politics, and Foreign Policy*. Stanford, CA: Stanford University Press.

Lyons, Thomas (1987). *Economic Integration and Planning in Maoist China*. New York: Columbia University Press.

Ma, Jun (2013). "Hidden Fiscal Risks in Local China." *Australian Journal of Public Administration* 72(3): 278–292.

Ma, Rong (2010). "The 'Politicization' of 'Culturalization' of Ethnic Groups." *Chinese Sociology and Anthropology* 42(4): 31–45.

MacFarquhar, Roderick (1983). *The Origins of the Cultural Revolution. Vol. 2: The Great Leap Forward 1958–1960*. New York: Columbia University Press.

MacFarquhar, Roderick (1999). *The Origins of the Cultural Revolution. Vol. 3: The Coming of the Cataclysm 1961–1965*. New York: Columbia University Press.

MacFarquhar, Roderick (2011). *The Politics of China: Sixty Years of the People's Republic of China*. 3rd ed. Cambridge, UK: Cambridge University Press.

MacFarquhar, Roderick and Michael Schoenhals (2008). *Mao's Last Revolution*. Cambridge, MA: Belknap Press of Harvard University Press.

Mackerras, Colin (ed.) (2011). *Ethnic Minorities in Modern China*. Critical Concepts in Asian Studies. London: Routledge.

Mackerras, Colin and Michael E. Clarke (2011). *China, Xinjiang and Central Asia: History, Transition and Crossborder Interaction into the 21st Century*. Routledge Contemporary China Series 38. London: Routledge.

Mann, Michael (1984). "The Autonomous Power of the State: Its Origins, Mechanisms and Results." *European Journal of Sociology* 25(2): 185–213.

Mao, Zedong (1937) [1961]. "On Guerrilla Warfare." In: *On Guerrilla Warfare*, trans. by Samuel B. Griffith. New York: Praeger.

Martin, Helmut (1982). *Cult & Canon: The Origins and Development of State Maoism*. Armonk, NY: M.E. Sharpe.

Martin, Michael F. (2007). *Hong Kong: Ten Years After the Handover.* June 29. Washington, DC: Congressional Research Service. https://www.fas.org/sgp/crs/row/RL34071.pdf. Accessed: January 21, 2016.

Maurer, Tim, Robert Morgus, and Isabel Skierka (2014). "The Anti-Surveillance Strategies That Could Ruin the Internet" *Time.* December 10. http://time.com/3628212/strategies-ruin-internet/. Accessed: July 30, 2015.

McGregor, Richard (2010). *The Party: The Secret World of China's Communist Rulers.* New York: Harper.

McKinnon, Ronald I. (1973). *Money and Capital in Economic Development.* Washington, DC: Brookings Institution Press.

McNally, Christopher A. (ed.) (2007). *China's Emergent Political Economy: Capitalism in the Dragon's Lair.* Routledge Studies in the Growth Economies of Asia. London: Routledge.

McNally, Christopher A. (2013). "Refurbishing State Capitalism: A Policy Analysis of Efforts to Rebalance China's Political Economy." *Journal of Current Chinese Affairs* 42(4): 45–71.

Mertha, Andrew C. (2008). *China's Water Warriors: Citizen Action and Policy Change.* Ithaca, NY: Cornell University Press.

Mertha, Andrew C. (2009). "'Fragmented Authoritarianism 2.0': Political Pluralization in the Chinese Policy Process." *The China Quarterly* (200): 995–1012.

Miller, Alice (2008). "China's New Party Leadership." *China Leadership Monitor* (23). http://www.hoover.org/sites/default/files/uploads/documents/CLM23AM.pdf. Accessed: March 31, 2015.

Miller, Alice (2013). "The Work System of the Xi Jinping Leadership." *China Leadership Monitor* (41). http://media.hoover.org/sites/default/files/documents/CLM41AM.pdf. Accessed: January 10, 2016.

Miller, Alice (2014). "More Already on the Central Committee's Leading Small Groups." *China Leadership Monitor* (44). http://www.hoover.org/sites/default/files/research/docs/clm44am.pdf. Accessed: January 10, 2016.

Ministry of Commerce 商务部. Foreign Investment Department 境外投资服务机构 (2016). "New Release of National Assimilation of FDI From January to December 2015." http://www.fdi.gov.cn/1800000121_49_4071_0_7.html. Accessed: February 1, 2016.

Mitter, Rana (2013a). *China's War with Japan, 1937–1945: The Struggle for Survival*. London: Allen Lane.

Mitter, Rana (2013b). *Forgotten Ally: China's World War II, 1937–1945*. New York: Houghton Mifflin Harcourt.

MOCA [Ministry of Civil Affairs] 民政部 (2013). 中国民政统计年鉴 2013 (China civil affairs statistical yearbook 2013). Beijing: Zhongguo tongji chubanshe.

MOCA [Ministry of Civil Affairs] 民政部 (2015). 中国民政统计年鉴 2015 (China civil affairs statistical yearbook 2015). Beijing: Zhongguo tongji chubanshe.

MOF [Ministry of Finance] 财政部, Fazhan gaigewei发展改革委. Renmin yinhang 人民银行 Yinjianhui, 银监会 et al. (2010). "关于贯彻国务院关于加强地方政府融资平台公司管理有关问题的通知相关事项的通知" (Implementing matters concerning the notice of the State Council on issues concerning strengthening the management of local-government financing platform companies). *Caiyu* 财预 (412). July 30. http://www.mof.gov.cn/zhengwuxinxi/caizhengwengao/2010nianwengao/wg2010diqiqi/201009/t20100927_340778.html. Accessed: July 4, 2015.

MOHRSS [Ministry of Human Resources and Social Security] 人力资源和社会保障部 (2015). "2014年度人力资源和社会保障事业发展统计公报" (Statistical communiqué on labor, social security, and employment in 2014). http://www.mohrss.gov.cn/SYrlzyhshbzb/dongtaixinwen/buneiyaowen/201505/t20150528_162040.htm. Accessed: January 11, 2016.

Mok, Ka-Ho and Ray Forrest (eds.) (2007). *Changing Governance and Public Policy in East Asia*. London: Routledge.

Montinola, Gabriella, Yingyi Qian, and Barry R. Weingast (1995). "Federalism, Chinese Style: The Political Basis for Economic Success in China." *World Politics* 48(1): 50–81.

Moore, Scott M. (2013). "China's Massive Water Problem." *The New York Times*. March 28. http://www.nytimes.com/2013/03/29/opinion/global/chinas-massive-water-problem.html?_r=0. Accessed: July 30, 2015.

Moore, Scott M. (2014). "Modernisation, Authoritarianism, and the Environment: The Politics of China's South–North Water Transfer Project." *Environmental Politics* 23(6): 947–964.

Mu, Rongping and Qu Wan (2008). "The Development of Science and Technology in China: A Comparison with India and the United States." *Technology in Society* 30(3–4): 319–329.

Mulvenon, James (2008). "The Chinese Military's Earthquake Response Leadership Team." *China Leadership Monitor* (25). http://media.hoover.org/sites/default/files/documents/CLM25JM.pdf. Accessed: January 10, 2016.

Naishul', Vitali A. (1991). *The Supreme and Last Stage of Socialism: An Essay*. New Series 2. London: Centre for Research into Communist Economies.

NAO [National Audit Office] 审计署 (2013). "全国政府性债务审计结果" (Audit report on government debt). December 30. http://www.audit.gov.cn/n1992130/n1992150/n1992500/n3432077.files/n3432112.pdf. Accessed: June 6, 2015.

Nathan, Andrew J. (2003). "China's Resilient Authoritarianism." *Journal of Democracy* 14(1): 6–17.

Nathan, Andrew J., Larry Diamond, and Marc F. Plattner (eds.) (2013). *Will China Democratize? Journal of Democracy* Book. Baltimore: Johns Hopkins University Press.

NationMaster (2010). "Rape Rate: Countries Compared." http://www.nationmaster.com/country-info/stats/Crime/Rape-rate. Accessed: February 6, 2016.

Naude, Wim, Amelia Uliafnova, Santos Paulino, and Mark McGillivrary (eds.) (2011). *Fragile States: Causes, Costs, and Responses*. UNU-WIDER Studies in Development Economics. Oxford, UK: Oxford University Press.

Naughton, Barry (1995). *Growing Out of the Plan: Chinese Economic Reform, 1978–1993*. Cambridge, UK: Cambridge University Press.

Naughton, Barry (2007). *The Chinese Economy: Transitions and Growth*. Cambridge, MA: MIT Press.

Naughton, Barry (2008). "A Political Economy of China's Economic Transition." In: Loren Brandt and Thomas G. Rawski (eds.). *China's Great Economic Transformation*, 91–135. Cambridge, UK: Cambridge University Press.

Naughton, Barry (2011). "China's Economic Policy Today: The New State Activism." *Eurasian Geography and Economics* 52(3): 313–329.

Naughton, Barry (2014). "'Deepening Reform': The Organization and the Emerging Strategy." *China Leadership Monitor* (44). http://www.hoover.org/sites/default/files/research/docs/clm44bn.pdf. Accessed: June 22, 2015.

Naughton, Barry and Dali L. Yang (eds.) (2004). *Holding China Together: Diversity and National Integration in the Post-Deng Era.* Cambridge, UK: Cambridge University Press.

NBS [National Bureau of Statistics] 国家统计局 (2010). 中国统计年鉴 2010 (China statistical yearbook 2010). Beijing: Zhongguo tongji chubanshe.

NBS [National Bureau of Statistics] 国家统计局 (2012). 中国农村贫困监测报告 2011 (Poverty monitoring report of rural China 2011). Beijing: Zhongguo tongji chubanshe.

NBS [National Bureau of Statistics] 国家统计局 (2013a). 中国农村统计年鉴 2013 (China rural statistical yearbook 2013). Beijing: Zhongguo tongji chubanshe.

NBS [National Bureau of Statistics] 国家统计局 (2013b). 中国统计年鉴 2013 (China statistical yearbook 2013). Beijing: Zhongguo tongji chubanshe.

NBS [National Bureau of Statistics] 国家统计局 (2014a).中国民族统计年鉴 2013 (China ethnic statistical yearbook 2013). Beijing: Zhongguo tongji chubanshe.

NBS [National Bureau of Statistics] 国家统计局 (2014b). 中国统计年鉴 2014 (China statistical yearbook 2014). Beijing: Zhongguo tongji chubanshe.

NBS [National Bureau of Statistics] 国家统计局 (2015a). 中国统计年鉴 2015 (China statistical yearbook 2015). Beijing: Zhongguo tongji chubanshe.

NBS [National Bureau of Statistics] 国家统计局 (2015b). 广东统计年鉴 2015 (Guangdong statistical yearbook 2015). Beijing: Zhongguo tongji chubanshe.

NBS [National Bureau of Statistics] 国家统计局 (2015c). "2014年全国农民工监测调查报告" (National monitoring report of migrant workers 2014). http://www.stats.gov.cn/tjsj/zxfb/201504/t20150429_797821.html. Accessed: February 4, 2016.

NBS [National Bureau of Statistics] 国家统计局 (2015d). 西藏统计年鉴 2015 (Tibet statistical yearbook 2015). Beijing: Zhongguo tongji chubanshe.

NBS [National Bureau of Statistics] 国家统计局. Department of Population and Employment Statistics 人口与就业统计司 (2015). 中国劳动统计年鉴2014 (China labour statistical yearbook 2014). Beijing: Zhongguo tongji chubanshe.

NDRC [National Development and Reform Commission] 国家发展和改革委员会 (2013). "物联网发展专项行动计划" (Special plan of action for the development of Internet of Things). http://www.sdpc.gov.cn/zcfb/zcfbghwb/201309/W020140221372854934790.pdf. Accessed: July 19, 2015.

Novaretti, Simona (2014). "Social Governance vs. Social Management: Towards a New Regulatory Role for Social Organizations in China?" Conference Paper. 5th ECPR Regulatory Governance Conference. Barcelona. June 25–27. http://reggov2014.ibei.org/bcn-14-papers/96-244.pdf. Accessed: July 10, 2015.

Nyberg, Albert and Scott Rozelle (1999). *Accelerating China's Rural Transformation.* Washington, DC: World Bank.

O'Brien, Kevin J. (ed.) (2008). *Popular Protest in China.* Harvard Contemporary China Series 15. Cambridge, MA: Harvard University Press.

O'Brien, Kevin J. and Rongbin Han (2009). "Path to Democracy? Assessing Village Elections in China." *Journal of Contemporary China* 18(60): 359–378.

O'Brien, Kevin J. and Lianjiang Li (2006). *Rightful Resistance in Rural China.* Cambridge Studies in Contentious Politics. Cambridge, MA: Harvard University Press.

OECD [Organisation for Economic Co-operation and Development] (2008). *OECD Reviews of Innovation Policy: China.* Paris: OECD Publishing.

Orlik, Tom (2012). *Understanding China's Economic Indicators: Translating the Data into Investment Opportunities.* Upper Saddle River, NJ: FT Press.

Osterhammel, Jürgen (1989). *China und die Weltgesellschaft: Vom 18. Jahrhundert bis in unsere Zeit.* Munich: Beck.

Pan, Wei 潘维 (2009). 中国模式: 解读人民共和国的60年 (The Chinese model: Decoding 60 years of the PRC). Beijing: Zhongyang bianyi chubanshe.

Pan, Ying 潘颖 and Lu Zhangping卢章平 (2012). "基于专利视角的中、美物联网产业比较研究" (On the Internet of Things in China and America: A comparative study based on the perspective of patents). *Journal of Intelligence* 情报杂志 31(9): 30–35.

PBOC [People's Bank of China] 中国人民银行 (2014). "2014中国区域金融运行报告" (Report on regional finance development). July 3. http://www.pbc.gov.cn/zhengcehuobisi/125207/125227/125960/126049/2169456/2891068/index.html. Accessed: January 10, 2016.

PBOC [People's Bank of China] 中国人民银行 and CBRC [China Banking Regulatory Comission] 中国银行业监督管理委员会 (2009). 关于进一步加强信贷结构调整 促进国民经济平稳较快发展的指导意见 (On further adjusting the credit structure to promote the rapid yet steady development of the national economy). Yinfa 银发 (92). http://www.gov.cn/gongbao/content/2009/content_1336375.htm. Accessed: January 10, 2016.

Pearson, Margaret M. (2011). "Variety Within and Without: The Political Economy of Chinese Regulation." In: Scott Kennedy (ed.). *Beyond the Middle Kingdom: Comparative Perspectives on China's Capitalist Transformation,* 25–43. Contemporary Issues in Asia and the Pacific. Stanford, CA: Stanford University Press.

Pearson, Margaret M. (2014). "China's Foreign Economic Relations and Policies." In: Saadia M. Pekkanen, John Ravenhill, and Rosemary Foot (eds.). *Oxford Handbook of the International Relations of Asia,* 160–178. Oxford, UK: Oxford University Press.

Peck, Jamie and Jun Zhang (2013). "A Variety of Capitalism...with Chinese Characteristics?" *Journal of Economic Geography* 13(3): 357–396.

Pei, Minxin (1994). *From Reform to Revolution: The Demise of Communism in China and the Soviet Union.* Cambridge, MA: Harvard University Press.

Pei, Minxin (1997). "'Creeping Democratization' in China." In: Larry Diamond, Marc F. Plattner, Yun-han Chu, and Hung-mao Tien (eds.). *Consolidating the Third Wave Democracies: Regional Challenges,* 213–227. Journal of Democracy Book. Baltimore: Johns Hopkins University Press.

Pei, Minxin (2006). *China's Trapped Transition: The Limits of Developmental Autocracy.* Cambridge, MA: Harvard University Press.

Peng, Jianmei 彭建梅 and Liu Youping 刘佑平 (2012). 美国NGO在华慈善活动分析报告 (Report on the philanthropic activities of international NGOs [US Section] in China). Beijing: China Charity and Donation Information Center. http://mat1.gtimg.com/gongyi/2012/2012earthhour/Americanreport.pdf. Accessed: January 11, 2016.

Peng, Liu (2010). "Tracing and Periodizing China's Food Safety Regulation: A Study on China's Food Safety Regime Change." *Regulation and Governance* 4(2): 244–260.

Perkins, Dwight H. (2013). *East Asian Development: Foundations and Strategies.* The Edwin O. Reischauer Lectures. Cambridge, MA: Harvard University Press.

Perry, Elizabeth J. (1993). *Shanghai on Strike: The Politics of Chinese Labor.* Stanford, CA: Stanford University Press.

Perry, Elizabeth J. (2012). *Anyuan: Mining China's Revolutionary Tradition.* Asia: Local Studies/Global Themes. Berkeley: University of California Press.

Perry, Elizabeth J. and Merle Goldman (eds.) (2007). *Grassroots Political Reform in Contemporary China.* Harvard Contemporary China Series 14. Cambridge, MA: Harvard University Press.

Pettis, Michael (2014). "The Four Stages of Chinese Growth." http://blog.mpettis.com/2014/06/the-four-stages-of-chinese-growth/. Accessed: July 27, 2015.

Pils, Eva (2014). *China schafft Arbeitslager ab, oder doch nicht? Artikel zum System der Umerziehung durch Arbeit.* Hongkong: Heinrich Böll Stiftung. March. https://www.boell.de/sites/default/files/epaper_laojiao_chinaarbeitslager_eva_pils.pdf. Accessed: January 10, 2016.

Potter, Pitman B. (2013). *China's Legal System.* China Today Series. Cambridge, UK: Polity Press.

Przeworski, Adam, Michael E. Alvarez, José Antônio Cheibu, and Fernando Limonji (2000). *Democracy and Development: Political Institutions and Well-Being in the World, 1950–1990.* Cambridge Studies in the Theory of Democracy 3. Cambridge, UK: Cambridge University Press.

Putnam, Robert D. (1988). "Diplomacy and Domestic Politics: The Logic of Two-Level Games." *International Organization* 42(3): 427–460.

Pye, Lucian W. (1988). *The Mandarin and the Cadre: China's Political Cultures.* Michigan Monographs in Chinese Studies 59. Ann Arbor: Center for Chinese Studies, University of Michigan.

Ramo, Joshua Cooper (2004). *The Beijing Consensus.* London: Foreign Policy Centre.

Ran, Ran (2009). "Environmental Politics at Local Levels in China: Explaining Policy Implementation Gap and Assessing the Implications." Dissertation. Universität Duisburg-Essen.

Rawski, Evelyn S. (2015). *Early Modern China and Northeast Asia: Cross-Border Perspectives.* Cambridge, UK: Cambridge University Press.

Reform Magazine: Thematic Research 改革杂志社专题研究部 (2013). "行政审批制度改革背景的地方操作: 京津沪渝证据" (The background to the reform of local operations of the administrative approval system: Evidence from four municipalities). *Reform* 改革 (5): 5-14.

Ren, Xianliang 任贤良 (2010). 舆论引导艺术: 领导干部如何面对媒体 (The art of guiding public opinion: How leading cadres handle the media). Beijing: Xinhua chubanshe.

Richter, Carola and Sebastian Gebauer (2010). "Die China-Berichterstattung in den deutschen Medien." Berlin: Heinrich-Böll-Stiftung. June 11. http://www.boell.de/sites/default/files/Endf_Studie_China-Berichterstattung.pdf. Accessed: January 10, 2016.

Rodríguez-Merino, Pablo Adriano (2013). "Violent Resistance in Xinjiang (China): Tracking Militancy, Ethnic Riots and 'Knife-Wielding' Terrorists (1978–2012)." Historia Actual Online (30): 135–149. http://www.researchgate.net/profile/Pablo_Rodriguez_Merino/publication/265597435_VIOLENT_RESISTANCE_IN_XINJIANG_(CHINA)_TRACKING_MILITANCY_ETHNIC_RIOTS_AND_KNIFE-_WIELDING_TERRORISTS_(1978-2012)/links/541437ef0cf2fa878ad3e583. Accessed: July 10, 2015.

Rozman, Gilbert, with Seizaburō Satō and Gerald Segal (eds.) (1992). *Dismantling Communism: Common Causes and Regional Variations.* Washington, DC: Woodrow Wilson Center Press; Baltimore: Johns Hopkins University Press.

Saich, Anthony (2008). *Providing Public Goods in Transitional China.* London: Palgrave Macmillan.

Saich, Anthony (2015). *Governance and Politics of China*. 4th ed. Comparative Government and Politics. London: Palgrave Macmillan.

Saich, Anthony and Biliang Hu (2012). *Chinese Village, Global Market: New Collectives and Rural Development*. London: Palgrave Macmillan.

Sautman, Barry and June Teufel Dreyer (eds.) (2006). *Contemporary Tibet: Politics, Development, and Society in a Disputed Region*. East Gate Book. Armonk, NY: M.E. Sharpe.

Sauvant, Karl P. and Victor Zitian Chen (2014). "China's Regulatory Framework for Outward Foreign Direct Investment." *China Economic Journal* 7(1): 141–163.

Scharpf, Fritz W. (1988). "The Joint-Decision Trap: Lessons from German Federalism and European Integration." *Public Administration* 66(2): 239–278.

Schier, Peter, Ruth Cremerius, and Doris Fischer et al. (1993). *Studentenprotest und Repression in China, April–Juni 1989: Chronologie, Dokumente, Analyse*. 3rd ed. Mitteilungen des Instituts für Asienkunde Hamburg 223. Hamburg: Institut für Asienkunde.

Schlaeger, Jesper and Min Jiang (2014). "Official Microblogging and Social Management by Local Governments in China." *China Information* 28(2): 189–213.

Schlichting, Svenja (2008). *Internationalising China's Financial Markets*. London: Palgrave Macmillan.

Schlinger, Karl and Günter Schucher (2014). *Mission: Impossible! Gewerkschaften und Arbeitsfrieden in China*. GIGA Focus Asien (8). Hamburg: GIGA [German Institute of Global Area Studies]. http://www.giga-hamburg.de/de/system/files/publications/gf_asien_1408.pdf. Accessed: July 4, 2015.

Schmidt, Dirk H. (2012). "'From the Charm to the Offensive': Hat China eine neue Außenpolitik?" *ASIEN* 122 (January): 34–56.

Schmidt, Dirk and Sebastian Heilmann (2010). "Dealing with Economic Crisis in 2008–09: The Chinese Government's Crisis Management in Comparative Perspective." China Analysis 77. Trier: Center for East Asian and Pacific Studies, Trier University. January. http://www.chinapolitik.de/studien/china_analysis/no_77.pdf. Accessed: July 4, 2015.

Schmidt, Dirk H. and Sebastian Heilmann (2012). *Außenpolitik und Außenwirtschaft der Volksrepublik China*. Wiesbaden: Springer VS.

Schmidt, Manfred G. (2000). *Demokratietheorien: Eine Einführung*. 3rd ed. Opladen: Leske + Budrich.

Schmidt-Glintzer, Helwig (1997). *China: Vielvölkerreich und Einheitsstaat*. Beck's Historische Bibliothek. Munich: Beck.

Schmidt-Glintzer, Helwig (1999). *Das neue China: Von den Opiumkriegen bis heute*. Beck'sche Reihe 2126. Munich: Beck.

Schubert, Gunter (2013). "Das politische System Hongkongs." In: Claudia Derichs and Thomas Heberer (eds.). *Die Politischen Systeme Ostasiens: Eine Einführung*, 233–253. Wiesbaden: Springer VS.

Schubert, Gunter (2014). "Political Legitimacy in Contemporary China Revisited: Theoretical Refinement and Empirical Operationalization." *Journal of Contemporary China* 23(88): 593–611.

Schubert, Gunter and Anna L. Ahlers (2012). *Participation and Empowerment at the Grassroots: Chinese Village Elections in Perspective*. Challenges Facing Chinese Political Development. Lanham, MD: Lexington Books.

Schucher, Günter (2012). *Chinas neues Entwicklungsmodell und die Herausforderungen an die Berufsbildungspolitik*. Chinesisch-Deutsche Projektleiter-Konferenz. Beijing. April 18–19. Munich: Hanns-Seidel-Stiftung. http://www.hss.de/fileadmin/china/downloads/Chinas_neues_Entwicklungsmodell_und_die_Herausforderungen_an_die_Berufsbildungspolitik.pdf. Accessed: May 28, 2015.

Schulte, Barbara (2014). "Chinas Bildungssystem im Wandel: Elitenbildung, Ungleichheiten, Reformversuche." In: Doris Fischer and Michael Lackner (eds.). *Länderbericht China*, 499–541. Schriftenreihe Bd. 351. Bonn: Bundeszentrale für politische Bildung.

Schulte-Kulkmann, Nicole, Lea Shih, and Sebastian Heilmann (2004). "Änderungen der Verfassung der Volksrepublik China (2004): Übersetzung und Kommentar." *Verfassung und Recht in Übersee (VRÜ)* 37(3): 345–361.

Schurmann, Franz (1968). *Ideology and Organization in Communist China*. 2nd ed. Berkeley: University of California Press.

Selden, Mark (1995). *China in Revolution: The Yenan Way Revisited*. Socialism and Social Movements. Armonk, NY: M.E. Sharpe.

Senger, Harro von (1985). "Recent Developments in the Relations Between State and Party Norms in the People's Republic of China." In: Stuart R. Schram (ed.). *The Scope of State Power in China*, 171–207. London: School of Oriental and African Studies.

Senger, Harro von (1994). *Einführung in das chinesische Recht*. Schriftenreihe Juristische Schulung. Ausländisches Recht 124. Munich: Beck.

Senger, Harro von (2002). *Strategeme: Die berühmten 36 Stragegeme der Chinesen*. 2nd ed. Bern: Scherz.

Senger, Harro von (2008). *Moulüe-Supraplanung: Unerkannte Denkhorizonte aus dem Reich der Mitte*. Munich: Hanser.

Shambaugh, David L. (2007). "China's Propaganda System: Institutions, Processes and Efficacy." *The China Journal* (57): 25–58.

Shambaugh, David L. (2008). *China's Communist Party: Atrophy and Adaptation*. Washington, DC: Woodrow Wilson Center Press; Berkeley: University of California Press.

Shambaugh, David L. (2011). *Charting China's Future: Domestic and International Challenges*. London: Routledge.

Shambaugh, David L. (2012). *Tangled Titans: The United States and China*. Lanham, MD: Rowman & Littlefield.

Shambaugh, David L. (2013). *China Goes Global: The Partial Power*. Oxford, UK: Oxford University Press.

Shao, Lei 邵雷 (2014). "中国监狱罪犯教育改造发展概况" (Short report on the re-education of prisoners in China). March 25. http://www.moj.gov.cn/jyglj/content/2014-03/25/content_5393650.htm?node=253. Accessed: July 5, 2015.

Shapiro, Judith (2012): *China's Environmental Challenges*. Cambridge, UK: Polity Press

Shi, Tianjian (2014). *The Cultural Logic of Politics in Mainland China and Taiwan*. Cambridge, UK: Cambridge University Press.

Shi, Weiping (2013). "Issues and Problems in the Current Development of Vocational Education in China." *Chinese Education and Society* 46(4): 12–21.

Shi, Yigong and Yi Rao (2010). "China's Research Culture." *Science* 329(5996): 1128.

Shi-Kupfer, Kristin (2014a). "China–Tibet." January 1. Bonn: Bundeszentrale für politische Bildung. http://www.bpb.de/themen/4GQA2G,0,China_Tibet.html. Accessed: July 10, 2015.

Shi-Kupfer, Kristin (2014b). "China–Xinjiang." January 1. Bonn: Bundeszentrale für politische Bildung. http://www.bpb.de/internationales/weltweit/innerstaatli-che-konflikte/54592/china-xinjiang. Accessed: July 10, 2015.

Shi-Kupfer, Kristin (2014c). "Menschenrechte in der Volksrepublik China: Fortschritte, Defizite, Herausforderungen." In: Doris Fischer and Michael Lackner (eds.). *Länderbericht China,* 327–350. Schriftenreihe Bd. 351. Bonn: Bundeszentrale für politische Bildung.

Shi-Kupfer, Kristin and Yi Zhu (2013). "'V-Leute' im Rampenlicht – Chinas virtuelle Meinungsmacht und ihre Macher." *MERICS China Monitor* (1). November 11. http://www.merics.org/fileadmin/templates/download/china-monitor/2013-11-18/china-monitor-v-leute.pdf. Accessed: July 10, 2015.

Shi-Kupfer, Kristin and Yi Zhu (2014). "Chinesische Träume: Wohin führt die Suche nach Werteorientierungen in der Volksrepublik?" *MERICS China Monitor* (5). February 28. http://www.merics.org/fileadmin/templates/download/china-monitor/China_Monitor_No_5_gesamt.pdf. Accessed: July 10, 2015.

Shih, Lea (2015). *Chinas Industriepolitik von 1978–2013: Programme, Prozesse und Beschränkungen.* Wiesbaden: Springer Fachmedien.

Shih, Lea and Moritz Rudolf (2014). "Machtzentralisierung im Eiltempo: Die Zentrale Reform-Führungsgruppe und die Neuorganisation der Entscheidungszentrale unter Xi Jinping." *MERICS China Monitor* (13). July 4. http://www.merics.org/fileadmin/templates/download/china-monitor/China_Monitor_No_13.pdf. Accessed: July 30, 2015.

Shih, Victor C. (2008). *Factions and Finance in China: Elite Conflict and Inflation.* Cambridge, UK: Cambridge University Press.

Shih, Victor C., Christopher Adolph, and Mingxing Liu (2012). "Getting Ahead in the Communist Party: Explaining the Advancement of Central Committee Members in China." *American Political Science Review* 106(1): 166–187.

Shirk, Susan L. (1993). *The Political Logic of Economic Reform in China.* California Series on Social Choice and Political Economy 24. Berkeley: University of California Press.

Shirk, Susan L. (2007). *China: Fragile Superpower.* Oxford, UK: Oxford University Press.

Shirk, Susan L. (ed.) (2011). *Changing Media, Changing China.* Oxford, UK: Oxford University Press.

Shue, Vivienne (2012). "Modern/Rural China: State Institutions and Village Values." In: Ane Bislev and Stig Thøgersen (eds.). *Organizing Rural China: Rural China Organizing,* 223–232. Lanham, MD: Lexington Books.

Shue, Vivienne and Christine Wong (eds.) (2007). *Paying for Progress in China: Public Finance, Human Welfare and Changing Patterns of Inequality.* London: Routledge.

Slaughter and May (2015). "Competition Law in China." http://www.slaughterandmay.com/media/879862/competition-law-in-china.pdf. Accessed: July 18, 2015.

Smolik, Milan W. (2012). *The Politics of Authoritarian Rule.* Cambridge Studies in Comparative Politics. Cambridge, UK: Cambridge University Press.

Song, Shiming 宋世明 (2013). "实现取消和下放行政审批事项数量质量的统: 写在国务院公布新一批取消和下放行政审批事项之际" (The number and quality of abolished and delegated test and approval processes: State Council announces next round of abolitions and delegations). December 10. http://www.gov.cn/jrzg/2013-12/10/content_2545552.htm. Accessed: July 21, 2015.

Spence, Jonathan D. (1990). *The Search for Modern China.* New York: Norton.

State Council国务院 (2007). "中华人民共和国政府信息公开条例" (Regulation of the PRC on the disclosure of government information) (492). April 5. http://www.gov.cn/zwgk/2007-04/24/content_592937.htm. Accessed: January 20, 2015.

State Council国务院 (2009). "国务院关于开展新型农村社会养老保险试点的指导意见" (Guiding opinions of the State Council on the trial of the new pattern of rural social endowment insurance). Guofa [2009] 32 hao. September 4. http://www.gov.cn/zwgk/2009-09/04/content_1409216.htm. Accessed: July 8, 2015.

State Council国务院 (2010). "国务院关于加强地方政府融资平台公司 管理有关问题的通知" (Notice of the State Council on strengthening regulation of local-government financing vehicle corporations) (19). June 13. http://www.gov.cn/zwgk/2010-06/13/content_1627195.htm. Accessed: July 8, 2015.

State Council国务院 (2014a). "国家新型城镇化规划 (2014–2020年)" (National new urbanization plan [2014–2020]). March 16. http://www.gov.cn/zhengce/2014-03/16/content_2640075.htm. Accessed: January 11, 2016.

State Council国务院 (2014b). "'一国两制'在香港特别行政区的实践白皮书" (White paper: The practice of the "One Country, Two Systems" policy in the Hong Kong Special Administrative Region). June 10. http://www.scio.gov.cn/zxbd/tt/Document/1372801/1372801.htm. Accessed: June 25, 2015.

State Council国务院. General Office 办公厅 (2013). 关于推进物联网有序健康发展的指导意见 (Guidelines for promoting the development of the Internet of Things industry). February 17. Guofa [2013] 7 hao. http://www.gov.cn/zwgk/2013-02/17/content_2333141.htm. Accessed: January 11, 2016.

Stepan, Matthias (2015). "Towards State Guaranteed Old-Age Income for All: The Transformation of the Pension System in China." Dissertation. Vrije University (Amsterdam).

Stewart, Vivien (2015). "Made in China: Challenge and Innovation in China's Vocational Education and Training System." Washington, DC: National Center on Education and the Economy. http://www.ncee.org/wp-content/uploads/2015/03/CHINA-VETFINAL1.pdf. Accessed: May 28, 2015.

Stockmann, Daniela (2013). *Media Commercialization and Authoritarian Rule in China*. Communication, Society, and Politics. Cambridge, UK: Cambridge University Press.

Sun, Yutao and Cong Cao (2014). "Research Funding: Demystifying Central Government R&D Spending in China." *Science* 345(6200): 1006–1008.

Suttmeier, Richard P. (2012). "China's Management of Environmental Crises: Risks, Recreancy, and Response." In: Jae-Ho Chung (ed.). *China's Crisis Management,* 108–129. London: Routledge.

Svensson, Marina (2002). *Debating Human Rights in China: A Conceptual and Political History.* Lanham, MD: Rowman & Littlefield.

Swiss Rail Industry Association (2011). *China Railway Market Study: Final Report.* Zurich: Osec Business Network.

Tai, Zixue (2006). *The Internet in China: Cyberspace and Civil Society.* London: Routledge.

Taleb, Nassim Nicholas and Gregory F. Treverton (2015). "The Calm Before the Storm: Why Volatility Signals Stability, and Vice Versa." *Foreign Affairs* 94(1): 86–95.

Tanner, Murray Scot and Eric Green (2007). "Principals and Secret Agents: Central versus Local Control Over Policing and Obstacles to 'Rule of Law' in China." *The China Quarterly* (191): 644–670.

Teets, Jessica C. (2014). *Civil Society under Authoritarianism: The China Model.* Cambridge, UK: Cambridge University Press.

Teiwes, Frederick C. (1995). "The Paradoxical Post-Mao Transition: From Obeying the Leader to 'Normal Politics.'" *The China Journal* (34): 55–94.

Teorell, Jan (2010). *Determinants of Democratization: Explaining Regime Change in the World, 1972–2006.* Cambridge, UK: Cambridge University Press.

TI [Transparency International] (2015). *Corruption Perceptions Index 2015.* https://www.transparency.org/cpi2015. Accessed: February 2, 2016.

Tianya shequ 天涯社区 (2013). "中国社会的阶层分析" (Chinese social class analysis). August 1. http://bbs.tianya.cn/post-develop-1406156-1.shtml. Accessed: April 24, 2015.

Tong, Yanqi and Shaohua Lei (2014). *Social Protest in Contemporary China, 2003–2010: Transitional Pains and Regime Legitimacy.* China Policy Series 35. London: Routledge.

Tsering, Shakya (1999). *The Dragon in the Land of Snows: A History of Modern Tibet Since 1947.* New York: Columbia University Press.

UN [United Nations]. Department of Economic and Social Affairs (2015). "2015 Revision of World Population Prospects." http://esa.un.org/unpd/wpp/index.htm. Accessed: July 7, 2015.

UNDP [United Nations Development Programme] (1997). *Human Development Report 1997.* New York: Oxford University Press.

UNDP [United Nations Development Programme] (1999). *The China Human Development Report.* New York: Oxford University Press.

UNDP [United Nations Development Programme] (2001). *Human Development Report 2001.* New York: Oxford University Press.

UNDP [United Nations Development Programme] (2008). *Human Development Report China 2007/08.* Beijing: China Translation and Publishing Corporation.

UNESCAP [United Nations Economic and Social Commission for Asia and the Pacific] (2008). "Implementation of the Hyogo Framework for Action in Asia and the Pacific: Case Study: The National Disaster Management System of China and Its Response to the Wenchuan Earthquake." Bangkok. March 27–29. http://www.unescap.org/idd/events/cdrr-2009/CDR_2E.pdf. Accessed: July 9, 2015.

Unger, Jonathan (ed.) (2002). *The Nature of Chinese Politics: From Mao to Jiang.* Contemporary China Books. Armonk, NY: M.E. Sharpe.

UNODC [United Nations Office on Drugs and Crime] (2011). "Global Study on Homicide: Trends, Contexts, Data." Vienna. http://www.unodc.org/documents/data-and-analysis/statistics/Homicide/Globa_study_on_homicide_2011_web.pdf. Accessed: July 10, 2015.

Vanhanen, Tatu (1997). *Prospects of Democracy: A Study of 172 Countries.* London: Routledge.

Vogel, Ezra F. (1989). *One Step Ahead in China: Guangdong under Reform.* Cambridge, MA: Harvard University Press.

Vogel, Ezra F. (2011). *Deng Xiaoping and the Transformation of China.* Cambridge, MA: Belknap Press of Harvard University Press.

Vogelsang, Kai (2013). *Geschichte Chinas.* 3rd ed. Stuttgart: Reclam.

Walmsley, Roy (2011). "World Prison Population List (9th Edition)." http://www.pris-onstudies.org/sites/default/files/resources/downloads/wppl_9.pdf. Accessed: July 7, 2015.

Walter, Andrew and Xiaoke Zhang (eds.) (2012). *East Asian Capitalism: Diversity, Continuity, and Change.* Oxford, UK: Oxford University Press.

Walter, Carl E. and Fraser J. Howie (2006). *Privatizing China: Inside China's Stock Markets.* 2nd ed. Singapore: John Wiley & Sons.

Walter, Carl E. and Fraser J. T. Howie (2011). *Red Capitalism: The Fragile Financial Foundation of China's Extraordinary Rise.* Singapore; Hoboken, NJ: Wiley.

Wang, Can, Jie Lin, Wenjia Cai, and Zhongxiang Zhang (2014). "Policies and Practices of Low Carbon City Development in China." FEEM Working Paper (9). Milan: Fondazione Eni Enrico Mattei. http://papers.ssrn.com/sol3/papers.cfm?abstract_id=2393317##. Accessed: July 30, 2015.

Wang, Gungwu (2003). *Ideas Won't Keep: The Struggle for China's Future.* Ethnic Studies. Singapore: Eastern Universities Press.

Wang, Hongying (2001). *Weak State, Strong Networks: The Institutional Dynamics of Foreign Direct Investment in China.* Oxford, UK: Oxford University Press.

Wang, Mark Y., Pookong Kee, and Jia Gao (eds.) (2014). *Transforming Chinese Cities.* Routledge Contemporary China Series 116. London: Routledge.

Wang, Peng (2013a). "The Increasing Threat of Chinese Organised Crime: National, Regional and International Perpsectives." *The Royal United Services Institute (RSI) Journal* 158(4): 6–18.

Wang, Peng (2013b). "The Rise of the Red Mafia in China: A Case Study of Organised Crime and Corruption in Chongqing." *Trends in Organized Crime* 16(1): 49–73.

Wang, Shaoguang (2009). "Adapting by Learning: The Evolution of China's Rural Health Care Financing." *Modern China* 35(4): 370–404.

Wang, Shaoguang and Angang Hu (2001). *The Chinese Economy in Crisis: State Capacity and Tax Reform.* Studies on Contemporary China. Armonk, NY: M.E. Sharpe.

Wang, Tong (2012). "The Power of Social Media in China: The Government, Websites and Netizens on *Weibo*." National University of Singapore. http://www.scholarbank. nus.edu.sg/bitstream/handle/10635/35804/Wang%20Tong_Master%20Thesis_ The%20Power%20of%20Social%20Media%20in%20China.pdf?sequence=1. Accessed: July 11, 2015.

Wang, Yuhua (2014). *Tying the Autocrat's Hands: The Rise of the Rule of Law in China*. Cambridge Studies in Comparative Politics. Cambridge, UK: Cambridge University Press.

Wasserstrom, Jeffrey N. and Elizabeth J. Perry (eds.) (1994). *Popular Protest and Political Culture in Modern China*. 2nd ed. Politics in Asia and the Pacific: Interdisciplinary Perspectives. Boulder, CO: Westview Press.

Wedeman, Andrew (2012). *Double Paradox: Rapid Growth and Rising Corruption in China*. Ithaca, NY: Cornell University Press.

Wenzel-Teuber, Katharina (2015). "Statistisches Update 2014 zu Religionen und Kirchen in der Volksrepublik China." *China heute* 34(1): 20–34. http://www.china-zentrum.de/fileadmin/redaktion/China_heute_185_Statistisches_Update_2014_zu_ Religionen_und_Kirchen_in_der_Volksrepublik_Chnia__Katharina_Wenzel-Teuber. pdf. Accessed: January 10, 2016.

Whyte, Martin King (2010). *Myth of the Social Volcano: Perceptions of Inequality and Distributive Injustice in Contemporary China*. Stanford, CA: Stanford University Press.

Wildau, Gabriel (2015). "China Data: Making the Numbers Add Up." *Financial Times*, September 28. http://www.ft.com/intl/cms/s/0/cb446e10-6057-11e5-97e9-7f0b-f5e7177b.html#axzz41AZD7umt. Accessed: February 25, 2015.

Williams, Pete (2014). "U.S. Charges China with Cyber-Spying on American Firms." http://www.nbcnews.com/news/us-news/u-s-charges-china-cyber-spying-american-firms-n108706. May 18. Accessed: July 26, 2015.

Wilson, Scott (2015). *Tigers Without Teeth: The Pursuit of Justice in Contemporary China*. State and Society in East Asia. Lanham, MD: Rowman & Littlefield.

Womack, Brantly (ed.) (2010). *China's Rise in Historical Perspective*. Lanham, MD: Rowman & Littlefield.

Wong, Christine (2010). "Fiscal Reform: Paying for the Harmonious Society." *China Economic Quarterly* 14(2): 20–25. http://chinastudies.unimelb.edu.au/sites/www.chinastudies.unimelb.edu.au/files/3%EF%BC%89Paying%20for%20the%20harmonious%20society.pdf. Accessed: January 16, 2015.

Wong, Christine (2011). "The Fiscal Stimulus Program and Public Governance Issues in China." *OECD Journal on Budgeting* 11(3): 1–22. http://www.oecd-ilibrary.org/governance/the-fiscal-stimulus-programme-and-public-governance-issues-in-china_budget-11-5kg3nhljqrjl. Accessed: June 11, 2015.

Wong, Christine (2013a). "Performance, Monitoring, and Evaluation in China." *PREMnotes* (23). World Bank. http://siteresources.worldbank.org/EXTPOVERTY/Resources/336991-1345145100025/Nuts&BoltsENG_23.pdf. Accessed: July 4, 2015.

Wong, Christine (2013b). "Reforming China's Public Finances for Long-Term Growth." In: Ross Garnaut, Cai Fang, and Ligang Song (eds.). *China: A New Model for Growth and Development,* 199–219. Canberra: ANU E Press. http://press.anu.edu.au/wp-content/uploads/2013/07/ch101.pdf. Accessed: January 19, 2015.

Wong, Christine and Richard M. Bird (2008). "China's Fiscal System: A Work in Progress." In: Loren Brandt and Thomas G. Rawski (eds.). *China's Great Economic Transformation,* 429–466. Cambridge, UK: Cambridge University Press.

Woo-Cumings, Meredith (1999). *The Developmental State.* Cornell Studies in Political Economy. Ithaca, NY: Cornell University Press.

World Bank (2009). "From Poor Areas to Poor People: China's Evolving Poverty Reduction Agenda." http://www-wds.worldbank.org/external/default/WDSContentServer/WDSP/IB/2009/04/08/000334955_20090408062432/Rendered/PDF/473490SR0CN0P010Disclosed0041061091.pdf. Accessed: January 10, 2016.

World Bank (2014). "Poverty Headcount Ratio at $1.90 a Day (2011 PPP) (% of Population). China." http://data.worldbank.org/indicator/SI.POV.DDAY/countries/CN?display=graph. Accessed: July 4, 2015.

World Bank (2015). "Data." http://data.worldbank.org/country/. Accessed: January 28, 2016.

World Bank (2016). "Population Growth (Annual %). http://data.worldbank.org/indicator/SP.POP.GROW. Accessed: February 4, 2016.

World Bank and DRC [Development Research Center of the State Council] (2013). "China 2030: Building a Modern, Harmonious, and Creative Society." http://www. worldbank.org/content/dam/Worldbank/document/China-2030-complete.pdf. Accessed: July 5, 2015.

Wu, Alfred M. (2014a). *Governing Civil Service Pay in China*. Governance in Asia Series 3. Copenhagen: NIAS Press.

Wu, Fei 吴飞 (2009). 新闻专业主义研究 (A study on journalistic professionalism). Beijing: Zhongguo renmin daxue chubanshe.

Wu, Harry X. (2014b). "China's Growth and Productivity Performance Debate Revisited: Accounting for China's Sources of Growth with a New Data Set." The Conference Board Economics Program Working Paper Series. January 14–01. https://www.conference-board.org/pdf_free/workingpapers/EPWP1401.pdf. Accessed: July 29, 2015.

Wu, Weiping and Piper Rae Gaubatz (2013). *The Chinese City*. London: Routledge.

Wübbeke, Jost (2014). "The Three-Year Battle for China's New Environmental Law." *China Dialogue*. April 25. https://www.chinadialogue.net/article/show/single/en/6938-The-three-year-battle-for-China-s-new-environmental-law. Accessed: July 16, 2015.

Xi, Jinping (2014). *The Governance of China*. Beijing: Foreign Languages Press.

Xia, Ming (2008). *The People's Congresses and Governance in China: Toward a Network Mode of Governance*. Library of Legislative Studies. London: Routledge.

Xiao, Yuefan (2013). "The Politics of Crisis Management in China." Dissertation. University of Warwick (UK). http://wrap.warwick.ac.uk/58953/1/WRAP_THESIS_Xiao_2013.pdf. Accessed: July 9, 2015.

Xinhuanet 新华网 (2009). "独家专访陆学艺: 中产阶级每年增长一个百分点" (Exclusive interview with Lu Xueyi: Middle class grows by 1 percent each year). August 17. http://news.xinhuanet.com/politics/2009-08/17/content_11894452.htm. Accessed: July 7, 2015.

Xinhuanet 新华网 (2013). "云南停止三类行为劳教审批: 对在教人员继续执行" (Yunnan suspends approval of three kinds of 're-education-through-labor' within the province: Continues implementation of the teaching staff). February 7. http://news.china.com/domestic/945/20130207/17674451.html. Accessed: January 21, 2016.

Xinhuanet 新华网 (2014). "习近平: 把我国从网络大国建设成为网络强国" (Xi Jinping: China must evolve from a large Internet nation to a powerful Internet nation). February 27. http://news.xinhuanet.com/politics/2014-02/27/c_119538788.htm. Accessed: January 20, 2015.

Xinhuanet新华网 (2015). "China to Raise Budget Deficit Ratio in 2016." December 28. http://news.xinhuanet.com/english/2015-12/28/c_134958916.htm. Accessed: February 12, 2016.

Xu, Chenggang (2011). "The Fundamental Institutions of China's Reforms and Development." *Journal of Economic Literature* 49(4): 1076–1151.

Xu, Guangchun 徐光春 (2011). "中国共产党新闻实践与新闻思想的与时俱进不断发展: 纪念中国共产党成立 90周年" (The continuous and up-to-date development of CCP press practices and ideology: On the occasion of the 90th year of the founding of the CCP). *Guangming Daily* 光明日报. June 28. http://media.people.com.cn/GB/40606/15019274.html. Accessed: January 21, 2016.

Xue, Lan and Kaibin Zhong (2010). "Turning Danger (危) to Opportunities (机): Reconstructing China's National System for Emergency Management after 2003." In: Howard Kunreuther and Michael Useem (eds.). *Learning from Catastrophes: Strategies for Reaction and Response,* 190–210. Upper Saddle River, NJ: Pearson Education.

Yahuda, Michael (2013). "China's New Assertiveness in the South China Sea." *Journal of Contemporary China* 22(81): 446–459.

Yang, Dali (2004). *Remaking the Chinese Leviathan: Market Transition and the Politics of Governance in China.* Stanford, CA: Stanford University Press.

Yang, Fengchun 杨凤春 (2014). 当代中国政治制度 (China's contemporary political system). Beijing: Zhongguo renmin daxue chubanshe.

Yang, Guangbin 杨光斌 (2003). 中国政府与政治导论 (An introduction to Chinese government and politics). Beijing: Zhongguo renmin daxue chubanshe.

Yang, Guobin (2013). "Contesting Food Safety in the Chinese Media: Between Hegemony and Counter-Hegemony." *The China Quarterly* (214): 337–355.

Yang, Jisheng (2012). *Tombstone: The Great Chinese Famine, 1958–1962,* translated by Stacy Mosher and Guo Jian. New York: Farrar, Straus and Giroux.

Yang, Po (2014). "Understanding Vocational Education Market in China." CEREC Working Paper (6). September. Tampere: Chinese Education Research & Exchange Centre.

Yin, Deyong (2009). "China's Attitude Toward Foreign NGOs." *Washington University Global Studies Law Review* 8(3): 521–543.

Yu, Kai, Andrea Lynn Stith, Li Liu, and Huizhong Chen (2012). *Tertiary Education at a Glance: China.* Global Perspectives on Higher Education 24. Rotterdam; Boston: Sense Publishers.

Yu, Li (2014). "Low Carbon Eco-City: New Approach for Chinese Urbanisation." *Habitat International* 44: 102–110.

Yuan, Yue 袁岳, Zhang Hui 张慧, and Jiang Jianjian 姜健健 (2013). "2013 中国城市居民生活质量指数报告" (Report on the quality of life in Chinese cities in 2013). In: Li Peilin 李培林, Chen Guangjin 陈光金, and Zhang Yi 张翼 (eds.). 2014 年中国社会形势分析与预测 (Analysis and forecast of China's society 2014), 152–174. 社会蓝皮书 (Blue book on Chinese society). Beijing: Shehui kexue wenxian chubanshe.

Zhang, Jun and Jamie Peck (2016). "Variegated Capitalism, Chinese Style: Regional Models, Multi-Scalar Constructions." *Regional Studies* 50(1): 52–78.

Zhang, Qianfan (2012). *The Constitution of China: A Contextual Analysis.* Constitutional Systems of the World. Oxford, UK: Hart Publishing.

Zhang, Yu (2014). "Homegrown Developers Look to Unseat Microsoft's Dominant OS." *Global Times.* October 22. http://www.globaltimes.cn/content/887716.shtml. Accessed: July 23, 2015.

Zhao, Bo 赵波 and Zhang Zhihua 张志华 (2013). "协同创新视角下的江苏物联网发展对策" (Measures to develop the Internet of Things in Jiangsu from the perspective of collaborative innovation). *Social Sciences in Nanjing* 南京社会科学 (7): 150–155.

Zhao, Lianfei 找联飞 and Tian Feng 田丰 (2013). "大学生生活与价值观: 基于12所高校学生调查数据的分析" (Living conditions and social attitudes of university students: A report based on a tracking survey of university students from 12 universities). In: Li Peilin 李培林, Chen Guangjin 陈光金, and Zhang Yi 张翼 (eds.). 2014 年中国社会形势分析与预测 (Analysis and forecast of China's society in 2014), 239–272. 社会蓝皮书 (Blue book on Chinese society). Beijing: Shehui kexue wenxian chubanshe.

Zhao, Yuezhi (1998). *Media, Market, and Democracy in China: Between the Party Line and the Bottom Line.* Urbana: University of Illinois Press.

Zheng, Yongnian (2007). "China's De Facto Federalism." In: Baogang He, Brian Galligan, and Takeshi Inogushi (eds.). *Federalism in Asia,* 213–241. Cheltenham, UK: Edward Elgar.

Zheng, Yongnian (2008). *Technological Empowerment: The Internet, State, and Society in China.* Stanford, CA: Stanford University Press.

Zheng, Yongnian (2010a). "Central-Local Relations: The Power to Dominate." In: Joseph Fewsmith (ed.). *China Today, China Tomorrow: Domestic Politics, Economy, and Society,* 193–222. Lanham, MD: Rowman & Littlefield.

Zheng, Yongnian 郑永年 (ed.) (2010b). 中国模式: 经验与困局 (The China model: Experiences and dilemmas). Hangzhou: Zhejiang renmin chubanshe.

Zheng, Yongnian and Joseph Fewsmith (eds.) (2008). *China's Opening Society: The Non-State Sector and Governance.* China Policy Series 2. London: Routledge.

Zhihu 知乎 (2013). "中国社会的阶层划分模型?" (A social class module for Chinese society?). August 16. http://www.zhihu.com/question/21491491. Accessed: April 27, 2015.

Zhong, Yang (2010). "Chinese Township Government: Between a Rock and a Hard Place." In: Jae Ho Chung and Tao-Chiu Lam (eds.). *China's Local Administration: Traditions and Changes in the Sub-National Hierarchy,* 147–173. London: Routledge.

Zhongguo xinxi bao 中国信息报 (2014). "为转型升级进程建立科学的量化标尺" (Implementation of scientific quantitative indicators to transform and optimize processes). September 16. http://www.stats.gov.cn/tjgz/tjdt/201409/t20140916_609968.html. Accessed: July 29, 2015.

Zhonghua luntan 中华论坛 (2013). "最近网络上出了一个最新中国社会的阶层划分模型" (A new class module for Chinese society recently found on the Internet). August 8. http://club.china.com/data/thread/1011/2763/01/56/4_1.html. Accessed: April 27, 2015.

Zhou, Hang (2014). "China's New Coast Guard: One Year after the Restructuring Plan." Paper presented at the SIPRI Maritime Forum. Stockholm. July.

Zhou, Kate Xiao (1996). *How the Farmers Changed China: Power of the People*. Transitions: Asia & Asian America. Boulder, CO: Westview Press.

Zhou, Nan, Gang He, and Christopher Williams (2012). "China's Development of Low-Carbon Eco-Cities and Associated Indicator Systems." Berkeley: Ernest Orlando Lawrence Berkeley National Laboratory. http://china.lbl.gov/sites/all/files/china_eco-cities_indicator_systems.pdf. Accessed: July 30, 2015.

Zhu, Jingwen 朱景文 (2013). 中国人民大学中国法律发展报告: 中国法律工作者的职业化 (Renmin University of China. Report on Chinese law development: Professionalization of China's legal workers). Beijing: Renmin daxue.

Zhu, Xufeng (2012). *The Rise of Think Tanks in China*. China Policy Series 28. London: Routledge.

Zou, Ximing 邹锡明 (1998). 中共中央机构沿革实录, 1921.7–1997.9 (A historical record of CCP central institutions, 1921/7–1997/9). Beijing: Zhongguo dang'an chubanshe.

10 Index

A

B

D

E

H

I

M

N

Urban Planning Society of China (UPSC) 377
urban population 47, 246, 254, 259, 264, 266, 267, 292
Urumqi 285, 324
Uyghurs 23, 31, 238, 282, 283, 285
    World Uyghur Congress 285

V

value-added tax (VAT) 106
Vanhanen, Tatu 418
Vatican 286
Venezuela 423
Vietnam 70, 295
villages 29, 49, 64, 101, 195, 256
vocational education 385
Vogelsang, Kai 26, 497
V people 324

W

wages 237, 251, 257, 271, 290
Walmsley, Roy 294
Walter, Andrew 43
Walter, Carl E. 188, 216
Wang Can 379
Wang Gungwu 39
Wang Hongying 418
Wang Huning 176
Wang Peng 294, 295
Wang Qishan 175, 186, 187, 227
Wang Shaoguang 43, 237
Wang Tong 324
Wan Li 129
Washington 177, 420, 426
Wasserstrom, Jeffrey N. 39
Way, Lucan 298
WeChat 313, 327, 328
Wedeman, Andrew 230, 231
Weingast, Barry R. 92

X

Updates and supplements
to this book
can be downloaded here:
www.merics.org/polsys

11 Contributors

The *Mercator Institute for China Studies (MERICS)* is an independent research and analysis institute established in 2013 and based in Berlin. It is an initiative of *Stiftung Mercator,* a major private European foundation. Now employing almost 35 people, MERICS has grown into one of the largest international think tanks for policy-oriented research and knowledge about contemporary China. MERICS research is focused on the practical – current and long-term – challenges of relations with China. The institute analyzes political, economic, social, technological, and ecological developments in China as well as their international impact. It provides relevant information to decision-makers in politics, business, and society, and enhances public discussions on China.

Nabil Alsabah is a research associate at MERICS.

Johannes Buckow is a research associate at MERICS.

Björn Conrad is Vice-President of research at MERICS.

Hauke Gierow is a MERICS Policy Fellow for Internet Governance and also works as an IT-security journalist with the German IT-news portal golem.de.

Sandra Heep is a research associate at MERICS.

Sebastian Heilmann is the founding president of MERICS, and Professor for the Political Economy of China at Trier University.

Marie Hoffmann is Executive Assistant to the President at MERICS.

Mikko Huotari is Head of the Geoeconomics and International Security Program at MERICS.

Elena Klorer is a research associate at MERICS.

Kerstin Lohse-Friedrich is Director of Communications at MERICS.

Mirjam Meissner is Head of the Economy and Technology Program at MERICS.

Moritz Rudolf is a research associate at MERICS.

Dirk H. Schmidt is tenured Senior Lecturer at the Chair for Comparative Government and Political Economy of China at Trier University. He is a MERICS Senior Policy Fellow for China's Foreign Political and Economic Relations.

Kristin Shi-Kupfer is Director of Research on Politics, Society, and Media at MERICS.

Lea Shih is a research associate at MERICS.

Matthias Stepan is Head of the Domestic Politics Program at MERICS.

Marc Szepan teaches at Saïd Business School and at Green Templeton College, University of Oxford. He is a MERICS Senior Policy Fellow for China's Political Economy.

Jost Wübbeke is Head of the Economy and Technology Program at MERICS.

Yi Zhu is a research associate at MERICS.